Great Lives from History
American Heroes

Great Lives from History

American Heroes

Second Edition

Volume 1

Aeronautics and Spaceflight
Art
Athletics
Business
Education
Entertainment
Environment
Exploration
Invention
Journalism

Editor
D. Alan Dean

SALEM PRESS
A Division of EBSCO Information Services, Inc.
Ipswich, Massachusetts

GREY HOUSE PUBLISHING

Cover photo: Chris Hurtt via iStock

Copyright © 2019 by EBSCO Information Services, Inc., and Grey House Publishing, Inc.

Great Lives from History: American Heroes, published by Grey House Publishing, Inc., Amenia, NY, under exclusive license from EBSCO Information Services, Inc.

All rights reserved. No part of this work may be used or reproduced in any manner whatsoever or transmitted in any form or by any means, electronic or mechanical, including photocopy, recording, or any information storage and retrieval system, without written permission from the copyright owner. For information, contact Grey House Publishing/Salem Press, 4919 Route 22, PO Box 56, Amenia, NY 12501.

∞ The paper used in these volumes conforms to the American National Standard for Permanence of Paper for Printed Library Materials, Z39.48 1992 (R2009).

**Publisher's Cataloging-In-Publication Data
(Prepared by The Donohue Group, Inc.)**

Names: Dean, Dewayne A., editor.
Title: American heroes / [editor, Dewayne A. Dean].
Other Titles: Great lives from history.
Description: [Second edition]. | Ipswich, Massachusetts : Salem Press, a division of EBSCO Information Services, Inc. ; Amenia, NY : Grey House Publishing, [2019] | Includes bibliographical references and index.
Identifiers: ISBN 9781642650587 (set) | ISBN 9781642653595 (v. 1) | ISBN 9781642653601 (v. 2) | ISBN 9781642653618 (v. 3)
Subjects: LCSH: Celebrities--United States--Biography. | Heroes--United States--Biography. | United States--Biography. | LCGFT: Biographies.
Classification: LCC CT214 .A47 2019 | DDC 920.073B--dc23

FIRST PRINTING
PRINTED IN THE UNITED STATES OF AMERICA

Contents

Publisher's Note vii
Introduction ix
Complete List of Contents xiii

Aeronautics and Spaceflight
Neil Armstrong 3
Bessie Coleman 8
Jimmy Doolittle 10
Amelia Earhart 13
John Glenn 16
Hazel Ying Lee 20
Shannon W. Lucid 22
Christa McAuliffe 25
Ellen Ochoa 27
Sally Ride 30
Alan Shepard 33
Sunita Williams 37
Orville and Wilbur Wright 39
Chuck Yeager 43

Art
Ruth Asawa 49
Judith F. Baca 51
Jean-Michel Basquiat 53
Barbara Carrasco 55
Keith Haring 56
Edmonia Lewis 58
Maya Ying Lin 60
Georgia O'Keeffe 63
Maria Tallchief 67
Martin Wong 70

Athletics
Muhammad Ali 75
Jack Dempsey 78
Lou Gehrig 82
Althea Gibson 85
Michael Jordan 88
Michelle Kwan 91
Martina Navratilova 94
Jack Nicklaus 97
Jesse Owens 100
Jackie Robinson 103
Bill Russell 106

Babe Ruth 108
Serena Williams 112
Babe Didrikson Zaharias 115

Business
Andrew Carnegie 121
Bill Gates 125
Andrea Jung 128
Indra Nooyi 130
John D. Rockefeller 132
Sheryl Sandberg 136
George Soros 138
Dave Thomas 140
Madam C. J. Walker 142

Education
Elizabeth Cabot Agassiz 149
Mary McLeod Bethune 151
Fabiola Cabeza
    de Baca Gilbert 155
Huping Ling 157
Juliette Gordon Low 159
Anne Sullivan 162
Booker T. Washington 165

Entertainment
Joan Baez 171
Lynda Carter 174
Ellen DeGeneres 176
Duke Ellington 177
Aretha Franklin 180
Katharine Hepburn 184
Billie Holiday 187
Nancy Kwan 190
Bruce Lee 192
Stan Lee 195
Dolly Parton 198
Prince 202
Fred Rogers 205
Selena 208
Nina Simone 209
James Stewart 211
Oprah Winfrey 215
Anna May Wong 218

Environment
Rachel Carson 223
Van Jones 226
Winona LaDuke 232
John Muir 234
Margaret Murie 237
Henry David Thoreau 239

Exploration
Robert D. Ballard 245
Daniel Boone 248
Richard Byrd 252
Meriwether Lewis and William Clark 255

Invention
Patricia Bath 263
Alexander Graham Bell 265
George Washington Carver 268

Lee De Forest 271
John Deere 276
Charles Richard Drew 279
George Eastman 282
Thomas Alva Edison 286
Thomas L. Jennings 290
Hedy Lamarr 293
Garrett Augustus Morgan 296

Journalism
Walter Cronkite 303
Ann Curry 306
Margaret Fuller 308
William Lloyd Garrison 311
Katharine Graham 316
Maria Hinojosa 319
Edward R. Murrow 321
Ida Tarbell 325

Publisher's Note

Great Lives from History: American Heroes joins the *Great Lives* series, which provides in-depth critical essays on important men and women in all areas of achievement, from around the world and throughout history. Titles in this series include *The Ancient World, The Middle Ages, The Renaissance & Early Modern Era, The 17th Century, The 18th Century, The 19th Century, Notorious Lives, The 20th Century, Inventors & Inventions, African Americans, The Incredibly Wealthy, Jewish Americans, Latinos, Scientists & Science, Asian & Pacific Islander Americans, American Women,* and *Great Athletes.* This new installment extends the series to 18 titles, 64 volumes, and more than 8,000 great lives.

Scope of Coverage

Great Lives from History: American Heroes features 297 biographies, some from earlier Great Lives titles and all reviewed and brought up to date. We've added dozens of brand new biographies of heroic men and women. This three-volume set includes artists, business giants, religious and political leaders, scientists, inventors, educators, and social activists. Each essay has been written specifically for this set, for which inclusion criteria includes historical significance, representation of a wide range of fields of endeavor, relevance to classroom curricula, and appeal to high school, undergraduate, and general readers.

Essay Length and Format

Each essay, 1,000 to 2,000 words in length, includes top matter information:
- **Name** by which the subject is best known, with pronunciation guidelines as needed;
- **Description** of each subject's contributions or occupation;
- **Birth, death dates** and **locations,** as available;
- **Alternative identifications**, such as alternative spellings, pseudonyms, and nicknames;
- **Areas of achievement** with which the profiled subject is most closely identified;
- **Synopsis** of the subject's historical or social importance.

The body of each essay is divided into the following three parts:
- **Early Life** provides facts about upbringing and the environment in which the subject was reared. When details are scarce, historical context is provided.
- **Life's Work**, the heart of the essay, consists of a straightforward, generally chronological account of how the subject gained recognition in their chosen field, emphasizing the most significant achievements in their life and career.
- **Significance** provides an overview of the long-range importance of the profiled subject's accomplishments, and why studying them is important.

Each essay includes **Further Reading**, an annotated bibliography that provides a starting point for further research.

Special Features
- **Editor's Introduction:** Offers an informative, detailed look at heroes and how they have been defined throughout history, in a variety of areas, and through numerous lenses.
- **Sidebars**: Highlight significant, high-point events and accomplishments of the profiled subject.
- **Photographs**: Approximately 650 photographs punctuate the volumes.
- **Complete List of Contents**: An alphabetical list of all of the individuals covered in this set appears in each volume.

Back matter includes the following appendixes and indexes of particular interest to those studying American heroes:
- **Chronological List of Entries** is arranged by year of birth;
- **Alphabetical List of Entries** is arranged by last name;
- **Subject Index** includes people, organizations, events, legislation, court cases, cultural movements, works, and concepts.

CONTRIBUTORS

Salem Press would like to extend its appreciation to Editor Dewayne A. Dean for his invaluable guidance and thoughtful introduction, and to all those involved in the development and production of this work. Contributors include scholars of history, humanities, the sciences, and other relevant disciplines. Without these expert contributions, a project of this nature would not be possible. Editor's bio and list of contributors and their affiliations appear at the end of the third volume.

INTRODUCTION

Heroes are not always role models, leaders, saints or other admirable people, but are often thought of in these ways. One way to understand a word's meaning is to look at how it is used by people in a variety of contexts—the way that dictionaries are compiled. A 2015 study published in *Frontiers in Psychology* interviewed 189 people regarding their thoughts on what heroes do. Responses were collated into 14 answers. Heroes: improve the world; do what no one else can or will do; help; give hope; are role models; protect; save; inspire; act against evil; motivate; exemplify morals and values; guide; improve morale; and remind people about what is good (Kinsella et al. 2015). We might quibble about terms or methodology, but this statement comprises as good a definition of *hero* as any, and it's one that comes with a claim to empirical validity.

To better understand the concept, it helps to have some historical background. "Hero" comes from the Greek ἥρως (hérōs), meaning "protector" or "defender." The word meant something very particular in the ancient world, yet it informs each of the answers above. In the classical world, heroes were figures from mythology who were human, either male or female, and who lived in an ancient past. Although human, they were endowed with extraordinary, and even superhuman, abilities. Heroes lived in a time known as the Heroic Age, and were descended from the gods. A most significant hero was the fighter Akhilleus, more commonly known as Achilles, and a most important text in classical Greece—Homer's *Iliad*—features Achilles as its main protagonist.

ANCIENT GREEK HEROES
According to legend, Achilles was destined to either 1. die a glorious warrior or 2. live a long life in obscurity. His mother, wanting him to be a glorious warrior, dipped her infant into the River Styx, to make him immortal. His only vulnerable spot was his heel—where she held him in the water. During his life, Achilles shows superhuman skill in battle, apparently, immortal. During the 10-year siege of Troy, Achilles sacked twenty-three cities, and was renowned for his courage and valor.

After Achilles slays Hector, a noble Trojan warrior, to avenge the death of his friend, Patroclus, Hector's brother, Paris shoots the arrow (guided by the god Apollo) that kills him, into the only vulnerable spot on Achilles's body—his heel. That vulnerability is a unique trait in humans compared to gods, and one that is perhaps essential to being considered a hero. If there is no vulnerability, there would be no opportunity to put your life on the line to defend everything you value.

Greek heroes, then, were literary and mythological figures, with important roles in the mythic origins of the Greek people themselves. They were known for their superhuman abilities, physical strength, and feats. They exemplified valor, honor, and pride. Further, heroes were worshiped in certain religious rites. And heroes were closely associated with Greek athletics, which had a strong civic and ritual component (as did ancient Greek drama). Athletes weren't themselves considered heroes by the Greeks, but they were understood to imitate what the heroes did -- excellence, glory, and worship.

"Hero" in classic sense was defined more narrowly than the word is today. Modern usage does, however, retain a strong memory of the Greek definition; for example, today's soldiers or police officers are more quickly called heroes than teachers or businessmen, despite the fact that these can be heroes too, as this work will show. Despite expanded, modern usage, "hero" retains memory of the virtues that were originally heroic—martial valor and physical strength—and the kind of person who was called heroic—primarily fighters. And, an important aspect of ancient heroism that has continued into the modern world is that heroes were non-divine, extraordinary figures who were worshiped and celebrated in ways that united a community.

ANCIENT CHRISTIAN HEROES
Christianity represented a near-reversal of Greek heroism, asserting that the holy could be found in powerlessness rather than in power. Christians worshiped a weak and suffering savior. Jesus was distinctly un-heroic in the classical sense. In his first letter to the Corinthians, Paul writes that the Christian is an "athlete," but

one contending for an imperishable crown rather than a perishable laurel. The use of tropes related to heroism would occur again and again in Christian literature, until the concept of "hero" was redefined. Christians adopted the Greek word used for athletic training—*askesis*—for their spiritual training. The ascetics who entered the desert and submitted themselves to fasting and prayer performed quiet and un-celebrated "feats" of spiritual work to enter the "kingdom" of God. The network of ideas and practices that linked athletic contests, public glory, myth, and state power was thus co-opted. After the adoption of Christianity by the Roman empire, thousands of Christians chose to separate themselves from official Roman Christianity. Entering the deserts of Egypt to live simple lives of asceticism and prayer, "asceticism was the new form of heroism...." (McNeill 5). In early monastic literature, which grows out of the desert movement, holy men are often called "athletes of Christ." Early Christians, in short, used tropes connected to pagan heroism in order to extol personal sanctity rather than physical strength. They also shifted the focus to *inner life* rather than *public life*.

A MORE MODERN HERO

"Hero" entered modern English with a history of Greek ideas and the dramatic extension of those ideas associated with Christianity. Samuel Johnson's great dictionary of 1755 defined "hero" this way: *1. A man eminent for bravery; 2. A man of the highest class in any respect.*

The first definition hearkens back to the Greeks; the second definition reflects expansion. No matter how much we try to ignore the first, it's always there, evident in classic essays on heroes and heroism, especially those from the nineteenth century: Thomas Carlyle's book, *On Heroes, Hero-Worship, and the Heroic in History*; and Ralph Waldo Emerson's "Heroism" (1841) in *Essays: First Series*, which also contains the famous essay "Self-Reliance." Emerson's understanding of heroism is broad and varied, but distinctly inflected, at first, with ancient Greek meaning. Heroes are called "prodigies of individual valor," and heroism is called a "wild courage" that is "not of the schools, but of the blood..." Heroism is a "military attitude of the soul" and a "warlike attitude" that is assumed "within the breast." It enables the hero to "cope single-handed" with enemies.

Emerson then moves away from the Greek definition to focus on modern, democratic, and American values: "Self-trust is the essence of heroism," he writes. "It speaks the truth, and it is just, generous, hospitable, temperate, scornful of petty calculations, and scornful of being scorned." And elsewhere: "The essence of greatness is the perception that virtue is enough. Poverty is its ornament. It does not need plenty, and can very well abide its loss."

Emerson began with the traditional language of heroism and proceeded with Transcendentalist language of individualism. Heroic "self-trust" was a virtue because, in an echo of Rousseau, Emerson believed that man's most natural state, and man's natural goodness, are found at the level of the individual. When self-trust is present—when you follow your own star, always speak the truth, bow to no man—then you are the kind of individual that democracy both allows to flourish and requires for its continuance -- a hero.

Importantly, the self-trust that the individual exemplifies inspires strong ties of solidarity with others in the community: "These men fan the flame of human love and raise the standard of civil virtue among mankind." Emerson is aware of the apparently universal need to elevate and idolize, or to have heroes that we can celebrate, and he knows that this inspires strong communal feelings. This is so even in a democratic society because the hero shows us how we each should be, or what we each should become.

Sociologist Robert Bellah, in his essay "American civil religion," discusses the relationship between heroes and American ideals. What bonds would unite the people of a fledgling nation without an ancient history, without ancient traditions, and without a king? The discourse of the Founding Fathers was established in large part to meet these symbolic requirements. No Founding Father was more significant in this regard—or was made to signify so much—as George Washington.

After Washington's death, some Americans sought to deify him reminiscent of classical mythology and religion. In 1840, American sculptor Horatio Greenough depicted Washington as Zeus, with a strikingly muscular, heroic body topped by Washington's head. Commissioned by Congress, many observers found the sculpture absurd, and, after several locations, it was eventually installed in the Smithsonian. The painting inside the dome of the United States capitol, *Apotheosis of George Washington,* was done in 1865 by Constantino Brumidi, depicting George Washington rising to the heavens in glory and flanked by female figures representing Liberty and Victory.

In another, more homely depiction, Washington is presented as a hero in the Christian sense, an example of personal integrity to emulate. George Washington and the cherry tree first appeared in Mason Locke Weems's *The Life of George Washington* in 1806. Weems set out to show that Washington's "unparalleled rise and elevation were due to his Great Virtues," and the stories illustrating these "Great Virtues" of Washington bear a strong relation to religious devotional literature. The tale of the cherry tree was picked up by William Holmes McGuffey, who included it in his textbooks for children called *McGuffey's Readers* first published in 1836, and in print for almost a century. Generations of Americans grew up learning the edifying tale of Washington's honesty, despite the tale not being true.

The painting at the Capitol focused on Washington's *public* accomplishments, fusing Greek ideas about heroes, Roman notions of statehood, and Christian religious symbolism in celebration of a hero for the nation; for the most part, this style of discourse has faded from view. The story of Washington's childhood honesty, focusing on *private* virtue and a tradition of moral and didactic discourse, survived for much longer.

LEADERS, ROLE MODELS & HEROES
Heroes today are both figures to admire—if not to apotheosize—and models for moral behavior. That dual function is a continuation of the history outlined above. They are idealized images (echoes of "mythological figures") who inspire us by their accomplishments, whether personal or public, and by their unique strengths and victories. They also perform a social function, forging in us bonds of fellow-feeling and shared values.

Kinsella, et al. who gave us the 14 fourteen definitions of hero indicates that leaders are generally understood to be people who organize and motivate others to achieve a common good. "Transformational leaders," in particular, are thought to be both inspiring and seeking to make the world a better place. In short, many of the things that are said about heroes are said about leaders. Using their 14-point schema, researchers showed how people think differently about leaders versus heroes—both heroes and leaders help, save, motivate, make the world better, guide, and do what others can't. However, heroes were rated much more likely than leaders to help, save, protect, and make the world a better place. Leaders, by contrast, were rated much more likely to motivate and to guide. The two have significant areas of overlap, but they remain distinct.

Role models, a term first used by Robert K. Merton in a Columbia University study, are generally more personable and more humble than those classed as "heroes." An individual has many roles within the social structure, and attached to those roles is a set of expected behavior (Holton 514). By modeling that expected behavior within their roles, individuals can help inspire and guide people to do the same. Role models are more likely to be people of the same generation or country or profession (10). Again, despite significant overlap, one of the specific functions of heroes is, indeed, to model morals and values.

The language of heroism reveals another way that distinguishes heroes from other figures. We speak about "hero worship," but not of "role model worship" or "leader worship." Heroes were worshiped in ancient Greek and Roman rites and public athletic contests. The admiration that we have for heroes often includes a historical element, and so differs somewhat from the admiration that we have for role models or leaders.

ELEVATION AND HEROES
The quasi-religious notion about the hero function is also worth noting because it connects heroes to a recent development of positive psychology, with implications for how we talk about admired figures. In 2003, social psychologist Jonathan Haidt published an influential article in which he argued that there is a distinct human emotion that we barely recognize -- uplift, or "elevation." Elicited by contemplating acts of "moral beauty," it is said to be related to awe, gratitude, and admiration. Like other emotions, it involves a physiological response, an aroused tingling or energy in the chest cavity. Haidt didn't discover elevation, but read about it in a letter that Thomas Jefferson wrote to a friend in 1771, describing the effect that is experienced when we either see or imagine great acts of "charity or of gratitude" that deeply impress us. The impression produces not only a response of warmth in the chest, it gives us an elevated feeling and a desire to perform fine deeds ourselves.

Following Haidt, other researchers have studied elevation as a "self-transcending" emotional response related to admiration and awe (Shiota 2014). More recent research by Haidt relates elevation to both gratitude and admiration, elicited in subjects by "witnessing excellence in action" (Algoe 2009).

Understanding elevation—and related responses like awe and wonder—is increasingly seen by psychologists to be important for our understanding of heroism and the admiration elicited in response to heroes. Knowing the history of heroes in the ancient world, we see links between the social function of heroism and hero worship in the past and the role that heroes play in societies today, as well as between the overtly religious aspect of heroism in ancient Greece and the quasi-spiritual, psychological response studied by modern scientists.

Defining a hero or heroism is ambiguous and many-layered, though so are their definitions. Words like excellence, inspiration, integrity, even morality, can change depending on your culture, age, gender, and your own personal values and beliefs, so that the interpretation of heroics is largely left up to the individual. This work includes individuals that have many or all of the 14 qualities the Kinsella's research attributes to heroes, tied to the American qualities of freedom, struggle, justice and hope, although such a list is sure to encourage disagreement. The multi-ethnic, multi-racial nature of America is one of its greatest strengths, and this work showcases heroes from all walks of life and backgrounds.

D. Alan Dean

References

Algoe, Sara; Jonathan Haidt (2009). "Witnessing Excellence in Action: The other-praising emotions of elevation, admiration, and gratitude." *Journal of Positive Psychology*. 4 (2): 105–127.

Bellah, Robert N. "Civil Religion in America." *Daedalus*, Vol. 96, No. 1, Religion in America (Winter, 1967), pp. 1-21.

Brelich, A. *Gli eroi greci: Un problema storico-religioso*. Rome: Edizioni dell'Ateneo, 1958.

Clark, Elizabeth A. *Reading Renunciation: Asceticism and Scripture in Early Christianity*. Princeton: Princeton University Press, 1999.

Emerson, Ralph Waldo. "Heroism." In *Ralph Waldo Emerson: Essays & Lectures*. New York: Library of America, 1983. pp. 371-381.

Gardella, Peter. *American Civil Religion: What Americans Hold Sacred*. New York: Oxford University Press, 2013.

Hadas, Moses and Morton Smith. *Heroes and Gods: Spiritual Biographies in Antiquity*. New York: Harper & Row, 1965.

Haidt, Jonathan. "Elevation and the Positive Psychology of Morality." In C.L.M. Keyes & J. Haidt (Eds.) *Flourishing: Positive Psychology and the Life Well-Lived*. Washington DC: American Psychological Association, 2003. pp. 275-289.

Gerald, Holton. "Robert K. Morton - Biographical Memoirs." *Proceedings of the American Philosophical Society*, vol. 148, no. 4, Dec. 2004, p. 514.Kinsella, Elaine L et al. "Lay perspectives on the social and psychological functions of heroes." *Frontiers in psychology* vol. 6 130. 17 Feb. 2015, doi:10.3389/fpsyg.2015.00130

Lengel, Edward. G. *Inventing George Washington: America's Founder in Myth and Memory*. New York: HarperCollins, 2010.

McNeill, John T. "Asceticism Versus Militarism in the Middle Ages." *Church History,* Vol. 5, No. 1 (Mar., 1936), pp. 3-28.

Nagy, Gregory. *The Best of the Achaeans: Concepts of the Hero in Archaic Greek Poetry*. 2d rev. ed. Baltimore: Johns Hopkins University Press, 1999.

Poliakoff, Clare, and Michael Poliakoff. "Jacob, Job, and Other Wrestlers: Reception of Greek Athletics by Jews and Christians in Antiquity." *Journal of Sport History*, vol. 11, no. 2, 1984, pp. 48–65. JSTOR, www.jstor.org/stable/43609021.

Shiota, Michelle; Thrash, T. M.; Danvers, A. F.; Dombrowski, J. T. (2014). "Transcending the self: Awe, elevation, and inspiration." In M. Tugade, M. Shiota & L. Kirby. *Handbook of Positive Emotions*. The Guilford Press. pp. 362–377.

COMPLETE LIST OF CONTENTS

Volume 1
Publisher's Note vii
Introduction ix
Complete List of Contents xiii

Aeronautics and Spaceflight
Neil Armstrong 3
Bessie Coleman 8
Jimmy Doolittle 10
Amelia Earhart 13
John Glenn 16
Hazel Ying Lee 20
Shannon W. Lucid 22
Christa McAuliffe 25
Ellen Ochoa 27
Sally Ride 30
Alan Shepard 33
Sunita Williams 37
Orville and Wilbur Wright 39
Chuck Yeager 43

Art
Ruth Asawa 49
Judith F. Baca 51
Jean-Michel Basquiat 53
Barbara Carrasco 55
Keith Haring 56
Edmonia Lewis 58
Maya Ying Lin 60
Georgia O'Keeffe 63
Maria Tallchief 67
Martin Wong 70

Athletics
Muhammad Ali 75
Jack Dempsey 78
Lou Gehrig 82
Althea Gibson 85
Michael Jordan 88
Michelle Kwan 91
Martina Navratilova 94
Jack Nicklaus 97
Jesse Owens 100
Jackie Robinson 103
Bill Russell 106

Babe Ruth 108
Serena Williams 112
Babe Didrikson Zaharias 115

Business
Andrew Carnegie 121
Bill Gates 125
Andrea Jung 128
Indra Nooyi 130
John D. Rockefeller 132
Sheryl Sandberg 136
George Soros 138
Dave Thomas 140
Madam C. J. Walker 142

Education
Elizabeth Cabot Agassiz 149
Mary McLeod Bethune 151
Fabiola Cabeza
    de Baca Gilbert 155
Huping Ling 157
Juliette Gordon Low 159
Anne Sullivan 162
Booker T. Washington 165

Entertainment
Joan Baez 171
Lynda Carter 174
Ellen DeGeneres 176
Duke Ellington 177
Aretha Franklin 180
Katharine Hepburn 184
Billie Holiday 187
Nancy Kwan 190
Bruce Lee 192
Stan Lee 195
Dolly Parton 198
Prince 202
Fred Rogers 205
Selena 208
Nina Simone 209
James Stewart 211
Oprah Winfrey 215
Anna May Wong 218

Environment
Rachel Carson 223
Van Jones 226
Winona LaDuke 232
John Muir 234
Margaret Murie 237
Henry David Thoreau 239

Exploration
Robert D. Ballard 245
Daniel Boone 248
Richard Byrd 252
Meriwether Lewis and William
    Clark 255

Invention
Patricia Bath 263
Alexander Graham Bell 265
George Washington Carver 268
Lee De Forest 271
John Deere 276
Charles Richard Drew 279
George Eastman 282
Thomas Alva Edison 286
Thomas L. Jennings 290
Hedy Lamarr 293
Garrett Augustus Morgan 296

Journalism
Walter Cronkite 303
Ann Curry 306
Margaret Fuller 308
William Lloyd Garrison 311
Katharine Graham 316
Maria Hinojosa 319
Edward R. Murrow 321
Ida Tarbell 325

Volume 2
Complete List of Contents vii

Literature
Mercedes de Acosta 331
Maya Angelou 333
James Baldwin 336

Complete List of Contents

Pura Belpré 339
Judy Blume 342
Giannina Braschi 344
Sandra Cisneros 347
Ta-Nehisi Coates 349
Martha P. Cotera 351
Emily Dickinson 353
Henry Louis Gates, Jr. 358
bell hooks 361
Zora Neale Hurston 363
Jhumpa Lahiri 365
Toni Morrison 368
Lola Rodríguez de Tió 370
Susan Sontag 372
Harriet Beecher Stowe 374
Walt Whitman 377
August Wilson 381

Medicine
Clara Barton 387
Martha Bernal 390
Elizabeth Blackwell 392
Deepak Chopra 396
Margaret Chung 398
Jane L. Delgado 399
Gertrude Belle Elion 402
Sanjay Gupta 405
David Ho 408
Joseph LeDoux 410
Antonia Novello 415
Susan La Flesche Picotte 417
Jonas Salk 420
Margaret Sanger 423
Nora D. Volkow 427

Military
Omar Nelson Bradley 435
Stephen Decatur 438
Mary A. Hallaren 442
Oveta Culp Hobby 444
Stonewall Jackson 447
Robert E. Lee 451
Chester W. Nimitz 455
John J. Pershing 458
Loreta Janeta Velázquez 462
Cathay Williams 464

Native American Leaders
Crazy Horse 469
Geronimo 474
Chief Joseph 477
Kamehameha I 480
Lili'uokalani 484
Wilma Mankiller 487
Nanyehi 490
Red Cloud 493
John Ross 496
Sacagawea 499
Sitting Bull 503
Sarah Winnemucca 506

Politics/Law
Madeleine Albright 511
Louis D. Brandeis 515
William J. Brennan 518
Ralph Bunche 521
Norma V. Cantú 524
Elaine L. Chao 525
Shirley Chisholm 527
Judy M. Chu 529
Clarence Darrow 531
Helen Gahagan Douglas 534
William O. Douglas 538
Tammy Duckworth 540
Geraldine Ferraro 542
Heather Fong 547
Benjamin Franklin 549
Ruth Bader Ginsburg 553
Al Gore 555
Nikki Haley 558
Alexander Hamilton 559
Learned Hand 564
Patrick Henry 567
Mazie Hirono 570
Charles Evans Hughes 572
Daniel Ken Inouye 577
Marí-Luci Jaramillo 580
Barbara Jordan 582
Robert F. Kennedy 586
Robert M. La Follette 590
Belva A. Lockwood 594
Huey Long 597
John Marshall 601
Thurgood Marshall 605

Vilma Socorro Martínez 608
Harvey Milk 610
Patsy Mink 613
Ralph Nader 615
Sandra Day O'Connor 617
Thomas Paine 622
Rachel Paulose 625
Colin Powell 626
Jeannette Rankin 630
Condoleezza Rice 633
Felisa Rincón de Gautier 636
Margaret Chase Smith 638
Sonia Sotomayor 642
Adlai E. Stevenson II 645
Norman Thomas 649
Earl Warren 654

Volume 3
Complete List of Contents vii

Presidents and First Ladies
Abigail Adams 661
John Adams 664
Dwight D. Eisenhower 668
Betty Ford 672
Andrew Jackson 675
Thomas Jefferson 678
John F. Kennedy 682
Abraham Lincoln 686
Dolley Madison 689
James Madison 692
Barack Obama 695
Eleanor Roosevelt 699
Franklin D. Roosevelt 702
Theodore Roosevelt 707
George Washington 710

Religion
Sister Thea Bowman 717
Mary Baker Eddy 718
Barbara Harris 724
M. Hasna Maznavi 726
Thomas Merton 728
John R. Mott 731
Sally J. Priesand 735
Zaid Shakir 737
Avi Weiss 738

Social Reform

Ralph David Abernathy............743
Jane Addams 746
Susan B. Anthony.....................750
Gloria Anzaldúa 753
Ella Baker.................................756
John Brown 758
Olympia Brown........................762
Luisa Capetillo 765
Mary Ann Shadd Cary 767
Lourdes Casal...........................769
César Chávez 771
Helen Fabela Chávez 774
Kimberlé Williams Crenshaw..775
Dorothy Day.............................777
Eugene V. Debs 780
Dorothea Dix............................784
Frederick Douglass 787
W. E. B. Du Bois......................790
Marian Wright Edelman 793
Sue Kunitomi Embrey..............797
Betty Friedan............................799
Marcus Garvey.........................803
Emma Goldman 806
Emma González 809
Fannie Lou Hamer 811
Harry Hay.................................814
Aileen Clarke Hernandez.........817
Samuel Gridley Howe..............820
Dolores Huerta.........................824
Larry Itliong 829
Jesse Jackson............................831
Marsha P. Johnson....................834
Mother Jones............................837
Frank Kameny..........................840
Helen Keller.............................843
Martin Luther King, Jr. 847
John L. Lewis...........................850
Malcolm X 854
Cherríe Moraga 857
Bree Newsome.........................859
Queen Noor 861
Rosa Parks................................863
Alice Paul.................................866
Elizabeth Peratrovich...............869
Ai-jen Poo 871
A. Philip Randolph 873
Sylvia Rivera............................877
Bayard Rustin 879
Edward Snowden 881
Elizabeth Cady Stanton............883
Mary Tape 888
Reies López Tijerina 890
Sojourner Truth 892
Harriet Tubman 895
Nat Turner 898
Ida B. Wells-Barnett.................899
Elie Wiesel 901

STEM

Benjamin Banneker..................907
Steven Chu...............................909
Albert Einstein 911
Grace Murray Hopper..............914
Edwin Powell Hubble 918
Mae C. Jemison........................921
Katherine G. Johnson...............923
Mary Golda Ross 925
Steve Wozniak..........................926
Chien-Shiung Wu.....................929

Appendixes

Chronological List of Entries...935
Alphabetical List of Entries 941
Subject Index 947

Aeronautics and Spaceflight

The term aeronautics originally meant *navigation* through the *air* (from Greek *nautikos*, "pertaining to sailing," plus *aero-*, "air"). The word was used to describe travel in hot air balloons—navigating through the air in the days before airplanes were invented. Today *aeronautics* refers to the science of flight in all its forms—from balloons to airplanes to rockets—and to the mechanics of flight. *Aviation,* which has to do with the activity of flying aircraft, is here considered a part of aeronautics.

America holds a privileged place in the history of modern aeronautics. Although balloons were developed in Europe in the eighteenth century, and the technology for gliders was developed in Germany in the nineteenth century, it was primarily in America that machines were first used successfully to assist humans in flight. In the 1890s, Samuel P. Langley, the director of the Smithsonian Institution, tried to add a motorized engine to a flying machine. His steam-powered "aerodrome" was heavy and not very successful in flight, but it paved the way for the work of Orville and Wilbur Wright. On December 17, 1903, the Wright brothers made four brief flights near Kitty Hawk, on the Outer Banks in North Carolina, with the first successful powered aircraft, a plane that they called the Flyer.

In the jet age, American achievements in the field of aeronautics led naturally to achievements in the field of *aerospace*. The Soviet Union during the Cold War devoted enormous resources to winning the "space race" against the United States, and they achieved many of the first milestones in space flight. These include the first human space flight in 1961 (Yuri Gagarin aboard Vostok 1) and the first spacewalk in 1965. Twenty-three days after Gagarin's achievement, Alan Shepard became the first American to reach suborbital space; John Glenn became the first American to orbit the earth nearly a year after Gagarin. Of course, when American astronauts Neil Armstrong and Buzz Aldrin walked on the moon in 1969, America essentially "won" the space race. No other achievement in aerospace, before or since, has been quite as dramatic as that.

Our selection of heroes in aeronautics includes Orville and Wilbur Wright, the duo who flew the first successful airplane, and Chuck Yeager, the first pilot to break the sound barrier. It also includes important women in the field such as Bessie Coleman, the first Native and African American woman to hold a pilot license, and Hazel Ying Lee, a Chinese-American who flew missions for the United States military during World War II. Among the astronauts included here are John Glenn, the first American in space, and Neil Armstrong, who landed on the moon. Also included are Sally Ride, the first American woman in space; Ellen Ochoa, who served on the Discovery and was later the director of the Johnson Space Center; and Shannon Lucid, the woman who once held the record for the longest duration stay in space by an American astronaut.

The space shuttle Discovery *at Kennedy Space Center under a full moon. (NASA)*

NEIL ARMSTRONG

Astronaut and aviator

Born: August 5, 1930; Wapakoneta, Ohio
Died: August 25, 2012; Cincinnati, Ohio
Areas of Achievement: Aviation and space exploration, science, invention and technology

Armstrong was the first person to walk on the Moon. He was commander of the Apollo 11 spacecraft, which made the first piloted lunar landing mission in history, and he had an early career as a test pilot.

EARLY LIFE

Neil Armstrong, the first person to set foot on the Moon, was born on a farm in Auglaize County near Wapakoneta, Ohio. He was the elder son of Stephen Armstrong and Viola Armstrong; his younger brother, Dean Alan, was born in Jefferson, Ohio, and had a long career with the Delco Division of General Motors Corporation at Anderson, Indiana; Neil also had a sister, June Louise. Stephen Armstrong was an auditor for the state of Ohio, and his work took the family across the state to many towns. The Armstrong's moved from Warren to Jefferson, to Ravenna, to St. Mary's, Upper Sandusky, and finally to a more permanent home in Wapakoneta. The Armstrong's were descendants of Scotch-Irish immigrants, while the mother's ancestors were of German background. Neil's father eventually was made the assistant director of mental hygiene and corrections of the state of Ohio.

Armstrong began his formal education in the public schools of Warren, Ohio, where he attended Champion Heights Elementary School. His advanced reading ability (he had read ninety books in the first grade) permitted him to skip the second grade. Known as a shy and modest boy, he played baseball and football with friends and enjoyed school activities.

Influenced by his father, Armstrong had an early interest in aviation. His family attended the National Air Races at the Cleveland airport, and as a six-year-old boy, he accompanied his father in a plane called a Tin Goose (Ford TriMotor) that provided air rides near their home in Warren. During the Great Depression, Armstrong developed a deep interest in building model airplanes, a hobby that soon filled his room with the smell of glue and balsa wood. He quickly advanced from hobby kits to creating bigger and more powerful models of his own, which he tested at the town park. During his high school years, to

Neil Armstrong (Wikimedia Commons)

improve his homemade planes, Armstrong built a seven-foot-long wind tunnel in the basement of his family's house. He was also an enthusiastic fan of science fiction, especially that of H. G. Wells.

One neighbor, Jacob Zint, owned a powerful telescope and often invited youngsters to look at the Moon, stars, and planets. Armstrong remembered these stargazing experiences as awe inspiring and began more study of the universe. He loved to learn; his schoolbooks, which his parents saved, reflect his thorough study and wide reading in the fields of science and mathematics. With his collection of the popular *Air Trails* magazine, he kept pace with aviation advancements. As a high school student, at the age of fifteen, he worked in stores to earn enough money to take flying lessons. On his sixteenth birthday, even before he had a driver's license, he was granted a student pilot's license. He later said that he had decided to become an aircraft designer and thought that a good designer needed to know how to fly.

Armstrong rode his bicycle day after day in 1946 to the Auglaize Flying Field at Wapakoneta, where flight instructor Aubrey Knudegard trained him to fly in an Aeronca 7AC Champion, built in Middletown, Ohio. The Aeronca Airplane Company had been a pioneer in the production of light, single-wing aircraft for private flying, and Armstrong learned to fly the plane with skill. Since the initial flights in 1903 of the Wright brothers at Kitty Hawk, North Carolina, the growth of aerospace research had been concentrated at the Wright-Patterson Air Force Base in Dayton, Ohio, and the Miami Valley had become a center of postwar aviation development and testing. Armstrong was flying from a local airfield not far from this national air base. He also became an Eagle Scout in the Boy Scouts of America.

In the fall of 1947, following his graduation from Wapakoneta High School, Armstrong entered Purdue University at Lafayette, Indiana, on a United States Navy scholarship. Enrolled in the College of Engineering, he had completed about two years of study when the navy ordered him to report to Pensacola, Florida, for special flight training. After the outbreak of the Korean War in July, 1950, Armstrong was the youngest member of his unit, Fighter Squadron 51, when it was sent overseas for active duty. He flew seventy-eight combat missions from the flight deck of the aircraft carrier the USS *Essex*. One mission nearly cost him his life: His Panther jet, damaged by antiaircraft fire, nicked a cable stretched across a North Korean valley; with grim determination and skill, he guided the plane back into South Korea before parachuting to safety. Armstrong won three Air Medals for his combat duty. (Author James Michener modeled his classic 1953 novel *The Bridges of Toko-Ri* after Armstrong and some other fliers in the squadron.)

On completion of his navy service in 1952, Armstrong returned to Purdue to finish his bachelor of science degree in aeronautical engineering and was graduated in 1955. On campus, he met Janet Shearon of Evanston, Illinois, who shared his love for flying; their college courtship led to marriage on January 28, 1956. Three children were born to the Armstrong's: Eric, born in 1957, Karen, born in 1959 (she died near the age of three), and Mark, born in 1963.

> "*Mystery creates wonder and wonder is the basis of man's desire to understand.*"

Armstrong had by then matured into a handsome aviator with a strong physical stature, standing nearly six feet tall. Reserved in speech but quite able to express himself, Armstrong had keen blue eyes that reflected the intensity of concentration and the good judgment of his mind.

Engineering the Possible

Intensely private and unassuming, Neil Armstrong avoided public appearances after his days as an astronaut, but on July 20, 1999, the thirtieth anniversary of the first lunar landing, he gave a lighthearted speech before the National Press Club in Washington, D.C., on behalf of the National Academy of Engineering. Describing the mission as one of humanity's greatest engineering achievements, he observed that while "science is about what is, engineering is about what can be."

Always a good listener, he had absorbed a remarkable amount of information about airborne flight and often drew vital information from that reservoir.

LIFE'S WORK

Armstrong went to work at the Lewis Flight Propulsion Laboratory in Cleveland, serving as a research pilot. After six months at Lewis, he transferred to the High Speed Flight Station at Edwards Air Force Base in California, where he served as an aeronautical research pilot testing many pioneering aircraft, including the X-15 rocket airplane (he took it to more than 200,000 feet above Earth's surface and flew at speeds of nearly four thousand miles per hour), the X-1, F-100, F-101, F-102, F-104, F5D, B-47, and the paraglider. In all, he flew more than two hundred different kinds of aircraft. While in California, he began his master of science degree in aerospace engineering at the University of Southern California, completing it in 1969.

Spurred by the Soviet Union's successful launching of the first Earth-orbiting satellite, Sputnik 1, on October 4, 1957, the United States in 1958 established the National Aeronautics and Space Administration (NASA) to coordinate all space research projects sponsored by the federal government. Soon the United States was sending its satellites skyward, and NASA began training spacecraft pilots called "astronauts" for orbital flights. Explorer 1 became the first successful American data-gathering space satellite, launched in January, 1958. It was Soviet cosmonaut Yuri Gagarin, however, who became the first human in space orbit, in April, 1961, aboard the Vostok 1; the United States sent its first piloted capsule into suborbital flight in May, 1961, with Alan B. Shepard, Jr., flying in

Freedom 7. That month, President John F. Kennedy, in an address to Congress, called for the nation to land the first person on the Moon by the end of the decade, a goal that was achieved.

While still working at NASA's facility at Edwards Air Force Base (consolidated into NASA), Armstrong applied to be one of the United States' astronauts. The requirements favored men from military units, but Armstrong was accepted in 1962; he was the first civilian admitted to the astronaut program by NASA. The Armstrongs moved to El Lago, Texas, and Armstrong joined the nation's second recruit class of astronauts in training at the new NASA Manned Spacecraft Center in Houston for a two-year intensive program of classroom study and training for space travel.

NASA developed three space programs while Armstrong worked as an astronaut. The first, designated Project Mercury, was to develop the technology and experience to send a person into Earth orbit. On February 20, 1962, the first piloted orbital flight launched by the United States carried John Glenn as pilot of a three-orbit space trip. The Gemini program, created in 1962, launched a series of two-person spacecraft in Earth orbit during 1965 and 1966, including two unpiloted and ten piloted ventures. Project Apollo, created in 1960, was redirected in 1962 to land on the Moon by 1970, using a three-person crew. Nine crewed Apollo missions of lunar orbit or landings were made by the end of that program in 1972.

Armstrong was assigned as a command pilot for the Gemini 8 mission launched on March 16, 1966. He successfully performed the first docking of two vehicles (one piloted, the other unpiloted) in space. He and David R. Scott found the two crafts pitching and spinning out of control; Armstrong detached their Gemini capsule, and then, as it began to roll even faster, brought it back under control and made an emergency landing in the Pacific Ocean. He also served as commander of the backup crew for Gemini 11 and late in 1966, at the request of President Lyndon B. Johnson, went on a twenty-four-day goodwill tour of South America with other astronauts.

It was as spacecraft commander of Apollo 11, the first piloted lunar landing mission in history, that Armstrong gained the distinction of being the first to land a craft on the Moon and the first to step on its surface, an event that was achieved on July 20, 1969, four days after the craft's launch. Michael Collins served as command module pilot of the *Columbia*, which orbited the Moon while Armstrong and Colonel Edwin E. Aldrin, Jr., aboard the four-legged lunar module called the *Eagle*, landed near the Sea of Tranquillity (at about 4:18 p.m., eastern daylight time) and explored the surface before the rendezvous with the *Columbia* for the return trip.

The next day, *The New York Times* ran the headline, "Men Walk on Moon: Astronauts Land on Plain; Collect Rocks, Plant Flag." Relating one of humanity's most historic moments, a journalist recounted,

> About six and a half hours [following the lunar landing], Mr. Armstrong opened the landing craft's hatch, stepped slowly down the ladder and declared as he planted the first human footprint on the lunar crust: "That's one small step for man, one giant leap for mankind."

His first step on the moon came at 10:56:20 p.m., as a television camera outside the craft transmitted his every move to an awed and excited audience of hundreds of millions of people on Earth.

Colonel Aldrin soon joined Armstrong and, in a two-and-a-half-hour stay outside the *Eagle*, the two set up a camera for live television transmission, conducted seismographic and laser experiments, planted a United States flag, and collected samples of Moon soil and rocks. After

The crewmen of the Apollo 11 lunar landing mission leave the Kennedy Space Center's (KSC) Manned Spacecraft Operations Building (MSOB) during the prelaunch countdown. (Wikimedia Commons)

twenty-two hours, they blasted off to rejoin the *Columbia*, climbed back into the command module, jettisoned the lunar *Eagle*, and returned to earth to splash down southeast of Hawaii and were personally welcomed by President Richard M. Nixon aboard the USS *Hornet*. Nixon said: "You have taught man how to reach for the stars."

For eighteen days after the splashdown, the three lunar astronauts were kept in isolation to avoid any contamination from the Moon's environment. New York City welcomed them with the greatest ticker-tape parade since Charles A. Lindbergh's solo flight to Paris in 1927. At the White House, they received the nation's highest civilian honor: The Medal of Freedom was given to each of them. In the next months, they visited twenty-two nations and were awarded medals and citations from governments and scientific organizations around the world.

Ticker tape parade for the Apollo 11 astronauts. Location is Manhattan, New York City on the section of Broadway known as the "Canyon of Heroes". Pictured in the lead car, from the right, are astronauts Neil A. Armstrong, Michael Collins and Edwin E. Aldrin, Jr. (Wikimedia Commons)

Armstrong was reassigned to the position of deputy associate administrator for aeronautics, Office of Advanced Research and Technology, NASA Headquarters, Washington, D.C. He was responsible for the coordination and management of NASA research and technology work related to aeronautics. Warned in his correspondence with Charles A. Lindbergh of the dangers of fame, he resolutely shunned the limelight and evaded reporters and photographers. From then on his name was among the best known on the planet, but he could travel anywhere without being recognized.

In the fall of 1971, at the urging of his friend, Paul Herget, astronomer and professor of space science, whose work in the field of minor planets and in satellite orbits had won world recognition, Armstrong accepted an appointment as professor of engineering at the University of Cincinnati, an interdisciplinary post he retained until 1980. After their return to Ohio, the Armstrong's lived on a farm near Lebanon, Warren County, where their sons were graduated from high school.

Between 1979 and 1981, Armstrong worked part-time for the Chrysler Corporation and appeared in a national advertising campaign for the Detroit car manufacturer. For a short time, he and his brother Dean owned and operated the Cardwell International Corporation, a producer and exporter of oil field equipment. He later headed CTA, an aviation company based in Charlottesville, Virginia.

Sought by many major corporations, Armstrong accepted positions on the board of directors of several companies, including Gates Learjet and United Airlines. In the 1980's, although carefully guarding his schedule, he became a popular speaker at national conventions and trade associations as well as a commencement speaker for many universities, some of which awarded him honorary degrees. He turned down offers from both major political parties to run for office.

Following the explosion of the *Challenger* space shuttle on January 28, 1986, in which seven astronauts lost their lives, President Ronald Reagan named William Rogers chair and Neil Armstrong vice chair of a presidential commission to investigate the causes of the *Challenger*'s failure. For the next six months, Armstrong served as an active member of that commission, appearing on television and before Congress with the chair to report on the findings of the body. After the Rogers Commission disbanded, Armstrong served on the board of directors of Thiokol, the corporation that had manufactured the rocket booster that caused the disaster.

In 1989 he was divorced from Janet. During a golf tournament in 1992, Armstrong met Carol Held Knight; they married two years later. In addition to creating difficulties in his first marriage, his fame sometimes caused him embarrassment and problems. He stopped signing autographs in 1994 after learning that the autographed items were being sold for thousands of dollars on such venues as the Internet company eBay, and he twice initiated lawsuits against those who used his name, words, or in one case hair without his permission or knowledge. He donated the settlements to charities.

Armstrong retired from business on May 7, 2002, resigning as chair of the board of EDO Corporation, an advanced technology firm serving defense, intelligence, and commercial markets in New York. He had become chair in 2000.

In 2005 a long-standing controversy was revived over what exactly Armstrong had said when he first stepped onto the Moon's surface. He always maintained that he had said "That's one small step for a man, one giant leap for mankind"; however, the "a" went unheard and the resulting statement, seemingly a mere redundancy, was sometimes ridiculed. A computer programmer in Australia, Peter Shann Ford, reprocessed the audio recording with advanced computer equipment and discovered that Armstrong was correct; an "a," only 35 milliseconds long, emerged from the reprocessing. Hidden in the static of the original transmission, the correct version reflected Armstrong's modest attempt to deflect attention from himself and include all humanity in the event.

Honors came early to Armstrong for his moon landing and continued throughout his life. The Boy Scouts gave him the Distinguished Eagle Scout Award and Silver Buffalo Award. He also received the Congressional Space Medal of Honor, Robert H. Goddard Memorial Trophy, and the National Aeronautics Association's Collier Trophy. Many places have been named after him, including a moon crater near his landing site, schools, streets, and, in 2004, the new engineering building at his alma mater.

Significance

When the three astronauts of Apollo 11 addressed a joint session of the United States Congress on September 16, 1969, Armstrong recalled how they had left a bronze plaque on the *Eagle*'s remnants. It declared: "Here men from the planet Earth first set foot upon the Moon. July 1969, a.d. We came in peace for all mankind." Such sentiments reflect the noble convictions of Armstrong: He saw his individual role in the gigantic space exploration mission as that of only one member of the nation's great team; his accomplishment as a victory for the whole of human endeavor: "a giant leap for mankind," "in peace for all mankind." Hence, he was able to return quietly to university and business activities after becoming the world's greatest explorer of all time.

Governor James A. Rhodes led a drive for the erection of a globelike museum honoring Armstrong on the edge of his hometown at Wapakoneta, which houses a vast collection of the awards, citations, gifts, and honors given the Ohio native. As a new American hero, a skillful and courageous commander in the tradition of Christopher Columbus, Ferdinand Magellan, and others, Armstrong confidently walked on the Moon first and confidently returned to work among his fellows. Through it all he remained unassuming about his achievement. He said in 2005, "I was elated, ecstatic and extremely surprised that we were successful."

Paul F. Erwin

Further Reading

Brinkley, Douglas. "The Man and the Moon." *American History* 39 (August, 2004): 26-78. A substantial, enjoyable article that discusses Armstrong's famous reticence and shyness, reluctant participation in the Johnson Space Center Oral History Project, ferocious ability to concentrate on whatever he is doing, and role in U.S. aerospace programs.

Crouch, Tom D. *The Giant Leap: A Chronology of Ohio Aerospace Events and Personalities, 1815-1969*. Columbus: Ohio Historical Society, 1971. A graphic story of human flight from the time of early balloons, aircraft, and dirigibles through to Apollo 11's splashdown in 1969.

Hansen, James R. *First Man: The Life of Neil A. Armstrong*. New York: Simon & Schuster, 2005. Highly acclaimed biography that recounts Armstrong's career in flying, portraying him as a great but reluctant hero.

Mallon, Thomas. "Moon Walker." *The New Yorker*, October 3, 2005. A shrewd, provocative review of Armstrong's career and examination of his character that came out, in part, as a review of James R. Hansen's biography.

Wagener, Leon. *One Giant Leap: Neil Armstrong's Stellar American Journey*. New York: Forge, 2004. A well-researched, balanced, and updated biography of Armstrong.

Westman, Paul. *Neil Armstrong: Space Pioneer*. Minneapolis, Minn.: Lerner, 1980. A preliminary biography of Armstrong in conversational style packed into sixty-four pages with fine black-and-white photographs largely supplied by NASA. Contains an appendix of all United States piloted space flights from Mercury 3 through Project Apollo.

Bessie Coleman

Aviator

Born: January 26, 1892; Atlanta, Texas
Died: April 30, 1926; Jacksonville, Florida
Areas of Achievement: Aviation and space exploration, theater and entertainment, civil rights, women's rights

Coleman was the first female African American pilot, performing stunts and aerial acrobatics before audiences in the United States and Europe. Facing explicit racism and ridicule from critics, she still earned a living with her skills as a flamboyant barnstorming flyer. She inspired many to pursue aviation at a time when that career was almost unthinkable for blacks, and for women. Her career preceded by several years that of aviator Amelia Earhart.

Early Life

Bessie Coleman was born to farm laborers George Coleman and Susan Coleman in Atlanta, Texas, near the Arkansas border. Three of her paternal great-grandparents were American Indian. When Coleman was two years old, her parents constructed a home in Waxahachie, Texas, south of Dallas. The racism the family faced because of their African and American Indian ancestry led George to move the family north to Indian Territory (now Oklahoma). Although George emphasized that the family would experience better socioeconomic conditions in Indian Territory, Susan stayed in Texas with several of her youngest children, including Coleman.

Intrigued by mathematics, Coleman walked several miles to the closest school for African American children when she did not have to pick cotton to earn wages for her family. Because her mother was illiterate, she read the Bible aloud to her family. Her mother encouraged literacy by subscribing to a bookmobile so her children had access to books. Coleman preferred biographies of notable African Americans such as Harriet Tubman. After completing eight grades, Coleman wanted an advanced education. By 1910, she enrolled in the Oklahoma Colored Agricultural and Normal University (now Langston University). Unprepared for college curricula, however, Coleman had to take basic courses. For a writing class, she read news accounts of pioneer male and female pilots.

Coleman returned to Texas in 1911 because she could not afford additional tuition. She started working as a housekeeper and launderer. The next year, she read a newspaper report that aviator Harriet Quimby (whom she admired), the first licensed U.S. female pilot and the first woman to fly across the English Channel, had died in an airplane crash.

Life's Work

In 1915, Coleman traveled by train to Chicago. Frustrated with her monotonous life in Texas, Coleman had written to her brothers, who were living in Chicago, about her plans to move there. She started working as a manicurist in a barber shop, tending to customers including Robert Abbott, publisher of the *Chicago Defender*, an African American newspaper. (Abbott would later support her financially.) While reading news articles, she learned about white female pilots who flew locally. She also read about African American World War I pilot Eugene Bullard. Coleman's brother, John, who had served in France during World War I, told her he had seen women aviators in that country. Aspiring to learn to fly, Coleman applied to flight schools in the United States but was refused admission because of her gender and race. Aware of Coleman's ambition, Abbott urged her to travel to France, where racism and sexism would not be as much of a

Bessie Coleman (Wikimedia Commons)

hindrance, offering to assist her financially. Preparing to travel overseas, Coleman took French language courses.

In November, 1920, Coleman sailed to France and went to Le Crotoy to study with Gaston Caudron and René Caudron at École d'Aviation des Frères Caudron(aviation school of the Caudron brothers). Although Coleman saw a fatal crash soon after she started instruction, she decided she would risk such hazards. In ground school, she learned mechanics and other basic skills before taking flying lessons in a Nieuport biplane.

On June 15, 1921, the French Fédération Aéronautique Internationale granted Coleman license #18310, the first license presented by the agency to an American woman. Moreover, she became the first African American woman to earn a pilot license anywhere. Coleman took additional lessons at Le Bourget Field in Paris until September, when she returned to the United States. Soon, the African American press was reporting her accomplishments on its front pages.

Coleman hoped for a career as a barnstormer, popular entertainment in the 1920's, needing to raise enough money to establish an aviation school for African Americans in the United States. Because stunt flying was so popular, Coleman sailed again to Europe in February, 1922, to learn aerobatics. She flew for six months in France, Germany, and Holland. Newsreels of her flights impressed American audiences and captured the attention of *The New York Times*, which published a brief article about her stunt flying in its August 14, 1922, edition. She had just arrived in New York to prepare for her first public flights in the United States.

On September 3, Coleman debuted at the Curtiss Field air show on Long Island, New York. Her next performance was held October 15 at Chicago's Checkerboard Airdrome, where her family watched. Later, Coleman offered to let people fly with her for five dollars. Also, she agreed to drop advertisements while she flew for the Coast Tire and Rubber Company, visiting executives in Oakland, California. After a visit to Los Angeles to examine military surplus aircraft, she purchased a Curtiss JN-4 biplane, flown during World War I.

On February 4, 1923, Coleman's engine in her recently acquired aircraft malfunctioned, causing her to crash in Santa Monica, California. While her fractured bones healed for three months, she continued her plans for what would be called the Coleman School of Aeronautics, placing advertisements in newspapers. After Coleman recovered, she barnstormed in Texas, including her hometown, and other cities in the South, Midwest, and New England. She spoke and showed films of her flights, and emphasized that aviation was a possible career for African Americans, especially women. Furthermore, she refused to fly at a show if its ticket sales and stands were segregated by race.

> *"The air is the only place free from prejudices. I knew we had no aviators, neither men nor women, and I knew the Race needed to be represented along this most important line, so I thought it my duty to risk my life to learn aviation..."*

Coleman prepared a media release that re-created her history, hoping to garner more media attention. African American newspapers published articles featuring Coleman, but other media often mocked her and her flying, if they mentioned her at all. Her stylish French flight clothing and showmanship attracted crowds who were astonished to see an African American aviator. To further her publicity, she permitted African American preachers to fly with her without cost, shrewdly realizing they would publicize her flights to their congregations.

In contrast to most pioneering female pilots, who were white and had money, Coleman had to seek sponsors and borrow or purchase used planes, which sometimes had technical problems. In early 1926, John Betsch, representing the Jacksonville, Florida, Negro Welfare League, invited Coleman to fly at a May festival. She also spoke at African American schools in Jacksonville, urging children to pursue their goals. Because Coleman was unable to lease a plane because of her race, a Florida patron provided her funds to buy and transport a plane from Texas. Mechanic William D. Wills flew the airplane to Jacksonville, commenting he had experienced some glitches in the air. Although aware of dangers, Coleman decided that performing to raise money merited the risks.

On Friday, April 30, Coleman and Wills took off from Paxon Field for a morning practice flight, during which Coleman surveyed the area for parachute landing sites while Wills piloted. Attaining an altitude of 3,000 feet, the airplane jolted into an unstoppable nosedive. Coleman, who had not fastened her safety belt, was ejected from the plane and fell approximately 1,500 feet to her death. The airplane plunged to the ground, killing Wills. Mourners in Florida and Chicago attended funerals for Coleman, who was buried in Chicago's Lincoln Cemetery.

Significance

In the face of racism and sexism, Coleman's perseverance inspired generations of pilots, including Willa Brown, the first African American woman to earn a commercial pilot license and who started a Chicago flight school, and Mae Jemison, the first African American female astronaut. Determined to fly, Coleman exulted in knowing that Jim Crow laws were not applicable in the air. Her efforts to educate and encourage African Americans about aviation led many to pursue careers as pilots or as professionals in other areas of aviation.

People began preserving Coleman's legacy soon after her death. In 1929, William J. Powell, a World War I veteran, started the Bessie Coleman Aero Club, a school in Los Angeles to teach flying. Bessie Coleman Aero Clubs soon formed around the country to promote African American aviation and stage air shows solely with African American pilots. Powell began distributing the Bessie Coleman Aero News in May, 1930. The Lambert-St. Louis International Airport depicted Coleman in its mural, Black Americans in Flight. On April 27, 1994, the U.S. Postal Service issued a stamp that featured Coleman, and in 2017, on the 125th anniversary of her birth, Google posted a Google Doodle in her honor.

Elizabeth D. Schafer

Further Reading

Freydberg, Elizabeth, and Amelia Hadley. *Bessie Coleman: The Brownskin Lady Bird.* New York: Garland, 1994. Based on the author's doctoral dissertation. Discusses contemporary women pilots, African American efforts to integrate flight, and popular culture and entertainment. Examines the importance of France to Coleman's training and career. Includes facsimiles of advertisements and correspondence.

Hardesty, Von, and Dominic Pisano. *Black Wings: The American Black in Aviation.* Washington, D.C.: Smithsonian Institution Press, 1987. Chronicles a 1984 National Air and Space Museum exhibition on black aviators. Includes a photograph of Coleman, a discussion of her significance as a pioneer African American pilot, and an examination of her influence on other minority aviators.

Lebow, Eileen F. *Before Amelia: Women Pilots in the Early Days of Aviation.* Washington, D.C.: Brassey's, 2002. Profiles pioneering European and U.S. female flyers, describing situations that Coleman and her contemporaries experienced regarding training and earning licenses, promoting barnstorming, enduring negative public opinion, and risking accidents and death. Illustrations, bibliographical essay, and appendix that provides license information.

Rich, Doris L. *Queen Bess: Daredevil Aviator.* Afterword by Mae Jemison. Washington, D.C.: Smithsonian Institution Press, 1993. Thoroughly researched account of Coleman's life and endeavors based on primary sources. Corrects errors perpetuated in other biographical accounts. Illustrations from Coleman's family, newspapers, and letters complement the text.

Walker, Mike. *Powder Puff Derby: Petticoat Flyers and Flying Flappers.* Chichester, England: John Wiley & Sons, 2003. Discusses Coleman in a chapter also examining the life of German test pilot Hanna Reitsch. Emphasizes their struggles and challenges and how Coleman overcame racial and gender discrimination

Jimmy Doolittle

Aviator

Born: December 14, 1896; Alameda, California
Died: September 27, 1993; Pebble Beach, California
Area of Achievement: Aviation and space exploration; military

Doolittle was a pioneer in American aviation, establishing numerous records and gathering data vital to aviation history. His defining accomplishment as a military pilot was an air raid on Tokyo in 1942 that shocked Japan during World War II. Also, as an aviation researcher, Doolittle combined test-flight information with laboratory data to prove that pilots needed visual aids to know wind and direction information. This was a major contribution to the knowledge of instruments and their use, making flying more precise and less dangerous.

Early Life

Jimmy Doolittle was born in Alameda, California. He was the only child of Frank Doolittle and Rosa Doolittle. While he was still an infant, his father left the family for Alaska in search of gold. After three years, the family was reunited in Nome, Alaska. The next eight years, in the most lawless town in Alaska, taught Doolittle independence and self-defense. A difficult relationship with his father, plus his mother's insistence that her son have better educational opportunities than those offered in

Alaska, led to a return to California in 1908. Now eleven years old, Doolittle lived with his mother in Los Angeles.

Reaching college age, Jimmy enrolled in the University of California, Berkeley, as a mine engineering major. His self-defense skills led him to amateur boxing. Although only five feet four inches tall, he became a West Coast bantamweight and middleweight champion. To earn extra money he briefly turned to professional boxing.

Jimmy was a college junior in 1917 when the United States entered World War I. Having already developed a strong interest in aviation, he enlisted in the U.S. Army's Signal Enlisted Reserve Corps as a flying cadet. Quickly earning his pilot's license, he became a second lieutenant in the Army Air Corps. He served in the Air Corps until 1930, leaving as a major.

During these early years, Doolittle served as an instructor pilot and engaged in air aerobatics, with the goal of breaking aviation records. His first record came in 1922 when he crossed the North American continent from Florida to California, becoming the first to do so in less than twenty-four hours. He finished his bachelor's degree at Berkeley the same year.

> "*There's nothing stronger than the heart of a volunteer.*"

LIFE'S WORK

In 1923, Doolittle, with a two-year leave of absence from the military, enrolled at the Massachusetts Institute of Technology. By 1925 he had earned both a master's degree and a Ph.D. in aeronautical engineering. His doctoral dissertation, "Wind Velocity Gradient and Its Effect on Flying Characteristics," disproved the assumption that pilots knew instinctively the direction and speed of the wind, as well as the direction in which their plane was flying. Doolittle combined test-flight information with laboratory data to prove that pilots needed visual aids to know wind and direction information. This was a major contribution to the knowledge of instruments and their use, making flying more precise and less dangerous.

Doolittle's daredevil feats reached their peak in the last half of the 1920's. By 1925 he had won all major racing trophies, including the Schneider Trophy for winning a seaplane race and flying his Curtiss Navy seaplane an average of 232 miles per hour. This feat earned Doolittle the nickname Lone Pilot. Taking another leave of absence from the Air Corps in April, 1926, he did demonstration flights in South America. On one occasion, after breaking his ankles in an accident unrelated to flying, he flew with his ankles strapped to the plane's rudders, leaving his parachute behind since he could not have bailed out in an emergency.

In 1927, after recovering from his injuries, Doolittle, at Wright Field in Dayton, Ohio, accomplished a feat previously thought impossible. In what was called an "outside loop," he dived in his Curtiss fighter plane from 10,000 feet, reached a speed of 280 miles per hour, bottomed out upside down, then climbed to complete the loop.

Major Doolittle left the Air Corps in 1930, but continued his record-setting exploits as a civilian. Working for Shell Oil Company in 1931, he established a new speed record, flying from Burbank, California, to Cleveland, Ohio. He set a new cross-county record the same year. In 1932 he averaged 252 miles per hour, with a top speed of 406 miles per hour, in winning the Thompson Trophy race in Cleveland.

Doolittle, despite his risky aerobatics, was dedicated to improving aviation safety. Based on the ideas of his doctoral dissertation, he became the first pilot to fly with total reliance on instruments, sometimes called "flying blind."

Following the German invasion of Poland in September, 1939, Doolittle reentered the Army Air Corps. Although the United States was not yet directly involved in the war, it was obvious that the nation would soon need experienced pilots. After the Japanese attack on Pearl Harbor, Doolittle was promoted to lieutenant colonel.

Just nineteen weeks after Pearl Harbor, Doolittle successfully carried out the plan that made his name a household word in the United States. His mission is best summarized by the headline that ran in newspapers across the country, "TOKYO BOMBED! DOOLITTLE DOOD IT!"

Early in 1942, Doolittle was chosen to lead a retaliatory, post-Pearl Harbor raid on Japan. The Seventeenth Bombardment Group was formed and began special and top-secret training. Sixteen specially equipped B-25 bombers, each with a five-person volunteer crew, were soon assigned to the mission. Two aircraft carriers also were involved: The USS *Hornet* was modified to carry and launch the bombers, and the USS *Enterprise* led a task force to provide support. Because of the large distance between the *Hornet* and the island of Japan, the plan was for the bombers, after dropping their bombs, to continue on and land in an area of China unoccupied by Japan instead of returning to the *Hornet* at sea.

On April 18, without the element of surprise because the Japanese unexpectedly sighted the *Enterprise*, the bombers were launched; they hit their military targets. Thirteen bombs were dropped around Tokyo, and three were dropped on as many Japanese cities. Although the physical damage was minimal, the psychological blow to Japan was tremendous. However, the planes failed to reach the safe airfields of China. Most crash-landed in the China Sea or in Japanese-occupied China. One landed in the Soviet Union. Five crew members were killed and eight were captured by the Japanese, who executed three. Another captured crew member died of his injuries. In total, seventy-one of the eighty men involved in the operation, including Doolittle, survived; most were saved by the Chinese, but some returned with life-altering injuries.

Shortly after the raid, Doolittle was promoted to brigadier general, skipping the rank of colonel. In May, 1942, President Franklin D. Roosevelt presented General Doolittle with the Congressional Medal of Honor.

During the remainder of the war, Doolittle commanded the Twelfth Air Force in North Africa and the Eighth Air Force in Europe and in the Pacific. He retired from active duty as a lieutenant general in 1959. He gave up action flying in 1961. Curiosity, however, led him to test-fly several new military aircraft, including the F-100, which was the first supersonic fighter, and the huge B-52 bomber. These were his last flights as first pilot, and, surprisingly, he said later that he never missed it.

As a civilian Doolittle was chair of the board of Space Technology Laboratories. He enjoyed his retirement years with Joe, his wife of more than seventy years. The two eventually took a trip to Alaska, a visit Doolittle had promised her long before. He died at the age of ninety-six in 1993.

Significance

The bombing of Tokyo and other cities in Japan caused the Japanese to accelerate their plans of expansion. A premature attack on Midway Island in June, 1942, designed to cripple the U.S. aircraft carrier fleet, ended with the loss of four of their own carriers and none from the U.S. Navy.

Doolittle's accomplishments in early aviation technology alone were enough to rank him as a legend, especially given his innovative idea that instrument flying was safe. His wartime activities led to honors by Great Britain, France, China, Belgium, Poland, and Ecuador.

His military service to his own country, before, during, and after World War II, led to numerous honors. The culmination of those honors came in 1985, when President Ronald Reagan presented him with an honorary promotion to the elite rank of four-star general.

Glenn L. Swygart

Further Reading

Larson, Ted W. *Thirty Seconds over Tokyo*. New York: Random House, 1943. Written by the pilot of plane seven of Doolittle's raid, who lost both of his legs crashing into the China Sea. Provides the most detailed account of the raid and the experiences of the crew after the raid, including those captured by the Japanese.

Murray, Williamson. *War in the Air, 1914-1945*. London: Cassell, Wellington House, 1999. Places Doolittle, the raid, and Doolittle's later World War II leadership in the context of early military aviation history. Reveals his impact on the bombing missions that became a vital part of World War II.

Nelson, Craig. *The First Heroes: The Extraordinary Story of the Doolittle Raid, America's First World War II Victory*. New York: Viking Press, 2002. Based on original accounts of aging survivors. Excellent photos of war leaders and events, including the listing and photos of all crew members of all planes involved in the raid.

Thomas, Lowell, and Edward Jablonski. *Doolittle: A Biography*. Garden City, N.Y.: Doubleday, 1976. Perhaps the best of several biographies of Doolittle, all of which repeat the same basic information, including Doolittle's autobiography *I Could Never Be So Lucky Again*, written with Carroll Glines in 1991.

Wilson, William R. "Jimmy Doolittle Reminisces About World War II." *American History*, August, 1997. Based on comments by Doolittle in about 1980. The author first met Doolittle about six months after the raid. Includes biographical and autobiographical information.

AMELIA EARHART

Aviator

Born: July 24, 1897; Atchison, Kansas
Disappeared: July 2, 1937; Pacific Ocean
Area of Achievement: Aviation and space exploration

By being the first woman to fly across the Atlantic and by establishing numerous other flying records, Earhart helped to promote commercial aviation and advance the cause of women in aviation.

EARLY LIFE

Amelia Earhart (eh-MEEL-yeh EHR-hahrt), the daughter of Amy Otis and Edwin Stanton Earhart, was born in the home of her maternal grandparents in Atchison, Kansas. Her grandfather was Alfred G. Otis, a pioneer Atchison settler who became a prominent lawyer, banker, and federal district court judge. Her father worked for a railroad as an attorney and claims agent.

Earhart's early childhood was spent in Kansas City, Kansas, where she and her younger sister learned to ride horseback. When her father accepted a job in Des Moines, Iowa, in 1905, Earhart and her sister remained for a year in Atchison, where she later recalled, "There were regular games and school and mud-ball fights, picnics, and exploring raids up and down the bluffs of the Missouri River." After joining her father in Des Moines, Earhart attended school and began reading the books that further encouraged her spirit of adventure. Sir Walter Scott, Charles Dickens, George Eliot, and William Makepeace Thackeray were her favorite authors, and she and her sister made up imaginary journeys while they played in an abandoned carriage.

When her father went to work for the Great Northern railroad, the Earharts moved to St. Paul, Minnesota, but Edwin's alcoholism grew worse, and her mother took her daughters to Chicago, where Earhart was graduated from Hyde Park High School in June, 1916. She attended the Ogontz School in Rydal, Pennsylvania, then went to Toronto, Canada, where her sister was in school. In Toronto, she saw wounded veterans of World War I and became a Red Cross volunteer. She worked at Spadina Military Hospital, where she came to know and admire the young fliers of the Royal Flying Corps. In 1918, she was ill with pneumonia and went to live with her sister in Northampton, Massachusetts. While her sister was enrolled at Smith College, Earhart took a course in automobile repair. In 1919, she moved to were chosen to study medicine at Columbia University but left after a year to join her parents in Los Angeles.

The aviation industry was just beginning to develop in Southern California, and Earhart was attracted to the air shows and flying demonstrations at local airports. She took her first airplane ride from the Glendale airport and soon convinced her parents to help her take flying lessons with a pioneer woman pilot, Neta Snook. In June, 1921, Earhart made her first solo flight in a Kinner Airster. One year later, she had saved two thousand dollars to buy a three-cylinder Kinner Canary, a plane in which she set a woman's altitude record of fourteen thousand feet. Her career as a pilot was launched.

LIFE'S WORK

Even in 1922, however, flying was expensive, and paid employment for women in aviation was limited. When her parents were divorced, Earhart sold her plane and returned to Massachusetts, where she taught English to immigrants and became a social worker at Denison House, a Boston settlement. She was able to combine her interests in social work and aviation, on one occasion flying over Boston and dropping leaflets announcing a Denison

Amelia Earhart (Library of Congress)

House street fair and on another judging a model airplane contest for the National Playground Association.

In 1928, she was selected by the publisher George P. Putnam to fly with pilot Wilmer Stutz and mechanic Lou Gordon in a Fokker trimotor across the Atlantic. The plane, named Friendship, had been purchased from the explorer Richard Byrd by Amy Phipps Guest, an American flying enthusiast who had married and settled in England. When Guest was unable to make the flight herself, she asked Putnam to find a young woman (he found Earhart) to represent her in the promotion of women in aviation. On June 3, Friendship left Boston for Halifax, Nova Scotia, and Trepassy, Newfoundland. Delayed by bad weather for several days, the plane left Trepassy on June 17 and landed the following day at Burry Port, Wales. Earhart was given a hero's welcome on her return to New York.

Because her flight came only a little more than a year after the solo flight by Charles A. Lindbergh, and because of her tall, slender build and short, blond hair, she was nicknamed Lady Lindy, but she preferred to be called "AE." Within a few months Putnam rushed her account of the flight, *Twenty Hours Forty Minutes* (1928), into print. The book is part autobiography, part journal of the flight, and part advocacy of flying in general. It is the third part that is most interesting because of her observations on the future of flying and on the role of women in aviation.

After stating that the remarkable thing about flying is that it is not remarkable, Earhart goes on to discuss the need for more attractive airports, a review of safety regulations, and better weather reporting. Women will have a role to play in all these areas, she asserts, because they have already had a major impact on the automobile industry. The airplane will be used for leisure and recreation, and the growing purchasing power of American women will help to shape the airline industry. Earhart concludes her book with a characteristically honest assessment of the ways in which her life has been changed by her sudden fame.

For the remainder of her life, Earhart campaigned tirelessly for the cause of women in flying. She participated in many cross-country air races, flew an autogyro (a forerunner of the helicopter), and was one of the founders of an organization of licensed women pilots, the Ninety-nine Club. In 1932, she was elected a member of the Society of Women Geographers. She also wrote a column on aviation for Cosmopolitan magazine. Her advice was sought by many airlines and airplane manufacturers, and she became a model for young women throughout the country.

In 1931, she married Putnam, who had been managing her career. Her second book, *The Fun of It,* was published in 1932. In it Earhart adds details about her childhood and further explains her attraction to flying, especially to unusual aerial maneuvers known as "stunting." I had fun trying to do [stunts] . . . so much so, in fact, I have sometimes thought that transport companies would do well to have a "recreation airplane" for their pilots who don't have a chance to play in the big transports or while on duty. If a little stunt ship were available, the men could go up 5000 feet, and "turn it inside out" to relieve the monotony of hours of straight flying.

Her assurance that flying was safe and fun and her example as the first woman to fly the Atlantic alone increased her popularity with the public. Earhart's solo flight from Harbor Grace, Newfoundland, to Culmore, Ireland, May 21-22, 1932, won for her the Distinguished Flying Cross from the Congress of the United States, an award from the French Legion of Honor, and a medal from the National Geographic Society.

In 1935, she became the first person to fly alone from Hawaii to California and the first to fly nonstop from Mexico City to Newark, New Jersey. The trustees of Purdue University purchased a twin-engine Lockheed Electra for her, and she began to plan a roundthe- world flight. After several false starts and minor accidents, Earhart and her navigator, Fred Noonan, took off from Miami, Florida, on June 1, 1937. A month of flying brought them across the Atlantic, Africa, and southern Asia to Lae, New Guinea. She and Noonan took off July 2, intending to land and refuel on tiny Howland Island in the middle of the Pacific Ocean. Several hours later, the Coast Guard cutter Itasca, anchored off Howland Island, heard a radio message from Earhart that she was lost and running low on fuel. Neither the plane nor its pilot and navigator were ever found.

Because the Japanese claimed many of the islands in the mid-Pacific, rumors grew that Earhart and Noonan had crashed on a Japanese-held island and been captured and killed. After World War II, attempts were made to find the wreckage and confirm the rumors, but no convincing evidence had come to light. However, in late 2014, the International Group for Historic Aircraft Recovery (TIGHAR) claimed that a small piece of aluminum plane wreckage discovered on a nearby island in 1991 could very well have belonged to Earhart's Electra. The group spotted a similar metal patch in the photograph of Earhart and her plane captured before taking off from Miami. They believe that the piece served as a modification in the field. To further support this connection, the group compared the patch's size, shape, and rivulet holes with an

Earhart reviewing maps and charts in Hawaii. (Wikimedia Commons)

Electra being restored in Kansas, deeming it a match. This discovery would bolster the theory that the pilot and her navigator were forced to land on Nikumaroro after running out of fuel rather than crashing in the Pacific. While TIGHAR wants to travel back to Nikumaroro to see if an earlier anomoly found close to the island on sonar could be more of the wreckage, critics and skeptics have argued that there are still too many variables involved to make this possible link definitive.

> "*Please know that I am aware of the hazards. I want to do it because I want to do it. Women must try to do things as men have tried. When they fail, their failure must be a challenge to others.*"

SIGNIFICANCE

Earhart was one of the most appealing heroes in an age of American hero worship. Like Lindbergh and Byrd, Earhart pioneered air travel by establishing flying records and opening new routes. Like Babe Didrikson Zaharias the athlete and Louise Arner Boyd the Arctic explorer, Earhart showed that women had a place in fields that were generally restricted to men.

Although she was criticized during her life for using her fame for profit at various times she promoted Lucky Strike cigarettes, luggage, and sports clothes Earhart remained essentially a private person. Because her parents believed that girls should have the same opportunities as boys, she was able to learn to fly. Because she believed that she should help others by sharing her experiences, she maintained a hectic schedule of flying and lecturing.

Once she had been given the opportunity to be the first woman to fly across the Atlantic, Earhart dedicated herself to flying. She was able to combine pleasure with business, and she worked hard at both. Success brought her into contact with other notable women from First Lady Eleanor Roosevelt to film star Mary Pickford. Earhart was also a celebrity, and her untimely death at the age of thirty-nine enshrined her in the hearts of her generation.

Earhart was a product of the social changes in the United States between the world wars. In many ways she epitomized her generation's desire to break with the past and to create a better world. She captured something of that spirit in one of her poems, which begins,

> Courage is the price that life exacts for granting peace.
> The soul that knows it not, knows no release
> From little things;
> Knows not the livid loneliness of fear
> Nor mountain heights, where bitter joy can hear
> The sound of wings.

Bernard Mergen

FURTHER READING

Backus, Jean L. *Letters from Amelia: 1901–1937.* Boston: Beacon, 1982. Print.

Earhart, Amelia. *The Fun of It: Random Records of My Own Flying and of Women in Aviation.* 1932. Reprint. Detroit: Gale Research, 1975. Print.

---. *Last Flight.* 1937. Reprint. Detroit: Gale Research, 1975. Print.

---. *Twenty Hours Forty Minutes.* 1928. Reprint. New York: Arno, 1980. Print.

Gillespie, Ric. *Finding Amelia: The True Story of the Earhart Disappearance.* Annapolis: Naval Inst., 2006. Print.

Loomis, Vincent V. *Amelia Earhart: The Final Story.* New York: Random, 1985. Print.

McCoy, Terrence. "The Metal Fragment That Could Solve the Mystery of Amelia Earhart's Disappearance." *Washington Post*. Washington Post, 30 Oct. 2014. Web.

Morrissey, Muriel Earhart. *Courage Is the Price*. Wichita: McCormick, 1963. Print.

Pellegreno, Ann Holtgren. *World Flight: The Earhart Trail*. Ames: Iowa State UP, 1971. Print.

Putnam, George Palmer. *Soaring Wings*. New York: Harcourt, 1939. Print.

Van Pelt, Lori. *Amelia Earhart: The Sky's No Limit*. New York: Forge, 2005. Print.

JOHN GLENN

Astronaut and US senator

Born: July 18, 1921; Cambridge, Ohio
Died: December 8, 2016; Columbus, Ohio
Area of Achievement: Aviation and space exploration, politics

On February 20, 1962, Glenn became the first American to orbit Earth in a flight that reduced the Soviet Union's early lead in the space race. Glenn later served as a US senator from Ohio in four consecutive terms from 1974 to 1998, made an unsuccessful bid for the presidency in 1984, and, in 1998, became the oldest person to fly in space during his flight aboard the space shuttle Discovery.

John Glenn (Wikimedia Commons)

EARLY LIFE

John Glenn was born in Cambridge, Ohio, to John and Clara Glenn. Glenn and his sister Jean grew up in New Concord, Ohio, a largely Presbyterian town of about two thousand inhabitants where their father ran a heating and plumbing business and, at one time, also owned a Chevrolet car dealership. Glenn was an honor student at New Concord High School and played several varsity sports. After graduating from high school in 1939, Glenn enrolled in Muskingum College (now Muskingum University) in New Concord, an institution affiliated with the Presbyterian Church. Glenn served in the choir of the local Presbyterian church, and later became a Sunday school teacher. When he was in the Mercury program, Glenn told the press, "I am a Presbyterian and I take my religion very seriously." Glenn played on the Muskingum football team and enrolled in a Navy-sponsored civilian pilot training program.

After the United States' entry into World War II, Glenn joined the Navy in March 1942. He took advantage of an opportunity to receive his commission in the Marine Corps at Corpus Christi Naval Air Training Center and, in March 1943, became a Marine lieutenant and Navy aviator. Returning briefly to New Concord, Glenn married Anna Castor (whom he had known since age six) in April 1943, before being shipped out to the Pacific theater. From February 1944 to February 1945, Glenn flew fifty-nine combat missions in F4U Corsairs for VMO-155, based at Roi-Namur and Kwajalein, against Japanese positions in the Marshall Islands campaign. His unit employed napalm bombs as its primary ordnance on the dive bomb missions. For his World War II service, Glenn earned two Distinguished Flying Crosses (DFCs) and ten Air Medals.

Glenn served at several Marine air bases in the United States from February 1945 to December 1946 and did patrol duty in northern China and Guam from 1947 to 1949. While in China, Glenn flew Corsairs with VMF-218, based near Beijing. The Glenns' first child, John David, was born in 1946, and their second, Carolyn, in 1947. Glenn served as flight instructor from 1949 to 1951 at Corpus Christi. He attended Amphibious Warfare School in Quantico, Virginia, in 1951–52, and a jet training course before requesting combat in the Korean War. Based primarily at P'ohang, Glenn flew for VMF-311, and, for a time, as an exchange pilot with the Air Force. In his ninety combat missions in Korea from February to September 1953, Glenn piloted F9F Panther jets and F86 Sabre jets (fighter-interceptors), and he shot down three enemy MIGs in the last nine days of the war. Some of his missions were along the Yalu River. Glenn earned two more DFCs and eight more Air Medals for his Korean War service.

> "*The most important thing we can do is inspire young minds and to advance the kind of science, math and technology education that will help youngsters take us to the next phase of space travel.*"

LIFE'S WORK

Glenn rose steadily in the ranks, becoming a captain in 1945, a major in 1952, and a colonel in 1959. He became a test pilot in 1954, and on July 16, 1957, as a pilot for Project Bullet, set a record for the first coast-to-coast nonstop supersonic flight in an F8U-1 Crusader jet (Los Angeles to New York). He received his fifth DFC for this event, and the attention he received from the transcontinental flight got him an invitation to be on the television show *Name That Tune*.

In the following year, Glenn volunteered for the National Aeronautics and Space Administration's (NASA) Project Mercury man-in-space program. On April 9, 1959, he was one of seven military test pilots (but the lone Marine) chosen to become the United States' pioneer astronaut corps, a group that became known to the public as the Mercury Seven. Glenn and his Project Mercury colleagues performed a variety of grueling physical and psychological simulations in preparation for the experience of single-person space flight. Glenn's technical expertise as a pilot enabled him to aid in the design of the Mercury cockpit and control system. Although he was the oldest of the Mercury astronauts, Glenn initiated a rigorous daily personal training regimen in addition to regular rounds of NASA tests. He visited his family only on weekends. The purpose of Project Mercury was to put astronauts in Earth orbit in short-duration, single-person flights as the preliminary stage toward the anticipated goal of lunar missions and to beat out the Soviet Union in the space race amid a climate of rising Cold War tensions.

Glenn was chosen to pilot the first Mercury orbital flight, originally scheduled for December 20, 1961. The Soviet Vostok program had already placed two cosmonauts in orbit by this time, and NASA, as well as the American public, regarded Project Mercury's first orbital flight as a means to cut the advantage held by the Soviets since their 1957 launch of the satellite Sputnik. Glenn's mission, however, had to be canceled ten times over the next two months because of technical problems and inclement weather.

Finally, on February 20, 1962, Glenn became the first American to orbit Earth. Glenn blasted off into orbit from Cape Canaveral, Florida, aboard his small, bell-shaped

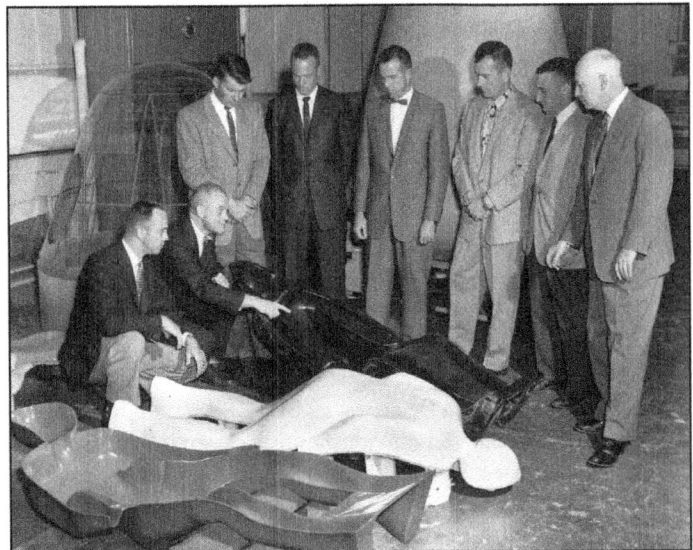

The Mercury 7 astronauts examine their 'couches.' Each astronaut's couch was molded to fit his body to help withstand the G-loads of the launch. Plaster casts of the astronauts were created in order to properly mold the couches. Left to right are Alan Shepard, John Glenn, Walter Schirra, Scott Carpenter, Gordon Cooper, Deke Slayton, Gus Grissom and Bob Gilruth. (Wikimedia Commons)

capsule, *Friendship 7*. Glenn's three orbits, covering 81,000 miles, lasted 4 hours and 56 minutes. His average altitude ranged between 99 and 162 miles. Flying backward, Glenn narrated his visual experiences through the capsule's small, overhead porthole. He performed a variety of experiments and, with the camera he brought along, also became a pioneer of space photography.

Toward the middle of the mission, Mercury Control's monitoring panels received a signal indicating that the heat shield on Glenn's capsule might have come loose from its securing connections. The flight directors feared that Glenn and his capsule might incinerate upon reentry if he jettisoned his retropack (attached to the outside of the heat shield) as planned. Glenn was instructed not to jettison the retropack and to fly the capsule manually during reentry. He saw pieces of the retropack break free and melt from the intense heat, but the heat shield held in place. There was an atmosphere of exceptional tension at Mercury Control during the four-minute-and-twenty-second blackout period.

Glenn splashed down 800 miles southeast of Bermuda in the Atlantic Ocean and was picked up by the USS *Noa*. He was called to the White House, and President John F. Kennedy presented him with a special medal. Glenn was cheered in victory parades by a quarter of a million people in Washington, DC, and by four million people in New York City. While addressing a special joint session of Congress, Glenn made contacts that would serve him well in his future political career. Although he wished to return to space, it was widely believed that NASA passed him by in the Gemini and Apollo programs because he was considered by the administration as too great of a national asset to risk in future missions.

Glenn retired from the Marine Corps in 1965 and served as an executive with Royal Crown International before being elected as a Democrat to the US Senate from Ohio in 1974. Glenn had previously unsuccessfully run for the Senate twice. In 1964, he was injured in a home accident and had to withdraw, and in 1970, he was defeated in the Democratic primary by Howard Metzenbaum. He won in 1974 by beating Republican contender Ralph Park, former mayor of Cleveland. He was reelected in 1980, 1986, and 1992, becoming the first senator from Ohio elected to four terms. In the Senate, Glenn served on the Governmental Affairs Committee, the Foreign Relations Committee, the Armed Services Committee, the

President John F. Kennedy receives a gift of an American flag from Glenn (right); Glenn carried the flag in his space suit during his orbital flight aboard Mercury-Atlas 6, also known as Friendship 7. (Wikimedia Commons)

Select Committee on Intelligence, and the Special Committee on Aging. In 1978, he coauthored the Nonproliferation Act.

Glenn ran for the presidency in 1984 after the release of a major film based on Tom Wolfe's book *The Right Stuff* (1980), an epic about the Mercury program. Glenn, however, lost in the Democratic Party's primary to former Vice President Walter Mondale. Glenn lent his support to fellow Democrat Bill Clinton in the 1992 presidential election and appeared live on television with the president in Ohio during Clinton's journey to the Democratic National Convention in 1996. On the thirty-fifth anniversary of his historic flight (February 20, 1997), Glenn announced that he would retire from the Senate at the end of his fourth term in 1998.

Glenn had been lobbying for a spot on a future space shuttle mission since 1996, and despite some criticism for preferential treatment, NASA announced in January 1998, that he would serve as a payload specialist on an October 1998 flight of the shuttle *Discovery* (STS-95). The detailed medical records on Glenn from Project Mercury were used as a yardstick to measure metabolic and bone density changes that occurred in zero-gravity conditions. Glenn noted before the mission that such a study was important because the changes that occur in young astronauts in zero-gravity are similar to those experienced by the elderly on Earth.

Glenn's flight on *Discovery* lasted for almost nine days, orbited Earth 134 times, and spanned 3.6 million miles. The seven-person international crew included astronauts from Japan and Spain. Glenn provided blood, urine, and saliva samples on the mission for study. The mission also provided Glenn with yet another record: at seventy-seven years old, he became the oldest human ever to undertake space flight.

In addition to performing age-related experiments involving Glenn, the crew deployed a "Spartan" satellite designed to photograph the sun (specifically the solar corona and solar winds), which orbited for two days until the crew retrieved it. They also deployed the Hubble Space Telescope Orbital Systems Test Platform. The experiments for which Glenn was responsible involved the separation and purification of biological materials. During the flight, Glenn exchanged e-mail with President Clinton. Glenn wrote in his memoirs that his shuttle flight at age seventy-seven should serve as evidence that elderly astronauts can "continue to go into space as active mission participants and research subjects."

On his return, Glenn and his six crew mates were honored with parades in Houston and New York City. He became one of only a few people (including Amelia Earhart) to receive more than one ticker tape parade in New York. Glenn published his memoirs in 1999 and helped found the John Glenn Institute of Public Service and Public Policy at Ohio State University in Columbus. The institute houses Glenn's archives and artifacts of his career. Glenn's boyhood home was restored at its original location and became a historic site. Both Glenn and his wife served on the board of trustees of their alma mater, Muskingum College. They lived in Columbus and maintained another home near Washington, DC. In 2010, Glenn received an honorary doctorate from Ohio Northern University. In 2012, Glenn was a part of the ceremonial transfer of *Discovery* from NASA to the Smithsonian, where it would be permanently displayed. Glenn openly criticized the discontinuation of the shuttle program, saying the grounding the crafts would impede research efforts.

Glenn died on December 8, 2016, after being hospitalized at the James Cancer Hospital of the Ohio State University Wexner Medical Center. He was ninety-five years old. After lying in state at the Ohio Statehouse, he was interred at Arlington National Cemetery.

Significance

Glenn's impressive political and military careers are usually overshadowed by his career as a pioneering astronaut as a member of the Mercury Seven, as the first American to orbit Earth, and as the oldest person to achieve space flight. His February 1962 orbital flight was, without a doubt, a crucial moment in the space race between the United States and the Soviet Union and was therefore also an important political moment in the Cold War confrontation between the two superpowers. At the time, Americans tended to regard Glenn's flight as a sign that the United States had caught up with the Soviets and would soon take the lead in the space race, fulfilling President Kennedy's 1961 claim that the United States would put a person on the moon by the end of the decade. Glenn, however, humbly insisted before his mission, "This is a technological problem, not a space race. Our primary concern is not to beat the Russians but to put a man up and bring him back safely." His February 1962 mission proved that this goal was indeed attainable. Glenn's October 1998 space flight aboard the shuttle *Discovery* broke another record: He became the oldest person to fly in space. The mission, however, was not intended simply to boost morale in the space program; the scientific data collected from the mission was employed in studies on aging and zero gravity.

William E. Watson

Further Reading

"A Rocket Man at 90." *People* 20 Feb. 2012: 100–106. Print.

Bell, Joseph N. *Seven into Space: The Story of the Mercury Astronauts*. London: Ebury, 1960. Print.

Carpenter, M. Scott, et al. *We Seven: By the Astronauts Themselves*. New York: Simon, 1962. Print.

Committee on Aeronautical and Space Sciences, United States Senate. *Project Mercury: Man-in-Space Program of the National Aeronautics and Space Administration*. Washington, DC.: GPO, 1959. Print.

Glenn, John, and Nick Taylor. *John Glenn: A Memoir*. New York: Bantam, 1999. Print.

Kluger, Jeffrey. "John Glenn's Friendship 7 Flight." *Time* 27 Feb. 2012: 17. Print.

Launius, Roger D. *Frontiers of Space Exploration*. Westport: Greenwood, 2004. Print.

McDougall, Walter A. *The Heavens and the Earth: A Political History of the Space Age*. New York: Basic, 1985. Print.

Shepard, Alan, Deke Slayton, Jay Barbree, and Howard Benedict. *Moon Shot: The Inside Story of America's Race to the Moon*. Atlanta: Turner, 1994. Print.

Wilford, John Noble. "John Glenn, American Hero of the Space Age, Dies at 95." *The New York Times*, 8 Dec. 2016, www.nytimes.com/2016/12/08/us/john-glenn-dies.html.

Winkler, David F. "Godspeed, John Glenn." *Sea Power* Feb. 2012: 48. Print.

Wolfe, Tom. *The Right Stuff*. New York: Bantam, 1980. Print.

HAZEL YING LEE

Pilot

Born: August 24, 1912; Portland, Oregon
Died: November 25, 1944; Great Falls, Montana
Also known as: Hazel Lee; Ah Ying
Areas of Achievement: Aviation, military, women's rights

The child of Chinese immigrants, Hazel Ying Lee became the first Asian American woman to fly for the United States Armed Forces, serving with one of the Army Air Force's first all-female flight divisions. She had attempted to join China's air force after the Japanese invasion but was prevented because of her gender. Instead, she served with the US Army Air Force civilian pilots' division, for which she delivered supplies and aircraft until her death in 1944.

Hazel Ying Lee (Wikimedia Commons)

EARLY LIFE

Hazel Ah Ying Lee was born in Portland, Oregon, in 1912, one of eight children born to immigrant parents from Canton (Guangdong), China. Lee came from an affluent family and enjoyed the benefits of that lifestyle, learning to drive a car and engaging in other activities that most Chinese women did not.

Following high school, Lee faced prejudice in finding a job. Asian Americans had been facing discrimination since the Chinese exclusion acts of 1882 and 1924, which restricted their immigration and employment. She had to settle for working as an elevator operator at H. Liebes & Co., a department store in Portland.

In 1932, Lee took her first flight in an aircraft, after which she became obsessed with learning to fly. Both Lee and her brother Victor took pilot's training and joined the Chinese Flying Club of Portland. Lee was a rarity as a woman pilot, as less than 1 percent of pilots in the United States were women.

LIFE'S WORK

Lee's experiences with racism left her with a strong sense of Chinese nationalism, and when Japan invaded Manchuria in 1933, Lee and her brother sailed to China and attempted to enlist as pilots. Lee's brother was accepted, but the Chinese air force rejected Lee because of her gender. Consequently, she moved to Canton and flew for a private airline. When Japan bombed Canton in 1937, Lee and her brother escaped to Hong Kong. Lee returned to the United States in 1938 and moved to New York, where she took a job shipping armaments to the Chinese Nationalist Army.

Following the 1941 Japanese attack on Pearl Harbor, the US Army Air Force was desperate for personnel and began recruiting civilian pilots. In 1943, the US Army Air Force created the Women Airforce Service Pilots (WASP), a division of female civilian pilots headed by pioneering aviators Nancy Harkness Love and Jacqueline Cochran, who personally selected pilots for the program.

> "*I held a moment in my hand, brilliant as a star, fragile as a flower, a tiny sliver of one hour. Ah! I didn't know, I held opportunity.*"

Lee was one of at least two thousand women who applied to join WASP. She was accepted to the fourth class, 43-W-4, and sent for a six-month training program at Avenger Field in Sweetwater, Texas. During her training, Lee met and married Major Lin Cheung "Clifford" Louie,

Lee reviews her performance after a training flight in 1944. (Wikimedia Commons)

a Chinese Nationalist pilot who was recovering after being wounded in action.

On one of her training flights, Lee was forced to make an emergency landing in a cornfield in Kansas. When the farmer mistook her for an invading Japanese pilot, he held her at bay with his pitchfork until his son called the base and confirmed her identity.

After training, Lee was assigned to the Air Transport Command's Third Ferrying Squadron at Romulus Army Air Base in Michigan. She was popular with her WASP colleagues and developed a habit of inscribing the Chinese characters of her fellow pilots' nicknames on the tails of their planes. Friends described her as humorous and fun loving, often playing practical jokes on the other pilots.

Lee attended Pursuit School in September 1944, qualifying her to fly single-engine fighter aircraft, including the P-39, P-47, P-63, and her favorite, the P-51 Mustang. In November 1944, Lee traveled to Niagara Falls, New York, to pick up a P-63 aircraft that was to be delivered to Great Falls, Montana. When she was making the return flight, on November 23, the Great Falls airstrip was crowded with an unusual number of returning aircraft. Lee and another pilot approached the strip at the same time and collided before either could pull away. Lee was pulled from the burning wreckage but died two days later from burns sustained in the accident.

Despite dying in performance of military duties, Lee was not given a military funeral, and her family was denied benefits usually given to the families of armed service members. In 1979,

Congress passed Public Law 95-202, which led to formal recognition of the contribution of women service

Women and World War II

Despite the overwhelming demand for women in the military during World War II, the Women's Army Corps (WAC) bill, which granted women equal status in the service, was not passed officially until the summer of 1943. During the ninety-day conversion period following WAC's passing, more than 60,000 women were given the option of remaining on as soldiers or going home. By this time, women were serving both stateside and abroad, in Japan, Iran, India, and parts of Africa.

Formed in September 1942, the Women's Auxiliary Ferrying Squadron (WAFS) became a bourgeoning branch of the Army during this time, partly because of efforts by pilots Jacqueline Cochran and Nancy Harkness Love. Cochran quickly established the Women's Flying Training Detachment (WFTD) in the Army Air Forces, and by November 28, the WAFS flew its first mission. Close to four hundred women graduated from the program in 1943, which led Cochran to merge the WAFS and WFTD to form the Women Airforce Service Pilots in August 1943. By the time that program disbanded in 1944, more than 120,000 women were serving in approximately four hundred of six hundred formerly off-limits military occupational specialties (MOS), including air-traffic controllers, instructors, and trainers of carrier pigeons and dogs.

pilots and conferred military status on Lee and the other women who served in the WASP division.

SIGNIFICANCE

Lee was the first Asian American woman to fly for the US military, making her a pioneer in both women's rights and Asian American achievement. In fall 2007, the Museum of Chinese in the Americas in New York opened a permanent exhibit about the life and career of Lee. She helped to open the door for other women who wished to serve their country in the United States Armed Forces. Her bravery and determination continue to inspire generations of women and Asian Americans.

Micah L. Issitt

FURTHER READING

Merry, Lois K. *Women Military Pilots of World War II: A History with Biographies of American, British, Russian, and German Aviators*. Jefferson, NC: McFarland, 2010. Print. Contains biographies of women military pilots, including a brief section on Lee and the WASP division.

Monahan, Evelyn, and Rosemary Neidel-Greenlee. *A Few Good Women: America's Military Women from World War I to the Wars in Iraq and Afghanistan*. New York: Random, 2011. Print. A collection of brief biographical accounts of women who fought in American military conflicts. Contains brief references to Lee and other members of the WASP division.

Weatherford, Doris. *American Women during World War II: An Encyclopedia*. New York: Routledge, 2010. Print. A collection of brief biographies of women who served in the armed forces and civilian services during World War II. Contains an entry describing Lee's contribution.

Wong, Kevin Scott. *Americans First: Chinese Americans and the Second World War*. Cambridge: Harvard UP, 2005. Print. A history of Chinese Americans who entered the US armed services and fought during World War II.

SHANNON W. LUCID

Astronaut

Born: January 14, 1943; Shanghai, China
Area of Achievement: Aviation and space exploration

Chosen by NASA as one of the first American female astronauts, Lucid was a mission specialist on five shuttle flights and lived for six months on Russia's Mir space station. Her time on Mir led to the US record for the most flight hours in orbit by a non-Russian and the international record for the most flight hours of any woman, a record held for more than a decade.

EARLY LIFE

Shannon W. Lucid (LEW-sihd) was born Shannon Matilda Wells in Shanghai, China, where her parents, Oscar and Myrtle Wells were serving as Baptist missionaries. During the Japanese occupation, Lucid and her parents, grandparents, aunts, an uncle, were interned by the Japanese in the Chapei Civil Assembly Center prison

Shannon W. Lucid (Wikimedia Commons)

camp. Early in 1944 they were evacuated aboard the Swedish ship *Gripsholm* in an exchange of noncombatant citizens of the warring nations. Lucid learned to walk onboard ship and received her first pair of shoes when the ship was docked in the port of Johannesburg on its way to the United States. The family spent the remaining years of the war in Fort Worth, Texas, where Lucid's younger sister, Ann, and brother, Joe, were born. The family later returned to China, where Lucid was enrolled in a Chinese-speaking school.

When the Communist Party took over China in 1949, Lucid and her family returned to the United States and settled in Bethany, Oklahoma, near Oklahoma City. As a young girl she was fascinated with airplanes and was influenced by a book about Robert H. Goddard, the founder of modern rocketry. After graduating from Bethany High School in 1960, she began college in Illinois at Wheaton, where she spent two years completing basic science and mathematics courses along with German, literature, and Biblical studies. In 1962, she transferred to the University of Oklahoma after taking summer courses there, and along with her work in chemistry, she learned to fly and earned a pilot's license. She completed a bachelor of science degree in chemistry in 1963 and remained for another year as a teaching assistant in the chemistry department.

LIFE'S WORK

During the next few years after graduation, Lucid held several positions in chemistry and obtained commercial, instrument, and multiengine ratings as a pilot. From 1963 to 1964 she served as a teaching assistant at Oklahoma, was a senior laboratory technician at the Oklahoma Medical Research Foundation from 1964 to 1966, and was a research chemist at Kerr-McGee in Oklahoma City from 1966 to 1968. While at Kerr-McGee, she met and married Michael F. Lucid of Indianapolis, Indiana, and they had two daughters, Kawai Dawn and Shandra Michelle, and one son, Michael Kermit. Lucid returned to the University of Oklahoma in 1969 as a graduate assistant in the university's Health Science Center, earning a master of science degree in biochemistry in 1970 and a doctor of philosophy degree in biochemistry in 1973. From 1974 to 1978, Lucid returned to the Oklahoma Medical Research Foundation as a research associate and began the application process for the space program as soon as women were recruited for the astronaut corps.

On January 16, 1978, Lucid was selected by the National Aeronautical and Space Administration (NASA) as one of thirty-five astronauts from a pool of more than two hundred finalists. She was one of six women in the first astronaut class that accepted women, a class that included Sally Ride, Judith Resnik, Anna Fisher, Margaret Seddon, and Kathryn Sullivan. After a period of intense training and rigorous physical and psychological testing, Lucid became an astronaut in August 1979, qualifying as a mission specialist on space shuttle flight crews. Although Lucid was not the first American woman in space, she is America's most experienced female astronaut.

Lucid's technical assignments include work with the Shuttle Avionics Integration Laboratory; the Flight Software Laboratory in Downey, California; and the Astronaut Office interface at Kennedy Space Center, Florida, on shuttle testing and launch countdowns. She also was a spacecraft capsule communicator at the Johnson Space Center, Mission Control, Houston, during many space shuttle missions. She was chief of Mission Support, chief of Astronaut Appearances, and chief scientist of NASA from 2002 to 2003.

Lucid was part of the crew of five spaceflights and logged 223 days in space, more than any other woman until surpassed by US astronaut Sunita Williams on June 16, 2007. Lucid's first space voyage was a seven-day mission on the space shuttle *Discovery* (STS-51-G) from June 17 to 24, 1985. On this mission the crew deployed

Lucid exercises on a treadmill which has been assembled in the Russian Mir space station Base Block module. (Wikimedia Commons)

three communication satellites and used the Remote Manipulator System to deploy and retrieve the *Spartan* satellite after its seventeen hours of x-ray astronomy observations. The crew also conducted biomedical experiments during *Discovery*'s 112 orbits of Earth, covering a distance of 2.5 million miles.

Lucid's next two orbital flights were both on space shuttle *Atlantis*. Her second shuttle flight was a five-day mission (STS-34) from October 18 to 23, 1989. On this flight she deployed the *Galileo* spacecraft to explore Jupiter and its moons, mapped atmospheric ozone using ultraviolet solar back-scattering, and conducted research on lightning, microgravity effects on plants, ice crystal growth in space, and many other secondary experiments during seventy-nine orbits. Her third shuttle flight was a nine-day mission (STS-43) from August 2 to 11, 1991. On this mission the crew deployed a tracking and data relay satellite (TDRS-E) and conducted during 142 orbits thirty-two science experiments related to extended space flights.

Lucid's fourth spaceflight was a fourteen-day mission on the shuttle *Columbia* (STS-58) from October 18 to November 1, 1993. This record-duration shuttle flight was considered the most successful Spacelab-related mission flown by NASA. The crew conducted sixteen engineering tests and twenty extended-duration medical experiments on themselves and on 48 rats during 225 orbits. Even before her record-breaking Mir flight, Lucid had logged 838 hours and 54 minutes in space, more than any other American woman.

> "*Basically, all my life I'd been told you can't do that because you're female. So I guess I just didn't pay any attention. I just went ahead and did what I could and then, when the stars aligned, I was ready.*"

On her last and most famous spaceflight, Lucid gained the US single-mission space-endurance record of 188 days while aboard Mir. After a year of training in Star City, Russia, she began her journey from Kennedy Space Center on March 22, 1996, aboard *Atlantis* (STS-76) and was transferred to Mir, where she served as board engineer 2 with Russian cosmonauts Yuri Onufrienko and Yuri Usachev. She conducted many science experiments during her six months in space, and became the first American to participate in extravehicular activity, or spacewalking, while stationed on Mir. Her return was scheduled for July 31 but was delayed nearly two months because of mechanical and weather problems with shuttle launches. She returned to Kennedy Space Center aboard *Atlantis* on September 26 after traveling more than 75 million miles in space.

From 2002 to 2003, Lucid worked in Washington, DC, as NASA's chief scientist. In the fall of 2003, she returned to Johnson Space Center to work in the Astronaut Office. She also served as a capsule communicator in the Mission Control Center for many missions before her retirement from NASA in January 2012.

Significance

Lucid's space career reaffirmed that female astronauts could equal or surpass their male counterparts. When no other astronaut seemed interested in an extended trip on the sparse Mir space station, she was the one who volunteered, and by doing so she established several space records. Given her six months of weightlessness on Mir, doctors thought that she would have to be carried off the shuttle upon her return to Earth. She surprised the experts, however, by walking on her own to the medical transporter. She became NASA's most important source for data on the effects of space on the human body and was monitored and tested for three years after her trip.

In addition to her many scientific experiments in space, Lucid helped to facilitate space exploration. She launched several satellites, contributed to the exploration of Jupiter by launching the Galileo spacecraft, and assisted with many aspects of the space program on the ground. In December of 1996, she became the tenth astronaut to receive the Congressional Space Medal of Honor and, in February of 1997, she won the Free Spirit Award from the Freedom Forum. On April 24, 2013, the US National Air and Space Museum awarded Lucid a current achievement Trophy Award. In 2014, Lucid was inducted into the United States Astronaut Hall of Fame.

Joseph L. Spradley

Further Reading

Atkins, Jeannine. *Wings and Rockets: The Story of Women in Air and Space*. New York: Farrar, 2003. Print. A children's book about pioneers in air and space travel that includes a chapter on Lucid.

"Briefly Noted." *Mechanical Engineering* 134.3 (2012): 11. *Academic Search Complete*. Web. 23 Dec. 2013.

Dailey, J. R. "And the Trophy Goes To." *Air & Space Smithsonian* 28.2 (2013): 2. *Academic Search Complete*. Web. 23 Dec. 2013.

Lucid, Shannon W. "Six Months on Mir." *Scientific American*, May 1998, 46–55. Print. A personal account of Lucid's life on Mir, including information on weightlessness, safety in space, and her experiments and other activities.

NASA. "Biographical Data: Shannon W. Lucid (Ph.D.)" *NASA: Lyndon B. Johnson Space Center*. NASA, Feb. 2012. Web. 23 Dec. 2013.

Shayler, David, and Ian Moule. *Women in Space Following Valentina*. New York: Springer, 2005. Print. A history of women in space, from balloonists to astronauts, with updated accounts based on interviews with women, including Lucid, with careers in flight.

Christa McAuliffe

High school teacher and astronaut

Born: Sepember 2, 1948; Boston, Massachusetts
Died: January 28, 1986; Cape Canaveral, Florida
Also known as: Sharon Christa Corrigan
Area of Achievement: Aeronautics; Education

In 1986, NASA's Challenger Space Shuttle exploded just one minute and thirteen seconds after liftoff, killing its seven-person crew. On board was Christa McAuliffe, a high school teacher and the first private citizen ever invited to join a NASA space mission. She had been selected through a well-publicized program called "Teacher in Space."

Christa McAuliffe (Wikimedia Commons)

Early Life

Christa McAuliffe was born on September 2, 1948 in Boston, Massachusetts, to Edward and Grace Corrigan. She was the oldest of their five children. As a bright and outgoing young girl, McAuliffe was active in the Girl Scouts of America and enjoyed skiing and other outdoor activities. Later she took piano lessons and performed in musicals at her high school in Framingham, Massachusetts. She graduated in 1966 and attended Framingham State College, where she majored in history. In 1970, with a bachelor's degree completed, she married the man who had been her boyfriend since high school, Steven McAuliffe, and the couple relocated to Maryland.

Life's Work

McAuliffe was hired for her first teaching position at a high school in Morningside, Maryland. Later she taught junior high school in Lanham, Maryland. While there, she took graduate courses in education at Bowie State College in Bowie, Maryland, earning a master's degree in 1978. Her first child, Scott, was born in 1976 and her second, Caroline, in 1979. In 1980, Steven McAuliffe was hired to be an assistant district attorney for the State of New Hampshire, and the family relocated to Concord, where Christa resumed teaching, first at Rundlett Junior High School, then at Bow Memorial School in Bow, New Hampshire, and finally at Concord High School where she taught social studies. In her teaching, McAuliffe liked to emphasize that ordinary people were a part of history and made history, too—it was not just about the lives of kings and generals.

McAuliffe was active in this period in her teacher's union, and she taught Catholicism to children at her parish church. She led a Girl Scouts troop, and she worked with inner city students as a volunteer with the Junior Service League. McAuliffe's solid resume as an upstanding—and also a fundamentally "ordinary"—member of her middle-class community would soon bring her an extraordinary opportunity.

In November 1984, Vice-President George Bush announced NASA's "Teacher in Space Project," a plan to

McAuliffe experiences weightlessness during a training session. (Wikimedia Commons)

involve an ordinary citizen—a teacher, in particular—in a space mission on the Challenger spacecraft. It would be the first time that a non-astronaut would be taken to outer space, and it came at a time when NASA was sharply increasing its launches and touting that a new era was dawning in which space missions were becoming routine.

McAuliffe was very excited by the news and filed an application—along with eleven thousand others—to be the teacher selected. The applications were narrowed down to 114, then down to ten. The ten finalists were invited to Washington, DC, to meet with a review board and undergo several days of physical, medical, and psychological testing. Although some other finalists had impressive accomplishments on their resumes that McAuliffe didn't have—a former fighter pilot, a published author—the board unanimously selected McAuliffe. Her exuberant and almost innocently optimistic personality was a decisive factor in winning them over. ("If you're offered a seat on a rocket ship, don't ask what seat. Just get on!" as she told Johnny Carson.)

McAuliffe spent the next six months in astronaut training and handling television appearances. The media attention for the "teacher in space" program was strong from the beginning. It had been seventeen years since the moon landing, but the spirit of excitement over the space program was still a palpable thing, especially for those, like McAuliffe, who were old enough to have watched—and, in a way, participated in—those national achievements on television.

By design, McAuliffe would do "teacherly" things in space. She was going to teach two lessons from the shuttle as it circled the earth's orbit to be broadcast live to school children across the nation. The lessons were going to be called "The Ultimate Field Trip" and "Where We've Been, Where We're Going, and Why." She was also given an experiment to perform in space growing hydroponic vegetables, and the cargo included experiments that were designed by teachers and school children from around the country that would observe the effects of weightlessness on things like a developing chicken's egg and the growth of crystals. Finally, she was going to keep a journal, she said, like a pioneer woman "on the Conestoga wagons."

The Challenger's launch was originally scheduled for January 22, 1986. It was delayed four times because of inclement weather and other issues. If these delays had any effect on McAuliffe's optimism, she never let on. The fourth attempt went as far as buckling the astronauts into their seats before the flight was canceled for mechanical repairs.

On the morning of January 28 the temperature was 27 degrees, still unusually chilly for Cape Canaveral, Florida, but NASA decided it was safe to proceed with the launch. Millions watched on television, including many school children. The shuttle was to burn through a two million gallon supply of rocket fuel in the so-called "booster rockets" on its way up. These were intended to lift the craft into space, then drop away. But seventy-three seconds after lift off, what remained of those millions of gallons of fuel exploded all at once. The craft had reached 48,000 feet when it burst into an orange ball of flame. There were no survivors, and debris from the explosion fell into the Atlantic Ocean for the next hour.

Thirty-eight days later, the remains of the crew of seven were recovered from the bottom of the ocean floor. McAuliffe was buried in Concord, New Hampshire.

> *"If I can get some student interested in science, if I can show members of the general public what's going on up there in the space program, then my job's been done."*

Significance

A presidential commission, called the Rogers Commission, determined that the accident was caused by the failure of rubber gaskets—O-rings—intended to form a tight seal for the rocket booster fuel. The rings failed to work properly in the cold weather and allowed fuel to leak. It was attributed to a design flaw, and the commission charged that the explosion was the result of NASA ignoring months of warnings about problems with the design. Investigations over the next year revealed that the leadership at NASA was dysfunctional, with Administrator James Beggs recently indicted on fraud charges, and key officials not even on speaking terms with other officials.

Journalist Michael Isikoff, writing in 1987 in the *Washington Post*, summarized a year's worth of independent investigations in a scathing indictment: "NASA of the mid-1980s was a confused and rudderless ship, hopelessly addicted to public relations extravaganzas to maintain its faltering claim on the public's attention."

The space program never really recovered from the Challenger incident. Whatever national excitement remained was severely chastened by both the explosion and the dreary results of the investigation. A few years after the disaster, the Soviet Union collapsed, making it easier to note the extent to which even the excitement of the early days of the program, in the 1960s, was a function of the Cold War and the international battle for hearts and minds.

In 2011, President Barack Obama announced an end to NASA's manned space shuttle missions. Today, the enthusiasm for space travel formerly associated with NASA (to quote McAuliffe again, "We'll have space post offices, space restaurants, space camps… space everything!") has found a home primarily in the pitches of private sector entrepreneurs.

Christa McAuliffe became a household name because she was unusually accessible and enthusiastic as a spokesperson for the mission. She was also a consummate teacher, a personality with an infectious enthusiasm. A *New York Times* review of Robert T. Hohler's book-length biography noted that McAuliffe's was "an uncynical life," a kind that is rarely the subject of books. Inspired by her example, a number of McAuliffe's students went on to become teachers themselves. Both of her two children became teachers as well.

D. Alan Dean

FURTHER READING

Brenneman, Rose. "Challenger's Legacy: Many of Christa McAuliffe's Students Are Now Teachers." *Education Week Blog*. https://blogs.edweek.org/teachers/teaching_now/2016/01/challenger-teacher-christa-mcauliffe-students-became-teachers.html.

Heitin, Liana. "25 Years After Challenger Tragedy, McAuliffe Continues to Inspire." *Education Week*, 30 No.18, January 26, 2011; pp. 6-7.

Hohler, Robert T. *"I Touch the Future…" The Story of Christa McAuliffe*. New York, NY: Random House, 1986.

Isikoff, Michael. "Challenger: Who Is to Blame?" *Washington Post*, Feb. 22, 1987. https://www.washingtonpost.com/archive/entertainment/books/1987/02/22/challenger-who-is-to-blame/ff9084b8-6259-4811-b081-fc095e21f65d/.

Kennedy, Mopsy Strange. "Ordinary in an Extraordinary Way." *New York Times*, March 15, 1987.

McDonald, Allan, and James Hansen. *Truth, Lies, and O-Rings: Inside the Space Shuttle Challenger Disaster*. University Press of Florida, 2009.

ELLEN OCHOA

American astronaut and inventor

Born: May 10, 1958; Los Angeles, California
Areas of Achievement: Aviation and space exploration, science and technology

Ochoa was the first Latina to become an astronaut. She had flown on four spaceflights by 2011 and holds three patents as an inventor or co-inventor of optical systems used for space imaging. Ochoa was named deputy director of Lyndon B. Johnson Space Center in Houston, Texas, in 2007.

EARLY LIFE

Ellen Lauri Ochoa (oh-CHOH-ah) was born May 10, 1958, in Los Angeles, California, to Rosanne Deardorff Ochoa, a homemaker, and Joseph Ochoa, the manager of a retail store. Ochoa grew up in La Mesa, California. The third of five children, Ochoa was an outstanding student who excelled in the sciences and mathematics. In her family, education was considered very important, and the children were encouraged in their intellectual activities. Ochoa had many interests. At age thirteen, she won the San Diego County spelling bee. She also played classical flute and was a member of the Civic Youth Orchestra in San Diego.

Ochoa's parents divorced when she was twelve years old. Even with the changes in her family life, she

Ellen Ochoa (Wikimedia Commons)

continued to excel academically and graduated with honors as the class valedictorian from Grossmont High School in La Mesa in 1975. Ochoa was offered a four year scholarship to Stanford University but turned it down to stay near home and help her mother raise her younger siblings.

Ochoa instead went to San Diego State University as a music major. She changed her major five times before graduating in 1980 as class valedictorian with a bachelor of science degree in physics. She then went to Stanford University on an engineering fellowship and received her master's degree in electrical engineering in 1981. Ochoa received an IBM Pre-Doctoral Fellowship from 1982 to 1984 and focused her work on designing optical systems for information processing. Her doctoral dissertation on the use of photorefractive crystals to filter images from space resulted in a patent in 1987. While at Stanford, Ochoa also played the flute and was an award-winning soloist in the Stanford Symphony Orchestra. In 1985, she received her doctorate in electrical engineering.

Life's Work

From 1985 to 1988, Ochoa was a researcher in imaging technology at the Sandia National Laboratories. She continued her work on optical systems used for filtering space images and developed an optical system to guide robots. After three years, Ochoa joined the National Aeronautics and Space Administration (NASA) at Ames Research Center and worked with a research team developing optical recognition systems as applied to space images. She also helped develop computer systems for aeronautical expeditions. Ochoa's work resulted in two additional patents as co-inventor of an optical object recognition system and a method for noise removal in images.

Although Ochoa became interested in the astronaut program while she was at Stanford, NASA was not accepting female candidates. After two other attempts, Ochoa was chosen in January, 1990, as one of five women and eighteen men to begin training at Lyndon B. Johnson Space Center in Houston, Texas. That year, she married Coe Fulmer Miles, a computer research engineer she met at Ames Research Center. They later had two sons, Wilson and Jordan.

> "What everyone in the astronaut corps shares in common is not gender or ethnic background, but motivation, perseverance, and desire - the desire to participate in a voyage of discovery."

In July, 1991, Ochoa finished training and qualified as a mission specialist. Her first mission was on the April 4-17, 1993, flight of the space shuttle *Discovery,* followed shortly thereafter by the *Atlantis* shuttle flight November 3-14, 1994. Both the May 27-June 6, 1999, *Discovery* flight and the April 8-19, 2002, *Atlantis* flight visited the International Space Station. In total, Ochoa logged more than 978 hours in space. She was awarded a 1995 NASA Outstanding Leadership Medal, four NASA Space Flight Medals, a 1991 NASA Group Achievement Award for photonics technology, a NASA Distinguished Service Medal, and NASA's Exceptional Service Medal in 1997.

While in the Astronaut Office, Ochoa served in various roles and became the deputy director of flight crew operations in December, 2002. In September, 2006, Ochoa was

Ochoa poses for a photo with Robonaut 2 (R2) during media day in the Space Vehicle Mock-up Facility at JSC. R2, who hitched a ride with the STS-133 crew members, was the first humanoid robot to travel to space and the first U.S.-built robot to visit the International Space Station. R2 will stay on the space station indefinitely to allow engineers on the ground to learn more about how humanoid robots fare in microgravity. (Wikimedia Commons)

named the director of flight crew operations, in which capacity she managed and directed the Astronaut Office and aircraft operations at Johnson Space Center. On September 17, 2007, Ochoa was named deputy director of Johnson Space Center, where her responsibilities include planning and organizing the day-to-day management of the space shuttle program.

Ochoa became director of the Johnson Space Center in 2012 upon the retirement of previous director Michael Coats. Her appointment made her the first Hispanic and second female director of the center.

Significance

In interviews, Ochoa has indicated that she never felt that her Latina heritage helped or hindered her. She has, however, served as a role model for minorities and women in the fields of science and engineering. She has talked with thousands of students, sharing her life experiences and encouraging young people to set goals and stay in school. Ochoa is passionate about encouraging students to follow their dreams and not be discouraged, thus inspiring young women to choose fields that challenge them and benefit society.

Ochoa has received numerous awards and honors, including having two schools named after her: Ellen Ochoa Middle School in Pasco, Washington, and Ellen Ochoa Learning Center in Cudahy, California. She also was the first woman to be named engineer of the year by the Hispanic Engineer National Achievement Awards Conference. The award, which she won in 2008, recognizes overall leadership and technical achievement in science, technology, engineering, and mathematics. Ochoa was inducted into the United States Astronaut Hall of Fame in 2017 along with Michael Foale.

Virginia L. Salmon

Further Reading

Hasday, Judy L. *Ellen Ochoa.* New York: Chelsea House, 2007. Offers basic biographical information and details Ochoa's space flights. Includes a time line, index, and bibliography.

Paige, Joy. *Ellen Ochoa: The First Hispanic Woman in Space.* New York: Rosen, 2004. Overview of Ochoa's life that explains many aspects related to space travel. Includes photographs, index, further reading, and glossary.

Schraff, Anne. *Ellen Ochoa: Astronaut and Inventor.* Berkeley Heights, N.J.: Enslow, 2010. Focuses on her astronaut career and includes a general discussion of the missions. Includes chronology, notes, index, and further reading.

Woodmansee, Laura S. *Women Astronauts.* Toronto: Apogee Books, 2002. A collection of interviews and histories of several female astronauts, including Ellen Ochoa.

Sally Ride

Astronaut

Born: May 26, 1951; Los Angeles, California
Died: July 23, 2012; La Jolla, California
Areas of Achievement: Aviation and space exploration, physics, education, science

NASA astronaut Ride was the first American woman to fly in space when she flew aboard space shuttle Challenger in 1983 as a mission specialist. She was one of the first of a new breed of astronauts who were, primarily, scientists, and who were called mission specialists. Ride later founded NASA's Office of Exploration.

Early Life

Sally Ride was born in Encino, a suburb of the city of Los Angeles. She was the older of two daughters born to Joyce Ride and Dale B. Ride, a member of the faculty at Santa Monica City College. Ride's parents were active as elders in their Presbyterian church, and Joyce often volunteered her time as an English tutor to students from outside the United States and as a counselor at a women's prison.

Ride's parents encouraged her competitive spirit in academics and in athletics. She was a born athlete and often played the rough-and-tumble games of football and baseball with the neighborhood boys. Ride began playing tennis, a less hazardous sport, at the request of her mother. Under the tutelage of tennis great Alice Marble, Ride quickly excelled in this sport and became proficient enough to rank eighteenth nationally. Her excellence in tennis earned her a partial scholarship to Westlake School for Girls (now Harvard-Westlake School), a private preparatory school in Los Angeles. At the preparatory school, Sally became interested in the study of physics through the influence of her science teacher, Elizabeth Mommaerts, and, for the next five years, science and tennis competed for Ride's time and attention.

In 1968, Ride enrolled at Swarthmore College in Pennsylvania as a physics major, but left after three terms to concentrate on her tennis game after winning a national collegiate tennis tournament. Although she was a top-ranked college player, she realized that she did not have the talent to advance to professional tennis. Ride returned to college in 1970 and completed a double major in English literature and physics at Stanford University in California in 1973. After graduation, she briefly considered studying Shakespeare in graduate school but settled on astrophysics to further her dream of working for the National Aeronautics and Space Administration, or NASA.

Life's Work

Ride began her path to fame while completing work on her doctoral dissertation at Stanford with research into free-electron laser physics. One day she read an announcement in the campus newspaper indicating that NASA was seeking young scientists to serve as mission specialists. Acting on impulse, she applied to join the astronaut program, which had lifted its long-standing policy against women astronauts to attract additional qualified scientists willing to forgo high salaries and work on the new space shuttle program. To Ride's surprise, she made it through the preliminary screening process to become one of the finalists. In 1977, she was flown to the Johnson Space Center outside Houston, Texas, for exhausting interviews and fitness and psychiatric evaluation tests. After three months of rigorous testing, Ride officially became an astronaut. In 1978, shortly after earning her Ph.D., she reported to the Johnson Space Center to begin the intensive training required of NASA mission specialists.

In the first year of training, Ride learned parachute jumping and water survival techniques, the latter for the possibility that the shuttle might have to be aborted into the ocean. She also acclimated to increased gravity forces, the force encountered during acceleration and

Sally Ride (Wikimedia Commons)

deceleration back to Earth, as well as to weightlessness. She had courses in radio communication and navigation and learned to fly a jet. Piloting a jet proved to be an enjoyable experience for Ride, and she eventually acquired a pilot's license. From 1982 until 1987 she was married to fellow astronaut Steven Hawley.

Throughout Ride's preparation time, NASA maintained its bureaucratic composure regarding its inclusion of women in the space shuttle program. There was no flamboyant talk about "one giant step for womankind." Indeed, team player that she was, Ride insisted that her participation in the flight was "no big deal." Whether she liked it or not, news of her flight brought her instant celebrity. Newspapers and television reporters interviewed her again and again, and U.S. president Ronald Reagan gave her extra attention at a White House luncheon. Composer Casse Culver wrote and recorded a song, "Ride, Sally, Ride," and T-shirts urged the same.

Ride was asked to join the shuttle program by U.S. Navy captain Robert L. Crippen, a veteran astronaut who had piloted the first shuttle mission in 1981. Crippen said, of his choice of Ride, that "she is flying with us because she is the very best person for the job. There is no man I would rather have in her place." Ride, in her unassuming manner, simply stated that she had not become an astronaut to become "a historic figure," and that she believed it was "time that people realized that women in this country can do any job that they want to do." Ride's special virtue was that she was so much like the male astronauts and so utterly and convincingly their equal. She was just as determined, just as disciplined, just as fearless, and just as predictable.

> "There are lots of opportunities out there for women to work in these fields... Girls just need support, encouragement and mentoring to follow through with the sciences."

On June 18, 1983, Ride blasted off from the Kennedy Space Center in Florida, aboard space shuttle *Challenger* (STS-7) as one of five crew members. On board, she had general mission duties in addition to performing her scientific work. She was chosen to sit behind mission commander Crippen and copilot Frederick Hauck to act as flight engineer during takeoff and landing. During the ninety-six orbits, she and her fellow mission specialist, John Fabian, worked in weightless conditions with the complex Canadarm a fifty-foot remote "arm" used to move payloads in and out of the shuttle cargo bay. Ride and Fabian trained for two years on the ground with the computerized arm and became experts in its operation. Another task on the mission was to start Anik-C, a Canadian domestic communications satellite, on its way to a geosynchronous orbit hovering above Earth's equator. This satellite was designed to handle thirty-two color television channels. A second communications satellite, named Palapa-B and owned by the Indonesian government, was launched into orbit to carry voice, video, and telephone signals to Southeast Asia.

Forty other experiments were conducted by the *Challenger* crew. These included studies of metal alloy manufacture, solar cell testing, growth of semiconductor crystals, and glass production. One experiment, devised by high school students, was a project sending 150 carpenter ants into orbit in the shuttle cargo bay to see how weightlessness affected their social structure. The California Institute of Technology sent an experiment in which radish seedlings were subjected to simulated gravity to find the right gravitational force for best growth. Purdue University's experiment investigated how sunflower seeds germinated in zero gravity. The highlight of the mission was the deployment of a huge free-floating satellite to document its position with the first in-space color photographs before recapturing it. The satellite was then released again and snared once more. The crew repeated this procedure for nine and one-half hours before Ride captured the satellite for the last time and stowed it in the cargo bay for the trip home. *Challenger* landed at Edwards Air Force Base in California on June 24.

Sally's ride (a pun often used by the media) marked major changes in what could no longer be called the United States "manned" space program. Much of the daredevil aspect was now gone from space travel. The object of the space program was not simply getting into orbit but working there. In fact, Ride had recommended to NASA administrator James Fletcher that space be used to study planet Earth.

Two Soviet women preceded Ride into space, but their feats did not leave a lasting mark. In 1963, in the early days of piloted spaceflight, twenty-six-year-old textile mill worker and amateur skydiver Valentina Tereshkova was put on a rocket by the Soviet Union in what was considered by many to be a propaganda coup. Reports of that flight indicate that Tereshkova was sick for most of the three-day flight. In August of 1982, the Soviets launched into space the second woman cosmonaut

Ride performs a number of functions simultaneously, proving the necessity for versatility and dexterity in space travel. (Wikimedia Commons)

thirty-four-year-old test pilot Svetlana Savitskaya. Her presence in space, however, was taken lightly by her colleagues.

Ride went into space a second time aboard the *Challenger* on October 5, 1984, as part of the seven-person crew of STS-41-G. Again, Crippen was the commander. She was joined by Kathryn D. Sullivan, marking the first time that two women had flown on the same space mission. Before landing on October 13, the crew deployed the Earth Radiation Budget Satellite, tested an orbital refueling system, and performed oceanography observations.

At the end of the trip Ride had 343 hours in space. Ride had been training for a third shuttle trip when the *Challenger* explosion occurred in January, 1986. She was named to the presidential commission that investigated the accident and was chair of a subcommittee on operations. She later worked at NASA's headquarters in Washington, D.C., as special assistant to Fletcher for long-range and strategic planning. As part of her research brief, she produced an influential report entitled "Leadership and America's Future in Space." She also founded NASA's Office of Exploration. In 2003 she served on the *Columbia* Accident Investigation Board, which studied the accident involving space shuttle *Columbia*.

Ride left NASA in 1987 to be part of Stanford University's Center for International Security and Arms Control. Two years later she moved to the University of California, San Diego (UCSD), as a professor of physics and director of the California Space Institute. Her research focused on the theory of nonlinear beam-wave interactions.

One of Ride's principal interests involved encouraging young people to study science. In 1999 she inaugurated and directed EarthKam, a program permitting schoolchildren to take photographs from space and download them to the Web. In 2001, she founded Sally Ride Science, a company dedicated to science education. Her programs encouraged girls in the fifth through eighth grades to pursue science, mathematics, and technology. The company sponsored science camps, a national toy-design competition, festivals, and workshops, and provided instruction for teachers, reading packets about individual sciences for public schools, and other publications. Ride also wrote five science books for children about astronomy and space exploration.

Ride received numerous awards and honors. Among them are the Space Flight Medal (twice), Von Braun Award, Lindbergh Eagle, Jefferson Award for Public Service, Theodore Roosevelt Award (the highest honor bestowed by the National Collegiate Athletics Association), and UCSD's Chancellor's Associated Recognition Award for Outstanding Community Service. She was inducted into the National Women's Hall of Fame, Astronaut Hall of Fame, International Scholar-Athlete Hall of Fame, and California Hall of Fame.

Ride died in 2012, after being diagnosed with pancreatic cancer. In 2013, the U.S. Navy named a research ship, the *RV Sally Ride,* in her honor and she posthumously received the Space Foundation's James E. Hill Lifetime Space Achievement Award. At "A National Tribute to Sally Ride" at the Kennedy Center in May 2013, President Barack Obama announced that Ride would be posthumously honored with the Presidential Medal of Freedom.

Significance

For all the merits of the scientific and experimental aspects of the voyages of the space shuttle *Challenger*, Ride was the one who provoked the world's curiosity. Cool, calm, and controlled in all circumstances, Ride hurtled through space aboard the one-hundred-ton white-and-blue shuttle, proving that she was certainly made of "the right stuff."

Ride's legacy as an astronaut-scientist also came to signify the ascendancy of the mission specialist over the pilot. The close-knit brotherhood of test and fighter pilots who made up the original astronaut corps was diluted by those having a new kind of skill the ability to do quadratic equations and conduct scientific experiments instead of fancy flying alone. Under these developing guidelines, Ride became the ideal candidate and the ideal NASA astronaut because of her scientific background and because she was able to learn and readily solve new problems.

Being a respected space pioneer was more important to Ride than achieving celebrity as a woman astronaut. Her space shuttle career earned for her the trust and high regard of her colleagues as well as the admiration of an entire nation. Following her work with the space shuttle program she worked to encourage young people, especially girls, to pursue careers in science.

Jane A. Slezak, updated by Micah L. Issitt

Further Reading

America's Space Shuttle: Shuttle Mission Reports and Astronaut Biographies, Documents on the Past, Present, and Future of the Shuttle. Mt. Laurel, N.J.: Progressive Management, 2001. A massive, 12,305-page CD-ROM collection of documents chronicling the history of the space shuttle program and shuttle astronauts. The disk includes the complete Johnson Space Center mission reports for each flight up to 2001.

Begley, Sharon. "Challenger: Ride, Sally Ride." *Newsweek,* June 13, 1983. An overview of Ride's life and the results of her crucial decision to join the elite NASA astronaut group in preparation for missions on the space shuttle.

Camp, Carole Ann. *Sally Ride: First Woman in Space.* Springfield, N.J.: Enslow, 1997. For young adult readers, this biography supplies a wealth of information about Ride's NASA career, emphasizing her dedication and the fascination of space flight. Includes a chronology and bibliographical references for further study.

Fox, Mary Virginia. *Women Astronauts: Aboard the Shuttle.* Rev. ed. New York: J. Messner, 1987. Chronicles the experiences of women selected for the space shuttle program. Aimed at young readers, this work discusses Ride's experiences as the first American woman to fly in space as well as the women who followed.

Golden, Frederic. "Sally's Joy Ride into the Sky." *Time,* June 27, 1983. In the magazine's section on space, Golden tells of Ride's experiences on the second orbiting flight of the space shuttle *Challenger* and includes Ride's observations regarding the public's reaction to her flight.

Harland, David M. *The Space Shuttle: Roles, Missions, and Accomplishments.* New York: John Wiley & Sons, 1998. Covers the complete history of the shuttle program up to the late 1990s, with a section on exploration and discussion of shuttle operations. Includes glossary, bibliography, and index.

Kevles, Bettyann. *Almost Heaven: The Story of Women in Space.* Cambridge, Mass.: MIT Press, 2006. Excellent history of female astronauts that provides details, photographs, and quotations from the astronauts about their pioneering accomplishments in space.

Ride, Sally, and Tam O'Shaughnessy. *Exploring Our Solar System.* New York: Crown, 2003. This splendidly vivid book exemplifies Ride's campaign to intrigue preteens and teens in science. It provides them with a tour of the solar system, emphasizing both fact and the adventure of discovery. Accompanied by more than one hundred color photographs and graphics.

Shayler, David, and Ian Moule. *Women in Space Following Valentina.* New York: Springer, 2005. A history of women in space, from balloonists to astronauts, with updated accounts based on interviews with women with careers in flight.

Alan Shepard

Astronaut

Born: November 18, 1923; Derry, New Hampshire
Died: July 21, 1998; Pebble Beach, California
Area of Achievement: Aviation and space exploration

Shepard flew the first U.S. piloted spaceflight in 1961 and became the only Project Mercury astronaut to walk on the Moon, only the seventh human to have done so.

Alan Shepard (Wikimedia Commons)

EARLY LIFE

Alan Shepard was born to Colonel Alan B. Shepard and Renza Shepard in East Derry, Hew Hampshire. After attending primary school in East Derry, Shepard graduated from Pinkerton Academy in Derry. He spent a year studying at Admiral Farragut Academy in Toms River, New Jersey, prior to his acceptance into the United States Naval Academy. After several years of distinguished military service, Shepard studied at the Naval War College in Newport, Rhode Island, graduating in 1958.

The National Aeronautics and Space Administration (NASA), created on October 1, 1958, received primary authority for Project Mercury, which attempted to send the first humans into space. As a result, astronauts were required. Military service files of test pilots were studied, invitations for application were sent, and NASA accumulated a large set of candidates. Following rigorous medical examinations, psychological tests, and personal interviews, seven individuals were selected as the original Mercury astronauts. Shepard was among that select group.

NASA announced on February 22, 1961, that three astronauts John Glenn, Gus Grissom, and Shepard had been selected to train for the first suborbital Mercury flight. Which astronaut would make that first flight was not revealed until Shepard emerged from the Astronaut Quarters on May 2, 1961, fully suited, only to have poor weather prevent launch that day. By that time, NASA had lost the race to send the first human into space. On April 12, 1961, Soviet cosmonaut Yuri Gagarin had orbited Earth once in Vostok 1 before landing within the Soviet Union.

> *"I realized up there that our planet is not infinite. It's fragile. That may not be obvious to a lot of folks, and it's tough that people are fighting each other here on Earth instead of trying to get together and live on this planet. We look pretty vulnerable in the darkness of space."*

LIFE'S WORK

Shepard's next launch attempt came on May 5, 1961. Before sunrise, Shepard rode out to Pad 5-6. Leaving his transfer van, he paused to look up at the Redstone rocket about to hurtle him down the Atlantic Missile Range. Shepard slipped into his Mercury-Redstone 3 (*Freedom 7*) spacecraft and was hooked up to life support and communications systems therein. Technicians bolted closed the hatch. Minor difficulties were encountered during the remainder of the countdown. Each was overcome, but each delayed liftoff. The last, a faulty pressure gauge reading, surfaced less that three minutes before liftoff. Once resolved, the countdown continued until, at 9:34 a.m. eastern daylight time (EDT), the Redstone rocket rose from its pedestal. Shepard was on his way. The Redstone exhausted its fuel a little over two minutes into flight. *Freedom 7* separated from the spent booster, and the escape tower jettisoned. Shepard assumed manual control and reoriented his spacecraft for retrofire.

Shepard briefly viewed the Earth below using a periscope extended from *Freedom 7*'s hull. He experienced five minutes of weightlessness before reentry, reaching a maximum altitude of 115 miles. Three retrorockets fired in turn, and then the retropack on which they were located separated from *Freedom 7*. The spacecraft hit the upper atmosphere at over five thousand miles per hour, slowing down to about three hundred miles per hour over the next minute, the result of which was to subject Shepard to ten times normal Earth gravity.

Shepard on the moon, next to the American flag. (Wikimedia Commons)

Parachute deployments occurred normally, and, at 9:50 a.m., *Freedom 7* splashed down about one hundred miles from Grand Bahama Island. NASA's first piloted spaceflight lasted fifteen minutes, twenty-two seconds. The spacecraft traveled 302 miles downrange from Cape Canaveral (now Cape Kennedy). Based on Shepard's success, a prior chimpanzee (Ham) flight, and a subsequent suborbital flight by Virgil "Gus" Grissom (*Liberty Bell 7*), NASA was confident to move ahead with orbital missions, beginning with John Glenn's three-orbit flight on February 20, 1962.

Later, as Project Gemini (the stepping stone between Mercury missions and Apollo lunar flights) evolved from design to test-flight stages, Shepard was considered for an early flight assignment. However, he was dropped from active astronaut status in 1963 and restricted to flying conventional aircraft only with a copilot, having developed Ménière's syndrome, an inner-ear condition capable of inducing nausea, ringing ears, and vestibular disturbances. Shepard assumed the role of chief of the Astronaut Office but clung to hopes of flying in space again. In 1968 he secretly underwent an experimental surgical procedure. Detailed postsurgical testing by NASA doctors found no evidence of Ménière's syndrome, and Shepard lobbied for active flight status restoration and assignment to a lunar landing. He received command of Apollo 13. NASA management did not approve and suggested that Shepard needed additional training time because he had been inactive so long. He and fellow crew members Edgar Mitchell and Stuart Roosa were bumped back to Apollo 14, and James Lovell, Fred Haise, and John Swigert moved up to the ill-fated Apollo 13 mission.

Apollo 13's lunar landing site, the Fra Mauro highlands, was considered too scientifically significant to be missed. Fra Mauro held promise for sampling bedrock material excavated from deep below the lunar surface during the formation of Cone Crater. Originally, Apollo 14 was to land near the crater Censorinus in Mare Tranquilitatis relatively close to where Apollo 11 landed. Fra Mauro became Apollo 14's landing site. Apollo 14 carried tremendous responsibility for continuing Moon flights in the aftermath of Apollo 13. Budget considerations had already cut three previously planned landings. NASA could not survive another aborted flight and maintain sufficient congressional support for the remaining Apollo missions.

Apollo 14 launched from Cape Canaveral at 4:03 p.m. on January 31, 1971, the thirteenth anniversary of Explorer 1, United States' first orbital satellite. Ascent into orbit and subsequent translunar injection to boost Apollo 14 toward the Moon were both normal. A series of serious problems arose shortly thereafter, the first when the command and service module (*Kitty Hawk*) attempted to dock with the lunar module (*Antares*). Contact was made, but not a latched mating. If the two vehicles could not rigidly dock, Apollo 14's lunar landing was impossible. On the sixth attempt, *Kitty Hawk* and *Antares* achieved hard dock and separated from their Saturn 5 rocket's spent third stage.

Apollo 14 entered lunar orbit on February 4 amid concern over a suspect docking apparatus. Examination of the command module's probe failed to relieve that concern or identify the cause of earlier difficulties. *Kitty Hawk* dropped down to an orbital low point of only eleven miles above the surface, the point from which *Antares* would begin its powered descent to touchdown.

On February 5, *Antares* separated from *Kitty Hawk*, but before its braking engine could fire, a major computer problem required resolution. A false signal was being sent to *Antares* guidance computer, one that would automatically trigger an abort twenty-six seconds after power descent initiation and send the astronauts back up to orbit. After two hours, Massachusetts Institute of Technology (MIT) computer specialists devised a software patch that circumvented that action. Then, as *Antares* steadily descended toward the lunar surface, the radar altimeter failed to lock on and provide critical altitude data to the guidance computer. After technicians recycled the radar's

Shepard and Ed Mitchell work with the MET in the KC-135 aircraft. (Wikimedia Commons)

circuit breaker, critical data started flowing at an altitude of just 2,500 feet.

Antares touched down at 4:17 a.m., resting in a small depression tilted 8 degrees. Five and one-half hours later, Shepard and lunar module pilot Mitchell stood on the surface at Fra Mauro to begin the first of two moonwalks, the primary focus of which was to assemble a small science station that would provide data for months after the astronauts returned home. One experiment required active data collection. Shepard and Mitchell fired small pyrotechnics while a seismometer registered subsurface vibrations. Before concluding the first moonwalk, there was time for collecting geological samples.

The second moonwalk began at 3:10 a.m. on February 6, this one dedicated to careful geological sampling during a traverse to the rim of Cone Crater. Shepard pulled behind him a special rickshaw-like transporter in which he stored tools and samples during the climb up Cone Crater's slope. The slope of the crater proved steeper than anticipated, and determination of position among the boulders and depressions was difficult. Shepard and Mitchell terminated their ascent and settled for sampling a promising boulder field just short of Cone Crater's rim. Before returning to *Antares*, Shepard, an avid golfer, took time to chip a pair of golf balls using a sample-collecting tool affixed with a club head. With limited moon-suit mobility, Shepard could only swing one arm, but the balls went quite far in the reduced lunar gravity.

Antares lifted off from the Moon carrying Shepard, Mitchell, and 108 pounds of lunar samples at 1:49 p.m. on February 6. This time, docking was trouble free, and the journey home was devoid of nagging problems. Apollo 14 ended after slightly more than nine days with a gentle ocean splashdown.

Shepard returned to his post of chief astronaut, remaining in that capacity from June, 1971, until August 1, 1974. Shepard retired simultaneously from NASA and the Navy (at the rank of rear admiral) to enter private enterprise, joining the Marathon Construction Company in Houston, Texas. Shepard had other business ventures in his post-Apollo period and served as president of Seven-Fourteen Enterprises in Houston. He was instrumental in several different efforts to both memorialize early spaceflights and educate young people. Shepard, along with the other Mercury, Gemini, and Apollo astronauts, was inducted into the Astronaut Hall of Fame in Titusville, Florida, where the *Kitty Hawk* is on display.

Shepard had planned to be present at the Kennedy Space Center to view his former colleague John Glenn's historic return to space after thirty-six years when the space shuttle *Discovery* launched in late 1998. Unfortunately, the United States' first human in space succumbed to leukemia and passed away at age seventy-four on July 21, 1998. That passing was noted by all major Western media news services with great nostalgia and respect for Shepard's contributions to the early years of the U.S. space program.

Significance

The name and contributions of Shepard loom large in the U.S. space program's early history. His laurels include being the original Mercury astronaut, the first American in space, the seventh human to walk on the Moon, and the first astronaut to be posted as chief of the Astronaut Office. Shepard's suborbital Mercury flight came three weeks after Russian cosmonaut Gagarin became the first human to orbit the Earth. Although Shepard's flight only lasted fifteen minutes, *Freedom 7* provided enough confidence for President John F. Kennedy to challenge the Soviets to achieve a piloted lunar landing before the end of the 1960's. That challenge was issued nine months before NASA was even able to match Gagarin's orbit with John Glenn's *Friendship 7* flight.

David G. Fisher

Further Reading

Caidin, Martin. *Man Into Space*. New York: Pyramid, 1961. Perhaps somewhat difficult to locate, this book provides an excellent account of the early days of the space program leading up to and including Shepard's suborbital *Freedom 7* flight told from that period's viewpoint. The author is a noted writer of historical spaceflight books for the general audience.

Carpenter, M. Scott, et al. *We Seven*. New York: Simon & Schuster, 1962. The original Mercury astronauts provided insight from personal experience as part of the first U.S. piloted space program. Four sections and one entire chapter were provided by Shepard. The chapter chronicles his *Freedom 7* suborbital flight.

Shepard, Alan, et al. *Moon Shot: The Inside Story of America's Race to the Moon*. Atlanta, Ga.: Turner, 1994. Plenty of texts chronicle the United States' race to the Moon from an engineering, exploration, or political viewpoint. Written by two astronauts instrumental in the rich story of Apollo, assisted by two of the most experienced space journalists, this book provides the inside story of NASA's golden age of piloted spaceflight, detailing Shepard's participation in and supervision of that effort. A video version of this material is also available.

Slayton, Deke, with Michael Cassutt. *Deke! U.S. Manned Space: From Mercury to the Shuttle*. New York: Forge, 1994. Although an autobiography of Deke Slayton, this book also provides plenty of insight into the life of Alan Shepard, who, like Slayton, was an original Mercury astronaut and suffered a long period during which a medical condition forced him off active flight status. Slayton and Shepard developed a close friendship working together in the Astronaut Office.

Thomson, Neal. *Light This Candle: The Life and Times of Alan Shepard, America's First Spaceman*. New York: Crown, 2000. Comprehensive biography based on exclusive access to Shepard's private papers and interviews with his family and fellow astronauts.

Sunita Williams

Astronaut

Born: September 19, 1965; Euclid, Ohio
Full name: Sunita Lyn Pandya Williams
Areas of Achievement: Science and technology, military

Sunita Williams (Wikimedia Commons)

United States Navy Captain Sunita Williams is a highly versatile pilot and astronaut who has set several milestones while in space as both a woman and an Asian American. She is best known for her work on the International Space Station and her space walks.

Early Life

Sunita Williams was born to Deepak N. Pandya, a neuroanatomist from the Indian state of Gujarat, and Ursuline "Bonnie" Zalokar Pandya, an x-ray technician of Slovenian ancestry from Cleveland, Ohio. When her father accepted a new appointment in Boston, Massachusetts, in 1966, the family moved to nearby Needham, where Williams was raised and graduated from high school in 1983. She was active in athletics, especially competitive swimming, and contemplated a career in veterinary medicine because she loved animals. When both Columbia University and the United States Naval Academy offered her admission, she selected the latter, in part because she could avoid assuming student loans, and in part because her brother Jay was already enrolled there. After graduating in the middle of her Naval Academy class in 1987, Williams attended flight school in Pensacola, Florida. In 1989, she joined a helicopter support squadron in Norfolk, Virginia, and was deployed to the Middle East as

Williams works with the Lab-on-a-Chip Application Development-Portable Test System (LOCAD-PTS) experiment in the Destiny laboratory of the International Space Station. LOCAD-PTS is a handheld device for rapid detection of biological and chemical substances onboard the station. (Wikimedia Commons)

part of Operation Desert Shield in 1990 and Operation Provide Comfort in 1991 during the first Gulf War.

In 1969, a nearly four-year-old Williams had watched Neil Armstrong and Buzz Aldrin walk on the moon, but never imagined that she might become an astronaut herself. However, after meeting several astronauts at the Johnson Space Center in Houston, Texas, Williams realized she had many of the skills necessary for piloting spacecraft. She graduated from the United States Naval Test Pilot School in Patuxent, Maryland, in 1993 and in 1995 earned a master's degree in engineering management from the Florida Institute of Technology. In 1998, NASA selected her for astronaut training.

> "When you're flying in space some of the things down on Earth seem trivial. Things like politics leave your mind. I didn't feel like I was a person from the United States, I felt like I was lucky enough to be a person from Earth."

Life's Work

As a new NASA astronaut, Williams received extensive training in additional skills, including water and wilderness survival techniques, piloting the supersonic T-38 training jet, and operating robotic arms. She lived underwater for eight days in NASA's Aquarius laboratory in 2002. As a result of working with the Russian Space Agency in Moscow, Williams learned to speak Russian, a talent that proved useful when she served with Russian flight engineers on board the International Space Station.

Williams first traveled into space in December 2006 on board the space shuttle *Discovery*. She brought with her a copy of the Hindu scripture *Bhagavad Gita* and a statue of Ganesha, the Hindu god of beginnings, from her Hindu father, as well as a Christian cross from her Slovenian Catholic grandmother. After docking with the International Space Station, Williams joined Expedition 14 and then remained with Expedition 15 until June 2007. In all, Williams spent 195 days on the station, establishing a record for space endurance by women that had not been broken by 2011. During these two expeditions, Williams also logged 29 hours, 17 minutes, of walking in space, setting a new record for women until it was broken by astronaut Peggy Whitson in 2008.

Several noteworthy events occurred during Williams's six months in space. Shortly after arriving, her long black hair was cut by fellow astronaut Joan Higginbotham and brought back to Earth, where it was donated to children who had lost their hair due to medical problems. In April 2007, while the Boston Marathon was taking place in her home state of Massachusetts, Williams became the first astronaut to run a marathon in space. Williams ran the 26.2 miles in 4 hours, 23 minutes, and 46 seconds, while strapped to a stationary treadmill inside the Space Station. In May 2007, she spoke with Queen Elizabeth II of Great Britain via video communication.

By 2011, Williams had logged more than three thousand flight hours as a Navy pilot in more than thirty different aircraft, rising in rank to captain. She served as a crew member on Expedition 32 and commander on Expedition 33 on board the International Space Station in 2012. While on the ISS, Williams became the first person to complete a triathalon in space, which coincided with the Nautica Malibu Triathalon held in Southern California. She used the ISS's treadmill, stationary bike, and the Advanced Resistive Exercise Device to do weightlifting and resistance exercises that approximated swimming in zero gravity. Williams finished with a time of 1 hour, 48 minutes, and 33 seconds, as she reported.

In July 2015, NASA announced Williams as one of the first astronauts for U.S. Commercial spaceflights. Subsequently, she has started working with Boeing and SpaceX to train in their commercial crew vehicles, along with other chosen astronauts. In August 2018 she was assigned to the first mission flight, CTS-1, to the International Space Station of the Boeing CST-100 Starliner.

Significance

By 2011, Williams was only the second female of Indian heritage to fly in space; she holds the record for the longest spaceflight for a woman. Her numerous honors include two Navy Commendation Medals, the Navy and Marine Corps Achievement Medal, and the Humanitarian Service Medal. She has also received international awards such as Russia's Medal of Merit in Space and India's Sardar Vallabhai Patel Vishwa Pratibha Award.

James I. Deutsch

Further Reading

Kanin, Zachary. "One Small Step." *New Yorker* 83.15 (2007): 47. Print. A humorous parody, written after Williams ran her own Boston Marathon on the International Space Station, in which author Kanin imagines some other feats Williams might accomplish in space.

Mahanti, Subodh. *Pioneer of Space Travel, Sunita Williams.* New Delhi: Indian Ministry of Information and Broadcasting, 2007. Print. Places Williams's achievements in the context of recent spaceflight history.

Seshadri, S., and Aradhika Sharma. *Astronaut Sunita Williams: Achiever Extraordinaire* New Delhi: Rupa, 2007. Print. Contains many details of Williams's personal life and Indian American identity, thanks to the cooperation of her parents.

ORVILLE AND WILBUR WRIGHT

Aeronautical engineers and inventors

Orville Wright
Born: August 19, 1871; Dayton, Ohio
Died: January 30, 1948; Dayton, Ohio

Orville and Wilbur Wright (Wikimedia Commons)

Wilbur Wright
Born: April 16, 1867; Millville, Indiana
Died: May 30, 1912; Dayton, Ohio

Areas of Achievement: Aviation and space exploration, invention and technology

The Wright brothers invented the first practical powered aircraft flown by a pilot, thereby initiating the age of aviation.

Early Lives

The Wright brothers belonged to a midwestern family of five children. Wilbur and Orville were the third and fourth boys, respectively; their younger sister, Katherine, was the only girl. Their father, the Reverend Milton Wright of the Evangelical United Brethren Church in Christ, had a large personal library, particularly of scientific and mechanical books. Their mother, née Susan Catherine Koerner, had been college educated and, with her husband, had invented several practical household items. As children, Wilbur, Orville, and Katherine established a closeness that became lifelong, especially after 1889, when Katherine took over running the home on their mother's

The Wright Flyer airborne during the first powered flight at Kitty Hawk, North Carolina in 1903. Orville is the pilot while Wilbur runs alongside. (Wikimedia Commons)

death. The Wright brothers initially fashioned and sold toys; later they made tools, including a lathe, a newspaper-folding device, and a printing press. Between 1889 and 1894, they used the latter to produce a small local journal; Wilbur did the writing. Since their father's calling required the family to move often, the boys attended public schools in Iowa, Indiana, and Ohio. Wilbur and Orville were the only Wright children not to attend college.

The two brothers shared a remarkable genius for mechanics and complemented each other so closely as to give the appearance of being practically of one mind. Both had serious, no-nonsense, and reserved personalities. Wilbur was more pragmatic, had a steadier business sense, read much, and wrote for his father's church bulletin. Orville was more meticulous, temperamental, and full of ideas; he became a fairly successful bicycle racer. Late in 1892, the two young men opened a shop for the sale and repair of bicycles, utilizing their own mechanical skills to ensure quality workmanship. They were so successful that within three years they had sold their printing press, had expanded their bicycle business, and had begun to assemble their own cycles, using improved designs and tools of their own making. Orville even devised a crude calculating machine. An early gift from their father of a toy helicopter stimulated a gradual interest in the rudiments of flight.

Lives' Work
By the mid-1890's, the Wright brothers were closely following the successful experiments of the German Otto Lilienthal with gliders, only to be stunned by news of his death in a gliding mishap in 1896. The tragedy, however, served as a catalyst for both men, who thereupon embarked on a common quest to solve the problem of piloted flight. At first they read the scanty scientific literature on aerodynamics. From 1899, they experimented with kites and gliders in their spare time, usually to the derision of witnesses. The task came to dominate both their lives, and neither one ever married. From 1900, Wilbur corresponded extensively with the French expert in gliders, Octave Chanute, who was endeavoring to discover where Lilienthal had erred. Chanute greatly encouraged the Wright brothers and promoted their work.

The approach of the Wrights toward mastering the air was novel. They differed from the experimenters in Europe who, ever since the adoption of the internal combustion engine to the automobile in the 1880's, had concentrated on developing power plants. Instead, the two brothers after observing birds in flight in 1899 believed that pilot control of a vehicle under wind power had to be established before mechanical power could be applied. Orville theorized that lateral balance held the key. (Lateral balance is the ability of the pilot to adjust air pressure against the wing tips to his right and left at different angles to the wind to bank to either side.) Wilbur provided the means: a twisting or "warping" of the wings at correspondingly opposing angles. They built and tested a small kite-like glider in 1899 that proved their thinking correct. They discovered that a piloted "aeroplane" not only had to be controlled simultaneously along the horizontal axis to bank right or left but also had to be steered vertically to climb or descend. The plane also had to be directed to turn right or left.

> "*If we all worked on the assumption that what is accepted as true is really true, there would be little hope of advance.*"

Concurrent control of flight along these three axes thus dominated the Wrights' subsequent experiments before a motor could ever be mounted. Solution of the three-axis control problem was their greatest contribution to the science of aerodynamics. Between 1899 and 1903, they constructed and tested a succession of biplane gliders, incorporating the horizontal wing-warping mechanism, a forward elevator for vertical control, and a movable rear rudder tail for turning. The latter became standard for all subsequent aircraft. Because existing tables of air pressure and drift proved inaccurate, Orville devised two small wind tunnels to make his own innumerable correct measurements of wing surfaces. Wilbur revealed these figures to the world of aeronautics in 1901. Though the Wrights' scientific work was undertaken at Dayton, their glider flights were made in the ideal breezes over the sand dunes on the beach at Kitty Hawk and nearby Kill Devil Hill, North Carolina.

By 1903 the brothers not only had solved the three-axis challenge but also had calculated the amount of engine power required to lift their most advanced biplane glider. Their talents as mechanics enabled them that year to build a superb, lightweight four-cylinder engine with approximately four horsepower. They also constructed an unprecedentedly efficient airscrew propeller for the engine to drive. They then joined these two inventions with bicycle chains, which drove two propellers mounted aft of the wings as pushers. Skids rather than wheels ensured stable landings. The entire flying machine was to be launched by a weight-dropping catapult. With Orville at the controls, the completed aircraft, the *Flyer I*, made its first flight at Kill Devil Hill on December 17, 1903. It flew 120 feet in twelve seconds, but by the end of the day Wilbur had achieved a flight of 852 feet. Only five other people, all local citizens, witnessed the epic event.

The world took no notice of the Wright brothers' monumental achievement, especially since the Wrights discouraged publicity until after their pending patents had been granted in 1906. Returning to Dayton, they devoted all of their time to creating and testing the first practical airplane. They were frustrated in their attempts to sell it to the United States or foreign governments; only in 1908 did their success become known. That summer, Orville dazzled U.S. Army observers at Fort Myer, Virginia, while Wilbur did the same in France for European observers. The effect was electric, and aviation enthusiasts now adopted the Wright method of aerodynamical control. Although a U.S. Army officer was killed and Orville seriously injured in a crash at Fort Myer, the Army accepted a Wright plane. European governments made similar purchases. In 1909, the Wright Company was incorporated, with Wilbur as president. Orville was content to be vice president and leave the business to his brother while he taught flying and improved aircraft designs.

Their fame assured, the Wrights now prospered, yet the adoption of their wing-warping techniques by competitors led them to institute legal action against many manufacturers. In the United States, their chief rival was Glenn H. Curtiss, who, like many other manufacturers, had adopted the European-invented aileron in preference to the full warped wing for lateral control. The Wrights protested that any wing-warping device owed ultimate credit to themselves. The bitter lawsuits did not endear them to the world's aviation community, and they absorbed much of their energies. Furthermore, after 1909, they were quickly bypassed by advancing technology in Europe, and several of their army planes suffered fatal crashes. Then, in May, 1912, Wilbur succumbed to typhoid fever, and this blow sapped much of Orville's enthusiasm.

Succeeding to the presidency of the company, Orville carried on. He continued to test every improvement to his planes, even though whenever a plane vibrated in flight he suffered pains stemming from his 1908 injuries. Because his interest was in research and not business, he sold out his interest in the company late in 1915 and gave his final flying lesson. Orville remained thereafter a consulting engineer with the company. The lawsuits, and countersuits, were not resolved until the United States entered World War I in 1917, at which time all the aircraft manufacturers agreed to a cross-licensing system whereby their patents were pooled to enable the United States to produce unlimited numbers of warplanes. Orville served as a major in the Army Air Service, primarily as a technological adviser at Dayton. He gave up flying in 1918 and spent the rest of his life devising aeronautical equipment, mechanical toys, and other ingenious gadgets. He also for many years lent his expertise as a member of the National Advisory Committee on Aeronautics (NACA).

Rival claims and ensuing controversies did not abate until the early 1940's. However, Wilbur and Orville Wright are firmly recognized as the undisputed inventors of the airplane.

SIGNIFICANCE

The Wright brothers exemplified the great era of individual invention that preceded the massive team research efforts funded by large corporations, foundations, governments, and universities. Their discovery of the key to piloted, powered flight pilot control over the free-flying aircraft stemmed largely from the mechanical "Yankee know-how" passed on to them by their parents and honed in their bicycle business. Their practical experiments, therefore, succeeded whereas those of the theoretical scientist Samuel Pierpont Langley (1834-1906) of the

Smithsonian Institution did not. Similarly, the bicycle and motorcycle racing and manufacturing of their major American competitor, Curtiss, yielded the same results as those of the Wrights after Curtiss profited from their basic discovery. Also, the Wrights did not succumb to the European fascination with engines until the fundamental aerodynamical problems had been solved; nor were they air sportsmen, like many enthusiasts of the day.

The historical timing was right. Technology and science were merging in all aspects of the rapidly industrializing Western world, enabling the Wrights to apply existing knowledge in the creation of the first airplane. In addition, the conquest of the air had become but one aspect of the last phase of public preoccupation with terrestrial exploration of the polar regions, remote jungles, and "lost" civilizations a preoccupation shared by the Wrights. They also exploited the public's craving for adventure with an exhibition team of stunt-flyers, though they did this only in response to competitors; by nature, neither man enjoyed popular hoopla of any kind. Finally, the drift of the European powers toward world war brought the Wrights the contracts they needed to continue their work with formal companies at home and in Europe.

The American military had no such sense of urgency and adopted early Wright flying machines only slowly, turning to the brothers to teach several officers to fly. The U.S. Army relied most heavily on Wright planes in the early years, 1908-1912, but several crashes led the Army to turn increasingly to other manufacturers. By contrast, the U.S. Navy initially preferred "hydroaeroplanes" that took off from and landed on the water, machines Curtiss provided since the Wrights opted for "landplanes." To compete in seaplanes, however, the Wright brothers subcontracted with the only other airplane manufacturer of the early days, W. Starling Burgess (1878-1947), who used Wright blueprints but designed his own pontoon floats. Still, the Wright control mechanism of levers proved too cumbersome and was eventually overshadowed by the Deperdussin method, another example of the brothers' failure to innovate beyond their basic design. Ironically, the Wright Company merged with the Curtiss firm in 1929 to become Curtiss-Wright.

The tragic aspect of the Wright brothers was their attempt, through litigation, virtually to patent powered flight itself with their claims over the wing-warping concept. Whatever the legal merits of their case, the airplane was one of those inventions that belonged to humanity as a whole and could not be controlled through patents. They did not object to others imitating their design, but they steadfastly opposed any who used it for profit without recompense to them. The ensuing lawsuits inhibited much aeronautical progress in Europe and the United States in the early years. The principal focus of their anger was Curtiss, a man of almost identical character, integrity, and mechanical genius whose seaplanes and flying boats provided the bulk of Allied naval aviation during World War I. Orville's resentment only deepened after Wilbur's untimely death, which he attributed partly to his brother's exhaustion from the dispute. Another source of irritation was the insistence of the Smithsonian Institution that its pioneer scientist, Langley, really deserved the credit for the key initial discoveries in aeronautics a claim not abandoned until World War II.

The Wrights solved the problems of piloted flight and by so doing initiated the air age, that essential historic bridge between the planet's surface and the ultimate leap into outer space.

Clark G. Reynolds

FURTHER READING

Adams, Noah. *The Flyers: In Search of Wilbur and Orville Wright.* New York: Crown, 2003. Adams, one of the hosts of the radio program *All Things Considered*, tells the story of the Wright brothers through their letters, diaries, and visits to the significant sites associated with their lives and work.

Crouch, Tom D., and Peter L. Jakab. *The Wright Brothers and the Invention of the Aerial Age.* Washington, D.C.: National Geographic and Smithsonian Air and Space Museum, 2003. The authors, curators at the Smithsonian Air and Space Museum, published this book to commemorate the one-hundredth anniversary of the Kitty Hawk flight. It includes biographical information, extensive descriptions of how the Wright brothers devised the airplane they flew at Kitty Hawk, and one hundred archival photographs.

Freudenthal, Elsbeth Estelle. *Flight into History: The Wright Brothers and the Air Age.* Norman: University of Oklahoma Press, 1949. An adequate popular biography of the two men.

Gibbs-Smith, Charles H. *Aviation.* London: Her Majesty's Stationery Office, 1970. A historical survey of flight from its origins in antiquity to the end of World War II, this work is the best single volume on the subject, giving a balanced treatment of the Wrights' key role. It is dedicated to them, their entry in the *Encyclopaedia Britannica* also being written by Gibbs-Smith.

---. *The Wright Brothers: A Brief Account of Their Work, 1899-1911.* London: Science Museum, 1963. A well-illustrated booklet on the crucial years.

Heppenheimer, T. A. *First Flight: The Wright Brothers and the Invention of the Airplane.* Hoboken, N.J.: Wiley, 2003. Heppenheimer, an aviation writer, provides a comprehensive look at the brothers' lives, the design and construction of the airplane flown at Kitty Hawk, the Kitty Hawk flight, and the bothers' subsequent business and technological ventures.

Kelly, Fred C. *The Wright Brothers.* New York: Harcourt Brace, 1943. The closest volume to an autobiography, this work was authorized by Orville Wright, who contributed heavily to it. It remains the standard work on their lives, though it is weak on the technological aspects and on the rivalry with Glenn Curtiss.

McFarland, Marvin W., ed. *The Papers of Wilbur and Orville Wright.* 2 vols. New York: McGraw-Hill, 1953. An exhaustive, meticulously annotated compendium of all papers relating not only to the Wrights' careers but also to that of Octave Chanute.

Renstrum, Arthur G., comp. *Wilbur and Orville Wright: A Further Reading Commemorating the Hundredth Anniversary of the Birth of Wilbur Wright.* Washington, D.C.: Library of Congress, 1968. An essential listing of books and articles.

Wright, Orville, and Wilbur Wright. *Miracle at Kitty Hawk: The Letters of Wilbur and Orville Wright.* Edited by Fred C. Kelly. New York: Farrar, Straus and Young, 1951. A very complete collection of the personal and technical correspondence of the brothers.

CHUCK YEAGER

Aviator

Born: February 13, 1923; Myra, West Virginia
Areas of Achievement: Aviation and space exploration; military

Yeager, one of the best-known American pilots of all time, was an accomplished wartime aviator during World War II and the first pilot to break the sound barrier in level flight.

EARLY LIFE

Born into a rural family, Chuck Yeager (YAY-gur) spent his early years working with his father in the family gas-drilling business near Hamlin, West Virginia. Like his father, Yeager was mechanically inclined, and he developed the skill to repair and maintain complex machinery, an

Chuck Yeager (Wikimedia Commons)

advantage that later served him well. Yeager lived a normal Depression-era existence, graduating from high school in Hamlin just as the United States entered World War II in December, 1941.

Yeager's first experience with aviation was rather inauspicious. As a teenager, he had observed a damaged airplane make an emergency landing near his home, leaving the future pilot unimpressed with the prospects of flight. With the United States at war, however, he enlisted in the US Army Air Forces (AAF) and became an airplane mechanic at a base in California. In 1942 he enrolled in the Flying Sergeant Program, a course designed to attract skilled enlisted men into the pilot ranks. Bored with repair work and attracted by the higher rank and monthly pay, Yeager entered the program, graduating in early 1943.

Initially, the AAF trained Yeager and the other pilots of his first unit, the 357th Fighter Squadron, to fly the P-39 Airacobra fighter. The P-39 proved an unsuccessful aircraft, however, and Yeager was reassigned to the 363rd Fighter Squadron equipped with the more successful P-51 Mustang fighter. In November 1943, Yeager arrived at his first combat base, a British Royal Air Force facility at Leiston, England.

LIFE'S WORK

Yeager flew his first combat mission in early 1944 in his P-51 that he nicknamed the Glamorous Glenn for his girlfriend back home, Glennis Dickhouse. On March 4, on his seventh combat mission, Yeager downed his first enemy aircraft, a German Messerschmitt Me 109 fighter. The next day, however, Yeager tangled with three German fighters in combat over Bordeaux, France, and was shot down. Evading capture by the Germans, Yeager made contact with the Maquis, an underground group resisting the German occupation of France. The Maquis hid Yeager from the Germans for nearly three weeks until late-winter snows melted and the group could move Yeager across the Pyrenees Mountains into neutral Spain. Yeager repaid the Maquis by instructing them how to fuse plastic explosives, one of the many mechanical skills Yeager had acquired as a youngster.

> "You don't concentrate on risks. You concentrate on results. No risk is too great to prevent the necessary job from getting done."

Once returned to England, Yeager found himself in a dilemma. Army rules forbade pilots rescued by the Maquis or other resistance groups from again flying combat missions. The Army feared that if a pilot was shot down a second time, the Germans might be able to extract information about the Maquis. Faced with losing his flight status, Yeager and another escaped pilot, Frederick Glover, pled their case to General Dwight D. Eisenhower, supreme commander of Allied forces in Europe. While Eisenhower pondered Yeager's fate, Yeager downed his second aircraft, a German Junkers Ju 88 bomber, over the English Channel. Eisenhower eventually returned both Yeager and Glover to duty, and Yeager returned to his squadron, now with the rank of lieutenant.

Once back in the war, Yeager added to his total of destroyed German planes. On October 12, 1944, he shot down five German fighters in a single day. A month later, he became one of the few Allied pilots to shoot down a fearsome German Me 262 fighter. The first jet fighter to enter combat, the Me 262 could fly 150 mph faster than Yeager's P-51, but Yeager caught the German fighter in its final airfield approach and shot the vulnerable German aircraft out of the sky.

With the air war starting to wind down, Yeager flew his final combat mission on January 14, 1945, and returned to the United States to report for duty at Wright Field, Ohio. Yeager, now a captain, married Glennis on February 26.

Uncertain about his future, Yeager assumed his duties at Wright Field. His primary task was to test-fly repaired aircraft, and he had the opportunity to demonstrate his flying skills in a number of different aircraft. His versatility and mechanical skills caught the attention of Colonel Albert Boyd, head of the Aeronautical Systems Flight Test Division at Wright Field, who invited Yeager to become a test pilot. Yeager accepted the invitation and transferred to Muroc Airfield (now Edwards Air Force Base) in California.

Among Yeager's early projects was the X-1, an experimental aircraft built by Bell Aircraft Corporation to study high-speed flight. The goal of the X-1 project was to break the sound barrier and fly beyond the speed of sound (supersonic speed). Bell Aircraft and its test pilot, Chalmers Goodlin, were initially in charge of the project, but the Air Force (the Army Air Force became the Air Force in 1947) believed the project was moving too slowly. When Goodlin demanded hazard pay for the risky flights, the Air Force took over the project and made Yeager the main test pilot.

The Air Force planned a flight to break the sound barrier on October 14, 1947. Two days before the flight, however, Yeager broke two of his

Jackie Cochran and Yeager being presented with the Harmon International Trophies by President Dwight D. Eisenhower. (Wikimedia Commons)

Yeager in front of the Bell X-1, which, as with all of the aircraft assigned to him, he named Glamorous Glennis (or some variation thereof), after his wife. The X-1 is the aircraft he flew when he broke the sound barrier. (Wikimedia Commons)

ribs in a horseback-riding accident. Afraid the Air Force would find another pilot, Yeager told only his wife, and project engineer-pilot Jack Ridley, about the injury. On the day of the flight above the Mojave Desert in Southern California, Ridley helped Yeager into the X-1 and provided part of a broom handle for Yeager to use as a lever to close the inside aircraft hatch. Yeager was able to secure himself into the aircraft and complete the flight, reaching a top speed of Mach 1.07 (700 mph). Due to national security concerns, the facts of Yeager's history-making flight did not become public for several months. Once the flight became public, Yeager became a national celebrity and was awarded both the MacKay and Collier Trophies for his achievement.

Although less newsworthy than breaking the sound barrier, Yeager had many other achievements during his Air Force career. During the Korean War, Yeager was one of a handful of pilots to test-fly a Soviet-built MiG 15 fighter that had been flown to South Korea by a defecting North Korean pilot. In 1953, Yeager participated in a number of research flights that continuously set new speed records, culminating with a flight that reached Mach 2.44 in October. For the rest of the 1950s, Yeager commanded US fighter squadrons based in Germany, France, and Spain.

Yeager's wife, Glennis, died in 1999. Yeager married his second wife, Victoria Scott D'Angelo, in 2003. In 2012, at the age of eighty-nine, he celebrated the sixty-fifth anniversary of breaking the sound bearing by doing it again, taking off from Nellis Air Force Base in Nevada in an F-15 Eagle. He lives in Penn Valley, California, near Sacramento.

Significance

With the US-Soviet space race just beginning during the 1950s, Yeager was primed to become the leading adviser to the National Aeronautics and Space Administration (NASA) and the space program itself. Although he was not an astronaut, he did serve as the first commanding officer of the Air Force Aerospace Research Pilot School, which provided trained pilots for NASA and the Air Force.

Yeager's test-flight days would end in 1963, when he was badly burned in an accident while flying an NF-104 aircraft, but he recovered enough from his injuries to fly once again during the Vietnam War. He commanded the 405th Fighter Wing in 1966, flying 127 combat missions over Vietnam with the rank of brigadier general. He then served in several administrative posts until his retirement from the Air Force in 1975. In 1986, U.S. president Ronald Reagan appointed Yeager to the investigative team looking into the explosion of the space shuttle *Challenger*.

Yeager, whose very name has become synonymous with risky, but necessary, flight, excelled at meeting challenges and accomplishing great feats. Moreover, he achieved notoriety by repeatedly risking his life in incredibly dangerous situations. Even when given the option of taking the safe path, such as the option of going home after being shot down in World War II, Yeager saw challenges as jobs to be done. By accomplishing his great tasks, Yeager furthered the causes of aviation and space travel in the late twentieth century, becoming a legend in the process.

Steven J. Ramold

Further Reading

Caygill, Peter. *Sound Barrier: The Rocky Road to Mach 1.0+*. Barnsley, Eng.: Pen & Sword, 2006. Print.

Courtwright, David. *Sky as Frontier: Adventure, Aviation, and Empire*. College Station: Texas A&M P, 2005. Print.

Darling, David J. *The Rocket Man: And Other Extraordinary Characters in the History of Flight*. London: Oneworld, 2013. Print.

"Get the Stuff Right." *Executive Leadership* 28.3 (2013): 6. *Business Source Complete*. Web. 12 Dec. 2013.

Hallion, Richard P. "The Air Force and the Supersonic Breakthrough." *Technology and the Air Force: A Retrospective Assessment*. Ed. J. Neufeld, G. M. Watson, and D. Chenoweth. Washington, DC: Air Force History and Museums Program, 1997. Print.

Hallion, Richard P., and Michael H. Gorn. *On the Frontier: Experimental Flight at NASA Dryden*. Washington, DC: Smithsonian, 2003. Print.

"Legends of Aviation." *Aviation History* 22.2 (2011): 21. *Academic Search Complete*. Web. 12 Dec. 2013.

Yeager, Chuck. *The Quest for Mach One: A First-Person Account of Breaking the Sound Barrier*. New York: Penguin, 1997. Print.

Yeager, Chuck, with Leo Janos. *Yeager: An Autobiography*. New York: Bantam, 1985. Print.

Art

Our ideas about *art* as a field for heroic endeavor date largely to the Romantic era—from the late eighteenth century through the nineteenth. In this period in Europe, and to a lesser degree in North America, the intellectual trend known as Romanticism swept away the neoclassical aesthetic. It introduced a new emphasis on the subjective, the visionary, the imagination, radical individualism, emotions, the sublime, and the transcendent. Eccentricity and even madness were claimed as signs of a new kind of greatness of soul. This was unlike anything known before in the West. If we think today that art can be a path to human fulfillment or transcendence, or if artists can dress or behave in ways that business leaders can't or wouldn't, these things are evidence that the Romantic paradigm still has power.

Recent scholarship by the great English Marxist critic Terry Eagleton (and others) has focused on the development of high culture in the Romantic era as an activity that might replace religion for modern people. Art in this period became something spiritually profound and transformative: art puts us in touch with what is transcendent yet resident in or accessible through the material world. It reaches to the unknown; it makes creation a near-sacred act; it is experienced in spaces that are like churches (the modern museum as shrine), and so on.

For Eagleton the project hasn't been successful. In large part, he thinks that this is because it was always an elitist project. Elitism led to the idea that paintings are luxury items for the world's elite consumers and to the excesses of the art market in the twentieth century. A great deal of late twentieth-century and early twenty-first century art can be understand only in relation to this development; the subway art of Keith Haring in the 1980s, for example, was pop art—by definition anti-elite—but it also did something that earlier pop art from the 1960s did not do: it gave itself away for free and it displayed itself in the subways of New York City. This was a reaction to commercialization in the art world in the 1980s.

However, the fact that Haring's paintings can still move us and inspire us today speaks to the continued vitality of the historical project that he identifies. Or consider the changing fortunes of Martin Wong, the Chinese-American artist who was active since the 1970s and who died in 1999. Wong achieved recognition in the national press following an important retrospective in 2015. Largely neglected by the art establishment during his lifetime, today he is hailed not only for his poetic realism, but as an exemplar of a simpler, less commercially-driven and more bohemian period in the art world. As long as our daily routines are as disciplined, routinized, and subjected to the rules of the market as they are in the twenty-first century, figures Wong—an example of the artist as a bohemian—will remain potent for us, and the legacy of the ideas of Romanticism will continue.

The Hunter's Return *by Thomas Cole, a landscape artist of the Hudson River School, heavily influenced by Romanticism.* (Wikimedia Commons)

Ruth Asawa

Artist, educator, and arts advocate

Born: January 24, 1926; Norwalk, California
Died: August 5, 2013; San Francisco, California
Area of Achievement: Art, education, and art advocacy

Ruth Asawa is best known in San Francisco for her arts advocacy and public sculptures. Her abstract looped- and tied-wire sculptures were considered pioneering in the mid-twentieth century and continue to influence artists throughout the world.

Early Life

Ruth Asawa, known as Aiko to her parents, was the fourth of seven children born to Japanese immigrant truck farmers in Norwalk, California. In addition to public school, she attended Japanese school on Saturdays, where she learned calligraphy and origami. When she was not attending school, she helped her parents with farm chores.

In 1942, during World War II, the US government began rounding up people of Japanese descent to put them in internment camps. Asawa's family was separated: her father was interned at a camp in New Mexico, while the rest of the family was placed in a camp in Santa Anita, where they were forced to live in horse stalls. Ruth made the best of the situation by taking advantage of art classes held there by animators from the Walt Disney Studios. Later, the family was moved to a permanent camp in Rohwer, Arkansas. Surrounded by barbed wire fencing and enduring harsh living conditions, Asawa continued to explore art with interned artists and persevered in the camp's high school, serving as the art editor for the yearbook. After graduation, she attended the Milwaukee State Teachers College (now the Wisconsin State University at Milwaukee) for three years, intending to become an art teacher; however, she was unable to complete the program because Japanese student teachers were unwelcome in the schools.

Asawa then discovered Black Mountain College, an experimental college located in North Carolina. She studied painting, drawing, and design there with German American artist Josef Albers, gaining additional inspiration from faculty and visiting scholars, including Buckminster Fuller, Merce Cunningham, and Jacob Lawrence. Considered one of the most talented students, she was selected to participate in a Black Mountain student exhibit held at the Addison Gallery in Andover, Massachusetts.

Asawa's San Francisco Fountain, featuring bas-relief scenes of San Francisco. (Wikimedia Commons)

Life's Work

In 1949, Asawa moved to San Francisco and married Albert Lanier, a Black Mountain student of architecture. During the 1950s, while raising their six children, she developed the first of her looped-wire sculptures using a crocheting technique learned on a visit to Mexico. She exhibited these and other works at the San Francisco Museum of Art, the Whitney Museum of American Art in New York City, and other major museums, rising to national and international prominence as an abstract artist. By the mid-1960s, Asawa was receiving commissions for large-scale sculptures for many public and commercial spaces in San Francisco and beyond. The bare-breasted mermaids Asawa portrayed in her sculpture *Andrea* (1968) generated much controversy upon installation at Ghirardelli Square. Asawa's other pieces included the Hyatt Hotel sculpture at Union Square (1973) and a fountain for Buchanan Plaza in Japantown (1976).

In 1968, Asawa cofounded the Alvarado School Arts Workshop at her children's school, where she had children craft masks and other artwork using a flour-based clay known as baker's clay. Asawa also used baker's clay to form molds from which she cast some of her bronze sculptures. The Arts Workshop program eventually led to the founding of the Ruth Asawa San Francisco School of the Arts.

In 1985, Asawa was diagnosed with the autoimmune disorder lupus, and her health began to deteriorate. Nevertheless, the following year, she designed *Aurora* for Bayside Plaza, a stainless steel fountain shaped like an origami waterwheel. She also designed the *Japanese American Internment Memorial Sculpture* (1994) at the

Various wire sculptures by Asawa. (Wikimedia Commons)

San Jose Federal Building and the Garden of Remembrance at San Francisco State University (2002).

> "*Sometimes good comes through adversity. I would not be who I am today had it not been for the internment, and I like who I am.*"

Asawa's awards include the Asian American Art Foundation's Golden Ring Lifetime Achievement Award (1995) and honorary doctorates from California College of Arts and Crafts, San Francisco Art Institute, and San Francisco State University. In 1998, the University of Wisconsin at Milwaukee awarded her a belated BFA degree. In 2005, the H. W. de Young Museum in San Francisco chose fifteen of Asawa's wire sculptures to grace its new wing. In 2010, the San Francisco School of the Arts was renamed the Ruth Asawa San Francisco School of the Arts in the artist's honor

Significance

Asawa's abstract sculptures are considered pioneering for their bridge between craft and art, as well as their linking of nature with urban space. Crocheted loosely in spheres, hourglasses, and other recognizable or freeform shapes so that the sculptures remain transparent, their play of light, shadow, and positive and negative space presents a unique sculptural approach.

As an advocate for art education, Asawa especially left her mark on the children of San Francisco, by democratizing art and empowering children with techniques to build self-esteem and encourage a sense of experimentation. Her cofounding of the Alvarado Art Workshop in 1968, at a time when funding for the arts was not a priority, led to an unprecedented citywide art program with major funding from the California Arts Council and several key foundations. The workshop model with residencies by established artists inspired many other such programs. Asawa is also known for designing public spaces and memorials intended to address the injustice of World War II Japanese internment camps. Ruth Asawa died at her San Francisco home on August 5, 2013.

Sally Driscoll, updated by Micah L. Issitt

Further Reading

Cornell, Daniel, et al. *The Sculpture of Ruth Asawa: Contours in the Air.* Berkeley: U of California P, 2006. Print. A good source for biographical information and images of Asawa's paintings, drawings, and sculpture.

Isenberg, Alison. " 'Culture-a-Go-Go': The Ghirardelli Square Sculpture Controversy and the Liberation of Civic Design in the 1960s." *Journal of Social History* 44.2 (Winter 2010): 379–412. Print. Details the late 1960s controversy surrounding Asawa's mermaid sculpture.

Koplos, Janet, and Bruce Metcalf. *Makers: A History of American Studio Craft.* Chapel Hill: U of North Carolina P, 2010. Print. A survey of the twentieth century arts and crafts movement, attesting to Asawa's prominence in innovative wire sculpture.

Ollman, Leah. "The Industrious Line." *Art in America* 95.5 (May 2007): 158. Print. A review of Asawa's first major retrospective exhibit at San Francisco's M. H. de Young Museum (2006–07), providing insight into the artist and her work.

Judith F. Baca

Muralist

Born: September 20, 1946; Los Angeles, California
Areas of achievement: Art; social issues; education

Baca brings together diverse communities through her participatory approach to mural production. An artist whose work has been exhibited worldwide, Baca also is a university professor, community activist, and founder of a nonprofit public art resource center.

Early Life

Judith Francisca Baca (BAH-kah) was born in Los Angeles, California, to Ortensia Baca. As a child, Baca and her mother moved to Watts, California, where they lived with Baca's grandmother and two aunts. Baca's biological father was absent from her youth. Ortensia never told Baca's father, who had been deployed by the Navy, about her pregnancy, and the two were never married. Baca later investigated and learned the identity and whereabouts of her biological father, Valentino Marcel.

Baca began painting as a kindergartener. A fluent Spanish-speaker, she had yet to learn English and could not participate fully in class lessons. In 1952, Baca's mother married an Italian American named Clarence Ferrari. The family moved to Pacoima, California, where Baca's stepsiblings Gary and Diane were born.

Baca was enrolled in public schools through junior high, then attended Bishop Alemany High School in Mission Hills. Compared with the public schools she previously had attended, the Catholic school had limited art resources. Baca practiced art informally, entertaining her high school peers by drawing on blackboards. She won popularity with her creative sketches and whimsical cartoons of nuns.

Although neither her mother, who worked at a tire factory, nor her stepfather, an upholsterer at Lockheed Martin, had completed college, Baca enrolled at California State University, Northridge (CSUN) after high school. She enjoyed taking courses in art, philosophy, and history. She earned a bachelor's degree in art in 1969 and ten years later received a master's in art education, both from CSUN. Baca married at age nineteen but was divorced six years later.

Life's Work

Baca's earliest jobs included working as a production illustrator at Lockheed Martin and teaching at her former high school. Baca's pivotal employment opportunity, however, arose in the early 1970's when she was hired to teach art classes at community centers in East Los Angeles. Here she befriended young local residents, primarily teenage boys, who would pass time at the parks. They chatted about tattoos and about their mutual artistic interests; a collaborative energy began to blossom. When Baca proposed that she and the youths paint together, her boss resisted, chiding her naïveté; partnership implied that the youth might be crossing rival gang territories. Undeterred, Baca began her grassroots efforts in muralism. In 1970, she and the teenagers collaboratively painted *La Abuelita* as a backdrop to the local open-air theater. The mural depicts a loving, dark-skinned grandmother with outstretched arms. Soon, local newspapers published articles applauding her transformative work organizing peace treaties among rival gangs. Shortly thereafter, Baca was promoted to director of Eastside murals. She initiated a citywide mural project that ultimately produced more than four hundred urban murals and employed more than one thousand residents.

> "*I really don't want to produce artwork that does not have meaning beyond simple decorative values. I want to use public space to create a public voice, and a public consciousness about the presence of people who are, in fact, the majority of the population but who are not represented in any visual way. By telling their stories we are giving voice to the voiceless and visualizing the whole of the American story.*"

During the summers of 1974 through 1984, Baca created one of her most famous murals, *The Great Wall of Los Angeles*. Located in the Tujunga Wash drainage channel in the San Fernando Valley, *The Great Wall of Los Angeles* is 2,754 feet long, making it one of the longest murals in the world. With powerful imagery grounded in a visual history of Los Angeles, the piece is most famous for its comparative representations of the city's ethnic history. The impact of Baca's work generated tremendous interest and sponsorship from various community agencies, leading her to cofound the Social and

Public Arts Resource Center (SPARC) in 1976 in Venice, California, with artist Christina Schlesinger and filmmaker Donna Deitch. Baca's leadership style solidified her democratic and innovative approach to art production. Former Los Angeles mayor Tom Bradley commissioned her to work on a series of public art displays in 1988 for the Great Walls Unlimited: Neighborhood Pride program, which put hundreds of young artists to work on more than eighty murals.

The magnitude, scope, and tremendous collaborative efforts involved in *The Great Wall of Los Angeles* earned Baca critical acclaim and set the tone for her increasingly ambitious future cultural projects. Baca's dramatic use of color juxtaposed with tranquil imagery is exemplified in *World Wall: A Vision of the Future Without Fear* (1990). This portable mural addressing world peace, spirituality, and social justice consists of numerous 10-foot-by-30-foot panels arranged in a semicircle. The exhibit has traveled around the globe, adding new panels by local artists in many of the countries it has visited. Baca's more recent work uses computer technology to draft initial concepts, create and arrange visual images, and prepare pieces for transfer to public spaces.

Baca's academic career kept pace with her artistic prominence, flourishing after she took a professorship in Visual Arts at the University of California, Irvine in 1981. Baca later served as vice chair at the University of California at Los Angeles (UCLA) César Chávez Center for Interdisciplinary Studies in 1996 and was appointed as full professor in UCLA's World Arts and Cultures department. Beyond teaching and painting, Baca forged new academic territory by establishing the visual and public art program at California State University, Monterey Bay, when she served as one of thirteen founding campus faculty members in 1995-1998.

In March 2010, Baca was part of a mural project in the East Bay, Northern California, the Richmond Mural Project. It is a five panel mural that featured different themes in each panel. The goal of the project was to connect the citizens, and share their wildly diverse backgrounds. She was also part of a group that successfully preserved her mural, *Danza Indigenas*, in Baldwin Park, after there were violent protests and vandalism towards the artwork. Baca has also had a huge part in the group Mural Rescue Program, which is a program that works to restore, preserve/stabilize, and conserve murals (both painted and digital) that have been painted or printed on substrates and walls built in public environments. One of Baca's most recent and ongoing projects is "new codex-Oaxaca- immigration and cultural memory" this project is

Beyond Mexican Muralism: Baca's Innovative Style

Judith F. Baca's murals are most heavily influenced by the work of Mexican muralist David Alfaro Siqueiros. Siqueiros is one of Mexico's three most famous muralists, along with Diego Rivera and José Clemente Orozco, who are known as "Los Tres Grandes" (the three great ones). Baca's artistic education in college did not, however, include their work. Rather, Baca learned about the Mexican muralists by chance. In the early 1970's, she received a book on Mexican muralism while she was working with inner-city youths in East Los Angeles. Inspired to learn more, Baca traveled to Mexico to see their murals. In 1977, she was one of twenty-five artists to participate in a muralism workshop hosted at Taller Siqueiros (Siqueiros's studio) in Cuernavaca, Mexico. There she mastered Siqueiros's artistic techniques, which incorporate musical ratios, creative spatial divisions, and visual connectivity. Baca departs from the style of Mexican muralists, however, in her participatory style of mural-making. Her murals are produced through intense collaboration with community affiliates. The historiography of her murals is intimately intertwined with the method in which they are produced. Unlike Los Tres Grandes, who produced art for the public, Baca produces art with the public, thereby empowering local communities to reclaim and take pride in their communal open spaces.

about sharing artwork and stories of those who are immigrating from Mexico (namely Oaxaca) to the US; why they are immigrating, what they are leaving behind, what's happening to make them leave, etc. Baca is involved in choosing the art pieces that are being displayed, community outreach to help come up with ways for these immigrants to have a stable outcome, and just getting a conversation started in the community, using these immigrants' artwork.

SIGNIFICANCE

A renowned artist and scholar, Baca remains grounded in community activism. Her cultural and artistic identity is infused with her Mexican American heritage. Her approach to art and the substance of her work exemplify a participatory-action approach to social awareness through murals. Baca's legacy is reflected in the art she produces and the young artists she trains. Her art depicts generational diversity and conveys respect for the elderly; the empowerment of women; familial bonds and unity; the value of education; and most importantly honor and respect for community practices and history. One of the persistent challenges faced by Baca is the lack of funding and political leverage to protect established murals in public spaces, which is why SPARC created Save L.A. Murals, an organization that raises awareness and preserves Los Angeles murals.

Michelle Madsen Camacho

Further Reading

Baca, Judith F. "The Human Story at the Intersection of Ethics, Aesthetics and Social Justice." *Journal of Moral Education* 34, no. 2 (June, 2005):153-169. A transcript of Baca's speech at the Association for Moral Education Conference in which she reflects on art and its relation to broader socio-political issues in the United States.

---. Official Web site. http://www.judybaca.com. Baca's professional Web site includes a biography, photos and video of her work, and many other useful resources.

---. "Oral History Interviews with Judith Baca." Interview by Amalia Mesa-Bains. *Archives of American Art, Smithsonian Institution* (August, 1986). Baca tells her life story to historian Amalia Mesa-Bains in 1986, at the beginning of Baca's academic career.

---. "World Wall: A Vision of the Future Without Fear." *Frontiers: A Journal of Women Studies* 14, no. 2 (1994): 81-85. This scholarly article provides Baca's own subjective analysis of her mobile mural *World Wall*.

---. "World Wall: A Vision of the Future Without Fear—An Interview with Judith F. Baca." Interview by Frances K. Pohl. *Frontiers: A Journal of Women Studies* 11, no. 1 (1990): 33-43. An interview by art historian Frances Pohl providing contextual background and analysis of Baca's mural *World Wall*.

Olmstead, Mary. *Judy Baca*. Chicago: Raintree, 2005. Written for a younger audience, this monograph provides an accessible biography of Baca.

Social and Public Art Resource Center. http://www.sparc-murals.org. Official Web site for Baca's nonprofit organization, which produces, preserves, and educates the public on murals.

Jean-Michel Basquiat

Artist

Born: December 22, 1960; Brooklyn, New York City
Died: August 12, 1988; New York, New York City
Area of achievement: Art and photography

A graffiti artist who blurred the line between high and trivial art, Basquiat shocked the 1980's art world with his meteoric rise and early death. He epitomized the excesses of the era, especially its out-of-control art prices and the nexus of music, fashion, art, and drugs.

Early Life

Jean-Michel Basquiat (ZHOHN-mee-SHEHL BAHSkee-AHT) was born December 22, 1960, to Haitian-born Gérard Basquiat and Matilde Basquiat, a Brooklyn native of Puerto Rican heritage. Basquiat grew up in the middle-class Park Slope section of Brooklyn as the only son of three children. While his father worked as an accountant, his homemaker mother took the boy to New York City museums. Basquiat later credited his mother and her parents for fostering his love of art and music, dedicating *Abuelita* (1981) to his Spanish-speaking grandmother. In 1968, Basquiat was struck by a car while playing in the street; his spleen had to be removed, and he suffered several other injuries. To help her son pass the time while hospitalized, Matilde gave him the classic anatomical book *Gray's Anatomy*. The repeated themes of internal organs and human skeletons in Basquiat's art undoubtedly owe much to the book, which he studied passionately.

> "*I don't listen to what art critics say. I don't know anybody who needs a critic to find out what art is.*"

Basquiat had little interest in formal schooling. He changed schools frequently after his parents divorced in 1968 and the children moved with their father to Flatbush and then to Boerum Hill in Brooklyn. When the family moved to Puerto Rico in 1974 for two years, Basquiat ran away from home for the first time. He later recalled that his art at the time reflected mostly anger. In 1976, the

Fans of Basquiat leave small offerings on his grave stone at Green-Wood Cemetary in Brooklyn, New York. (Wikimedia Commons)

family returned to Brooklyn but Basquiat's relationship with his father remained troubled.

In 1977, Basquiat drew a comic for his school paper about a young searcher for truth who wants to find a modern and stylish form of spirituality and who struggles to escape the falsity of established religions. Basquiat signed the comic SAMO, the name of his invented pure religion. SAMO became the famous pseudonym with which Basquiat signed his graffiti in New York's SoHo neighborhood. In 1978, he dropped out of school and left home for good.

Life's Work

With a blond Mohawk, Basquiat quickly became a fixture on the New York City nightclub circuit. He played in a band called Gray, worked as a disc jockey, and made additional money by selling painted T-shirts. He met many of the most prominent artists of the 1980's as well as Mudd Club owner and filmmaker Diego Cortez. Basquiat's first exhibition, the 1980 "Times Square Show," resulted from his friendship with Cortez. He acted in the 1981 film *New York Beat* and then opened a studio at the film production office. His early paintings reflect the theme of big-city life and clearly show the influence of French primitive painter Jean Dubuffet. American graffiti artist Cy Twombly was another strong influence, but Basquiat gained fame for his unconventional mingling of various visual ideas and sources.

Basquiat's reputation continued to grow throughout 1981 as he participated in shows and garnered critical acclaim in the magazine *Artforum*. He held his first one-man show that year in Modena, Italy, under the name SAMO.

Basquiat's first one-man show in the United States came in March, 1982, at Annina Nosei's gallery. The show featured his silkscreen prints titled *Anatomy*. His work was exhibited in Los Angeles and throughout Western Europe. While staying in Los Angeles, Basquiat produced the record "Beat Bop" (1983). Upon returning to New York in 1983, he developed a friendship with his idol, pop artist Andy Warhol.

By 1984, Basquiat had become a major artist. His continued his early themes but also began to comment through his paintings on the absurd prices charged for art. At the time, Basquiat's paintings were selling for twenty thousand dollars in Europe. Basquiat had little interest in money and strongly objected to his exploitation as an artist, once referring to himself as a "gallery mascot." When the Basquiat-Warhol collaborative show in 1985 received a near-unanimous critical panning, Warhol pulled away from the younger artist. Warhol's 1987 death left Basquiat inconsolable. He held a few more shows but gradually gave up on his life. He announced an intention to abandon painting. Basquiat died from an overdose August 12, 1988, in the Great Jones Street studio that he had rented from Warhol. He is buried in Greenwood Cemetery in Brooklyn.

Significance

Basquiat produced art to make statements, not to make money. He protested his exploitation as an artist at the same time that he represented the excesses of the 1980's. His death is generally attributed to his disappointment and disillusionment with the art scene's obsession with money.

Simplistically labeled the "Black Picasso," Basquiat ultimately proves too complex for easy classification. Critical and scholarly treatment of his work declined in the 1990's while the prices paid for it continued to rise. In 2002, Sotheby's auctioned Basquiat's *Profit I* for $5.5 million.

Caryn E. Neumann

Further Reading

Emmerling, Leonhard. *Basquiat*. Los Angeles: Taschen, 2003. A heavily illustrated short biography of Basquiat, this book is a superb introduction to the artist.

Fretz, Eric. *Jean-Michel Basquiat: A Biography*. Westport, Conn.: Greenwood Press, 2010. Part of a biographical series, this work covers Basquiat's impact on the contemporary art world.

Hoban, Phoebe. *Basquiat: A Quick Killing in Art*. New York: Penguin, 1998. A very readable biography of the artist that also explores the art market of the 1980's, including the graffiti movement and the out of control auction houses.

Marshall, Richard, ed. *Jean-Michel Basquiat*. New York: Harry N. Abrams and Whitney Museum of Art, 1992. Published in conjunction with an exhibition of Basquiat's work, this is a collection of scholarly essays about the artist and his art.

Mayer, Marc, ed. *Basquiat*. London: Merrell, 2010. This book focuses more on Basquiat's art than his life, with detailed examinations of his works, including many rarely exhibited pieces.

Mercurio, Gianni, ed. *The Jean-Michel Basquiat Show*. New York: Skira, 2007. This coffee table book is a comprehensive examination of Basquiat and the 1980's New York City art scene.

BARBARA CARRASCO

Artist and educator

Born: 1955; El Paso, Texas
Area of Achievement: Art, education, social issues

Carrasco is an award-winning artist and muralist whose works have been exhibited in museums and at conventions worldwide. Carrasco's work is particularly displayed in the Unites States, Europe, and Latin America. Aside from creating artwork, Carrasco has also taught at multiple American universities.

EARLY LIFE

Barbara Carrasco (kah-RAHS-koh) was born in 1955 in El Paso, Texas. As a child, she was raised in the predominantly Mexican American, African American, and immigrant housing projects of Culver City, California. From first grade through eighth grade, she attended a Catholic school, where she felt the nuns treated white students better than Latino students. At this young age, Carrasco became aware of the difficulties she would face in life because of her skin color, ethnicity, and gender.

After graduating high school, Carrasco began attending West Los Angeles College. During this time, it was rare for Chicanas to receive any education beyond high school and even more rare for Chicanos to study art. Much of the art produced by Chicanos was considered primitive; however, many well-known Latino and Chicano artists now hold advanced degrees in the arts.

In 1976, Carrasco graduated from West Los Angeles College with her associate of arts degree. She immediately enrolled at the University of California at Los Angeles, from which she earned her bachelor of fine arts degree in 1978. After graduating, Carrasco traveled to Mexico, where she was able to meet many of renowned artist Frida Kahlo's students and read Kahlo's biography. This trip made a huge impact on Carrasco's life and served as a major source of inspiration for the young artist.

She was heavily influenced by Kahlo's self-portraits and began drawing pictures of her own face. Carrasco sees this as a way to explore her autobiography while simultaneously repossessing her Chicana heritage. Her self-portraits also often examine her Catholic upbringing with satire and humor.

> "*I think that's the best part of mural making, meeting people in the community, because you don't get a chance to really do that. I think a good muralist makes an effort to meet people. Because when it's a historical mural, when it's a mural period, it's not your personal work. It's a public work of art and it should involve the public.*"

LIFE'S WORK

Although she took a break from school after receiving her bachelor's degree, Carrasco soon resumed her education. In 1991, she graduated from the California Institute of the Arts with a master of fine arts degree. From 1976 to 1991, Carrasco created banners for the United Farm Workers. She later produced a well-known portrait of UFW leader Dolores Huerta (Dolores, 1999). Carrasco also has painted murals in Leningrad and Armenia for the Union of Soviet Socialist Republics (1985 and 1987) and created the computer-animated piece PESTICIDES! for the Spectacolor light board in Times Square (1989). Since her graduation in 1991, Carrasco has exhibited her work not only in the United States but also in Europe and parts of Latin America.

Carrasco's style of work includes painting and murals that display and represent Chicano art, U.S. contemporary political art, U.S. public art, and women's cultural production. Carrasco often emphasizes skin color in her paintings to depict her experiences as a light-skinned Chicana stuck in a racial limbo. One piece in particular, Self-Portrait (1994), addresses Carrasco's feelings about her light skin.

Carrasco has received a number of awards, honors, and grants, including a fellowship from the J. Paul Getty Fund for the Visual Arts (1988); a Window Grant for Literature from the Los Angeles Cultural Affairs Department (1990); a Rockefeller Foundation artist grant (1992); an Andy Warhol Foundation artist grant (1992); and the Los Angeles Cultural Affairs Department's City of Los Angeles award (2000).

In 1993, Carrasco married writer, photographer, and video artist Harry Gamboa, with whom she had a daughter in 1994. One year later, Carrasco received a diagnosis of lymphoma; she underwent a bone-marrow transplant in 1996. Her illness briefly put a halt to her work, but in 1999, Carrasco returned to active participation in the art world. She also has worked as an art professor at the University of California, Riverside; University of California, Santa Barbara; and Loyola Marymount University.

Significance

Carrasco has exhibited her work around the world. After battling cancer, she reflected on her illness and mortality in a survey exhibition at the Vincent Price Art Museum at East Los Angeles College titled "Barbara Carrasco: A Brush with Life" (2008). Through her work, Carrasco examines issues of race, gender, identity, politics, class, sexuality, and social injustices. Known for her ballpoint-pen drawings as well as her large-scale murals and paintings, Carrasco is an activist and contributor to the iconography representing Chicana feminists.

Macey M. Freudensprung

Further Reading

Brown, Betty Ann. "Autobiographical Imagery in the Art of Los Angeles Women." In *Yesterday and Tomorrow: California Women Artists*, edited by Sylvia Moore. New York: Midmarch Arts Press. 1989. Describes Carrasco's youth and how it influenced her art career.

Shorris, Earl. *Latinos: A Biography of the People*. New York: W. W. Norton, 1992. Notes the origins and history of Latino culture from the first arrivals in America through the close of the twentieth century; includes information on Carrasco's role and significance.

Venegas, Sybil. "Brush with Life: Barbara Carrasco Powerfully Mixes Art with Race, Class, and Gender Politics." *Ms.*, Spring, 2008. This account of Carrasco's life and work includes many images of her artwork.

Keith Haring

Artist and activist

Born: May 4, 1958; Reading, Pennsylvania
Died: February 16, 1990; New York City, New York
Area of Achievement: Art

One of the most iconic American artists of the second half of the twentieth century, Keith Haring died of AIDS at the age of thirty-one.

Early Life

Keith Haring was born May 4, 1958 in Kutztown, Pennsylvania. He grew up in Reading, Pennsylvania, not far from Philadelphia. His father, Allen Haring, was an engineer with an interest in cartoon art, and his mother Joan encouraged Keith's early interest in making drawings. By the time Keith was a teenager, he had developed not only a passion for drawing but an interest in activism and a concern for others that would remain with him even at the height of his celebrity.

When he was still a teen, using his own money to purchase supplies, Haring led informal, open-air, free art

Keith Haring (Wikimedia Commons)

workshops for children in an inner-city neighborhood near where he grew up. Haring also went through an intense religious phase when he was an adolescent; for a time, he was involved in the "Jesus Movement" in the early 1970s.

Later, in high school, Haring hitchhiked across the country, experimenting with drugs and selling T-shirts with his own designs. In 1976, Haring moved to Pittsburgh, Pennsylvania, to attend the Ivy School of Art where he studied commercial art. He stayed in Pittsburgh for two years, then moved to New York City to study painting at the School of Visual Arts. He worked at the popular nightclub Danceteria as a busboy.

> "Art should be something that liberates your soul, provokes the imagination and encourages people to go further."

Large outdoor mural by Haring in Collingwood, a suburb of Melbourne, Australia. The mural was painted in 1984 on a cement panel over a wall of the former Collingwood Technical School. (Wikimedia Commons)

LIFE'S WORK

Haring arrived in New York City when he was twenty years old. Immersing himself in the trendy downtown scene, he absorbed influences from figures as diverse as William S. Burroughs, Jean Dubuffet, Pierre Alechinsky, Andy Warhol, Christo and the popular culture of New York City at that time. Shortly after arriving in New York, he met and befriended other emerging artists like Jean-Michel Basquiat and Kenny Scharf. Through the late seventies and into the 1980s, there was a lively underground scene that sometimes overlapped with the club and punk scenes in New York, and Haring found plenty of opportunities to show his work in alternative spaces across that spectrum.

Haring, riding the subways in New York, saw empty advertising boxes on the subway walls filled with black paper inserts. In 1980, inspired by the profuse graffiti art in New York City at that time, he took white chalk and began drawing on the black paper inserts as if they were blackboards. He had to work quickly to avoid being arrested. (Over the next several years he was arrested many times for defacing public property.) His unique, bold, style and his quirky, elusive iconography were immediately recognizable. His art became widely known and talked about before anyone knew the identity of the artist.

Haring produced hundreds of images for world to enjoy in this period, and he did it anonymously. On some days, he did as many as forty subway drawings. Many of the familiar pictographic elements of Haring's work were developed in this period, including the so-called "radiant baby," groups of dancing figures, the barking dog, and figures with television sets for heads.

Haring's subway drawings were influenced by a cohort in the arts world who were interested in merging elements from intellectual culture, like *semiotics*, which Haring studied in art school, with counter-cultural themes of personal, spiritual, and socio-political transformation. (Semiotics studied culture as a system of *signs*.) William S. Burroughs, a pervasive influence on the American underground and avant-garde from the 1940s until his death in the 1990s, was a hero to Haring and perhaps the single most important influence on Haring's thinking. Burroughs had promulgated an influential idea that an artist could break the codes through which the "control society" constructed and influenced us, as if the semiotic elements of mass culture were, he imagined, like Mayan hieroglyphs that could be re-arranged with subversive intent. This meshed well with Haring's interest in drawing iconic and pictographic imagery, and it was one of the inspirations for his suggestive style in which the meaning was elusive but full of energy and even urgent. Haring was strongly influenced by Burroughs, and his famous barking dog pictograph is sometimes even described as appearing "Mayan." The two collaborated on several projects in the 1980s.

In 1981, Haring had his first solo New York exhibition at the Westbeth Painters Space. The next year was a watershed: he showed at the prestigious Tony Shafrazi Gallery, and Tony Shafrazi would represent Haring for the rest of his career. Also in 1982, Dan Rather did a segment on the national news profiling Haring. Haring became a highly visible figure in the downtown social scene, befriending the likes of Madonna, Andy Warhol, Yoko Ono, and Boy George. Over the next several years until his early death in 1990, Haring was commissioned to paint 50 public murals around the world. Perhaps the most famous of these are "Crack is Wack" along FDR Drive in New York City and a 300-foot mural on the Berlin Wall.

By the mid-1980s, Haring was painting canvases in acrylic and oil and producing sculptures. During his lifetime, his paintings sold for as high as $350,000. He also painted interiors for New York City nightclubs, backdrops for music concerts, and sets for MTV. In 1986, he opened a store in Manhattan called the Pop Shop that sold his merchandise.

Haring was active in a number of social and political causes in the 1980s, including the fight against apartheid in South Africa. His primary interest, however, was AIDS activism in the United States. He founded the Keith Haring Foundation to provide financial support to AIDS patients as well to promote art education among disadvantaged children. In 1988, Haring announced that he had AIDS. Drugs to treat the disease in that period were still dangerous and unreliable, and Haring died in 1990. He was only thirty-one years old.

Significance

Keith Haring has become one of the most iconic artists of the late twentieth century. His energetic art, inspired by commercial art, animation, pop art, and other sources, has proven to have tremendous staying power. A spirit of generosity and vitality animated not only his art but the way that he shared it, too; Haring created hundreds of images for free and for the enjoyment of everyone who rode the New York City subway. Haring was especially fond of children, and he reportedly liked to sit at the "kids' table" whenever his friends invited him to dinners. This generosity also inspired his involvement in socio-political movements.

Haring has rightly been understood as consistently counter-cultural. There was always, too, a boyishness that was more than the fact of his relative youth. These are elements that make Haring, on the one hand, an accessible and delightful artist, but, on the other, something of a permanent cipher. His art was both serious (represented by a gallery) and casual (MTV sets and subways). It was freely given but expensively sold, extremely successful but counter-cultural, radical but maybe just radical chic. He was threading a needle.

In 1997, the Whitney Museum held a retrospective of Haring's art, a watershed moment in terms of legitimacy in the art world. At the time of the retrospective, Haring's father, still living in Kutztown, may have put his finger on something essential when he told an interviewer, "Keith doesn't need art-world legitimacy. He found a much more interesting legitimacy. He invented an audience for himself. There's nothing better than that."

D. Alan Dean

Further Reading

Buchhart, Dieter. *Keith Haring: The Political Line*. New York: Prestel, 2014.

Deitch, Jeffrey, and Julia Gruen. *Keith Haring*. New York: Rizzoli, 2014.

Haring, Keith. *Journals*. New York: Penguin Classics, 2010.

Kolossa, Alexandra. *Keith Haring, 1958–1990: A Life for Art*. New York: Taschen, *Köln*, Germany, 2004.

Mercurio, Gianni. "Keith Haring: In the Moment." In *The Keith Haring Show by Gianni Mercurio and Demetrio Paparoni*. Milan, Italy: Skira, 2005.

Phillips, Natalie E. "The Radiant (Christ) Child: Keith Haring the Jesus Movement." *American Art, 21, no. 3 (October 15, 2007): 54-73.*

Sussman, Elisabeth, et. al. *Keith Haring*. New York : Whitney Museum of American Art, 1997.

Edmonia Lewis

Artist

Born: July 21, 1845; Greenbush, New York
Died: Unknown, after 1909; possibly Rome, Italy
Also known as: Mary Edmonia Lewis; Wildfire Edmonia Lewis
Area of Achievement: Art and photography

Best known for her sculptures of African, African American, and American Indian figures and subject matter, Lewis was widely considered the first African American woman sculptor to achieve national and international critical acclaim.

Early Life

Mary Edmonia Lewis was born July 21, 1845, in Greenbush, New York. Her father was an African American

Edmonia Lewis (Wikimedia Commons)

(possibly Haitian) fugitive slave, and her mother was a Mississauga Ojibwe. She had an older brother, Samuel. Lewis's mother was a traditional weaver skilled in Native American crafts, skills that she passed down to her daughter. At around the age of nine, Lewis lost both of her parents. She and her brother were raised by her mother's sisters in the area around Niagara Falls and Buffalo, New York. As a child, she hunted, fished, and sold Native American crafts. Her brother attended boarding school for a time and is said to have taken part in the California gold rush. He returned from California with some wealth, which he used to pay Lewis's tuition at New York Central College. She was dismissed from the school for wildness, however, and moved to Oberlin College in Ohio in 1859.

Lewis's first two years at Oberlin were unremarkable except for a course in linear drawing that constituted her first formal art training. In 1862, she was accused of poisoning two of her roommates. The case caused a minor sensation and led to Lewis being physically assaulted (the incident was never investigated). She was arrested and formally charged with poisoning her classmates, but she was exonerated. Lewis was later charged with minor thefts, but she was exonerated again. In her final term at Oberlin, her application for registration was not accepted.

Life's Work

Lewis left Oberlin frustrated but determined to pursue a career in art. She had a letter of recommendation from famed abolitionist William Lloyd Garrison to study sculpture with Edward A. Brackett. Brackett tutored Lewis and allowed her to use his famous bust of the abolitionist John Brown as a model. She later sold small plaster relief medallions of John Brown and Union colonel Robert Gould Shaw. Her sculpture and sales were successful enough that in 1864, possibly with her brother's financial assistance, Lewis was able to start her own studio in Boston. Her sales and commissions for marble busts of Shaw and temperance leader Dr. Dioclesian Lewis earned her the money to travel to Florence, Italy, in 1865.

In Florence, Lewis met Hiram Powers and Thomas Ball. The two sculptors introduced her to the American Neoclassical style that characterized much of her later work. After some months in Florence, Lewis moved to Rome in the beginning of 1866. There, she became part of an influential group of American female artists. From 1866 to 1870, Lewis created some of her most famous sculptures, including depictions of Anna Quincy Waterston, Mary and Jesus, Hiawatha, Minnehaha, Hagar, and Henry Wadsworth Longfellow. She created her most famous sculpture, *Forever Free*, in 1867-1868 to celebrate the Emancipation Proclamation. On August 20, 1870, Lewis's *Hagar* (1868) was exhibited in Chicago's Farewell Hall. In 1871, she traveled to the Boston for the presentation of *Forever Free*.

> "*There is nothing so beautiful as the free forest. To catch a fish when you are hungry, cut the boughs of a tree, make a fire to roast it, and eat it in the open air, is the greatest of all luxuries. I would not stay a week pent up in cities if it were not for my passion for art.*"

Between 1871 and 1877, Lewis created a number of other sculptures with subjects such as Abraham Lincoln, Ulysses S. Grant, Moses, and the Greek goddess Hygieia. She also made the pieces *Cupid Caught*, *The Wedding of Hiawatha*, *Awake*, *Asleep*, and *The Old Arrow-maker and His Daughter*. In 1875, she produced a two-ton, life size sculpture titled *The Death of Cleopatra*, which gained critical acclaim at the 1876 Centennial Exposition in Philadelphia and a show in Chicago (the statue was stored and forgotten until the 1970's, when it was rediscovered and

Lewis' sculpture Death of Cleopatra. This piece was first exhibited to great acclaim at the Centennial Exhibition in Philadelphia in 1876 and critics raved that it was the most impressive American sculpture in the show. Not long after its debut, however, Death of Cleopatra was presumed lost for almost a century—appearing at a Chicago saloon, marking a horse's grave at a suburban racetrack, and eventually reappearing at a salvage yard in the 1980s. (Wikimedia Commons)

restored; it was donated to the Smithsonian in 1994). Lewis's last known commission was an 1883 sculpture of the baby Jesus and the three wise men for a Baltimore church; the work was lost. In 2007, a forty-eight-inch sculpture titled *The Veiled Bride of Spring*, dated 1879, was discovered and attributed to Lewis.

While *The Veiled Bride of Spring* is Lewis's latest surviving sculpture, there is a record of her working as late as 1887, when Frederick Douglass's diary reports that he visited her studio in Rome. Little is known about Lewis from this time until her death. U.S. Embassy records show that she was alive in 1909, but the year and place of her death are unknown.

Significance

Lewis is considered the first African American female sculptor to gain international prominence. Her work, although widely acclaimed, also was sometimes criticized for its neoclassical style. Her choice of subjects reflected her American Indian ancestry and abolitionist beliefs and represented women as strong and regal despite their oppression.

Idris Kabir Syed

Further Reading

Bearden, Romare, and Harry Henderson. *A History of African American Artists from 1972 to the Present*. New York: Pantheon Books, 1993. Includes a chapter on Lewis that critically examines her life and work. Contains useful photos, including pictures of works that have been lost.

Bontemps, Arna Alexander, and Jacqueline Fonvielle-Bontemps. "African American Women Artists: An Historical Perspective." In *Black Feminist Cultural Criticism*, edited by Jacqueline Bobo. Malden, Mass.: Blackwell, 2001. Important critical analysis of Lewis's work, focusing on her racial identity and how it is expressed in her subject matter.

Buick, Kirsten Pai. *Child of the Fire: Mary Edmonia Lewis and the Problem of Art History's Black and Indian Subject*. Durham, N.C.: Duke University Press, 2010. This book is the most exhaustive analysis of Lewis and her sculpture to date. It both challenges and draws upon traditional racial and gender analyses of Lewis's work and life.

Wolfe, Rinna Evelyn. *Edmonia Lewis: Wildfire in Marble*. Parsippany, N.J.: Dillon Press, 1998. The first book dedicated to the work of Lewis, offering details of her life and a list of her known sculptures.

Maya Ying Lin

Artist, architect, and writer

Born: October 5, 1959; Athens, Ohio
Area of Achievement: Architecture and design, art

During her senior year at Yale University, Maya Ying Lin achieved fame by winning the national design competition for the Vietnam Veterans Memorial in Washington, DC. Besides elegant, unconventional memorials and monuments, Lin has created art installations, sculptures, and architecture that express her deep interest in nature and environmentalism.

Maya Ying Lin (Wikimedia Commons)

EARLY LIFE

Maya Ying Lin was born in Athens, Ohio, on October 5, 1959. Her father, Henry Huan Lin, was a prominent ceramist and school administrator in China who came to America in 1948. He became a teacher at the University of Washington in Seattle and later dean of the fine arts program at Ohio University in Athens. Lin's mother, Julia Chang, was the daughter of a prominent Shanghai physician. She immigrated to the United States in 1948 and attended graduate school at the University of Washington, where she met Henry Lin. They married and settled in Athens, Ohio. Julia Lin became a professor of English and Oriental literature at Ohio University.

Maya Lin's older brother Tan was born in 1956 and Maya followed on October 5, 1959. Tan became a teacher and a published poet. Maya, on the other hand, enjoyed making pottery in her father's studio and constructing things. There were few Asians in Athens, but she never felt ostracized because of her ethnicity. She chose to be a loner and preferred family activities to outside friendships and social activities. Lin was a shy but excellent student who enjoyed reading. She spent much of her time watching the wildlife in her backyard. In the woods behind her house, she explored streams, hills, and Native American burial mounds. This love of nature and the environment became an essential part of her art.

LIFE'S WORK

Lin enrolled at Yale University in 1977 where she first majored in zoology and switched to a major in architecture the next year. During her junior year, she spent a semester in Denmark and travelled throughout Europe. In November 1980, the Vietnam Veterans Memorial Fund, a nonprofit organization started by Jan Scruggs, announced a nationwide design competition for a memorial honoring the over 58,000 Americans who were killed or missing in action during the Vietnam War. The sponsors required that the monument be harmonious with its environment near the Mall in Washington DC; it also needed to include the names of all fallen soldiers, be apolitical, and help promote reconciliation in the country.

Lin saw the contest announcement posted at Yale and visited the proposed site. She immediately conceived of the design she would submit: a horizontal, polished black granite V-shaped wall cut into the earth to provide a quiet, safe place to contemplate the inscribed names as well as one's own reflection in the smooth stone. Unlike traditional figurative and heroic monuments, Lin's memorial would be modern and abstract.

> "*Nothing is ever guaranteed, and all that came before doesn't predicate what you might do next.*"

A jury of eight experts in architecture and art decided the winner. In May 1981, Lin's design was unanimously awarded first place out of 1,421 submissions. The design was controversial. Many veterans felt that the color black was inappropriate and that the simplicity of the monument's design was belittling to the soldiers' sacrifice. Other critics objected to the selection of a Chinese artist to design a Vietnam War memorial. A compromise was eventually reached in which a traditional bronze statue—*The Three Soldiers*—would be placed at the entrance to the memorial. The memorial was dedicated on Veterans Day in 1982.

After graduating from Yale in 1981, Lin moved to Washington, DC, to work as a consultant on the memorial. In the fall of 1982, she began graduate studies in architecture at Harvard University but left after a year in order to work for a Boston architectural firm in early 1983. In the

> **Maya Lin's Vietnam Veterans Memorial**
>
> In 1979, when decorated and wounded Vietnam War veteran Jan Scruggs watched the movie *The Deer Hunter,* he was inspired to build a memorial to all American soldiers killed or missing in action in the Vietnam War. He founded the non-profit Vietnam Veterans Memorial Fund, which eventually raised $8.4 million in private donations.
>
> In July 1980, Congress approved a site in Constitution Gardens near the Mall and the Lincoln Memorial, and a national design contest was announced. By the deadline on March 31, 1981, 1,421 designs had been submitted, each identified by number only, with the designer's name in an envelope taped to the back. On May 6, 1981, a jury of eight sculptors and architects unanimously chose the winner: number 1026, a design by Maya Ying Lin, a twenty-one-year-old architecture student at Yale University.
>
> The memorial is divided into two walls forming a V, each wall stretching over 246 feet, long. It reaches ten feet high at its center. There are 58,267 names carved into the Memorial wall. Although initially there were objections to the non-traditional design, black color, and the choice of an Asian designer, the emotional and aesthetic effectiveness of Lin's design eventually became obvious. A universally honored landmark and popular tourist attraction, the Memorial was ranked tenth on the American Institute of Architects' (AIA) 2007 list of America's Favorite Architecture.

fall of that year, she enrolled in the master's program at the Yale School of Architecture and graduated in 1986.

In 1988, Lin designed the Civil Rights Memorial (1989) for the Southern Poverty Law Center in Montgomery, Alabama. The memorial consists of a curved black granite wall engraved with a quotation from Martin Luther King Jr. and a fountain with water flowing over a circular black granite table carved with the dates of major civil rights events and the names of forty individuals, including children, who gave their lives in the struggle for civil rights.

Beginning in the 1990s, Lin's artwork was inspired by nature and reflected her interest in environmentalism. In her Wave Field installation series—consisting of The Wave Field (1995; Ann Arbor, Michigan), Flutter (2005; Miami, Florida), and Storm King Wavefield (2009; Mountainville, New York)—she created grass-covered earthen mounds that mimic the swells of ocean waves.

Incorporating sustainable solutions throughout a former machine shop, Lin designed the new 14,000 square foot Museum of Chinese in America (MOCA) in New York City. Its opening in September 2009 marked the emergence of a leading national museum of Chinese history and culture. Other notable large-scale works include a topiary park called Topo (1991) in Charlotte, North Carolina; The Women's Table (1993), a commemorative sculpture at Yale; and Groundswell (1993), an installation in Columbus, Ohio, consisting of forty-three tons of shattered automobile safety glass.

In 2009, Lin began what she called her last memorial, *What Is Missing?* (2010), which is an ambitious, worldwide project encompassing multiple sculpture and multimedia installations, both permanent and temporary, and traveling exhibits. While memorializing the extinction of species and habitats, the project also raises consciousness about global efforts to preserve the natural environment. The first piece, called *Listening Cone*, is a sculptural work of metal lined with reclaimed redwood at the California Academy of Sciences in San Francisco; the second piece, *The Empty Room*, is an interactive multimedia environment and touring exhibit that debuted at the Beijing Center for the Arts in China.

Throughout Lin's career, her sculptures have been shown in museums worldwide. Her architectural designs have included a library and a chapel for the Children's Defense Fund, a park for Ohio University, and corporate offices in New York City. Lin was also a member of the selection jury for the World Trade Center Site Memorial Competition. She published the book *Boundaries* in 2000 and has been awarded honorary doctorate degrees from Yale and Harvard, as well as Smith College and Williams College. In 2013, Lin's largest installation work, *A Fold in a Field*, was completed in Auckland, New Zealand. The installation, covering 3 hectares, features a series of sculpted, earthen mounds, covered in grass. Lin's next project, *Under the Laurentide*, debuted at Brown University in 2015. The sculpture, carved in granite, reproduces the form of the water flowing across the underwater structure of Narragansett Bay.

Vietnam Veterans Memorial, West end of Constitution Gardens (Wikimedia Commons)

The Maya Lin Studio, which Lin owns and operates, is located in New York City where Lin lives with her husband, Daniel Wolf, and their two daughters, Rachel and India.

Significance

Maya Lin's radical, nonfigurative design for the Vietnam Veterans Memorial changed the basic concept of memorials in the United States. Her controversial design also survived objections to an Asian designer, and she became an internationally recognized artist before she had reached her mid-twenties. In 2005, the American Institute of Architects (AIA) gave the Memorial its Twenty-Five-Year Award, which recognizes architecture of enduring value.

In 1995, Freida Lee Mock's film *Maya Lin: A Strong Clear Vision* won the Academy Award for best documentary. Lin's *What Is Missing?* radically changed the meaning and design of memorials once again. In February 2010, Lin received a National Medal of Arts from President Barack Obama, the United States government's highest award presented to artists and art patrons. In 2016 she was given the Presidential Medal of Freedom, again by President Barack Obama, the highest notation awarded to civilians. In 2014, Lin was the recipient of the Dorothy and Lillian Gish Prize in Art, a $300,000 prize given to artists whose work is seen as having significant impact in modern culture.

Alice Myers, updated by Micah L.Issitt

Further Reading

Lashnits, Tom. *Maya Lin.* New York: Chelsea, 2007. Print. Biography that covers Lin's life through 2006.

Lin, Maya. *Boundaries.* New York: Simon, 2006. Print. An illustrated book that explores Lin's creative processes and the existence of her art between various boundaries, such as between urban and natural and Asian and American.

O'Brien, Tim. *The Wall: 25th Anniversary Commemorative.* Newton, MA: Boston Publishing, 2007. Print. An illustrated history of the Vietnam Veterans Memorial that includes the story of the memorial's design and construction.

Scruggs, Jan C., and Joel L. Swerdlow. *To Heal a Nation: The Vietnam Veterans Memorial.* New York: Harper, 1985. Print. Describes the construction of the Vietnam Veterans Memorial.

Georgia O'Keeffe

Painter

Born: November 15, 1887; Sun Prairie, Wisconsin
Died: March 6, 1986; Santa Fe, New Mexico
Area of achievement: Art

Breaking with European traditionalism, O'Keeffe pointed to new ways to perceive the world, creating precise and sometimes stark depictions of nature and of urban scenes.

Early Life

For her first twenty-eight years, Georgia O'Keeffe was an artistic revolution waiting to erupt. Georgia, the second of seven children born to Francis O'Keeffe and Ida Totto O'Keeffe, was fascinated by art. By age ten, she wanted to be a painter, although she did not know what that entailed. When people pressed her to tell them what kind of painter she wanted to be, she invariably replied, "A portrait painter."

O'Keeffe's early training in art began with a local art teacher and continued in a parochial school. When the nun who taught art told the impressionable child that she was painting things too small, Georgia obliged by painting her subjects large, sometimes so large that her pictures overflowed their boundaries, as many of her later floral paintings would.

In 1905-1906, O'Keeffe attended the Art Institute in Chicago, where she was embarrassed to paint nude men

Georgia O'Keeffe (Library of Congress)

and where she was schooled in an ultraconservative, highly traditional European style of painting. She spent the following year at the Art Students League in New York City, where, as had been the case in Chicago, her painting received favorable comments and won prizes.

O'Keeffe, however, was not receiving the kind of instruction she needed. Unwilling to go through life painting dead rabbits and pastoral scenes, she gave up painting in 1908, becoming a commercial artist in Chicago. She designed the rosy-cheeked girl who still graces cans of Dutch Cleanser. O'Keeffe hated commercial art but, needing to earn a living, she stayed with it until she fell ill, suffering a temporary impairment to her vision. She returned to her family, who had relocated in Virginia in 1903.

During this interval, O'Keeffe took a summer course at the University of Virginia, which did not admit women but allowed them to study in summer school. The instructor, Alon Bement, was a disciple of Arthur Dow of Columbia University, an artist who, influenced by Asian art, had broken away from European artistic conventions. O'Keeffe eventually studied with Dow, who changed forever the way she saw things and recreated them.

From 1912 to 1914, O'Keeffe taught art in Amarillo, Texas, where she was intrigued by the big sky and the broad, seemingly endless plains. In 1915, she spent an abortive semester teaching at Columbia College in South Carolina, but the following fall she became an art instructor at West Texas State Normal School in Canyon. It was during this teaching stint that O'Keeffe sent some of her charcoal drawings to her New York friend Anita Pollitzer, who showed them to photographer Alfred Stieglitz. He exhibited them in 1916 without O'Keeffe's knowledge or consent at his 291 Gallery. This showing marked the beginning of Georgia O'Keeffe's future as an artist.

LIFE'S WORK

When O'Keeffe, recently arrived from Texas to continue her studies with Arthur Dow, learned that Stieglitz had shown her work without authorization, she stormed into his studio to confront him. When the two met, however, Stieglitz's enthusiastic assessment of her work mollified her.

Stieglitz, whose reputation in the art world was solid, held another exhibition of O'Keeffe's work in 1917. She was in Texas when this exhibition was held, but Stieglitz won O'Keeffe's heart by rehanging the entire exhibition for her alone when she arrived in New York shortly after the closing.

During her years in west Texas, O'Keeffe imbibed its stark landscape and intense colors, regularly painting the nearby Palo Duro Canyon, a favorite subject. Her artwork, always precise, began to show a new depth and originality in both its use of light and its angularity.

O'Keeffe was developing one of her most significant skills, an ability to paint something as static as a tree or flower yet imbue the painting with incredible motion and dynamism. Nothing in an O'Keeffe still life is at rest; everything moves. The charcoal sketches that first attracted Stieglitz's attention reflect this motion, but as O'Keeffe experimented with color and light, the motion in her still lifes became explosive.

> *"I've been absolutely terrified every moment of my life - and I've never let it keep me from doing a single thing I wanted to do."*

By 1918, O'Keeffe was ready to leave west Texas. When Stieglitz arranged for her to receive a subvention in

Red Canna, *1919* (Wikimedia Commons)

support of her painting, she willingly moved to New York and soon was living with Stieglitz. Her years in west Texas did much to shape O'Keeffe's later work. She had discovered the unique quality of light in the southwestern desert. Also, in search of objects for her students to paint, she stumbled on the notion of using sun-bleached animal bones, which were plentiful in the surrounding desert.

Although she did not herself begin to paint animal skulls and pelvises until more than a decade later, she had gained an appreciation for the kind of patina that sun-drenched bones acquire and for their translucence. For the next decade, however, O'Keeffe, who had first visited Santa Fe, New Mexico, just before her return to New York, remained in the East. In 1924, she was married to Stieglitz, now divorced from the wife he had left in 1918.

The life O'Keeffe and Stieglitz had established in 1918 summers at the Stieglitz family home at Lake George in New York's Adirondack Mountains, winters in New York City continued throughout the 1920s. O'Keeffe, Stieglitz's favorite model, spent much of her time and creative energy posing for his photographs, which he exhibited widely.

O'Keeffe was finding subjects for her own painting both at Lake George and in New York City. In 1925, the couple moved into an apartment on the thirtieth floor of Lexington Avenue's Shelton Hotel, which gave O'Keeffe a view that extended to the East River. Here she painted her famed New York cityscapes. Her paintings of industrial scenes along the East River and of various buildings in New York City marked a new direction in O'Keeffe's career as an artist and reflected the influence of John Marin, whose paintings of industrial scenes impressed her when she first saw them in 1915.

In the 1920s, O'Keeffe also painted many still lifes particularly flowers and scenes from the Lake George summers. Perhaps the most interesting of her urban paintings is *The Shelton with Sunspots* (1926). The towering building in which O'Keeffe and Stieglitz lived springs from the bottom of the canvas like the prow of a ship, many of its details obscured by blinding sunspots that bounce off the hotel's windows. O'Keeffe imbues this painting of a bland, commonplace skyscraper with conflict. It has been suggested that O'Keeffe, who suffered from migraine headaches, replicated in this picture the play of light that sometimes accompanies that malady.

In 1929, Mabel Dodge Luhan invited O'Keeffe, who by now was well known, to visit her ranch in Taos, New Mexico. Because Stieglitz refused to venture west of the Hudson River, O'Keeffe went to New Mexico alone, remaining at the Luhan ranch from April until August. This trip heralded a new direction in O'Keeffe's life and work.

From that point on, she would spend most of her summers in New Mexico, doing so until 1946, when Stieglitz died. O'Keeffe moved permanently to Abiquiu, north of Santa Fe, in 1949. She had bought a house at Ghost Ranch, fifteen miles north of Abiquiu, in 1940 and occupied both houses until encroaching feebleness necessitated her final move to Santa Fe in 1984.

In Taos, O'Keeffe learned to drive and bought a car. Every day during her New Mexican summers, she packed her equipment into her car, which rode high off the ground, and drove into the desert to paint. When the desert heat oppressed O'Keeffe, she stretched out beneath the car's chassis.

The desert paintings represent a large portion of O'Keeffe's most celebrated work. Her paintings of animal bones *Cow's Skull: Red, White, and Blue* (1931), *Ram's Head with Hollyhock* (1937), and *Pelvis with Moon* (1943) representing an extended period in her artistic career, are among her most puckish works.

O'Keeffe enjoyed painting the soft, flowing lines and angles of adobe buildings, as seen in such paintings as her *Ranchos Church* (1930) or *Black Patio Door* (1955), to which such Lake George paintings as her *Stables* (1932) and *Barn with Snow* (1933) contrast sharply.

After Stieglitz's death, O'Keeffe became a world traveler. Many thought she had now entered her abstract period. Actually, many of the paintings she produced between 1946 and 1980 were photographically realistic representations of scenes she observed from more than 30,000 feet up as she jetted across the sky. Among her most famous paintings of this period is an enormous canvas, *Sky Above Clouds II* (1963).

Living to be nearly a hundred, O'Keeffe painted until failing eyesight forced her into a brief retirement with her companion, Juan Hamilton, and his family in Santa Fe. There she died on March 6, 1986.

Significance

Georgia O'Keeffe always insisted that she was an artist, not a woman artist. She denied that gender had much to do with accomplishment and, from her earliest exhibitions, demonstrated that she could hold her own with her masculine competitors. Indeed, as an artist, she was superior to most of them.

During nearly a century of life, O'Keeffe continually grew professionally. She constantly tried new things. She considered no subject lacking in artistic potential, as her preoccupation with bones, paper flowers from New Mexican graveyards, conventional urban buildings, and scenes of smokestack industries clearly demonstrates.

O'Keeffe saw things as no one else saw them. Many subsequent artists have tried to imitate her floral paintings, for example, producing huge flowers crammed into canvases too small to accommodate them. Somehow, O'Keeffe could do that and, in the process, communicate something about the essence of a flower that no one had captured before. Her imitators end up with crowded canvases that look cramped. Perhaps an artist's imitators suggest more accurately than words can the true greatness of the artist they seek to copy. In O'Keeffe's work, one finds the zeal for life that so well characterized her as a person. She left a legacy of hope to artists in all fields who dare to deviate drastically from artistic convention. She neither disparaged her predecessors nor imitated them. She was truly and completely her own person.

R. Baird Shuman

Further Reading

Ciboire, Clive, ed. *Lovingly, Georgia: The Complete Correspondence of Georgia O'Keeffe and Anita Pollitzer.* New York: Simon & Schuster, 1990. Georgia O'Keeffe maintained a correspondence with Anita Pollitzer, a classmate at Columbia University, for more than forty years. Much of it is reproduced here.

Drohojowska-Philp, Hunter. *Full Bloom: The Art and Life of Georgia O'Keeffe.* New York: W. W. Norton, 2004. Exhaustively detailed biography.

Eisler, Benita. *O'Keeffe and Stieglitz: An American Romance.* New York: Doubleday, 1991. Eisler provides crucial insights into the sometimes stormy but always symbiotic relationship that existed between O'Keeffe and Stieglitz for the forty years they knew each other. Contains many of Stieglitz's photographs of O'Keeffe.

Lisle, Laurie. *Portrait of an Artist: A Biography of Georgia O'Keeffe.* Albuquerque: University of New Mexico Press, 1986. A sensitive and accurate biography of O'Keeffe. The author understands the artist's artistic orientation and how she uses her environment artistically.

Messinger, Lisa Mintz. *Georgia O'Keeffe.* New York: Metropolitan Museum of Art, 1988. This book, aside from O'Keeffe's autobiography, contains the best reproductions of O'Keeffe's work. It offers reproductions of the twenty-nine works in the collection of the Metropolitan Museum of Art. Well written and insightful.

O'Keeffe, Georgia. *Georgia O'Keeffe.* New York: Viking Press, 1976. If one could read only one book relating to O'Keeffe, this autobiography would be the sensible choice. An indispensable book for anyone seriously interested in O'Keeffe.

Peters, Sarah Whitaker. *Becoming O'Keeffe: The Early Years.* Rev. ed. New York: Abbeville Press, 2001. Peters offers a sensitive and spirited look into the making of an artist. Excellent illustrations.

Pyne, Kathleen. *Modernism and the Feminine Voice: O'Keeffe and the Women of the Stieglitz Circle.* Berkeley: University of California Press, 2007. Describes how O'Keeffe and the other women in Alfred Stieglitz's circle developed their artistic voices and how Stieglitz's image of O'Keeffe as the pure "woman in art" affected her self-identity.

Robinson, Roxana. *Georgia O'Keeffe: A Life.* New York: Harper & Row, 1989. The most comprehensive biography of Georgia O'Keeffe to date. Well written and amply illustrated. The illustrations, however, do not include reproductions of O'Keeffe's work, which are readily available in the autobiography.

Shuman, R. Baird. Georgia O'Keeffe. Vero Beach, Fla.: Rourke, 1993. Intended for the nonspecialist, this book contains excellent illustrations, a chronology, and an annotated bibliography. Accurate coverage of O'Keeffe's life and work.

Maria Tallchief

Ballet dancer

Born: January 24, 1925; Fairfax, Oklahoma
Died: April 11, 2013; Chicago, Illinois
Area of Achievement: Dance, theater and entertainment

Prima ballerina of the New York City Ballet for fifteen years, Tallchief symbolized American ballet for an entire generation of theater and television audiences.

Early Life

Maria Tallchief was born Elizabeth Marie Tall Chief in Fairfax, Oklahoma, a small community on the Osage Indian Reservation. Oil discovered on the reservation and the tribal leaders' insistence on holding their mineral rights in common had made the Osage the wealthiest tribe in the United States. Tallchief's father, Alexander Tall Chief, a full-blooded Osage, was a well-to-do real estate executive whose grandfather, Chief Peter Big Heart, had negotiated the tribe's land agreements with the federal government. Her mother, Ruth Porter Tall Chief, came from Irish, Scottish, and Dutch ancestry. Her paternal grandmother, Eliza Big Heart Tall Chief, often took her to secret tribal dance ceremonies (the government had outlawed these "pagan" rituals at the turn of the century), but it was Ruth Tall Chief's culture and ambitions that ultimately prevailed.

Tallchief began taking piano and ballet lessons at age three; by the time she started school, she was performing before nearly every civic organization in Osage County. In her 1997 autobiography, *Maria Tallchief: America's Prima Ballerina,* she wrote of her childhood that she was intensely shy, although a good student at Sacred Heart, a Catholic school, and loved to be outdoors in her backyard: "I'd also ramble around the grounds of our summer cottage hunting for arrowheads in the grass. Finding one made me shiver with excitement. Mostly, I longed to be in the pasture running around where the horses were."

Tallchief's mother, however, wanted a more structured, directed life for her. Concerned about the lack of educational and artistic opportunities on the reservation, Ruth Tall Chief convinced her easy-going husband to move the family to Beverly Hills, California, in 1933. There, her daughter began a rigorous program of piano lessons and ballet classes, the latter taught by Ernest Belcher (whose talented daughter, Marge, would later team up with dancer-choreographer Gower Champion). Ruth Tall Chief was determined to groom her daughter for a career as a concert pianist, but it was dance that captivated both Tallchief and her younger sister Marjorie. In 1938, Tallchief and Marjorie began intensive training with David Lichine, Lichine's prima ballerina wife Tatiana Riabouchinska, and Bronislava Nijinska. Sister of the legendary dancer Vaslav Nijinsky, Nijinska was one of the foremost ballet teachers and choreographers in the United States.

> *"A ballerina takes steps given to her and makes them her own. Each individual brings something different to the same role."*

With Nijinska, Tallchief learned rigorous discipline and total dedication to dancing in fact, to think of dancing so thoroughly as to sleep like a ballerina and even stand like a ballerina while waiting for a bus. "We understood what she meant," Tallchief later told an interviewer. "Ballet is your life. Everything else doesn't mean that much." Both sisters impressed Nijinska, who cast them in her ballet *Chopin Concerto*, which was performed at the Hollywood Bowl in 1940.

Life's Work

After her graduation from Beverly Hills High School in 1942 at age seventeen, Tallchief made her professional debut with the New York-based Ballet Russe de Monte Carlo, one of the two leading ballet companies in the country at that time. (The other, Ballet Theatre, hired Marjorie Tallchief two years later.) It was early in her five-year association with Ballet Russe that Tallchief had changed her name to Tallchief (from Tall Chief). Advancing rapidly from the corps de ballet to solo parts, she attracted favorable critical notice in a variety of classical productions, including Bronislava Nijinska's *Chopin Concerto* in 1943 and Michel Fokine's *Schéhérazade* and George Balanchine's *Gentilhomme and Danse Concertante* in 1944. By 1946, Tallchief's repertoire also included principal roles in Léonide Massine's *Gaîté Parisienne* and two more Balanchine ballets, *Baiser de la Fée* and *Ballet Imperial*. Critics and audiences alike now recognized her as a rising star in the ballet theater.

Balanchine's brief stint as ballet master with the Ballet Russe (1944-1946) marked a turning point in Tallchief's career. Trained in the Russian Imperial School of Ballet, Balanchine was one of the most brilliant choreographers and teachers of the twentieth century. His School of American Ballet, founded in 1936, trained many of the best performing artists on the American stage. He quickly recognized the young dancer's potential, made Tallchief his protégée, and created roles designed to exploit her strength, agility, and great technical proficiency. On August 16, 1946, Tallchief was married to the forty-two-year-old Balanchine. The following spring, she made her European debut with the Paris Opera (a first for an American), where her husband was guest choreographer. When she returned to the United States, Tallchief joined Balanchine's new company, the Ballet Society, which in 1948 became the New York City Ballet (NYCB).

From 1947 to 1965, Tallchief was the prima ballerina of the NYCB and created roles in most of Balanchine's repertoire. Two of these roles were destined to become classics of the ballet theater. In 1949, composer Igor Stravinsky revised his score especially for Balanchine's new version of *The Firebird*, with Tallchief in the title role. Her electrifying performance as the mythical bird-woman dazzled critics and audiences alike; for the rest of her career, she would be more closely identified with this role than with any other. In 1954, Balanchine choreographed the NYCB's most popular and financially successful production, a full-length version of Peter Ilich Tchaikovsky's *The Nutcracker*, with Tallchief as the Sugar Plum Fairy, which is regarded as the most difficult role in a classical dancer's repertoire. Tallchief's Sugar Plum Fairy earned for her the title of "America's prima ballerina" and helped establish The Nutcracker as an annual Christmas season favorite in cities all over the country. Among the other works in which Balanchine created roles for her were *Symphony in C* (1948), *Orpheus* (1948), *Bourèes fantasque* (1949), *Sylvia Pas de deux* (1950), *Jones Beach* (1950), *Caracole* (1952), *Scotch Symphony* (1952), *Pas de dix* (1955), *Allegro brillante* (1956), and *Gounod Symphony* (1958). In 1999 she described his choreographic technique: "He would show us how to walk, how to run, how to present your foot. He wasn't technical. He would just say things so that your whole body becomes very poetic. Being vulnerable is the most important thing of all, and he taught us how to be vulnerable."

During the 1950s and early 1960s, Tallchief reached the pinnacle of her success as a classical dancer. She toured Europe and Asia with the NYCB, accepted guest engagements with other ballet companies, and gave numerous television performances on programs such as *Omnibus, Hallmark Hall of Fame,* and *The Ed Sullivan Show*. She played the famous Russian ballerina Anna Pavlova in a 1953 film, *Million Dollar Mermaid*, dancing the Dying Swan role from Balanchine's version of *Swan Lake*. She also taught in the School for American Ballet.

Among her many honors, none pleased Tallchief more than those conferred by her home state: June 29, 1953, was declared Maria Tallchief Day by the Oklahoma State senate, while the Osage Nation staged a special celebration during which she was made a princess of the tribe and given the name Wa-xthe-Thonba, Woman of Two Standards. That same year President Dwight D. Eisenhower dubbed her Woman of the Year. A triumphal tour of Russia in 1960 with the young Danish ballet sensation Erik Bruhn cemented her international stardom. In 1961, Tallchief won for a second time (the first came in 1949) the coveted annual Dance Award. She resigned from the NYCB in 1965 and retired from the stage a year later.

Tallchief's marriage to Balanchine (though not her friendship or their professional association) was annulled in 1952, on the grounds that he did not want children. By her own admission, their age difference and his obsession with Tallchief the artist rather than the woman doomed their marital relationship. A brief second marriage to airline pilot Elmourza Natirboff ended in divorce in 1954 when Natirboff insisted that she give up her career. In June, 1956, Tallchief was married to Henry D. "Buzz" Paschen, a Chicago construction company executive who accepted her career ambitions. She gave birth to their only child, Elise Maria, in 1959. Retirement in 1966 allowed Tallchief to settle permanently in Chicago with her husband and daughter.

During the 1970s and 1980s, Tallchief brought to the Chicago artistic world the same energy and determination that had characterized her own dancing. In 1974, she formed the Ballet School of the Lyric Opera, where she passed on to younger dancers the Balanchine techniques and traditions that had shaped her own success. The school's original purpose was to provide a corps of dancers for the Chicago Lyric Opera. When financial problems forced the elimination of ballet from the opera's budget, Tallchief engineered, in 1980, the creation of the Chicago City Ballet (CCB), using $100,000 in seed money from the state of Illinois and a building donated by her husband. Marjorie Tallchief, retired from her own highly successful career in Europe, moved to Chicago to direct her sister's school, while Maria became artistic co-director (with Paul Mejia) of the new ballet company. Following the demise of the CCB in 1988, Tallchief returned to the Lyric Opera to direct its ballet activities. In 1989, she appeared in *Dancing for Mr. B.: Six Balanchine Ballerinas*, a documentary film for PBS. Later she became artistic director for the Von Heidecke's Chicago Festival Ballet, directed by Kenneth von Heidecke.

Despite her assimilation into European-American culture, Tallchief remained proud of her American Indian heritage. In 1967, she received the Indian Council of Fire Achievement Award and was named to the Oklahoma Hall of Fame. A longtime member of the Association on American Indian Affairs, she frequently spoke to American-Indian groups about Indians and the arts, and participated in university programs to educate students about the first Americans. In 1991, Tallchief became a charter member of the honorary committee of the National Campaign of the National Museum of the American Indian, whose members raised funds to assist the Smithsonian Institution in building the new museum on the National Mall in Washington, D.C. In 1998, Tallchief was among five Native American ballerinas designated Oklahoma Treasures in a ceremony at the state capitol. Tallchief was inducted into the National Women's Hall of Fame in 1996 and received Kennedy Center Honors. President Bill Clinton presented to her the National Medal of the Arts in 1999, and in return she gave him foam rubber for his daughter Chelsea's ballet shoes to make them more comfortable.

Tallchief's husband died in 2003. She remained in Chicago near her daughter Elise Paschen Brainerd, a poet and former executive director of the Poetry Society of America, and two granddaughters. The Metropolitan Museum of Art in New York hosted "A Tribute to Ballet Great Maria Tallchief" on November 7, 2006, and in 2007 the Public Broadcasting Service aired a retrospective program about her career. In 2011, Tallchief received the Making History Award for Distinction in the Performing Arts from the Chicago History Museum. Tallchief died in 2013, after suffering a broken hip in December of 2012. At the time of her death, she had been serving as artistic adviser to the Chicago Festival Ballet.

SIGNIFICANCE

Tallchief's primary contribution to American culture rests on her role as the first truly American prima ballerina. Four other American Indian ballet dancers enjoyed distinguished careers during Tallchief's era Rosella Hightower (Choctaw), Yvonne Chouteau (Cherokee), Moscelyn Larkin (Shawnee), and Marjorie Tallchief but none left her mark on American ballet theater as did the elder Tallchief sister. Ballet as an art form in the United States was relatively new, and until the late 1940s, it relied heavily on European dancers.

Even the Ballet Russe, with whom most of the "Indian ballerinas" began their careers, was a European company in exile, staffed largely with artists trained abroad. Not until the 1950s, when the NYCB came into its own as a major ballet company, did American ballet reach the standards set by the prestigious national ballets of France, England, and, especially, Russia. "Until then," Tallchief remarked, "the Russians thought Americans could only slap their fannies, chew gum, and tap dance." If it is true that Balanchine and the NYCB created Tallchief's prima ballerina status, it is equally true that she, in turn, contributed significantly to that company's critical and financial success. American-born and American-trained, Tallchief fascinated audiences with her exotic beauty and her unmatched technical brilliance.

Gifted and driven, Tallchief made personal sacrifices to pursue her demanding career as a performing artist. Then, at age forty and still in peak form, she left the stage to devote more time to rearing her daughter. Like a number of Balanchine's former protégées, she ultimately went on to teach what she had learned from the master. She modeled her Chicago school after Balanchine's School of American Ballet in New York, and until his death in 1983, her former husband frequently hired dancers trained by Tallchief. A teacher, lobbyist, fundraiser, and publicist for the arts, Tallchief remains a commanding force in the world of ballet.

Constance B. Rynder, updated by Micah L. Issitt

Further Reading

Gourley, Catherine. *Who Is Maria Tallchief?* New York: Grosset & Dunlap, 2002. Meant for high school readers, this short biography outlines Tallchief's life and offers sidebars explaining the history of ballet. With illustrations.

Gruen, John. *Erik Bruhn: Danseur Noble.* New York: Viking Press, 1979. Somewhat gossipy in tone, this biography of the superb Danish dancer contains useful insights into the artistic partnership (and alleged personal relationship) of Tallchief and Bruhn in the 1960s. It is especially useful in the absence of any Tallchief biography, assessing her off-stage persona and later ballet achievements.

---. "Tallchief and the Chicago City Ballet." *Dance Magazine*, December, 1984. Examines the progress of the CCB as a major American ballet company in the Balanchine tradition, including Tallchief's work with her artistic co-director, Paul Mejia, and NYCB star Suzanne Farrell (Mejia's wife).

Hardy, Camille. "Chicago's Soaring City Ballet." *Dance Magazine*, April, 1982. Details the origins of Tallchief's ballet company, focusing on the CCB's premiere of Mejia's Cinderella.

Kufrin, Joan. *Uncommon Women: Gwendolyn Brooks, Sarah Caldwell, Julie Harris, Mary McCarthy, Alice Neel, Roberta Peters, Maria Tallchief, Marylou Williams, Evgenia Zukerman.* Piscataway, N.J.: New Century, 1981. One of nine performing artists profiled through extensive interviews, Tallchief speaks candidly about her career as a dancer, her professional debt to Balanchine, and her continuing commitment to ballet through teaching and creating the Chicago City Ballet.

Lang, Paul. *Maria Tallchief: Native American Ballerina.* Springfield, N.J.: Enslow, 1997. A short biography intended for young adult readers, this book, part of a series on Native Americans, emphasizes her roots. With bibliography and chronology.

Mason, Francis. *I Remember Balanchine: Recollections of the Ballet Master by Those Who Knew Him.* New York: Doubleday, 1991. Tallchief's contribution to this collection reveals her undiminished admiration for Balanchine's genius. She discusses their early association at Ballet Russe, describes the creation of her most famous role, The Firebird, and incorporates anecdotes of their life together.

Maynard, Olga. *Bird of Fire: The Story of Maria Tallchief.* New York: Dodd, Mead, 1961. An incomplete and dated biography that lacks objectivity but gives the fullest account available of the dancer's early life and rise to stardom.

Myers, Elisabeth. *Maria Tallchief: America's Prima Ballerina.* New York: Grosset & Dunlap, 1966. A sentimental handling of Tallchief's stage career, based largely on the Maynard biography. Like Maynard's work, it reveals little about Tallchief the woman and nothing about her career after leaving the stage.

Tallchief, Maria, and Larry Kaplan. *Marie Tallchief: America's Prima Ballerina.* New York: Henry Holt, 1997. In her autobiography, Tallchief recalls her shy rural girlhood and transformation into an international ballet star, providing readers with an insider's acquaintance with many of the leading personalities in the art along the way.

Martin Wong

Chinese-Mexican-American Artist

Born: July 11, 1946; Portland, Oregon
Died: August 12, 1999; San Francisco, California
Area of achievement: Art

Affiliated with Nuyorican arts movement in New York City, Martin Wong was a painter whose work combined influences from the West Coast in the 1960s and New York City in the 1970s. Since his death in 1999, he has been recognized as a major artist of the period.

Early Life

Martin Wong was born in Portland Oregon, the only child of Benjamin and Florence Wong. When Martin was still an infant, his parents moved to San Francisco where they both worked for the Bechtel Corporation, and Wong was raised in that city in the Chinatown district. His mother painted as a hobby, and she encouraged her son's early interest in art. A series of self-portraits that survive from Wong's teenage years chart his development as a young man from about the age of thirteen until his graduation from high school in 1964. Wong attended Humboldt State

University in California where he studied art with a focus on ceramics.

LIFE'S WORK

After college, Wong was determined to become an artist. He managed to win a competition in ceramics in 1970 and had his work shown at the de Young museum in San Francisco as a result. However, shortly after that, he abandoned ceramics and devoted himself to painting. Remaining in San Francisco for most of the 1970s, Wong collected and sold Asian art, an area in which he had taught himself enough to find work as a consultant as well. He painted posters for the gender-bending theatrical troupe the Cockettes. He also performed with, and created elaborate sets for, an off-shoot of the Coquettes, a troupe called the Angels of Light. His art from this period was influenced by psychedelic and Asian motifs. At times, Wong could also be found in the 1970s painting "instant" portraits for a few dollars apiece on street corners in San Francisco.

In 1979, hoping for serious recognition and seeking to enjoy New York City's downtown scene, Wong moved East. For a time, he lived in a rundown hotel where he had found an inexpensive room. Eventually, he rented an apartment on Ridge Street in Manhattan's Lower East Side where he became friends with other artists and bohemians in the neighborhood. At that time, the Lower East Side was notably rough around the edges, a place where artists, addicts, bums, and bohemians all lived side by side—and often enough overlapped in those roles. The neighborhood was also home to a sizable Puerto Rican population, many of whom lived in the neighborhood's housing projects. Wong began showing his work in small spaces, including on the walls of a Japanese restaurant near his new home. He also joined the cohort of graffiti artists who were at that time finding some publicity, riding subways and "tagging" buildings, walls, and subway cars around the city.

To support himself, Wong took a job uptown as a cashier in the gift shop at the Metropolitan Museum of Art. Downtown, he befriended many of the people involved with the Nuyorican Poets Café, including one of its co-founders, Miguel Piñero, a Puerto Rican ex-convict who had found new life as an actor and writer after his release from Sing-Sing. The Nuyorican Movement, represented above all by the successful and lauded Poets Café, celebrated and explored the Puerto Rican experience in New York City. Because Wong's father was of Chinese and Mexican heritage, Wong at this time referred to himself "Chino-Latino." Wong and Piñero lived together and were sometimes lovers, until Piñero's death in 1988 from cirrhosis of the liver. He was only 41 years old.

In 1984, the Metropolitan Museum purchased a painting from Wong, now recognized to be one of his most iconic works, *Attorney Street (Handball Court with Autobiographical Poem by Piñero)*. The painting incorporates many of Wong's characteristic motifs. He once said, "Everything I paint is within four blocks of where I live and the people I know and see all the time." This painting, a scene of a handball court on Attorney Street in the Lower East Side, is no exception to that description. Wong often painted scenes of dilapidated urban environments, and his insistent rendering of brickwork is an immediately recognizable element in many paintings. This painting also incorporates strong textual elements, and Wong playfully painted a frame of trompe l'oeil wood around the picture. These illustrative features, together with the urbanism of his street scenes, contribute to the dynamic, unpretentious impact of the work. Wong incorporated words spelled out in the sign language alphabet, each stylized hand emerging from a white shirt cuff with a cuff link. This, too, is highly characteristic of Wong's works from the 1980s. In fact, he was recognized by the city of New York at the time for creating "inclusive" art, and he was dubbed the artist in residence at New York City's Department of Transportation, where he worked with the sign shop to produce a multi-site artwork called *Traffic Signs for the Hearing Impaired*.

Wong had his first solo show in 1984 at Barry Blinderman's Semaphore Gallery in New York. The show, called *Urban Landscapes*, included *Attorney Street* and other works, and brought Wong a taste of art world respectability. Later in the 1980s, Wong and a friend established the Museum of American Graffiti in the East Village. Because of financial difficulties, the museum closed after six months. Wong later donated his collection of graffiti art, one of the best collections then in private hands, to the Museum of the City of New York.

Wong was diagnosed with AIDS in 1994. Soon thereafter he moved back to San Francisco. Effective treatments for HIV/AIDS in that era were still being developed, and Wong—like more than a hundred thousand other gay men in the United States—didn't live long enough to access the better treatment options that have since become routine. In 1998, the New Museum of Contemporary Art in New York held a retrospective of his work, and Rizzoli published the catalogue, titled *Sweet Oblivion: The Urban Landscape of Martin Wong*. His health continued to deteriorate over the next year. Wong's aging parents nursed him at home until his death at age 53 in 1999.

Significance

"Hybridity" is a word that appears from time to time in appreciations of Wong: he was a Chinese-Mexican-American who affiliated with the Nuyorican Movement. In addition, his career united multiple, unrelated art trends in a similarly hybrid manner. His work combined influences from the psychedelic art scene of the 1960s and 1970s in San Francisco with the darker, nihilist world of New York City in the 1970s and 1980s. Because of this hybridity, Wong is a figure who did not come easily into focus until the passage of time. Largely neglected by the art establishment during his lifetime, critical appreciation for Wong's work has grown tremendously in the years since his death in 1999. Today, Wong is hailed for his poetic realism, as one of the premier artists of the East Village scene in the 1980s, and as an exemplar of a simpler, less commercially-driven and more bohemian art world. Wong's work is held not only by New York's Metropolitan Museum but by the Museum of Modern Art, the Whitney Museum, and other notable institutions across the country. A 2015 retrospective of his paintings at the Bronx Museum of the Arts earned positive reviews in prominent publications and did more than any other previous exhibition to bring his name to the world's attention.

D. Alan Dean

Further Reading

Bessa, Antonio Sergio (Ed.) *Martin Wong: Human Instamatic*. New York: Black Dog Publishing, 2016.

Cotter, Holland. "Martin Wong, an Urban Visionary With a Hungry Eye." *New York Times*. Nov. 19, 2015. https://www.nytimes.com/2015/11/20/arts/design/martin-wong-an-urban-visionary-with-a-hungry-eye.html

Heartney, Eleanor. "Street Life." *Art in America*. January 29, 2016. https://www.artinamericamagazine.com/news-features/magazines/street-life/

McCormick, Carlo. "Martin Wong: Bronx Museum of the Arts, New York." *ArtForum*. March 2016.

Schjeldahl, Peter. "A Bohemian's Triumphant Return." *The New Yorker*. November 16, 2015. https://www.newyorker.com/magazine/2015/11/16/city-scenes

Wong, et al. *Sweet Oblivion: The Urban Landscape of Martin Wong*. New York: Rizzoli, 1998.

Athletics

In the modern world athletes are iconic bearers of heroic virtues, displaying courage, valor, strength, and other praiseworthy qualities. The idea that a sports figure is a natural role model, especially for young people, may seem obvious, but it wasn't always so. According to some sports historians, the perception has everything to do with the rise of sports as mass entertainment in the twentieth century. In the 1920s, according to historian Mark Dyreson, sports figures were praised for their singular physical accomplishments—for the feats that they performed, like Babe Ruth hitting fifty-four home runs in 1920.

In the following decades, as mass media like radio and then television changed the way that we participate in sports as viewers, the ways in which we talk about sports figures began to change, too. By the late twentieth century, athletes were widely expected to be role models, and their life stories—overcoming poverty and other hardships on the road to victory—often became important parts of their heroism. On the one hand, this can be attributed to the ease with which sport lent itself to didactic purposes such as illustrating the values of hard work or persistence using figures that young people already knew and admired. But it was also a function of the massification of images in the new media, which were capable of expanding the audience for a live sports match from hundreds of people to millions.

The association of athletes with heroism has even deeper roots than this twentieth-century phenomenon, however. Ancient Greece was a society in which physical and martial prowess were highly praised, and athletes were important figures. Athletes in the time of Plato or Socrates recalled the struggles of Greece's ancient heroes, figures shrouded in myth but at the foundation of Greek civilization and Greece's ideas about its own history and identity. The strong civic, didactic, and moral component that was present in ancient Greek athletics was revived naturally with the revival of the Olympics in 1896, and its influence contributed to the development of the modern discourse described above.

A packed Petco Park in Dan Diego, California, where the San Diego Padres play. (Wikimedia Commons)

Muhammad Ali

Boxer

Born: January 17, 1942; Louisville, Kentucky
Died: June 3, 2016; Scottsdale, Arizona
Also known as: Cassius Marcellus Clay, Jr. (birth name); Cassius Clay; the Greatest
Areas of Achievement: Athletics: boxing; Athletics: Olympics

Ali is widely considered not only the best boxer of all time but one of the greatest athletes who ever lived. After winning a gold medal at the 1960 Summer Olympics, Ali went on to an outstanding professional career, winning the world heavyweight championship three times. He retired in 1981 with a professional record of fifty-six wins and five losses, including thirty-nine knockouts.

Early Life

Muhammad Ali (muh-HAHM-mad ah-LEE) was born Cassius Marcellus Clay, Jr., on January 17, 1942, in Louisville, Kentucky. He lived on the middle-class west side of town with his father, a sign painter, and his mother, who cleaned houses. The family attended Mount Zion Baptist Church, where young Ali was baptized a Christian. His boxing career began almost by chance. One night at the age of twelve, Ali and his friends went to a local auditorium. Upon leaving, Ali realized his bike had been stolen. The nearest police officer was Joe Martin, who worked as a trainer at a boxing gym in the auditorium's basement. Rushing to report his stolen bike, Ali proclaimed to Martin that he was going to find the person who had stolen his bike and beat him up. Martin, impressed by the boy's energy, invited him to learn to box at the gym. Within six weeks, Ali had his first amateur fight.

> "My soul has grown over the years, and some of my views have changed. As long as I am alive, I will continue to try to understand more because the work of the heart is never done."

As a teenager, Ali dreamed of becoming world heavyweight champion. He was not a good student and spent most of his high school years boxing. In his first professional fight, on the television show *Tomorrow's*

Muhammad Ali (Library of Congress)

Champions, Ali was awarded a split decision. Martin noticed that although Ali did not have good technique, he had great drive and never stopped punching. Reality set in when Ali lost his first Golden Gloves bout to a boy with excellent technique. Ali realized he needed a coach who could teach him the science of boxing. After joining trainer Fred Stoner's gym at Grace Community Center, Ali realized he was learning boxing techniques and a style that would become his trademark in all his future fights. While Martin taught Ali to box, it was Stoner who molded him into a great fighter.

Life's Work

Ali's amateur career spanned 108 fights, 100 of which he won. He won six Kentucky Golden Gloves championships and two national titles. His last amateur fight came at the 1960 Summer Olympics in Rome, where he won a gold medal as an eighteen-year-old. After winning the gold medal, Ali decided to turn professional. He chose Angelo Dundee as his coach and manager. Dundee remained with him for all of his sixty-one professional career bouts.

Ali's first professional fight was on October 29, 1960, and he won easily. After nineteen professional bouts, he

Ali lands a stunning right hook on Brian London, August 6, 1966. (Wikimedia Commons)

was ready to challenge Sonny Liston for the world heavyweight title. Liston was said to be unbeatable, but that did not deter Ali, who went on television and told reporters and fans, "I am the greatest. I can't be beat." His statements made the fight one of the most anticipated heavyweight bouts in history. Ali also did something before that fight that he would become known for: He predicted the round in which he would beat his opponent. Ali told the television audience, "Sonny Liston is great— he will fall in eight." Fans from around the world took notice of the flamboyant twenty-two-year-old from Louisville. The fight, on February 25, 1964, went almost as Ali had called it. At the start of the seventh round, an exhausted Liston did not get up from his stool when the bell rang. Ali became the heavyweight champion of the world, his teenage dream fulfilled.

After winning the world heavyweight title, Ali announced that he had converted to Islam and changed his name from Cassius Clay to Muhammad Ali. He faced a backlash from a public that did not want to accept the fact that their "great white hope," Liston, had been beaten and that a Black Muslim held the heavyweight title. Another fight between Ali and Liston was scheduled for May 25, 1965. The fight lasted less then one round; Ali felled Liston with a hard, straight right to the head. It was called the "phantom punch" because it was so fast that virtually no one in the audience saw it.

The religion that brought Ali hope and joy almost ended his career. Due to his faith, he refused induction into the U.S. Army during the Vietnam War and was barred from boxing for three and a half years (from 1967 to 1970). Although he was at the top of his sport, his stance against the war was seen as unpatriotic and he was ostracized by boxing promoters. Ali was in his twenties, his prime years athletically, when he refused to be drafted, leaving many people to wonder what could have been during those lost years. In 1970, a federal court ruling lifted the ban and Ali reentered the boxing world.

Ali returned to boxing in October, 1970, against Jerry Quarry, whom he defeated in the third round. That December, he fought Oscar Bonavena at Madison Square Garden, bringing him the publicity to challenge the undefeated heavyweight champion Joe Frazier in 1971. In a bout called the "Fight of the Century," Ali experienced his first loss, by unanimous decision in fifteen rounds. Frazier, who had lost his title to George Foreman, lost a rematch to Ali some three years later. Thus, Ali got a shot at the title against Foreman in 1974. Ali prevailed in eight rounds, exhausting Foreman by employing what came to be known as the "rope-a-dope," a strategy in which he covered up and let his opponent tire. Ali went on to win ten straight fights, including a third against Frazier, before losing to twenty-six-year-old Olympic champion Leon Spinks in 1978. Seven months later, Ali regained his heavyweight boxing title in a rematch against Spinks.

Ali is named the victor against Zbigniew Piertrzykowski at the 1960 Rome Olympics. Commons)

> ### Ali's Conversion to Islam
>
> Early in Muhammad Ali's life, he encountered racism and segregation while growing up in Louisville. At school, he found a newspaper called *Muhammad Speaks*, which was about the Nation of Islam. Ali realized that Islam appealed to him and matched his personal beliefs. He wanted to be a part of a religion that he saw as promoting black rights and standing up for equality in the world. Although Ali was reading the teachings of Nation of Islam leader Elijah Muhammad and attending mosques, he did not publicly proclaim his Muslim faith until after he won his heavyweight title fight against Sonny Liston. In America in the 1960's, Muslims were seen as radical and even dangerous; Ali's ties to Islam could have cost him a chance at the heavyweight title. Soon after winning the championship, he changed his name from Cassius Clay to Muhammad Ali in honor of Elijah Muhammad. His faith led him to refuse to be drafted into the U.S. Army in 1967. Because of his refusal, he was briefly incarcerated and banned from professional boxing. For three and a half years, the former champion could not compete during his trial for draft dodging. Eventually, the charge was dismissed and his boxing license restored. Ali had earned a reputation as a man who lived his faith and stood up for what he believed in.

After losing his last two fights in 1980 and 1981, Ali retired.

After his boxing career, Ali remained a devout Muslim and a humanitarian who supported many causes. In 1982, he was diagnosed with Parkinson's disease. He has been featured in hundreds of publications, including being on the cover of *Sports Illustrated* thirty-seven times, has inspired several feature films, and has a star on the Hollywood Walk of Fame. His boxing gloves are on display in the Smithsonian Institution. Ali died on June 3, 2016 in Scottsdale, Arizona after being hospitalized with a respiratory illness. He was 74 years old.

SIGNIFICANCE

Ali is one of the greatest African American sports figures of all time. During his rise to the top of the boxing world, he changed the face of the sport forever. Ali took the spotlight away from promoters and managers and made himself—the fighter—the focus. This revolutionized media coverage of boxing and spilled over to other sports. Ali also is known worldwide as an activist against racism. He was the first heavyweight to win the world title three times, but he is also known as the athlete who threw his Olympic gold medal into a river to express his disgust over racism. Ali is the consummate showman and never hesitated to speak his mind. He put aside his boxing career and risked jail to stand by his opposition to the Vietnam War. Fans around the world embrace him as "The Greatest." Interestingly, his daughter Laila has developed a successful career in women's professional boxing.

Timothy M. Sawicki

FURTHER READING

Ali, Muhammad, and Richard Durham. *The Greatest: My Own Story*. New York: Random House, 1975. Ali tells the story of his life, showing his humorous side and addressing the racism he encountered as he rose to the top of the sporting world.

Bolden, Tonya, and Gregory Christie. *The Champ: The Story of Muhammad Ali*. New York: Alfred A. Knopf, 2004. Biography of Ali, from his early years to winning an Olympic gold medal to carrying the Olympic torch in Atlanta in 1996.

Brunt, Stephen. *Facing Ali: The Opposition Weighs In*. Toronto: Alfred A. Knopf, 2002. Tells the stories of fifteen men who faced Ali in the ring, including Foreman and Frazier.

Conklin, Thomas. *Muhammad Ali: The Fight for Respect*. Brookfield, Conn.: Millbrook Press, 1991. Takes quotations and observations from Ali and his friends and interweaves them with books and newspaper articles about him. Focuses mostly on his career. Hauser, Thomas. *Muhammad Ali: His Life and Times*. New York: Simon & Schuster, 1991. Comprehensive biography by a onetime boxer and award-winning writer. Details Ali's life inside and outside the ring and how he influenced the world around him.

Kindred, Dave. *Sound and Fury*. New York: Free Press, 2006. Details the early meetings between Muhammad Ali and sportscaster Howard Cosell and how their on-air relationship developed.

Remnick, David. *King of the World*. New York: Random House, 1998. Discusses the many sides of Ali, his rise to boxing supremacy, his showmanship, and his support of Islam.

Jack Dempsey

Boxer

Born: June 24, 1895; Manassa, Colorado
Died: May 31, 1983; New York City, New York
Area of Achievement: Athletics: boxing

Dempsey was one of the greatest sports personalities of the so-called golden age of sports (the 1920's) and the first boxer to make major contributions to sporting life in the United States.

Early Life

Jack Dempsey (DEHMP-see), one of eleven children, was of Indian, Irish, and Scottish ancestry. The son of Hyrum Dempsey and Celia Dempsey, he became accustomed to a nomadic existence early in life, a primary requisite for a boxing career. Hyrum had converted to the Church of Jesus Christ of Latter-day Saints and had moved to Manassa in 1880 because it was a center of Mormon life. Hyrum, however, never was a successful businessman and was regarded as something of a dreamer. The family began a succession of moves from Manassa when Jack was four or five years old; the longest stay was at a ranch near Montrose, Colorado, for two years.

Jack permanently left his family in 1911, when they were living in Lakeview, Utah, and he was sixteen years old. He had already been attracted to the sport that made him famous, for he had begun to fight at about ten years of age, and it had become a way of life. This was a type of boxing in which there were no holds barred, and the biggest and toughest competitors usually won. As a preventive against cuts (which might interfere with his vision and hence his ability to hit and block blows), the budding boxing great bathed his face and hands in beef brine. Cuts were lessened this way, and his hands were toughened as well.

Dempsey was never large, especially if compared to boxers of the late twentieth century. In his prime as an adult, Dempsey stood six feet one and a half inches tall and weighed from 180 to 187 pounds; in his earlier years, he often weighed less than 150. From 1911 to 1916, Dempsey led the life of what one could legitimately call a hobo, a traveling worker seeking gainful employment. During this time he also fought and sharpened his skills and techniques. His was a rather brutal existence, an existence that forced Dempsey to remain aloof from most other men in his situation because of his fear of attacks

Jack Dempsey (Library of Congress)

from older, stronger individuals or groups. This in itself was good training for a boxer; once he is in the ring, a boxer is completely on his own, simply one individual who is pitted against another.

Dempsey was not the only man of his family to box. At one time, his older brother Bernie was fighting under the name of Jack Dempsey. This Jack was one of the more popular earlier middleweights and was known as "The Non-pareil." One night, William Harrison substituted for his older brother in the ring and used the name Jack Dempsey. This fight in Denver gave him his permanent professional name.

Dempsey needed two more ingredients for a really successful boxing career. Most successful boxing careers are shaped, if not made, by a manager, and an astute boxing promoter of matches can make or break a career. Dempsey's fights in the West gave him these, for he was introduced to the men who would be the two most important figures in his professional life. John Leo McKernan, or Jack Kearns, was the epitome of the fight manager: a master storyteller whom Nat Fleischer, editor of *The Ring*, credited with having invented the art of "ballyhoo." The promoter was George L. "Tex" Rickard, who was to develop boxing's first million-dollar gates, with Dempsey as the prime attraction.

Kearns was the most successful manager in the history of boxing, until the 1970's, for producing revenue for his boxers and himself. He managed six world champions, four of whom have been elected to *The Ring*'s Hall of Fame. Dempsey, Kearns, and Rickard were also lucky: They were at the right place at the right time. Boxing had only recently been legalized in the state of New York, opening the largest populated area of the country to mass spectator sports. For the first time, boxing was being taken from small, seedy arenas that housed only a few hundred or a thousand seats, to the sporting meccas of America.

> "*A champion is someone who gets up when he can't.*"

Dempsey's first two managers were Jack Price and John "the Barber" Reisler. It was not until 1917, when he was twenty-two, that Dempsey met Kearns and began his rise to fame. By the time he met Kearns, he had knocked out practically every opponent he had faced, but without recognition and the good paydays that went with that accomplishment. By the time he won the heavyweight championship of the world in 1919 from Jess Willard, he had knocked out twenty-one opponents in the first round, and newspapers had begun calling him the "Manassa Mauler" and "Jack the Giant Killer." From 1917 until 1919, he suffered only one defeat, and by 1919 he had won more than eighty victories.

Dempsey had also married by this time. His first wife, Maxine Gates, was a saloon piano player whom he had met during his early days in the West. He then married Estelle Taylor, an actor, whom he had met after becoming heavyweight champion. They were later divorced and Dempsey married a singer, Hannah Williams. They had two daughters, Joan in 1934 and Barbara in 1936, but again he was divorced, in 1943. Dempsey was given custody of the children. He was married for the fourth time in 1958, to Deanna Piatelli, who survived him. Dempsey also adopted his fourth wife's daughter from a previous marriage, who took the name Barbara Piatelli Dempsey. She later helped him to write his 1977 autobiography, *Dempsey*.

LIFE'S WORK

Dempsey's status as a serious contender was established when he knocked out Fireman Jim Flynn in one round. In July, 1918, he knocked out Fred Fulton in twenty-three seconds of the first round. Dempsey threw the only punch, a right. This got him a title fight with Jess Willard, who had won the title in 1915 but who had defended it only once since then, in a no-decision match with Frank Moran in 1916.

The championship bout with Willard, on July 4 in Toledo, Ohio, made Dempsey a national hero. Willard was five inches taller and seventy pounds heavier, and was the overwhelming favorite. The fight was held in a specially made outdoor arena constructed of rough-hewn planks, a Rickard trademark. Although the ring was set up on the shores of Maumee Bay, it was blisteringly hot. Dempsey began to stalk Willard; he had to stand on his tiptoes to reach the champion. Reach the champion he did, however, for Dempsey knocked him down seven times in the first round, breaking Willard's jaw in twelve places. Both Dempsey and Kearns left the ring at the end of the first round, believing the fight won. Dempsey had to reenter the ring, but at the end of the fourth round, Willard retired, after taking a frightful beating. Dempsey was now champion.

What is not generally known about Dempsey, however, is that this time of his life was not a particularly happy one. He was not immediately accepted by the public as a champion; indeed, he did not become a real hero until he lost the crown to Gene Tunney. A large part of this lack of acclaim was because of questions concerning his role in the war effort during World War I. Supposedly doing essential work in a Philadelphia shipyard, he had posed for a news photograph while holding a riveting gun and wearing overalls. He was also, however, wearing patent leather dress shoes. The photograph convinced many that he had evaded fighting, and the sobriquet "draft dodger" was hung on him. Partly as a result of this unfavorable publicity, Rickard matched Dempsey with Georges Carpentier, the light-heavyweight champion. Carpentier was advertised as the archetypal hero; he had been decorated while serving in the French armed forces during the war. Rickard shrewdly surmised that many fans would buy tickets hoping to see Dempsey lose. Rickard built one of his stark wooden arenas in an area of Jersey City known as Boyle's Thirty Acres. A crowd of 80,183 paid $1,789,238 to see the fight it was the first of the legendary million-dollar gates. Carpentier, however, did not stand a chance. He was knocked out in the fourth round.

Dempsey (left), Harry Houdini (center), and Benny Leonard (right) spar at a publicity event. (Library of Congress)

There were some unpleasantries associated even with the Willard fight. Dempsey maintained that he never received any funds from the proceeds of his share of the fight. Kearns reportedly bet ten thousand dollars on Dempsey to win in a first-round knockout. When Dempsey had to return to the ring, he lost the bet. The rest of the money supposedly went for training expenses. This was the first intimation that all was not well between Dempsey and Kearns. Kearns later claimed that Dempsey's pounding of Willard was a result of his wrapping of Dempsey's hands with plaster of paris the previous night, actually a common ploy then used by fighters, especially those employed by circuses and traveling carnivals, who regularly took on all comers. Generally, if the challenger lasted three rounds, he was declared the winner. Most did not, thanks to such ploys.

Dempsey's next fight after Carpentier was held in Shelby, Montana. This fight is still cited as an example of what small-town promoters should not do: hock the family jewels for a bit of national recognition. Kearns had received a guarantee of $250,000 for Dempsey to fight Tommy Gibbons in Shelby. The fight was held in the oil-rich town, but very few people came to witness Dempsey's victory in a five-round decision. Nevertheless, Kearns collected the entire guarantee; one of the most fabled stories of sports and gambling concerns Kearns's foresight in hiring a locomotive and caboose to whisk the Dempsey entourage out of town.

Dempsey actually fought only six fights defending the championship. During this period, there were no boxing commissions or organizations mandating that champions defend their title at least twice a year. He won the title in 1919, then in 1920 defeated, for the second time, Billy Wiske and Bill Brennan, before meeting Carpentier in 1921. It had taken Dempsey twelve rounds to dispose of Brennan by knockout. He did not defend the title in 1922. In 1923, he defeated Gibbons and then fought the famous battle with Luis Angel Firpo of Argentina in New York City. This short fight probably contained more action than any other heavyweight championship bout. Early in the first round, Dempsey was stopped by a right to the jaw, but he was able to knock Firpo down four times. Firpo then knocked Dempsey into the press row. Reporters broke his fall and helped push him back into the ring. Dempsey then knocked Firpo down for the fifth time and all this happened in the first round. The second round was all Dempsey's, and he finished Firpo off by knocking him down twice.

Dempsey did not fight again for three years. Then came his two losses to Gene Tunney. Tunney, a former marine, won the title from Dempsey on September 23, 1926. More than one hundred thousand spectators witnessed the bout. Dempsey lost by a ten-round decision. By this time, Kearns was no longer Dempsey's manager and was suing Dempsey for his share of the Tunney purse. A year later, Dempsey challenged Tunney for the title. Dempsey was soundly outboxed, except for the long-count seventh round. Dempsey knocked Tunney down but refused to go to a neutral corner as newer rules mandated. Dempsey stood over the fallen Tunney for at least four seconds before moving to a neutral corner. Only after Dempsey had done so did the referee begin his count. Tunney recovered, and any hope that Dempsey would win was lost.

Dempsey made a comeback in August of 1931, but a loss to Kingfish Levinsky in August of 1932 convinced him to retire again. In 1940, he returned to the ring once again, but only to knock out three stiffs.

During his career, Dempsey fought sixty-nine professional bouts. He won forty-seven by knockout, seven by decision, and one by foul; in five of his fights there was no decision, and four were declared a draw; he lost four by decision and was knocked out once.

While champion, Dempsey had been attracted to the glamour and charisma of the stage and screen. His featured role in a Broadway play was, to say the least, not outstanding. The female lead was played by his second wife, Estelle Taylor, a star of silent films whom he had met while in Hollywood. His Hollywood career was a disaster, however, as was the film *Manhattan Madness* (1925), in which he appeared.

After the Tunney bouts, Dempsey refereed bouts and tended to his business interests. During World War II, he was unable to enlist in the U.S. Army but joined the Coast Guard as director of its physical fitness program. He held the rank of commander, ending his service in November, 1945.

Dempsey was the first winner of the New York Boxing Writers Association's Edward J. Weil Memorial Plaque, in 1938, and was elected to the Boxing Hall of Fame in 1954. By this time, his popularity was at an all-time high, and he was generally regarded as the best boxer in history until the postwar period. Probably the most important reason for this public acclaim was Dempsey's mellowing personality. His successful restaurant on Broadway in New York City kept him in the public eye, for he was always willing to greet a customer and have his picture taken with him or her. He died on May 31, 1983, in New York City.

Significance

Dempsey is a sports legend, along with such epic American sports heroes as Harold "Red" Grange and the Four Horsemen of Notre Dame, of football fame, and the other greats of sports' Golden Age. Although his record in the ring is possibly overrated, his fights were marked by a ferocity seldom encountered elsewhere in boxing. His long life enabled him to become a genial host in the most populous city in the United States, a position that continued to keep him in the national limelight. The champ thus came to personify much that was good in American life.

Henry S. Marks

Further Reading

Bromberg, Lester. *Boxing's Unforgettable Fights*. New York: Ronald Press, 1962. Bromberg graphically depicts the fights with Willard, when Dempsey won the championship, the Carpentier and Firpo fights, and the two Tunney fights. Interesting reading.

Cavanaugh, Jack. "The Long Count Is a Long Memory." *The New York Times*, September 22, 2002, sec. 8, p. 9. Recounts the 1927 boxing match between Dempsey and Gene Tunney, in which Tunney was knocked out in the seventh round but eventually won the fight.

Dempsey, Jack, with Barbara Piatelli Dempsey. *Dempsey*. New York: Harper & Row, 1977. The official autobiography by Dempsey, who was assisted by his adopted daughter. Should be read with care and compared to other sources.

Fleischer, Nathaniel S. *Fifty Years at Ringside*. New York: Fleet, 1958. Fleischer, editor and publisher of *The Ring* in its heyday, was considered "Mr. Boxing" after World War II. Provides an excellent evaluation of Dempsey, compared to other ring greats such as Jack Johnson and Joe Louis. Fleischer always considered Johnson to be the greatest champion.

---. *The Heavyweight Championship*. New York: G. P. Putnam's Sons, 1949. Includes excellent comparisons between Dempsey and Tunney, and captures the reasons for which Dempsey was so popular with the public after his defeats by Tunney.

Heimer, Mel. *The Long Count*. New York: Atheneum, 1969. Focuses on the long-count knockdown in the second Dempsey-Tunney bout; provides good insights into the private life as well as the career of Dempsey.

Dempsey landing a right punch to the jaw of Jess Willard in Toldeo, Ohio. (Library of Congress)

Kahn, Roger. *A Flame of Pure Fire: Jack Dempsey and the Roaring '20's*. New York: Harcourt Brace, 1999. A biography placing Dempsey in the context of his times. Kahn describes Dempsey as a "wild and raucous champion of the wild and raucous 1920's."

Kearns, Jack, with Oscar Fraley. *The Million Dollar Gate*. New York: Macmillan, 1966. An "as-told-to" autobiography providing Kearns's version of his life with Dempsey. Anti-Dempsey, it should be read in conjunction with Dempsey's own autobiography.

Roberts, Randy. *Jack Dempsey: The Manassa Mauler*. Baton Rouge: Louisiana State University Press, 1979. The best source for beginning to understand Dempsey's problems both in and outside the ring.

Smith, Red. "Jack Dempsey Is Dead." *The New York Times*, June 1, 1983, sec. 2, p. 4. In-depth obituary of Dempsey, prepared by Smith, who was a noted sports columnist for the *Times*.

Lou Gehrig

Baseball player

Born: June 19, 1903; Manhattan, New York City
Died: June 2, 1941; Bronx, New York City
Area of Achievement: Athletics: baseball

Gehrig was the bulwark of the New York Yankees baseball dynasty of the 1920's, including the famed Murderer's Row team of 1927. He played in 2,130 consecutive major league games, an endurance record unsurpassed until 1995.

Lou Gehrig (Wikimedia Commons)

Early Life

Lou Gehrig (GEHR-ihg) was born in New York's upper East Side. His parents, Heinrich and Christina Gehrig, were German immigrants whose two other children died at a very young age. They spoke no English on their arrival in New York, and their lives were filled with deprivation and poverty. Lou's father was never able to work consistently at his craft and often drank beer and played pinochle at the neighborhood tavern. Lou's mother was the dominating force of his life. She worked at many jobs, such as domestic, cook, and laundress, and Lou often helped and ran her errands. Christina Gehrig's driving ambition was to provide Lou with an education so that he might become an engineer and escape the cycle of poverty that had engulfed her and her husband.

As he grew up on the East Side, Lou was a profoundly shy "momma's boy." He wore hand-me-down clothes and spoke with a German accent, leading his peers to taunt him. This formative period of his life left him with a lack of self-confidence that he would never overcome completely. His mother, however, emphasized the idea that hard work and dedication to his studies were keys to success in America. Lou was so proud of his perfect attendance record in elementary school that he would not allow pneumonia to keep him out of school.

Gehrig was a good and attentive student, but he excelled in sports. His father once gave him a right-handed catcher's mitt for Christmas. Although he was a southpaw, Gehrig was very proud of the glove and played ball with neighborhood children. He was big and awkward, not a natural-born baseball player. Yet his father helped him to build up his physique and muscle coordination, and Gehrig became very active in school sports, particularly track, shot put, and baseball. His proudest moment occurred when he helped his team win New York's Park Department League baseball championship.

At the High School of Commerce, and despite his mother's fears that sports would distract her son from his studies, Gehrig became the star of the school's basketball, soccer, and baseball teams. Commerce's soccer team, for example, won the city's championship three consecutive years. Gehrig played first base for the baseball team and became the team's leading slugger. During his senior year, the baseball team won the city's championship, which entitled them to play Lane High School, the champions of Chicago. Gehrig hit a grand-slam home run to help his team emerge victorious.

Gehrig's baseball exploits at Commerce enabled him to enter Columbia University in 1921 on an athletic scholarship. His parents were employed at a fraternity house, and Gehrig helped out by waiting on tables. When he had some spare time, he played baseball with members of the fraternity. He inadvertently jeopardized his scholarship, however, when he signed a contract with the New York Giants under manager John McGraw, who sent him to Hartford, Connecticut, in the Eastern League. When Gehrig's professional contract became known, Columbia University officials attempted to strip him of his amateur status. Friends intervened on behalf of Gehrig, however, and his amateur ranking was restored on the condition that he sit out his freshman year.

LIFE'S WORK

By this time, Gehrig was six feet tall with massive shoulders and weighed two hundred pounds. He played fullback on Columbia's football team and pitched and played first base on the baseball team. He was called "Columbia Lou" as his hitting exploits received increasing attention from fans. During the spring of 1923, Paul Krichell, a scout for the New York Yankees, was so impressed with Gehrig's hitting that he predicted that he would become another Babe Ruth. Gehrig was offered a bonus and a contract to complete the 1923 season with the Yankees. The money was so good that even his mother approved of his withdrawal from Columbia. Thus, at the age of twenty, Gehrig began his professional baseball career.

During the early 1920's, Yankee manager Miller Huggins sought to build a nucleus for a baseball dynasty. Babe Ruth was the heart of the team, and Gehrig found it difficult to find a place for himself. First base was Gehrig's position, but veteran Wally Pipp was at the height of his career and had a lock on it. Accordingly, Gehrig spent most of the 1923 and 1924 seasons in Hartford, where he hit well over .300 and drove out sixty-one home runs over two years.

> "*There is no room in baseball for discrimination. It is our national pastime and a game for all.*"

In 1925, Gehrig's break finally came. On June 1, 1925, he pinch-hit for the shortstop. On June 2, 1925, Pipp was hit in the head by a fastball during batting practice and was unable to start the game. Huggins inserted Gehrig into the starting lineup, and Pipp never played first base for the Yankees again. Gehrig started every game for fourteen years, a total of 2,130 consecutive games. He became the Iron Horse of the New York Yankees.

Gehrig enjoyed a solid rookie year. He hit .295, with twenty home runs, twenty-three doubles, nine triples, and sixty-eight runs-batted-in (RBI's), for a seventh-place team. In 1926, the Yankees won the American League pennant, and Gehrig proved to be a major factor in that season with a .313 average, 107 RBI's, and twenty triples. Gehrig hit cleanup, between Ruth and outfielder Bob Musil. In 1927, that trio formed part of Murderer's Row, perhaps the greatest baseball team in history. The team's statistics were awesome: a 110-44 won-lost record, a .307 team batting average, and an earned run average of 3.20.

What also caught the fans' imagination were the exploits of Ruth and Gehrig. For good or ill, Ruth was the dominant personality on the team. In many ways, he was an oversized boy who challenged authority to its limits. Gehrig, in contrast, was the organization man, obedient, quiet, noncontroversial, and hardworking. Gehrig's quiet, passive personality may explain his inability to escape Ruth's shadow fully. In 1927, Gehrig hit .373 and Ruth .356; Gehrig led the league with 175 RBI's, and Ruth came in second. Yet Ruth led Gehrig in slugging percentage; in the most spectacular race of all, he and Gehrig were neck and neck for the home-run title. Finally, in the last weeks of the season, Ruth pulled ahead to hit sixty home runs, a record that was to last until Roger Maris of the Yankees hit sixty-one in 162 games in 1961. Few people recall that Gehrig finished second with forty-seven home runs.

During the early 1930's, the Yankees were once again in the process of reconstructing their team under manager Joe McCarthy. Ruth was desperately unhappy under McCarthy's discipline, and age began to blunt his skills. By 1935, Ruth was gone, traded to the Boston Braves. Gehrig

Gehrig scores head first in the 4th inning as Joe Harris' throw gets away from catcher Hank Severeid of Senators, August 16, 1925. (Library of Congress)

thrived under McCarthy and, at last, emerged from Ruth's shadow. Moreover, he became more independent of his mother when he married Eleanor Twichell of Chicago late in December, 1933. Eleanor Gehrig provided her husband with a happy and contented home life. The results were obvious: In 1934, Gehrig had his best year, winning baseball's coveted Triple Crown: forty-nine home runs, 165 RBI's, and a .363 batting average. Gehrig's days in the Yankee sun, however, were few. In 1935, his performance did not match that of 1934. In 1936, the Yankees acquired center fielder Joe DiMaggio from the Pacific Coast League, and DiMaggio would dominate the team through the 1940's. Even so, 1936 was one of Gehrig's best years, as he hit .354 and led the league in home runs (forty-nine). He came through again in 1937, with 159 RBI's, thirty-seven home runs, and a .351 average. The following year, however, was extremely disappointing. Only thirty-four years old, he appeared to be on the decline, although his .295 batting average and 114 RBI's were quite respectable. His defensive play at first base was below his usual standards; he played in constant pain, pain so severe that he had to leave games in the late innings. Gehrig suspected that he had lumbago, but his doctors diagnosed the problem as a gallbladder condition. He was treated on that basis during the winter months.

The 1939 spring training season in St. Petersburg, Florida, revealed that Gehrig was very ill. His muscle coordination had deteriorated over the winter. During the early part of the regular season, Gehrig had only four hits in twenty-eight times at bat for a .143 average. Finally, in Detroit in early May, he requested that McCarthy take him out of the lineup, thus terminating his legendary consecutive-game streak. Gehrig later flew to the Mayo Clinic in Rochester, Minnesota, where doctors diagnosed his condition as amyotrophic lateral sclerosis, an incurable and deadly form of paralysis. At the insistence of his wife, Eleanor, doctors did not inform Gehrig of the implications of his disease.

Gehrig ultimately returned to the Yankees as a coach for the remainder of the 1939 season. On July 4, 1939, the team held a Lou Gehrig day in Yankee Stadium, and more than sixty thousand fans came out to honor the Iron Horse. Gehrig was deeply moved by the fans' display of affection and respect; in a moving and heartfelt speech, he declared that he was "the luckiest man on the face of this earth." Eleanor made the last days of Gehrig's life as useful and happy as possible. She arranged to have New York mayor Fiorello La Guardia appoint Gehrig as a member of the parole board. They attended as many cultural events as they could. Finally, on June 2, 1941, Gehrig died at home, quietly, at ten o'clock in the evening, only two weeks short of his thirty-eighth birthday.

SIGNIFICANCE

Gehrig played in 2,164 major league games, of which 2,136 were at first base, nine in the outfield, and one at shortstop. He had 8,001 official at bats and collected 2,721 hits, including 525 doubles, 162 triples, and 493 home runs. He hit a home run every 6.2 times at bat. His lifetime batting average was .340. He scored 1,888 runs, batted in 1,191 runs, struck out 789 times, and walked to first base 1,528 times. His lifetime slugging percentage was .632. In World Series play, his record was equally impressive. Gehrig played in thirty-four World Series games; in 119 at bats, he had forty-three hits, of which eight were doubles, three were triples, and ten were home runs. He scored thirty runs and knocked in thirty-five runs against the best teams that the National League had to offer. His career World Series batting average was .361, and his slugging percentage, .731.

For all their impressive effect, these statistics do not reveal Gehrig the human being. He represented the American dream to hard-pressed citizens of the late 1920's and 1930's. He was an inspiring role model for American youth in a way that Babe Ruth could never have been. He represented basic American values that were the bedrock of the baseball mystique: honor, sportsmanship, duty, and work. However, Gehrig fulfilled this role without visible effort. It was as much a part of his character and personality as were the grace and dignity of his play in a child's game. He never complained that life had been unfair to him. The courage and humility of his last days were so inspiring that amyotrophic lateral sclerosis became popularly known as Lou Gehrig's disease. In 1939, the Baseball Writers Association of America did him honor by waiving the required waiting period to vote Gehrig into baseball's Hall of Fame

Stephen P. Sayles

FURTHER READING

Allen, Mel, and Ed Fitzgerald. *You Can't Beat the Hours: A Long, Loving Look at Big League Baseball, Including Some Yankees I Have Known*. New York: Harper & Row, 1964. A general and popular account of the New York Yankees by their radio broadcaster of a quarter of a century. Covers the team from the era of Ruth and Gehrig to the era of Mantle and Maris. A very readable and entertaining book.

Anderson, Dave, Murray Chass, Robert Creamer, and Harold Rosenthal. *The Yankees: The Four Fabulous Eras of Baseball's Most Famous Team*. New York: Random House, 1979. A fascinating account of the Yankee dynasties from the perspectives of the dominating players of each era. Many photographs.

Eig, Jonathan. *Luckiest Man: The Life and Death of Lou Gehrig*. New York: Simon & Schuster, 2005. A balanced and interesting profile of Gehrig, including information about his relationships with his family, wife, and Babe Ruth.

Fleming, G. H., ed. *Murderer's Row*. New York: William Morrow, 1985. A collection of photographs, newspaper clippings, and articles by the major sportswriters of the 1920's, linked by Fleming's commentary to form a day-by-day narrative of the 1927 season. A major theme is the home-run duel between Ruth and Gehrig.

Gehrig, Eleanor, and Joseph Durso. *My Luke and I*. New York: Thomas Y. Crowell, 1976. A moving, personal account of the public and private lives of Lou and Eleanor Gehrig. Particularly revealing are insights into Gehrig's personality, the rivalry between Gehrig's mother and his wife for his affections, and the stability of Gehrig's life following his marriage.

Kashatus, William C. *Lou Gehrig: A Biography*. Westport, Conn.: Greenwood Press, 2004. This biography of Gehrig also focuses on his wife, Eleanor, who devoted her life to finding a cure for amyotrophic lateral sclerosis.

Rubin, Robert. *Lou Gehrig: Courageous Star*. New York: G. P. Putnam's Sons, 1979. An admiring popular biography of the Iron Horse. Written by a Miami newspaper sportswriter. Emphasizes the impact of Gehrig's formative years and his struggle to emerge from the shadow of Babe Ruth, only to be overshadowed by the young Joe DiMaggio.

Sultans of Swat: The Four Great Sluggers of the New York Yankees. New York: St. Martin's Press, 2006. Using sports reporting from *The New York Times*, the book re-creates the careers of Gehrig, DiMaggio, Ruth, and Mantle.

ALTHEA GIBSON

Tennis player

Born: August 25, 1927; Silver, South Carolina
Died: September 28, 2003; East Orange, New Jersey
Areas of Achievement: Civil rights; Athletics: golf and tennis

The first African American to compete in the major tennis tournaments, Gibson was responsible for the desegregation of the sport. She was the world's top-ranking tennis player during the late 1950's and won five Grand Slam singles titles, including the U.S. Open and Wimbledon.

EARLY LIFE

Althea Gibson (al-THEE-ah) was born in Silver, South Carolina, to Daniel Gibson and Annie Bell. Her parents were sharecroppers who moved to Harlem during the Great Depression. The eldest of five children, Gibson was a headstrong child who frequently skipped school and ran away. At the age of ten, she was enrolled in an athletic program for problem children. A natural athlete, Gibson

Althea Gibson (Library of Congress)

began to win paddleball competitions. Bandleader Buddy Walker, a volunteer recreation supervisor, introduced her to tennis professional Fred Johnson at the Cosmopolitan Tennis Club in Harlem. Gibson's talent impressed members, who collected money to cover her coaching.

Gibson dropped out of school after eighth grade and worked at menial jobs. In 1942, she won the New York State girls' championship of the all-black American Tennis Association (ATA). She also won the ATA National Junior Championships in 1944 and 1945. Although she lost her first women's tournament in 1946, she attracted the attention of two wealthy ATA members, Drs. Walter Johnson and Hubert Eaton. In September, 1946, Gibson moved to Wilmington, North Carolina, to live with the Eaton family. There, she attended high school and trained on their private tennis court. In the summers, she toured the tennis circuit with Johnson, who later coached Arthur Ashe. After finishing high school in 1949, Gibson enrolled at Florida Agricultural and Mechanical University on a tennis scholarship.

Life's Work

Gibson won the ATA ladies' national singles title for ten consecutive years starting in 1947. Her success attracted the attention of the white tennis community, and she was invited to the Eastern Indoor Championships of the U.S. Lawn Tennis Association (USLTA) in 1949. She won the event the following year. However, in order to qualify for the USLTA's U.S. Open at Forest Hills, New York, Gibson needed to be invited to one of the preliminary outdoor tournaments. Here, she faced a racial barrier. Alice Marble, a former U.S. Open and Wimbledon champion, wrote a piece in *American Lawn Tennis* magazine criticizing the USLTA for excluding Gibson because of her race. In 1950, Gibson was finally invited to play at Forest Hills, where she lost to Wimbledon champion Louise Brough. The next year, Gibson was invited to play at Wimbledon but lost in the first round.

After graduating from college in 1953, Gibson taught physical education at Lincoln University in Missouri. Frustrated by her failure to win major titles, she contemplated giving up tennis. She was encouraged to persevere and began training with coach Sydney Llewellyn. In 1955, Gibson was invited to represent the United States on a tour of Southeast Asia, which boosted her confidence and renewed her commitment to tennis. An extremely tall player with a powerful serve, Gibson perfected her game and, in 1956, she won the singles title at the French Open. She also took the doubles title with partner Angela Buxton. Back at Wimbledon, Gibson lost in singles but won the doubles title. She also lost at Forest Hills that year but won singles titles at the Italian Open and the Asian Championships.

> "*No matter what accomplishments you make, somebody helped you.*"

By 1957, Gibson had reached the top of her game. She won the Wimbledon singles title and defended the doubles title. Upon her return to New York City, Gibson was greeted with a ticker-tape parade on Broadway. In September, Gibson won the women's singles tournament at Forest Hills as well as the women's doubles and mixed doubles titles. She defended her titles at Wimbledon and Forest Hills in 1958. Gibson became the number one woman tennis player in the world and published an

Statue of Gibson in Branch Brook Park, Newark, NJ. (Wikimedia Commons)

autobiography, *I Always Wanted to Be Somebody* (1958). It came as a surprise, therefore, when she announced her retirement from amateur tennis. Despite her fame, she was unable to earn a decent living in the sport; unlike her white counterparts, she received little income from endorsements.

For a time, Gibson toured with the Harlem Globetrotters, playing exhibition tennis matches. A talented singer, she performed on *The Ed Sullivan Show* in May, 1958, and recorded an album, *Althea Gibson Sings*, the next year. She also appeared in the film *The Horse Soldiers* (1958) with John Wayne. Seeking a more reliable source of income, Gibson took up professional golf and played on the ladies' circuit from 1963 to 1977. However, she did not enjoy the same success as at tennis and earned little from the tours.

Gibson married businessman William Darben in 1965 and settled in East Orange, New Jersey. When the major tennis tournaments were opened to professionals in 1968, she attempted a comeback, but her age worked against her. During the 1970's and 1980's, Gibson was a tennis coach at several private clubs. In 1975, she was named New Jersey state athletic commissioner, the first woman in the United States to hold such a position. She also served on the state governor's council on physical fitness. Gibson and Darben were divorced in 1976. In 1983 she married her former coach, Llewellyn; they divorced in 1988.

Gibson's later life was plagued by poor health and financial problems. In 1994, a stroke left her confined to her home, bitter and almost penniless. This prompted a

Gibson's Role in the Integration of Tennis

When Althea Gibson began her career, other major sports were beginning to admit black players—but it took a player of Gibson's caliber to overcome barriers in tennis. As the United States Lawn Tennis Association (USLTA) did not admit African Americans, they could only compete in tournaments organized by the American Tennis Association (ATA), its black equivalent. Gibson was only the second black player to play in the USLTA National Indoor Championships and the first African American invited to the USLTA Grass Championships. Gibson also became the first African American to compete in the major international tennis tournaments.

Although she received sponsorship and encouragement from other African Americans, including boxers Sugar Ray Robinson and Joe Louis, Gibson faced a solitary crusade. She paved the way for later generations of black players, some of whom she mentored. The ATA initiated a junior development program that produced players such as Arthur Ashe. However, in contrast to other sports, Gibson's achievements did not open the floodgates for African Americans in tennis. It was not until 1990 that another African American woman, Zina Garrison, reached the finals at Wimbledon. Despite her poor health, Gibson traveled to London to cheer on Garrison. Gibson also took pleasure in the success of Venus and Serena Williams, who, like her, had grown up in poverty. Gibson's legacy continues through the Althea Gibson Foundation, set up to support urban students and enable them to excel at tennis and golf.

group of female athletes, including her former doubles partner, Buxton, to raise funds for her. In 1997, Gibson was honored at the dedication of the Arthur Ashe Stadium in New York City but did not attend the ceremony. She died of respiratory failure in 2003 at age seventy-six.

SIGNIFICANCE

Gibson overcame racism, sexism, and her humble beginnings to triumph in tennis at a time when it was almost unknown for African Americans to compete in the sport. Her exceptional talent opened up the game, and she won major titles at previously segregated clubs and tournaments. Gibson was also the first African American to play on the women's professional golf circuit. In 1957-1958, she became the first black woman to be named the Associated Press's female athlete of the year. She was elected to the International Tennis Hall of Fame in 1971 and to the International Women's Sports Hall of Fame in 1980.

Christine Ayorinde

FURTHER READING

Gibson, Althea. *I Always Wanted to Be Somebody*. New York: Harper, 1958. Gibson's autobiography provides a personal and colorful account of her life through her second victory in the women's singles competition at Wimbledon.

Gray, Frances Clayton, and Yanick Rice Lamb. *Born to Win: The Authorized Biography of Althea Gibson*. Hoboken, N.J.: Wiley, 2004. Co-written by Gray, a friend of Gibson and cofounder of the Althea Gibson Foundation, this work describes Gibson's journey to sporting success.

Harris, Cecil. *Charging the Net: A History of Blacks in Tennis from Althea Gibson and Arthur Ashe to the Williams Sisters*. Chicago: Ivan R. Dee, 2007. A comprehensive history of the black experience in tennis, examining racism in the game.

Schoenfeld, Bruce. *The Match—Althea Gibson and Angela Buxton: How Two Outsiders—One Black, the Other Jewish—Forged a Friendship and Made Sports History*. New York: Amistad, 2004. Documents the relationship between Gibson and Buxton, both of whom were viewed as outsiders in the tennis world.

MICHAEL JORDAN

Basketball player

Born: February 17, 1963; Brooklyn, New York
Also known as: Michael Jeffrey Jordan; M.J.; Air Jordan
Areas of Achievement: Business; Athletics: baseball; Athletics: basketball; Athletics: Olympics

Jordan performed at a level unmatched in National Basketball Association (NBA) history. He won five most valuable player awards and an unprecedented ten NBA scoring titles, leading the Chicago Bulls to six NBA championships in the 1990's. He made numerous theatrical game-winning shots.

EARLY LIFE

Michael Jeffrey Jordan was born on February 17, 1963, in New York, the fourth of five children of James Jordan, a General Electric equipment supervisor, and Deloris Peoples Jordan, a United Carolina Bank employee. Both parents inspired his strong work ethic and drive for

Michael Jordan (Wikimedia Commons)

excellence. He attended Wilmington, North Carolina, schools and loved baseball, pitching a two-hitter in the Little League eastern regionals and earning most valuable player honors with his Babe Ruth League state championship team. Jordan honed his basketball skills with his older brother, Larry, on the backyard court that his father built. Jordan was brokenhearted when he failed to make the varsity basketball team as a sophomore at Emsley A. Laney High School. He averaged 28 points per game as a point guard for the junior varsity team that year. Jordan averaged 20.8 points for the varsity team at power forward as a junior and competed in baseball and football. He grew to 6 feet 4 inches by his senior year and averaged 29.2 points, 11.6 rebounds, and 10.1 assists for 19-4 Wilmington. In the summer of 1980, Jordan performed impressively at Dean Smith's University of North Carolina basketball camp and Howard Garfinkel's Five-Star Basketball Camp in Pittsburgh, Pennsylvania.

After graduating from high school in 1981, Jordan enrolled at North Carolina and became a rare freshman starter for coach Smith. Smith liked Jordan's quickness, jumping ability, competitiveness, and defensive potential. Jordan garnered Atlantic Coast Conference (ACC) freshman of the year honors. He hit four consecutive jump shots to help North Carolina edge the University of Virginia, 47-45, for the ACC title. Jordan's clutch 15-foot corner jump shot with fifteen seconds left lifted the top-ranked 32-2 Tar Heels to a 63-62 victory over Georgetown University for the National Collegiate Athletic Association (NCAA) crown. The title was also the first of Smith's career. In 1982-1983, Jordan led the ACC in scoring (averaging 20 points) and recorded 78 steals as the Tar Heels finished tied for first place in the ACC. He sparked top-ranked North Carolina to an undefeated conference record and title in 1983-1984, averaging 19.6 points, 5.3 rebounds, 4 assists, and 3 steals. He was designated the *Sporting News* college player of the year and consensus All-American in 1983 and 1984, and received the Naismith Award and Wooden Award in 1984. During his college career, Jordan led North Carolina to an 88-13 record and three NCAA appearances, scored 1,754 points (17.4 average) in 101 regular-season games, and tallied 165 points in ten NCAA Tournament games. He made the 1982 NCAA All-Tournament Team, NCAA Final Four All-Time Team, and the All-Decade Team of the 1980's. Jordan also won a gold medal as a member of the 1984 U.S. Olympic basketball team.

LIFE'S WORK

Jordan left North Carolina to enter the 1984 National Basketball Association (NBA) draft. The Chicago Bulls selected Jordan with the third overall pick and signed him to a seven-figure, five-year contract. Jordan revived fan interest in the foundering Chicago franchise, mesmerizing crowds with his blinding speed, physical artistry, and gravity-defying slam dunks. Jordan was named rookie of the year and led the NBA with 2,313 total points. Jordan broke a bone in his left foot in November, 1985, and played just 18 games that season. In the 1986 NBA play-offs, he averaged 43.7 points in a series against the Boston Celtics and tallied an NBA-record 63 points in a double overtime loss in game 2 on April 20. In 1986-1987, Jordan won his first NBA scoring crown (averaging 37.1 points), becoming only the second NBA player to tally 3,000 points and first to record 200 steals and 100 blocked shots in a season. He scored 61 points in a playoff loss to the Atlanta Hawks on April 16, 1987, made his first All-NBA first team, and finished second in the most valuable player (MVP) balloting. Jordan won a second scoring title in 1987-1988 and led the NBA in steals. He repeated as slam-dunk champion and tallied 40 points en route to being named MVP of the All-Star Game. The NBA MVP and defensive player of the year, Jordan made his initial first team all-defensive squad and averaged 45.2 points in the play-offs against the Cleveland Cavaliers.

> "I've missed over 9,000 shots in my career. I've lost almost 300 games. 26 times I've been trusted to take the game-winning shot and missed. I've failed over and over and over again in my life. And that is why I succeed."

In 1988-1989, Jordan paced the NBA with 32.5 points per game and averaged a career-best 8 assists and 8 rebounds. Jordan placed second in the MVP balloting and made a last-second shot to eliminate Cleveland from the play-offs. In the Eastern Conference Finals, however, the Detroit Pistons intimidated Jordan and ousted Chicago. Phil Jackson became the Bulls' head coach in 1989-1990, and molded Jordan into more of a team player within Jackson's "triangle" offense. Jordan repeated as NBA scoring champion, led the NBA in steals, and tallied a career-high 69 points against Cleveland on March 28. When Chicago lost to Detroit again in the seven-game Eastern Conference Finals, however, critics charged that Jordan's

Jordan goes up for a dunk. (Wikimedia Commons)

brilliant individual performance had not elevated teammates' play or brought the Bulls an NBA title.

In 1990-1991, Jordan won his second MVP award and paced the NBA again in scoring (31.5 points). Chicago captured its first NBA crown, dominating the Los Angeles Lakers to win the NBA Finals in five game. Jordan was named the NBA Finals most valuable player. The Bulls continued their domination in 1991-1992, and Jordan bagged another MVP trophy. He led the NBA in scoring in the regular season and play-offs, averaging 34.5 points in the latter. Chicago defended its NBA title in six games over the Portland Trail Blazers, with Jordan snagging another NBA Finals MVP nod. His 35 first-half points highlighted game 1. The "Dream Team" of NBA superstars, including Jordan, breezed to a gold medal at the 1992 Olympics in Barcelona, Spain. In 1992-1993, Jordan's Bulls became the first team to win three consecutive NBA titles since the mid-1960's. Chicago vanquished the Phoenix Suns in six games, as Jordan's 41-point average set an NBA Finals record. Jordan became the first NBA player to earn three straight NBA Finals MVP awards.

Jordan retired from basketball in October, 1993, citing diminished motivation. He briefly pursued a baseball career but struggled in the minor leagues. In March, 1995, Jordan rejoined the Bulls. In 1995-1996, Chicago rolled to seventy-two victories, the best single-season total in NBA history. Jordan captured the regular-season, All-Star Game, and NBA Finals MVP awards and snagged his eighth straight scoring title. Chicago bested the Seattle Super Sonics in the six game NBA Finals. Jordan led the Bulls to a fifth NBA championship in 1996-1997 and became the second quickest NBA player to reach 25,000 career points. He averaged 32.3 points in the NBA Finals, as the Bulls conquered the Utah Jazz in six games. Jordan won game 1 with a buzzer-beating jump shot. In game 5, which came to be called "The Flu Game," Jordan scored 38 points and hit a game-winning three-pointer despite battling a fever and dehydration.

After earning a fifth NBA Finals MVP award, he signed an unprecedented thirty-three-million dollar, one-year contract. In 1997-1998, Jordan led the NBA in scoring for a record tenth time, secured his fifth regular-season MVP award and third All-Star Game MVP, and made his tenth All-NBA first team and ninth NBA All-Defensive team. Chicago recorded another three-peat, vanquishing Utah in the NBA Finals. In the deciding game 6, Jordan gave perhaps the greatest clutch performance in NBA Finals history. He stole the ball from the Jazz's Karl Malone and sank a dramatic shot with less than ten seconds left, giving the Bulls an 87-86 victory and sixth NBA championship. Jordan averaged 32.4 points in the NBA Finals, including 45 in game 6, and earned a record sixth NBA Finals MVP Award.

Jordan retired from the Bulls on January 13, 1999. In January of the following year, he became part owner and president of basketball operations for the Washington Wizards NBA team. He played with the Wizards from 2001 to 2003 and retired with 32,292 career points, third on the NBA's all-time scoring list. In June of 2006, he bought a stake in the Charlotte Bobcats NBA team; in March of 2010, he bought the team from majority owner Robert L. Johnson. On September 11, 2009, Jordan was enshrined in the Naismith Memorial Basketball Hall of Fame.

Jordan has been almost as prolific an endorser as he was a scorer. He was his generation's most effectively marketed athlete, broadening the NBA's appeal to corporate America and overseas. He endorsed numerous commercial products, most notably Nike's Air Jordan footwear. Jordan married Juanita Vanoy in September of 1989 in Las Vegas, Nevada. They had three children—Jeffrey, Marcus, and Jasmine—before their 2006 divorce.

SIGNIFICANCE

Among the best-known and wealthiest athletes in organized sports history, Jordan won ESPY Awards for Athlete of the Century, Male Athlete of the 1990's, Pro Basketball Player of the 1990's, and Player of the Decade. The Associated Press ranked him the second greatest athlete of the twentieth century. In 2003, *SLAM Magazine* named him the NBA's all-time best player. In 2016, President Barack Obama honored Jordan with the Presidential Medal of Freedom. Noted for his theatrical game-winning shots, Jordan led North Carolina to an NCAA championship and the Chicago Bulls to six NBA titles. He paced the NBA in scoring a record ten times and compiled the highest career scoring average in league history. The five-time MVP and six-time Finals MVP propelled the NBA to stratospheric success and international visibility. Jordan was a born scorer whose physical strength and agility allowed him to drive inside, convert 20-foot jumpers, pass, rebound, and defend tenaciously. Most important, he had an inexhaustible will to win.

David L. Porter

FURTHER READING

Halberstam, David. *Playing for Keeps*. New York: Random House, 1999. The fullest biographical account of Jordan's life, this powerful narrative brimswith human drama, revealing anecdotes, and penetrating insights.

Jackson, Phil, and Hugh Delehanty. *Sacred Hoops*. New York: Hyperion, 1995. Describes how Jackson integrated Jordan into the "triangle" offense and made Jordan more of a team player—a strategy that paid off in six championships for the Chicago Bulls.

Jordan, Michael. *Driven from Within*. Edited by Mark Vancil. New York: Atria Books, 2005. Jordan describes the personal qualities—work ethic, leadership, competitiveness—that made him successful.

LaFeber, Walter. *Michael Jordan and the New Global Capitalism*. New York: W. W. Norton, 2002. Examines Jordan's influence beyond basketball, adroitly assessing how his numerous commercial endorsements changed the global marketplace.

Porter, David L. *Michael Jordan: A Biography*. Westport, Conn.: Greenwood Press, 2007. Discusses Jordan's mystique, the many phases of his remarkable career, and his enduring legacy.

Smith, Dean, with John Kilgo and Sally Jenkins. *A Coach's Life*. New York: Random House, 1999. Describes how Smith instilled discipline and other values in Jordan and how Jordan affected North Carolina's basketball program.

Smith, Sam. *The Jordan Rules*. New York: Simon & Schuster, 1992. Analyzes Jordan's 1990-1991 season. Jordan disliked the Bulls' triangle offense, frequently played by his own rules, and often clashed with management.

MICHELLE KWAN

Figure skater

Born: July 7, 1980; Torrance, California
Also known as: Michelle Wing Kwan
Area of achievement: Athletics: figure skating

Michelle Kwan is the most decorated figure skater in the history of the sport. The winner of nine US Figure Skating Championships, five World Figure Skating Championship titles, and two Olympic medals, she continued her mastery of the sport for ten years, becoming one of the most admired athletes both on and off the ice.

EARLY LIFE

Michelle Wingshan Kwan was born on July 7, 1980, in Torrance, California. She is the third and youngest child of Danny and Estella Wing Kwan, immigrants who moved from Hong Kong to California after they were married. Michelle Kwan began ice skating at age five after watching her older brother, Ron, play hockey. She and her sister, Karen, were finally allowed to take skating lessons, which placed a heavy financial burden on the family.

To finance the sisters' training, the family sold their house and moved to a house in Torrance owned by Danny's parents. Michelle and Karen began skating practice at three o'clock in the morning and were back on the ice again after school. In 1991, Michelle won a gold medal in the United States Figure Skating Association's Southwest Pacific Junior Championship, and in 1992, she won the bronze medal in the Pacific Coast Junior Championship.

Michelle's wins earned her a scholarship to pay for a coach and rink fees at Ice Castle, an exclusive training center. Karen (who was also admitted to the program),

Michelle Kwan (Wikimedia Commons)

Michelle, and their father moved to Lake Arrowhead, California, for the girls to begin working with noted skating coach Frank Carroll.

At the age of thirteen, Michelle Kwan competed as the youngest skater at the 1993 US Figure Skating Championships. She placed sixth. At the Olympic Festival later that year, she won the gold medal. In the 1994 US Championships in Detroit, Kwan placed second behind Tanya Harding, who was later disqualified for her involvement in an attack on competitor Nancy Kerrigan. Kwan went on to the World Figure Skating Championships, where she placed eighth and was named alternate at the 1994 Olympic Games in Lillehammer, Norway. However, she did not compete.

For the 1996 season, Kwan assumed a more mature look, achieved more expressive artistry, improved both her speed and her jumps, and developed stronger choreographic techniques. She perfected the change-of-edge spiral, a turn in which her weight shifted from the inside to the outside edge of the skate, which became her signature move. She swept both the US Championships and the World Championships in 1996 and became the brightest new skating star.

While beginning her promising career as a figure skater, Kwan maintained her schooling. She graduated from Rim of the World High School in 1999 and attended the University of California, Los Angeles. She dropped out after one year to pursue her skating career.

Life's Work

Kwan's career suffered some setbacks in 1997. Hampered by new skates that she was under contract to wear as an endorsement, she fell twice and faltered in her free skate in the US Championships, losing to Tara Lipinsky. With a stress fracture in her foot, Kwan entered the 1998 US Championships in which Lipinsky was the favorite. However, Lipinsky fell in the short program, opening the way for Kwan to be the first woman to earn a perfect score in the US Championships. Altogether she received seven 6.0 marks from the judges. In the long program, she was given seven out of nine possible perfect scores, making her presentations the best ever seen at the US Championships.

Following her 1998 success, Kwan elected to skate on programs for television but continued to enter competitions whose wins would retain her eligibility for the Olympics. In 1999, Kwan won the US Championships, but her competition in the 2000 US Championships brought forth numerous complaints about her program, which was seen to be easier than those of her competitors. However, she fell on the questionable jump and finished third. Undeterred, she returned the following year to win the 2001 US Championships.

> "You see figure skaters fall all the time. It's the way you pick yourself back up and keep going. Sports provides that tool kit to be successful in life. Because it's not always going to be smooth sailing."

In 2001, Kwan and coach Frank Carroll ended their longtime association, and with no plans to engage another coach, Kwan arrived at the 2002 US Championships on her own, aiming to "take responsibility" for her skating. Winning the US Championships, she placed third in the 2002 Olympic Games in Salt Lake City and second in the World Championships. Desperate for the opportunity to compete in the Olympic Games again in 2006 for the gold medal, Kwan continued entering competitions whose wins conferred Olympic eligibility. Still an amateur, she was given a lucrative contract with the Disney Corporation as spokesperson and performer.

Kwan, under the guidance of her new coach, Scott Williams, won all competitions she entered in 2002–03

> **Michelle Kwan's Olympic Medals and World Championship Titles**
>
> Much of Michelle Kwan's career was devoted to pursuing the elusive Olympic Gold Medal, but she was continually frustrated. In 1998 at Nagano, Japan, Kwan was the gold-medal favorite, having defeated Tara Lipinski earlier in the year. However, in the closely contested match, Lipinski skated the most technically difficult program and edged Kwan for the gold. At Salt Lake City in 2002, Kwan entered the Olympic Games again as the favorite, but Sarah Hughes executed a technically flawless program, while Kwan fell on a triple flip jump. Hughes placed first, Russian skater Irina Slutskaya was second, and Kwan won the bronze medal.
>
> Kwan won her first World Championship in 1996, beating China's Lu Chen. With seven flawless triple jumps and a last-minute triple toe jump, Kwan triumphed in the closest competition in the history of the event. Kwan won the 1998 World Championship following her loss in the Olympic Games. During the 2000 World Championship, Kwan fell behind Russian skaters Maria Butyrskaya and Irina Slutskaya after the short program but performed superbly in the free skate to win. Kwan also won the World Championship in 2001, coming from behind to excel in the free skate. In 2003, Kwan won the World Championship for the fifth time, becoming the only woman ever to regain the title three times.

and regained her world title. In 2003, Kwan engaged famed technician Rafael Arutunian to help advance her technical expertise. Kwan skated well in the 2003 US Championships and won. Intent upon qualifying for the 2006 Olympic Games in Turin, Italy, Kwan suffered a hip injury in a fall in 2005, which forced her to withdraw from all planned competitions before the Olympic Games. An abdominal injury in December 2005 forced Kwan ultimately to withdraw from the 2006 Olympic Games.

That same year, Kwan decided to pursue her education and her interest in foreign policy. She enrolled at the University of Denver to finish her undergraduate work. She was also appointed the first US public diplomacy envoy by Secretary of State Condoleeza Rice. She traveled around the world, working with students on leadership and social issues. Upon graduation from the University of Denver, Kwan decided to put off the 2010 Winter Olympics to enroll at Tufts University in Medford, Massachusetts, for postgraduate work in international studies, although she did commentate for *Good Morning America* during those Olympics.

Kwan wrote her autobiography at age seventeen and an inspirational book for children, *The Winning Attitude: What It Takes to Be a Champion*, in 2001. In 2002, Kwan was awarded the prestigious James E. Sullivan Award for America's best amateur athlete. Ten years later, in 2012, Kwan was inducted into the US Figure Skating Hall of Fame.

SIGNIFICANCE

Michelle Kwan's exceptional performances on ice were the result of personal and family dedication to the development of her talent. The years of training instilled in her ideals of fine skating—the importance of athleticism, precision, skills, and good sportsmanship—but Kwan's uniqueness came from the blending of these basic elements with her own innate qualities. Never content to skate by numbers or merely exhibit correctness, Kwan sought to connect with the audience and invite them to join her on an emotional journey. Her musical accompaniments intensified the experience as she dazzled audiences with her expressive artistry and exquisite techniques. Even in defeat, she won the audiences' affection for her graciousness and continued to enjoy great admiration and popularity.

Mary Hurd

FURTHER READING

Koestler-Grack, Rachel A. *Michelle Kwan*. New York: Chelsea, 2007. Print. Asian Americans of Achievement. Emphasizes the story of Kwan's Chinese immigrant family, their financial hardships and commitment to hard work, as well as Kwan's serious appreciation of her role model status.

Kwan, Michelle, and Laura M. James. *Michelle Kwan: My Story–Heart of a Champion*. New York: Scholastic, 1988. Print. A memoir written by Kwan for young audiences, emphasizing her family, the sacrifices they made for her training, and her feelings during competition. Includes a glossary of skating terminology and full-color photographs.

Milton, Steve. *Figure Skating's Greatest Stars.* Buffalo: Firefly, 2009. Print. Focuses on sixty of the best representatives of figure skating, including Kwan. Contains informative essays on each with sidebars noting significant events and achievements.

Martina Navratilova

Czech-born tennis player

Born: October 18, 1956; Prague, Czechoslovakia
Area of Achievement: Athletics: tennis

As a leading figure in women's tennis from the mid-1970s into the twenty-first century, Navratilova was instrumental in demonstrating the professionalism of women's sports and that women athletes deserved comparable financial rewards. She followed Billie Jean King in coming out as lesbian at a time when being an openly lesbian or gay athlete was considered impossible.

Early Life

Martina Navratilova (mahr-TEE-nah nav-RAH-teeloh-VAH) was born in Prague, Czechoslovakia (now the Czech Republic). Her parents divorced when she was three years old, and her mother then married Mirek Navratil. Navratilova lived a robust outdoor life in the Krkno Mountains until the age of five, when her family moved to Revnice near the capital city of Prague. She started skiing before she was three years old and within a couple of years became an excellent skier. She preferred playing rough games such as soccer with boys rather than playing with girls. From earliest childhood she exhibited exceptional strength and athletic ability. Her mother and stepfather were concerned about her "unfeminine" behavior but were impressed by her physical gifts; they believed she would become a champion if she could find the right sport on which to focus her energies.

In the densely populated urban environment near Prague, Navratilova found that opportunities for vigorous physical activity were limited. Nevertheless, the city offered ample facilities for playing tennis. Her whole family played the game. Her maternal grandmother, Agnes Semanska, had been a national champion before World War II. Both of Navratilova's parents competed in amateur tournaments and served as tennis administrators for the Czech government. They were on the courts practically

Martina Navratilova (Wikimedia Commons)

every day and brought Navratilova with them. Her stepfather cut down an old racket for Navratilova to use, and he became her first tennis instructor. She immediately became enthusiastic about tennis and was competing in junior tournaments by the age of eight. Soon she was beating players five and six years older than herself. All the while she had to attend school full time and watch over her younger sister.

By age sixteen, Navratilova had won three national women's championships with her aggressive play. She was ecstatic when selected by the Czechoslovakian Tennis Association to tour the United States in 1973 with a team of the best men and women players. She was enchanted by the freedom she found in the United States, which was so different from the repressed spirit of her Communist-dominated homeland. Fascinated by American music, fashions, and food, she returned home twenty pounds heavier. Her first trip to the United States made an impression that changed her life. She realized that many of the negative things she had heard about the United States were merely Communist propaganda.

Navratilova became pregnant when she was seventeen and had an abortion. She later said that she regretted the whole affair because she had not truly been in love. She eventually acknowledged that she felt a strong sexual attraction to women. Indeed, after she gained U.S. citizenship, she became candid about her sexuality, which would have been impossible to acknowledge in ultraconservative Czechoslovakia.

While still a teenager, Navratilova asked the U.S. government for political asylum and applied for citizenship. For years she lived in fear of being kidnapped by her government's secret police because she was creating negative publicity for the whole Communist system. In defecting to the United States, Navratilova knew she was cutting herself off from home and family, because she would not be allowed to visit her homeland after becoming an American citizen. She bravely faced the future in a strange new land with a limited knowledge of the English language.

Navratilova has been universally called Martina. In her autobiography *Martina* (1985), she explains her preference for being called by her first name because Americans, including sports announcers, have so much trouble pronouncing her surname. She wrote that her last name should be pronounced with emphasis on the second and last syllables.

> "Labels are for filing. Labels are for clothing. Labels are not for people."

LIFE'S WORK

Once Navratilova discovered tennis, she devoted her life to it with the intensity that was her outstanding characteristic. Women's tennis had been a game of finesse until Navratilova burst on the scene. She turned it into a game of speed and power one that was less "ladylike" than it had been in the past but far more interesting to spectators. Navratilova brought to professional tennis a cannonball serve that was clocked at a higher speed than the serves of some of the better professional male players. She was left-handed, which is considered an asset in tennis, and was noted for her powerful forehand as well as her aggressive charges to the net.

Navratilova's rivalry with Chris Evert became legendary. For years, the two battled for first place at the world's most important tournaments: the Australian Open, the U.S. Open, the French Open, and Wimbledon in England. Navratilova won so many titles on the grass courts of the historic All English Lawn Tennis and Croquet Club (Wimbledon) that people said she owned the tournament there. Despite their rivalry, Evert and Navratilova became good friends and often played as partners in doubles matches. Navratilova's record at doubles became almost as impressive as her singles record.

Navratilova was not a popular player when she entered professional tennis. Because she possessed a steely determination and demeanor unmatched since Helen Wills Moody was champion, spectators thought of Navratilova as an iceberg. Her limited knowledge of English made it difficult for her to communicate with the press, and she had a subtle sense of humor that did not translate easily into English. Because of her size and strength, she gave the impression that she beat other women players simply by overpowering them. This was not true, although she could hardly be blamed for making the most of her physical assets. At five feet eight inches tall and about 145 pounds, she was tall enough to serve and volley well yet small enough not to strain her joints excessively. This matter of strain was crucial, because an extremely high level of conditioning powered her performance.

Navratilova quickly became wealthy from prize money and endorsements. She brought her parents to the United States and gave them a beautiful house near her own home in Texas. She continued to pursue an active professional schedule into the 1990s, one that included travel, public appearances, and all sorts of athletic activities. Navratilova also began exploring other interests, and she signed a contract with a New York publisher to write mystery novels; she co-wrote three during the 1990s. Her leisure time remained intensely active, as she enjoyed ice hockey, mountain biking, scuba diving, skiing, snow boarding, basketball, golf, and horseback riding. She also earned a pilot's license and took up photography, shooting in Africa and exhibiting her work in Prague.

Navratilova established an example for women who are not considered feminine in the conventional sense. She proved that there are as many different types of women as there are different types of men, and that each woman has the option to develop to her fullest potential.

In the midpoint of her professional tennis career, Navratilova had become one of the most popular personalities in the game. She was the number-oneranked female player in the world for seven years, and in 1984 she secured a record for the longest consecutive string of match wins (74). It was a tearful crowd that saw her play her tennis matches at Wimbledon in 1993. She made it to the semifinals but had to bow to talented younger players, such as Monica Seles and Steffi Graf, who were only half her age and had learned to play her aggressive style of tennis. In 2003, however, she tied Billie Jean King's record of twenty Wimbledon titles when she won the mixed doubles crown with Leander Paes. The same year she

Navrátilová meets with UK prime minister David Cameron to sign the Charter for Action to tackle homophobia and transphobia in sport. (Wikimedia Commons)

In 1994, shortly before Navratilova announced her retirement from professional tennis, she had won her 167th singles title by defeating Julie Halard of France in the Paris Women's Open (with a prize of $400,000). This set an all-time record for career singles championships for women as well as men. Navratilova had also earned more money in prizes than any other male or female tennis player in history. In addition to more than $21.4 million in prize money, she had received a huge amount of funds for sponsoring various products. This was a fantastic achievement, considering that when she entered professional tennis the lion's share of the big prizes as well as the lucrative advertising fees went to men.

In 2004, Navratilova returned to singles play for two years. By the time she retired completely in 2006 she had won 1,442 games and lost 219. This record includes 167 singles titles and 177 doubles titles, of which eighteen of the singles and forty-one of the doubles were Grand Slam titles. Her last Grand Slam title came in 2006 when she took the mixed doubles title at the U.S. Open with Bob Bryan.

Navratilova was placed nineteenth on the list of the 100 Greatest Athletes of the Century by sports television network ESPN and second among the 40 Greatest Players of the Tennis Era listed by *Tennis* magazine. In 2000 she was inducted into the International Tennis Hall of Fame. Still, the greatest testimony to her athletic prowess came from the many fellow professionals who consider her abilities unmatched. King stated it simply when she said that Navratilova was "the greatest singles, doubles, and mixed doubles player who's ever lived."

Significance

Navratilova contributed greatly to women's tennis and to women's sports in general by demonstrating that women could compete just as fiercely as men and could play with as high a degree of technical excellence. Many sportswriters suggested that she was sufficiently strong and aggressive to compete with the best male players. Shrugging off such speculations, she helped to popularize women's tennis as a spectator sport, thereby attracting larger crowds as well as broader television coverage.

Navratilova also had a tremendous impact on lesbian and gay rights. She was one of the few public figures who was out as lesbian or gay as well as politically active. She captured the only Grand Slam victory that had escaped her: She won the mixed doubles title and was the oldest player ever to win a Grand Slam competition.

Success had made Navratilova feel more relaxed and amiable, while at the same time the public had come to understand that her impassive exterior concealed a sensitive temperament. Like Jimmy Connors and John McEnroe, two of the greatest male tennis players of all time, she was disliked at the beginning of her career but came to be adored for her courage and dedication to excellence.

As an international superstar, Navratilova's personal life has been a subject of great media interest. She soon realized that it was impossible to conceal her sexuality or her intimate relationships with women. One of the biggest news stories had to do with the so-called palimony suit involving Judy Nelson, who sued Navratilova for half of the money Navratilova earned during the years they had lived together. The suit was finally settled out of court, with Nelson receiving a house in Aspen, Colorado, and an undisclosed amount of cash. Navratilova later brought suit to oppose anti-lesbian and anti-gay legislation in Colorado, spoke out against scientific research trying to show that homosexuality can be treated as a disease, and donated money in support of the search for a cure for acquired immunodeficiency syndrome (AIDS).

called for greater public understanding and tolerance. Navratilova married her longtime girlfriend Julia Lemigova in December of 2014. Her charities have included the Rainbow Endowment, which supports lesbian and gay causes and research on AIDS; the Laureus World Sports Academy; the Sierra Club; Save the Rhino, a retirement home for horses; and People for the Ethical Treatment of Animals. Her efforts on behalf of gay and lesbian rights and for children brought her the 2000 National Equality Award from the Human Rights Campaign. She was one of the first inductees to the National Gay and Lesbian Sports Hall of Fame in 2013.

The publicity generated by Navratilova on and off the tennis court increased as well the use of professional women athletes as product endorsers (and increased their salaries), but she also led the charge for professional women athletes to be compensated at the same level as men in their respective sports.

Bill Delaney, updated by Micah L. Issitt

FURTHER READING

Blue, Adrianne. *Martina: The Lives and Times of Martina Navratilova.* New York: Crown, 1995. This biography covers Navratilova's life until her first retirement, focusing on the obstacles she faced in becoming a professional tennis player and living as an out lesbian. Blue argues that no other sports champion was so involved with the sexual politics of the times. Includes photographs.

Faulkner, Sandra, with Judy Nelson. *Love Match: Nelson Versus Navratilova.* New York: Carol, 1993. A full-length book about the notorious palimony suit brought against Navratilova by her former partner, Judy Nelson. Brings out much information about Navratilova's character away from public view.

Henry, William A., III. "The Lioness in Winter." *Time*, November 30, 1992. A brief retrospective article on Navratilova's career and her feelings about professional sports, lesbian and gay rights, and life in general as she was approaching the end of her illustrious tennis career.

Howard, Johnette. *The Rivals: Chris Evert Versus Martina Navratilova: Their Epic Duels and Extraordinary Friendship.* New York: Broadway Books, 2005. The eighty tennis matches between Navratilova and rival Evert were among the most popular sports spectacles of tennis's golden age, but, despite their fierce competition, the two remained friends. Howard discusses their intertwined careers and their combined effect on tennis. Includes photographs.

Kort, Michele. "Ms. Conversation." *Ms.*, February, 1988. An interesting interview with both Navratilova and another great tennis player, Billie Jean King, who discuss their views on women's tennis, their personal lives, and other subjects.

Navratilova, Martina. *Shape Your Self: My Six-Step Diet and Fitness Plan to Achieve the Best Shape of Your Life.* Emmaus, Pa.: Rodale Books, 2006. Navratilova relates personal stories to illustrate her program that small changes in habits (such as eating natural foods), fun exercise, and greater mental focus lead to health and fitness. Affords a glimpse into how she prepared herself during her career.

_____, with George Vecsey. *Martina.* New York: Alfred A. Knopf, 1985. A frank and revealing autobiography in which Navratilova describes her unhappy childhood and conflicts about her sexuality. Displays her sympathetic and human personality, in dramatic contrast to the cold, aggressive image she projected on the tennis courts.

Vecsey, George. "Martina's Last Bow? 1993 Wimbledon." *Tennis*, July, 1993. Discusses Navratilova's anticipated appearance in the 1993 Wimbledon tennis tournament and the unsurpassed record she established at this prestigious event, beginning in 1974. Paints a word picture of the historical Wimbledon as well. Includes photographs.

JACK NICKLAUS

Golfer

Born: January 21, 1940; Columbus, Ohio
Area of Achievement: Athletics: golf

One of the greatest golfers in the history of the sport, Nicklaus ended his remarkable career after seventy-three Professional Golf Association (PGA) victories, which included a record eighteen wins in major championships. He was named Golfer of the Century by the PGA in 1988 and received the Presidential Medal of Freedom in 2005. Additionally, he designed hundreds of golf courses and clubs around the world.

EARLY LIFE

Jack Nicklaus (NIHCK-luhs) and his younger sister, Marilyn, were the only children of Charlie and Nellie Nicklaus, growing up in the Columbus suburb of Upper

Jack Nicklaus (Wikimedia Commons)

Arlington. His father was a pharmacist who established a string of Columbus-area stores named Nicklaus Drugs.

Nicklaus would develop his father's passion for all sports, but it took a doctor's advice to his father, who had broken his ankle, to walk for exercise that landed Nicklaus and his father on a golf course. Golfing would become a regular event for the two. At the age of nine, Nicklaus began playing locally at Scioto Country Club, and he was encouraged by Scioto Club professional Jack Grout to join the club's junior program. Under the tutelage of Grout, who Nicklaus credits with teaching him how to play golf, Nicklaus won the Scioto Club juvenile trophy at the ages of ten and eleven. He went on to win a series of state junior championships in his early teens and was considered the best junior golfer in Ohio in the 1950s.

Even though Nicklaus excelled at other sports in high school and had aspirations of one day playing with Ohio State University's football team, virtually all his free time was devoted to golf. From an early age, Nicklaus played golf with his father's friends, and in tournaments he defeated older boys regularly. After winning the Ohio Open at the age of sixteen, Nicklaus knew that golf had become his sport.

After graduating from Upper Arlington High School in 1957, Nicklaus enrolled at Ohio State to pursue a degree in pharmacy. During his freshman year he met Barbara Bash. They were married on July 23, 1960. His golf success led him to decide to leave Ohio State before graduating.

Life's Work

Nicklaus's success as a golfer spanned six decades. At Ohio State, he helped the Buckeyes win the Big Ten golf championship in 1961 as the individual medalist. That same year, he was the individual medalist at the NCAA championships. Even more important to his career was winning the US Amateur Championship in 1959 and 1961; he was a member of the US Walker Cup team that played at Muirfield in Scotland in 1959, and he led the United States to victory in 1960 at the World Amateur Championship.

Nicklaus's decision to turn professional was not an easy one, in part because Nicklaus's hero, Bobby Jones, remained an amateur golfer his entire career and because Nicklaus's father had always envisioned his son as Jones's heir apparent. Contributing to Nicklaus's decision to turn pro was the birth of his first child, Jack William Nicklaus II, on September 23, 1961, and the need to practice and play full time rather than part time while selling insurance, which he had started doing while in college. On November 8 he officially became a professional golfer. To be the best golfer possible and to support his family, Nicklaus needed to become a member of the PGA Tour.

> "*Success depends almost entirely on how effectively you learn to manage the game's two ultimate adversaries: the course and yourself.*"

Before Nicklaus made his professional debut on the tour in 1962, he signed a management agreement with Mark McCormack, who was already the agent for Arnold Palmer and Gary Player. McCormack and his agency, International Management Group (IMG), were instrumental in Nicklaus's achievements off the golf course. Endorsements and speaking engagements became the norm for Nicklaus as a result of his association with IMG in the 1960s.

While his pro career began uneventfully, it was Nicklaus's eleventh tournament, the 1962 US Open at Oakmont Country Club in western Pennsylvania, that changed everything for him. Paired with Palmer, Nicklaus, who was ten years younger, defeated the "King of Golf" forty miles from Palmer's hometown of Latrobe. Later, nicknamed Golden Bear for his build and prodigious drives off the tee, Nicklaus would win thirty-eight tournaments, including seven majors during his first eight years on the tour.

Always a colorful dresser on the links, Nicklaus enhanced his image and popularity by shedding extra pounds during the year following his father's death from cancer in 1970. His most memorable stretch of the 1970s was when he won the PGA championship in 1971 and the Masters and the US Open in 1972; he lost the British Open in 1972 to Lee Trevino by one stroke. Nicklaus considered this loss the most devastating of his career. Of the thirty-seven tournaments he won in this decade, eight were majors.

Entering his third decade on the PGA tour, Nicklaus won the US Open and the PGA Championship again in 1980. His eighteenth and final victory in a major was the Masters in 1986. He was forty-six years old, the oldest golfer to win the Masters. Nicklaus continued to play on the PGA Tour after joining the PGA Senior Tour (now known as the Champions Tour) in 1990. His final appearance in a major was the British Open at the Old Course at St. Andrews, Scotland, in 2005. Complementing his individual accomplishments was his participation as a member of the US Ryder Cup teams that competed against golfers from Europe. He served as team captain in 1987.

A significant challenge for Nicklaus beyond the tour was fulfilling his dream of building a golf course in his home state. Increasingly interested in designing golf courses and inspired by Augusta National, the home of the Masters tournament in Georgia, Nicklaus spent time and money on developing the Country Club of Muirfield Village and Muirfield Village Golf Club, home to the annual Memorial Tournament in Dublin, Ohio, a suburb of Columbus where the Nicklaus family maintains a home. The Muirfield courses opened in 1974, and the first Memorial Tournament was held there in 1976. He also decided to break from McCormack and IMG and established his own business, Golden Bear, near his Florida home in Palm Beach.

Equally important for Nicklaus was the continuous support of his wife, Barbara, and their five children. Beginning with the 1982 US Open, sons Jackie and Gary often caddied for their famous father, and the Nicklaus family received the Golf Family of the Year Award from the National Golf Foundation in 1985. In 1999 he was named Male Sportsman of the Century by *Sports Illustrated* magazine.

Nicklaus walks up to his ball on the 9th hole of the par-3 course at Augusta National Golf Club during the 2006 par-3 contest. Nicklaus was playing along with Andy North and Tom Watson as a non-competitor in the contest. (Wikimedia Commons)

Nicklaus has remained active in retirement. His interest in golf-course design has only intensified, and his courses are considered some of the finest in the world. In fact, in 2011, fourteen of his designed courses were part of *Golf Digest*'s "75 Best Golf Resorts." In 2008, he became a global ambassador for golf and was a key spokesman for the return of golf to the Summer Olympics in 2016, the first time golf was part of the Olympic Games since 1904.

On May 19, 2014, the United States House of Representatives voted to pass H.R. 2203, a bill that would award Nicklaus the Congressional Gold Medal "in recognition of his service to the nation in promoting excellence and good sportsmanship." The bill says that Nicklaus' "magnetic personality and unfailing sense of kindness and thoughtfulness have endeared him to millions throughout the world."

Significance

Although he earned a total of $5.7 million as a player, less than the amount of the average single-tournament purse for most PGA events today, Nicklaus took professional golf to a new level. A worldwide ambassador of the game, he epitomized the sportsmanship and etiquette of golf's rich history. His style of play and golf swing have been emulated and written about extensively, and his relationship with other players, fans, and the media remained positive throughout his career. As a young player in the 1960s, Nicklaus was befriended by the great golfer Jones;

like Jones, Nicklaus, too, befriended another young golfing great, Tiger Woods.

Nicklaus's interest in golf-course architecture and his ability to design quality courses made him a major part of the development of nearly four hundred courses around the world. The success of his company, now called Golden Bear International, enabled Nicklaus to continue marketing his own line of equipment and apparel and to offer golf academies for budding golfers from around the country. Nicklaus's legacy continues into the twenty-first century.

Kevin Eyster

Further Reading

Andrisani, John. *The Nicklaus Way: An Analysis of the Unique Techniques and Strategies of Golf's Leading Major Championship Winner*. New York: HarperCollins, 2003. Print.

Barrett, Connell. "Jack the Ripper." *Golf Magazine* 55.4 (2013): 108. *Academic Search Complete*. Web. 18 Dec. 2013.

Barrett, Connell, and Joe Passov. "No.1 Player of All Time Jack Nicklaus." *Golf Magazine* 54.10 (2012): 88. *Academic Search Complete*. Web. 18 Dec. 2013.

Boyette, John. *The 1986 Masters: How Jack Nicklaus Roared Back to Win*. Guilford, CT: Lyons, 2011. Print.

Clavin, Thomas. *One for the Ages: Jack Nicklaus and the 1986 Masters*. Chicago: Chicago Review, 2011. Print.

Jacobs, Timothy, ed. *Golf Courses of Jack Nicklaus*. New York: Gallery, 1989. Print.

Nicklaus, Jack. *Jack Nicklaus: My Story*. New York: Simon, 1997. Print.

Nicklaus, Jack, with Ken Bowden. *Jack Nicklaus: My Most Memorable Shots in the Majors*. Trumbull, CT: Golf Digest, 1988. Print.

Nicklaus, Jack, with David Shedloski. *Jack Nicklaus: Memories and Mementos from Golf's Golden Bear*. New York: Stewart, 2007. Print.

Nicklaus, Jack, with Herbert Warren Wind. *The Greatest Game of All: My Life in Golf*. New York: Simon, 1969. Print.

Shaw, Mark. *Jack Nicklaus: Golf's Greatest Champion*. New York: Sports, 2002. Print.

Sounes, Howard. *The Wicked Game: Arnold Palmer, Jack Nicklaus, Tiger Woods, and the Story of Modern Golf*. New York: HarperCollins, 2004. Print.

Jesse Owens

Track-and-field athlete

Born: September 12, 1913; Oakville, Alabama
Died: March 31, 1980; Tucson, Arizona
Also known as: James Cleveland Owens; J. C. Owens; the Buckeye Bullet
Areas of Achievement: Athletics: Olympics; Athletics: track and field

Owens achieved international fame at the 1936 Berlin Olympics, winning four gold medals and defying Nazi leader Adolf Hitler's contentions of white supremacy. He won the 100- and 200-meter dashes, the long jump, and the 4-by-100-meter relay. His significant role as a trailblazer for racial equality helped changed the social landscape of America.

Early Life

James Cleveland Owens was born September 12, 1913, in Oakville, Alabama, to Henry and Emma Alexander. He was the seventh of eleven children. Owens's father was a

Jesse Owens (Wikimedia Commons)

sharecropper and his grandfather was a slave. When Owens was nine years old, the family moved to Cleveland, Ohio. The first day at his new school, the teacher asked him his name. Owens replied, "J. C.," but because of his southern accent, she thought that he said "Jesse." The name stuck with him for the remainder of his life.

Owens first started to run track in junior high school. Because he had a job at a shoe repair shop after school, the coach let him practice before school. At East Technical High School in Cleveland, Owens developed into an elite performer, tying the national high school record of 9.4 seconds in the 100-yard dash, and setting records in the 220-yard dash and long jump.

Owens was heavily recruited by colleges, and although Ohio State University could not offer him a scholarship, the school provided a job for Owens's father. Thus, Owens ended up at Ohio State, where he became known as the "Buckeye Bullet." He also worked several jobs, such as an elevator operator, a waiter, and gas station attendant, to support himself and his wife, Ruth.

One of the greatest sporting achievements ever occurred at the Big Ten Conference championship meet in Ann Arbor, Michigan, on May 25, 1935. In a span of just forty-five minutes, Owens set three world records and tied a fourth. Owens was a dominant sprinter and long jumper in college. He won a record four gold medals in the 1935 National Collegiate Athletics Association (NCAA) championships and duplicated the feat the following year.

> "The road to the Olympics, leads to no city, no country. It goes far beyond New York or Moscow, ancient Greece or Nazi Germany. The road to the Olympics leads — in the end — to the best within us."

A Day for the Record Books

At the 1935 Big Ten Conference Track and Field Championships in Ann Arbor, Michigan, Jesse Owens rewrote the college track and field record books. In forty-five minutes, the twenty-one-year-old sophomore from Ohio State University tied the world record in the set world records in three events and tied the world record in another. After falling down a flight of stairs a few days before the meet while roughhousing with fraternity brothers, Owens was uncertain that he would even be able to compete but decided to try. In his first event, the 100-yard dash, Owens finished in 9.4 seconds, tying the world record. Only ten minutes later, he went to the long-jump pit for his second event. His first jump was 26 feet, 8¼ inches—a mark that broke the world record by more than six inches. The record would stand for twenty-five years. Next, Owens lined up for the 220-yard dash, which he ran in 20.3 seconds, bettering the previous world record by 0.3 seconds. Finally, he ran the 220-yard low hurdles. Owens was not a particularly accomplished hurdler, but his unmatched speed between the hurdles helped him to beat opponents who were technically superior. He finished the race in 22.6 seconds, the first time the 23-second mark had been broken.

LIFE'S WORK

Owens's phenomenal success at Ohio State gave him confidence that he could compete at the international level. The 1936 Summer Olympics were held in Germany, led by Adolf Hitler and his Nazi Party. Hitler espoused a belief that Aryan people (that is, white Germans) were the dominant race and superior to people of color. The Germans had high expectations that their athletes would dominate the Games. In a remarkable display of athletic ability, Owens became the first track-and field athlete to win four gold medals in a single Olympics. At a time when segregation and racism were pervasive, Owens's performance discredited Hitler's master race theory.

Owens's first event in the Olympics was the 100-meter sprint, in which he defeated American teammate Ralph Metcalfe. The next day, he struggled in the long jump until German competitor Luz Long gave him some advice that helped him advance and ultimately win the event. Owens next won the 200 meters and anchored the 4-by-100-meter relay team to another gold medal. Adi Dassler, the founder of Adidas, approached Owens in the Olympic village and gave him shoes; this event marked the first sponsorship deal for a male African American athlete. In medal ceremonies on the opening day of competition, Hitler shook hands with only the German victors. When advised by Olympic officials to great each medalist or none at all, Hitler skipped all further medal presentations.

Owens at start of record breaking 200 meter race during the Olympic games 1936 in Berlin. (Library of Congress)

Despite Hitler's attitude, Owens was hailed as a hero by the German spectators, who cheered him loudly and sought his autograph. Owens was even allowed to travel with whites and stay in the same hotels, which he could not do in the United States at the time. In Berlin, a street near the Olympic stadium was later renamed Jesse Owens Allee.

After the Olympic Games, Owens returned to the United States and tried to capitalize on his success by pursuing commercial opportunities. However, American athletic officials wanted him to compete in Sweden at a post-Olympic meet. When Owens declined, the officials withdrew his amateur status. Olympic athletes did not receive significant product endorsements and advertising deals in those days, and Owens did not receive the offers he had expected. To earn a living, he became an athletic entertainer, putting on shows by giving local sprinters a head start and then beating them in the 100-yard dash. He also competed against racehorses in short sprints, winning most of the races. Owens also worked at various jobs, including running a dry-cleaning business. At one point, he served as a playground director in Cleveland, beginning many years in which he worked with underprivileged youths. He became a board member and director of the Chicago Boys' Club. In 1955, the State Department named him America's ambassador of sports, and he spent two months traveling through India, Singapore, Malaysia, and the Philippines to meet with government officials and underprivileged children. In 1956, he was the personal representative for President Dwight D. Eisenhower at the Olympic Games in Australia. Owens became a consultant to many corporations, including the United States Olympic Committee. He was in high demand as an inspirational speaker.

Owens's achievements brought him many awards and honors. President Gerald Ford awarded him the Medal of Freedom, the highest civilian honor in the United States, in 1976. President Jimmy Carter presented him with a Living Legend Award in 1979. He was inducted into the U.S. Olympic Hall of Fame and National Track and Field Hall of Fame. In 1981, U.S.A. Track and Field established the Jesse Owens Award, which is presented to each year's most outstanding American male and female track and field performers. Owens died of complications from lung cancer at age sixty-six.

Significance

Owens achieved international fame by winning four gold medals in the 1936 Olympics in Berlin. In a time of racial segregation and deep-seated prejudice, he disproved Hitler's theory of Aryan racial superiority. Many experts call his four world records at the Big Ten Track and Field Championships the greatest sporting achievement ever in one day. Later in life, Owens worked to provide opportunities to underprivileged youths.

Mark Stanbrough

Further Reading

Baker, William J. *Jesse Owens: An American Life*. New York: Free Press, 1986. An introduction to the life and accomplishments of Owens.

Braun, Eric. *Jesse Owens*. Mankato, Minn.: Capstone Press, 2006. This book is designed for early readers and describes and illustrates the life of Owens.

Nuwer, Hank. *The Legend of Jesse Owens*. New York: Franklin Watts, 1998. Owens is presented as a talented, hardworking athlete with both good and bad personal traits. The social history of the African American Great Migration, segregation, the racial overtones of World War II, and the Civil Rights movement are examined.

Schaap, Jeremy. *Triumph: The Untold Story of Jesse Owens and Hitler's Olympics*. New York: Houghton Mifflin, 2007. Schaap adds previously unreported details and corrects historical misconceptions about the 1936 Olympics Games.

Streissguth, Thomas. *Jesse Owens*. Minneapolis, Minn.: Lerner, 2005. Biography chronicling Owens's life from his childhood in Alabama to the 1984 Olympic memorial service that honored him.

JACKIE ROBINSON

Baseball player

Born: January 31, 1919; Cairo, Georgia
Died: October 24, 1972; Stamford, Connecticut
Also known as: Jack Roosevelt Robinson, the Dark Destroyer, the Colored Comet
Areas of Achievement: Athletics: baseball; Athletics: miscellaneous; Civil rights

A talented athlete who excelled in four sports in college, Robinson broke the color line in Major League Baseball when he made his debut for the Brooklyn Dodgers in 1947. Subjected to close scrutiny and brutal racism, he endured with grace and made a notable contribution to the Civil Rights movement.

EARLY LIFE

Jack Roosevelt Robinson was born on January 31, 1919, in Cairo, Georgia, to a family of sharecroppers. He was the youngest of five children. In 1920, after his father left the family, the Robinsons moved to a predominantly white, suburban part of Pasadena, California. At an early age, Robinson learned what it was like to be an outcast and how to work within that social environment.

As Robinson grew up, he began to become interested in sports. His first forays into athletics came as he started high school during the mid-1930's. His brothers Frank and Mack—a silver medalist in the 1936 Summer Olympics—encouraged him to pursue sports. At John Muir High School, Robinson played on the football, basketball, track, tennis, and baseball teams.

When Robinson enrolled at Pasadena Junior College (later Pasadena City College) after graduating from high school, he continued playing most of the same sports. He talents were apparent, and he received widespread recognition. Robinson also excelled in the classroom and in 1938 was named to the Order of the Mast and Dagger, an honor recognizing exemplary service to the school. The fact that Robinson accomplished this at a predominantly white school makes his feat more remarkable.

Robinson's next move was to enroll at the University of California at Los Angeles (UCLA) in 1939. At UCLA, he played baseball, basketball, football, and track, becoming the first athlete in school history to earn varsity letters in four sports. He was one of four African American players on the UCLA football team, one of the most integrated teams of its era.

During Robinson's senior year, two significant events occurred. The first was that Robinson met Rachel Isum, who would become his wife. The second was that, during the spring semester, he left school without finishing his degree to become an assistant athletic director with the National Youth Administration (NYA), an organization run by the federal government. His division of the NYA soon halted operations, and by 1941, Robinson was looking for ways to make ends meet. He usually did so by playing semiprofessional football.

> "*Many people resented my impatience and honesty, but I never cared about acceptance as much as I cared about respect.*"

Jackie Robinson (Library of Congress)

Robinson with Eleanor Roosevelt (third from left) at the Manhattan School for Boys. (National Archives and Records Administration)

Life's Work

Robinson was drafted into the U.S. Army in 1942. He initially began service in Fort Riley, Kansas, where he served with and befriended heavyweight boxing champion Joe Louis. After he completed officer training, Robinson was transferred to Fort Hood, Texas. It was there that his military career fell apart. Refusing to follow a bus driver's command to move to the back of the bus, Robinson was arrested by the military police. Although he was exonerated by an all-white panel, the court-martial proceedings ensured that he never saw combat. After becoming a coach for Army athletics, Robinson was honorably discharged in 1944.

Although Robinson's Army career was unsuccessful, it introduced him to a former baseball player for the Kansas City Monarchs of the Negro American League, a meeting that proved fortuitous. The player encouraged Robinson to write to the Monarchs for a tryout. Before he got the chance to try out, however, Robinson moved to Sam Houston College to coach the basketball team.

Robinson's job as a basketball coach did not last long; the Monarchs sent Robinson an offer to play for them in 1945. While he was happy to be playing baseball, his experience was a frustrating one. Robinson found the league disorganized and was troubled by its embrace of gambling. His aggravations did not curtail his ability to produce as a player, however, and Robinson was named to the Negro League All-Star Game.

During the season, Robinson attended tryouts to attempt to join a Major League Baseball (MLB) team. While his tryout with the Boston Red Sox was largely a charade, the one with the Brooklyn Dodgers was more promising. The Dodgers at that time were run by Branch Rickey, a cunning man who understood the game of baseball and what it would take for an African American player to break baseball's color line. At a meeting that has become famous, Rickey grilled Robinson for more than three hours, trying to determine whether Robinson could handle the scrutiny and derision that would accompany his playing in the all-white major leagues. Rickey was looking for a player who was courageous enough to withstand the barrage without lashing out. In Robinson, he found his man.

On October 23, 1945, the Dodgers announced they had signed Robinson to a contract and that he would play for their minor-league affiliate the Montreal Royals for the 1946 season. Although Robinson was not the best Negro League player of his time, and some of his peers were angered that he was signed before them, Robinson became the first African American major leaguer since the 1880's.

Robinson and Rachel got married at the start of the 1946 season. Then Robinson went to spring training in Florida, a state with immense racial tension. Robinson was unable to stay with the team, and local police padlocked stadiums or threatened to cancel games. However, on March 17, 1946, Robinson finally got the chance to play, taking the shortstop position. By the time the Royals played their season opener, he had moved to second base and his statistics began to improve. Although fans on the road would often yell disparaging remarks, the fans in Montreal were mostly welcoming and supportive.

Six days before the start of the 1947 season, the Dodgers called up Robinson from the Royals. His first game, on April 15, 1947, effectively broke the color barrier in Major League Baseball. He played first base throughout the season and finished with 12 home runs, 29 steals, and a .297 batting average. His efforts were good enough to win him the inaugural MLB rookie of the year award.

Reaction to Robinson playing in the major leagues was mixed. Robinson often got a better reception from fans than from players—on his own team as well as on opposing teams. It was his play that helped win over people,

> ### Robinson's Accomplishments in Other Sports
>
> Although Jackie Robinson is best known for his accomplishments as a baseball player, he was in fact an excellent all-around athlete. At Pasadena's John Muir High School, he earned varsity letters in football, basketball, track, and baseball. In addition, he also was a member of the tennis team and won the Pacific Coast Negro Tennis Tournament singles title in 1936.
>
> At Pasadena Junior College, Robinson excelled in basketball, football, baseball, and track. In football he was a quarterback and safety and in baseball he played shortstop. His older brother Mack, who won a silver medal in the 1936 Summer Olympics, had set the school record in the broad jump; Robinson bested it.
>
> When Robinson entered the University of California at Los Angeles (UCLA) in 1939, he continued competing in baseball, basketball, football, and track. At the school he became the first athlete to be awarded varsity letters in four sports. In 1941, he was named an All-American in football.

as once they saw what he could do, they could not deride him for his skills.

The next year was a somewhat easier one for Robinson as other African American players joined the league, notably Larry Doby and Satchel Paige. The Dodgers also added three more African American players to their roster. Feeling more comfortable and having switched back to second base, Robinson put together another respectable season. Before the 1949 season, Robinson sought hitting help from George Sisler, who gave him tips on how to approach different pitches. The coaching brought Robinson's batting average up almost 50 points and improved his hitting overall. He was voted to the All-Star Game, the first to include African American players, and was also named the National League most valuable player (MVP).

From 1949 to 1954, Robinson was a player to be reckoned with, but after winning his only World Series in 1955, his skills began to diminish. In addition to his age, Robinson was suffering from the effects of undiagnosed diabetes. After the 1956 season, he retired from baseball. After his baseball career was over, Robinson remained a trailblazer. He became the first African American vice president of a major company when he joined Chock Full o'Nuts. Later, he became a broadcaster for ABC's baseball coverage—again, he was the first African American to do so. Robinson also was active in politics and the Civil Rights movement, serving on the board of directors of the National Association for the Advancement of Colored People (NAACP).

In 1962, Robinson became a first-ballot inductee to the Baseball Hall of Fame. However, he did not live to see his number, 42, retired by every team in MLB in 1997. He died on October 24, 1972, of a heart attack.

SIGNIFICANCE

Robinson's integration of baseball was one of the iconic events of the early Civil Rights movement. It took a strong man to become the first and only African American in the game, and a talented one to defy doubters and prove he belonged in the major leagues. Robinson's courage is as much a part of his legend as his athletic skill. In the ten years that Robinson played for the Dodgers, he established himself as one of the best players in the game. He is still remembered for his contributions, as each year Major League Baseball celebrates Jackie Robinson Day on April 15.

P. Huston Ladner

FURTHER READING

Dorinson, Joseph, and Joram Warmund, eds. *Jackie Robinson: Race, Sports, and the American Dream*. Armonk, N.Y.:M. E. Sharpe, 1998. This book is a collection of essays that offer different perspectives about Robinson. The entries vary from remembrances to media scrutiny to examining Robinson's impact on society.

Eig, Jonathan. *Opening Day: The Story of Jackie Robinson's First Season*. New York: Simon & Schuster, 2007. Offers a thorough examination of Robinson's first season in professional baseball, detailing the different extremes that Robinson faced and offering insight into his courage.

Robinson, Jackie, and Alfred Duckett. *I Never Had It Made: An Autobiography of Jackie Robinson*. 1972. Reprint. New York: HarperCollins, 2003. Robinson's autobiography goes beyond baseball and instead focuses on his inspirational role in American history.

_____, and Carl T. Rowan. *Wait Till Next Year: The Life Story of Jackie Robinson*. New York: Random House, 1960. This early biography details what Robinson endured when he joined the major leagues.

Robinson, Sharon. *Jackie's Nine: Jackie Robinson's Values to Live By*. New York: Scholastic, 2001. Written by Robinson's daughter, this book is aimed at young adults but offers an inside perspective on Robinson's character.

BILL RUSSELL

Basketball player and coach

Born: February 12, 1934; Monroe, Louisiana
Birth Name: William Fenton Russell
Areas of Achievement: Athletics: basketball; Athletics: Olympics

As the cornerstone of one of the most successful sports dynasties in history, Russell was the consummate team player. He went on to become the first African American coach in professional sports and has served as a thoughtful commentator on race, society, sports, and other issues.

EARLY LIFE

William Fenton Russell was born in Monroe, Louisiana, in the midst of the Great Depression, to Charles and Katie Russell. When Russell was eight, his family moved to Oakland, California. Four years later, Katie Russell died.

As a child, Russell was not successful athletically—unlike his older brother, Charlie, who was a star football player. Russell played two years on his school's varsity basketball team but was only a mediocre player. After his senior season, though, Russell was selected to join a touring team. Over the next weeks, he carefully studied the moves of better players and then copied them. Suddenly, Russell saw success on the basketball court for the first time. He also found that his skills—including excellent jumping ability—were best suited to playing defense.

Offered a scholarship to the University of San Francisco (USF), Russell seized the opportunity to go to college. There he met guard K. C. Jones, who became a lifelong friend. The two constantly discussed basketball, exploring the best way to approach different situations on the court. In three years with the varsity team, Russell averaged 20.7 points and 20.3 rebounds a game. The team thrived. The USF Dons managed fifty-five consecutive wins over those two seasons and captured two National Collegiate Athletic Association (NCAA) championships.

Bill Russell (Wikimedia Commons)

The year they won their first NCAA title, 1955, Russell was voted the tournament's most outstanding player.

Russell's defensive skill had caught the eye of Red Auerbach, the coach and general manager of the Boston Celtics. Auerbach made a trade with the St. Louis Hawks so he could select Russell in the National Basketball Association (NBA) draft. With Russell's arrival—and that of Jones—a dynasty was born. Before that dynasty could take shape, though, Russell and Jones went to Australia to win the Olympic gold medal in men's basketball.

LIFE'S WORK

Russell and Jones joined the Celtics with the 1956-1957 season underway. Russell made his mark immediately, leading the league in rebounding. The Celtics met the Hawks in the NBA Finals that year. In a thrilling triple-overtime seventh game, Boston won its first championship.

Russell led the league in rebounding each of the next two years and captured the league's most valuable player (MVP) award for the 1957-1958 season. The first of those seasons ended in disappointment, though, as Russell was injured in the third game of the finals and the Celtics lost to the Hawks. The setback was temporary.

The Celtics won the next eight NBA championships, a run of success unequaled in American professional sports. During that time, Russell captured four consecutive MVP awards.

Despite all the success, Russell occasionally had to endure slights and worse because of his race. He was outspoken about racial injustice when it occurred, behavior that led to a sometimes prickly relationship with Celtics fans.

After the 1965-1966 season, Auerbach retired as coach and named Russell the team's player-coach, making the center the first African American coach in the NBA. The Celtics won the Eastern Conference again the next year, but they lost in the play-offs to the Philadelphia 76ers, led by Russell's rival, Wilt Chamberlain.

The Celtics returned to form and won NBA titles the next two years. Russell played at a high level until the end of his career. In the 1968-1969 season, he averaged 42.7 minutes and 19.3 rebounds a game. To win another championship that year, Russell and the Celtics had to defeat Chamberlain's 76ers, then the Los Angeles Lakers. The Celtics won game seven in Los Angeles as Russell, at age thirty-five, collected 21 rebounds. He retired with eleven championship rings.

The 1959-60 Boston Celtics team that won its 3rd NBA title. Russel is number 6, standing in center. (Wikimedia Commons)

> "To me, one of the most beautiful things to see is a group of men coordinating their efforts toward a common goal, alternately subordinating and asserting themselves to achieve real teamwork in action. I tried to do that, we all tried to do that, on the Celtics. I think we succeeded."

A few years later, Russell returned to the NBA as general manager and coach of the Seattle SuperSonics. He lasted four years, but when the team finished below .500 in the last of those years, Russell resigned. He had difficulty getting players to accept his views on how basketball should be played, views shaped by his experience with the Celtics.

After a few years as a sportscaster on NBA broadcasts, in 1987 Russell returned briefly to coaching. He took charge of the Sacramento Kings that year, but in the first two-thirds of the eighty-two-game season, the Kings managed only seventeen wins. Russell was fired.

Russell received several honors and awards, which he did not always embrace. When the Boston Celtics retired his uniform number in 1972, he did not attend the ceremony. Similarly, when he was elected to the Naismith Memorial Basketball Hall of Fame, he refused to attend the ceremony. He was on hand, however, in 1999 when the Celtics, opening their new arena, held a second number- retiring ceremony. In 1996, when the NBA marked its fiftieth anniversary, he was named one of its best fifty players in history.

On Saturday, February 14, 2009, during the 2009 NBA All-Star Weekend in Phoenix, NBA Commissioner David Stern announced that the NBA Finals MVP Award would be named after Russell. Russell was named as a 2010 recipient of the Presidential Medal of Freedom. On June 15, 2017, Russell was announced as the inaugural recipient of the NBA Lifetime Achievement Award.

Russell Versus Chamberlain

The rivalry between National Basketball Association (NBA) star centers Bill Russell and Wilt Chamberlain was one of the most famous in all of sports. The two legends played against each other for ten seasons. Russell, the defensive-minded center, was about four inches shorter and about sixty pounds lighter than Chamberlain, who was an offensive force and a superb rebounder himself. Much was made of the rivalry between the two, but they were, in fact, friends—off the court—for much of that time. On the court, both were dominating forces, but Chamberlain, no matter how effective he was against the rest of the league, could not overmatch Russell. With the exception of the 1967 season, Russell always ended up the champion. Chamberlain often seemed to hesitate before taking shots against Russell, as though he were waiting for the Celtic to stop him.

Significance

Russell was a perennial champion as a basketball player. He won two college championships in his four years at the University of San Francisco. He won an Olympic gold medal. He won eleven championships in thirteen years in the NBA.

The Celtics won so consistently because they had a potent offense coupled with tenacious defense; they had skilled players who complemented one another; they cared about winning more than they cared about individual statistics; but most of all, they won because of Russell. He was the only player involved in all eleven championship teams between 1957 and 1969.

At only 6 feet, 9 inches tall and 220 pounds, Russell was not an intimidating physical presence, but his carefully honed skills and jumping ability made him an intimidating presence on the court. He was the first center to dominate the game defensively.

Dale Anderson

Further Reading

Goudsouzian, Aram. *King of the Court: Bill Russell and the Basketball Revolution.* Berkeley: University of California Press, 2010. Goudsouzian makes the case that Russell was as much a pioneer in the NBA as Jackie Robinson was in baseball. He also explores Russell's role as an outspoken critic of racism.

Johnson, James. *The Dandy Dons: Bull Russell, K. C. Jones, Phil Woolpert, and One of College Basketball's Greatest and Most Innovative Teams.* Lincoln: University of Nebraska Press, 2009. Johnson chronicles the University of San Francisco team on which Russell played, telling the story not only of their success on the court but also of the racist attitudes they had to contend with.

Russell, Bill. *Red and Me: My Coach, My Lifelong Friend.* New York: HarperCollins, 2009. Russell recounts his long, successful association with Auerbach, the mastermind behind the Celtics dynasty.

_____ and Taylor Branch. *Second Wind: The Memoirs of an Opinionated Man.* New York: Random House, 1979. Russell and Branch do more than describe Russell's brilliant basketball career; they explore living with race, celebrity, and one's own values in American society.

Taylor, John. *The Rivalry: Bill Russell, Wilt Chamberlain, and the Golden Age of Basketball.* New York: Ballantine Books, 2006. Taylor describes one of the most storied rivalries in sports history while vividly describing the early years of the NBA and offering an in-depth look at two very different athletes and men.

Babe Ruth

Baseball player

Born: February 6, 1895; Baltimore, Maryland
Died: August 16, 1948; Manhattan, New York City
Area of Achievement: Athletics: baseball

A remarkably talented athlete with a great flair for showmanship, Babe Ruth has come to symbolize baseball, the American national pastime.

Early Life

George Herman Ruth, Jr., later known as Babe Ruth, was the son of George H. Ruth, Sr., and Kate Schamberger Ruth. Some confusion exists about the younger Ruth's actual date of birth. For many years, George Ruth believed that he had been born on February 7, 1894, but his birth certificate gives February 6, 1895, as his date of birth. George Ruth was the eldest of the eight children born to the Ruths, although only he and a sister (later Mrs. Wilbur Moberly) survived to adulthood. George Ruth's mother

Babe Ruth (Wikimedia Commons)

(whose maiden name is sometimes spelled Schanberg) lived until her eldest son was thirteen. His father survived until young George's second year in Major League Baseball.

The Ruths attempted to support their family through the operation of a barroom. Of his childhood, the dying Ruth told his biographer Bob Considine in 1947, "I was a bad kid. I say that without pride but with a feeling that it is better to say it." Having discovered that their eldest child, George, was a fractious youth, George and Kate enrolled him in St. Mary's Industrial School in Baltimore, Maryland, in 1902. Under the direction of the Xaverian Catholic Brothers, St. Mary's served as a vocational school as well as an orphanage, boarding school, and reform school. It was at St. Mary's that young Ruth studied to become a tailor and also learned to play baseball. Brother Matthias of St. Mary's would hit fungoes to Ruth, who quickly seized on the game as a release from the studies and chores at St. Mary's as well as a chance to demonstrate what Brother Matthias recognized as a remarkable skill in the popular game. To Ruth, Brother Matthias was not only a fielding, hitting, and pitching coach, but also "the father I needed." Years later, at the height of his fame and popularity, Babe Ruth never forgot St. Mary's or the Xaverian Brothers who had taught him so well.

In Baltimore, in 1914, there was a professional baseball team named the Orioles. At the time, the Orioles were a minor league team, owned and managed by Jack Dunn, who, after learning about Ruth's great baseball promise, signed the young athlete to a contract. Ruth discovered that he did not have to become a tailor; he could make a living doing what he enjoyed most: playing baseball. On February 27, 1914, George Ruth left St. Mary's to join the Baltimore team. During his first few days of spring training, Jack Dunn's new "babe" was the subject of some good-natured baseball pranks. Eventually, the new arrival on the team became Babe Ruth, arguably the greatest and most colorful player in the history of the sport he loved so well.

LIFE'S WORK

Young Babe Ruth was a left-handed pitcher, and the high prices being offered for Ruth's pitching ability soon proved too tempting for the financially distressed Orioles to resist: Ruth was sold to the Boston Red Sox in July, 1914. On July 11, 1914, Babe Ruth pitched and was victorious in the first major league baseball game he had ever played. With his tremendous speed and sharp breaking ball, Ruth impressed Red Sox manager Bill Carrigan. Still, it was clear by August that the Red Sox would not win the American League pennant from Connie Mack's Philadelphia Athletics. Ruth was therefore sent down to the Red Sox minor league team in Providence, Rhode Island, to help them win the International League pennant. Providence manager "Wild Bill" Donovan was credited by Ruth for his effective pitching coaching, later of value to Ruth in his Red Sox career.

Throughout his long and colorful career, Ruth was criticized for financial, gastronomic, and sexual excesses. As with other legendary personalities, however, his sins as well as his successes may have been exaggerated. In his major league career, spanning 1914 to 1935, the Babe (as he was called) was an exciting, intelligent, and astonishingly well-rounded ballplayer, suggesting that the tales about his endless hedonism were largely, if not entirely, fictitious. On October 17, 1914, Babe Ruth married Helen Woodford, a waitress whom he had met in 1914, while with the Red Sox. In 1922, the Ruths adopted a baby girl named Dorothy. In 1926, the Ruths separated; in January, 1929, Helen Ruth was killed in a tragic fire. Three months later, Ruth married a beautiful woman named Claire Merritt Hodgson and adopted her daughter, Julia. Ruth remained with his second wife until his death in August, 1948.

In 1915, the Boston Red Sox won the American League pennant, winning 101 games, of which Ruth had won 18, and losing only 50. In the 1915 World Series, the

Ruth scoring the first home run of the game, April 21, 1924. (Library of Congress)

Red Sox defeated the Philadelphia Phillies, four games to one. In 1916, Ruth won twenty-three games a figure he matched in 1917. Overall, Babe Ruth won ninety-two games as a pitcher, and lost only forty-four; his earned run average was a remarkable 2.24. Ruth pitched for Boston in three World Series: 1915, 1916, and 1918. He won three World Series games, lost none, and sported an earned run average of 0.87. Had he continued as a pitcher, Ruth's pitching record could have been as remarkable as his hitting record.

> "*For ball players know that it isn't individuals who count. It's the way a team plays as a whole that determines its offensive power or its defensive strength.*"

The Red Sox now faced a problem with Ruth. In 1918, Ruth was recognized as one of the finest pitchers in baseball. He also hit eleven home runs, knocked in sixty-four runs, and batted .300. Ruth was too good a hitter to pitch every four days, resting between starts. He was too good a pitcher, however, to play the outfield or first base every day. It is some indication of Ruth's phenomenal baseball ability that from 1914 to 1919, while he was principally a pitcher, Ruth had 342 hits in 1,110 at-bats, with 49 home runs and 230 runs batted in. He simply had become too powerful as a hitter to keep as a pitcher. He also had become too expensive. Babe Ruth's 1917 salary was five thousand dollars, in 1918 it was seven thousand, and by 1919, it had grown to ten thousand. In January, 1920, Babe Ruth was sold again this time by the Red Sox to the New York Yankees. The price tag was $100,000 and a loan of $350,000.

The season of 1920 was a turning point in the history of baseball. In that season, Ruth smashed an incredible 54 home runs, driving in 137. A new national hero was born, and the game of baseball began to change from a short game (meaning a game of bunts, sacrifices, and steals) to a long game (meaning home runs and big-scoring innings). There had been great concern for the future of the national pastime when it was revealed that some Chicago White Sox players had been bribed in the 1919 World Series, which they lost to Cincinnati. Ruth's amazing feats, however, drove the 1919 scandal from fans' minds. As *The New York Times* reported: "Inside of a fortnight the fandom of the nation had forgotten all about the Black Sox, as they had come to be called, as its attention became centered in an even greater demonstration of superlative batting skill by the amazing Babe Ruth." In 1921, Ruth hit an astounding 59 home runs and drove in 170, while batting .378. Ruth's Yankees won ninety-eight games in that season and beat their crosstown rivals, the New York Giants, five games to three, in the World Series. It was no wonder, *The New York Times* reported, that "the baseball world lay at his feet."

The Yankees won the pennant again in 1922, 1923, 1926, 1927, 1928, and 1932; they won the World Series in 1922, 1923, 1927, 1928, and 1932. In the World Series games in which he played as a Yankee, Ruth hit fifteen home runs, drove in twenty-nine runs, and hit .347. Obscured by his extraordinary totals as a hitter (and pitcher) are Ruth's fielding, throwing, and baserunning abilities. Numerous baseball fans and analysts testify to Ruth's superb skills as an outfielder and daring, aggressive base runner. Ruth's attempted steal of second base in the final game of the 1926 World Series, which the St. Louis Cardinals won, is part of baseball folklore. With two outs in the ninth inning of the deciding Series game, Ruth walked. Trailing 3-2 in the ninth inning, the Yankees had two outs, but powerful Bob Meusel was at bat. With one strike on Meusel, Ruth attempted a delayed steal of second but was thrown out. The game was over, and the Cardinals were world champions. Baseball fans still argue the wisdom of Ruth's attempted steal. There is another Ruth legend associated with the 1926 World Series, the validity of which is still debated by baseball mythologists. A young boy, John Sylvester, was seriously ill during the 1926 Series. When he asked his father for a ball autographed by Ruth, the older Sylvester wired that request to the Babe. Players of both teams autographed balls that were sent to the Sylvester home. Johnny Sylvester did recover, but reports that Ruth promised to hit a home run for Johnny that, when executed, led to the boy's recovery, are in error.

In 1927, the New York Yankees, led by Ruth's herculean hitting (60 home runs, 164 runs batted in, batting average of .356), won the World Series in a four-game sweep of the Pittsburgh Pirates. The 1927 Yankees are properly regarded by baseball historians as the greatest of all baseball teams. Ruth had by that time accumulated 416 home runs, batted in 1,274, and was batting .349. He was regarded as the great turnstile whirler, and it seemed as though people everywhere knew of Babe Ruth. In 1927, the Yankees paid Ruth an unbelievable seventy thousand dollars a figure they matched in 1928 and 1929. In 1930 and 1931, he received eighty thousand dollars per season. Ruth's earnings over twenty-two seasons in the majors were estimated to be $896,000, in addition to World Series shares of $41,445 and approximately one million dollars from endorsements and barnstorming tours. Despite the high cost, Ruth was an asset to the Yankees: He attracted so many fans to Yankee Stadium, which opened in 1923, that it was nicknamed the House That Ruth Built.

Although 1927 will always be associated in sports history with Babe Ruth, the years 1928-1933 are equally, perhaps even more, impressive. In those years alone, Ruth batted .341, hit 270 home runs, and drove in 852 runs. It was spectacular. It was the golden age of sports, and Babe Ruth came to symbolize it all. Americans needed a diversion: The Depression had hit, and Prohibition was not repealed until December, 1933. The public followed Ruth's successes and his failures, his heroics and his occasional misconduct, with enthusiasm.

In 1934, Babe Ruth spent his last full year in the major leagues. His average sank to .288; he hit twenty-two home runs and batted in eighty-four. It would have been an excellent season for most players, but it signaled the end for Babe Ruth. In 1934, the Yankees failed again (as in 1933) to win the pennant. Ruth left the Yankees and signed on for the 1935 season with the Boston Braves of the National League. He played in only twenty-eight games for the Braves, hitting six homers, driving in twelve runs, and batting .181. Ruth never attained his goal of becoming a major league manager, although he did coach in 1938 for the Brooklyn Dodgers. Statistics do not always reliably convey the value of a ballplayer, but, in Ruth's case, the evidence is clear: In his major league career, he played in 2,503 games; he batted 8,396 times and had 2,873 hits, of which 714 were homers. His lifetime batting average was .342. At the time of his death in 1948, Babe Ruth held fifty-four major league records. Although some of those records have now been captured by more recent players, Babe Ruth, the famous Number Three of the Yankees, is still the standard against which ballplayers are measured.

In June, 1948, Ruth, a dying man, stood in Yankee Stadium to say good-bye to thousands of fans. About two months later, he died of cancer at a New York City hospital. On the evening of August 17, 1948, Ruth's body lay inside the main entrance to Yankee Stadium. It is estimated that more than 100,000 fans passed by to pay their respects. The Babe was dead, but, as Marshall Smelser put it, "one with ears tuned and eyes alert will hear or read his name almost monthly. Even without any imposing monument his memory will last in this country till memory be dead."

SIGNIFICANCE

In March, 1944, during the bitter fighting on Pacific Islands, Japanese soldiers attacked U.S. Marine positions, screaming in English, "To hell with Babe Ruth." Babe

The 1921 New York Yankees wearing team sweaters. Ruth is standing third from right. (Wikimedia Commons)

Ruth had come to symbolize not only American baseball but also America. As Robert Creamer, the baseball historian, reported, Ruth once said of himself: "I swing big, with everything I've got. I hit big or I miss big. I like to live as big as I can." Here was an indigent boy who rose from the obscurity of a Maryland boys' home to become one of the most famous Americans, whose death was reported in the headlines of *The New York Times*. Although he died when he was only fifty-three, Ruth's life seemed curiously long and complete. Ruth had a remarkable flair for the spectacular and the flamboyant. He lived his life with a zest that his countrymen seemed able to share. As he was dying, he told Considine that "I want to be a part of and help the development of the greatest game God ever saw fit to let man invent Baseball." Smelser summarized the importance of Babe Ruth in American life thus: "[H]e is our Hercules, our Samson, Beowulf, Siegfried. No other person outside of public life so stirred our imaginations or so captured our affections."

James H. Toner

FURTHER READING

Creamer, Robert W. *Babe: The Legend Comes to Life*. New York: Penguin Books, 1974. A very well-written and well-researched biography. A balanced account of Ruth's life, neither iconoclastic nor hagiographic. Probably the best general account of Ruth's life, although there is little documentation for the close reader.

Montville, Leigh. *The Big Bam: The Life and Times of Babe Ruth*. New York: Doubleday, 2006. Comprehensive biography based on new documents and interviews in which Montville separates the facts from the myths of Ruth's life.

Reisler, Jim. *Babe Ruth: Launching the Legend*. New York: McGraw-Hill, 2004. Recounts the 1920 baseball season, Ruth's first season with the Yankees, to examine the team's impact on the game of baseball.

Ruth, Babe. *Babe Ruth's Own Book of Baseball*. New York: G. P. Putnam's Sons, 1928. No credit is given in this volume to any assistant writer, although there very probably was at least one. This is an interesting book because it contains details about Ruth's life as well as about his baseball beliefs which are rarely referred to elsewhere. Anecdotal. It provides an interesting view of baseball strategy in the 1920's.

Ruth, Babe, as told to Bob Considine. *The Babe Ruth Story*. New York: E. P. Dutton, 1948. A surprisingly well-done and frank account of Babe's life, written in the last months of that life. Although bowdlerized, the book contains the Babe's views of many important episodes in his life and is enjoyable reading for the Ruth fan.

Smelser, Marshall. *The Life That Ruth Built*. New York: Quadrangle/New York Times Books, 1975. By far the best study of Ruth yet to emerge. Balanced account, if rather forgiving of Ruth in certain areas. Superbly researched and documented. Thoughtful and analytical. Thorough. Attempts to place Ruth into his historical context. Indispensable for those wishing a deeper study of the Ruth legend.

Wagenheim, Kal. *Babe Ruth: His Life and Legend*. New York: Praeger, 1974. A very good popular account, overshadowed by Creamer's when both appeared at about the same time. Although this volume is not as thorough as Creamer's and certainly not as thorough as Smelser's it is a useful and readable account.

Weldon, Martin. *Babe Ruth*. New York: Thomas Y. Crowell, 1948. A book appearing about the same time as *The Babe Ruth Story*, this book was never given close attention, but it is a short, readable account without documentation. Tends to be rather flattering of the Babe. This book, like Claire Ruth's memoir *The Babe and I* (with Bill Slocum), published by Prentice-Hall in 1959, becomes a philippic against organized baseball for not embracing Babe as a manager after his playing career was done. Useful if read with other accounts.

SERENA WILLIAMS

Tennis player

Born: September 26, 1981; Palm Beach Gardens, Florida
Areas of Achievement: Athletics: tennis

Williams reached the top of the professional tennis world in singles and doubles with her sister Venus. She also branched out into fashion design and entertainment. As African Americans excelling at a sport historically dominated by upper-class whites, the Williams sisters attracted much attention throughout their careers.

EARLY LIFE

Serena Jameka Ross Evelyn Williams was born in Saginaw, Michigan, the youngest of five daughters of Richard, part-owner of a security business, and Oracene Price Williams, a nurse. The family soon moved to

Serena Williams (Wikimedia Commons)

Compton, California, a poor and crime-ridden suburb of Los Angeles. Richard coached Williams and her sister Venus on the local public tennis courts and entered Williams in her first tournament when she was four years old. Over the next five years, Williams gained national attention for her performance in the junior tournament circuit.

By 1991, Williams had become the highest ranked ten-year-old tennis player in Southern California. Her father removed his daughters from the circuit and enrolled them in Rick Macci's tennis academy in Florida. This move was controversial at the time, as the tournament circuit was considered to be the best venue for success in the sport. The girls were homeschooled while they attended Macci's academy. In 1995, Richard returned to coaching his two daughters in tennis and also published newsletters on their progress. In October 1995, at the Bell Challenge in Vanier, Quebec, fourteen-year-old Williams debuted as a professional tennis player. Over the next couple of years, she was overshadowed by her sister's abilities, but in 1997, she went from being ranked number 453 to number 99. She placed well at the Ameritech Cup tournament later that year.

LIFE'S WORK

Williams participated in the Australian Open, her first Grand Slam tournament, in January 1998. She lost to her sister Venus in the second round. Six months later, Williams paired with Max Mirnyi of Belarus and won the mixed double tournament at Wimbledon. Her ranking soon jumped to number 21 and garnered her a twelve million-dollar contract with Puma. Williams won her first Women's Tennis Association (WTA) championship at the Open Gaz de France in 1999 and her second one at the US Open later that year. She and her sister also won the doubles championship at the US Open. After several injuries and illnesses forced her out of competitions in 1999 and 2000, Williams had a string of wins. She was bested by her sister in March at the Lipton Championships in Florida, but still earned a top-ten ranking. The duo won the doubles title at Wimbledon in 2000; Williams won in singles at the Faber Grand Prix; and then the sisters earned a gold medal at the Summer Olympics in Sydney.

> "*Luck has nothing to do with it, because I have spent many, many hours, countless hours, on the court working for my one moment in time, not knowing when it would come.*"

The 2001 tennis season brought mixed results for Williams. After her sister withdrew, Williams won the singles title at Indian Wells, California. She lost in the Australian Open, but the sisters won the doubles championship. Williams then was bested at the French Open, Wimbledon, and the US Open. In 2002, a sprained ankle forced Williams to withdraw from the Australian Open. Later that year, Williams earned the number-one ranking in women's tennis. She won the singles title at Wimbledon in 2003, but a knee injury at the US Open forced Williams to skip the rest of the year's major tournaments. That year, she signed a forty-million-dollar contract with Nike that included her own signature clothing line, Aneres.

When she returned to the WTA circuit, Williams won the 2004 NASDAQ-100 Open, the 2005 China Open, and the 2006 Australian Open. After a six-month hiatus, Williams won the singles titles at the 2007 Australian Open, the 2007 Sony Ericsson Open, the 2008 Hopman Cup, and the 2008 US Open. She and her sister also won the doubles title at Wimbledon and a second Olympic gold medal at the Beijing Olympics. In 2009, Williams overpowered Venus for the singles title at Wimbledon and accompanied her in the doubles title.

At the U.S. Open in 2009, Williams's angry outburst against a line judge resulted in a fine and two years' probation. Despite this incident, Williams and her sister won the tournament's doubles crown. In November, Williams won the Sony Ericcson Championship. In December, 2009, Williams was named Associate Press Female Athlete of the Year, and the International Tennis Federation named her a world champion in singles and doubles. She continued her dominance of women's tennis in 2010, winning Wimbledon and the Australian Open.

Williams's other interests include fashion designing and entertainment. She attended the Art Institute of Fort Lauderdale and designed her own clothing line. In 2005, she debuted in a television series, *Venus and Serena: For Real*; she also made guest appearances on many talk shows and television programs. Williams became part-owner of the Miami Dolphins football team in 2009.

In 2011 Williams experienced a number of health setbacks. She had a blood clot in her lung and underwent a series of surgeries and was required to take a several-month break from tennis. She returned for the US Open in September, but did not walk away with the title. At the 2012 French Open, Williams lost in the first round of play for the first time in her career. She bounced back to win the singles title at Wimbledon that year and won two gold medals at the Summer Olympics in London in singles and in doubles with her sister, Venus. She won another grand slam title at the US Open that fall.

In 2013 Williams won the singles title at the French Open and the US Open. She took the US Open title again in 2014, and the French Open and Wimbledon singles titles in 2015. After a disappointing start to the 2016 season in which she lost a number of grand slam titles, including one to newcomer Angelique Kerber at the Australian Open, Williams won the singles title at Wimbledon, defeating Kerber in straight sets for the victory. She and her sister then secured the doubles title as well. However, the two faced a disappointing loss in the 2016 Olympic Games in Rio de Janeiro, Brazil, and Williams missed much of the rest of the season due to a shoulder injury.

In January 2017, Williams defeated her sister to secure the Australian Open title for a record-setting seventh time. After withdrawing from her next two competitions, she announced in April 2017 that she was pregnant and would be missing the rest of the season. Since she was 20 weeks pregnant in April, she was pregnant when she played in and won the Australian Open in January. By the time of her exit from the 2017 season, Serena Williams had thirty-nine grand slam titles to her name, twenty-three of them singles titles. This surpassed the previous record of

Williams after winning her 6th Wimbeldon title. (Wikimedia Commons)

twenty-two singles titles set by German tennis player Steffi Graf.

Williams gave birth to a daughter, Alexis Olympia Ohanian, in September 2017. She suffered from many complications during labor, including a blood clot in her lungs, and in August 2018 revealed that she was suffering from postpartum depression. Williams did return to tennis after giving birth, but faced many issues, including her postpartum depression, poor performance, and seeding controversy. Williams was consistently seeded higher than her rank, notably in the US Open, where she was seeded 17th despite being ranked 26th. Williams made it to the finals, but lost to Japanese player Naomi Osaka in a controversial match where Williams was fined for breaking her racket and verbally abusing the chair umpire.

Significance

Williams rose from humble beginnings to become top-ranked in the WTA. While at times she was overshadowed by her sister, Williams became a champion through talent and determination. She also used her success to promote outreach to inner-city youths. She supported middle school and high school mentoring programs and helped found the Venus and Serena Williams Tutorial/Tennis Academy and the Serena Williams Secondary School in Matooni, Kenya.

Earning almost $29 million in prize money and endorsements, Williams was the highest paid female athlete in 2016. She repeated this feat in 2017 when she was the only woman on Forbes' list of the 100 highest paid athletes with $27 million in prize money and endorsements.

Cynthia J. W. Svoboda

FURTHER READING

"Australian Open 2017: Serena Williams Beats Venus Williams to Set Grand Slam Record." *BBC Sport*, 28 Jan. 2017. Accessed 8 May 2017.

Rodgers, R. Pierre, and Ellen B. Brogin Rodgers. "'Ghetto Cinderellas': Venus and Serena Williams and the Discourse of Racism." In *Out of the Shadows: A Biographical History of African American Athletes*. Fayetteville: University of Arkansas Press, 2006. Print.

Williams, Serena, and Daniel Paisner. *On the Line*. New York: Grand Central Publishing, 2009. Print.

---. *My Life: Queen of the Court*. New York: Simon, 2009. Print.

Williams, Venus, Serena Williams, and Hilary Beard. *Venus and Serena: Serving from the Hip—Ten Rules for Living, Loving, and Winning*. Boston: Houghton Mifflin Harcourt, 2005. Print.

BABE DIDRIKSON ZAHARIAS

Athlete

Born: June 26, 1911; Port Arthur, Texas
Died: September 27, 1956; Galveston, Texas
Areas of Achievement: Athletics: basketball; Athletics: Olympics; Athletics: softball; Athletics: track-and-field

Participating in numerous sports in which she excelled and set several records, Zaharias is recognized as the greatest woman athlete of the first half of the twentieth century.

EARLY LIFE

Babe Didrikson Zaharias (bayb DEE-drihk-sehn zeh-HAR-ee-ehs) was born Mildred Ella Didriksen in Port Arthur, Texas. Her mother, née Hannah Olson, was born in Norway and immigrated to the United States in 1908; her father, Ole Didriksen, also born in Norway, came to Port Arthur in 1905 and worked as a sailor and carpenter. Throughout her adult life she was known as Babe Didrikson Zaharias, taking the name Babe from the sports hero Babe Ruth and the spelling of her surname, Didrikson, to emphasize that she was of Norwegian rather than Swedish ancestry.

After the 1915 hurricane that devastated Port Arthur, the family, which included Zaharias's sister and two brothers, moved to nearby Beaumont. Growing up in the rugged south end of the city, Zaharias was a tomboy who shunned feminine qualities and excelled at a variety of athletic endeavors. She was slim and of average height but had a muscular body and was exceptionally well coordinated. Her hair was cut short and she usually wore masculine clothing. As a youth, she had a belligerent personality and was constantly involved in fights and scrapes.

At Beaumont High School, Zaharias was outstanding at a number of sports, including volleyball, tennis, baseball, basketball, and swimming, but she was not popular with her classmates. She was a poor student, usually passing only enough courses to remain eligible for athletic competition. All of her energy was directed toward accomplishment on the athletic field, where she had no equal. Her best sport was basketball, which was the most popular women's sport of the era. During her years with Beaumont, her high school team never lost a game largely because of her aggressive, coordinated play.

> *"Study the rules so that you won't beat yourself by not knowing something."*

LIFE'S WORK

In February, 1930, Colonel Melvin J. McCombs of the Casualty Insurance Company recruited Zaharias to play for the company's Golden Cyclone basketball team in Dallas. She dropped out of high school in her junior year and took a job as a stenographer with the company with the understanding that she would have time to train and compete in athletics. During the next three years, 1930-1932, she was selected as an All-American women's basketball player and led the Golden Cyclones to the national championship in 1931. She often scored thirty or more points in an era when a team score of twenty for a game was considered respectable. While in Dallas, she competed in other athletic events, including softball. She was an excellent pitcher and batted over .400 in the Dallas city league. Increasingly, however, her interest was drawn to

Babe Didrikson Zaharias (Wikimedia Commons)

track and field and she became a member of the Golden Cyclone track team in 1930. Profiting from coaching provided by the Dallas insurance company and relying on her innate athletic ability, she soon became the premier women's track-and- field performer in the nation.

Between 1930 and 1932, Zaharias held American, Olympic, or world records in five different track-and-field events. She stunned the athletic world on July 16, 1932, with her performance at the national amateur track meet for women in Evanston, Illinois. She entered the meet as the sole member of the Golden Cyclone team and by herself won the national women's team championship by scoring thirty points. The Illinois Women's Athletic Club, which had more than twenty members, scored a total of twenty-two points to place second. In all, Zaharias won six gold medals and broke four world records in a single afternoon. Her performance was the most amazing feat by any individual, male or female, in the annals of track-and-field history. The outstanding performance at Evanston put her in the headlines of every sports page in the nation and made her one of the most prominent members of the United States Olympic team of 1932.

Although Zaharias had gained wide recognition in her chosen field of athletics, many of her fellow athletes resented her. They complained that she was an aggressive, overbearing braggart who would stop at nothing to win. During the trip to Los Angeles for the Olympic Games, many of her teammates came to detest her, but her performance during the Olympiad made her a favorite among sportswriters and with the public. At Los Angeles, she won two gold medals and a silver medal, set a world's record, and was the coholder of two others. She won the javelin event and the eighty-meter hurdles and came in second in the high-jump event amid a controversy that saw two rulings of the judges go against her. She came very close to winning three Olympic gold medals, which had never been accomplished before by a woman. She became the darling of the press, and her performance in Los Angeles created a springboard for her lasting fame as an athlete.

After the 1932 Olympic Games, Zaharias returned to Dallas for a hero's welcome. At the end of 1932, she was voted Woman Athlete of the Year by the Associated Press, an award that she won five additional times, in 1945, 1946, 1947, 1950, and 1954. After a controversy with the Amateur Athletic Union concerning her amateur status, she turned professional in late 1932. She did some promotional advertising and briefly appeared in a vaudeville act in Chicago, where she performed athletic feats and played her harmonica, a talent she had developed as a youth. Struggling to make a living as a professional athlete, she played in an exhibition basketball game in Brooklyn, participated in a series of billiard matches, and talked about becoming a long-distance swimmer. In 1933, she decided to barnstorm the rural areas of the country with a professional basketball team called Babe Didrikson's All-Americans. The tour was very successful for several years, as the team traveled the backroads of America playing against local men's teams. In 1934, she went to Florida and appeared in major-league exhibition baseball games during spring training and then played on the famous House of David all the men on the team sported long beards baseball team on a nationwide tour. As a result of her many activities, she was able to earn several thousand dollars each month, a princely sum during the depths of the Depression.

During the mid-1930s, Zaharias's athletic interests increasingly shifted to golf. Receiving encouragement from sportswriter Grantland Rice, she began intensive lessons in 1933, often hitting balls until her hands bled. She played in her first tournament in Texas in 1934 and a year later won the Texas Women's Amateur Championship. That same year, she was bitterly disappointed when the United States Golf Association (USGA) declared her a professional and banned her from amateur golf. Unable to make a living from the few tournaments open to professionals, she toured the country with professional golfer Gene Sarazen, participating mainly in exhibition matches.

On December 23, 1938, Zaharias married George Zaharias, a professional wrestler; they had no children. Her marriage helped put to rest rumors that she was a man and other attacks on her femininity. Her husband became her manager, and under his direction she won the 1940 Texas and Western Open golf tournaments. During World War II, Zaharias gave golf exhibitions to raise money for war bonds and agreed to abstain from professional athletics for three years to regain her amateur status. In 1943, the USGA restored her amateur standing.

After the war, Zaharias emerged as one of the most successful and popular women golfers in history. In 1945, she played flawless golf on the amateur tour and was named Woman Athlete of the Year for the second time. The following year, she began a string of consecutive tournament victories, a record that has never been equaled by any man or woman. During the 1946-1947 seasons, Zaharias won seventeen straight tournaments, including the British Women's Amateur. She became the first American to win the prestigious British championship. In the summer of 1947, Zaharias turned professional once again, with Fred Corcoran as her manager. She earned an estimated $100,000 in 1948 through various promotions and exhibitions but only $3,400 in prize money on the professional tour, despite a successful season. In 1948, Corcoran organized the Ladies Professional Golfer's Association (LPGA) to help popularize women's golf and increase tournament prize money. During the next several years, the LPGA grew in stature, and Zaharias became the leading money winner on the women's professional circuit.

In the spring of 1953, doctors discovered that Zaharias had cancer, and she underwent radical surgery in April. Although many feared that her athletic career was over, she played in a golf tournament only fourteen weeks after the surgery. She played well enough the remainder of the year to win the Ben Hogan Comeback of the Year Award. In 1954, she won five tournaments, including the United States Women's Open, and earned her sixth Woman Athlete of the Year Award. During 1955, doctors diagnosed that the cancer had returned, and she suffered excruciating pain during her final illness. Despite the pain, Zaharias continued to play an occasional round of golf and through her courage served as an inspiration for many Americans. She died in Galveston, Texas, on September 27, 1956.

SIGNIFICANCE

Zaharias was a remarkable woman in many respects. Her place in American sports history is secure in her athletic accomplishments alone: In addition to her six Woman Athlete of the Year Awards, she was named the Woman Athlete of the Half Century by the Associated Press in 1950. No other woman has performed in so many different sports so well. She is arguably one of the greatest athletes, female or male, of all time.

Beyond this, however, Zaharias was a pioneer who struggled to break down social customs that barred women from various segments of American life. During an era when society dictated that women conform to a particular stereotype, Zaharias persisted in challenging the public's view of women's place in society. She not only insisted on pursuing a career in sports but also participated in sports considered in the male domain. In her dress, speech, and manner, Zaharias refused to conform to the ladylike image expected of female athletes. She did it successfully because she was such an outstanding athlete. It nevertheless took courage, because she was subjected to the most insidious rumors and innuendos concerning her gender and femininity, attacks that she endured without outward complaint.

During her final illness, Zaharias displayed the kind of strength and courage that was a trademark of her career. She was a great athlete, but beyond that she was a courageous pioneer blazing a trail in women's sports that others have followed.

John M. Carroll

FURTHER READING

Gallico, Paul. *The Golden People*. Garden City, N.Y.: Doubleday, 1965. A moving tribute to Zaharias is part of this anthology by a sportswriter who covered her career.

Hutchison, Kay Bailey. *American Heroines: The Spirited Women Who Shaped Our Country*. New York: William Morrow, 2004. Hutchison, a U.S. senator, provides profiles of women who made history, including Zaharias.

Johnson, William O., and Nancy P. Williamson. *Whatta-Gal: The Babe Didrikson Story*. Boston: Little, Brown, 1975. This popular biography offers the fullest account of Zaharias's life but tends to be uncritical.

Miller, Helen Markley. *Babe Didrikson Zaharias: Striving to Be Champion*. Chicago: Britannica Books, 1961. A juvenile book aimed at high school students; glorifies Zaharias's life.

Rader, Benjamin G. *American Sports: From the Age of Folk Games to the Age of Spectators*. Englewood Cliffs, N.J.: Prentice Hall, 1983. Gives an overview of American sports history, in the context of which Zaharias's career can be best understood. Rader attempts an assessment of her place in history.

Schoor, Gene. *Babe Didrikson: The World's Greatest Woman Athlete*. Garden City, N.Y.: Doubleday, 1978. Strictly a popular account that adds a few details and stories omitted by Johnson and Williamson.

Warren, Patricia Nell. *The Lavender Locker Room: Three Thousand Years of Athletes Whose Sexual Orientation Was Different*. Beverly Hills, Calif.: Wildcat Press, 2000. This book about lesbian and gay athletes includes the chapter "Babe Didrikson Zaharias: Golfing Amazon of the Newsreels."

Wimmer, Dick, ed. *The Women's Game: Great Champions in Women's Sports*. Short Hills, N.J.: Burford Books, 2000. A compilation of magazine articles, interviews, and book excerpts about great women athletes, including a chapter about Zaharias.

Zaharias, Babe Didrikson, with Harry Paxton. *This Life I've Led: My Autobiography*. New York: A. S. Barnes, 1955. Avoids the rough spots in Zaharias's life but is good on her family and personality. Useful when read in conjunction with other sources.

Business

It wasn't until the second half of the nineteenth century that business leaders were spoken of in heroic terms or elevated into role models. This was the period of the so-called "captains of industry"—men like John D. Rockefeller, Cornelius Vanderbilt, Andrew Carnegie, Henry Ford, J.P. Morgan and Thomas Edison. As business firms increased in size and scope into entities much larger than anything that had been seen before, the presidents and owners of these firms became themselves titanic figures. They also became enormously rich.

The transformation of the American landscape and American society that occurred under the leadership of these industrialists was profound. The Second Industrial Revolution, roughly from 1870 to 1914, was a period of rapid change. It occurred as a result of growing synergy between iron, steel, railroads, and coal. These technologies themselves were all developed in the First Industrial Revolution. The railroads allowed cheap transportation of materials and products across the nation, while the railroads themselves were dependent upon the steel and coal industries. Another factor in the rise of the great industrialists was the rapid process of consolidation that occurred in many branches of industry, such as the steel industry. The first billion-dollar corporation in history was United States Steel, formed in 1901 by J.P. Morgan when he bought and consolidated several other steel firms, including those of Andrew Carnegie.

The power and money of these men was unprecedented. It was a far cry from the kind of thrifty capitalism that had been expounded by Benjamin Franklin or enshrined as an expression of the Protestant work ethic or Protestant sobriety. For these reasons—for the excess of it all and the in-egalitarianism—these men were also called America's "robber barons." Not unlike today, they were "job creators" and they expanded access to commodities for consumers, but they also engaged in highly unscrupulous behaviors in order to become wealthy. In this period and with these men, and in part in reaction to growing opposition to what they represented, many of the virtues that are now associated with great capitalist leaders were developed and consolidated in popular discourse. These include praise for their determination, strong wills, and their "vision."

At the same time, and out of the same mix of motives, there emerged a now-familiar type: the successful entrepreneur who becomes a great philanthropist. This was largely the work of Andrew Carnegie, whose "The Gospel of Wealth" from 1889 spells out the responsibility of the wealthy, and whose own philanthropy is still legendary. Today, when we praise the accomplishments and the philanthropy of men like Bill Gates, or marvel at the rags-to-riches story of Wendy's founder Dave Thomas, we are engaged in a very American kind of hero worship, one that has spread to other parts of the world but that originated right here with the figures described above.

One of the over 2,500 public libraries that Andrew Carnegie established, this one at Syracuse University in upstate New York. (Wikimedia Commons)

Andrew Carnegie

Financier and philanthropist

Born: November 25, 1835; Dunfermline, Scotland
Died: August 11, 1919; Lenox, Massachusetts
Area of Achievement: Business

One of the wealthiest men in the world at the time of his retirement, Carnegie achieved great fame for his business success and for his many benefactions, which became the chief interest of his later years.

Early Life

Andrew Carnegie was born in Scotland, where his father, William Carnegie, was a prosperous handloom weaver at the time of his birth. However, his father could not compete with the new technology of steam looms and fell into poverty as Andrew grew older. Andrew's mother, Margaret Morrison Carnegie, proved under these circumstances to be the bulwark of the family. Ambitious for her two sons, Andrew and younger brother Thomas, she organized a family move to the United States in 1848, when Andrew was thirteen.

The Carnegies settled in Allegheny, Pennsylvania, where they had relatives and attempted to rebuild the family's fortunes. Although William Carnegie was never again a success, the family got by through hard work and timely assistance from the Pittsburgh area's close-knit Scottish community. Working long, hard hours in factories, Andrew improved his skills, learning double-entry bookkeeping in night school, and in barely a year left factory work to become a telegraph messenger in 1849, an operator in 1851, and in 1853, secretary and personal telegrapher to Tom Scott, superintendent of the Pennsylvania Railroad's western division.

Life's Work

Carnegie remained with the Pennsylvania Railroad for a dozen years, acquiring managerial skills and a sharp insight into the economic principles of the capitalist economy, and forming close personal relationships with several entrepreneurs who were to prove instrumental in his own success. Scott, who delegated increasing responsibility to the resourceful Carnegie, became vice president in 1859; he then named Carnegie superintendent of the western division, perhaps the most challenging position of its kind with any railroad in the United States. The demands of the Civil War would vastly increase his responsibilities, but Carnegie proved equal to them. At Scott's behest, he organized the movement of Union troops into beleaguered Washington in April, 1861, restored regular rail service between Washington and the north, and stayed in the capital for some months as Scott's assistant in charge of railroads and telegraph services. (Scott had been appointed assistant secretary of war with special responsibility for railroads.) Carnegie then returned to Pittsburgh to resume his duties with the Pennsylvania Railroad.

Carnegie was already losing interest in a salaried position. On a tip from Scott, he had purchased six hundred dollars' worth of stock in the Adams Express Company in 1856. The first dividend check he received was a revelation, and legend has it that Carnegie, thrilled to realize that he could earn money without physical toil, exclaimed, "Here's the goose that lays the golden eggs." More investments followed: in the Woodruff Sleeping Car Company, the Columbia Oil Company, and the Keystone Bridge Company, in which Carnegie held a one-fifth interest, enough to make him the dominant shareholder.

By 1863, Carnegie was earning more than forty thousand dollars annually from his investments, several times his salary, and left the Pennsylvania Railroad at the end of the Civil War to devote more of his time to the management of Keystone and to the Union Iron Mills, which was a principal supplier of Keystone. Carnegie left the operating decisions to experts in bridge construction, while concentrating on sales and finances. With Keystone, he secured contracts to sell materials to such projects as the

Andrew Carnegie (Library of Congress)

Eads Bridge at St. Louis, the Ohio River bridges at Cincinnati and Point Pleasant, West Virginia, and the Brooklyn Bridge.

Carnegie's involvement in finance required that he travel often to Europe, and his lifestyle changed. Always interested in the world of ideas, he never allowed his lack of formal education to keep him from broadening his knowledge. He read extensively and cultivated friendships in Europe and in were chosen, to which he moved with his mother in 1867. A bachelor throughout these years, Carnegie enjoyed the companionship of women and led an active social life. He also actively sought the company of intellectuals and eventually would count among his friends the British statesman William Gladstone and literary figures such as Matthew Arnold, Richard Watson Gilder, John Morley, Herbert Spencer, and Mark Twain. A man of much personal charm, the small-statured Carnegie—he stood but five feet, three inches tall—was equally at ease discussing ideas with the learned and business with financiers or potential customers.

Carnegie was still not content with his lot in life, for he believed that he had become too involved in financial speculation and wished instead to turn to manufacturing, which he considered a more constructive and respectable pursuit. His familiarity with the needs of railroads made him believe that there were large profits to be made in steel, for improved rails would be needed in immense quantities. In 1872, he organized a partnership, drawing on Pittsburgh business acquaintances of long duration to establish Carnegie, McCandless and Company to manufacture steel by the Bessemer process. After several reorganizations involving many different combinations of partners over the years, this firm would become known as Carnegie Steel Company, Limited, in 1892.

By 1874, the gigantic new Edgar Thomson Works was under construction, its development supervised by Alexander Holley, the foremost American expert on the Bessemer process, and its operations turned over to Bill Jones, who brought in top-notch department heads from other companies. Characteristically, Carnegie turned over the day-to-day operations to experts such as Jones, while he concentrated on sales and finances, employing the efficient cost-based management techniques learned in the railroad business.

Always alert to technological improvements that would lower the cost of production and lead to increased sales and profits, within a decade, Carnegie introduced to his plants the open-hearth steel production process. Carnegie's business philosophy led him to expand and diversify. During the mid-1880's, his organization acquired the massive Homestead Works and developed a major new market by selling steel structural members to the elevated railways and skyscrapers that were beginning to appear in major American cities.

In 1880, Carnegie met Louise Whitfield, the twenty-three-year-old daughter of a prominent New York merchant. Louise endured the tribulations of a relationship troubled by Carnegie's frequent and extended business travel. Moreover, he initially refused to marry, out of deference to his mother's wishes. The two were finally married in 1887, less than a year after the death of Carnegie's mother. The couple had one daughter.

At the time of his marriage, Carnegie was a millionaire several times over. The 1890's brought more prosperity, as well as some of Carnegie's greatest disappointments. The prosperity came in substantial measure from Carnegie's faith in the continued growth of the American economy and the business acumen of Henry Clay Frick. Chairman of the company since 1889, Frick conducted an aggressive campaign of expansion and cost-cutting that led to one of the bitterest episodes in American labor history, the Homestead Strike of 1892. During this period, Carnegie remained in virtual seclusion in Scotland, giving Frick authority to handle negotiations with the Amalgamated Association of Iron and Steel Workers. The labor-management strife led to intense press criticism of Carnegie in both England and the United States and, along

Andrew Carnegie (front row, center) and Robert C. Ogden (front row, far left) visiting faculty members of the Tuskegee Institute in Tuskegee, Alabama. Booker T. Washington and his wife Margaret James Murray are sitting between Carnegie and Ogden. (Library of Congress)

with other issues, precipitated a split between Carnegie and Frick.

Carnegie, who held an interest of more than 50 percent in the firm, resumed a more active role in company affairs, forcing Frick out as chief operating executive at the end of 1894 and leading the business to its most profitable years. The key was Carnegie's success in increasing the firm's share of the market during the depression of the 1890's, acquiring ownership of more of its basic raw materials, its own railroads and its fleet of ore-carrying ships, and its modernizing facilities. Carnegie Steel's annual profits grew 800 percent between 1895 and 1900. In Charles Schwab, a brilliant executive totally loyal to Carnegie, the company at last had a worthy successor to Frick.

At the end of the 1890's, new troubles arose from competitors. On one hand, Carnegie relished a fight; on the other hand, he was willing to sell out, provided the price was right. It was—nearly $500 million, of which Carnegie's share was $300 million in 5 percent first-mortgage bonds in the successor company, United States Steel. The investment banker J. P. Morgan, who had handled the transaction, said that Carnegie was "the richest man in the world." While a similar claim has been made for Carnegie's contemporary, John D. Rockefeller, there is no doubt that Carnegie had built one of the most formidable business enterprises of the nineteenth century; Carnegie Steel produced more than the combined output of the entire steel industry of Great Britain.

> "*No man will make a great leader who wants to do it all himself or get all the credit for doing it.*"

Carnegie devoted his remaining years to philanthropy. It was, however, philanthropy with a difference. In Carnegie's hands, philanthropy, a term that he disliked, itself became big business. In two articles published in 1886, Carnegie, a widely published author, had called for an understanding of the needs of the working man and for the acceptance of unions. The bitterness of the Homestead Strike had inevitably made Carnegie appear a hypocrite, and Carnegie was determined to demonstrate to the world that he was not insensitive to the needs of the less privileged. In an essay entitled "Wealth," first published in 1889 and often reprinted as "The Gospel of Wealth," he had set forth the essentials of his views on charitable giving. He held that the man of means should spend his fortune during his own lifetime in ways that would advance society. The millionaire, he argued, was but a trustee who should approach philanthropy scientifically and endow institutions such as universities, public libraries, and recreational areas for the masses.

On a relatively small scale, he had begun to dispense grants at the end of the 1880's, increasing the number and size of his benefactions as the years passed. In retirement, Carnegie had the time to systematize his giving. While he did provide some money for medical facilities, his usual response to a request for support from a hospital or medical school was to say "That is Mr. Rockefeller's specialty." The great bulk of Carnegie's support went to libraries and the support of education. He ultimately provided more than fifty million dollars to establish twenty-eight hundred public libraries, the vast majority in the United States and Great Britain. Carnegie ordinarily provided funds for the buildings only, for he expected the communities concerned to provide the revenues needed for books and maintenance. Fond of the limelight, Carnegie often appeared at the dedication of his libraries.

Carnegie also gave large amounts of money to Edinburgh University and three other

Carnegie, pictured with assembled dignitaries, oversees the laying of the foundation stone of the Waterford Free Library at Lady Lane - one of five free libraries in Waterford that Carnegie sponsored. (Wikimedia Commons)

universities in Scotland, and he established the Carnegie Institute of Technology in Pittsburgh (later the Carnegie-Mellon University) and the Carnegie Institution in Washington, D.C., which subsidized basic research in several disciplines. Another substantial sum went to the Carnegie Foundation for the Advancement of Teaching. Ostensibly a pension plan for college faculty, in practice the foundation did much to set standards that raised the quality of higher education in the United States. The largest sum of all, $125 million, was used in 1911 to endow the Carnegie Corporation of New York, which had the mission of advancing knowledge through the promotion of schools, libraries, research, and publication.

Carnegie dispensed still more money to causes designed to promote international peace, while he spent various amounts on such diverse items as church organs; the Hero Fund, which recognizes valorous deeds performed in everyday life; New York City's Carnegie Hall; and pensions for the widows of United States presidents and for tenant farmers on his Scottish estate, Skibo Castle.

During his lifetime, Carnegie had succeeded in giving away slightly more than $350 million, utilizing the Carnegie Corporation as his principal means of organizing the distribution of his fortune. Its establishment indicated Carnegie's recognition that it was impossible for a single individual as wealthy as he to supervise personally the administration and meaningful use of his own fortune, the tenet he had advocated in "The Gospel of Wealth." After his death at his summer home in Lenox, Massachusetts, in 1919, his will revealed that there were but thirty million dollars left to distribute; he had already made provisions for his wife and daughter. Praise for his generosity in the press was widespread.

Significance

Andrew Carnegie was a man of contradictions. Despite having little formal education himself, he had a great respect for knowledge, writing books and essays on several topics, reading widely, and making it possible for countless others to read through the thousands of libraries he established. A ruthless businessperson, he made platitudinous statements about the dignity of labor but denied many workers that dignity through the practices of his company, a denial that culminated in the Homestead Strike. However, as a businessperson, he must be remembered as an outstanding success, for, in three separate fields, he showed mastery.

Carnegie's first triumph was with the Pennsylvania Railroad, in whose employ he rose from secretary to one of its most responsible executives at a time when railroads were at the forefront of establishing patterns of modern business management. His next and greatest triumph was in building the giant Carnegie Steel Company. Finally, the practices that had served him so well in the business world enabled him to organize philanthropy on an almost unprecedented scale, as he spent his fortune generously and, on the whole, wisely. To many, he symbolized widely shared values in American culture: generosity combined with the success ethic.

Lloyd J. Graybar

Further Reading

Bridge, James Howard. *The Inside History of the Carnegie Steel Company*. New York: Aldine, 1903. Written by a man who assisted Carnegie in some of his writing endeavors. The author knew not only Carnegie but also most of his key associates. Tends to see the management controversies of the 1890's from Frick's perspective.

Carnegie, Andrew. *The Autobiography of Andrew Carnegie*. Boston: Houghton Mifflin, 1920. Published the year after Carnegie's death, this book contains a wealth of interesting information but tends to be self-serving.

---. *Triumphant Democracy: Or, Fifty Years' March of the Republic*. New York: Charles Scribner's Sons, 1886. Carnegie wrote several books, even more essays, and still more letters that appeared in newspapers under his name. This book and "The Gospel of Wealth" are perhaps his best-known works. Makes clear his ardent faith in capitalism, democracy, and opportunity.

Hendrick, Burton J. *The Life of Andrew Carnegie*. 2 vols. Garden City, N.Y.: Doubleday, 1932. Written in a vigorous style by a man who had a chance to talk with Carnegie's widow and many of his business associates.

Hessen, Robert. *Steel Titan: The Life of Charles M. Schwab*. New York: Oxford University Press, 1975. The best study of any of the hard-driving executives who did so much to put Carnegie Steel at the top of American industry. The first half of this biography deals with Schwab's early life and his years with Carnegie. The latter part discusses Schwab's own considerable success after he left United States Steel.

Hogan, William T. *Economic History of the Iron and Steel Industry in the United States*. 5 vols. Lexington, Mass.: D.C. Heath, 1971. The first two volumes of this five-volume work provide invaluable information on the steel industry during the years in which Carnegie was its dominant personality.

Krass, Peter. *Carnegie*. New York: John Wiley & Sons, 2002. A well-reviewed, detailed and thorough examination of Carnegie's life, career, and personality.

Krooth, Richard. *A Century Passing: Carnegie, Steel, and the Fate of Homestead*. Lanham, Md.: University Press of America, 2002. Krooth said this study of the 1892 Homestead Strike "describes how greed devastated a nineteenth century town and a great steel mill. The conflict foretold the death of vibrant national industry, perhaps basic U.S. industry itself."

Livesay, Harold C. *Andrew Carnegie and the Rise of Big Business*. Edited by Oscar Handlin. Boston: Little, Brown, 1975. Brief but invaluable biography that places Carnegie's business accomplishments in the context of developments in nineteenth century business management.

McHugh, Jeanne. *Alexander Holley and the Makers of Steel*. Baltimore: Johns Hopkins University Press, 1980. Biography of the man generally considered to be the foremost American expert in the Bessemer process. Attempts to place its subject in the context of the late nineteenth century technological revolution in steelmaking.

Swetnam, George. *Andrew Carnegie*. Boston: Twayne, 1980. While Carnegie will always be remembered as an industrialist and philanthropist, he became an author even earlier. This valuable, brief book examines his interest in writing and his best-known works.

Wall, Joseph Frazier. *Andrew Carnegie*. New York: Oxford University Press, 1970. More than a thousand pages in length, this is the definitive biography of Carnegie and is likely to remain so for many years.

BILL GATES

Philanthropist and businessman

Born: October 28, 1955; Seattle, Washington
Areas of Achievement: Business and industry; computers and technology; social issues

With his wife, Melinda Gates, he established one of the largest charitable organizations in the world, the Bill & Melinda Gates Foundation. Gates cofounded Microsoft Corporation, the world's largest software company, and served as Microsoft's chair, CEO, and chief software architect.

Bill Gates (Wikimedia Commons)

EARLY LIFE

Born in Seattle, Washington, Bill Gates was the second of three children and only son of Bill Gates Sr., an attorney, and Mary Gates, a University of Washington regent. As a baby, Gates often rocked himself, a trait for which he became well known as an adult. Intellectually curious from a young age, Trey, as his family called him, reportedly read the lion's share of his family's encyclopedia at age seven or eight.

Gates preferred skiing and activities with the Boy Scouts over team sports, and he was extremely competitive during family card games. Small in stature and socially awkward as a child, he was frequently teased by his classmates, which prompted him to assume the role of class clown. His parents sent him to a psychologist when he was in the sixth grade because of his stubborn, rebellious nature.

In the seventh grade, Gates transferred to Lakeside School, an elite private institution. It was at Lakeside that he first used a computer, which was actually a teletype machine connected by telephone to a mainframe computer in a local office of General Electric. He spent endless hours in the computer room, writing his first software program, a game of tic-tac-toe, at age thirteen. He formed a close friendship with Paul Allen, a likeminded student two years his senior. Gates, Allen, and several others formed the Lakeside Programmers, a club that earned money by writing payroll and traffic data programs. Gates surprised some classmates by landing the lead role in a school play.

Gates entered Harvard University in 1973 as a prelaw major, but he remained focused on computers. He frequently skipped his classes and studied at the last minute for exams. On the social side, he became friends with fellow student Steve Ballmer and often participated in all-night poker games.

Life's Work

The turning point in Gates's life occurred when he was in his second year at Harvard. While Allen was visiting him on campus, Allen discovered a magazine article featuring the first microcomputer, the Altair 8800, which was manufactured by Micro Instrumentation and Telemetry Systems (MITS). However, the computer lacked software. Sensing a groundbreaking opportunity, Gates and Allen informed MITS that they had software for the computer, even though that was not yet the case. For approximately five weeks during the winter of 1975, the pair worked around the clock to adapt a program from Beginners All-purpose Symbolic Instruction Code (BASIC). After Allen successfully demonstrated the program at MITS's New Mexico headquarters, the company agreed to distribute it with the Altair 8800 pursuant to a royalties agreement. It was under these circumstances that Gates and Allen established their business, Micro-Soft, later known as Microsoft Corporation.

While Allen temporarily went to work for MITS, Gates took a leave of absence from Harvard, briefly returned, and then permanently dropped out and moved to New Mexico, where Micro-Soft was based. Known to work sixteen-hour days, Gates raced his car around the nearby desert to relieve stress. In 1979, Gates relocated the business to Bellevue, Washington, a Seattle suburb. Through the promise of stock options, he persuaded Ballmer to join the company in a top position.

In 1980, International Business Machines (IBM) asked Microsoft to write a program for its new personal computer (PC). At the time, it was commonly believed that software played a subservient role to hardware. However, Gates had a contrary opinion. He purchased an existing operating system for $75,000 and adapted it for IBM's PC. Called the Microsoft Disk Operating System, or MS-DOS, it was sold with every IBM PC. Pursuant to the licensing agreement, Microsoft was also entitled to sell its software to other companies. The operating system quickly became the computer industry standard. By the end of 1982, Microsoft sold approximately $32 million worth of software.

Gates was left in charge of Microsoft when Allen left the company in 1983 because of health concerns. Early on, Gates had often been underestimated because of his youthful, unkempt appearance. As Microsoft grew and Gates matured, he acquired a reputation as a savvy businessman and a ruthless competitor, the latter of which resulted in numerous enemies. Known for recruiting the brightest college graduates, Gates often sat in on interviews. His employees dressed casually and had flexible hours, but the work environment was intense and competitive. Gates himself continued to work long hours and had little time for vacations. He was often rude and arrogant, and he did not easily tolerate those whose technological knowledge failed to match his. However, he preferred sweaters to suits and only agreed to a reserved parking spot so he could leave on time for the airport.

> "*Success is a lousy teacher. It seduces smart people into thinking they can't lose.*"

Under Gates's leadership, Microsoft continued to expand its product offerings, with sales topping $140 million in 1985. In 1986, Microsoft's shares were traded on the stock exchange, and Gates soon became the world's youngest billionaire. By 1987, Microsoft became the planet's largest software company. It was a point of pride that Gates had never borrowed money from his family to finance his business.

Gates's immense wealth did not slow him down. In 1990, he launched the operating system Windows 3.0, which was a huge success because it allowed several different applications to run at the same time and was more user-friendly with its point-and-click mouse. Gates continued to release new versions of Windows, with each version an improvement over the last. Although he initially failed to recognize the importance of the Internet, Gates subsequently released Internet Explorer (IE), Microsoft's web browser, with the operating system Windows 95. IE would become the dominant web browser for a time.

Although Gates devoted long hours to Microsoft, he still found time to have several girlfriends, most notably businesswoman Ann Winblad, with whom he still

U.S. Secretary of State John Kerry and Ambassador Eric Goosby, the U.S. Global AIDS Coordinator, not pictured, meet with Gates at the U.S. Department of State in Washington, D.C., on March 13, 2013. (Wikimedia Commons)

maintains a friendship. In 1987, Microsoft hired a manager, Melinda French, who attracted his attention. They were married in Hawaii on January 1, 1994, and soon had three children. The family later lived in a forty-five-room house on Lake Washington in Medina that cost more than $50 million to build.

On May 18, 1998, the US Department of Justice and twenty states commenced an antitrust suit against Microsoft, alleging, among other things, that Microsoft bullied other companies into using Microsoft's web browser over that of competitors. Gates did not personally testify at the trial. Instead, attorneys played his taped deposition, during which he denied knowledge of important company matters. His reputation suffered somewhat because many did not believe that he had been unaware of Microsoft's business dealings. Although the trial judge ordered Microsoft to be split into two companies, the order never took effect because of a reversal on appeal and a settlement by the parties.

Gates was Microsoft's chair and chief executive officer (CEO) until 2000. At that time, Ballmer became CEO while Gates remained chair and assumed the title of chief software architect. On June 15, 2006, Microsoft announced that, effective July 2008, Gates would no longer be involved in the company's daily operations. However, he would retain the role of chair as well as advise the company on certain projects under development. In 2014, he stepped down as chairman, becoming a technology advisor and supporting the transition of Satya Nadella to CEO.

After reducing his role at Microsoft, Gates devoted extensive time to the Bill & Melinda Gates Foundation, a philanthropic organization he formed with his wife in 2000. The foundation is dedicated to improving health and education and reducing poverty, among other goals. It supports work throughout the United States and in more than one hundred countries. By 2014, the foundation had an endowment of more than $40 billion. In addition to his work with the Bill & Melinda Gates Foundation, Gates, along with more than one hundred of the world's wealthiest individuals, has taken the Giving Pledge, a pledge to donate at least half of his wealth to charitable causes during his lifetime or after his death.

An important focus of Gates's advocacy in the 2010s has been climate change and alternative energy. In 2015 Gates pledged $2 million for clean energy research and development and called for governments and private investors alike to put more money into the issue, arguing that speeding the pace of clean energy research is the only way of preventing disastrous climate change. In a later interview he specifically suggested that the US government increase its energy research budget from $6 billion over five years to $12 billion a year.

In late 2016, Bill and Melinda Gates were awarded Presidential Medals of Freedom for their work through the Gates Foundation.

Significance

While the industry was still in its infancy, Gates envisioned widespread use of computers and recognized the critical importance of software. His products made it easier for the average person to use a computer and for businesses to communicate with each other. These factors, in turn, made it easier to access information on a previously unimaginable scale.

Coupling astute business sense with superior technological knowledge, Gates embodies the traits that are necessary to survive and thrive in the modern global economy. Dedicated to philanthropic work, he has challenged others to donate a larger percentage of their fortune to charitable causes. Notwithstanding one's opinion of Gates as a person, his influence on the world cannot be denied.

Diane S. Carter

Further Reading

Allen, Paul. *Idea Man: A Memoir by the Cofounder of Microsoft*. New York: Penguin, 2012. Print.

Becraft, Michael B. *Bill Gates: A Biography*. Santa Barbara: Greenwood, 2014. Print.

Brinkley, Joel, and Steve Lohr. *U.S. v. Microsoft*. New York: McGraw, 2001. Print.

---. *The Road Ahead*. New York: Penguin, 1995. Print.

--- and Lisa Rogak. *Impatient Optimist: Bill Gates in His Own Words*. London: Hardie Grant, 2012. Print.

---. "The Bill Gates Interview: An Energy Miracle Is Coming, and It's Going to Change the World." Interview by Drake Baer. *Tech Insider*. Business Insider, 22 Feb. 2016. Web. 5 Apr. 2016.

---. "Bill Gates Talks Climate Peril and Election 2016 (Oh, and Beyonce)." Interview by Davey Alba. *Wired*. Conde Nast, 22 Feb. 2016. Web. 5 Apr. 2016.

---. "We Need an Energy Miracle." Interview by James Bennet. *Atlantic*. Atlantic Monthly Group, Nov. 2015. Web. 5 Apr. 2016.

Klein, Maury. *The Change Makers*. New York: Holt, 2003. Print.

Lowe, Janet. *Bill Gates Speaks*. New York: Wiley, 1998. Print.

Rogak, Lisa, ed. *Impatient Optimist: Bill Gates in His Own Words*. Chicago: B2, 2011. Print.

Watson, Ian. *The Universal Machine: From the Dawn of Computing to Digital Consciousness*. New York: Springer, 2012. Print.

Andrea Jung

Business executive

Born: September 18, 1958; Toronto, Canada
Area of Achievement: Business

Andrea Jung's storied rise from consultant to chief executive officer (CEO) at Avon Products Inc. paints a compelling portrait of women's empowerment in the workplace. Her success in steering the world's largest direct-selling retailer and her advocacy for the advancement of women in business have contributed to her status as one of the most prominent Asian American women executives of her generation.

Early Life

Andrea Jung was born in Toronto, Ontario, in 1958. Her parents were first-generation Chinese immigrants to Canada. Her father, an architect, was born in Hong Kong, and her mother, a chemical engineer, was born in Shanghai, China. The family's Asian upbringing left Jung and her younger brother, Mark, with a strong sense of traditional values, including an emphasis on education and achievement. Jung's parents moved the family to the United States from Canada and settled in Wellesley, Massachusetts, after her father accepted a teaching position at the Massachusetts Institute of Technology (MIT). In 1979, Jung graduated magna cum laude from Princeton University with a BA in English literature. Jung, who has married and divorced twice, had a daughter with her first husband. She married her second husband, Bloomingdale's CEO Michael Gould, in 1993, and they adopted a son together.

Fluent in Mandarin, Cantonese, French, and English, Jung pursued a career in retail marketing after graduating from Princeton. Her family, dubious about her chosen career path, tried to dissuade her from embarking on this route, but Jung joined Bloomingdale's, an iconic US

Andrea Jung (Wikimedia Commons)

retailer, as a management trainee. She soon discovered that her strong business acumen coupled with creativity could help her succeed within the retail industry. To build her skill set, she aligned herself with mentor Joan Vass, a senior executive at Bloomingdales who dexterously managed her own professional career and family life. Jung's exceptional performance at Bloomingdales saw her move to merchandising manager and then to vice president. In 1987 she followed her mentor to upscale retailer I. Magnin, and was based in San Francisco, California, for the next five years.

LIFE'S WORK

She quickly ascended the corporate ladder at I. Magnin, going from general merchandising manager to senior vice president. Her success there paved the way for a senior vice president appointment in 1991 at Neiman Marcus, a much larger department store chain specializing in luxury goods. Jung was based in Dallas, Texas, for the following two years. Somewhat disillusioned with Neiman Marcus's business model, she left the company to consult for Avon Products in 1993. This step would mark the beginning of an illustrious corporate footprint.

Jung's tenure at Avon both defined and legitimized her global status as an iconic businesswoman and powerful role model. Within seven months of joining Avon as a consultant, she was appointed president of the marketing group in the United States. She introduced innovative product lines that attracted new customers and increased revenue among existing clients. She also retired the company's marketing initiatives and introduced a new advertising campaign along with a trendier, more elegant packaging design. Her bold marketing campaigns included Avon's ubiquitous presence at the 1996 Olympic Games in Atlanta, Georgia. That same year Jung was promoted to head of global marketing. In 1997, she was promoted to executive vice president of the company, and two years later, in 1999, she became president and CEO. In five years she had worked her way up from consultant to the top position in the organization.

Following Jung's appointment as CEO, Avon's earnings tripled, share prices shot up, and the company's growth rate exceeded 10 percent over the next six years. Sales spikes were noted in various regions of the world where Avon's products were marketed. In 2005, however, Avon encountered a sales slump, and the share price rapidly declined. The company's sales were also buffeted by the fallout from the 2007–09 global financial crisis. Jung employed aggressive cost-cutting strategies to stave off serious consequences to the brand, successfully steering the organization through these challenging times.

Despite these successes, Avon's stock price sagged again through 2011, and the company has been beset by government investigations into allegations of bribery of foreign officials by Avon executives. With investor concern mounting, the company announced in December 2011 that, after twelve years on the job, Jung would step down as CEO of Avon as soon a replacement could be found. However, Jung continued serving the company for two more years as executive chairwoman.

In addition to her responsibilities as the CEO of Avon Products, by 2011, Jung was also serving on the board of directors for General Electric and Apple, as a member of the New York Presbyterian Hospital Board of Trustees, as chairwoman of the World Federation of Direct Selling Associations, and as a director of Catalyst, a nonprofit organization engaged in building inclusive workplaces and improving opportunities for women in business.

> "*There are pros and cons of experience. A con is that you can't look at the business with a fresh pair of eyes and as objectively as if you were a new CEO. Fire yourself on a Friday night and come in on Monday morning as if a search firm put you there as a turn-around leader. Can you be objective and make the bold change?*"

SIGNIFICANCE

Jung's career trajectory is an example for all women in business, particularly Asian American women. By 2011, Jung was the longest-serving female CEO on the Fortune 500 list of companies, heading the world's largest direct seller with operations in more than one hundred countries. As the first female CEO of Avon Products, Jung's appointment was a significant milestone in the history of the company. Her efforts to promote gender equality and women's empowerment in the workplace continued well into her tenure as Avon CEO and on the board at Catalyst. In addition to being a firm proponent of expanding opportunities for women in business, Jung has been directly involved in the Avon Foundation for Women, a philanthropic organization dedicated to promoting women's causes, especially breast cancer research and working to end domestic violence.

Jeff Naidoo

Further Reading

Byrnes, Nanette. "Avon: More Than Cosmetic Changes." *BusinessWeek* 12 Mar. 2007: 62–63. Evaluates Jung's reorganization of Avon after its slump in 2005.

Setoodeh, Ramin. "Calling Avon's Lady." *Newsweek* 27 Dec. 2004: 98–101. Focuses on Jung's contributions as CEO of Avon.

Tarquino, J. Alex. "Selling Beauty on a Global Scale." *New York Times*. New York Times, 31 Oct. 2008. Web. 20 Feb. 2012. Interview with Jung in which she discusses Avon's global expansion and how its business model can help women in the developing world.

Zong, Wubing. "Business Leaders." *Chinese American Forum* 16.2 (Oct. 2000): 2–5. Discusses Jung's career and significance in US business history, also including entries for other Chinese American businesspeople.

Indra Nooyi

Indian-born business executive

Born: October 28, 1955
Full name: Indra Krishnamurthy Nooyi
Area of Achievement: Business

Indra Nooyi S appointment as chief executive officer (CEO) and chairperson of PepsiCo Inc. was a highlight of her corporate career. Her work has been characterized by determination, adroit negotiation, and visionary endeavors. Prestigious business publications such as Fortune and U.S. News & World Report have described Nooyi as one of the most powerful businesswomen of the early twenty-first century.

Early Life

Indra Krishnamurthy Nooyi (IHN-druh KRIHSH-nah-MOOR-tee NOO-ee) was born into a conservative, middle-class family in Chennai (formerly known as Madras), Tamil Nadu, India. After graduating from the Holy Angels Anglo Indian Higher Secondary School in Chennai, she attended Madras Christian College for her undergraduate studies. She obtained her bachelor's degree in physics, chemistry, and mathematics in 1974. Nooyi subsequently attended the Indian Institute of Management in Calcutta (now Kolkata), where she received her M.B.A., with specializations in finance and marketing. Notwithstanding her conservative upbringing and devout Hindu faith, Nooyi played cricket, a sport traditionally reserved for males, and was a member of an all-girl rock band. She later married Rajkantilal Nooyi, a management consultant, with whom she had two daughters.

After earning her M.B.A., Nooyi remained in India for two years, working as a brand manager for two major corporations. Her first position was with a British textiles company with a substantial presence in India at the time, and her next appointment was at Johnson & Johnson in their offices in Bombay (now Mumbai). Nooyi, however, had much greater ambitions, and she eventually convinced her parents to let her go to the United States. She enrolled at the Yale School of Management in 1978 and graduated with a master's degree in public and private management in 1980.

Life's Work

After completing her degree at Yale, Nooyi was recruited by the Boston Consulting Group as director of international corporate strategy projects. She remained at the company for six years before leaving for Motorola, where she started as a member of the automotive division development team in 1986. After two years, Nooyi was promoted to vice president and director of corporate strategy and planning. In 1990, she left Motorola, having accepted a position at the Swiss automation technology company Asea Brown Boveri (ABB) as senior vice president of

Indra Nooyi (Wikimedia Commons)

strategy, planning, and strategic marketing.

Nooyi's outstanding contribution in providing strategic direction for ABB brought her much acclaim from peers, headhunters, and other corporate executives. Consequently, Jack Welch, acclaimed businessman and leader of General Electric, attempted to woo her away from ABB in 1994. Around the same time, Wayne Calloway, chief executive officer (CEO) of PepsiCo, began to court her for his company. Calloway's more compelling offer resulted in Nooyi joining the company as senior vice president of corporate strategy and development in 1994.

An exacting negotiator and visionary, Nooyi championed some radical strategic maneuvers at PepsiCo, which earned her widespread respect. She aggressively advocated for the divestiture of certain underperforming subsidiaries and actively encouraged other strategic acquisitions. Two such acquisitions were Tropicana and Quaker Oats Company, both of which proved to be very lucrative undertakings for PepsiCo. After serving as senior vice president for approximately five years, she was promoted to chief financial officer in February 2000. The following year, she was promoted to president, a position she held for almost six years. PepsiCo's board of directors appointed Nooyi as CEO in 2006, and she also assumed the role of chairperson in 2007.

Nooyi visits Indian Prime Minister, Shri Narendra Modi, in New Delhi on December 10, 2015. (Wikimedia Commons)

> "*Just because you are CEO, don't think you have landed. You must continually increase your learning, the way you think, and the way you approach the organization. I've never forgotten that.*"

As of February 2012, Nooyi had been at the helm of one of the world's most formidable multinational corporations for nearly half a decade. Nooyi has been ranked on Forbes list of America's most powerful women and most powerful women in business since 2006. She was ranked 2nd on the *Forbes* list of the 100 Most Powerful Women in 2015.

In 2018, PepsiCo confirmed that Nooyi would step down as CEO and Ramon Laguarta, a 22-year veteran of the company, would take her place. Nooyi will continue to serve as chairwoman of the company until early 2019. During her tenure at the company, sales grew 80%. Her tenure is also noted for its length: at 12 years as CEO, Nooyi served 7 years longer than the average CEO at large companies.

Significance

Nooyi's business skills and determination have made her a legendary corporate executive. Her appointments as CEO and chairperson of PepsiCo were particularly telling, as she was selected over other competitors who had more typical demographic profiles for a chief executive of a large multinational corporation. Nooyi's accomplishments as a successful female executive serve as inspiration to many businesswomen and Asian Americans in the corporate world. A well-rounded and broadly engaged member of society, Nooyi has applied her business expertise to such diverse organizations as the board of the International Rescue Committee, the advisory board of the Greenwich, Connecticut Breast Cancer Alliance, and the board of trustees for the Convent of the Sacred Heart School.

Jeff Naidoo, updated by Micah L. Issitt

Further Reading

Kim, David J. "Nooyi, Indra K." *Current Biography* 67.11 (Nov. 2006): 68-74. Offers biographical information about Nooyi, including notes on her education and experiences in the business world.

"The Pepsi Challenge." *Editorial. Economist* 380.8491 (2006): 51-52. Discusses aspects of Pepsi CEO Steve

Reinemund's early retirement and his replacement by Nooyi.

Sellers, Patricia, and Corey Hajim. "It's Good to Be the Boss." *Fortune* 154.8 (2006): 134-42. Presents profiles of top women executives in the United States in 2006, including a section detailing Nooyi's business accomplishments.

Wells, Melanie. "A General in Waiting?" *Forbes* 121.2 (2003): 74. Details Nooyi's career development before coming to PepsiCo, including statements about her business strategies by company executives such.

JOHN D. ROCKEFELLER

Industrialist and philanthropist

Born: July 8, 1839; Richford, New York
Died: May 23, 1937; Ormond Beach, Florida
Areas of Achievement: Business, patronage of the arts

One of the major industrialists and philanthropists in American history, Rockefeller pioneered in raising the scale of business organization through his phenomenally successful Standard Oil Company; he also raised the scale of philanthropic giving.

John D. Rockefeller (Wikimedia Commons)

EARLY LIFE

John Davison Rockefeller was the son of Eliza Davison and William Avery Rockefeller. His father owned a farm and traded such commodities as salt and lumber. The family, which included John's older sister, two younger sisters, and two younger brothers, moved frequently: first to Moravia, New York; then to Owego, New York; and finally, to Cleveland, Ohio. John's education was irregular, but he studied hard and did have two years at Cleveland High School. His father, who by that time had become a wandering vendor of patent medicine, encouraged him to go into business. John especially liked mathematics, and he took a three-month course in bookkeeping at Folsom's Commercial College.

In selecting a job, Rockefeller was not as much interested in the salary as he was in the possibilities a position offered for learning about the business world. He selected a large and diversified merchant firm and started as a bookkeeper at a salary of $3.50 per week. After three and a half years, he left to form his own wholesale grain and grocery business with Maurice B. Clark. Together, the two had only four thousand dollars; during their first year, however, they grossed $450,000 and netted a fourteen-hundred-dollar profit. The following year, the Civil War began. The war gave Rockefeller, along with a number of other leading postwar industrialists, the opportunity to make his initial pile of money. Business at Cleveland-based Clark and Rockefeller boomed with major orders coming in from the army, other cities, and Europe. Rather than miss these business opportunities fighting in the Civil War, Rockefeller avoided the draft by paying for a substitute to fight in his place.

During these early business years, Rockefeller displayed the character traits and personal lifestyle that would be with him throughout his life. A devout Baptist, Rockefeller remained active in that church, even after becoming fabulously successful in business. For years, he taught Sunday school and served on church boards with streetcar conductors and other working-class people. He also took seriously the biblical injunction to give away one-tenth of what he earned, even when starting out at a low salary. He lived simply, had few pleasures, and was devoted to his family.

In 1864, Rockefeller married Laura Celestia Spelman, whose father was a prosperous businessperson. Eventually, they had four children who lived to adulthood: three daughters, Bessie, Alta, and Edith, and a son, John D. Rockefeller II, of whom his father was quite proud. The family lived in a large, comfortable, but not ostentatious house in Cleveland until moving to New York during the 1880's. Rockefeller instilled a sense of industry and public responsibility in his offspring that extended down to the third and fourth generations, producing one vice president (Nelson) and three state governors (Nelson of New York, Winthrop of Arkansas, and John D. IV of West Virginia). Of all the leading American industrial families, the Rockefeller dynasty became the most remarkable.

> "I do not think that there is any other quality so essential to success of any kind as the quality of perseverance. It overcomes almost everything, even nature."

LIFE'S WORK

It was possible for John D. Rockefeller to gain a monopolistic fortune in the oil business because of certain conditions that existed at that time. Oil was first used for medicinal purposes. Oil strikes in Pennsylvania during the 1850's greatly increased the supply. To find other uses for the product, the Pennsylvania Rock Oil Company hired Yale chemist Benjamin Silliman, Jr. Silliman discovered that oil could be distilled into kerosene for burning in lamps, and he also noted its lubricating qualities. At the time, oil was obtained by skimming off what floated on the surface of water-filled ditches and springs.

With other uses, however, drilling quickly became economically productive. Independent oil wells and small-scale refineries sprang up in great profusion in northwestern Pennsylvania, and refineries also proliferated in Cleveland. The oil business was chaotic, with numerous small operators, overproduction, cutthroat competition, and alternating periods of boom and bust. Rockefeller perceived that whoever could bring order to this industry could make a fabulous fortune.

In 1863, Rockefeller began his involvement with the oil business. He and his wholesale grocery partners, along with refining expert Samuel Andrews, built a refinery in Cleveland. His wholesale grocery partners proved too cautious for Rockefeller's taste. In 1865, he decided to buy out the three Clark brothers, get entirely out of the wholesale grocery business, and devote himself to oil. By the end of the year, the firm of Rockefeller and Andrews had an oil refinery that was producing at least twice as much as any other single refinery of Cleveland's nearly thirty refineries.

Rockefeller prospered more than his competitors because of his foresight, attention to detail, emphasis on efficiency, lack of toleration for waste, and growing reputation as a successful businessperson. These qualities allowed him to borrow heavily from bankers and to attract partners who brought additional capital to his firm. Henry M. Flagler joined Rockefeller in 1867, bringing with him a substantial amount of money and the ability to negotiate ever lower railroad shipping rates. Railroad rates were unregulated then, with railroads commonly giving favored shippers rebates on their publicly stated rates. The larger the shipper, the more favorable the rate. Rockefeller was able to play two railroads off against each other and water transportation off against the railroads. In turn, his lower shipping rates allowed him to undersell his competitors, steadily driving them out of business.

Meanwhile, Rockefeller implemented a policy of vertical integration. To cut his firm's dependence on related businesses, he began making his own barrels and then bought his own timber tracts to supply his cooperage plant. He owned his warehouses, bought his own tank cars, and, to the extent possible, owned or produced the raw materials and transportation he needed to operate. Finally, he fought waste by using kerosene by-products to become the oil industry's leading producer of paraffin and machine lubricants.

In 1870, to accommodate additional growth, Rockefeller converted his partnership into a joint-stock corporation, the Standard Oil Company of Ohio. Meanwhile, Thomas A. Scott of the Pennsylvania Railroad began organizing certain railroads, oil refiners, and well owners into the infamous South Improvement Company. The purpose was to form a monopoly and get rebates on their competitors' shipments. The public reaction was hostile, and the South Improvement Company quickly lost its charter. Rockefeller had been part of this scheme, which badly tarnished his reputation. However, through the South Improvement Company, he acquired another wealthy partner, Cleveland refiner Oliver H. Payne.

Furthermore, Standard Oil decided to proceed on its own to create a monopoly in the oil business. Early in 1872, Rockefeller offered to buy out nearly all remaining

Rockefeller with his son in 1915. (Library of Congress)

Cleveland oil refineries. Owners could either accept a cash offer, take the offer in Standard Oil stock, or be driven out of business. With the South Improvement Company still a live entity and given the size of Standard Oil itself, most refiners sold out. Some claimed that they had been pressured into taking less than their businesses were worth, but those who acquired Standard stock did make small fortunes. Rockefeller accomplished this takeover of his Cleveland competitors in three months. From Cleveland, Standard then proceeded to acquire refineries in Pittsburgh, in Philadelphia, and on Long Island. By 1875, the firm was refining half of the oil products in the United States. Rockefeller's next step was to gain control of pipelines, oil terminals, kerosene distributors, and additional plants. He also attracted rival oilman John D. Archbold to his firm. By 1878, Rockefeller had secured his monopolistic position.

During the 1880's, Standard Oil continued to grow. The firm acquired new oil fields, built new refineries, and developed new refining methods. Under the direction of John's brother, William Rockefeller, the firm also expanded into the international market. Standard Oil products were a familiar sight in Asia, Africa, South America, and even Central Europe, where Standard encountered stiff competition from cheap Russian oil. Also, Standard Oil pioneered in corporate organization. Rockefeller employed the best legal talent to devise the concept of the trust. That meant that the stock of Standard's subsidiaries and related companies was combined with Standard's stock, new certificates were issued, and an executive committee with Rockefeller at the head assumed control. During 1883-1884, he transferred the corporate headquarters to New York City. However, Standard Oil never took total control of the oil industry. While accounting for 80-90 percent of oil produced in the United States and making substantial profits, Standard did lower the price of its products. Rockefeller had stabilized a chaotic industry.

In the process, Rockefeller became powerful and was feared and vilified. The lack of railroad rate regulation did much to make his monopoly possible. Unfair railroad rates upset many more people than Rockefeller's business competitors. The public began agitating for railroad rate regulation, first at the state level and then for the Interstate Commerce Act, passed in 1887. Because that law was largely ineffective, agitation continued until railroad rates were finally effectively regulated in the twentieth century. Throughout this agitation, the outstanding example of how unregulated railroad rates could lead to powerful monopolies was Standard Oil.

The New York legislature investigated Standard Oil in 1879 and again in 1888. Henry Demarest Lloyd published an exposé in the *Atlantic Monthly* in March, 1881. Congress sought to dampen the public's concern with the Sherman Antitrust Act of 1890. When that law went initially unenforced, muckrakers again attacked. The best-known exposé was Ida M. Tarbell's *History of the Standard Oil Company* (1904). Rockefeller always refused to respond directly to these attacks. His attitude was that his products spoke for themselves. Not until 1905 did Standard Oil hire its first public relations expert. Nevertheless, the federal government proceeded to prosecute Standard Oil for violating the Sherman Antitrust Act. Under court order, the company broke into smaller, separate companies in 1911.

Rockefeller's wealth at one point approached $900 million. What to do with all this money posed a dilemma. He invested in the stock market and, during the 1890's, gained control of the Mesabi Range, the richest iron ore

Rockefeller playing golf in 1932. (Wikimedia Commons)

field in the United States. Within a few years, however, he sold his Range holdings to Andrew Carnegie. Increasingly, his interests were turning to philanthropy, where his impact was tremendous.

At first, Rockefeller's gifts to hospitals, colleges, and other institutions were haphazard, and his gifts were sometimes misused. Soon, however, he began to apply some of his principles for making money—of attention to detail and organization—to giving money away. He virtually made the University of Chicago with a founding gift in 1889 of $600,000 and later gifts (some from his son) totaling $80 million. He created the Rockefeller Institute for Medical Research in 1901 and the General Education Board in 1902. The latter helped to revolutionize medical education, fought the spread of hookworm, and worked to improve southern agriculture. His philanthropy was further systematized with the creation of the Rockefeller Foundation in 1913. He gave away more than a half billion dollars, and the influence of his philanthropic institutions has continued to grow after his death. Rockefeller had turned over active leadership of the Standard Oil Company in 1897 but lived until 1937, dying at the age of ninety-seven.

SIGNIFICANCE

John D. Rockefeller succeeded as a businessperson and a philanthropist in part because of his personal qualities and in part because of his times. He had an uncanny ability to identify and secure leading executive talent. The extreme care with which he made decisions was accompanied by a boldness of action and accuracy of vision unmatched in his field. Furthermore, he had the steadiness to compete in a rough, competitive, "survival of the fittest" environment where there were few laws and regulations. Indeed, he turned this freewheeling environment to his advantage.

Rockefeller was able to build Standard Oil because of such conditions as the general absence of effective railroad rate regulation and lack of an income tax. He went into the oil business at a time when it was taking off, and good luck was with him when the gasoline-powered automobile came along to increase demand. He regarded himself as a trustee of his wealth and became, perhaps, the outstanding philanthropist in the United States. Finally, he instilled an obligation for public service in his descendants. Of all the "robber barons" of his generation, his long-range impact may have been the greatest.

Judith Ann Trolander

FURTHER READING

Abels, Jules. *The Rockefeller Billions: The Story of the World's Most Stupendous Fortune*. New York: Macmillan, 1965. Scholarly, readable, with a good selection of photographs of Rockefeller, his family, business associates, and houses. Generally, Abels is favorably disposed toward Rockefeller.

Carr, Albert A. *John D. Rockefeller's Secret Weapon*. New York: McGraw-Hill, 1962. Focuses on the role that the Union Tank Car Company, established by Rockefeller and the key to his transportation system, played in the success of Standard Oil. In 1891, the company became a separate corporation from Standard Oil in response to the Sherman Antitrust Act. Carr covers the history of Union Tank Car up to 1961.

Chernow, Ron D. *Titan: The Life of John D. Rockefeller, Sr*. New York: Random House, 1998. Well-written, meticulously researched biography based on newly acquired archival materials. Chernow recounts the details of Rockefeller's life and career, describing his human side as well as his misdeeds.

Collier, Peter, and David Horowitz. *The Rockefellers: An American Dynasty*. New York: Holt, Rinehart and Winston, 1976. The bulk of this book is on John D. Rockefeller's descendants, down through his great-grandchildren, the impact his fortune has had on them, and their sense of public responsibility.

Hawke, David F. *John D.: The Founding Father of the Rockefellers*. New York: Harper and Row, 1980. A chatty, popular account, this slim volume is not too extensively footnoted but is based on archival sources along with more detailed secondary sources, especially Nevins's 1940 biography.

Josephson, Matthew. *The Robber Barons: The Great American Capitalists, 1861-1901*. New York: Harcourt, Brace, 1934. Reprint. Harcourt, Brace, and World, 1962. In this critical account, Rockefeller is only one among many late nineteenth century industrialists, but the book is excellent for setting him in the context of his time. Josephson is critical of the business practices and extensive power of Rockefeller and his associates.

Nevins, Allan. *John D. Rockefeller: The Heroic Age of American Enterprise*. New York: Charles Scribner's Sons, 1940. Nevins is the scholarly authority on Rockefeller. This two-volume work was the most comprehensive, carefully researched, and balanced source on Rockefeller until Nevins's 1953 book appeared.

---. *Study in Power: John D. Rockefeller, Industrialist and Philanthropist*. New York: Charles Scribner's Sons, 1953. More of a second biography of his subject than a revision, this book incorporates material based on a large amount of documents not available to Nevins in his earlier biography; it also reflects a maturing of Nevins's analysis. Both Nevins biographies can be profitably consulted.

SHERYL SANDBERG

Tech executive and author

Born: August 28, 1969; Washington, D.C.
Area of Achievement: Business

Sandberg is a leading technology executive, a rare woman at the top of power in Silicon Valley. Although she says she is not a feminist, her book, Lean In: Women, Work, and the Will to Lead (2013), encourages women to stop trading their power for approval. She is the Chief Operating Officer of Facebook.

EARLY LIFE

Executive tech pioneer Sheryl Kara Sandberg was born in Washington, D.C. on August 28, 1969. Her family, which includes two siblings, moved to North Miami Beach, Florida when she was 2. Her father, Joel, is an ophthalmologist and her mother, Adele, is a former teacher. Sandberg was educated in public schools and graduated ninth in her high school class in 1987.

At Harvard University, Sandberg graduated Phi Beta Kappa and with a bachelor's degree in economics and earned the school's John H. Williams Prize for the top graduating student in economics. She met Lawrence Summers, who became an early career mentor, during her junior year of college when she took the then-professor's Public Sector Economics class. He became her thesis advisor her junior year. During her undergraduate years, she founded a group called Women in Economics and Government which, she told *The New Yorker*, was aimed at getting "more women to major in government and economics."

LIFE'S WORK

Sandberg went to work as a research assistant for Summers, who had become the World Bank's chief economist. During this era, Sandberg married, then divorced after a year. She moved on to Harvard Business School and earned her M.B.A. with high honors in 1995. For a year she worked as a management consultant for McKinsey & Co. Then Summers joined the U.S. Treasury Department as Deputy Treasury Secretary, and Sandberg became his Chief of Staff. She remained in the position

Sheryl Sandberg (Wikimedia Commons)

when he was elevated to U.S. Secretary of the Treasury in the Clinton Administration.

In 2001, Sandberg left Washington after Republican George W. Bush came into office, and joined Google as general manager of its business unit. At that time, the company was a three-year-old light of the dotcom boom with 260 employees. Sandberg moved on to become Google's vice president of global online sales & operations, and oversaw the company's online advertising strategies AdWords and Adsense, boosting the company's earnings. She also helped to launch the company's philanthropic arm, Google.org. In 2004, she married Yahoo executive David Goldberg, a fellow Harvard alumnus. The couple had two children.

In 2008, Facebook successfully wooed Sandberg to take on the company's number two executive position as chief operating officer under the company's then-24 year old founder Mark Zuckerberg. At the time, *The New York Times* reported that Sandberg would help the social media pioneer "expand overseas and develop and advertising network that will help justify its $15 billion valuation...oversee Facebook's marketing, human resources and privacy departments–essentially guiding how Facebook presents itself and its intentions to the outside world." Today, Sandberg oversees the company's sales, marketing, business development, human resources, public policy and communications.

Senator Stabenow and other woman members of the Senate meet with Sandberg, standing fourth from left. (Wikimedia Commons)

> "We can each define ambition and progress for ourselves. The goal is to work toward a world where expectations are not set by the stereotypes that hold us back, but by our personal passion, talents and interests."

In 2010, Sandberg delivered a TEDtalk called "Why We Have Too Few Women Leaders" that went to the heart of the professional world's dearth of women at the top. Not only do women face harder choices than men between professional success and personal fulfillment, she said, but women are dropping out. "My talk today is about what the messages are if you do want to stay in the workforce, and I think there are three. One, sit at the table. Two, make your partner a real partner. And three, don't leave before you leave." She went on to analyze her three points. Rather than joining decision makers at the table, women systemically underestimate their own abilities and do not negotiate for themselves in the workforce, she said.

Studies show that success and likeability are positively correlated for men, and negatively correlated for women. Making a partner a real partner means bringing partners fully into the housework and daycare chores if a woman is working full-time. And if a man is staying home with the kids, the "other mommies" need to understand he's doing the hardest job in the world. As for not leaving before you leave: women pondering a pregnancy have a way of checking out, of not going for a promotion, of sitting back and not pursuing new opportunities.

"I have a fve-year-old son and a two-year old daughter," she said. "I want my son to have a choice to contribute fully in the workforce or at home, and I want my daughter to have the choice to not just succeed, but to be liked for her accomplishments."

The talk's huge success evolved into the book, *Lean In: Women, Work, and the Will to Lead*, as well as the arrival of Lean In (leanin.org), an organization to encourage women to pursue their ambitions and change "the conversation from what we can't do to what we can." The book prompted a great deal of discussion of Sandberg's philosophy, given the immensely wealthy and professionally successful life she inhabits, and the single-minded focus on corporate success through individual effort that she espouses. The book was the subject of a number of critiques from feminist leaders like bell hooks and Susan Faludi.

In March 2014, LeanIn.org sponsored the Ban Bossy campaign, which criticized the use of the word "bossy" to describe assertive girls and women. The campaign claimed the word was stigmatizing and discouraged girls from seeking positions of leadership in order to avoid the moniker. The campaign was co-sponsored by the Girls Scouts and featured many celebrity advocates, including Beyoncé Knowles, Jennifer Garner, Jane Lynch, Condoleezza Rice, Anna Maria Chávez, among others. Several video spots were produced along with a website that offered school training material and leadership tips.

Significance

Sandberg sits at the near-top of a male-dominated technology world, and she has garnered a massive fortune in the process. Sandberg eschewed the label "feminist," even as she made a point of reaching out to women to help them succeed with her book, *Lean In, Women Work and the Will to Lead*. She has since claimed the term, but her book was notable as much for the discussion about the values of feminism that it provoked as for its popularity. Her professional success and personal wealth are often cited.

Allison Blake

Further Reading

Auletta, Ken. "A Woman's Place," *The New Yorker*, July 11, 2011. A significant profile of Sandberg written three years after she joined Facebook, as the company arrived at dominance in the social media realm.

Isaacson, Walter. *The Innovators: How a Group of Hackers, Geniuses, and Geeks Created the Digital Revolution* (New York: Simon & Schuster, 2015). From Steve Jobs's biographer, a look at tech innovators reaching back to nineteenth-century Ada Lovelace, whose mathematics Isaacson traces to the computer's development. (Lovelace was Lord Byron's daughter).

---. *Lean In: Women, Work, and the Will* (New York: Knopf, 2013). Sandberg's appeal to women to step up for themselves to move into positions of power. The book drew wide praise and debate upon its release and went on to bestselling status.

George Soros

Hungarian-born American financier and philanthropist

Born: August 12, 1930; Budapest, Hungary
Area of Achievement: Business; philanthropy

A self-made multibillionaire from financial investment and speculation, Soros became one of the world's most important philanthropists and championed the idea of an open society, a society governed as non-authoritarian, transparent, flexible, representative, and responsive to the needs of its citizens.

Early Life

Born György Schwartz in Hungary to a Jewish family on August 12, 1930, George Soros (SOHR-ohs) and his family evaded capture when Nazi Germany invaded Hungary in 1944. Soros was raised speaking Esperanto. At the age of fourteen, he witnessed the deportation of Jews from Budapest but was able to avoid deportation himself by posing as the godson of a Christian family. In 1946, he escaped the Soviet occupation of his homeland by leaving the country to participate in an Esperanto youth congress. He immigrated to London in 1947, studied at the London School of Economics with German philosopher Karl Popper, and received a BA degree there. He began work at the merchant bank Singer and Friedlander before moving to New York City in 1956, where he took a job as a money manager on Wall Street.

Soros began his financial career as an arbitrage trader and an analyst. From 1963, he worked at Arnhold and S. Bleichroeder, an international investment management firm, and eventually became the company's vice president. In 1967, the firm set up an offshore investment fund, First Eagle, at his urging. He was then given the task of running the new fund.

Life's Work

In 1970, Soros, with investor Jim Rogers, founded the hedge fund Quantum Fund. During the next ten years, the fund returned 3,365 percent. Soros reorganized Quantum Fund in 2000. Most spectacularly, he made his name in financial circles by short-selling the British pound in 1992 on Black Wednesday with protégé Stanley Druckenmiller. They profited from the Bank of England's failure to raise its interest rates to levels that were comparable to those of other countries of the European Exchange Rate

George Soros (Wikimedia Commons)

Mechanism and the Bank of England's failure to float its currency. Soros netted more than $1 billion because of the bank's errors.

Soros's financial investments were not always astute. He lost several hundred million dollars, for example, investing in the Russian telecom firm Svyazinvest, which privatized in the late 1990s. In 1997, during the Asian financial crisis, he was accused by the Malaysian prime minister of exploiting a situation in which the Association of Southeast Asian Nations was struggling to prop up its new member, Burma (Myanmar). In France, Soros was convicted of insider trading in a takeover bid of the French bank Société Générale in 1988. However, nearly twenty years later, in 2006, he appealed to Europe's court of human rights, claiming that he did not receive a fair hearing because of the fourteen-year delay in bringing the case to trial.

Soros advocated the model of a mixed economy, in which a strong, centralized government could correct excesses resulting from self-interest. Aware of appearing hypocritical in light of this model, Soros distinguished between a businessperson participating in the market and a businessperson working to change the rules, thus absolving himself of the consequences of his financial actions.

In 2015, *Forbes* magazine named Soros one of the world's richest individuals with an estimated net worth of $26 billion as of September 18, 2015. As a major philanthropist, he has given away more than $10 billion since the early 1990s, primarily through his Open Society Foundations, which promote human rights, social reform, and democratic principles. In 1991 his financial support helped create Central European University, an international, accredited, graduate university in Budapest, which focuses on the social sciences and the humanities and the development of open societies.

An open society is one governed as non-authoritarian, transparent, non-secretive, flexible, representative, and responsive to the needs of its citizens. In part because human and political rights form the foundation of all open societies, Soros has promoted the establishment of open societies in former communist countries. Because of his advocacy, he has been credited by some for helping to hasten the fall of communism in Eastern Europe. Soros also contributed to high-profile political campaigns. In the 2004 presidential campaign, Soros spent an estimated $27 million trying to unseat Republican US President George W. Bush. Following Bush's reelection, however, Soros and other liberal political donors helped to found Democracy Alliance, an informal fundraising group. Leading up to the 2010 elections, Soros donated $1 million in support of California Proposition 19, an ultimately unsuccessful attempt to legalize marijuana in that state. In 2012, Soros donated $1 million to Priorities USA Action, a political action committee that supported the reelection of US president Barack Obama.

"I would value it much more highly than any business success if I could contribute to an understanding of the world in which we live or, better yet, if I could help to preserve the economic and political system that has allowed me to flourish as a participant."

Soros also openly criticized US intervention in Iraq, arguing that Iraq's power as an enemy of the United States had been overstated. Internationally, his funding and behind-the-scenes networking among opposition parties in the Georgian Rose Revolution of 2003, which displaced Georgian president Eduard Shevardnadze, was considered by some observers to have been crucial to the revolution's success, although Soros has said his role was "greatly exaggerated." Soros also promoted a common

European foreign policy and studied the integration of Muslim residents in eleven European cities. He has spoken out against the powerful Washington lobby group American Israeli Public Affairs Committee (AIPAC), arguing for the need for an alternative to AIPAC, which supported the US invasion of Iraq in 2003 and the 2006 Israeli attack on Hezbollah forces in Lebanon.

Soros's first written work while an arbitrage analyst in New York was a Popperian treatise on philosophy, "The Burden of Consciousness: A Study of the Relationship between Thinking and Society," which has not been published. His first popular publication, however, was *The Alchemy of Finance* (1987), which started out as an exposition of financial strategies and instruments in real-time and included the development of a philosophy of reflexivity, also based on Popper's ideas. Reflexivity, as embraced by Soros, is the belief that a person's self-awareness cannot be considered separate from that person's immediate environment: a person's actions can disrupt economic equilibriums and, thus, disable the progression of free market systems.

Other books by Soros, namely *The Age of Fallibility* (2006), concentrate on broader, philosophical issues. Soros once thought that the United States was the world's best example of an open society. However, in *The Age of Fallibility*, he concludes that the United States cannot quite fill that role because its founding documents, replete with Enlightenment language, fail to incorporate a more modern skepticism that recognizes the limitations of the human mind. In his book *Financial Turmoil in Europe and the United States* (2012), Soros analyzes the national and international policies that contributed to the global financial crisis of 2007–2010.

Soros has received honorary doctorates from several institutions, including the New School for Social Research in New York City, Oxford University, the Budapest University of Economics, and Yale University. He also received a finance award from the Yale School of Management as well as the Laurea Honoris Causa, the highest honor bestowed by the University of Bologna.

SIGNIFICANCE

From firsthand experience of penury, genocide, and hyperinflation on the streets of Budapest at the end of World War II, Soros made himself into a multibillionaire through his skills in financial management. As a business leader, he has been keen to delegate authority to local managers rather than micromanage his foundations. Soros also is a major philanthropist, primarily concerned with civil society issues, but he also has branched out to fund organizations focused on the problems of world poverty, environmental protection, drug policy reform, public health, and education.

Stefan Halikowski Smith

FURTHER READING

Freeland, Chrystia. "The Imperfect World of George Soros." *Foreign Policy* 197 (2012): 61–62. Print.

Kaufman, Michael T. *Soros: The Life and Times of a Messianic Billionaire*. New York: Knopf, 2002. Print. A biography written with Soros's cooperation.

Preston, Caroline. "At 80, George Soros Looks ahead to His Legacy." *Chronicle of Philanthropy* 23.13 (2011): 21. Print.

Slater, Robert. *Soros: The Unauthorized Biography, The Life, Times, and Trading Secrets of the World's Greatest Investor*. New York: Irwin Professional, 1997. Print.

"The World's Billionaires: #29 George Soros." *Forbes.com*. Forbes.com, 18 Sept. 2015. Web.

DAVE THOMAS

Fast food entrepreneur

Born: July 2, 1932; Atlantic City, New Jersey
Died: January 8, 2002; Fort Lauderdale, Florida
Also known as: Rex David Thomas
Area of achievement: Business

An orphan who dropped out high school when he was fifteen years old, Dave Thomas went on to become a highly successful businessman in the fast food industry. He also became one of the most recognized pitchmen in television advertising history.

EARLY LIFE

Rex David Thomas was born in Atlantic City on July 2, 1932. His birth mother, whom he never knew, was unable to raise him. He was adopted at six weeks of age by a couple from Kalamazoo, Michigan. His adoptive mother, Auleva Thomas, died when he was five years old. Subsequently, Thomas had two step-mothers, both of whom died before he was ten years old. With his father, Thomas lived an itinerant life, as his father struggled to find work and permanent housing. A bright spot in his childhood was the time spent with his adoptive grandmother, Minnie Sinclair, who lived in Maine. Thomas spent many summers in Maine with his grandmother, and he enjoyed eating lunch with her often at the counter of the five-and-dime store. When Thomas was ten years old, his father moved the family to Fort Wayne, Indiana. Thomas began working various jobs, first as a paperboy, then as a grocery store delivery boy, a golf caddy, and a soda jerk at a Walgreen's. At age fifteen, he began working in a restaurant. When his father wanted to move again, Thomas decided to stay in Fort Wayne, drop of school (he was in the tenth grade), and work in the restaurant full-time.

LIFE'S WORK

Thomas served in the Army during the Korean War, managing a club for enlisted men, then he returned to Fort Wayne. He looked up his old boss at the restaurant, Phil Clauss, who by then owned several franchises of a new chain called Kentucky Fried Chicken in and around Columbus, Ohio. The stores were failing; Clauss made a deal with Thomas to turn them around. If he succeeded, Clauss would give Thomas 40 percent ownership. Thomas packed up and moved to Columbus, where, relying on old-fashioned salesmanship, good business savvy, and high quality control, Thomas succeeded in saving the stores. He sold his share of the franchise some years later for $1.5 million.

> "Share your success and help others succeed. Give everyone a chance to have a piece of the pie. If the pie's not big enough, make a bigger pie."

Thomas was soon recognized as a major player in the fast food industry. He worked as a regional director for Kentucky Fried Chicken, and he helped found Arthur Treacher's Fish and Chips. In 1969, he opened the first Wendy's Old-Fashioned Hamburgers in Columbus—his own store and his own concept, named after his daughter. More than most other fast food restaurants, Wendy's was marketed to adults; the stores had salad bars, which were then a new concept, and their décor featured old-fashioned bentwood chairs and Tiffany-style glass lamps. Each square hamburger was made fresh to order, with every topping selected by the customer—also an innovative practice for a fast food hamburger chain.

The franchise grew quickly; within less than a decade, there were over one thousand stores in the United States. In 1982, Thomas retired from overseeing day-to-day operations of the business. Within a few years, however, he returned and assumed an active role in running the company.

Perhaps his most momentous decision was to appear in television commercials as the spokesman for the company he founded. Other fast-food entrepreneurs had done the same; perhaps the most famous was Colonel Sanders. The first Wendy's ad featuring Dave Thomas aired in 1989. His demeanor was somewhat stiff, and most advertising critics were not impressed. The following year, however, his performances improved significantly with consultation from advertising experts. He now appeared folksy, relaxed, and self-effacing. During the 1990s, Thomas appeared in almost every Wendy's advertisement that aired, and Dave Thomas became a household name in the United States. One survey showed that ninety percent of Americans recognized him when shown a photograph.

In the same period, the 1990s, Thomas began devoting time to the cause of adoption. Aware of his personal story, in 1990, President George Bush asked Thomas to be a national spokesperson for adoption issues. In 1992, Thomas founded the Dave Thomas Foundation for Adoption, which focuses on helping older and disabled children find adoptive parents. He was quickly recognized as a leading figure for the cause of adoption of foster children. Thomas also lobbied the government for legislation that would encourage adoption. In 1997, he testified before Congress in support of a bill that would give a tax credit to parents who adopt; it was signed into law by President Bill Clinton.

In 1993, at the age of sixty, Thomas worked with a tutor to prepare for the G.E.D. high school equivalency exam. The Coconut Creek High School in Fort Lauderdale, Florida, where Thomas resided, decided to made him a part of their senior class. Thomas attended the graduation ceremony, where he was awarded a diploma along with the other students. Thomas even attended senior prom; he and his wife were voted prom king and queen.

SIGNIFICANCE

Thomas came from humble beginnings, but he achieved an extraordinary level of business success. An orphan, he went to work at age twelve, and he dropped out of high school at age fifteen. A living embodiment of the value of a strong "work ethic," Thomas applied old-fashioned salesmanship techniques in his stores, practiced high quality control, and held his staff to high standards. As a teenager he was impressed with his boss at a Fort Wayne restaurant who wasn't too proud to mop the floors while wearing a three-piece suit; Thomas modeled the same behavior for his staff, a mindset he called a "mop bucket" attitude.

D. Alan Dean

Further Reading

"Dave's Legacy." *Wendys.com.* https://www.wendys.com/daves-legacy. Accessed February 12, 2019.

Martin, Douglas. "Dave Thomas, 69, Wendy's Founder, Dies." New York Times. January 9, 2002. https://www.nytimes.com/2002/01/09/business/dave-thomas-69-wendy-s-founder-dies.html

Nocera, Joseph. "Wendy's Burger King." *Esquire,* November 1989. https://classic.esquire.com/article/1989/11/1/wendys-burger-king

Thomas, Dave. *Dave's Way: A New Approach to Old-Fashioned Success.* New York: Putnam, 1991.

Madam C. J. Walker

Entrepreneur and hair stylist

Born: December 23, 1867; Irvington-on-Hudson, New York
Died: May 25, 1919; Delta, Louisiana
Also known as: Sarah Breedlove
Area of Achievement: Business and industry; civil rights; philanthropy

Walker created hair care products that have been used by thousands of women both in the United States and abroad. More significantly, she developed business and marketing strategies that allowed women, particularly African-American women, to become financially independent.

Early Life

Madam C. J. Walker was born Sarah Breedlove to Owen and Minerva Anderson Breedlove; she was the fifth of six children. She was the couple's first child born outside slavery. Sarah became an orphan at the age of seven. She and her sister survived by working in cotton fields in both Louisiana and Mississippi. Sarah had very little formal education, but she improved her reading and writing skills through tutoring by women at the African Methodist Episcopal church she attended in St. Louis. At the age of fourteen, she married Moses McWilliams, largely to escape abuse from her sister's husband. When McWilliams died two years later, she moved to St. Louis with her only child, Lelia (born June 6, 1885), to join her four brothers, who were establishing themselves as barbers. Making only $1.50 per day, she managed to educate her young daughter. She also took jobs as a washerwoman and a cook to help support herself and Lelia.

Life's Work

During the 1890s, Sarah began to suffer from a scalp ailment that caused her to lose most of her hair. She began to experiment with both homemade remedies and store-bought products. In 1905, she moved to Denver, Colorado, where she married Charles Joseph Walker, and she became known as Madam C. J. Walker. Eventually, she created Madam Walker's Wonderful Hair Grower from a recipe she claimed had been revealed to her by a man in a dream. Her husband felt that she should be satisfied with making ten dollars per day; she disagreed, and the two were divorced. Madam Walker began to build her company: She was solely responsible for the sales, marketing, development, and distribution of her hair and skin care

Madam C. J. Walker (Wikimedia Commons)

products—a feat unheard of at the time for any woman, let alone an African-American woman.

While Walker's hair grower was a great invention, it was not the first of its kind. Walker worked for a short period for Annie Malone, an African-American entrepreneur who had a hair care product before Walker invented her own. Walker's product line eventually expanded beyond her hair grower: She invented other hair care products as well as skin creams. She ended up with a complete line of beauty products to fit the needs of black women throughout the world. Understanding that her beauty products need to be utilized appropriately, Walker made sure that her sales force trained women in the proper use of her products, creating the "Walker System." She emphasized customer service, wanting her clients to feel pampered and important. Walker's products included not only locally available ingredients but also ingredients imported from all over the world, includ - ing African countries. Unique to Walker's enterprise were the business and marketing strategies she implemented in the sale of her products. She started by selling her line door-to-door, demonstrating the proper use of her beauty products to black women in the southern and southeastern United States. This market had previously been ignored or misunderstood, and these women appreciated not only products designed for their needs but also the attention of a beautifully coifed black woman capable of showing them how to use the products. Walker's success grew.

In 1908, Walker moved to Pittsburgh, Pennsylvania, where she opened Lelia College. There she trained individuals she named "hair culturists," who began to sell her products. In 1910, she moved to Indianapolis, Indiana, where she built a factory, hair and manicure salon, and another training school. By creating the sales force and venues through which her products would be sold, Walker increased brand loyalty.

Walker then organized her independent sales agents in local and state clubs, a practice still utilized today be companies such as Mary Kay, Tupperware, and Avon. The agents not only sold the products but also used the products themselves. As walking endorsements of the Walker line, these saleswomen built brand loyalty; as homemakers and single mothers—women who had much in common with the women to whom they sold Walker's line—they demonstrated the feasibility of earning one's own money and making a living. These sales agents were not simply employees of Walker's company; they were themselves entrepreneurs who could enjoy the fruits of business ownership. Hence, Walker's Marketing, directdirect-marketing method became a popular small-business strategy, used to this day. The women Walker recruited and trained became part of a national sales force, who then went on to recruit and train other women to

Independent Business Operation

Madam C. J. Walker is noted to have invented the concept of independent business operators, whom she called hair culturists. These women independently sold products in the community in which they lived. As a result, Walker's products reached a broad market while retaining the sense of being a local product. This early version of "thinking globally and acting locally" created a strong following for Walker's products: Those who purchased Walker's hair care line and beauty creams learned how to use them in their own homes.

Madam Walker trained her culturists well and emphasized their participation in the company by holding the Madam C. J. Walker Hair Culturist Union of America Convention, the first national meeting of businesswomen in the United States. The convention sought not only to motivate the saleswomen but also to encourage their political and social activism within their communities.

Another benefit of this type of product distribution is the development of brand loyalty. By owning the product formula, the factories that produced the products, the schools utilized to train sales associates in the use and sale of the products, and the salons in which individuals could have the products professionally applied could always be assured of receiving a genuine Madam C. J. Walker hair tonic or cream, not an impostor. They were welcome to tour the factory and watch "their" products being created. They knew that they were getting the "real thing," and they had the sense that it was created just for them. This type of brand management and brand loyalty became the foundational principle of the marketing of all sorts of products, from automobiles to breakfast cereals.

establish beauty shops in their homes, keep business records, and practice exceptional customer service.

A visionary when it came to protecting her brand, Walker owned the formulas for making her hair care products, the factories in which they were made, the training facilities to teach her hair culturists to use and sell the products, and the salons in which her products could be used. This created "two brands in one": Walker's hair care products could be used both at home, by the layperson, and by professionals who set the example of how the products should be used to give women an elegant look.

> "*I am not merely satisfied in making money for myself, for I am endeavoring to provide employment for hundreds of women of my race. ... I want to say to every Negro woman present, don't sit down and wait for the opportunities to come. Get up and make them!*"

In a move employed by many of the largest companies in the world today, in 1917 Walker held a convention of the Madam C. J. Walker Hair Culturist Union of America in Philadelphia, considered the first national meeting of businesswomen in the United States. At this convention, Walker went beyond simply motivating her hair culturists to sell more of the Walker line of products. She also encouraged them to get engaged in political and social activism in the communities in which they lived. Walker led by example in this area, visiting the White House after a white mob had lynched three African Americans in Illinois. She donated one thousand dollars to the building fund of a "colored" YMCA in Indianapolis, and she contributed five thousand dollars to the anti-lynching movement of the National Association for the Advancement of Colored People (NAACP). In another brilliant marketing strategy, Walker popularized the use of famous spokespersons by having her product used and touted by Josephine Baker, one of the most popular African-American entertainers in the world at that time.

Walker's company was in operation from 1905 to 1985, when the right to manufacture products using the Walker name was sold to another company. She died from complications of hypertension on May 25, 1919, in New York State at the relatively young age of fifty-one. She left a sizable estate and a business that continued to function and provide good jobs for more than six decades after her death.

SIGNIFICANCE

Walker is often quoted as saying, "I got my start by giving myself a start." She took this concept further by not only giving herself a start but also giving a start to countless other African Americans through her innovative business practices and high-quality products that produced the results they promised. She brought beauty into the lives of women who where often working hard just to make ends meet. Some complained that she was trying to make African-American women's hair look like that of white women. Walker retorted that she was simply trying to promote the proper care of hair for women.

While Walker invented a number of products and developed many business and marketing strategies, she is often credited with inventions that were not hers. She did not, for example, invent the straightening comb, although she did popularize its use. She did not create the first African-American hair care product available for purchase; she in fact got her start working for an earlier inventor of hair care products for African Americans. Walker is, however, noted as the first self-made female millionaire in the United States. At her death, her estate had an estimated value of between $600,000 and $700,000 (approximately

The Madam C. J. Walker Manufacturing Company factory, Indianapolis, Indiana. (Wikimedia Commons)

$6 million to $7 million today). The value of her personal and business assets combined is believed to have exceeded $1 million. She also achieved such prominence that she counted such eminent social and political figures as W. E. B. Du Bois among her acquaintances.

The impact of Walker's work on the field of business is threefold. First, she changed the practice of direct marketing. Bypassing the "middleman," Walker brought the supplier directly to the customer and vice versa. This allowed feedback on the product line that led to quick corrections of product flaws as well as new products tailored to changing customer demands. Walker's second area of influence included the creation of a large galley of "business owners" and the concept of franchising products, as opposed to having a large cadre of employees. The result was not only financial independence and wealth for a large number of people but also the Walker company's freedom to focus on business products and services as opposed to employer-employee issues. Walker's third major contribution was the concept of woman-as-owner, a contribution that went beyond business to improve society as a whole. In a time when few women, and fewer African Americans, owned a business, Walker not only owned a company but also helped others to do so.

Doresa A. Jennings

FURTHER READING

Bundles, A'Lelia. *Madam C. J. Walker*. New York: Chelsea House, 1991. A biography of the African-American businesswoman by her great-granddaughter. Well illustrated.

---. *On Her Own Ground: The Life and Times of Madam C. J. Walker*. New York: Scribner, 2001. The most comprehensive, historically accurate account of the life of Walker published to date.

Lasky, Kathryn. *Vision of Beauty: The Story of Sarah Breedlove Walker*. Cambridge, Mass.: Candlewick Press, 2000. A chronicle of the life of Walker.

Lathan, Charles C. "Madam C. J. Walker and Company." *Traces of Indiana and Midwestern History* 1, no. 3 (Summer, 1989): 29-40. Lathan, while working at the Indiana Historical Society, processed eighty-seven boxes and forty-nine ledgers of material on Walker and used this information to write his article. The article contains much useful and reliable information, particularly about Walker's real estate purchases, donations to charities, the intricacies of her will, and her company's progress after her death.

Lommel, Cookie. *Madam C. J. Walker*. Los Angeles, Calif.: Melrose Square, 1993. A biography of the African-American businesswoman.

Lowry, Beverly. *Her Dream of Dreams: The Rise and Triumph of Madam C. J. Walker*. New York: Alfred A. Knopf, 2003. Lowry uses primary-source materials to chronicle Walker's life and career.

McKissack, Patricia, and Fredrick McKissack. *Madam C. J. Walker: Self-Made Millionaire*. Hillside, N.J.: Enslow, 1992. Covers the business ventures of Walker.

Education

Educators are a special class of heroes. From the age of five or younger, we spend thousands of hours of our young lives in schools, and our teacher have an enormous influence on the shape of our thinking and on our character. All those who have been touched by great teachers in their lives understand the appropriateness of calling them heroes.

Before the nineteenth century, most learning occurred at home. The first public schools were founded in a few cities and towns in the United States in the first half of the nineteenth century, and the first mandatory and free public school system was founded in Massachusetts in 1852. From that point onward, the link between education, democracy, and freedom was firmly established. It wasn't until 1918 that all children in America were able to—were expected to—attend school through at least the elementary grades. The history of expanding access to equal educational opportunities reached another milestone in 1954, when *Brown vs. Board of Education* declared segregation in public schools to be unconstitutional. Today the debate over charter schools is understood on both sides to turn on the axis of that same link, the one between educational opportunity, democracy, and individual freedom.

The expansion of educational opportunities has recently been expanding in the area of higher education. In twenty states today, students can attend either state colleges or community colleges tuition-free. Some proposals at the national level, like the "College for All" Act, would expand access even further. As a college degree is becoming the new high school degree, the role or meaning of a college education has changed dramatically. The liberal arts model upon which four-year colleges operated for most of the nineteenth and twentieth centuries has receded or been entirely replaced in some quarters by a jobs training model. This is said to be necessary in order to provide workers for today's economy. It's an historic shift in our understanding of the purposes of higher education. In this regard, we might do well to recall the words of Anne Sullivan, the great educator who was Helen Keller's teacher: "The immediate future is going to be tragic for all of us unless we find a way of making the vast educational resources of this country serve the true purpose of education: truth and justice."

Young students displaced by Hurricane Katrina learn in a Federal Emergency Management Agency (FEMA) funded building. (Robert Kaufmann/FEMA)

ELIZABETH CABOT AGASSIZ

Educator and science writer

Born: December 5, 1822; Boston, Massachusetts
Died: June 27, 1907; Arlington, Massachusetts
Area of Achievement: Education, science and technology

One of the founders and the first president of Radcliffe College, Agassiz was an influential pioneer in higher education for women and was also noted for her writings on natural history and her work with her husband, naturalist Louis Agassiz.

EARLY LIFE

Born Elizabeth Cabot Cary, Elizabeth Cabot Agassiz (ah-gah-see) was a member of a well-connected Massachusetts family. The second of the seven children of Thomas and Mary Cushing Perkins Cary, she received no formal education because of her physical weakness and fragile health as a child. Instead, she was taught at home by a governess who tutored her in languages, music, and art. However, the overall scope of her schooling was somewhat haphazard. During her youth, she exhibited no particular interest in science, which would become one of her keenest interests later in life.

At the age of twenty-eight, Elizabeth met Louis Agassiz, a Swiss professor of natural history employed at Switzerland's University of Neuchâtel. Agassiz had recently been widowed and left with his three children. When he met Elizabeth, he was on his first trip to the United States on a speaking engagement at Harvard. Shortly after returning home, he decided to emigrate to the United States to accept a position at the prestigious Harvard University as chair of natural history in the Lawrence Scientific School. Elizabeth married him in April, 1850, and became mother to his children. They had no children together.

To help support her family and to promote education among girls, Elizabeth opened the Agassiz School for Girls in her Cambridge, Massachusetts, home in 1856. During the seven years that she operated her school, she never taught in it herself but oversaw its management and day-to-day operations. Her husband, however, taught natural history to her students, in addition to his work at the university. Elizabeth often attended his classes and developed a keen interest in natural sciences. Her notes from

Elizabeth Cabot Agassiz (Wikimedia Commons)

her husband's lectures became the basis for much of his published work in later years.

After the school closed in 1863, Elizabeth devoted herself to supporting her husband's field expeditions. She organized and traveled with him on his field trips and collaborated with him on the documentation of the marine and biological life that he observed. Louis Agassiz was not only a naturalist but also a man who left his mark as an innovator in educational methods. Scholars remember him as a brilliant educator as well as a famed naturalist because he used an innovative approach to learning natural history by interacting with nature rather than studying it only in books. In Europe, he was recognized as one of the foremost ichthyologists of his time. He also put forth the idea of the ice age. Elizabeth contributed significantly to his success in both areas.

LIFE'S WORK

Elizabeth Agassiz organized, managed, and accompanied her husband on the Thayer expedition to Brazil in 1865-1866 and the Hassler expedition to the Strait of Magellan in 1871-1872. She and her husband founded the Anderson School of Natural History, a marine laboratory on Penikese Island in Buzzards Bay, Massachusetts. She attempted to write in a way that made scientific inquiry accessible and interesting to nonscientists. Multiple printings of her books attested to her success in achieving this goal. Her own writings included *A First Lesson in Natural History* (1859), *Geological Studies* (1886), and an article in the *Atlantic Monthly* recounting her husband's expedition to the Pacific Ocean. She also coauthored, with her stepson Alexander Agassiz, the popular textbook and field guide *Seaside Studies in Natural History* (1865). With her husband, she coauthored *A Journey in Brazil* (1867).

> "We have to show that the wider scope of knowledge and the severer training of the intellect may strengthen and enrich a woman's life," she said, "and help her in her appointed or chosen work, whatever that may prove to be, as much as it helps a man in his career."

In 1873, soon after her husband's death, Agassiz began writing an insightful biography of her famed partner, *Louis Agassiz: His Life and Correspondence,* that was was published in 1885. The "correspondence" to which the book's title alludes involved insights selected from a large collection of mostly personal letters Louis Agassiz had written over time to a friend and fellow naturalist, Arnold Guyot, as well as letters to his wife and son.

With her husband gone, Elizabeth Agassiz devoted herself to the care and nurturing of her grandchildren, as well as the book about her husband. Through this initial writing effort, she became recognized as a gifted author. Her work proved to be invaluable to her husband's career. About four years after completing her husband's memoirs, she took up a dream she had had since her husband's death: founding a college for women taught by the faculty of Harvard University. She believed that this would open up extensive resources and opportunities for women that up to that time had been accessible only to men.

Agassiz worked with Arthur Gilman and Alice Longfellow to help develop the "Harvard Annex," which was incorporated as the Society for the Collegiate Instruction of Women in 1879. Agassiz herself was appointed its first president. In 1894, the new institution was renamed Radcliffe College in honor of Ann Radcliffe Mowison, who had founded the first Harvard scholarship in 1643. Agassiz remained president until 1899, when she was seventy-six years old. On her retirement, she was given the title of honorary president.

Significance

Agassiz was mostly self-taught—an incredible accomplishment—in a society where this was not encouraged. Her academic achievements gave credence to the importance of educating women, and the potential value of women's contributions in the field of science. Her unique ability to make scientific notions accessible, interesting, and animated to the nonscientific reader was an important contribution to scientific education.

During World War II, four decades after Agassiz retired, Harvard and Radcliffe signed an agreement allowing women to attend classes at Harvard for the first time. The implementation of the joint instruction began in 1943. This agreement legitimized the education of women both at Harvard and, later, other institutions of higher education, and was, perhaps, the ultimate achievement of Elizabeth Cabot Agassiz.

Peggy J. Anderson

Further Reading

Agassiz, Elizabeth Cabot Cary, ed. *Louis Agassiz: His Life and Correspondence.* 2 vols. Bristol, England: Thoemmes Continuum, 2002-2003. Originally published in 1885, this book contains a biography of Elizabeth's husband and copies of his correspondence with many of the leading scientists of his day.

_____, and Alexander Agassiz. *Seaside Studies in Natural History.* New York: Arno, 1865. Reprint 1970. A textbook and field guide for zoologists.

Howells, Dorothy Elia. *A Century to Celebrate: Radcliffe College, 1979-1979.* Cambridge, Mass.: Radcliffe College, 1978. A history of the college, describing how its founding aimed to increase educational opportunities for nineteenth century women.

Lurie, Edward. *Louis Agassiz: A Life in Science.* Chicago: University of Chicago Press, 1960. A persuasive interpretation of the life of the husband of Elizabeth Agassiz, Louis Agassiz, and an exhaustive study of his papers. Lurie acknowledges Agassiz's weaknesses and pictures a genius with faults.

Paton, Lucy A. *Elizabeth Cary Agassiz: A Biography. 1919.* Reprint. New York: Arno Press, 1974. Still the only full-length biography of Elizabeth Cabot Agassiz, this book provides that details on her collaborative writing efforts with her husband and stepson and her role as a pioneer in the education of women.

Tharp, Louis Hall. *Adventurous Alliance: The Story of the Agassiz Family of Boston.* Boston: Little, Brown, 1959. Describes the lives and work of Elizabeth and Louis Agassiz, Elizabeth's family's connections in Boston, and her contributions to women's education.

MARY MCLEOD BETHUNE

Educator and social reformer

Born: July 10, 1875; Mayesville, South Carolina
Died: May 18, 1955; Daytona Beach, Florida
Area of Achievement: Education, social reform, civil rights

A leading voice and activist for democratic ideals before World War I and up to the early years of the Civil Rights movement, Bethune was instrumental in founding organizations to advance the education and rights of African Americans, inspiring others as she was herself inspired.

EARLY LIFE

Mary McLeod Bethune (meh-CLOWD bay-THYEWN) was born in Mayesville, South Carolina, to Sam and Patsy McLeod, who were former slaves. She was the seventeenth child to be born to the couple and the first to be born free. Her father was a farmer and her mother, Patsy, probably did laundry to supplement the family income in addition to her own work on the family farm. Many of the older McLeod children were either married or on their own, but the younger children assisted with the support of the family by picking cotton. By her own report, Bethune, at nine years of age, could pick 250 pounds of cotton a day.

One incident in particular is reputed to have inspired Bethune's determination to become educated. While she was in a neighboring house being shown around by the white family's young daughters, they happened into a room with books. Bethune picked up one of the books and was examining it when one of the girls spoke sharply to her about putting the book down, reportedly telling her "You can't read, so you shouldn't even handle a book!" Shocked at this response and perhaps vaguely aware of the insult, Bethune became determined to read. As it happened, a young black woman was in the neighborhood to start a school for black children. This teacher approached the McLeods about having Bethune attend. The likelihood of one of the children of this poor family being

Mary McLeod Bethune (Wikimedia Commons)

allowed to go to school seemed remote. Nevertheless, Bethune's desire to go was so strong and apparently so heartfelt that her mother convinced her father to let her go. When she was able to read the Bible to her parents as a result of this schooling, they all, parents and child, came to appreciate the benefits of education.

Bethune did well at the little country school. Her teacher recommended her for further schooling, and her tuition was paid in part by Mary Chrissman, a white dressmaker from Denver, Colorado. The new school, known as Scotia School, was located in Concord, South Carolina. Bethune contributed to her education by doing odd jobs at the school. Having done well in her studies at Scotia, she was again recommended by her teachers for scholarships to continue her studies. She was accepted as a student at the Moody Bible Institute in Chicago, Illinois, and received additional financial support from Chrissman.

At the Moody Institute, Bethune became a member of the Gospel Choir Team that preached and sang throughout Illinois. She had hoped to become a missionary in Africa on completion of her studies, but because she was so young, she was not considered a suitable candidate. Instead, she took a teaching assignment at Haines Normal and Industrial Institute in Augusta, Georgia, where she met a black woman who was to affect her life in important ways: Lucy Laney, the school's principal and founder and a trailblazer in the education of blacks. Sympathizing with Bethune's compassion for the uneducated black children of the neighborhood around the school, Laney allowed Bethune to teach them on Sunday afternoons. Soon, Bethune had the children singing familiar songs, and she encouraged them to listen to Bible stories later.

The sponsoring Presbyterian Board of Haines Institute sent Bethune to other schools nearby. One of those schools was the Kendall Institute in Sumter, South Carolina. It was here that she met Albertus Bethune, also a teacher, whom she married in May of 1898. Their son, Albert McLeod Bethune, was born a year later. The family soon moved to Palatka, Florida, where Mary Bethune established a Presbyterian mission school. Her husband did not share her enthusiasm for missionary work, however, and the couple was eventually separated.

Bethune with girls from the Literary and Industrial Training School for Negro Girls in Daytona, circa 1905. (Wikimedia Commons)

> "*We have a powerful potential in our youth, and we must have the courage to change old ideas and practices so that we may direct their power toward good ends.*"

Life's Work

Having been born in the South during Reconstruction undoubtedly saddled Bethune with many adversities. She was black, poor, and female, none of which made her more remarkable than other young women alive during the same period. What did distinguish her was her ability to conquer those misfortunes, to share her accomplishments with others, and to choose to devote her life to acts of service to others. From the time she read the Bible to her parents, she seemed to recognize and become inspired by the power of words and their effects on others.

Bethune's lifework began in Daytona Beach when she saw other young black women in need of all varieties of education. Her ambition to provide a place for their schooling took the form of grasping at any possibilities, becoming inventive as the needs arose: discarded, crumpled paper could be smoothed out to write lessons on; burned wooden twigs could become charcoal for pencils; cracked plates or broken chairs anything that could be salvaged was recycled and returned to useful service. Her crowning achievement in these salvage operations was an area in the city that had been used as a garbage dump, but which she saw could be used for a school. Selflessness and determination proved to be the hallmarks of Bethune's character. She had a dollar and a half as her original budget, but she made do and found creative ways to recruit both students and community assistance for her projects.

The years following the founding of the school with five students on October 3, 1904, led to the rapid growth of her program of education for blacks. By 1906, Bethune had 250 students and employed a few teachers who worked for salaries of fifteen to twenty-five dollars a month. To lessen the drain on the meager finances and to become more independent, she stopped renting and began to buy land for her needs. By 1925, Bethune School merged with the Cookman School for boys to become Bethune-Cookman College. The merged institution included a grade school, high school, and college. Because southern policies of segregation at the time extended to the care of hospital patients, Bethune was led to erect a hospital near the college in 1911 to provide better treatment for the black community. It was named for her father and proved to be another example of her vision.

During the years of the Wilson administration, Bethune became more active in social organizations devoted to protest and social reform. She served on the executive board of the Urban League as well as on committees resisting the discriminatory policies of the Young Women's Christian Association (YWCA). Since many of the positions taken by the YWCA were either condescending or blatantly biased, Bethune became one of several women opposing the racist stance of that association. She was also active in the formation of the National Association of Wage Earners, an organization dedicated to informing women of their rights as workers.

In 1921, Bethune was one of the executive leaders of the International Council of Women of the Darker Races of the World. The intention of this group was to raise the esteem and awareness of darker peoples about themselves and others from what has been called the Third World and what is best called the developing world.

She continued her activities on behalf of black children and women to combat the injustices and inequities they faced. Founding the National Association of Negro Women in 1935 and working with the Franklin D. Roosevelt administration, Bethune directed the Negro branch of the National Youth Administration. She was also founder and president of the National Association of Colored Women's Clubs.

Although she served as president of Bethune-Cookman College from 1904 to 1942 and was one of its trustees until her death in 1955, her influence was not exclusively focused on education. She was a special assistant to the secretary of war during World War II and served on the Committee for National Defense under President Harry S. Truman. She also served as a consultant to the conference that drafted the United Nations charter. These activities and her many honorary degrees and medals never caused her to abandon her main concern: the education of every black child.

Bethune's imagination was not restricted to what she, or anyone, could see immediately. She was known to say "just because you can't see a thing, does not mean that it does not exist." During many of her talks, Bethune would frequently compare the peoples of the world to flowers. Some students would remark that there were no black flowers in the world's gardens. At first, she had only her visionary remark to offer, since there appeared to be no way to rebut the observation. On one of her trips to Europe, however, she was presented with a "black" tulip by one of her hosts in the Netherlands. She later planted the tulips on her campus as proof of her maxim.

Bethune's ability to maintain her lofty vision allowed her to endure in the face of great challenges. The black community was hard hit by the era's wars, economic depressions, riots, and lynchings. For the most part, there was little government intervention on behalf of black victims. Protests by black organizations went unheard, were ignored, or were suppressed. The activities of racist organizations such as the Ku Klux Klan were accepted, permitted, or even encouraged while blacks were denied their civil rights despite their achievements as responsible citizens. Poverty and ignorance, combined with racism, did much to inhibit black people. None of these conditions could dampen Bethune's spirit. Working with Eleanor Roosevelt and some of the nation's top businesspeople, Bethune enhanced her effectiveness as a representative of the black community and as an individual educator. She died of a heart attack in 1955 and was buried on the campus of her beloved college.

SIGNIFICANCE

During times when being an African American often meant being invisible, being disheartened, and being denied chances to achieve intellectually, especially if female, Bethune became a person whose entire life disproved such stereotypes. By white American standards, she possessed little physical beauty, but by any standards her spirit, her energy, and her compassion were evidence of great inner beauty. Bethune's drive to give women access to worlds that had been closed to them, to give all blacks intellectual choices that had been denied them, and to give children an example to follow in providing service to others made her one of the most notable African

The Mary McLeod Bethune Memorial in Washington, D.C. (Library of Congress)

American leaders of her time. Before her death, she had lived to see Bethune-Cookman become one of the finest of the historically black colleges in the country. She had left her mark on the administrations of two American presidents. Using her keen understanding of human behavior and harnessing her ability to negotiate change in the face of great opposition, Bethune became one of the most influential voices in the struggle for racial equality.

In 1973, Bethune was inducted into the National Women's Hall of Fame. The next year, on what would have been her 99th birthday, the Mary McLeod Bethune Memorial was erected in Lincoln Park in Washington, D.C., designed by the artist Robert Berks. It was the first monument honoring an African American or a woman to be installed in a public park in the nation's capital. Over 18,000 people attended the unveiling ceremony, including Shirley Chisholm. The National Council of Negro Women raised the funds for the memorial, and the inscription on the bottom reads:

> I leave you love. I leave you hope. I leave you the challenge of developing confidence in one another. I leave you a thirst for education. I leave you a respect for the use of power. I leave you faith. I leave you racial dignity. I leave you a desire to live harmoniously with your fellow men. I leave you a responsibility to our young people.

Maude M. Jennings

FURTHER READING

Bethune, Mary McLeod. *Mary McLeod Bethune: Building a Better World Essays and Selected Documents*. Edited by Audrey Thomas McCluskey and Elaine M. Smith. Bloomington: Indiana University Press, 1999. Contains seventy of Bethune's writings and other documents dating from 1902 through 1955.

Carruth, Ella Kaiser. *She Wanted to Read: The Story of Mary McLeod Bethune*. New York: Abingdon Press, 1966. A biography written for juveniles that presents a portrait of Bethune's early years. Also includes some coverage of her involvement as a presidential adviser as well as her activities as an organizer and founder of groups concerned with women's rights and labor relations.

Hanson, Joyce A. *Mary McLeod Bethune and Black Women's Political Activism*. Columbia: University of Missouri Press, 2003. Hanson examines Bethune's political activism in the context of the activism of African American women in her time.

Lerner, Gerda, ed. *Black Women in White America: A Documentary History*. New York: Pantheon Books, 1972. Contains excerpts of works and speeches by notable black women including Bethune. Extremely useful for accurate firsthand accounts of her life and her activities in entries such as "A College from a Garbage Dump," "Another Begging Letter," and "A Century of Progress of Negro Women."

McKissack, Patricia, and Fredrick McKissack. *Mary McLeod Bethune: A Great Teacher*. Hillside, N.J.: Enslow, 1991. Another biography directed at juvenile readers that provides an excellent introduction, broadly describing Bethune's life and achievements in fighting bigotry and racial injustice. Focuses much of its attention on Bethune's courage in overcoming adversity. Illustrated.

Salem, Dorothy. *To Better Our World: Black Women in Organized Reform, 1890-1920*. New York: Carlson, 1990. Salem's work is the fourteenth volume in Carlson's Black Women in United States History series. Provides a chronological narrative of the efforts made by black women's organizations to improve the lives of African Americans in the United States. A well-researched historical account that provides insights into the backgrounds of black women reformers, highlighting their resiliency of character in the face of failures as well as successes.

Smith, Elaine M. "Mary McLeod Bethune and the National Youth Association." In *Clio Was a Woman: Studies in the History of American Women*, edited by Mabel E. Deutrich and Virginia C. Purdy. Washington, D.C.: Howard University Press, 1980. An excellent assessment of Bethune's work in supervising the activities of the National Youth Administration with respect to African Americans. Although aimed at a scholarly audience, this essay is accessible to general readers and helps place Bethune's accomplishments within the context of her own time as well as the larger field of women's studies.

Fabiola Cabeza de Baca Gilbert

American educator, home economist, and writer

Born: May 16, 1894; Las Vegas, New Mexico
Died: October 14, 1991; Albuquerque, New Mexico
Area of Achievement: Education, cooking, agriculture

Born into prosperity, Gilbert dedicated her life to helping the poor people of rural New Mexico. Working primarily among Hispanics and Native Americans, she taught the children of farmers and improved the lives of women by instructing them to apply modern methods of home economics to traditional domestic chores.

Early Life

Fabiola Cabeza de Baca Gilbert (FAH-bee-OH-lah kah-BEH-zah deh BAH-kah GIHL-bahr) was a descendant of sixteenth-century Spanish explorer Álvar Núñez Cabeza de Vaca and a niece of Ezequial Cabeza de Baca, New Mexico's second governor. She was one of four children born to Graciano Cabeza de Baca y Delgado and his wife, Indalecia Delgado. Fabiola and her siblings—Luis, Guadalupe, and Virginia—grew up in San Miguel County on a large, prosperous land-grant cattle ranch, Llano Estacado (Staked Plain) that had been in the family since the 1820's. Her mother Indalecia died when Fabiola was four years old, and the Cabeza de Baca children were then cared for by their grandparents, Tomas and Estefana, who lived in a large, elegant stone mansion in Las Vegas, New Mexico.

Fabiola attended school at Loretto Academy, a Catholic school in Las Vegas, and spent summers at the ranch, riding her own pony and working alongside her father, especially during branding season. She soon left Loretto (allegedly after a confrontation with a nun) and transferred to a public school. In 1906, she traveled to Spain for a year of Spanish language study before returning home. Fabiola graduated in 1913 from a high school run under the aegis of New Mexico Normal School (now New Mexico Highlands University), having earned a teaching certificate. In 1916, she began teaching the Spanish-speaking children of Hispanic and Indian homesteaders at a rural school in Guadalupe County. During a ten-year teaching career, she also was an instructor at schools in Santa Rosa and El Rita. In 1921, she earned a bachelor's degree in education at New Mexico Normal School, and afterward she returned to Spain to conduct genealogical research. Back in New Mexico, she resumed teaching and was assigned to instruct her students in the relatively new subject of home economics. Intrigued by the possibilities of bringing the modern methodology of family and consumer sciences to traditional domestic chores, in 1929 Gilbert returned to her studies and earned a bachelor's degree in home economics from New Mexico State University in Las Cruces.

Life's Work

Gilbert immediately put her new degree to good use, landing a position as a home demonstration field agent with the New Mexico Agricultural Extension Service in 1929. For the next thirty years, Gilbert, who at the time of her hiring was the only agent who spoke Spanish, as well as two Pueblo Indian dialects, drove throughout the mostly rural and heavily Hispanic Rio Arriba and Santa Fe Counties, bringing the benefits of modern home economics to the wives of isolated, often poverty-stricken farmers. She instructed the women in nutritional values and in techniques of food preparation and preservation, such as how to dry and can fruits or vegetables, and she showed them how to apply new advances in gardening and livestock care to their advantage. She translated useful government bulletins into Spanish for distribution. She also taught wives how to use sewing machines to make traditional craft items, such as quilts and *colcha* (embroidered coverlets), and helped market the finished products to enable impoverished families to earn extra income during the depths of the Great Depression.

In 1931, Fabiola married insurance agent Carlos Gilbert, who was a member of the League of United Latin American Citizens (LULAC), an organization formed to oppose discrimination against Hispanics, especially in the American Southwest. The couple eloped to Mexico; since Carlos had been married before, Fabiola knew her traditionally oriented father would not approve of the union. Though Fabiola would remain active with LULAC for many years—later serving as a national trustee and as president of a local chapter—the marriage did not last. The Gilberts, who had no children, divorced in the early 1940's.

Tragedy struck Fabiola in 1932. A train smashed into her car in Las Vegas, scarring her face and mangling her leg so severely that it had to be amputated. It took two years for her to recover, during which time she wrote extensively on home economics, food preparation, folklore, traditions, and other subjects. After recuperation, she

> ### Historic Cookery
>
> Fabioloa Cabeza de Baca Gilbert's first book, *Historic Cookery* (1939), originated in 1931, when Gilbert created a brief New Mexico Agricultural Extension pamphlet in which she compiled traditional and modern recipes from Spanish, Mexican, Indian, and Anglo cuisines. Gilbert had closely observed native cooks at work, and she carefully tested each of their recipes in her own kitchen, recording exact measurements of ingredients—customarily a pinch of this or a dash of that—for easy duplication. A popular publication, the pamphlet was reprinted several times before it was released as a book in 1939. *Historic Cookery* sold more than 100,000 copies before the copyright was bought in the 1970's for reprinting. New Mexico governor Thomas J. Mabry, who was in office from 1947 through 1951, helped boost distribution of the book by sending copies to officials of other states as a promotion for New Mexico.
>
> *Historic Cookery* is the first cookbook detailing the cuisine of the upper Rio Grande region and contains recipes for a variety of chili-based sauces, corn and meat dishes, cheese and egg preparations, salads, soups, breads, desserts, and more. The book, which emphasizes the concept of *guisar*—putting the finishing touch to prepared foods—is widely credited for popularizing New Mexican cuisine in general, and chili in particular.

returned to her job as an extension agent with renewed vigor, wearing a wooden leg.

Gilbert not only continued doling out valuable domestic advice to her housewife clients, but also she began gathering information from them. She collected prized family recipes, tidbits of folklore, natural home remedies passed down over the generations, details of religious celebrations, incidents from oral history, and other items of interest from Hispanic and Native American heritages. She used the data she collected to publish many articles in local newspapers and magazines. She also hosted a bilingual radio program about home economics. In 1939, she published the first of three books, *Historic Cookery*, which provided recipes for traditional dishes. In 1949, she released *The Good Life: New Mexican Food*, a fictional account of a typical Hispanic family that explained traditions and rituals and contained recipes for dishes associated with particular festive events. A third book, *We Fed Them Cactus* (1954), was a history of her family during four generations.

In 1951, through the auspices of the United Nations Educational, Scientific, and Cultural Organization (UNESCO), Gilbert was sent to Mexico to teach home economics to Tarascan Indians. She also trained more than fifty students from Bolivia, Costa Rica, Ecuador, El Salvador, Guatemala, Haiti, Honduras, Mexico, and Peru in modern home-economics techniques. Gilbert retired from the Agricultural Extension Service in 1959, but she kept busy. Always interested in learning about and preserving native customs and traditions, she became an active participant in the Folklore Society of Santa Fe. She lectured widely, wrote copiously, and during the 1960's served as a consultant in home economics to Peace Corps volunteers in training. Still alert and active late in life, Gilbert died in a retirement home in Albuquerque at the age of ninety-seven.

SIGNIFICANCE

Linked by her ancestors to the land for more than four hundred years, Fabiola Cabeza de Baca Gilbert is an important figure in New Mexico's history. She played a pivotal role in the survival of poor Hispanic and Indian residents by giving their children the rudiments of education and by teaching adults efficient methods of home economics designed to improve life during the Great Depression and afterward. Working in both domestic and foreign venues, Gilbert brought the advantages of good nutrition and effective food preparation to the Western Hemisphere, and, through her Peace Corps instruction, to the world. Her writings have preserved traditions and customs that would otherwise have been lost

Jack Ewing

FURTHER READING

Gilbert, Fabiola Cabeza de Baca. *The Good Life: New Mexican Food*. Drawings by Gerri Chandler. Santa Fe, N.Mex.: San Vincente Foundation, 1949. A fictional account of a typical Hispanic family, including recipes for foods associated with particular holidays.

---. *Historic Cookery*. 1939. Reprint. Santa Fe, N.Mex: Ancient City Press, 1970. Gilbert's first published book, containing recipes for traditional New Mexican dishes.

---. *We Fed Them Cactus*. Drawings by Dorothy L. Peters. Albuquerque: University of New Mexico Press, 1954. A four-generation history of Gilbert's family.

Locke, Liz, Theresa A. Vaughan, and Pauline Greenhill, eds. *Encyclopedia of Women's Folklore and Folklife*. Westport, Conn.: Greenwood, 2008. This well-researched, painstakingly documented, two-volume work discusses Gilbert's written works in conjunction with women's traditional occupations, such as cooking, and the relationship of her writings to the preservation of folklore and culture.

Melzer, Richard. *Buried Treasures*. Santa Fe, N.Mex.: Sunstone Press, 2007. Honors notable people in New Mexico's history. Includes a biography of Gilbert that recognizes her work as a cultural preservationist.

Schenone, Laura. *A Thousand Years over a Hot Stove: A History of American Women Told Through Food, Recipes, and Remembrances*. New York: W. W. Norton, 2004. An interesting compendium of cooking history that encompasses a variety of cuisines, including Native American and Hispanic, complete with recipes.

Huping Ling

Writer, scholar, and educator

Born: 1956; Taiyuan, Shanxi Province, China
Birth name: Linghu Ping
Areas of achievement: Literature, education, research

Huping Ling is a leading scholar on Chinese American women's history and Asian American community studies. As an internationally renowned historian and prolific writer, Ling's scholarly influence and public service span the Pacific and represent the contributions of post-1965 Asian professional migrants to American culture and society.

Early Life

Ling was born in 1956 into a well-educated family in Taiyuan, the capital city of Shanxi province in China. Her father, Linghu Pu, participated in the national movement of resistance against Japan's invasion and became a high-ranking nationalist government official at Shanxi province after 1945. Ling's mother, Ma Huiyuan, was versed in literature and music; she came from a well-established family in Taiyuan and her own mother was among the earliest Chinese women to receive modern education. After the communist takeover of mainland China in 1949, Ling's family was under constant scrutiny and endured economic hardship. At the age of three, Ling was sent to a boarding school where she learned self-discipline and independence. Despite her family background, Ling's diligence and talent earned her respect from her peers and teachers. She entered college in 1977, the first year of the restoration of the college entrance examination after the Cultural Revolution, and started publishing scholarly articles on President Franklin D. Roosevelt's foreign policies when she was a junior. After graduating top in her department, Ling was appointed as an assistant professor of history by Shanxi University while she continued her research on American history. Ling was selected as a visiting scholar at Georgetown University in 1985. She went on to earn her master's degree at the University of Oregon in 1987 and her doctorate at Miami University in 1991.

Huping Ling (Wikimedia Commons)

She began teaching history at Truman State University in 1991.

> *"I noted that there is a severe under-representation of Asian Americans in the Midwest, and that Asian American studies have traditional been coast-centered. To try to fill the void, I have devoted much of my time and energy to research on Asian Americans in the Midwest. I interviewed more than 200 Asian Americans in the region, from both small towns and metropolises such as St. Louis."*

Life's Work

Ling published *Surviving on the Gold Mountain: A History of Chinese American Women and Their Lives* in 1998. It is considered the first comprehensive history of Chinese American women. It revises the conventional characterization of Chinese American history and compares Chinese women with women of other immigrant groups. Her book *Chinese in St. Louis: From Enclave to Cultural Community* (2004) develops a new theoretical model of "cultural community" that defines immigrant communities based on common cultural practices and beliefs rather than physical concentrations or territorial boundaries.

Her book *Chinese Chicago: Race, Transnational Migration, and Community since 1870* (2012) has been praised for its insight into the links between local and global communities. Using transnational, comparative, and interdisciplinary frameworks, Ling extended her research interests to Asian American communities. She has also authored *Voices of the Heart: Asian American Women on Immigration, Work, and Family* (2007) and edited books that cover a wide variety of Asian American ethnic groups (including understudied groups such as Burmese, Hmong, Indonesians, Kashmiri, Laotians, Mong, Romani, Thai, and Tibetans). Examples include *Emerging Voices: Experiences of Underrepresented Asian Americans* (2008), *Asian America: Forming New Communities, Expanding Boundaries* (2009), and *Asian American History and Culture: An Encyclopedia* (2010). By early 2012, Ling had published eleven books and over one hundred articles and reviews. In recognition of her significant contributions to the field, she was elected Executive Editor of the *Journal of Asian American Studies* in 2008.

Ling founded the Asian studies minor program at Truman State University in 2001–one of the first programs in the United States to offer an undergraduate degree in Asian and Asian American studies. She was the chair of the history department from 2004 to 2006 and was recommended for the position of provost and vice president for academic affairs at the university in 2010.

Ling's scholarly influence extends beyond the United States. The Chinese version of her book on Chinese American women's history–*Jinshan Yao: A History of Chinese American Women*–won the Ford Foundation Award in 1998 and is used as a textbook for graduate programs in American studies across China. The book *Ping Piao Mei Guo: New Immigrants in America* (2003) was a nonfiction best seller in China. Ling has lectured widely in Asia and has been a visiting professor at Chinese universities. She has also served as a consultant to the Women Writers Association in Shanxi province and to the Overseas Chinese Affairs Office of Guangdong Provincial Government.

Significance

As the first foreign-born and first female editor of the *Journal of Asian American Studies*, Ling represents the contributions of foreign-born scholars to the field and is thus able to enhance dialogues with Asian Americanists and American scholars. In that sense, she has contributed significantly to Asian American studies as an expanding and multicultural collaborative enterprise. Ling's international career also symbolizes the burgeoning cultural, economic, and social exchanges across the Pacific at the turn of the twenty-first century and highlights the active role of Asian American scholars in strengthening and expanding the discussions of migration, gender, race, ethnicity, community, and identity beyond national boundaries.

Lisong Liu

Further Reading

Han, Jeff. "Professor Linghu Ping Chronicles Chinese American Histories." *The World Journal* (Shijie Ribao) 2 Feb. 2012: A9–11. Print. An interview on Ling's scholarly contributions.

Ling, Huping. *Chinese Chicago: Race, Transnational Migration, and Community Since 1870*. Stanford: Stanford UP, 2012. Print. A comprehensive and comparative history of Chinese Chicago.

---. *Chinese St. Louis: From Enclave to Cultural Community.* Philadelphia: Temple UP, 2004. Print. Detailed study of the Chinese community in St. Louis, Missouri.

---. *Ping Piao Mei Guo: New Immigrants in America.* Shanxi, China: Beiyue Literature and Art, 2003. Print. An autobiography of family history and a transnational journey.

---. *Surviving on the Gold Mountain: A History of Chinese American Women and Their Lives.* Albany: State U of NY P, 1998. Print. A comprehensive study of Chinese American women's history.

JULIETTE GORDON LOW

Educator

Born: October 31, 1860; Savannah, Georgia
Died: January 18, 1927; Savannah, Georgia
Area of Achievement: Education, philanthropy

The principal founder of the Girl Scouts of the United States of America, Low spent the last fifteen years of her life working for an organization that would be similar to, but independent of, the Boy Scouts of America.

EARLY LIFE

Juliette Gordon Low, the second of six children and the second of four daughters, was born in the middle of the secession crisis of 1860. Low's mother, Eleanor Lytle Kinzie Gordon, a Chicago native, had learned about the frontier experience from her father, who was a government agent to the Indians. Low's father, William Washington Gordon II, was a cotton broker who served during the Civil War as an officer in the Confederate army and later served as a general and peace negotiator for the United States in the Spanish-American War.

Full of energy, quick of wit, and blessed with an artistic nature, Low displayed much of the wit and charm attributed to her mother. She early exhibited the strong will and organizational abilities of her father, often taking charge of the childhood activities that she, her sisters, and more than a dozen cousins engaged in every summer at the Cliffs, the home of her aunt in northern Georgia. The Gordon girls and their cousins swam, camped, and sometimes hunted, and they often acted in and wrote several plays. Daisy, as Low was called by her family, usually acted several parts in each play.

Low attended private schools in Georgia, Virginia, and New York. The private school in New York City, nicknamed the Charbs by its students, was a finishing school run by the Charbonnier sisters, two extremely circumspect French women who had emigrated to the United States following the Franco-Prussian War. While in New York City, Low wrote additional plays, acted in amateur productions, and studied painting. Once her formal education was finished, Low began dividing her time between living in the United States and visiting Britain and the European continent, a pattern she would continue until her death.

While on one of her visits to Britain, Low fell in love with William Mackay Low, the son of a wealthy Englishman with Savannah connections. After a four-year courtship, which she attempted to conceal from a doting and protective father who viewed William as a social playboy, Juliette and William were married in Savannah, Georgia, in December of 1886. Juliette Gordon Low became part of the social elite in Britain, where her multimillionaire husband owned substantial property and was a close friend of the Prince of Wales and his entourage. The Lows hunted at their own estate in Scotland and entertained extensively in England and the United States. In

Juliette Gordon Low (Wikimedia Commons)

addition, Juliette was presented at Court to Queen Victoria.

Beneath the surface, however, all was not well. Increasingly Low was left alone as her husband went throughout the world on game-hunting expeditions and engaged in other gentlemanly pursuits. Kept even from her favorite pursuit of horseback riding by an injury, Low took up sculpting and oil painting to fill the lonely hours. She also carved a mantle-piece for the smoking room at her Warwickshire estate, forged a pair of iron gates for the entrance to the Wellesbourne property, and often traveled without her husband (but always properly with a female companion). When the Spanish-American War began in 1898, Low helped her mother operate a hospital for soldiers in Miami, Florida.

Meanwhile, Low's marriage continued to disintegrate. In 1902 she consented to a separation and, after her husband's affair with an attractive widow became common knowledge to English society, agreed to begin proceedings for a divorce. William died before the divorce was concluded, leaving his estate to his lover.

After several months of tense negotiations with estate lawyers, Low was granted a settlement of approximately $500,000, making her financially secure for the remainder of her life. Low resumed her active social life, alternating her time between London and Scotland while wintering in Savannah and other parts of the United States.

LIFE'S WORK

A turning point in Low's life came in 1911, when she met Sir Robert Baden-Powell, the hero of the defense of Mafeking in the Boer War and the founder of the Boy Scouts. She admitted later that she had disliked Baden-Powell before she met him, believing that he had received public acclaim at the expense of some of her friends who had participated in the rescue of Mafeking during the Boer War. However, she and Baden-Powell soon became close friends and quickly discovered they had much in common. She shared with him a book that her mother had written about the frontier experiences of Juliette's maternal grandfather; he introduced her to his sister, who had founded the Girl Guides in England.

Low had found the rewarding service she had been seeking throughout her life. She organized a troop of Girl Guides in Scotland and two troops of Girl Guides in London before deciding to expand the movement to include girls in her native country. On her return to the United States, Low established a Girl Guide unit on March 12, 1912, consisting of sixteen young girls in two troops that met in the carriage house in the rear of the garden of her house in Savannah, Georgia. The first Girl Guide was her niece, Margaret Eleanor (Daisy) Gordon. The young girls, dressed in middy blouses, dark blue skirts, light blue ties, and dark cotton stockings, wearing large black ribbons in their hair, engaged in camping and other sports and were soon the envy of the young girls of Savannah. Low rapidly moved to make the Girl Guides a national organization.

Girl Scout Troop #1, with Low standing and saluting at right. (Library of Congress)

> "*My purpose... to go on with my heart and soul, devoting all my energies to Girl Scouts, and heart and hand with them, we will make our lives and the lives of the future girls happy, healthy and holy.*"

William Gordon's death, although a serious blow to his worshipful daughter, caused only a slight delay in Low's plans. After a year abroad in England with her mother, Low returned to the United States and resumed her efforts to make the Girl Guides a national organization. At first, she hoped to merge the existing Campfire Girls organization, founded in 1910, with her Girl Guides organization and call the new organization the Girl Scouts, but the merger fell through. Undaunted, Low continued her dream of a national organization. She began organizational efforts in various states, created a national headquarters, and enlisted prominent Americans to serve on the national board. In 1915, the Girl Scouts of the United States of America was incorporated, with Low serving as its first president. By early 1916, more than 7,000 young women in the United States had registered as Girl Scouts.

Although World War I did not appear to affect Low's travels between the United States and Britain, it did take its toll on her finances. She had been the major financial supporter of the Girl Scouts before the outbreak of the war; with the increasing success of the organization, however, she discovered that even her substantial finances were insufficient to keep pace with the growth of the organization. She adopted little economies to save money for her Girl Scouts. Her famous teas began to feature cakes that were recycled until either they were eaten or ingeniously disposed of by her guests. She refused to permit the electric lights to be turned on in her home until half past five, regardless of how dark the day might be. Her friends and relatives claimed that she was saving pennies while spending hundreds of dollars on the Girl Scouts. Others suspected that her "economies" were a ruse to encourage donors to give more generously to the cause of Girl Scouting.

With the advent of their nation's entry into World War I, the Girl Scouts performed valuable services for their country, donations increased, and the organization soon grew too large to be staffed by volunteers alone. Low, recognizing that her responsibilities could be handled by a new generation of leaders, resigned as the president of the Girl Scouts in 1920, but remained active in her support and was granted the title The Founder. Diagnosed with cancer in 1923, Low continued to demonstrate the energy and will she had exhibited throughout her life. She attended the World Camp of the Girl Scouts in England the following year and soon became involved in plans to hold the World Camp of 1926 in New York State. When told by a friend to wait until 1928 to bring the World Camp to the United States, Low responded that she would not be around in 1928.

Although she found it difficult to conceal the increasing pain of her illness, Low summoned the energy to engage in the weeklong meeting of the World Camp in New York State in 1926. Following the World Camp's closing, she sailed for England, bidding her farewells to friends who were unaware of her condition, and returned to her beloved Savannah, where she died on January 18, 1927.

Low pins a badge on a Girl Scout. (Wikimedia Commons)

SIGNIFICANCE

Low would not be surprised by the size and importance of the Girl Scout movement today. She had faith in her abilities and the abilities of the young women she attracted to the Girl Scouts. Her indomitable will, boundless energy, and belief that physical challenges, such as her own increasing hearing impairment, only slowed advances, never stopped them, proved to be an inspiration both to the young girls fortunate enough to know her personally and the young women who would follow in their footsteps. The last message that she received from the national headquarters of the Girl Scouts shortly before her death adequately sums up her life: She was, the telegram read, "not only the first Girl Scout," she was "the best Scout of them all."

Robert L. Patterson

Further Reading

Choate, Anne Hyde, and Helen Ferris, eds. *Juliette Low and the Girl Scouts: The Story of an American Woman, 1860-1927*. Garden City, N.Y.: Doubleday, 1928. Rev. ed. New York: Girl Scouts of America, 1960. First published for the Girl Scout organization shortly after Low's death, this collection of reminiscences by friends and family members is filled with anecdotal information about the eccentricities of the Girl Scout founder. The revised edition, prepared by Ely List, who was the assistant to the director of the public relations department of the Girl Scouts, is an updated and shortened version of the Choate collection.

Degenhardt, Mary, and Judith Kirsch. *Girl Scout Collector's Guide: A History of Uniforms, Insignia, Publications, and Memorabilia*. 2d ed. Lubbock: Texas Tech University Press, 2005. This guide to Girl Scout uniforms and other collectibles includes several chapters chronicling the organization's history, including information on Low.

Kludinski, Kathleen. *Juliette Gordon Low: America's First Girl Scout*. New York: Viking Children's Books, 1988. Designed for juveniles, this brief book provides a useful introduction to the life of Low.

Saxton, Martha. "The Best Girl Scout of Them All." *American Heritage* 33 (June-July, 1982): 38-47. Although brief, this article could be used as an introduction to an examination of Low's life.

Schultz, Gladys D., and Daisy Gordon Lawrence. *Lady from Savannah: The Life of Juliette Low*. New York: J. B. Lippincott, 1958. Although it does not have either a bibliography or an index and nearly half of it concentrates on the Kinzie and Gordon family histories, this book continues to be useful as the most thorough treatment of the life of Low.

Strickland, Charles E. "Juliette Low, The Girl Scouts, and the Role of American Women." In *Women's Being, Women's Place: Female Identity and Vocation in American History*, edited by Mary Kelley. Boston: G. K. Hall, 1979. Strickland uses Erik Erikson's life-cycle model to analyze the reasons why Low became the founder of the Girl Scouts of the United States. Although designed for specialists in gender and child development studies, this essay can be read with benefit by the nonspecialist. Contains useful bibliographical references.

Anne Sullivan

Educator

Born: April 14, 1866; Agawam, Massachusetts
Died: October 20, 1936; Queens, New York City
Area of Achievement: Education, social reform

With patience, determination, and knowledge of the manual alphabet for the hearing impaired, Sullivan taught Helen Keller to communicate. Encouraged by Keller's quick intelligence, Sullivan devoted her entire life to living and working with Keller in a partnership that inspired many and championed the causes of the blind and the deaf.

Early Life

Anne Sullivan, born Joanna Mansfield Sullivan, experienced a childhood almost as difficult and tragic as that of her famous pupil Helen Keller. Sullivan, the oldest child of Irish immigrants Thomas and Alice Sullivan, had trachoma, a bacterial infection that damaged her eyesight, when she was about five years old. When she was nine years old, her mother died of tuberculosis, leaving her alcoholic father to attempt to care for his three remaining children. Before long, Sullivan and her brother, Jimmie, who suffered from a tubercular hip, were sent to the Tewksbury Almshouse, where Jimmie died a few months later.

Jimmie's death meant that Sullivan was the only child at Tewksbury, an institution infamous for its slovenly living conditions. Despite almost total blindness, Sullivan was determined to escape, and in 1880 she caught the attention of the visiting chair of the Massachusetts Board of Charities, Frank B. Sanborn. Shortly thereafter, Sullivan was sent to the Perkins School for the Blind in Boston. She initially felt humiliated by her ignorance, and her temper caused friction with her teachers and fellow students, but eventually she settled down to her studies.

The significance of Sullivan's time at the Perkins School cannot be overstated. It was there that she came to know Laura Bridgman, a deaf-blind resident of Perkins for over forty years who communicated through the manual hand alphabet. In addition, a summer job that the school arranged for Sullivan led to her meeting the doctor who performed the first successful operation on her eyes, restoring some of her lost vision. Sullivan applied herself

Anne Sullivan (Wikimedia Commons)

to her studies as never before, and graduated from Perkins in 1886 as the valedictorian of a class of eight. Perkins director Michael Anagnos wrote to Sullivan about a job opportunity as governess for a deaf-mute (a common term at the time), and blind young woman named Helen Keller.

> "The immediate future is going to be tragic for all of us unless we find a way of making the vast educational resources of this country serve the true purpose of education, truth and justice."

Life's Work

Sullivan arrived at the Keller home in Tuscumbia, Alabama, in March, 1887, having spent the preceding weeks reading teaching accounts by Samuel Gridley Howe, the first director of Perkins, who had taught Bridgman. Sullivan was relieved to find that Keller, who was not quite seven years old, was a robust if unruly child rather than frail and seriously disabled as she had feared.

Sullivan soon realized that she needed to calm Keller's robustness without breaking her spirit, before she could begin meaningful attempts to teach her language skills. Keller's family, however, was accustomed to giving the child her way, so Sullivan persuaded Keller's father to let the pair work together in a garden cottage away from the main house. Her initial progress with Keller was slow, but just over a month later, a breakthrough was reached when Sullivan finger-spelled the word "water" into Keller's hand while water from a pump poured over the girl's fingers, a scene that was famously re-created in the stage play *The Miracle Worker* (1956) by William Gibson, which also was produced as a play for television (1957) and as a film (1962).

Once Keller understood that the words Sullivan communicated represented objects, she progressed quickly, and Sullivan was able to convey to Keller not only nouns but also verbs, adjectives, and even abstract concepts. Sullivan concluded that she was meant to devote her life to Keller, and she soon accompanied the girl first on a visit to the Perkins School in Boston, then two years at the Wright-Humason School for the Deaf in New York City, and eventually to Radcliffe College, from which Keller would graduate in 1904. During these years, Sullivan spent several eye-straining hours every day either reading to Keller or helping her write her autobiography, *The Story of My Life*, which was published in 1903 with assistance from Harvard professor John Macy.

In 1904, Keller and Sullivan purchased a farmhouse in Wrentham, Massachusetts, thus formalizing their increasingly interdependent relationship. During this period, Macy courted Sullivan, but she initially rejected his proposal, believing that her relationship with Keller would hurt any marriage, and vice versa. In 1905, Macy finally persuaded Sullivan to marry him, but her prediction proved correct. He eventually left Sullivan in 1914 after several strained years and faded out of her life, although she always cared for him.

In the meantime, in 1913, Sullivan and Keller had begun a lecture tour throughout New England. Partly because of Sullivan's poor health, the pair engaged Polly Thomson in 1914 as a secretary to Keller, taking some of the burden from Sullivan, who had weak eyes. Public interest in Keller continued unabated. Although Keller tried to direct some of the attention toward her teacher, Sullivan felt she did not deserve any special acclaim. Nonetheless, in 1915, she and Keller were both awarded

Teacher's Medals at the Panama-Pacific Exposition in San Francisco.

In 1918, the trio traveled again to California to film *Deliverance*, a movie about Keller's life that was critically received but not commercially successful. In 1920, Sullivan and Keller went on the vaudeville circuit, making appearances in which Sullivan asked prepared questions and Keller answered with witty comments. Again, however, Sullivan's health suffered, and they were forced to give up the tour. After a period of rest, all three women accepted positions with the American Foundation for the Blind, for which they gave speeches and raised public awareness of blindness. Thomson and Sullivan also continued to help Keller write and edit books, interspersed with trips abroad to improve Sullivan's health. In 1932, Sullivan reluctantly accepted an honorary degree from Temple University, which had been trying to bestow the honor upon her for more than a year.

Sullivan's failing eyesight and other maladies greatly depressed her; even the publication of Nella Braddy Henney's biography Anne Sullivan Macy (Henney) (1933) did little to cheer her. Because she now felt assured that Thomson was a dependable companion for Keller, she almost seemed to welcome death, but she lived another three years before passing away on October 20, 1936, in Forest Hills, New York, due to a heart-related condition. Shortly before her death she dictated farewell messages to Keller and Thomson and spoke of her desire to see again her beloved husband, who had died a few years earlier, and her long-deceased brother.

Significance

Although Sullivan had difficulty accepting the value of her contributions to society, the fact remains that with little formal training, she both utilized and improved upon the teaching techniques of those who came before her. In addition, although she herself was shy, she selflessly provided the means by which Keller could bask in the public's attention, thus offering thousands of disabled Americans the chance to see a shining example of what they themselves might achieve.

As testament to the skills Sullivan provided Keller, and in tribute to her teacher, Keller wrote the biography *Teacher: Anne Sullivan* (1955). Sullivan believed that any teacher could have achieved the same feats with Keller, but Sullivan's inherent abilities, which allowed Keller not only to naturally acquire language skills the same way other children did but also to determine the direction of her own education, were truly miraculous.

Amy Sisson

Further Reading

Garrett, Leslie. *Helen Keller: A Photographic Story of a Life*. New York: DK, 2004. Although this juvenile biography focuses primarily on Keller, it does address Sullivan's early life and contains many photographs of the teacher as well as facsimile reproductions of announcements pertaining to Sullivan's and Keller's many public appearances.

Henney, Nella Braddy. *Anne Sullivan Macy: The Story Behind Helen Keller*. Garden City, N.Y.: Doubleday, Doran, 1933. Although somewhat difficult to locate, this book is considered the definitive biography of Sullivan. The author's close relationship with Sullivan and Keller allowed her to examine and analyze the dynamics of the pair's relationship.

Keller, Helen. *The Story of My Life*. New York: W. W. Norton, 2003. Newly edited and published on the hundredth anniversary of the original edition, this autobiography by Keller, which provides extensive insight on her relationship with her teacher, also contains "supplementary accounts" by Sullivan and by John Macy. Includes an extensive index and a list for further reading.

---. *Teacher: Anne Sullivan Macy, a Tribute by the Foster-Child of Her Mind*. Garden City, N.Y.: Doubleday, 1955. The last of Keller's published books, this volume consists of Keller's perceptions of the woman she called Teacher for the almost fifty years they lived and worked together.

Lash, Joseph H. *Helen and Teacher: The Story of Helen Keller and Anne Sullivan Macy*. 1980. New ed. New York: Addison-Wesley, 1997. In addition to an exhaustive examination of Keller and Sullivan's relationship, this book also discusses the influences of John Macy and Polly Thomson on the pair's lives. Includes a chronology and extensive index.

Booker T. Washington

Educator and activist

Born: April 15, 1856; near Hale's Ford, Virginia
Died: November 14, 1915; Tuskegee, Alabama
Also known as: Booker Taliaferro Washington
Areas of Achievement: Education; Social issues

Born into slavery on a tobacco farm, Washington became a famous educator and spokesman for African Americans during the trying period after the end of Reconstruction in the South. From 1890 to 1915, he was the best-known African American in the United States. He was able to raise significant educational funds from wealthy white supporters because of his belief that African Americans should temporarily accept institutional racism while developing their farming and industrial skills.

Early Life

Booker Taliaferro Washington spent his first nine years as a slave on the small tobacco-producing Burroughs plantation. He grew up in a one-room log cabin with a dirt floor and slept on a bed of old rags. His mother, Jane, was the cook for the Burroughs family and their one room also served as the plantation's kitchen. All that Washington ever revealed about his father was that he was a white plantation owner.

In April, 1865, a proclamation was read on the Burroughs Plantation announcing that slavery was at an end. Soon Washington left with his family for Maiden, West Virginia, to join his stepfather. The family moved into another rundown shack. Washington later said that he was thankful that slaves learned how to do many things on the plantation, and he pitied the former slave owners and their families who had not mastered the skills necessary for survival.

Life in Maiden for the nine-year-old Washington meant work in the salt furnace and coal mines, often starting early in the morning. He received some schooling in the afternoons, whenever possible. It was at school that he made up the name Washington, since he was the only student in the class who did not have a surname. An opportunity for some improvement came when he was selected as a houseboy for a wealthy local woman who encouraged Washington to further his education. According to Washington, this experience also provided him with the values of frugality, cleanliness, and personal morality, which he would carry with him for the rest of his life. In

Booker T. Washington (Library of Congress)

1872, he left for a new school for black students, the Hampton Institute, one of the earliest freedmen's schools focusing on industrial education. Like many Hampton students, he paid his tuition by working, mostly as a janitor.

> *"In any country, regardless of what its laws say, wherever people act upon the idea that the disadvantage of one man is the good of another, there slavery exists. Wherever, in any country the whole people feel that the happiness of all is dependent upon the happiness of the weakest, there freedom exists."*

Life's Work

After graduating with honors in 1875, Washington taught school in Maiden for two years and then attended Wayland Seminary in Washington, D.C. He returned to Hampton in 1879 as an instructor and organized a night program to train seventy-five American Indian students. This program was used as a model for his founding of the

BOOKER WASHINGTON AND SOME OF HIS DISTINGUISHED GUESTS.
From left to right, George T. McAneny, Robert C. Ogden, J. G. Phelps Stokes, Booker T. Washington, Dr. Lyman Abbott, President H. B. Frissell of Hampton Institute, and President Charles W. Eliot of Harvard.
(From Stereograph, Copyright, 1906, by Underwood & Underwood, New York.)

Washington, standing, center, with (front row) George T. McAneny, Robert C. Ogden, an unidentified man, and George W. Eliot, President of Harvard College, (2nd row) J.G. Phelps Stokes, Dr. Lyman Abbott, and Hollis B. Frissell, President of Hampton Institute. Photo taken at the Tuskegee Silver Jubilee. (Library of Congress)

Tuskegee Institute in Tuskegee, Alabama, in 1881. The state legislature gave Washington two thousand dollars a year for the school. He started holding classes in an old church and a run-down building. When it rained, one of the taller students would hold an umbrella over the teacher's head to keep him dry. Washington led Tuskegee Institute for the final thirty-four years of his life. At the time of his death in 1915, the institution's endowment was two million dollars.

The school reflected the Washington credo of self-reliance born of hard work. His students made the brick and built most of the buildings on the original campus. The school, which stressed industrial training rather than traditional academic learning, also embodied Washington's willingness to accommodate segregationist policies. For Washington, freedom from economic servitude was the first step before later civil rights could be achieved. He stated his position in his "Atlanta Compromise" address of 1895, which accepted temporary segregation and voting-rights restrictions if whites would support African American economic and educational advancement: "In all things that are purely social we can be as separate as the fingers, yet one as the hand in all things essential to mutual progress." Washington was a handsome man and a dynamic speaker, and this speech at the Cotton States and International Exposition in Atlanta catapulted him into the national spotlight and gained him fame as the leading spokesperson for African Americans.

Few whites were threatened by Washington's "accommodationist" attitudes, and most African Americans were highly respectful of his rising national prestige. He was able to gain financial support from powerful white supporters such as John D. Rockefeller, Andrew Carnegie, and Henry H. Rogers, a particularly close friend who was also one of the richest men in the United States. Their philanthropy helped Washington establish thousands of small community schools and institutes for African Americans. The Tuskegee Institute grew from two undersupplied buildings to more than one hundred well-equipped buildings. He was a celebrated dinner guest of President Theodore Roosevelt in 1901, becoming the first African American invited into the White House. That same year, Washington's autobiography, *Up from Slavery*, became a widely read work. Soon, he became a political adviser to Roosevelt and President William H. Taft, influencing a multitude of political patronage positions. He also served on the board of trustees for both Fisk and Howard universities. Washington helped found the National Negro Business League in 1900 with the support of Carnegie. Tuskegee Institute, under his guidance, emerged as a national center for industrial and agricultural training as well as a center for training black teachers.

As new African American leadership came to the fore in the Niagara Movement (1905-1909) and under the auspices of the National Association for the Advancement of Colored People (NAACP), beginning in 1909, Washington's ideas were openly challenged. A chief critic was the Harvard sociologist and writer W. E. B. Du Bois, who found Washington's silence on racial oppression and disenfranchisement to be reprehensible. The Washington-Du Bois clash of ideas became one of the great debates in American political life. In his later years, Washington denounced the increasing number of lynchings in the South and advocated making "separate but equal" facilities

UP FROM SLAVERY

After its publication in 1901, Booker T. Washington's autobiography, *Up from Slavery*, quickly became the most influential book ever published by an African American. Washington's memoirs provide a vivid account of his life as a slave and cite education as the main driver of his career. His early education came from working in various capacities on the farm, and to this experience he attributes his unshakable belief in hard work and self-reliance.

Although slaves were uneducated, Washington wrote that they were remarkably well informed about national developments. Frequent reports were passed along in whispers about the latest developments in the Civil War, picked up from the post office or from overheard conversations in the "big houses." Washington recalled that he had never met a slave who did not want freedom, nor did he ever meet an African American who wanted a return to slavery.

Up from Slavery also details Washington's transition from student to teacher and outlines his development as an educator and founder of the Tuskegee Institute in Alabama. Washington tells the story of Tuskegee's growth from humble beginnings to a two-thousand-acre campus with modern buildings. In the final chapters of the book, Washington describes his career as a public speaker and fund-raiser, and how he pursued African American betterment in the racial climate of the times. Since his "accommodationist" approach was the subject of much controversy, Washington's autobiography is an invaluable source for understanding his motivations and perspective on African Americans' place in American society.

more equal. He also wrote under assumed names to denounce Jim Crow laws and racial violence directed toward African Americans. However, his central belief was that once African Americans developed needed skills and proved to be responsible citizens, fuller participation in American life would follow. Patience, industry, thrift, and usefulness were the qualities that he felt would lead to eventual equality.

Washington died at Tuskegee on November 14, 1915, at the beginning of both the Great Migration from the rural South to the urban North and World War I, two events that would transform the remainder of the twentieth century. An autopsy performed in 2006 confirmed that the fifty-nine-year-old Washington had died of hypertension. His third wife, Margaret J. Murray, whom he married in 1893 following the deaths of his first two wives, outlived him by ten years. She was instrumental in raising Washington's two sons from his previous marriages.

SIGNIFICANCE

Washington rose from slavery to become the nation's most influential African American and remains a pioneer on the long journey toward racial equality. He was one of America's great self-made men, and his theme of self-reliance would be repeated for many succeeding generations. However, critics found fault with his acceptance of racial segregation and emphasis on vocational merit as a substitute for political and social equality. His undeniable legacy, though, is as one of America's foremost educators. His birthplace in Franklin County, Virginia, was designated a national monument in 1956.

Irwin Halfond

FURTHER READING

Bontemps, Arna W. *Young Booker: Booker T. Washington's Early Days*. New York: Dodd and Mead, 1972. Traces the events of Washington's youth and early career that led to his emergence as a famous educator.

Harlan, Louis R. *Booker T. Washington: The Making of a Black Leader, 1856-1901*. New York: Oxford University Press, 1972. A scholarly study of Washington's life and his rise to a national leadership position.

Smock, Raymond W. *Black Leadership in the Age of Jim Crow*. Chicago: Ivan R. Dee, 2009. An analysis of Washington's life and works within the context of the time in which he lived. Written by the editor of fourteen volumes of Washington's private papers.

Thornbrough, Emma. *Booker T. Washington*. Englewood Cliffs, N.J.: Prentice Hall, 1969. A standard biography of Washington.

Verney, Kevern. *Booker T. Washington and Black Leadership in the United States, 1881-1925*. New York: Palgrave Macmillan, 2009. A study of the subtle ways in which Washington tried to undermine the foundations of white supremacy.

Washington, Booker T. *Up from Slavery: An Autobiography*. 1901. Reprint. Mineola, N.Y.: Dover, 1995. Washington's landmark autobiography details his life experiences and philosophies.

Entertainment

Our entertainment category covers music, movies, television, and theater, and it includes figures as diverse as Stan Lee, Nina Simone, and Ellen DeGeneres. Role models and heroes from the entertainment industry are plentiful, probably more so today after nearly a century of radio and television than at any other point in human history. They are important to us for what they bring into our ordinary lives and how they transform our ordinary moments; art and entertainment—even when the medium is a comic book—is "one of the most important things in people's lives," as Stan Lee affirms.

Unlike some classes of heroes and role models, entertainment figures aren't required to illustrate particular virtues or to have life stories that follow any pattern. By contrast, think of business leaders, who almost always illustrate specific virtues for us, like determination or grit, and who are almost always expected to become philanthropists later in life in order to be moral leaders. The relative freedom of entertainment figures from similar constraints is significant. More than any other category in this book, entertainment figures model for us uniqueness, freedom, and creativity.

Take Billie Holiday, for example. She died in 1959, and many of her greatest recordings date from the 1930s. But her unique voice is still fresh and surprising; it is a living testament to her statement that "no two people on earth are alike, and it's got to be that way in music or it isn't music." This power of affirmation and of the unique finds a special witness in Fred Rogers. He was in many ways unlike anyone else in this category. Rogers was never exactly a star, and his plain and soft-spoken demeanor, like his children's show, was worlds apart from a glamorous Hollywood aesthetic. Nevertheless, when he spoke about the importance of personal affirmation and appreciation, Rogers gives philosophical and even theological heft to what Stan Lee and Billie Holiday both were pointing to. The power of affirmation and appreciation is also a key to what each of their special lives—ordinary and extraordinary at the same time—might mean for us. The joy brought by entertainers might be a small thing, like a popular song, a movie scene, a glance, or a gesture. Yet this can simultaneously be "one of the most important things in people's lives."

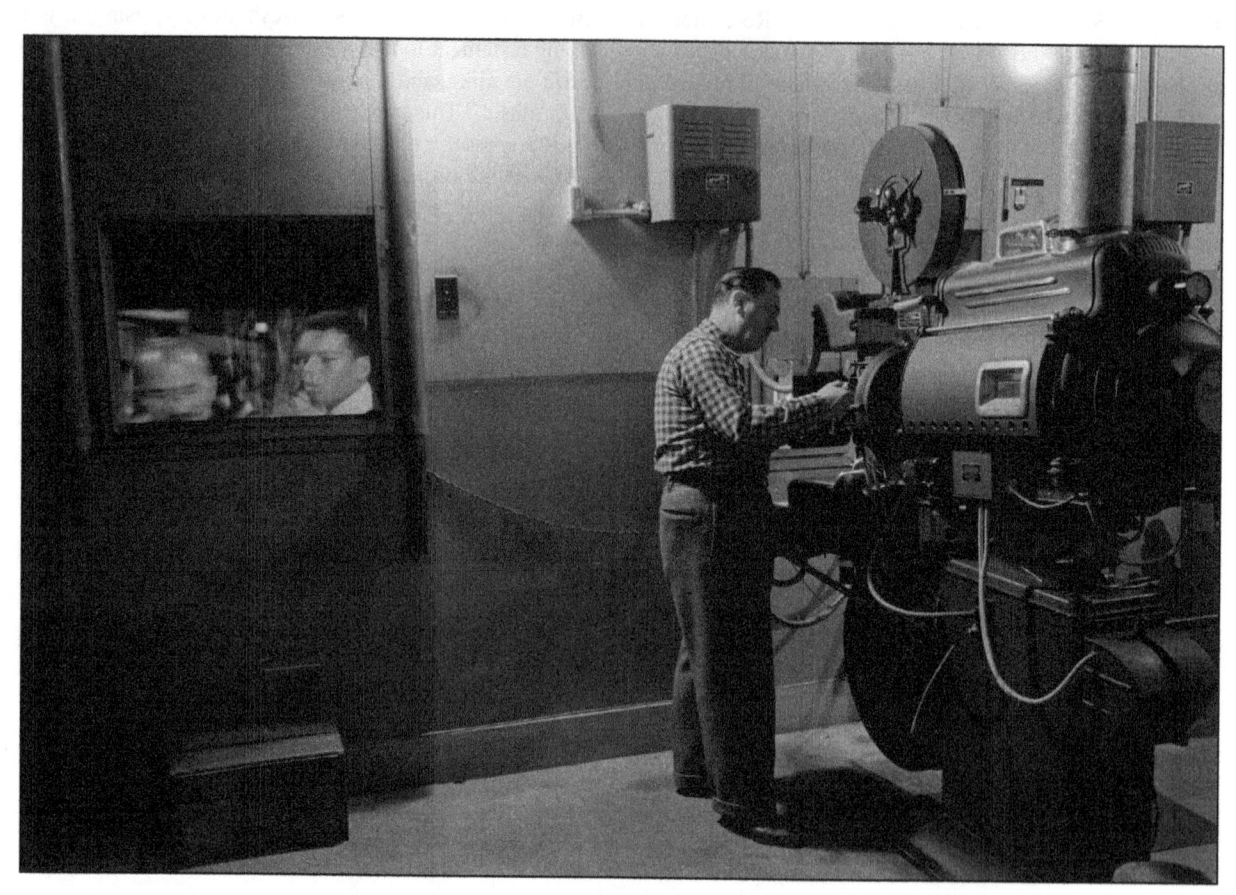

A man works on a film projector in a movie theater. (Library of Congress)

Joan Baez

Folk singer and activist

Born: January 9, 1941; Staten Island, New York
Area of Achievement: Music, activism, social issues

A pioneer in the American folk music revival of the late 1950's and 1960's, Baez blended pacifist and progressive views with her talent as a singer and guitarist to become one of the best-known social, political, and human rights activists of the era. Her protest songs galvanized a generation fighting for civil rights and against the Vietnam War.

Early Life

Joan Chandos Baez (BI-ehz) was born on Staten Island, New York, to physicist Albert V. Baez, a native of Puebla, Mexico, and Joan Bridge Baez, who was born in Edinburgh, Scotland. Albert and the elder Joan had three daughters, Pauline, Joan, and Mimi, who married American writer and folk singer Richard Fariña. Because Albert worked as a university professor, the family moved frequently and lived in various locations nationally and internationally, including Redlands, California; Baghdad, Iraq; and Belmont, Massachusetts, near Boston.

Baez's parents held progressive social and political views and raised their children as Quakers. When she was a junior high school student in Redlands, Baez was ostracized by her white classmates because of her dark skin and Mexican surname. Her first act of civil disobedience occurred when she was a student at Palo Alto High School. She refused to leave her desk during an air raid drill because she was opposed to the arms buildup during the Cold War. School officials punished her, and her fellow students shunned her because of her pacifist beliefs. Feeling isolated, Baez took refuge in music and began to develop her distinctive soprano voice. Her interest in traditional folk music was awakened when she was exposed to Pete Seeger's work. Other influences included Harry Belafonte and Odetta.

After Baez finished high school in 1958, her father accepted a teaching position at the Massachusetts Institute of Technology and moved his family to the Boston area. Baez briefly attended Boston University but dropped out when she discovered the vibrant folk music community flourishing in the Harvard Square coffee houses. Her career as a folk singer began when she became a regular at Club Mt. Auburn 47 (also known as Club 47) in Cambridge. She became more widely known when folk artist Bob Gibson invited her to perform at the Newport Folk Festival in 1959. A record contract with Vanguard followed in 1960.

Joan Baez (Wikimedia Commons)

> "*I think music has the power to transform people, and in doing so, it has the power to transform situations - some large and some small.*"

Life's Work

By 1961, Baez was the reigning queen of folk music, but she had not yet engaged in the high-profile activism that would mark her later career. When she met Bob Dylan at Gerde's Folk City in New York City, she was primarily known as a traditional folk singer. The two were part of a larger folk revival that included Carolyn Hester, Eric Von Schmidt, Jim Kweskin, Dave Van Ronk, Maria and Geoff

Muldaur, Bob Neuwirth, Mimi and Richard Fariña, and other musicians who lived in New York and Boston.

Baez and Dylan's meeting and subsequent love affair led to one of the most fruitful professional partnerships of the 1960's. At the time he first met Baez, Dylan was establishing his reputation as a writer of popular protest songs. Deeply impressed by his socially conscious lyrics, especially those in "With God on Our Side," Baez began to include such songs in her own repertoire. One of the highlights of their collaboration occurred when they appeared together during the March on Washington for Jobs and Freedom held on August 28, 1963. Organized by Martin Luther King, Jr., among others, the rally for civil and economic rights for African Americans drew more than 250,000 people. The two ardent young artists singing "We Shall Overcome" inspired other young activists of the 1960's.

Although Dylan and Baez ended their relationship in 1965, their partnership left its mark on Baez's personal and professional life. In 1965, she recorded *Farewell Angelina*, which included several of Dylan's songs. In 1968, she released an album of Dylan covers titled *Any Day Now*. In 1975, she recorded her acclaimed album *Diamonds and Rust*. The title song was a reflection on her star-crossed affair with Dylan.

Baez continued her work for social justice throughout the turbulent 1960's. In 1965, she joined King on his civil rights marches, most notably the journey from Selma to Montgomery, Alabama. In 1966, she supported César Chávez in his efforts to secure fair wages and safe working conditions for migrant farm workers in California. A passionate opponent of the Vietnam War, she founded the Institute for the Study of Nonviolence in 1964 and participated in numerous antiwar protests. In 1967, Baez was arrested in Oakland, California, for obstructing the doorway of the Armed Forces Induction Center. While serving a month long sentence in the Santa Rita Jail, she met David Harris, a fellow antiwar protester, whom she married in March, 1968.

Shortly after their marriage, Harris refused to be drafted and was arrested in July, 1969. Pregnant with their son, Gabriel, Baez continued to perform. She wrote a number of songs in honor of Harris, including "A Song for David" and "Fifteen Months," which was the term of Harris's imprisonment. She also released a tribute recording titled *David's Album* in 1969. Harris's imprisonment took a toll on their relationship, however, and they divorced in 1973.

Although the folk music revival waned in the late 1960's, Baez continued to record and perform. She

---

Hispanic Influences in Baez's Music

Joan Baez has featured some Spanish songs on her English-Language albums, including "El Preso Numero Nueve" ("Prisoner Number Nine") on *Joan Baez* (1960) and "Dida" on *Diamonds and Rust* (1975). Both songs appear on *Gracias a la vida: Joan Baez canta en español (Here's to Life: Joan Baez Sings in Spanish*, 1974), a work she has called "my gift to the Spanish people." Offering selections from Mexico, Cuba, Spain, and other Hispanic countries, the song list for the 1974 release was suggested by a group of exiled Chileans who had suffered under the repressive government of Augusto Pinochet, the successor of the murdered Salvador Allende. The title track was contributed by Chilean Violetta Parra, and "Te recuerdo Amanda" ("I Remember You, Amanda") was written by her countryman, Victor Jarra, who was killed during the 1973 coup d'état. Other selections include the protest song "No nos moveran" ("We Shall Not Be Moved") and Catalan folk song "El rossinyol" ("The Nightingale"). Latin rhythms prevail, and two songs are performed by a traditional mariachi band. The album sold moderately well in the United States but was a best seller in Spain and Latin America.

---

regularly released albums and toured nationally and internationally. In December, 1972, she traveled to North Vietnam with a peace delegation. She experienced the horrors of war firsthand when the United States engaged in eleven days of carpet bombing over Hanoi. She also witnessed human rights violations on the part of the North Vietnamese. Her experiences led her to found her own human rights organization, Humanitas International, and launch an American branch of Amnesty International. In addition to Vietnam, she has spread her message of peace and justice to many countries throughout Europe and Latin America.

For many years, Baez refused to sing in Spain because she disagreed with the oppressive policies of dictator Francisco Franco. After his death in 1977, as she toured the country, she paid tribute to those who were murdered under his regime. Although she does not speak fluent Spanish, during her concerts she sang some songs in Spanish, including "No nos moveran" ("We Shall Not Be

President Barack Obama, the First Family, Vice President Joe Biden and others in the audience applaud Joan Baez after her singing "We Shall Overcome" at the "In Performance At The White House: A Celebration Of Music From The Civil Rights Movement" concert in the East Room of the White House, Feb. 9, 2010. (Wikimedia Commons)

Moved"), an anthem of resistance that had not been sung publicly in Spain during Franco's rule. Her willingness to sing in the native language of the country demonstrated her solidarity with the Spanish people.

Baez also fought for human rights on behalf of the residents of several Latin American countries, including Brazil, Venezuela, Argentina, and, in particular, Chile. Disturbed about alleged Central Intelligence Agency involvement in the assassination of Salvador Allende on September 11, 1973, Baez gave a series of concerts sponsored by Amnesty International in support of Chileans who were repressed by the new regime. Her work gave birth to Baez's only Spanish-language album, *Gracias a la vida: Joan Baez canta en español* (*Here's to Life: Joan Baez Sings in Spanish*), released in 1974.

Baez performed at the White House in 2010, during a concert to celebrate the music of the Civil Rights Movement. She was honored in 2011 with the establishment of the Joan Baez Award from Amnesty International. She also performed at the Occupy Wall Street protests in November of 2011. Baez honored Apple Computer founder Steve Jobs, whom she dated in the 1980s, with a performance at Jobs' memorial held in 2011.

On April 4, 2017, Baez used Facebook to release her first song in twenty-seven years, "Nasty Man", a protest song against US President Donald Trump; it became a viral hit. On April 7, 2017, she was inducted into the Rock and Roll Hall of Fame. On March 2, 2018, she released a new studio album entitled Whistle Down the Wind, and has been undertaking her "Fare Thee Well Tour" to support the album.

Significance

An artist whose work is inextricably linked to her philosophical and political beliefs, Baez was an icon of the 1960's and 1970's counterculture and protest movements. Although her vocal opposition to war and violence and support of various human-rights causes made her a controversial figure at times, she remained steadfast in her dedication to activism. Baez's music was part of a rich tapestry of protest music that defined a generation and continues to speak to the antiwar fervor of new generations of activists.

Pegge Bochynski, updated by Micah L. Issitt

Further Reading

Baez, Joan. *Daybreak*. New York: Avon, 1970. Baez's first autobiography offers an inside look at her family life and Quaker upbringing.

---. *And a Voice to Sing With: A Memoir*. New York: Simon & Schuster, 2009. Baez's second memoir presents an honest, no-holds-barred account of her life, from her childhood in a progressive household through her long career as a singer, songwriter, and activist.

Fuss, Charles, J. *Joan Baez: A Bio-Bibliography*. Westport, Conn.: Greenwood Press, 1996. A concise biography, plus detailed entries that include release dates, songs, songwriters, musicians, production credits, review excerpts, and critical commentary offer a comprehensive look at Baez's life, career, and activism.

Hajdu, David. *Positively 4th Street: The Lives and Times of Joan Baez, Bob Dylan, Mimi Baez Fariña, and Richard Fariña*. New York: Farrar, Straus and Giroux, 2001. An illuminating account of the key roles Baez, Dylan, and the Fariñas played in the rise of the folk era in the mid-1960's.

Lynda Carter

Actor and singer

Born: July 24, 1951; Phoenix, Arizona
Area of Achievement: Radio and television; music

Best known as the title character from the television series Wonder Woman, Carter became a role model for girls and women through her portrayal of a strong, proactive female character. She also has received recognition for her singing, appearing in a number of television variety specials in the 1980's and releasing a critically acclaimed jazz and blues album in 2009.

Early Life

Lynda Jean Córdova Carter was born in Phoenix, Arizona, to Juana Córdova and Colby Carter. She was the youngest of three children. Carter's mother was of Mexican and Spanish ancestry, while her father was Irish American. Carter realized at a young age that she enjoyed performing, and she began participating in talent shows and taking ballet lessons while still in elementary school.

> "Wonder Woman is much more than a cartoon character. She's fighting for truth and justice and the secret self that exists in all women and girls. There's a moral fiber and a goodness about her that all women have."

Carter's parents divorced when she was ten years old, which had a negative financial impact on the family. Carter began working as a waitress in her early teens, but at age fourteen she found that she could make more money singing and joined a band called the Relatives that played at local restaurants. After a single semester in college, she joined another band, the Garfin Gathering, and began performing in Las Vegas and touring the United States. Carter took a break from touring to compete in a local beauty pageant in 1972, then went on to win the Miss World USA title. She reached the semifinals in the Miss World pageant. After she fulfilled her beauty pageant obligations, Carter moved to Los Angeles, California, to try her luck at acting.

Lynda Carter (Wikimedia Commons)

Life's Work

During her first few years in Los Angeles, Carter landed only a handful of guest roles on minor television shows such as *Starsky and Hutch*. She auditioned for but did not win the lead role as Wonder Woman in a 1974 television film that ultimately starred Cathy Lee Crosby. Just as Carter was about to move back to Arizona because of a lack of money, however, ABC decided to shoot a new version of the *Wonder Woman* series pilot in 1975, and producers chose Carter from among hundreds of actors to take over the role. The new pilot was a ratings success, and Carter won strong reviews for her portrayal of the strong yet vulnerable female action hero. Although it lasted for only three seasons before being canceled in 1979, the series—and Carter herself—gained something of a cult following over the subsequent decades.

In 1977, Carter married her agent, Ron Samuels, who encouraged her to market her career more aggressively. This strategy eventually led to starring appearances on several successful variety shows that allowed Carter to showcase her singing talent. In 1983, Carter starred in a television film biography of legendary actor Rita Hayworth, with whom Carter felt a great deal of kinship due

Carter in costume as Wonder Woman. (Wikimedia Commons)

in part to their shared Hispanic roots. Carter and Samuels divorced in 1982, and Carter met and married an attorney, Robert Altman, in 1984. The couple moved to the Washington, D.C., area for the sake of his work. During the following years, Carter and Altman had two children, and Carter pursued a variety of projects, making several made-for-television films and becoming a commercial spokesperson for companies such as Maybelline and Lens Express.

In 1991, Altman was accused of banking and securities fraud, resulting in a lengthy and highly publicized trial, but he ultimately was found not guilty. Nonetheless, Carter continued to work. In 2002, she appeared in the comedy film *Super Troopers*, following it with small comedic roles in the 2005 films *The Dukes of Hazzard* and *Sky High*. In 2008, she received a Lifetime Achievement Award from the National Museum of Women in the Arts, and in 2009, her jazz and blues album *At Last* reached number six on the *Billboard* Top Jazz Albums chart.

In a June 4, 2008 interview with *People* magazine, Carter stated that she had in the past entered a rehabilitation clinic for treatment of alcoholism and that she had been sober for nearly 10 years. When she was asked what the recovery process had taught her, Carter explained that the best measure of a human being is "how we treat the people who love us, and the people that we love". Through her inspiring story, Carter shares the power and grace of vulnerability, faith, and surrender that she believes nourish lasting recovery. Celebrating over 20 years of sobriety, Carter continues to guest speak at various health and well-being events. Her recovery story, and its message of hope, is directed to every member of the family. It is a strong reminder that family support can make a huge difference to a recovering addict or alcoholic.

In 2017, Carter explained her perspective of portraying the Diana Prince/Wonder Woman character. Carter says she got the role back in 1975 largely because she looked the part, which was both a blessing and – as one of the show's producers warned her – a curse: "Oh, women are going be so jealous of you"... "Well, I said, 'Not a chance. They won't be, because I am not playing her that way. I want women to want to be me, or be my best friend!". As Carter describes Wonder Woman, "There is something about the character where in your creative mind for that time in your life where you pretended to be her, or whatever the situation was, that it felt like you could fly."

During production of the 2017 Wonder Woman feature film, director Patty Jenkins approached Carter to appear in a cameo role in the film, as Carter confirmed, "Patty asked me to do a cameo in this. She was in England, and I was doing my concerts", Carter said, explaining she had singing engagements that made her unavailable. "At that time we couldn't get our timing together. So, this next time, if she writes me a decent part, I might do it".

SIGNIFICANCE

Although Lynda was not widely known as a Latina actor during the height of *Wonder Woman*'s popularity, several Latinas in the entertainment industry have cited Carter as a role model. In addition to singing and acting, Carter has been active throughout her career in charitable causes such as the Susan G. Komen Foundation for breast cancer research.

Amy Sisson

FURTHER READING

Jarvis, Jeff. "Lynda Carter Plays Rita." *People* 20, no. 19 (November, 1983). Discusses Carter's starring role in the television film *Rita Hayworth: The Love Goddess*, highlighting the many parallels between the two women's careers, including their Latino heritage.

Marquez, Sandra. "Still Flying High." *Hispanic* 18, nos. 6/7 (June/July, 2005): 22. Retrospective interview that discusses Carter's Hispanic heritage and her significance as a role model to other Latino actors as well as to young women in general.

Wallace, David. "Lynda Carter: The Real Thing." *The Saturday Evening Post* 255, no. 4 (May/June, 1983): 42-45. Discusses Carter's early life, her success in the role of Wonder Woman, her marriage to and divorce from Ron Samuels, and her religious views.

Ellen DeGeneres

Television show host

Born: January 26, 1958; Metairie, Louisiana
Area of Achievement: Film and television

Although DeGeneres is a comedian who is known for her quick wit and dry humor, she is also an advocate for serious issues including gay and lesbian rights, sexual abuse of teenage girls, and animal rights.

Early Life

Ellen Lee DeGeneres was born in Louisiana. Her mother and father were Betty DeGeneres (née Elizabeth Jane Pfeffer) and Elliott Everett DeGeneres. Her mother worked as a speech therapist and her father was an insurance agent. DeGeneres was raised as a Christian Scientist as a child. When she was 15, her parents divorced. Not long after, her mother married a salesman named Roy Gruessendorf, and they moved to Texas.

In 1976, when DeGeneres graduated from high school, she moved back to Louisiana and attended the University of New Orleans, majoring in communications. But she didn't stay in college long. After one semester, she left and began working a series of jobs. First, she worked in a law firm with a cousin doing clerical tasks. Later, she worked at J.C. Penney and as a waitress at T.G.I. Friday's.

Around this time, DeGeneres became involved in stand-up comedy, and she performed at small clubs and several coffee houses in New Orleans. Soon, by the early 1980s, DeGeneres began to tour nationally on the comedy circuit.

Life's Work

After her sitcom, *Ellen* (1994–98) and *The Ellen Show* (2001–2), Ellen DeGeneres launched *The Ellen DeGeneres Show* in 2003. The show won the Daytime Emmy Award for Outstanding Talk Show in 2004 and 2006–8.

Ellen DeGeneres (Wikimedia Commons)

DeGeneres also won People's Choice Awards in 2005–8 for Favorite Daytime Talk Show Host and Favorite Funny Female Star. The year 2003 was also marked by the release of the popular animated Pixar film *Finding Nemo*, in which DeGeneres voiced Dory the fish, Marlin's friend. She also performed her stand-up comedy routine "Here and Now" in cities across the United States.

In addition to her success as a comedian and television personality, DeGeneres has also found success in 2003 as an author. Her second book, *The Funny Thing Is. . .* , a collection of comedic essays, became a *New York Times* best seller. Since then she has published a third book, *Seriously . . . I'm Kidding* (2011).

DeGeneres's humorous views about everyday experiences—evident both in her stand-up comedy and in her books—and her experience as a talk show host have helped her land prominent emcee positions, most notably as host of the Emmy Awards (2001) and the Academy Awards (2007). She also judged one season of Am*erican Idol*, the popular reality television singing competition, in 2009.

In 1997, she famously came out of the closet on her television show as a lesbian. She began dating actor Portia de Rossi in 2004. The couple wed on August 16, 2008, in

California, where same-sex marriage had recently been legalized. Both DeGeneres and de Rossi have worked for the cause of animal rights. In 2009, the couple were jointly awarded the Wyler Award, a Humane Society honor given to public figures who publicly support animal rights.

In 2014 DeGeneres and Warner Bros. released ellentube, a website and iOS app that features video clips from the show and its fans. DeGeneres voiced the starring role of Dory in *Finding Dory*, the 2016 sequel to 2003's *Finding Nemo*. Also in 2016, she was awarded a Presidential Medal of Freedom by President Barack Obama.

> "*Here are the values that I stand for: honesty, equality, kindness, compassion, treating people the way you want to be treated and helping those in need. To me, those are traditional values.*"

SIGNIFICANCE

The *Ellen DeGeneres Show* has received over thirty-five Daytime Emmy Awards, and maintains an audience of 2.5 million people per episode. Critics have praised DeGeneres for her ability to bring humor to everyday experiences. DeGeneres' honesty and self-awareness around both her sexual orientation and her early experiences as a teenager have helped others facing similar challenges. Additionally, her animal rights advocacy has brought nationwide awareness to the issue.

Gina Kuchta

FURTHER READING

Albiniak, Page. "Ellen DeGeneres Launches New Digital Video Site, ellentube." *Broadcasting & Cable*. NewBay Media, 30 Oct. 2014. Web. 27 June 2016.

DeGeneres, Ellen. *Seriously . . . I'm Kidding*. New York: Grand Central, 2011. Print.

"Ellen DeGeneres." Celebrity Central: Top 25 Celebs. *People*. Time, Inc., 2012. Web. 9 July 2012.

"Ellen DeGeneres Molested as Teen." *CBS News*. CBS News Entertainment, 11 Feb. 2009. Web. 6 Aug. 2012.

James, Meg. "For Ellen DeGeneres, Things Are Going Along Nicely." *Los Angeles Times*, 5 Apr. 2013. Web. 27 June 2016.

DUKE ELLINGTON

Jazz musician, composer, and bandleader

Born: April 29, 1899; Washington, D.C.
Died: May 24, 1974; New York, New York
Also known as: Edward Kennedy Ellington
Areas of Achievement: Music and film

In a career spanning nearly sixty years, Ellington was one of the most influential and innovative figures in jazz. The scope of his musical work ranged from orchestral swing and big band to bebop and cool jazz. He composed and arranged jazz standards and large symphonic jazz works.

EARLY LIFE

Edward Kennedy Ellington was born in 1899 in Washington, D.C., during the heyday of ragtime. He was the son of Daisy Kennedy Ellington and James Edward Ellington. He was exposed to the piano and different kinds of music at an early age since both of his parents played; his mother opted for parlor standards while his father preferred classical music. Ellington was raised at home by

Duke Ellington (Wikimedia Commons)

his mother and her parents while his father worked as a butler for Dr. Middleton F. Cuthbert, a white physician. Ellington was known as a mild-mannered and even-tempered young man with exceptional manners, fine command of language, and a love of elegant clothes and luxury, probably because of his father's influence. These personality characteristics led to his nickname, "Duke," and served him well later on as an entertainer, a bandleader, and artistic collaborator. He began piano lessons early, although he did not favor studying music until his teens, just after hearing rag and stride pianists perform.

> "How can anyone expect to be understood unless he presents his thoughts with complete honesty?"

At age fifteen, Ellington took a job as a soda jerk in the Poodle Dog Café. "Soda Fountain Rag," also known as "Poodle Dog Rag," may have been his first composition (a year earlier, he may have written some incidental music by ear to accompany a street magician). This experience led quickly to his first arranging experience: He experimented with changing the rhythm of the song within the parameters of ragtime style and then rewriting the song in the style of a waltz, tango, and other kinds of dance music. Ellington focused on music (including music theory), particularly piano, under Dunbar High School music teacher Henry Lee Grant. He also continued playing ragtime by ear and eventually played in nightclubs and cafés throughout Washington, D.C. For employment reasons, Ellington also studied commercial art. He turned down an art scholarship to the Pratt Institute in Brooklyn and then dropped out of the Armstrong Manual Training School to pursue his music career. In the meantime, he studied briefly at Howard University and worked gigs as a solo pianist and with small ensembles. In 1917, Ellington established his first music ensemble, the Duke's Serenaders, who played for both white and black audiences. The ensemble broke up when the drummer, Sonny Greer, joined the Wilber Sweatman Orchestra in New York City. Ellington decided to move there, too—not to follow Greer, but because he was drawn to the Harlem Renaissance and its potential to help him develop as a bandleader, composer, musician, and artist.

Ellington's Contributions to Jazz

Many of Duke Ellington's compositional techniques influenced the evolution of jazz. In his swing band years, Ellington wrote songs with specific soloists in mind and used a collaborative compositional process with members of his orchestra. When a soloist left his orchestra, Ellington arranged or rearranged a song to feature the strengths of other soloists; thus his orchestra rarely had an excuse to stop playing a particular song. This practice led to renewed popularity for certain songs and demonstrated Ellington's and his orchestra's tastes in musical styles, textures, and harmonies. Major hits that appeared in different guises throughout his life included "Mood Indigo" (1931), "It Don't Mean a Thing (If It Ain't Got that Swing)" (1932), "Sophisticated Lady" (1933), and "Solitude" (1934). Other orchestras and musicians also rearranged Ellington's standards into hits of their own. Ellington led one of the first mixed race orchestras in the United States, and early on he appreciated the contributions to jazz by composers and musicians of all races and ethnicities. He employed orientalism and elements of Latin music that led to the development of Latin jazz, exemplified in "Caravan" (1936) and "Perdido" (1942). The sound of his orchestra in the 1940's, with more jagged melodic contours, produced original standards like "KoKo" (1940). These songs predated and inspired bebop and later cool jazz musicians (for example, Charlie Parker). Ellington astonished some jazz musicians and critics when he joined bebop founders Charles Mingus (bass) and Max Roach (drums) as pianist to record versions of his standards on *Money Jungle* (1962). Intended more for the western art music repertory, Ellington wrote several symphonic works and film scores. These included "Black, Brown, and Beige" (1943) and film music for *Anatomy of a Murder* (1959).

Ellington at the Aquarium club in New York city, circa 1946. (Library of Congress)

LIFE'S WORK

Although Ellington's first visit to New York was a failure and he returned to Washington, D.C., he moved back again to New York City in 1923. He followed Fats Waller's advice and joined Elmer Snowden's band, the Washingtonians (Greer was the band's drummer). That year, the Washingtonians played at the Hollywood Club and the Club Kentucky. Ellington took over as bandleader when Snowden left. Their songs included "East St. Louis Toodle-oo" (1926) and "Black and Tan Fantasy" (1927). Bubber Miley, who was well known for his growling trumpet sound as well as muting techniques, joined the orchestra briefly at this time. He worked with Ellington on composing "Black and Tan Fantasy." Their successful run at the Hollywood Club and Club Kentucky led to an engagement from 1927 to 1930 at the Cotton Club in Harlem, where Louis Armstrong and King Oliver performed. At the time, Ellington's orchestra included clarinetist Barney Bigard, alto saxophonist Johnny Hodges, trumpeter Cootie Williams, trombonist Juan Tizol, and drummer Greer. They recorded songs like "The Mooche" (1928) and "Mood Indigo" (1930). Their Cotton Club show became so famous that the orchestra was asked to appear in the Hollywood film *Check and Double Check* in 1930. Some of the lighter-skinned members were asked to wear dark makeup in the film. "Mood Indigo" became extremely popular worldwide.

From 1933 until 1939, the band toured the United States and overseas. Irving Mills, Ellington's agent and publisher, arranged the orchestra's travels so its members would spend their nights on trains rather than in hotels. (Ellington's contract agreement gave Mills authorship to his music as well as what would later be considered too large a share of Ellington's profits.) During the 1930's, members of Ellington's orchestra made hundreds of recordings in studios in New York and Los Angeles. Mills owned Master Records, which had a cheaper label known as Variety. Sound recordings that employed the entire orchestra were made for Master while ensemble recordings were destined for Master or Variety. During Ellington's career, other labels (such as Brunswick, Decca, RCA-Victor, Capitol, and Columbia) also recorded Ellington and his orchestra.

The period from 1932 to 1942 is widely considered Ellington's most creative decade. He continued to compose symphonic works as well as staged works and released a string of hits, including "It Don't Mean a Thing (If It Ain't Got That Swing)" (1932), "Solitude" (1934), and "Take the 'A' Train" (1941). "'A' Train" initiated a longtime collaboration with lyricist, arranger, composer, and pianist Billy Strayhorn. In the 1940's and 1950's, Ellington made several recordings for Victor. Some songs from this period are "Don't Get Around Much Anymore" (1942), "I'm Beginning to See the Light" (1945), "Come to Baby, Do" (1946), a new rendition of "Caravan" (1951) with percussive piano effects that mimicked the sound of a steam locomotive, and "Satin Doll" (1953). Although Greer, Hodges, and trombonist Lawrence Brown left in 1951, and Strayhorn followed soon afterward, Ellington and his orchestra managed a hit with "Satin Doll" and appeared in some of the earliest televised videos of an ensemble.

Ellington also drew critical acclaim for his group's performance of a new version of "Diminuendo and Crescendo in Blue" (composed in 1937 but this time featuring tenor saxophonist Paul Gonsalves) at the 1956 Newport Jazz Festival. Ellington signed a contract with Columbia, which released the recording of the performance a year later. The Newport appearance and the LP, which became a best seller, led to an enthusiastic reception at the first Monterey Jazz Festival in 1958. On his return, Ellington went on a tour of the United States that included participating in United Service Organizations (USO) musical productions such as *Rolling Along* (1959) at Fort Dix. With Strayhorn, who returned to the orchestra, Ellington scored the films *Anatomy of a Murder* (1959) and *Paris Blues* (1961).

Ellington reunited with musicians such as Brown, Tizol, and Williams in the early 1960's. He took his orchestra on worldwide tours yet managed to remain involved in the evolution of jazz. In 1962, he recorded *Money Jungle* with bassist Charles Mingus and drummer Max Roach. It received mixed reviews but proved to be a fascinating hybrid of hot jazz and bebop. It also demonstrated that Ellington was still a fine pianist. His final recordings included lengthy works like *The Far East Suite* (1966), *New Orleans Suite* (1970), and *The Afro-Eurasian Eclipse* (1971).

Ellington died from pneumonia as a result of lung cancer on May 24, 1974. Two years after his death, singer Stevie Wonder had a hit with "Sir Duke," a tribute to Ellington.

Significance

Ellington influenced countless jazz composers and musicians by assuming the role of mentor, bandleader, manager, collaborator, and friend. His musical output consisted of thousands of compositions; many were jazz standards, award-winning songs, and larger works. His orchestral hits that ranked number one on U.S. charts included "Three Little Words" (1930), "Cocktails for Two" (1934), and "I Let a Song Go Out of My Heart" (1938). His symphonic works gave the lasting impression that jazz could be serious music. Suites included *Reminiscing in Tempo* (1935), *Bluetopia* (1944), *Far East Suite* (1964), *New Orleans Suite* (1971), and *Togo Brava Suite* (1971). Notable film scores included *Symphony in Black* (1935), *The Asphalt Jungle* (1950), *Anatomy of a Murder* (1959), and *Paris Blues* (1961). In 1965, Ellington was nominated for the Pulitzer Prize in Music; he received a Pulitzer Prize Special Citation in Music in 1999. By 2010, thirteen of Ellington's sound recordings had earned Grammy Awards and nine had received Grammy Hall of Fame status in recognition of their historical significance. Ellington won the Grammy Lifetime Achievement Award in 1966.

Melissa Ursula Dawn Goldsmith

Further Reading

Dance, Stanley. *The World of Duke Ellington*. 2d ed. New York: Da Capo Press, 2000. Based on interviews with musicians who performed with Ellington. Dance was a jazz historian, critic, and friend of Ellington.

Ellington, Duke. *Music Is My Mistress*. Garden City, N.Y.: Doubleday, 1973. Ellington's autobiography reveals his perspective on his own life, compositional output, and music.

George, Don. *Sweet Man: The Real Duke Ellington*. New York: Putnam, 1981. This biography contains lyricist George's recollections of collaborating with Ellington, his close friend.

Hasse, John Edward. *Beyond Category: The Life and Genius of Duke Ellington*. New York: Simon & Schuster, 1993. A biography of Ellington's life and career, based on research in the Ellington archives at the Smithsonian Institute.

Howland, John. *"Ellington Uptown": Duke Ellington, James P. Johnson, and the Birth of Concert Jazz*. Ann Arbor: University of Michigan Press, 2009. Howland discusses Ellington's extended symphonic concert model and his cultural and artistic milieu during his years in New York.

Morton, John Fass. *Backstory in Blue: Ellington at Newport '56*. New Brunswick, N.J.: Rutgers University Press, 2008. This study is one of few detailed accounts of Ellington's late career as a conductor, composer, and festival concert performer.

Tucker, Mark, ed. *The Duke Ellington Reader*. New York: Oxford University Press, 1993. This anthology contains writings about Ellington in addition to the composer's own writings, especially during his early years.

Aretha Franklin

Singer

Born: March 25, 1942; Memphis, Tennessee
Died: August 16, 2018; Detroit, Michigan
Area of Achievement: Music: gospel, Music: rhythm and blues, Music: soul

Heralded as the "Queen of Soul," Franklin is best known for her powerful and emotional singing style, which features a wide vocal range and improvisational nuance. Her award-winning contributions to a wide variety of musical genres have helped to express and define the African American female experience.

Early Life

Aretha Louise Franklin (ah-REE-thah) was born in Memphis, Tennessee, to the Reverend Clarence La-Vaughn

Aretha Franklin (Wikimedia Commons)

Franklin, a prominent Baptist minister, and Barbara Siggers, a singer and nurse's aide who died early in her daughter's life. Franklin's upbringing was greatly influenced by her father's religious career and provided a foundation in gospel music and faith that would inform her adult life. After moving the family to Detroit during the 1940's, Clarence's charismatic preaching style increasingly drew the attention of dignitaries from the African American community, who traveled across the country to meet him and attend his services. The Franklin house was often filled with African American leaders and celebrities, including famous gospel singers Mahalia Jackson and Clara Ward, both of whom became close family friends and guided the young Franklin's musical training.

Franklin's musical talent was obvious, and by the age of twelve she was a pianist and featured soloist with the choir at her father's church. During the summers, she traveled the country with her father's gospel revival show, and it was on one of these tours that Franklin was first recorded by Chess Records, which regularly recorded her father's sermons. In 1956, her first album, *Songs of Faith*, was released by Chess. It featured the fourteen-year-old singing renditions of gospel songs and hymns. Although her early years were dedicated to devotional and spiritual song traditions, Franklin gradually turned her attention to the more widely popular rhythm-and-blues styles of secular singing, especially those popularized by Sam Cooke and Dinah Washington.

This period of musical transition also saw a number of personal—often difficult—changes in the singer's life, including the birth of her first two children by the time she was seventeen years old. Franklin dropped out of high school to care for them. She continued to create music, however, and after leaving her children in the care of her Detroit family, in 1960 she moved to New York City to pursue a career in music.

"*Being the Queen is not all about singing, and being a diva is not all about singing. It has much to do with your service to people. And your social contributions to your community and your civic contributions as well.*"

Life's Work

Soon after moving to New York, Franklin signed with Columbia Records. Under the guidance of producer John Hammond, she released her first secular album, *Aretha* (1961), which sold poorly. Over the next six years with Columbia, Franklin recorded a dozen albums in a variety of secular genres, including rhythm and blues, pop, and jazz, although she did not release any significant hits. She earned some status in the national rhythm-and blues scene because many of her songs were popular on the radio, although the records did not sell well. Her popularity also was helped by her public performances, including those on television, at clubs and festivals, and at major civil rights events, including fund-raising concerts with Martin Luther King, Jr., another friend of the Franklin family.

With her musical reputation growing, Franklin remained focused on her career. In late 1966, under the supervision of her manager and husband of five years, Ted White, she began working with producer Jerry Wexler at Atlantic Records, a label known for its focus on rhythm-and-blues sound. Franklin started recording her first Atlantic album in Muscle Shoals, Alabama, on January 24, 1967, and immediately enjoyed more musical and creative freedom than she had with Columbia, including being able to write, improvise, and play her songs at the piano while she sang, backed by the studio rhythm band. However, she returned to New York after recording only one full song because of a conflict between White and the studio.

Wexler moved the studio's band to New York and continued to work on Franklin's album. In the meantime, he released the sole recorded song from Muscle Shoals, "I Never Loved a Man (the Way I Love You)," which became Franklin's first commercial hit. With the addition of the female gospel group the Sweet Inspirations as background singers, the finished album *I Never Loved a Man the Way I Love You* (1967) also contributed other important U.S. hits, including "Respect" and "Baby, I Love You."

"Respect" was originally recorded by Otis Redding; Franklin covered the song in an improvised soul style on February 14, 1967. "Respect" was her most famous and enduring song; its immediate significance went beyond its financial success as a number-one hit on both the pop and rhythm-and-blues charts. The song's lyrical message, delivered in a powerful vocal style, addressed the contemporary struggle over the inherent equality of all people, regardless of race or gender, and it was adopted as an anthem by the Civil Rights and women's movements.

Building on her rapid success, Franklin's second Atlantic album, *Aretha Arrives* (1967), was released immediately, and three more albums followed in 1968. With each album gaining in popularity, Franklin became emblematic of the soul movement, a major contemporary force in African American popular music, and she was increasingly honored as a featured performer at major events such as the 1968 Democratic National Convention and the funeral of King.

With popularity, however, came unwelcome scrutiny of Franklin's personal life. Particularly devastating to Franklin was a profile published in *Time* magazine (June 28, 1968) that repeated sensational rumors and misinformation about the singer's mother and marriage. Although Franklin's marriage did dissolve soon after the article was published, its portrayal of White as abusive and the claim that her mother abandoned the family when Franklin was six years old led her to deeply distrust popular media. She subsequently refrained from giving much of her career. However, she still garnered ample media attention, especially for her fashion and lavish stage attire.

The early 1970's were a successful period for Franklin, who produced five more albums, including *Young, Gifted, and Black* (1971), an exuberant expression of African American pride. Franklin then returned to her gospel roots, releasing *Amazing Grace* the next year. The double album recorded in a church, featured gospel singer James

Franklin sings "My Country 'Tis Of Thee'" at the U.S. Capitol during the 56th presidential inauguration in Washington, D.C., January 20, 2009. (Wikimedia Commons)

Cleveland and the Southern California Community Choir and quickly became the best-selling gospel album of its time. Both albums won Grammy Awards in 1972; by 1974, Franklin had won the Grammy Award for Best Female R&B Vocal Performance an unprecedented eight years in a row.

With her popularity waning, Franklin switched to Arista Records in 1980 in hopes of reviving her career. Her work with Arista proved successful and was aided by her appearance in the popular film *The Blues Brothers* (1980), in which she performed her 1968 hit "Think." Her work throughout the 1980's focused on collaborations with other artists and further gospel inspired music. After not recording for much of the 1990's, she released *A Rose Is Still a Rose* in 1998. On that album, her use of urban contemporary music in combination with her soulful and expressive vocal style affirmed her ability to adapt her music to changing times.

Franklin continued working on new musical projects throughout the 2000s. She recorded an album under her own label, Franklin Records, in 2011, *Aretha: Falling Out of Love,* and performed on the Late Show with David Letterman in 2014. In December of 2015, Franklin performed "A Natural Woman," at a Kennedy Center Honors presentation honoring singer and songwriter Carole King. In November 2017 she released the album "A Brand New

> ### Franklin's Awards and Honors
>
> By the mid-1990's, Aretha Franklin's long career and classic songs had made her one of the most honored artists in the history of recorded music. She began accumulating accolades in 1967, when she received two Grammy Awards for "Respect" and numerous Female Singer of the Year honors. From 1967 to 2010, Franklin received seventeen total Grammy Awards, including a Grammy Legends Award (1990), and Lifetime Achievement Award (1994), which made her the most decorated female artist in Grammy history. She also received numerous awards from the American Music Association and was the first woman inducted into the Rock and Roll Hall of Fame (1987). Franklin also recieved a number of honorary doctoral degrees in music and musicology, including one conferred by Yale University in 2010. Later in her career, Franklin received commendations for her work's influence on awareness of racial and social issues. She accepted the Presidential Medal of Freedom from President George W. Bush in 2005, and the Vanguard Award from the National Association for the Advancement of Colored People in 2008. She also performed at the inaugurations of Presidents Jimmy Carter (1977), Bill Clinton (1993), and Barack Obama (2009).

Me" with the Royal Philharmonic Orchestra which included archived recordings of Franklin. The album peaked at number 5 on the Billboard Top Classical Albums chart.

Franklin passed away on August 16, 2018 at the age of 76 due to complications from pancreatic cancer. Her memorial service was held at New Bethel Baptist Church in Detroit, and her "Homegoing Service" was attended by dozens of celebrities and politicians, including Ariana Grande, Bill Clinton, Rev. Al Sharpton, Chaka Khan, Stevie Wonder, and Smokey Robinson. Franklin was interred at Woodlawn Cemetery in Detroit.

SIGNIFICANCE

Franklin is one of the most highly regarded singers of her time. Although her prominent family provided her with many social and artistic opportunities, the personal challenges she overcame throughout her career lent her music a sense of experience and hope, rooted in faith and hard work. While she was never overtly political or activist in nature, she emerged as a major voice of the Civil Rights era. The timeless appeal and significance of Franklin's music was evident in her performance of "My Country, 'Tis of Thee" at the inauguration of the first African American U.S. president, Barack Obama, in 2009. The following year, Franklin was awarded an honorary degree from Yale University and she received an honorary Doctor of the Arts degree from Harvard University in 2014. In August of 2012, Franklin was inducted into the Rock and Roll Hall of Fame, becoming the first woman to be inducted by the organization. She is regularly recognized by music journalists and magazines as one of the most influential artists in history.

Danielle M. Kuntz, updated by Micah L. Issitt

FURTHER READING

Awkward, Michael. *Soul Covers: Rhythm-and-Blues Remakes and the Struggle for Artistic Identity.* Durham, N.C.: Duke University Press, 2007. Includes a chapter on Franklin's tribute album to Dinah Washington and examines it in the context of African American rhythm-and-blues artists' struggle for authenticity

Bego, Mark. *Aretha Franklin: The Queen of Soul.* Cambridge, Mass.: Da Capo Press, 2001. Provides a detailed account of Franklin's life and career and is based on personal interviews with the singer.

Franklin, Aretha, and David Ritz. *Aretha: From These Roots.* New York: Villard, 1999. Franklin chronicles her life and rise to musical fame in this autobiography.

Nathan, David. *The Soulful Divas.* New York: Billboard Books, 1999. Profiles the personal and professional lives of seventeen African American female musicians, including Franklin, and focuses on their collective contributions to soul and rhythm-and-blues music.

Werner, *Craig. Higher Ground: Stevie Wonder, Aretha Franklin, Curtis Mayfield, and the Rise and Fall of American Soul.* New York: Crown, 2004. Describes the contributions of Franklin and other soul musicians to the Civil Rights movement.

Katharine Hepburn

Actor

Born: May 12, 1907; Hartford, Connecticut
Died: June 29, 2003; Fenwick, Connecticut
Area of Achievement: Film, theater and entertainment

With a career spanning most of the twentieth century, Hepburn embodied wit, independence, and charm. She was one of the first actors to break down Hollywood's stereotype of women, facing not only a shocked public but also condemnation from film critics. Nevertheless, she was a model of grit and beauty throughout her career.

Early Life

Katharine Hepburn was born the second of six children of Katharine "Kit" Hepburn and Thomas Hepburn. Her mother was part of a well-known New England family, the Houghtons. Encouraged by her dying mother to acquire an education for herself and her sisters, Kit eventually earned a bachelor's degree from Bryn Mawr (1899) and a master's degree from Radcliffe (1900). Houghton's upbringing encouraged her to value independence, education, and social responsibility, three qualities that dominated her life. Because of her mother's interests, Hepburn had a childhood that was characterized by her family's deep involvement in many social causes of the day: the suffrage movement, the presence of brothels in their home city of Hartford and the associated spread of sexually transmitted diseases, and the efforts to provide safe birth control to women. The latter cause was led by Margaret Sanger, a friend of the Hepburns.

The Hepburn family's social conscience was not, however, guided solely by Kit. Thomas Hepburn was a young medical student when he first met Kit, and his sense of social awareness was as acute as hers. He chose to specialize in urology, an unmentionable subject in the polite society of that time. His practice led him to understand the horrors of syphilis, which was devastating the populations of all social classes. He chose to speak out about this taboo disease, at one point even paying for the printing and distribution of a play (*Damaged Goods*, by French dramatist Eugène Brieux) on the subject.

Another feature of Hepburn's childhood was her family's emphasis on physical activity. From ice-cold baths to swinging on a homemade trapeze strung from the trees to playing tennis and golf, the family's active life was the

Katharine Hepburn (Wikimedia Commons)

result in large part of Thomas's belief that a sluggish body led to a sluggish mind.

This closely knit family did suffer one early tragedy that also shaped Hepburn's growth: the accidental death by hanging of the oldest child, Tom, who was especially close to his sister Katharine. (For some seventy years afterward, she used Tom's birthday as her own, not revealing her true birthday until she published her autobiography in 1991.) Soon after her brother's death, Hepburn and her four siblings formed the Hepburn Players, an assortment of neighborhood children who put on performances with their own staging and direction. Even here, the family's social consciousness dominated: All proceeds from their production of Beauty and the Beast went to benefit the children of the Navajo Indians in New Mexico. Hepburn played the beast.

Like her mother and grandmother before her, Hepburn attended Bryn Mawr, where she took part in many of the school theatricals. Her parts ranged from playing a young man in one performance to playing Pandora in The Woman in the Moone. These experiences seem to have led to her decision to become an actor; just before the end of her senior year, she approached Edwin H. Knopf, a director of a local theater company, armed with a letter of introduction and asking for work. She graduated from

Bryn Mawr with a bachelor's degree in history and philosophy in 1928. The same year she married Ludlow Ogden Smith, a businessman. Although they divorced in 1934, they remained lifelong friends.

LIFE'S WORK

In 1928, just before her graduation from Bryn Mawr, Hepburn's persistence overrode Knopf's objections, and he hired her to play one of six ladies-in-waiting in a production of The Czarina (1928). Hepburn's early years on the stage were marked by many struggles and ups and downs. She was, as she later said, "a quick study": She could read a part wonderfully and impress the director. When she was hired, however, she lacked the training and experience to carry through a full performance.

> "*Love has nothing to do with what you are expecting to get - only with what you are expecting to give - which is everything.*"

In 1932, Hepburn played the supporting role of Antiope, an Amazon warrior, in the Broadway production of *The Warrior's Husband*. Her entrance staggered Broadway: Wearing a short tunic, a helmet, a breastplate, and leggings, and carrying a dead stag over her shoulder, Hepburn leapt down a steep ramp and onto a platform, where she hurled the stag at Hippolyta's feet. Her stature enhanced the effect: At five feet seven inches, she was tall for actresses of the era. The performance led to an offer of a screen test for Hepburn.

On the basis of this screen test, Hepburn was awarded her first role in Hollywood, playing Hillary Fairfield in the 1932 film *A Bill of Divorcement* with the famous John Barrymore. This role led to her instant fame, although her second film in Hollywood, Christopher Strong, was neither a popular nor a critical success. Hepburn's popularity returned after her third picture, *Morning Glory* (1933), for which she was awarded her first Academy Award for Best Actress. Hepburn's next film role, Jo in *Little Women* (1933), was critically acclaimed, but she was not to be part of another popular film until *Stage Door* in 1937.

After she received her Academy Award, Hepburn's appeal was so great that she was offered the lead in the stage production of *The Lake* (1934). The play began disastrously, with a hard director apparently trying to browbeat Hepburn into buying out her contract. In her famous review of the play, critic Dorothy Parker gibed that Hepburn had "run the gamut of emotions from A to B." Hepburn stuck to her work, however, and struggled so hard to improve each performance that, by the time the play closed, she was turning in excellent performances. Soon after this experience, Hepburn returned to Hollywood.

In 1938, Hepburn's second film with the talented Cary Grant, *Bringing up Baby*, was released. Though it was not enormously popular upon first release, *Bringing up Baby* later came to be considered the finest of the "screwball comedies" that were so popular during the 1920's and 1930's. In the meantime, her fiery outspokenness, cutting wit, and unconventional life soured many filmgoers of the times. Like her parents she was a firm liberal, and she was a feminist, advocating then socially unacceptable issues such as birth control. Moreover, her relation with the press was often hostile. Once, asked whether she and her husband had any children, she shot back, "Yes, two white and three colored." In her role in the unsuccessful Sylvia Scarlet she dressed as a boy during the majority of scenes, which made audiences uncomfortable. In 1938 she was voted "box office poison" in a film industry poll.

Hepburn persevered nevertheless and enjoyed success in dealing with Hollywood on her own terms, and despite her previous difficulty with *The Lake*, often returned to the stage. One of her most successful theatrical runs was in *The Philadelphia Story* (1939). As well as starring in the play, Hepburn was involved in all aspects of its production, from writing to casting to arranging financing. She was as deeply involved in the writing and production of the film version of *The Philadelphia Story* (1940), in which she repeated her role from the stage version. It did much to erase her reputation as "box office poison."

Another Hepburn film, *Woman of the Year*, was released in 1942. This picture marked Hepburn's first screen work with the superb actor Spencer Tracy, and it initiated what became the longest screen partnership in history as well as a legendary Hollywood romance. They went on to make nine films together, including such comedy classics as *Adam's Rib* (1949), *Pat and Mike* (1952), and *Desk Set* (1957). As critics have noted, most of the plots were variations on William Shakespeare's *The Taming of the Shrew*, pitting a sharp-tongued woman against a determined, often exasperated, but loving man. Hepburn and Tracy worked together until 1967, when their ninth and last film together, *Guess Who's Coming to Dinner*, was completed shortly before Tracy's death. Hepburn's work in this film earned for her a second Academy Award, which she believed must have been meant for both Tracy and herself.

Hepburn, Cary Grant & James Stewart perform The Philadelphia Story *for the Victory Theater radio program in 1942.* (Wikimedia Commons)

The African Queen (1951), made with Humphrey Bogart on location in Africa, saw the transition in Hepburn's career from a young Hollywood actor who the studios had tried to portray as a starlet to the mature Hepburn, who was able to show film audiences the confidence and competence she had possessed all along. As one of her biographers, Sheridan Morley, explained, with the role of the missionary Rose Sayer, Hepburn transcended the "battle-of-the-sexes . . . comedies . . . and the old high-society romps" of her early career to become a great dramatic actor. This picture (for which Bogart won the Academy Award for Best Actor) was a critical and financial success for all concerned. She received Academy Award nominations for her leading roles in *Summertime* (1955), *Rainmaker* (1956), and *Suddenly Last Summer* (1959, adapted from a play by Tennessee Williams).

The film that brought Hepburn the greatest critical acclaim was *Long Day's Journey into Night* (1962), in which she gave a compelling performance of a woman sinking into the depths of drug addiction. According to many critics, this performance was the pinnacle of her career, a review that was a bit premature, since Hepburn continued to work. She won her next two Academy Awards for Best Actress for her portrayal of Eleanor of Aquitaine in *The Lion in Winter* (1968) and for her portrayal of Ethel Thayer in *On Golden Pond* (1981). In the meantime, she continued to take leading parts on stage, for instance in *The Madwoman of Chaillot* (1969), Euripides' *The Trojan Women* (1971), and Edward Albee's *A Delicate Balance* (1973). Also in 1973, she appeared in a television production of Williams's *The Glass Menagerie* and in 1975 earned an Emmy Award for her leading role in *Love Among the Ruins*. Her role as a straitlaced spinster in the cowboy film *Rooster Cogburn* (1975), playing opposite John Wayne, was widely popular with fans, if not with critics. All these performances clearly demonstrated to the studios and critics that the American public would not only pay to see but also relish quality films starring mature, competent actors.

Hepburn continued to act in films, plays, and television adaptations until 1994, when she appeared in the films *One Christmas*, *This Can't Be Love*, and *Love Affair*. In 1999 the American Film Institute placed her above all other woman actors of the last one hundred years in its Greatest American Screen Legends list. She continued an active life into her last years, riding her bicycle, gardening, and swimming in the ocean. On June 29, 2003, at the age of ninety-six, Hepburn died in Fenwick, her house in Old Saybrook, Connecticut. Memorial honors soon followed. The lights of Broadway were dimmed for an hour, and in 2004, New York City redesignated the corner of East 4th Street and 2nd Avenue as Katharine Hepburn Way. In 2006, Bryn Mawr College dedicated the Katharine Houghton Hepburn Center and inaugurated the Katharine Hepburn Medal, first awarded to actors Lauren Bacall and Blythe Danner.

Significance

Throughout her career, Hepburn pushed her own limits and those of the motion picture industry and the medium of film. Her stage work, from her struggles with *The Lake* to her success in *The Philadelphia Story* to her frequent Shakespearean roles, bear testimony to her determination not to rest on her laurels. Her four Academy Awards for Best Actress attest to her talent as an actor and to the admiration of her colleagues.

Although initially audiences did not know what to make of her early performances (which were far from Hollywood stereotypes of women), and despite more than her share of critical attacks, Hepburn would come to epitomize honesty, independence, and intelligence, and she was idolized by millions of filmgoers. Hepburn's biographer, Gary Carey, quoted Richard Watts of the *Herald Tribune* as saying, "Few actresses have been so relentlessly assailed by critics, wits, columnists, magazine editors, and other professional assailers over so long a period of time, and even if you confess that some of the abuse had a certain amount of justification to it, you must admit she faced it gamely and unflinchingly and fought back with courage and gallantry."

Hepburn also would "fight back" in her films with Tracy. Indeed, she believed that in her films with Tracy, the two actors epitomized a type of American couple that appealed to the nation from the 1940's on: Both intelligent and forceful, the woman challenging the man with her wit. The man might be the ultimate boss, but his kingdom, as Hepburn would say, "isn't an easy kingdom for him to maintain."

Katherine Socha

FURTHER READING

Andersen, Christopher. *Young Kate*. New York: Henry Holt, 1988. Based on conversations with Hepburn, this book chronicles her parents' lives, vividly recounts what it was like to grow up in the Hepburn family, and provides a detailed family chronology as well as a bibliography of supplementary references.

Berg, A. Scott. *Kate Remembered*. New York: G. P. Putnam's Sons, 2003. Berg relates anecdotes and opinions that he collected during twenty years of conversations with Hepburn.

Carey, Gary. *Katharine Hepburn: A Hollywood Yankee*. New York: St. Martin's Press, 1983. After a brief discussion of her childhood and college years, this book provides a general survey of Hepburn's career from her first theater job through her work in the early 1980's. Includes a chronology of her films from her first in 1932 to On Golden Pond in 1981.

Considine-Meara, Eileen. *At Home with Kate: Growing Up in Katharine Hepburn's Household*. Hoboken, N.J.: John Wiley & Sons, 2007. Written by the daughter of Hepburn's cook of thirty years, this memoir tells intimate inside stories about Hepburn's life at home, complete with the recipes that she loved and numerous photographs, movie stills, and cartoons.

Hepburn, Katharine. *The Making of "The African Queen": Or, How I Went to Africa with Bogart, Bacall, and Huston and Almost Lost My Mind*. New York: Alfred A. Knopf, 1987. This is Hepburn's writing at its best as she recalls the making of The African Queen. Discusses her first awareness of the project through the trials of working on location in Africa, the completion of the film in the studio, and Bogart's Academy Award.

---. *Me: Stories of My Life*. New York: Alfred A. Knopf, 1991. This book lives up to its title, providing stories of Hepburn's life from childhood through 1990. Written in a warm, readable, almost telegraphic style, the book discusses her career, her films and plays, and her family. Includes many photographs.

Kanin, Garson. *Tracy and Hepburn*. New York: Viking Press, 1971. This personal chronicle of the work and lives of Hepburn and Tracy is based on the author's long friendship with both and tells many stories of their lives together, both privately and professionally.

Mann, William J. *Kate: The Woman Who Was Hepburn*. New York: Henry Holt & Sons, 2006. Based upon interviews with Hepburn's family and friends, Mann traces the evolution of her career as a movie star, the various artistic and ideological influences on her, and her complicated, much misrepresented love affair with Tracy.

Morley, Sheridan. *Katharine Hepburn*. Boston: Little, Brown, 1984. This thorough retrospective of Hepburn's career, written by the son of one of her former colleagues, provides detailed information about the progress of Hepburn's career and each of her pictures. A filmography provides thorough documentation (to 1984) of her films, television work, and her stage work.

BILLIE HOLIDAY

Jazz singer

Born: April 7, 1915; Philadelphia, Pennsylvania
Died: July 17, 1959; Manhattan, New York City
Area of achievement: Music: jazz

One of the most famous jazz singers of all time, Holiday influenced generations of musicians. Her recording of "Strange Fruit" was a landmark in the civil rights struggle. After her death, she became an almost mythic figure whose music remained relevant into the twenty-first century.

EARLY LIFE

On April 7, 1915, Billie Holiday was born to Sarah (Sadie) Julia Harris, a domestic worker, in Philadelphia, Pennsylvania. Although he was not listed on the birth certificate, her father was Clarence Holiday, a professional

Billie Holiday (Library of Congress)

guitarist who later played in Fletcher Henderson's orchestra.

Holiday was taken to her mother's hometown of Baltimore to be cared for by Martha Miller, the mother-in-law of Sadie Harris's half-sister. Holiday's mother returned to Baltimore in 1918 but Holiday moved constantly among various caretakers until the age of nine. In 1924, Holiday and her mother moved into a house together. In January, 1925, Juvenile Court found Holiday guilty of truancy and sent her to a reform school, the Catholic House of the Good Shepherd. After she was released on parole in October, 1925, she returned to live with her mother. In December, 1926, eleven-year-old Holiday was raped by a neighbor and sent back to the reform school. She was released in February, 1927.

Holiday's mother moved to New York in 1928. Holiday joined her the next year and they lived in Florence Williams's brothel in Harlem. After a night raid in May, 1929, Holiday and her mother were arrested for prostitution and Holiday was sentenced to one hundred days on Welfare Island. After her release in October, 1929, she moved in with her mother in Brooklyn. Around this time, Holiday realized that she wanted to become a professional jazz singer. She sang along with recordings by Louis Armstrong and Bessie Smith and was greatly influenced by their music. She and saxophonist Kenneth Holton began performing together. In early 1930, she got her first professional engagement at the Grey Dawn cabaret in Queens. For her stage name, she took her father's surname and adopted "Billie" in honor of silent film actor Billie Dove.

In 1930, Holiday and her mother moved back to Harlem, where Holiday worked as a waitress and sang for tips in various clubs. Although she could not read music and had no formal music instruction, she became well-known in jazz circles for her intense emotional expression, subtle inflections, and unique rhythms.

Life's Work

Holiday was discovered in 1933 at Monette's Supper Club in Harlem by legendary music critic and producer John Hammond. At her first commercial recording session, she recorded "Riffin' the Scotch" and "Your Mother's Son-in-Law" accompanied by Benny Goodman, Gene Krupa, Buck Washington, and others.

In 1937 and early 1938, Holiday sang with Count Basie's Band, which, as the embodiment of the Kansas City style of jazz, was the ideal musical environment for her singing. In particular, the very light, driving rhythm section, in which only the bass and acoustic guitar maintained the quarter-note pulse, created space for the improvisers and vocalists. The musicians were very flexible because they did not rely heavily on notation and were able to modify the arrangements easily. In Holiday's case, this encouraged her to refine another of her trademark techniques; the manipulation of timing. She could hold back or push forward to add a dimension of excitement to her delivery and use her own sense of tempo to return to the exact metrical point in the original phrase.

Aside from Basie himself, one of her most important colleagues in the Kansas City style was tenor saxophonist Lester Young, who had developed a cool, almost detached approach that was the perfect complement to Holiday's vocal phrasing. Young, nicknamed "Prez" for "President," proclaimed Holiday "Lady Day." The moniker was in keeping with the jazz community's practice of creating its own royalty, which included a Duke, Count, and Lady holding court.

Another Holiday technique was the use of inflections to alter or even subvert the lyrics of a song. Her melodic embellishments could turn an assertion into a question or add a sudden fall to turn a cheerful, silly rhyme into a mournful sob. Using these techniques, she was even able to transform even trite songs into masterpieces of expression.

Also, as an improviser, Holiday would vary her techniques with each performance, depending on her mood, the audience, and the other musicians. Her fellow musicians deeply respected her skills, even though she did not attempt to imitate their own practices by scat singing like many other jazz vocalists.

In March, 1938, Holiday joined Artie Shaw's allwhite band, but left in December after encountering racism on tours. In 1939, she headlined at Barney Josephson's Cafe Society, a racially integrated nightclub in Greenwich Village. Holiday boldly risked ruining her career by by singing "Strange Fruit," an emotional song condemning racial lynching. Abel Meeropol, a Jewish high school teacher, had written the song to protest the horrors of lynching, and graphically described the gruesome killings. "Strange Fruit" became one of Holiday's signature songs and a part of all her live performances. Because of its controversial content, her label, Columbia Records, would not record the song. Holiday recorded "Strange Fruit" for Commodore Records, an alternative jazz label, and the song became one of her best-selling classics, eventually selling over a million copies. In 1978, Holiday's "Strange Fruit" was inducted into the Grammy Hall of Fame. In 2002, the Library of Congress added her recording to the National Recording Registry.

Holiday at Club Bali in Washington with Al Dunn (drums), Bobby Tucker (piano) and Benny Fonsville (bass). (Wikimedia Commons)

> "*No two people on earth are alike, and it's got to be that way in music or it isn't music.*"

In 1939, Holiday introduced a second masterpiece, "God Bless the Child," which she had cowritten with Arthur Herzog, Jr. Her recording of the song on the Okeh label was inducted into the Grammy Hall of Fame in 1976. The song inspired a children's book, *God Bless the Child* (2002), illustrated by the celebrated African American artist Jerry Pinkney.

In 1944, Holiday left Columbia Records to sign with Decca Records. During the 1940's, she became addicted to heroin but continued to perform. In 1946, she headlined at New York's Town Hall and starred with Louis Armstrong in the film *New Orleans*. In May, 1947, she was arrested on drug charges, imprisoned, and released on March 16, 1948. On March 27, she performed a sold-out comeback concert at Carnegie Hall.

From 1952 to 1957, Holiday recorded more than one hundred songs for Verve Records, and in 1954, she toured Europe. In 1957, she appeared in the CBS television program, *The Sound of Jazz*, which included her highly acclaimed rendition of "Fine and Mellow" with instrumental solos from jazz greats Young, Gerry Mulligan, and Coleman Hawkins. She recorded the celebrated *Lady in Satin* on Columbia Records in 1958.

On May 31, 1959, Holiday was admitted into Metropolitan Hospital in Manhattan. On June 12, Holiday was charged with possessing narcotics and arrested in her hospital bed. She died on July 17, 1959. More than three thousand mourners attended her funeral at St. Paul the Apostle Roman Catholic Church on July 21, 1959.

Significance

Since her death, Holiday has become iconic. A classic in African American literature, Holiday's autobiography, *Lady Sings the Blues* (1956), supported the mythology of the tragic, talented, and tortured artist. In 1972, Diana Ross portrayed Holiday in *Lady Sings the Blues*, a film based on the autobiography.

Holiday moved audiences and revolutionized American popular music with her unique voice, innovative rhythms, and deeply personalized songs. She inspired generations of artists, including Lena Horne, Etta James,

Joni Mitchell, Dianne Reeves, Nina Simone, and Frank Sinatra.

Holiday overcame many gender and racial obstacles. She was one of the first black women to sing with a white band. Her signature song, "Strange Fruit," helped advance the Civil Rights movement and was named the Song of the Century by *Time* magazine in 1999.

In 1988, the band U2 recorded a tribute to Holiday, "Angel of Harlem." A commemorative postage stamp in her honor was issued on September 17, 1994. In 2000, she was inducted into the Rock and Roll Hall of Fame. A memorial statue erected in Baltimore in 1985 was rededicated in 2009 on the fiftieth anniversary of Holiday's death.

Alice Myers

Further Reading

Blackburn, Julia. *With Billie: A New Look at the Unforgettable Lady Day.* New York: Pantheon Books, 2005. More than 150 previously unpublished interviews with people who knew Holiday offer multiple perspectives on her personal and professional life. Illustrated. Index and bibliography.

Clarke, Donald. *Billie Holiday: Wishing on the Moon.* Cambridge, Mass.: Da Capo Press, 2002. Based on interviews from the 1970's, this readable, wellresearched biography covers Holiday's entire life. Illustrated and index.

Griffin, Farah Jasmine. *If You Can't Be Free, Be a Mystery: In Search of Billie Holiday.* New York: Ballantine Books, 2002. Challenging many Holiday myths and the stereotype of the emotional black female vocalist, the author presents a view of Holiday as a disciplined music virtuoso who overcame serious obstacles. Illustrated. Bibliography and index.

Holiday, Billie, and William Dufty. *Lady Sings the Blues.* New York: Harlem Moon, 2006. This is the fiftieth-anniversary edition of Holiday's candid autobiography, whose title was taken from one of her most famous songs. Includes revised discography.

Margolick, David. *Strange Fruit: The Biography of a Song.* New York: Ecco Press, 2001. A detailed account of a signature Holiday song, which attacked racial lynching and helped shape the Civil Rights movement. Illustrated and discography.

O'Meally, Robert G. *Lady Day: The Many Faces of Billie Holiday.* New York: Da Capo Press, 2000. This enthralling biography emphasizes Holiday's jazz artistry and is beautifully illustrated with photographs throughout the book. Discography and bibliography.

Nancy Kwan

Hong Kong-born actor

Born: May 19, 1939; Hong Kong
Full name: Nancy Ka Shen Kwan
Area of Achievement: Film, theater, dance

Nancy Kwan is an Asian American actor best known for her films The World of Suzie Wong and Flower Drum Song. Her success in Hollywood paved the way for future generations of Asian and Asian American actors.

Early Life

Nancy Ka Shen Kwan was born on May 19, 1939, in Hong Kong to Kwan Wing Hong and Marquita Scott. Her mother was a Scottish fashion model. Her father was a successful architect who escaped the 1941 Japanese invasion of Hong Kong with Nancy and her older brother, Ka Keung. When Nancy was two years old, her parents divorced, and her mother left for England. Her father remarried and had five more children with his second wife.

Nancy Kwan attended Maryknoll Convent School in Hong Kong and Kingsmoor School in England. Her love of dance led her to the Royal Ballet School in London,

Nancy Kwan (Wikimedia Commons)

where she appeared in performances of *Swan Lake* and *Sleeping Beauty* at Covent Garden.

During a summer recess, Kwan visited her uncle's studio, which was holding auditions for a film production, *The World of Suzie Wong* (1960). She was invited to do a screen test and later offered a contract with the project. When actress France Nuyen dropped out of the film, Kwan was cast as Suzie Wong, opposite actor William Holden. In 1961, she was nominated for a Golden Globe Award for her performance in the film.

> "*I don't have that [need] to prove myself. I have a passion to do good roles but luckily I don't have to do it for economic reasons. I'm not a big spender and I don't need a lot of frills.*"

Life's Work

After meeting Hollywood producer Ross Hunter at a party, Kwan was cast in her second film, *Flower Drum Song* (1961). *Flower Drum Song* was one of the first Asian American–themed musicals and introduced audiences to a new generation of Asian American actors. Featuring music and lyrics by Rodgers and Hammerstein and the talents of an all-Asian cast, *Flower Drum Song* became a huge commercial success and earned five Academy Award nominations. Although it and *The World of Suzie Wong* were criticized for portraying negative Asian stereotypes, Kwan was proud of her work.

In 1962, Kwan married Austrian businessman Peter Pock. The couple had a son, Bernhard Pock, in 1963, but later divorced. Kwan married filmmaker David Giler in 1970. In 1972, Kwan divorced again and moved to Hong Kong with her son to attend to her ailing father. After nearly eight years in Hong Kong, Kwan and her son returned to California. She married her third husband, Austrian filmmaker Norbert Meisel.

Kwan's professional legacy includes over eighty credits in film, television, theater, and other projects. In the late 1960s, she co-starred with leading men such as Tony Curtis in *Arrivederci, Baby!* (1966), Dick Van Dyke in *Lt. Robin Crusoe, U.S.N.* (1966), and Dean Martin in *The Wrecking Crew* (1969). On television, Kwan was a guest star on *Hawaii Five-O* (1968–69), *Kung Fu* (1974), *Fantasy Island* (1978), *Knots Landing* (1984), *The A-Team* (1986), and *ER* (2000), among other shows.

Kwan's beauty and charm captivated international media. She appeared on over sixty magazine covers, including *Life*, *Esquire*, *Parade*, and *Screen Stories*. In 1963, Vidal Sassoon was asked to cut Kwan's hair for *The Wild Affair*. The resulting bob, known as the Nancy Kwan cut, became a symbol of 1960s style.

Besides portraying Asian characters, Kwan also played a Tahitian in *Tamahine* (1964), a Native American in *The McMasters* (1970), and Caucasian American singer Joni Mitchell in her son's film, *Rebellious* (1997). With her production company, Nancy Kwan Films, she produced, directed, and wrote for numerous projects, including several television commercials and films in Asia.

During the 1980s, Kwan mostly worked in theater, television, and independent films. She appeared in infomercials for Oriental Pearl Cream and an instructional video about the martial-arts technique tai chi chuan. In 1993, she played a restaurant owner in the semi-biographical film *Dragon: The Bruce Lee Story*. However, Kwan turned down a role in the film *The Joy Luck Club*, based on the novel by Amy Tan, because the script criticized *The World of Suzie Wong*.

Kwan's theatrical work includes *A Midsummer Night's Dream*, *Arthur and Leila*, and *Who's Afraid of Virginia*

Kwan at the premiere of the 1961 film Flower Drum Song *with Kwan Wing Hong, her father, and her step-mother.* (Wikimedia Commons)

Woolf? In 2004, she reunited with James Shigeta from *Flower Drum Song* in the play *Love Letters*.

In 1996, Kwan's son died of AIDS. Kwan compiled his poems and drawings in the book *Celebration of a Life: Memories of My Son* (1997) and dedicated all proceeds from the project to AIDS organizations. Kwan is also active in the Asian American community and a spokesperson for the Asian American Voters Coalition.

Significance

Kwan has been honored as a pioneer in Hollywood. She received a 1961 Golden Globe for Most Promising Newcomer, a 2001 Historymakers Award from the Chinese American Museum, and a 2009 Lifetime Achievement Award from the City of Los Angeles. She was interviewed for Arthur Dong's documentary *Hollywood Chinese* (2007) and is the subject of the documentary *To Whom It May Concern: Ka Shen's Journey* (2010), directed by Brian Jamieson. Kwan's success in Hollywood and among the mainstream media helped pave the way for new generations of Asian and Asian American actors in the film industry. Kwan was the recipient of a Lifetime Achievement Award at the San Diego Asian Film Festival in 2011 and, in 2015, was also given a Lifetime Achievement Award from New York's Museum of Chinese in America.

Jenny Cho, updated by Micah L. Issitt

Further Reading

Hamamoto, Darrell Y. *Countervisions: Asian American Film Criticism*. Philadelphia: Temple UP, 2008. Print. Presents a discussion of Kwan's work in film.

Lee, Joann Faung Jean. *Asian American Actors: Oral Histories from Stage, Screen, and Television*. Jefferson: McFarland, 2000. Print. Contains a section in which Kwan reflects on her life and the film industry.

McGurn, William. "Suzie Wong Revisited." Wall Street Journal 4 June 1990: A10. Print. Features an interview with Kwan.

Pock, Bernie, and Nancy Kwan. *A Celebration of Life: Memories of My Son*. Sherman Oaks: N & N, 1997. Print. Contains Pock's poems and drawings and an essay by Kwan.

Bruce Lee

Actor and martial artist

Born: November 27, 1940; San Francisco, California
Died: July 20, 1973; Hong Kong
Also known as: Lee Siu Lung; Lee Xiao Long; Little Dragon
Areas of achievement: Film, martial arts

Best known for his exciting depiction of kung fu on screen, Bruce Lee realized his ambition of showing the world authentic Chinese martial-arts culture through his films. A gifted athlete, he created his own style of martial art, which he named jeet kune do (way of the intercepting fist).

Early Life

Bruce Lee was born in San Francisco on November 27, 1940, to Lee Hoi Chuen and Grace Lee. His father was a famous Cantonese opera star from Hong Kong, while his mother, Grace, was of German and Chinese descent. Grace Lee gave her son the name Lee Jun Fan, which means "to return again," because she thought that he would one day return to his place of birth.

Lee's father arranged for him to appear onscreen as a

Bruce Lee (Wikimedia Commons)

three-month-old for a scene in a Chinese movie filming in San Francisco. Shortly after this early screen appearance, the Lee family moved back to Hong Kong. There, young Bruce lived with his parents, brothers Peter and Robert, and sisters Agnes and Phoebe, as well as his father's sister-in-law and her five children. The family home was crowded, and Bruce spent a lot of time on the streets of Hong Kong as a teenager, hanging out with street gangs and looking for fights.

During the 1940s, Japan occupied Hong Kong. It is said that Lee would shake his fist and yell at Japanese war planes that would fly over his home. He would also pick fights with British schoolchildren from King George V School when he enrolled at nearby La Salle College at the age of twelve. Around this time, he told his parents that he needed to defend himself at school and asked to study kung fu. His mother agreed, and at thirteen, he began to study wing chun kung fu under the famous master Yip Man.

Lee had a considerable career as a child star in Hong Kong films. His first role in a Hong Kong film was in *The Beginning of a Boy* (1946) at the age of six. By the time he was eighteen years old, he had appeared in twenty films. He began using the stage name Lee Siu Lung at age eight, which means "little dragon" in Cantonese.

> "*To grow, to discover, we need involvement, which is something I experience every day—sometimes good, sometimes frustrating. No matter what, you must let your inner light guide you out of the darkness.*"

Lee attended St. Xavier Francis High School for a time, but when he was eighteen, his parents decided to send him to the United States to live with a family friend. He was an American citizen by birth, and his parents felt that he could have a better life in America. He arrived in San Francisco in 1959 and shortly after began working as a waiter in a restaurant owned by a family friend in Seattle, Washington.

Lee earned a high school diploma at Edison Technical School and enrolled at the University of Washington in May 1961 to study philosophy. There, Lee met his future wife, Linda Emery, when she was a student in his kung fu class. The couple married in August 1964. Although Lee was a good student, he would not make a career out of academics. He left the University of Washington at the end of his junior year.

LIFE'S WORK

Lee's real passion in life was the practice, study, and analysis of the art of Chinese kung fu. Lee decided that he would make his living teaching kung fu. Along with his friend and fellow Chinese martial artist James Lee, Bruce Lee established the Jun Fan Gung Fu Institute in Oakland, California, in June 1964.

Shortly after opening the kung fu school, Lee received a formal challenge from a Chinese martial artist. The challenge, written in Chinese, stated that if Lee lost the

---

Bruce Lee in *Enter the Dragon*

Enter the Dragon (1973) was the first Hollywood movie to star a Chinese actor. It was also the first joint production between a major Hollywood studio, Warner Bros., and a Hong Kong film company, Bruce Lee's Concord Productions. *Enter the Dragon* was the realization of Lee's lifetime ambition to become a Hollywood star. Lee's relationship with Warner Bros. began when he was developing a kung fu Western television series with the studio in 1971. While in Hong Kong, he was informed on December 7, 1971, by Warner Bros. that he would not get the lead in the series. Despite this, Warner Bros. said they were committed to developing a feature film project for Lee. They offered him the lead in *Enter the Dragon* while he was shooting *Game of Death* in late 1972. *Enter the Dragon* began filming in Hong Kong in early 1973. The film was directed by Robert Clouse, who was recommended by Bruce after he saw Clouse's independent film *Darker than Amber* (1970). *Enter the Dragon* was a true co-production, with American and Hong Kong crews working side by side to make the film. Lee choreographed all of the fight scenes. He worked closely with Robert Clouse, putting all his efforts into making the best film possible. He died shortly before the film premiered in the United States in August 1973. *Enter the Dragon* was a great success and is still considered one of the best martial arts films ever made.

fight, he had to close down his school and stop teaching white people. Lee felt that he should be able to teach kung fu to anyone who wanted to learn, regardless of race. Lee fought the challenger and won the match, although he was disappointed that it took him three minutes to beat his opponent.

Because of this encounter, Lee reappraised his approach to martial arts and, in the process, created his own style that he would later name jeet kune do, meaning "way of the intercepting fist" in Cantonese. Jeet kune do combines elements of Western boxing and fencing, as well as the high kicking of tae kwon do and other martial arts such as wing chun.

Lee received an invitation to perform at the International Karate Tournament in Long Beach, California, on August 2, 1964. Ed Parker, founder of American kenpo karate, organized the event. Lee's demonstration, which Parker recorded on sixteen-millimeter film, captivated the audience. Parker showed the footage to television producer William Dozier, who invited Lee come to Twentieth Century Fox Studios for a screen test in early 1965. Dozier was impressed with Lee and cast him as the character Kato in the television show *The Green Hornet*.

The Green Hornet only lasted one season, airing from 1966 to 1967, but it was important to Lee's life and career because it marked a professional shift from kung fu instruction to acting. Lee believed work in film and television would help him bring Chinese kung fu to the world. Lee's work in television brought him into contact with the world of Hollywood, and he soon became friends with actor Steve McQueen and screenwriter Sterling Siliphant. Lee went back to Hong Kong in 1970 to visit with his son, appearing on local television. While there, Lee was surprised to learn that he was recognized everywhere he went as Lee Siu Lung from *The Kato Show*. Hong Kong had been rerunning *The Green Hornet* as *The Kato Show* to great success.

Lee managed to get bit parts in American television and film after *The Green Hornet*, but he wanted to be a star in Hollywood with his own television series. With a growing family to support, Lee began looking for a starring role. He had begun to develop a Western-style kung fu series with Warner Bros. in 1971, with the idea that he would be the star. However, Lee began to grow frustrated with Hollywood when it looked as though he might not get the part.

Because of the excitement generated by Lee's return to Hong Kong, several producers wanted to make films with him for Hong Kong audiences. The Hong Kong film company Golden Harvest offered him a deal in 1971 to star in

Van Williams as the Green Hornet and Lee as Kato from The Green Hornet. *(Wikimedia Commons)*

two Chinese films. Lee took the offer and started filming of *The Big Boss* in Thailand in July 1971. The movie became the highest-grossing film in Hong Kong history, breaking the record held by the American musical *The Sound of Music* (1965). Shortly after the release of *The Big Boss*, actor David Carradine took the lead role in the Western kung fu series called *Kung Fu*. The television network felt that Lee was too Chinese to star in an American television series.

Lee's next film, *Fist of Fury* (1972), featured his character fighting against the occupying Japanese in Shanghai in 1908 and broke the sales record previously set by *The Big Boss*. Because of his success, Lee was able to form his own satellite company within Golden Harvest, Concord Pictures, in 1972. His first film for Concord Pictures was *Way of the Dragon* (1972), which he wrote, produced, and directed himself; it broke the Hong Kong box office record set by *Fist of Fury*.

Hollywood began taking notice of Lee's record-breaking success. In 1972, while Lee was shooting his next self-directed film, *The Game of Death* (1978), Warner Bros. offered him a starring role in *Enter the Dragon*, a film to be shot in Hong Kong. The film, which was released in the United States in August 1973 and earned over $200 million worldwide, would be the last of Lee's career.

On May 10, 1973, Lee suffered a blackout while recording dialogue for the Warner Bros. film. He went to California to receive a full medical checkup and received a clean bill of health. However, Lee suffered another blackout episode on July 20, 1973. Doctors were unable to revive him and pronounced him dead. The official cause of death was ruled a cerebral edema, or swelling of the brain. He left behind his wife, Linda, and their two children, Brandon and Shannon.

Significance

The influence of Bruce Lee is far reaching. He has become more than just a film star or a great martial artist. Lee's early death, the success of *Enter the Dragon*, and the popularity of kung fu as a martial art in entertainment all helped make Lee a cultural icon. Audiences all over the world identify with his films and with the heroic image of Lee triumphing over racism and oppression. Lee has become a hero to many Asian Americans for countering the offensive stereotypes of Asian people that existed in American popular culture before him. He helped introduce Hong Kong cinema to the world and remains the most popular Hong Kong actor of all time. Movie stars such as Jackie Chan and Jet Li have followed Lee's lead, helping to establish martial-arts movies as a separate genre of film.

Lee also continues to have a profound influence on the world of martial arts. Many of his fans are quick to point out that he was a genuine martial-arts practitioner, not just an actor. Jeet kune do, the system of martial arts envisioned by Lee, has practitioners throughout the world.

Eric Pellerin

Further Reading

Bordwell, David. "Two Dragons: Bruce Lee and Jackie Chan." *Planet Hong Kong: Popular Cinema and the Art of Entertainment*. Cambridge: Harvard UP, 2000. Print. Discusses Lee's significance to Hong Kong and international film. Includes recommended studies on Lee in the notes section.

Bowman, Paul. *Theorizing Bruce Lee: Film-Fantasy-Fighting-Philosophy*. New York: Rodopi, 2010. Print. A scholarly examination of the influence Lee had on film and popular culture through the frameworks of cultural theory and philosophy. Includes a filmography.

Clouse, Robert. *The Making of "Enter the Dragon."* Burbank: Unique, 1987. Print. Details how Warner Bros. made the film *Enter the Dragon* on location in Hong Kong. Includes over two hundred behind-the-scenes photos. Written by the film's director.

Lee, Bruce, and John Little, ed. *Jeet Kune Do: Bruce Lee's Commentaries on the Martial Way*. Boston: Tuttle, 1997. Print. A treatise on jeet kune do written by Lee in 1970.

---. *Letters of the Dragon: Correspondence, 1958–1973*. Boston: Tuttle, 1998. Print. Traces Lee's life in his own words, including his journey to San Francisco in 1959.

Lee, Linda. *The Bruce Lee Story*. Santa Clarita: Ohara, 1989. Print. A biography of Lee written by his widow.

Stan Lee

Comic book writer and editor

Born: December 28, 1922; New York City, New York
Died: November 12, 2018; Los Angeles, California
Also known as: Stanley Martin Lieber
Area of achievement: Entertainment

A driving force at Marvel Comics from 1939 until his retirement in the 1990s, Stan Lee revolutionized comic books in the early 1960s and paved the way for blockbuster superhero movies in the twenty-first century.

Early Life

Comic book impresario Stan Lee was born Stanley Martin Lieber on December 28, 1922 in New York City. His parents were both Romanian Jewish immigrants, and his father worked as a dress cutter. The Great Depression had a powerful impact on the family; they had lived on the Upper West Side and in Washington Heights before moving to a modest apartment in the Bronx, where Lee shared the apartment's only bedroom with his brother while his parents slept in the living room.

A teenager ambitious to better his circumstances, Lee was an enterprising youth who sought out opportunities in the city. While he was still in high school, he worked numerous part-time jobs in Manhattan: as an office boy, an obituary writer, a salesman, and a delivery boy. He graduated from high school early, when he was only sixteen years old. Young Lee aspired to become a serious

Stan Lee (Wikimedia Commons)

writer—a novelist. In the meantime, however, he had to earn a living.

> "*I used to be embarrassed because I was just a comic-book writer while other people were building bridges or going on to medical careers. And then I began to realize: entertainment is one of the most important things in people's lives. Without it they might go off the deep end. I feel that if you're able to entertain people, you're doing a good thing.*"

Life's Work

Thanks to a connection made through his uncle, Lee became an office assistant at a small comic-book company called Timely Comics, located in the iconic Empire State Building. By a curious coincidence, his first day on the job was also the day that the first issue of "Captain America" went to press. His job began small—filling inkwells, picking up lunch for the staff, and other errands. However, within two years, despite his young age, he was named an editor. The honor was a mixed blessing. Lee had ambitions to become a respectable writer, and comic books were distinctly low-class "pulp" publications marketed to children. Adopting the pseudonym Stan Lee for his first published effort (writing text for "Captain America Foils the Traitor's Revenge" in 1941), Lee planned on using his real name when he turned to serious writing.

Tracing Stan Lee's career in comics charts a virtual history of the comics industry itself. The company he worked for, Timely—later called Atlas Comics and later still, Marvel—was a leader in what historians of comics now call the Golden Age of comic books, a brief era that spanned the late thirties through the 1940s. A defining feature of Golden Age comics was the superhero. Superman was introduced to the world in 1938 by rival company Action Comics, while Timely had Captain America and others. In the 1940s, the industry was booming. By the 1950s, a new class of comics had appeared that featured gory tales, crime, and darker figures in place of the Golden Age's shiny superheroes—prominent among the newer comics were lines from the company EC with titles like "Tales From the Crypt." In 1954, Tennessee Democratic senator Estes Kefauver led a Senate subcommittee on the deleterious social and moral effects of comic books on children. The industry quickly reined itself in, but the result was a dramatic loss of readership. In this period, Lee struggled financially and considered leaving the industry entirely.

Comics in this period also faced competition from new media like television. The industry could have disappeared altogether. However, in the late 1950s, DC Comics spearheaded a revitalization of comic books by taking older superhero material—beginning with a reboot of the Flash in 1956—and updating its sensibility. Although DC Comics is credited with initiating what is called the "Silver Age" in comics history, it was Stan Lee's company—now called Marvel—that is most associated with the era. In 1961, working with fellow comics founding figure Jack Kirby, Lee's Marvel created in rapid succession the Fantastic Four, Spider-Man, the X-Men, and the Hulk.

At least three characteristics of Marvel's output in this period show Lee's trademark influence. First, the comics employed wit and clever language. Second, they often have a real-worldly focus. And third, Marvel's new style of superhero came with a backstory and a personal complexity that made them, as Lee once said, not quite three-dimensional characters but at least *two-dimensional*—in contrast to the one-dimensional superheroes of the 1930s.

Spider-Man is a case in point: he's a teenage nerd, he worries about girls, he gets melancholy, and so on. Also, throughout the 1960s, Lee and his team of writers and artists began developoing socially-conscious content that addressed timely themes like racial prejudice, the Vietnam War, and drugs.

Lee became the editorial director and the publisher of Marvel Comics in 1972. As the 1970s wore on, the potential for expanding the Marvel characters into media like television and movies became apparent. Successful animated television shows were developed for a number of Marvel characters such as Spider-Man, and a live-action television series based on the Hulk was also produced. In 1981, Lee moved to Los Angeles to pursue the television and movie angle further. It was slow going at first, with more failures than successes, but Lee stayed the course. In the 1990s, the animated Fox television series *X-Men*, which ran from 1992 to 1997, paved the way for the live-action blockbuster film, *X-Men* (2000). In the first decade of the twenty-first century, movie franchises based on the Marvel stable of characters were thriving. It was a long way from the relatively small world of 1950s comic books, whether measured in terms of cultural presence or the sums of money involved. Lee, who had been an employee at Marvel rather than its owner, negotiated with Marvel for a cut of the profits from their lucrative licensing deals with Hollywood studios. In 2005, Lee was awarded a ten million dollar settlement from Marvel.

Thanks to the popularity of the Marvel Comics Universe films in the twenty-first century, Lee became a greater celebrity in his old age than he had ever been as a younger man. The place of comic books—and of Marvel's superheroes—in American popular culture was secured and has become a widely-studied phenomenon. Thanks to changes in taste, in technological capacities, and perhaps in contemporary consciousness, films based on material originally intended for an adolescent audience are filmed today with surprising sophistication and intelligence. In some respects, a capping stone in this development, at least with respect to Marvel, is *Black Panther* (2018). The film was not only politically relevant and a watershed for African-American representation in film, it was the first superhero blockbuster ever to be nominated for a Best Picture at the Academy Awards. It joins Christopher Nolan's *The Dark Knight* (2008) as one of the most critically-acclaimed films of the superhero genre.

SIGNIFICANCE

Stan Lee wanted to become a novelist, and he spent much of life worried that the comics he shepherded into existence over a career of more than sixty years were cultural schlock. However, beginning in the early 1960s, Lee began to develop a more sophisticated and clever, if still childlike, style in comics that would have profound consequences. First, the newer comics explored politically relevant themes and presented characters with more complicated human lives than the first generation of superhero comics did. Marvel's innovations became foundational to the development of the graphic novel in the 1970s and 1980s, a genre that won respectability in 1986 when Art Spiegelman's *Maus* won a Pulitzer Prize. Second, Lee's expanding sense of what comics could be like, begun in the Marvel office at the Empire State Building, initiated a trajectory whose arc we are still tracing today with the increasing sophistication and widening appeal of superhero mythologies in twenty-first century American cinema.

More technically, Lee and his colleagues—especially Jack Kirby—developed an influential working model for developing comics now known as the Marvel method. The method is highly collaborative: rather than a writer presenting the artists with a full script to be illustrated, the

Lee in his studio, wearing his Army uniform. (Wikimedia Commons)

Lee shouting his motto, Excelsior!, at the 2015 San Diego Comic Con. (Wikimedia Commons)

writer begins the process by presenting a general outline of the story that the artists freely use to sketch panels. The final product is a result of one or more such cycles between the writers and artists. (Because of the collaborative nature of the process, Lee has come under fire from some in the industry for taking all the credit rather than sharing it.)

Stan Lee died on November 12, 2018 in Los Angeles. He may have never written a novel, but what he left behind has been far more influential on American culture than the work of the vast majority of successful novelists. Over and above the individual characters and story lines, it was Lee's efforts to develop smarter comics has had the most durability. And this work, like the Marvel method itself—and unlike novel writing—continues to take shape as a profoundly collaborative process.

Lee has delighted fans since 1989 by appearing in nearly every adaptation of Marvel comics, either on television or on film. In the Marvel Cinematic Universe he appeared in every movie since 2008. His last cameo will posthumously appear in *Avengers: End Game*, set to be released in 2019.

D. Alan Dean

Further Reading

Batchelor, Bob. *Stan Lee: The Man Behind Marvel.* New York: Rowman & Littlefield, 2017.

Harvey, Robert C. *The Art of the Comic Book: An Aesthetic History.* Jackson: University Press of Mississippi, 1996.

Heer, Jeet, and Kent Worcester. *A Comics Studies Reader.* Jackson: University Press of Mississippi, 2009.

Lee, Stan & George Mair. *Excelsior! The Amazing Life of Stan Lee.* New York: Simon & Schuster, 2002.

Dolly Parton

Singer-actor

Born: January 19, 1946; Pittman Center, Tennessee
Area of Achievement: Music, film, theater and entertainment, television

Parton, a highly successful crossover country and pop singer, brought women to the forefront of country music and also fashioned a successful career in pop music as well as in films and television.

Early Life

A true child of Appalachia, Dolly Parton was born in eastern Tennessee, in the foothills of the Smoky Mountains, the fourth of twelve children. The family's one room cabin had no electricity, running water, or indoor plumbing. Parton's father, Robert Lee Parton, was a farmer and construction worker, and although the Parton family was quite poor, this did not doom the young Parton to an unhappy life. Her mother, Avie Lee Owens Parton, was a singer of ballads and old-time songs, and as a very young child, Parton made up songs for her mother. It was when she was age three that she first invented lyrics for a song about a doll, "Little Tiny Tassletop," which her mother wrote down.

At the age of nine, Parton took up playing the guitar and banjo on the local radio and, later, on television in nearby Knoxville. She later learned to play the Autoharp, piano, and drums as well. She had appeared on the Grand Ole Opry as a child and thereafter knew what she wanted to do with the rest of her life. Parton was nothing if not determined, so in June of 1964, immediately after she graduated from high school the first member of her family to do so she took a bus to Nashville to make her name in country music.

Life's Work

With her move to Nashville, Parton struggled to make herself a star. The way for women to succeed in country music had been demonstrated by Kitty Wells, Patsy Cline, and Loretta Lynn. At first, Parton lived with her uncle,

Dolly Parton (Wikimedia Commons)

Bill Owens, with whom she wrote songs. She wrote songs for Hank Williams, Jr., and Skeeter Davis in late 1965, but her career received a boost when, in 1966, Bill Phillips made a minor hit of her composition "Put It off Until Tomorrow," with Parton singing harmony. Soon after, the record company Monumental Records agreed to have her sing country music.

Parton married Carl Dean, a businessman, in 1966; while shunning the limelight, her husband always played a supportive role in helping her professional career. Although they had no children of their own, the couple helped raise several of Parton's younger siblings. Her performing career took off in 1967, when she had hits with two novelty songs: "Dumb Blonde" and "Something Fishy." That same year, she joined *The Porter Wagoner Show* on television as a female soloist and frequent duet partner with Porter Wagoner.

During this part of her career, Parton sang as a high soprano; there was a sharp contrast between the lyrics she sang, which were about hardship and pain, and her delicate singing voice. In a short time, Porter and Dolly, as they were known to their legions of fans, became country music's top duo, winning national awards in 1968, 1970, and 1971.

Wagoner helped Parton secure a contract with RCA records, and she began to fashion her career as a recording artist. By the mid-1970s she became a star, singing songs she claimed she had made up while trying to survive growing up in grinding poverty. Her sensitive lyrics and fragile vocal styling turned her into the singing star she had always hoped to be. At this point in her career, she was trying to find her own style, and she explored a wide variety of themes and sounds. Among her early recordings were conventional hymns, moral tales, and the usual country music stories of love lost. She seemed to be trying everything and anything that had worked for women in country music since the days of Wells, whom Parton had admired.

> "*The way I see it, if you want the rainbow, you gotta put up with the rain.*"

Parton was a real country artist. The petite (five feet two inches) blond woman, with her towering wigs and skin-tight fashions, epitomized that curious mixture of hillbilly fashion and heartfelt singing that Nashville likes to project. As a recording artist, Parton, however, moved ever further into the heart of the pop-music tradition, abandoning her earlier pure country style, much to the sorrow of many critics. These traditional critics argue, though, that to appreciate Parton's genius fully one has to go back to two path breaking albums from the early 1970s: *Coat of Many Colors* and *My Tennessee Mountain Home*.

Parton's song "Coat of Many Colors" carefully tells the tragic story of a rag coat that her mother made for Parton as a poor young child one winter. The album also includes a dark song dealing with madness, "If I Lose My Mind," and a pondering of religion, mountain style, in "The Mystery of the Mystery." *My Tennessee Mountain Home* presents a wonderfully engaging oral history lesson complete with a vision of Nashville ("Down on Music Row"), a pair of musical essays about hard times and grinding poverty ("Daddy's Working Boots" and "In the Good Old Days"), and a trio of lyrical oral histories ("Dr. Robert F. Thomas," "I Remember," and "My Tennessee Mountain Home").

However, Parton was not satisfied with being atop the country music charts. She set out to map territory that only Cline before her had explored stardom in pop music. She left Wagoner in 1974 and a few years later made her move with a series of Los Angeles-influenced albums. In 1977, when Parton recorded *Here You Come Again*, written by veteran New York City pop music writers Barry Mann and Cynthia Weill, the title song rose to number three on the mainstream pop charts and set in motion a whole new career for Parton after the album became her first to sell more than a million copies.

Parton wanted to put behind her the traditional country associations she had worked so successfully to build up in the years with Wagoner. No one mistakes her later duets with Kenny Rogers and the Bee Gees for hardcore hillbilly music. The new Parton was aimed directly at mainstream musical tastes.

Parton's new goal was to become a film star. In the late 1970s, she hired an agent, and soon she was appearing regularly on *The Tonight Show with Johnny Carson*. She formally began working in films in 1980, when she gave an engaging performance as a Southern secretary opposite Lily Tomlin and Jane Fonda in *Nine to Five*. Parton also wrote and sang the film's title song, which earned for her an Oscar nomination, a Grammy Award, and a hit album on both country and pop charts. Her acting performance brought her a Golden Globe nomination.

The film's hit song "9 to 5" has a big-band introduction and two basic melodies as it liltingly expresses working-class frustration. A full studio backup band (no country music combo here) beats at a disco-like pace. This song, the ultimate crossover hit, contains elements of most forms of pop music of the late 1970s and early 1980s, from disco to country-pop. Thereafter, Parton continued to work regularly in Hollywood, starring (and frequently singing as well) in *The Best Little. Whorehouse in Texas* (1982), *Rhinestone* (1984), and *Steel Magnolias* (1989).

As her career prospered, Parton took full control of her business, creating, with her former manager Sandy Gilmore, Sandollar Production Company and, in 1986, opening her own theme park, Dollywood, and adjacent water park, Dolly's Splash Country, located in the Smoky Mountains not far from where she was born. Parton regularly graced the covers of *Redbook, Vanity Fair*, and

Parton sits with other Kennedy Center honorees, conductor Zubin Mehta (left) and Smokey Robinson (right). (Wikimedia Commons)

People magazines. She was as famous as any Hollywood personality during the last years of the twentieth century. After twenty years recording with RCA, she switched to Columbia Records in 1987.

Parton even had her own television series from late September of 1987 through May of 1988 on the ABC television network. The network brass was looking for someone to revive the variety show genre, which had been moribund since the demise of *The Carol Burnett Show*. ABC made a two-season, $44 million commitment to Dolly, believing that Parton could cross over the generation gap and make a hit. She sang from her rustic living room, complete with a roaring fire, and Dolly seemed to be the perfect show for the nostalgic Reagan era of the 1980s. Unfortunately for both ABC and Par- ton, the glitzy, big-budget hour finished forty-seventh in the ratings for its first and only season. If anything, Parton's considerable talents and appeal were overused; she appeared in every segment, singing duets with guest stars and performing in comedy skits. Indeed, except for a four-man vocal harmony group called the A Cappellas, Parton was the lone show regular.

In 1991, Parton starred in a critically acclaimed made-for-television film about battered women: *Wild Texas Wind*. In 1992, she starred in and helped to produce the film *Straight Talk*. Parton's duet with James Ingram in "The Day I Fall in Love" for the film *Beethoven's 2nd* (1993) received an Oscar nomination, and they sang it during the Academy Awards ceremonies. Her composition "Travelin' Thru" for the film *Transamerica* also was nominated for an Academy Award in 2005, and it won a Golden Globe for Best Original Song.

Parton continued to give concerts and release new albums and singles, including duets with young country singers such as Randy Travis, Ricky Van Shelton, and Billy Ray Cyrus; some of her songs were produced as videos that aired on VH-1 and The Nashville Network. She also teamed up with veteran singers, such as Rod Stewart in 2004 and George Jones in 2005. In 2007, *The Very Best of Dolly Parton* was issued in two compact disc volumes.

HarperCollins published her autobiography, *Dolly*, in the fall of 1994. In addition to her theme park and Sandollar Productions, her business ventures include her own wig factory, a chain of dinner theaters called the Dixie Stampedes, and astute management of the rights to her songs. This close control helped make her a millionaire many times over. For instance, she turned down an offer by Elvis Presley to include "I Will Always Love You" on an album of his when he demanded that she grant him half of the publishing rights. When Whitney Houston produced a version of the same song in 1992 and it became the best-selling hit ever written and performed by a woman, Parton, because she had retained the rights, reaped huge profits. Returning to her musical roots, she made an acoustics-only compact disc *The Grass Is Blue*, which won the International Blue- grass Music Association's Album of the Year award in 1999.

Parton's 2008 album *Backwoods Barbie* reached 2nd place on Billboard's list of hit country songs. She released a collaborative album with Billy Ray Cyrus, *Brother Clyde* in 2010. Parton's next studio album, *Better Day*, was released in 2011, and Parton toured performing in 49 concerts to promote the album. Parton's 2014 album, *Blue Smoke*, reached 6th on the Billboard charts, making it one of her most successful albums to date. During her Blue Smoke World Tour, Parton appeared in 40 concerts in Europe, Australia, and the United States.

Parton holds major music awards, more than most country singers: seven Grammy Awards, ten awards from the Country Music Association (including Entertainer of the Year), and five awards from the Academy of Country Music. She was inducted in the Nashville Songwriters Hall of Fame in 1986 and into the Country Music Hall of Fame in 1999. She also received the National Medal of Arts from President George W. Bush in 2005. In 2006 the Kennedy Center for the Performing Arts included her among its honors recipients for her lifetime contribution to music.

Parton's philanthropy also has been recognized. Her Imagination Library, a literacy program that provides books to children, began in Tennessee and spread into other states and Canada. Because of her work with this library, the Association of American Publishers named her to its honors list in 2000, and she received the Good Housekeeping Seal of Approval in 2001. She also donated money to wildlife and medical causes. In 2016, in response to the Great Smoky Mountains wildfires, Parton participated in two telethons, one hosted by herself, raising around $9 million for support of the victims.

Parton also maintained several residences around the country: a house in the Nashville suburb Brentwood and an apartment in her office complex in the city, three residences in the Los Angeles area, a cabin in the Smoky Mountains (her childhood home refurbished), and apartments at Dollywood and in New York City.

SIGNIFICANCE

Parton's life embodied for many the American dream of success, of moving from rags to riches. As the so-called Cinderella of the South, Parton started with almost nothing, save her talent and iron will to succeed. Before she turned thirty years old, she had become a national star. By the time she was forty years old, she was a millionaire.

Parton sings on stage during a Grand Ole Opry live broadcast in Nashville, Tennessee, April 23, 2005 as U.S. soldiers watch the show via a video feed in Iraq. (Wikimedia Commons)

She became a tough businesswoman, a talented songwriter and singer, and a television and film star. In the long term, Parton should be remembered as a songwriter whose lyrics expressed the feelings of children and women in rural and urban American society.

A major force in bringing women to the forefront of country music, Parton followed the styling of Wells and Cline. Fashioning a smooth sound to traditional country music instrumentation, she created a popular commercial product intended to appeal to a national pop-music audience. In turn, she inspired a score of country-pop female singers, including Emmylou Harris and Linda Ronstadt, with whom she recorded the highly successful album *Trio* in 1987.

People who know little about country music frequently underestimate Parton. She embodied conservatism, the all-American virtues of family, and down-home music, but she was able to become a pop culture icon. Country stars before her have become famous, but few have matched her range and level of success as a performer.

Douglas Gomery, updated by Micah L. Issitt

Further Reading

Bufwack, Mary A., and Robert K. Oermann. *Finding Her Voice: The Saga of Women in Country Music*. New York: Crown, 1993. A well-documented history of the impact of women in country music. The bibliography is extensive. Chapter 14 is an excellent piece about the latter part of Parton's career. Well illustrated.

Dunn, Jancee. "Dolly Parton." *Rolling Stone*, October 30, 2003. This marvelous article reveals Parton at her most plain-speaking: "I patterned my look after the town tramp." It discusses her childhood, style, appearance, and determination to bring her recordings and performances back into the mainstream of American music.

Grant, Meg. "Dolly Lets Her Hair Down." *Reader's Digest*, January, 2006. Grant reports on an interview in which Parton reflects on her retrospective album *Those Were the Days*, her desire to do more oldtime material, and her work on a musical theater version of the film Nine to Five.

Malone, Bill C. *Country Music U.S.A.* Rev. ed. Austin: University of Texas Press, 1985. The standard one-volume scholarly history of country music. Its detailed bibliography and guide to recordings ought to be required reading for anyone seriously interested in this genre of popular music. The career of Parton is treated in considerable detail.

Nash, Alanna. *Dolly*. Rev. ed. New York: Cooper Square Press, 2002. A popular biography with a number of color photographs, a score of black-and-white photographs, and a short discography only reference material is lacking. An excellent full biography of Parton that brings readers up to the revival of her career in the late 1990s, concentrating on her business acumen as well as her performances and recordings.

O'Dair, Barbara. *Trouble Girls: The Rolling Stone Book of Women in Rock*. New York: Random House, 1997. Places Parton among the "hillbilly fillies" who were the trailblazers of country music. Its lively, intriguing text supplies useful background information on Parton's success. Includes a discography and bibliography.

Parton, Dolly. *Dolly*. New York: HarperCollins, 1994. Parton's autobiography is a frank account of the singer's life one that, if not entirely revealing, at least provides a glimpse of the hardship and challenges that Parton overcame in her quest to succeed in the world of country music and entertainment in general.

Prince

Singer, musician, and entertainer

Born: June 7, 1958; Minneapolis, Minnesota
Died: April 21, 2016; Chanhassen, Minnesota
Also known as: ⚥ ("Love Symbol"), Alexander Nevermind, The Artist, The Artist Formerly Known as Prince (TAFKAP), Camille, Christopher Tracy, Jamie Starr, Joey Coco, Tora Tora, The Kid
Area of Achievement: Music

Prince was an iconic figure of American popular music, known for his blend of funk, soul, pop, and rock and roll. This unique combination of genres brought his work to a racially diverse audience, his popularity with which was amplified by his overtly sexual productions and androgynous, extravagant, and often controversial persona.

Early Life

Prince was born Prince Rogers Nelson in Minneapolis, Minnesota, to musicians John Nelson and Mattie Shaw on June 7, 1958. His name was drawn from his father's stage name. John was the pianist and composer for the Prince

Prince (Wikimedia Commons)

Rogers Trio, a jazz group well known in Minneapolis. Prince was surrounded by music throughout his childhood, playing and composing on his father's piano in the family living room and attending his father's jazz performances in clubs and theaters throughout the city. As a teenager, he learned to play guitar; joined his first band, Grand Central (later known as Champagne); and learned to produce studio recordings. With his own early recordings, Prince began looking for a record label shortly after high school.

When he signed a contract with Warner Bros. Records in 1977, nineteen-year-old Prince negotiated an exceptional amount of creative independence from the label, including sole primary control over recording and production. At a time when most major record labels, including Warner Bros., were run by white executives and marketed black musicians according to racial stereotypes, this contract was unprecedented. Prince's parents had moved to liberal Minnesota to escape the racial turmoil of the South, and Prince eschewed racial stereotyping throughout his upbringing. He was careful to emphasize his diverse capabilities as an artist, not an "African American artist." Thus, in 1978, he alone recorded and produced his debut album, *For You*. Despite its middling success, the album revealed Prince's early artistic focus on blending various genres, including funk and pop, and overt emphasis on sexual, highly eroticized lyrical themes.

> "*Art is about building a new foundation, not just laying something on top of what's already there.*"

LIFE'S WORK

With a clear artistic vision, Prince developed a touring band comprising both black and white musicians, male and female, and produced an album each year for the next four years. Although none was a smash hit, the sexual themes that permeated his albums, especially the aggressively erotic *Dirty Mind* (1980), attracted a lot of attention. Prince's androgynous image and flamboyant fashion sense sparked further interest.

When "Little Red Corvette" from the album *1999* (1982) was put into regular rotation on MTV, Prince became only the second black musician—after Michael Jackson—to have his video featured on the channel. The song was a widespread hit and expanded Prince's fan base beyond African Americans. It featured funksoul vocals over a relaxed pop tone and rock-style guitar solos. After *1999*, Prince's major breakthrough came with his semiautobiographical feature film *Purple Rain* (1984) and its accompanying sound track, featuring the work of Prince and his new band, the Revolution. Several singles from the sound track, including "When Doves Cry," "Let's Go Crazy," and "Purple Rain," reached the top of the charts. The sound track and film garnered critical acclaim and brought Prince international fame, three Grammy Awards, and an Oscar. In 1985, in collaboration with Warner Bros., Prince built his own record studio complex, called Paisley Park, just outside Minneapolis. From there he produced his next eight albums and increased his work as a promoter of other artists—mostly female—such as Sheena Easton and Carmen Electra.

In the early 1990s, Prince's relationship with Warner Bros. Records disintegrated over contract disputes and conflicts regarding Paisley Park. Prince waged a high-profile battle against the label, appearing at an interview

Prince playing with Levi Seacer, Jr. (Wikimedia Commons)

with the word "slave" scrawled across his cheek, invoking the problems of black artists in a white-controlled industry, and legally changing his name to an unpronounceable symbol (✝). When he eventually was released from his Warner Bros. contract, Prince released an album titled *Emancipation* (1996), underscoring his earlier references to slavery. He later returned to using his original name. Despite a series of personal struggles in the late 1990s and 2000s, including two divorces and the deaths of his newborn son and parents, Prince continued to tour and produce albums.

The early 2000s were a period of musical experimentation for Prince; he produced several jazz and funk albums which were not commercially successful. He made a comeback with the pop album *Musicology*, released in 2004. On the tour for *Musicology*, he experimented with including the album with concert ticket purchases. Prince was inducted into the Rock and Roll Hall of Fame in 2004. He released *Planet Earth* in 2007, and *20Ten* in 2010. Prince performed at the Super Bowl halftime show in 2007.

In 2014 Prince released two albums simultaneously, *Art Official Age* and *Plectrumelectrum*. *Art Official Age*, which critics considered the more successful of the two, was a return to the height of his eighties sound, while *Plectrumelectrum* was more experimental funk rock. Prince continued to tour and released his final two albums through Jay Z's streaming service, Tidal. The tandem albums, *HitnRun Phase 1* and *HitnRun Phase 2* showcased Prince's unique brand of soul-funk with elements of rock and EDM.

In his last few years, Prince's health was beginning to fail him. He passed away on April 21, 2016, at his home of an accidental drug overdose of fentanyl, an opioid drug. Prince had been battling a secret addiction for some time. Only a week before, he had been hospitalized after losing consciousness on his private jet, which had to make an emergency landing.

Significance

Prince was one of the main figures in American popular music, rivaling the popularity of contemporary artists Madonna and Michael Jackson, and creating some thirty albums from the late 1970s to 2016. What made Prince's music such a sensation was its unique sound: More than any other artist before him, Prince sought to fuse a variety of musical styles, most notably pop- and funk-inspired bass grooves, rock-and-roll guitar playing, and soul-derived, sexually driven vocals. His fusion of music genres typically marketed to whites—rock and pop—with characteristically black genres—funk and soul—and his early insistence on full artistic control of his albums significantly altered perceptions of African American artists in the music industry and helped his work appeal to a large and racially diverse audience. Beyond his music, Prince's flamboyant persona explored issues of sexuality and gender and ensured his iconic status as a creative visionary.

Danielle M. Kuntz

Further Reading

Draper, Jason. *Prince: Life and Times*. London: Jawbone, 2009. Print.

Hahn, Alex. *Possessed: The Rise and Fall of Prince*. New York: Billboard, 2003. Print.

Morton, Brian. *Prince: A Thief in the Temple*. Edinburgh: Canongate, 2007. Print.

Pareles, Jon. "Prince, an Artist Who Defied Genre, Is Dead at 57." *New York Times*. New York Times, 21 Apr. 2016. Web. 23 June 2016.

Perone, James E. *The Words and Music of Prince*. Westport: Praeger, 2008. Print.

FRED ROGERS

Children's television host

Born: March 20, 1928: Latrobe, Pennsylvania
Died: February 27, 2003; Pittsburgh, Pennsylvania
Area of achievement: Entertainment; education

Creator and host of the long-running show Mister Rogers' Neighborhood, *Fred Rogers's study of child psychology, together with his views on Christian love, shaped his life's work and provided the ethos for his much-loved television program.*

EARLY LIFE

Fred McFeely Rogers was born on March 20, 1928, in Latrobe, Pennsylvania, about forty miles from Pittsburgh. His father, James Rogers, was the president of McFeely Brick Company, and Fred grew up in a large brick mansion with his parents in Latrobe. He was an only child until his parents adopted a girl, Elaine, when Fred was eleven years old. As a child, Fred was introverted; he was also frequently home-bound with various illnesses. He spent a lot of time alone with his collection of puppets, including a ventriloquist's dummy, or reading books, or playing the piano. Rogers was also overweight when he was a child. In school, he was often bullied and called "fat Freddy."

> "I believe that appreciation is a holy thing, that when we look for what's best in the person we happen to be with at the moment, we're doing what God does; so in appreciating our neighbor, we're participating in something truly sacred."

Rogers felt uncomfortable around his peers because his parents were the wealthiest family in the neighborhood. Later, as an adult, he deliberately chose not to stand out from others in this way; he preferred to live modestly and simply. In high school, Rogers made some friends early on who helped him overcome his social awkwardness, including the head of the football team. Aided by his new confidence, Rogers became a member of the National Honor Society, became president of the student council, and was the editor of the school's yearbook.

Fred Rogers (Wikimedia Commons)

He graduated from high school in 1947. After attending Dartmouth College for one year, Rogers transferred to Rollins College in Winter Park, Florida, where he studied musical composition. He graduated in 1951. In the following year, he married his college girlfriend, Sara Joanne Byrd.

LIFE'S WORK

In 1951, Rogers saw a television for the first time after his parents had purchased one for their home. By that year, the number of television sets in American homes had risen to 12 million from only six thousand in 1946. (The growth would continue so that by 1955 half of all homes in the United States had a television set.) Rogers was not pleased by what he saw. He later recalled that the first thing he witnessed on his parents' television was people throwing pies at one another. To Rogers, this was crass entertainment, playful violence, and he later recalled, "I went into television because I hated it so...." He thought that the medium could be used differently, in a manner that connected with viewers humanely and nurtured what was best in them. He moved to New York City in 1951 where he began working in television production. Although young, he was capable and bright, and he quickly became the floor director of prominent shows like *Your Hit Parade* and *The Kate Smith Hour*. Within two years, he was an assistant producer for *The Voice of Firestone*.

In 1953, Rogers received a call that changed his life and the course of television history. In Pittsburgh, close to his hometown of Latrobe, a new concept in television was being developed: community-sponsored educational television. This was fourteen years before the birth of the Public Broadcasting System (PBS). Rogers was asked if he'd like to be involved, and he jumped at the chance. WQED began broadcasting on January 1, 1954. Its lineup included *The Children's Corner*, a show for which Rogers developed puppets and wrote music. *The Children's Corner* was successful and won a national award, after which, in 1955, it was picked up by NBC for national distribution on their network.

In Pittsburgh, Rogers began giving form to what he felt was a calling. Working for WQED during the days, in the evenings he attended the University of Pittsburgh's Graduate School of Child Development as well as the Pittsburgh Theological Seminary. Pittsburgh in that period was an important center for child psychology. In the 1950s, such luminaries as Dr. Benjamin Spock, Erik Erikson, T. Berry Brazelton, and Margaret McFarland were among the professors at the university. Margaret McFarland, in particular, became an important mentor and an advisor for his television work. They met when she supervised his counseling of a child while he was studying counseling as part of his training at the seminary. In 1963, Rogers completed a divinity degree and became an ordained Presbyterian minister.

Also in 1963 Rogers moved to Canada to develop a show called *Misterogers* for the Canadian Broadcasting Corporation (CBC). The show aired from 1963 to 1967. In it, Rogers appeared in front of the camera for the first time in his career. Many aspects of his later PBS series were developed in *Misterogers,* including several puppet characters and many conceptual and stylistic elements. Rogers acquired the rights to *Misterogers* and returned to Pittsburgh in 1967; he even brought with him the sets from *Misterogers*. In Pittsburgh, he began developing *Mister Rogers' Neighborhood*, which first aired in 1968.

President George W. Bush presents the Presidential Medal of Freedom Award to Rogers on July 9, 2002. (Wikimedia Commons)

The difference between Rogers's approach to children's programming and the approach that was ascendant at the time was immediately apparent. He eschewed flash, valued slowness, and the show was carefully crafted by a team of writers and advisors that included child psychologists. His friend and mentor Margaret McFarland emphasized to Rogers that his relationship to the children watching him was a real relationship, even if it was mediated by television. This idea affected him profoundly, and the seriousness with which he took it to heart may account for the unusually strong impact that the show had on many of its young viewers.

For thirty years, each episode unfolded with the same repeated elements; for example, Mister Rogers entering the set through the door and changing into sneakers and a sweater; at a later point in every episode, it was time to feed the fish. These elements were carefully thought out, and were designed not only to model comforting adult behaviors and routine but to create a warm "holding environment," to use a phrase from child psychologist Donald Winnicott—a space that fosters a sense of emotional cohesiveness and in which one can bear one's feelings without fragmenting. Rogers, who dealt sometimes on the show with difficult emotional material like the experience of divorce or Bobby Kennedy's assassination, said that he wanted to teach children that their feelings are both "mentionable and manageable." The show was honored with four Emmy awards over the course its long run. In addition, Rogers was presented with a Lifetime Achievement

Rogers broke ground by inviting African American Officer Clemmons to wash his feet with him in the same kiddie pool. (Wikimedia Commons)

Award from the National Academy of Television Arts in 1997.

Rogers was a lifelong advocate for public television. In 1969, he testified before the United States Senate Subcommittee on Communications asking them to support funding for PBS at a time when budget cuts were on the table; his brief, heartfelt testimony was credited by the chairman of the subcommittee, John O. Pastore, a Democrat from Rhode Island, with giving him goosebumps. In 1979, Rogers testified before the Supreme Court in favor of home use of VCR equipment, saying that any technology that gave people more control over their viewing habits was "healthy" and "important."

Significance

Fred Rogers has long been respected as a television icon of a special sort: a United States Senate Resolution, passed unanimously in 2003, honored him for his "spirituality." A similar resolution passed in the House in the same year praised him for "demonstrating the power of compassion" and "spreading kindness through example." Morgan Neville's documentary, *Won't You Be My Neighbor?* (2018), marked a turning point in public dialogue about Fred Rogers. (It also became the highest grossing biographical documentary in film history.) The question in the film's title highlighted the divisive social and political atmosphere in the United States at the time of its release. The film was noteworthy for showing the extent to which Christianity undergirded the show's message and style, a point that was not widely known before; even the term "neighbor," for Rogers, was suffused with Christian significance derived from the New Testament use of that word. In Rogers's Christianity, unconditional and unflinching human love for the other—the kind that Rogers modeled—is practiced in response to the knowledge of God's similarly unconditional love and furthers that love in the world.

Through unparalleled, thoughtful attention to details of script and presentation, his television show created a safe space that allowed for a deeply personal connection with his young audience; this was documented as early as 1969 in an *Atlantic* article that noticed how often young children responded out loud to Mister Rogers's questions, as if he were actually present. A champion of the importance of kindness, authenticity, and presence to others, Rogers positively affected the lives of tens of millions of young children.

D. Alan Dean

Further Reading

Collins, Mark and Margaret Mary Kimmel, eds. *Mister Rogers' Neighborhood: Children, Television, and Mister Rogers*. Pittsburgh: U of Pittsburgh Press, 1996.

King, Maxwell. *The Good Neighbor: The Life and Work of Fred Rogers*. New York: Abrams Press, 2018.

Levin, Robert A., and Laurie Moses Hines. "Educational Television, Fred Rogers, and the History of Education." *History of Education Quarterly*, vol. 43, no. 2, 2003, pp. 262–275. JSTOR, www.jstor.org/stable/3218313.

Morris, Norman. "What's Good About Children's TV." *The Atlantic*. August 1969. https://www.theatlantic.com/magazine/archive/1969/08/whats-good-about-childrens-tv/305127/

Phillips, Adam. *Winnicott*. Cambridge: Harvard University Press, 1989.

Selena

American singer

Born: April 16, 1971; Lake Jackson, Texas
Died: March 31, 1995; Corpus Christi, Texas
Also known as: Selena Quintanilla-Pérez
Areas of achievement: Music; fashion; business

Hailed as the "Queen of Tejano music," Selena was among the first female performers to succeed in the male-dominated genre by conquering the hearts of Tejano and Latin American audiences. A successful singer, fashion designer, and entrepreneur, she was preparing to make her debut in the English-language pop market at the time of her death.

Early Life

Selena Quintanilla-Pérez (seh-LEE-nuh KEEN-tah-NEE-yah-PEH-rehz) was born on April 16, 1971, in Lake Jackson, Texas, to Abraham Quintanilla and Marcella Ofelia Samora. Her father performed with the Tejano group Los Dinos in his youth but eventually retired from music to work at the Dow Chemical plant in Lake Jackson. He provided his children with instruments and taught them to play as a family activity and they became Selena y Los Dinos: her brother A. B. played bass, sister Suzette played drums, and Selena acted as lead singer. The band started performing regularly at the family restaurant, Papagayo's, in 1980, as well as in clubs, local restaurants, and outdoor festivals, making a series of independent recordings starting with *Selena y Los Dinos* (1984). An excellent student, Selena had to be home schooled because of the demands and time commitment of touring throughout the Southwest when the band became the family's main source of income. After winning awards for female vocalist of the year and performer of the year at the 1987 Tejano music Awards, Selena was signed to EMI Records and released her first major-label album, *Selena*, in 1989.

Guitarist Chris Pérez joined the band in 1989, and he and Selena began dating two years later. They were married in 1992. Major-label albums and music videos allowed Selena to reach greater popularity, and her biggest success came with the 1994 release of *Amor prohibido*. Her appeal rested on the combination of her humble personality, powerful voice, spirited dance moves, and provocative outfits. Even at the peak of her career, the band remained a family affair, with her father acting as manager, brother A. B. writing and producing songs, and her sister and husband playing in the band. Selena designed the band's costumes. Her strong family ties coupled with her loyalty to her Texan working-class roots made her relatable to fans and earned her their devoted admiration.

Selena (Getty Images)

Life's Work

Despite having grown up speaking only English, Selena worked on her Spanish and managed to gain the acceptance of Mexican audiences, who often were unforgiving of Mexican Americans' Anglo backgrounds. Her popularity spread throughout Latin America and led her to tour Mexico and Central and South America. After the success of *Amor prohibido*, Selena started branching out into other projects, which included appearances in the Mexican telenovela *Dos mujeres, un camino* and the film *Don Juan de Marco* (1994), as well as musical collaborations with the group Barrio Boyzz and singer Alvaro Torres. She also began designing a clothing line and distributing it at her Selena Etc. boutiques throughout Texas. Her star status was clear when she performed at the Houston Astrodome for more than sixty-five thousand people.

Selena met Yolanda Saldivar in 1990 when Saldivar approached her with the idea of starting a fan club. Selena agreed, and Saldivar became the fan club's president, as well as manager of the Selena Etc. boutiques. In March, 1995, Selena's father discovered that Saldivar had been embezzling money from the boutiques. While Saldivar denied the accusations, the family decided to fire her. On

March 31, Selena met with Saldivar at a Corpus Christi hotel to break the news to her and retrieve important documents that Saldivar had taken; the two argued, and as Selena was leaving, Saldivar shot her in the back. She died later at the hospital. Meanwhile, Saldivar locked herself in her truck in the hotel parking lot for nine hours before surrendering to police. She was convicted of first-degree murder and sentenced to life in prison.

At the time of her death, Selena had been working on songs for her English-language debut album, set to be released that summer. The album, titled *Dreaming of You* (1995), included songs in both Spanish and English and debuted at number one on the Billboard charts. The album sold well, making Selena a crossover success in the mainstream U.S. market.

> "*Music is not a very stable business. It comes and it goes, and so does money, but your education stays with you for the rest of your life. When you have that education, and you have nothing to fall back on, you can get a get a job anywhere.*"

Selena's memory is kept alive through myriad commemorations; the events of her life have been the subject of the musical *Selena Forever* (2000) and the film *Selena* (1997) starring Jennifer Lopez. Immediately after her death, *People* magazine produced a commemorative issue dedicated to her, only the third of its kind after issues devoted to Audrey Hepburn and Jacqueline Kennedy Onassis. George W. Bush, then governor of Texas, declared Selena's birthday, April 16, Selena Day. The family recording studio in Corpus Christi have been converted into museums and a life-size statue of the singer was erected at the Mirador de la Flor memorial in Corpus Christi. The iconic outfit she wore at her Astrodome performance has even toured the country as part of the Smithsonian traveling exhibit America's Smithsonian.

Significance

Selena reached millions of people with her music, many of them Latinas who saw her as a role model. By effectively melding her Anglo American upbringing and Mexican background, without renouncing her Texan working-class roots, she was seen as exemplary of what Latinas could accomplish. Likewise, musically she was able to bridge her two heritages by performing songs steeped in the traditional music of Mexico, yet also infused by elements of Anglo American rock and roll and pop. The public display of her fans' mourning brought visibility to Hispanic groups in the United States, and her success has been heralded as the beginning of the musical Latin invasion of the late 1990's.

Georgina Chinchilla-Gonzalez

Further Reading

Koegel, John. "Crossing Borders: Mexicana, Tejana and Chicana musicians in the United States and Mexico." In *From Tejano to Tango*, edited by Walter Aaron Clark. New York: Routledge, 2002. Considers the contributions of female performers to the Tejano genre and Selena's unique role in the genre's development.

Novas, Himilce, and Rosemary Silva. *Remembering Selena: A Tribute in Pictures and Words/Recordando Selena: Un tributo en palabras y fotos*. New York: St. Martin's Press, 1995. Bilingual account of Selena's life and career featuring photos and stories from Selena's family.

Paredez, Deborah. *Selenidad: Selena, Latinos, and the Performance of Memory*. Durham, N.C.: Duke University Press, 2009. A scholarly exploration of the emergence of Selena as a Latina icon as seen through diverse practices of memorialization.

Patoski, Joe. *Selena: Como la flor*. Boston: Little, Brown, 1996. This detailed biography based on personal interviews and newspaper articles recounts Selena's life and career and remains an authoritative source.

Richmond, Clint. *Selena! The Phenomenal Life and Tragic Death of the Tejano Music Queen*. New York: Pocket Books, 1995. Bilingual biography that provides the English and Spanish translation side by side and contains previously unreleased photographs.

Nina Simone

Singer, musician, and activist

Born: February 21, 1933; Tyron, North Carolina
Died: April 21, 2003; Carry-le-Rouet, France
Area of Achievement: Civil rights, Music: blues, Music: classical and operatic, Music: jazz

Simone was one of the leading musical artists of the Civil Rights movement. Although she started out with the goal of becoming a famous classical pianist, her musical career transcended and informed several genres of music, including folk, jazz, blues, and protest music.

Nina Simone (Wikimedia Commons)

Early Life

Nina Simone was born Eunice Kathleen Waymon in the segregated town of Tryon, North Carolina, on February 21, 1933. Although the Great Depression made subsistence difficult, her parents, John Divine Waymon and Kate Waymon, managed to feed and clothe their eight children. The Waymons demonstrated to their children the importance of using hard work to overcome racism. Simone's father worked as a truck driver and later opened his own dry-cleaning business. Her mother was ordained as a minister in St. Luke's Christian Methodist Episcopal Church. By age six, Simone had begun playing the church organ, an early harbinger of her future as a pianist.

Recognizing Simone's talent, her parents began paying for piano lessons with a white benefactor. By age ten, she was serving as the pianist at her mother's church and a fund had been established to further her classical training. African Americans in the area took pride in the young musical prodigy.

Simone learned early on that, despite her best efforts, race would always be a factor in life. While she was preparing for a recital in Tryon, her parents were ushered to the back of the room. Simone objected and even refused to play before the white audience until her parents received front-row seats. In another incident, Simone and another African American purchased ice cream from a drugstore on a sweltering day in Tryon but were not allowed to sit inside to eat it.

Simone graduated from Tryon's segregated high school and attended Allen High School, a private, all-black girls school in Asheville, North Carolina. There, she continued piano lessons. Her dream was to become a classical pianist. However, Simone faced a daunting challenge. After completing her studies at Allen, she auditioned for admission to the Curtis Institute of Music. She was devastated when the renowned classical music school did not admit her. Determined to win admission, she gave recitals and taught other students to earn money for more lessons. Eventually, however, Simone gave up on her dream of becoming a classical pianist.

Life's Work

To cover her growing living expenses, Simone began playing in Philadelphia nightclubs in 1954. She chose the stage name "Nina Simone." "Nina" came from a Latino boyfriend and "Simone" from the French film star Simone Signoret.

After several weeks of playing piano at the Midtown Bar, the owner urged Simone to sing; customers wanted a piano player and a singer. Simone agreed, although she had little tolerance for rude bar patrons and refused to play while they talked. She gradually learned to sing.

Simone recorded her first album, *Little Girl Blue*, in 1957. It was a modest success and she moved to New York for bigger audiences and paydays. In New York, she continued classical training at the Juilliard School of Music and married Don Ross, her manager. By 1959, Simone's career had blossomed. She was in demand at small, intimate clubs and played concerts around New York, Philadelphia, Atlantic City, and Washington, D.C. She also enjoyed her greatest hit that year, "I Loves You, Porgy" from George Gershwin's *Porgy and Bess*. The song stayed on the charts for nearly four months and the album reached number eight. Her music attracted a small but loyal following.

Several more hits followed in the 1960s, including "I Put a Spell on You," "To Be Young, Gifted, and Black," and "Four Women." Although Simone had a strong following in northern metropolitan cities, she often received negative reviews from white music critics who were unable to characterize her music.

As the Civil Rights movement unfolded during the 1960s, Simone became involved, both personally and musically. She did benefit concerts for civil rights groups, donated money, befriended leading members of the movement, and addressed racial injustices in her music. After the murder of National Association for the

Statue of Simone by Zenos Frudakis in Tryon, NC. (Wikimedia Commons)

Advancement of Colored People (NAACP) field secretary Medgar Evers in 1963, she wrote "Mississippi Goddam." Some radio stations refused to play the song, especially those in the South.

> "I'll tell you what freedom is to me: no fear. I mean really, no fear!"

After the 1960s, Simone spent most of her time in Barbados, parts of Africa, and Europe, where she found peace and appreciative audiences. Europeans especially recognized her deft blend of jazz, blues, folk, and protest music. Throughout the 1970s, with a new husband and manager, Don Stroud, she played in the United States only when necessary. Their marriage produced a daughter named Lisa.

Although Simone's career declined in the early to mid-1980s, she experienced a revival between 1989 and 1993. *I Put a Spell on You: The Autobiography of Nina Simone* was published in 1991; she produced her last album, *A Single Woman*, two years later to good reviews. However, Simone struggled with depression. Her mother died at the age of one hundred in 2001; Simone overcame a bout of breast cancer. She performed her last concert in Poland in June, 2002. Soon after, Simone had a stroke in France and died six months later on April 20, 2003.

SIGNIFICANCE

Simone was a talented musician who refused to surrender to racism. Although she did not succeed in becoming a classical pianist, she did much more. She became an icon of the civil rights era and left an enduring legacy of jazz, blues, folk, and protest music.

Jackie R. Booker

FURTHER READING

Bratcher, Melanie E. *Words and Songs of Bessie Smith, Billie Holiday, and Nina Simone*. New York: Routledge, 2007. Contains analysis of Simone's music along with a discography and a short biography.

Cohodas, Nadine. *Princess Noire: The Tumultuous Reign of Nina Simone*. New York: Pantheon Books, 2010. The most complete biography of Simone, supported by voluminous research and personal remembrances from friends, family members, and supporters.

Grass, Randall. "Nina Simone: The High Priestess of Soul." In *Great Spirits: Portraits of Life-Changing World Music Artists*. Jackson: University Press of Mississippi, 2009. A very readable narrative of Simone's life and career.

Simone, Nina. *I Put a Spell on You: The Autobiography of Nina Simone*. Cambridge, Mass.: Da Capo Press, 1991. Simone's autobiography covers her upbringing in the segregated South, classical-music ambitions, and experiences in the Civil Rights movement.

JAMES STEWART

Actor

Born: May 20, 1908; Indiana, Pennsylvania
Died: July 2, 1997; Beverly Hills, California
Area of Achievement: Film

Stewart was one of the most successful and enduring actors in the history of American motion pictures. His most famous role was in the holiday classic It's a Wonderful Life, *from 1947.*

EARLY LIFE

James Stewart was born in the small town of Indiana, Pennsylvania. His father, Alex, owned a hardware store where Stewart worked as a young man. His mother, Elizabeth, was a homemaker and church organist. Stewart's only contact with the theater in his youth was the plays he

James Stewart (Wikimedia Commons)

staged in the family basement with his two younger sisters, Mary and Virginia. As a child, he attended Indiana's Model School, then Mercersburg Academy. On graduation from high school, he went to his father's alma mater, Princeton University, to study architecture.

While at Princeton, Stewart met future theatrical writer-producer Josh Logan, who encouraged him to appear in university main-stage productions. Shortly after graduation in 1932, Stewart accepted Logan's invitation to join him at a local theatrical group, the University Players, and played a number of small roles in summer stock productions. At the end of the summer, Princeton University offered Stewart a scholarship to pursue a master's degree in architecture. Instead, he traveled to New York with the University Players to appear in the Broadway opening of *Carry Nation*, a play loosely based on the life of the outspoken nineteenth century temperance leader. Though the play closed shortly after it opened, Stewart never returned to Princeton University.

LIFE'S WORK

Stewart stayed in New York after *Carry Nation* closed. He spent the next two years looking for stage work to help pay rent for the small apartment he shared with fellow struggling actors Josh Logan and Henry Fonda. Stewart's first successful stage appearance was as Sergeant O'Hara, a soldier volunteer for Walter Reed's malaria experiments, in *Yellow Jack*. Though *Yellow Jack* was also short-lived, Stewart received good critical reviews. He also received favorable notice from critics for his performance in *Divided by Three*. It was during the run of *Divided by Three* that a talent scout for Metro-Goldwyn-Mayer (MGM), the largest and most prestigious film studio in California, spotted Stewart's performance and arranged for a series of screen tests. Stewart signed a contract with MGM for $350 per week and moved to California.

> "*Never treat your audience as customers, always as partners.*"

In June of 1935, Stewart arrived in Hollywood and once again shared rent with Fonda and a series of other newly arrived actors. Over the next few years, Stewart appeared in a wide variety of roles while MGM tried to find a character type that would succeed with film audiences. He played a fugitive on the run in *Rose Marie* (1936), Jean Harlow's boyfriend in *Wife vs. Secretary* (1936), a murderer in *After the Thin Man* (1936), a sewer worker in *Seventh Heaven* (1937), a botany professor in *Vivacious Lady* (1938), and even sang a couple songs in *Born to Dance* (1936). He was also paired with former University Player Margaret Sullivan in a series of popular romantic comedies, including *The Shopworn Angel* (1938), *The Shop Around the Corner* (1940), and *The Mortal Storm* (1940). During this time, Stewart was also a frequent voice on radio, performing shortened versions of popular films and plays.

Stewart's screen personality the sweet, small-town, dependable good guy developed during the late 1930's. He made his mark with film critics in 1938 when he played Tony Vanderhoff in the screen adaptation of George Kaufman's Pulitzer Prize-winning play *You Can't Take It with You*. The film won the Academy Award for Best Picture, and Stewart's characterization of Tony charmed film audiences. In 1939, Stewart was paired with boisterous Marlene Dietrich as a sheriff in a comedy Western *Destry Rides Again*, which showed off Stewart's comedic flair. He received critical acclaim for holding his own against Dietrich's enormous screen presence.

In 1939, Stewart was cast as Jefferson Smith in *Mr.*

Smith Goes to Washington, directed by Frank Capra. His performance as young and idealistic Jefferson Smith cemented Stewart's good-guy image. In the film, Smith is a small-town boy elected to serve in the United States Congress who is unjustly accused of criminal activity. Smith discovers corruption and loses his political innocence while sponsoring a bill to establish a boys' camp. The film was popular with audiences and critics alike, and Stewart received his first Best Actor Oscar nomination.

In 1940, Stewart appeared in *The Philadelphia Story* with Katharine Hepburn and Cary Grant. Hepburn played Tracy Lord, a rich divorcé on the eve of her second marriage who has difficulty deciding among her fiancé, her former husband, and Mike Conner, a visiting reporter played by Stewart. *The Philadelphia Story* was a huge box-office success, and Stewart received the 1940 Academy Award for Best Actor for his performance.

As Stewart's acting career reached new heights, his life took an unexpected turn. When conflicts that precipitated World War II erupted in Europe, Stewart enlisted in the U.S. Army. Initially turned down for service because he was underweight, Stewart went on a high-calorie diet and reported for duty on March 22, 1941. Already a licensed pilot, he was assigned to the Army Air Corps. Stewart received his wings and commission as a second lieutenant within weeks of the Japanese attack on Pearl Harbor that brought the United States into World War II. He received heavy-bomber instruction at Kirkland Field in New Mexico and trained as a B-17 commander at Hobbs Air Force Base. In 1943, Captain Stewart was transferred to Boise, Idaho, where he trained young bomber pilots. He also appeared on recruiting tours, traveled on bond drives to raise funds for the war effort, and made instructional films for the Army, a project he would continue for the next four decades.

In 1943, Stewart was transferred to Tibenham, England, to command the 703d Squadron of the 445th Bombardment Group of B-24 Liberators. He led nearly twenty bombing missions against the Germans in a total of eighteen hundred flying hours and was promoted to the rank of major. For his wartime service, Stewart was awarded the Air Medal, an Oak Leaf Cluster for leadership, the Distinguished Flying Cross, and the French Croix de Guerre. Early in 1944, Colonel Stewart became operations officer for the 453d Bombardment Group before returning to the United States in August of 1945. After the war ended, Stewart remained in the Air Force Reserve and eventually achieved the rank of brigadier general.

Stewart returned to Hollywood after the war unsure of

Lt. Gen. Valin, Chief of Staff, French Air Force, awarding Croix De Guerre with palm to Stewart. (Wikimedia Commons)

the status of his acting career. In 1946, he quickly accepted an invitation from director Frank Capra to star in a small black-and-white film for Radio-Keith-Orpheum (RKO). At the time of its release, the film received some critical favor but only mediocre audience response, yet years later, Stewart proclaimed *It's a Wonderful Life* (1947) to be his favorite motion picture. Stewart played George Bailey, a small-town man who longs for adventure but is seemingly stuck in an uneventful life. Matters degenerate, and George contemplates suicide before an angel named Clarence shows George what his family and friends would be like if he had never been born.

In the summer of 1948, Stewart met Gloria Hatrick at a dinner party given by Gary Cooper. Hatrick was a recently divorced mother of two small boys. Stewart and Hatrick were married on August 9, 1949, at the Brentwood Presbyterian Church, ending the career of Hollywood's most eligible bachelor and beginning a long, successful marriage. In addition to Hatrick's two boys, the Stewarts had twin girls in 1951.

After the release of *It's a Wonderful Life*, Stewart tried to find his place in postwar American film by playing a variety of characters through the late 1940's. He was a newspaper reporter in *Call Northside 777* (1948), a public relations man in *Magic Town* (1947), and a detective in *Rope* (1948), which teamed him with director Alfred Hitchcock for the first time.

Stewart was the summer Broadway replacement for Frank Fay, who played the part of Elwood P. Dowd in *Harvey* twice during the later 1940's. Stewart enjoyed the role and successfully campaigned to play Dowd in the 1950 film version. *Harvey* marked the beginning of the most successful decade of Stewart's life. Dowd is a quiet, tipsy man who spends his day with his best friend, an invisible rabbit named Harvey. Stewart received another Oscar nomination for the role and for years to come was associated with the harmless eccentric and his rabbit friend.

Stewart appeared in a number of Westerns during the 1950's and 1960's. The sweet, small-town man became a hardened cowboy, and audiences loved it. Stewart appeared in *Winchester '73* (1950), *Bend of the River* (1952), *The Naked Spur* (1953), *The Far Country* (1955), and *The Man from Laramie* (1955). Stewart teamed with director John Ford for *The Man Who Shot Liberty Valance* (1962) and played Wyatt Earp in *Cheyenne Autumn* (1964). For every Western, Stewart insisted on working with his favorite horse, Pie, whom he credited with making him look like a real cowboy. In 1965, he played a stoic Virginia farmer determined to keep his six sons out of the Civil War in the popular film *Shenandoah*. The film was the number-one box-office draw for the year. He also portrayed a number of real-life heroes: He appeared as popular band leader Glenn Miller in *The Glenn Miller Story* (1954); baseball player Monty Stratton, who lost his leg in a hunting accident, in *The Stratton Story* (1949); and Charles A. Lindbergh in *The Spirit of St. Louis* (1957).

In 1954, Stewart and Hitchcock made the hugely successful film *Rear Window*. Stewart played a photojournalist who breaks his leg. Housebound and bored, he takes interest in the lives of the neighbors he watches through his rear window. Convinced that one neighbor has murdered his wife, he involves his nurse (who is also his girlfriend), played by Grace Kelly, in the intrigue. He teamed with Hitchcock again for *The Man Who Knew Too Much* (1956), in which Stewart played Dr. Ben McKenna, a vacationer in North Africa who finds himself thrust into murderous events over which he has little control. He played a former police officer plagued by a fear of heights in *Vertigo* (1958) and received another Oscar nomination

Stewart, Donna Reed, and Karolyn Grimes in the final scene of It's a Wonderful Life (1946). (Wikimedia Commons)

for the role of a small-town lawyer in *Anatomy of a Murder* (1959), directed by Otto Preminger.

Stewart appeared in fewer films during the 1970's and 1980's but starred in the television detective series *Hawkins*. He made frequent appearances at award ceremonies in his honor. He received an honorary Academy Award, was inducted into the American Film Institute, and was honored by the Kennedy Center. As a frequent guest on *The Tonight Show* with Johnny Carson, Stewart sometimes read poems he had written. They were so popular with audiences that he published a book of his poetry called *Jimmy Stewart and His Poems* (1989). Stewart's last film role was the voice of Wylie Burp in the animated *An American Tail 2: Fievel Goes West* (1991). Stewart's wife, Gloria, died of cancer in 1994, and Stewart remained reclusive until his death in 1997 at the age of eighty-nine.

Significance

Stewart, one of the most beloved actors of the twentieth century, gained extra notoriety through theater revivals and videotapes. *It's a Wonderful Life* was rediscovered in the 1970's and became a traditional Christmas favorite. Stewart's portrayal of small-town good guy George Bailey is perhaps his most memorable performance and creates a new legion of Stewart fans each year.

Leslie Stricker

Further Reading

Bingham, Dennis. *Acting Male: Masculinities in the*

Films of James Stewart, Jack Nicholson, and Clint Eastwood. New Brunswick, N.J.: Rutgers University Press, 1994. Bingham studies different acting styles and male portrayals among three leading actors.

Coe, Jonathan. *Jimmy Stewart: A Wonderful Life*. New York: Arcade, 1994. Coe focuses this work on Stewart's film and stage career.

Dewey, Donald. *James Stewart: A Biography*. Atlanta: Turner, 1996. This book studies Stewart's life from his small-town upbringing to his life as an actor, father, and Army Air Corps pilot.

Eliot, Marc. *Jimmy Stewart: A Biography*. New York: Harmony Books, 2006. An exhaustive and generally admiring account of Stewart's life and career based on newly conducted archival research.

Fonda, Henry, with Howard Teichmann. *Fonda: My Life*. New York: New American Library, 1981. This book, written by Stewart's best friend, gives special insight into Stewart's personal life.

Munn, Michael. *Jimmy Stewart: The Truth Behind the Legend*. London: Robson, 2005. Munn seeks to debunk Stewart's image by citing the less pleasant aspects of his character. He maintains that Stewart was a "secret agent" for the Federal Bureau of Investigation (FBI) as part of an effort to crack organized crime in Hollywood and was manipulated into "flushing out" alleged Communists from the film industry.

Pickard, Roy. *Jimmy Stewart: A Life in Film*. New York: St. Martin's Press, 1992. Pickard focuses on Stewart's film work with a good chronology of film and television appearances.

OPRAH WINFREY

Talk-show host and entrepreneur

Born: January 29, 1954; Kosciusko, Mississippi
Area of Achievement: Business; film; television

A television icon, Winfrey is one of the wealthiest and most successful entertainers in the world. Her long-running talk show, The Oprah Winfrey Show, became a powerful forum that is credited with launching the careers of other media personalities, turning books into best sellers, and drawing major attention to charitable causes. Winfrey also has produced several films and won praise for her acting ability.

EARLY LIFE

Oprah Gail Winfrey (OH-pruh gayl WIHN-free) was born to Vernon Winfrey and Vernita Lee in the winter of 1954 in the small southern town of Kosciusko, Mississippi. Vernon and Vernita were young and unmarried; Vernon soon relocated to Nashville, Tennessee, while Vernita moved to Milwaukee, Wisconsin, to find work. Winfrey was left in the care of her grandparents, Earlist and Hattie Mae Lee, on their farm. She spent her early years in poverty but was well loved by her strict grandmother, who taught Winfrey to read at age three and took her to church to recite scripture. Winfrey's natural speaking ability would prove to be an asset to her as an adult. At age six, Winfrey moved to Milwaukee to live with her mother and half-sister, Patricia. Vernita worked long hours as a housekeeper and had little time for her children. The conditions pushed Winfrey into independence at an early age, but her life was painful and unstable.

At age nine, she was molested by her mother's nineteen-year-old cousin. Other abuses followed, leaving Winfrey with deep emotional scars. Winfrey found her escape in education, where she excelled. An avid reader, she especially enjoyed books about African Americans such as Harriet Tubman and Sojourner Truth. Winfrey's

Oprah Winfrey (Wikimedia Commons)

abilities were noted by her teachers at Lincoln Middle School. One caring teacher helped her secure a scholarship to Nicolet High School in Glendale, a suburb of Milwaukee, where she could participate in the progressive Upward Bound program. She was the only African-American student at the school. Winfrey continued to struggle at home, however.

> "What I learned at a very early age was that I was responsible for my life. And as I became more spiritually conscious, I learned that we all are responsible for ourselves, that you create your own reality by the way you think and therefore act. You cannot blame apartheid, your parents, your circumstances, because you are not your circumstances. You are your possibilities. If you know that, you can do anything."

After running away from her mother's home at age fourteen, Winfrey moved to Nashville to live with her father, Vernon, a barber with a strong work ethic, and stepmother, Zelma. This disciplined environment provided Winfrey with much-needed stability. Her father stressed the importance of education and work and held Winfrey to high standards. Zelma also was supportive and encouraged Winfrey to excel. Winfrey's life began to change for the better. One of her favorite books, Maya Angelou's *I Know Why the Caged Bird Sings* (1969), helped inspire her to believe in her own innate worth. She represented her high school at the White House Conference on Youth held in Colorado and won an Elks Club oratorical contest that provided her a four year college scholarship.

During Winfrey's senior year in high school, she needed a business sponsor for the March of Dimes Walkathon. She contacted a local radio station, WVOL, and met acting director Joe Heidelberg, an African-American disc jockey. He liked her voice and offered her part-time work reading the news on the radio. In 1971, at age seventeen, Winfrey represented the radio station in a local beauty pageant run by the Nashville Fire Department; she won the title of Miss Fire Prevention.

LIFE'S WORK

In 1972, Winfrey entered college at Tennessee State University in Nashville, focusing on speech, English, and drama. That same year, she was crowned Miss Black Tennessee. Her sophomore year, 1973, she took a job as a news anchor at WTVF-TV, a CBS affiliate. At nineteen, she was the youngest person and the first African-American woman to anchor the news at the station.

After college, Winfrey moved to Baltimore to work at WJZ-TV. She was assigned local morning news updates and progressed to a morning talk show. High ratings brought her the opportunity to audition for WLSTV, an ABC affiliate in Chicago, where she became the first African-American female anchor for *A.M. Chicago* in 1983. Winfrey tailored her show to include controversial issues and current events; the show was renamed *The Oprah Winfrey Show* in 1985. The popularity of *The Oprah Winfrey Show* quickly led to national syndication, and it immediately displaced *Donahue* as the country's highest-rated talk show. The show eventually expanded into more than one hundred other countries and won numerous Emmy Awards. Because she holds an ownership stake in the show, Winfrey became a millionaire when it began airing nationally in 1986.

In 1985, Winfrey was cast as Sofia in Steven Spielberg's film *The Color Purple*, based on Alice Walker's 1982 novel of the same name. In 1986, she received an Academy Award nomination for Best Supporting Actress. Winfrey's only previous acting credit was in the 1978 one-woman show *The History of Black Women Through Drama and Song*. In 1988, she founded Harpo Productions and produced and costarred in a miniseries, *The Women of Brewster Place*, based on Gloria Naylor's 1982 novel, which aired in early 1989; the follow-up series, *Brewster Place*, was shown in 1990. She has produced several other film adaptations of books by African-American women authors, including a 1998 feature version of Toni Morrison's *Beloved* (1987) and a 2005 television movie based on Zora Neale Hurston's *Their Eyes Were Watching God* (1937).

In 1996, Winfrey used her national stature to launch a reading initiative, Oprah's Book Club. Drawing on her love of books and her belief in the power of reading, Winfrey initiated monthly discussions that sent each book she selected to the top of the best-seller lists. In 2000, she launched *O, The Oprah Magazine*, a lifestyle publication that targets affluent and middleclass women. Winfrey also used her influence to address social justice issues and political concerns. In 1998, she testified on behalf of the National Child Protection Act, also known as the "Oprah Bill," which ultimately was signed into law by President Bill Clinton. In 2005, "Oprah's Child Predator Watch List" targeted child predators and offered rewards of $100,000 to apprehend fugitives wanted by the Federal Bureau of Investigation (FBI). In 2008, Winfrey asked her viewers to support U.S. Senate Bill 1738, dubbed the "Protect Our Children Act" which addressed child pornography on the Internet; the bill passed in the fall of 2008. That year, she also made headlines by endorsing Barack Obama's presidential campaign, a major test of her influence.

In 2009, Winfrey announced that she would end her talk show in 2011, at the end of its twenty-fifth season. She turned her attention to launching her own cable network, OWN: The Oprah Winfrey Network, which debuted on January 1, 2011. Though Winfrey had not appeared in a live film role since the acclaimed 1998 *Beloved*, she returned to the screen for the hit 2013 film *The Butler*, for which she was nominated for a BAFTA for Best Supporting Actress as well as numerous other awards. She also acted in the critically acclaimed 2014 film *Selma*, which was nominated for Best Picture. In addition to performing a key supporting role in the film, Winfrey was also the producer of the biopic, which focused on the life of Martin Luther King, Jr. Because of her success in many different media, Winfrey became the first black woman billionaire. According to *Forbes*, her net worth topped $1 billion in 2003 and had risen to $2.9 billion by 2014. Winfrey has been called the greatest philanthropic African American of all time.

In 2005, *BusinessWeek* listed her among its top fifty philanthropists with an estimated $303 million in donations; she was the first African American to be included on the list. In 1998 Winfrey started Oprah's Angel Network, which raised more than fifty million dollars before Winfrey dissolved it in 2010. The Angel Network raised eleven million dollars in 2005 to aid victims of hurricanes Katrina and Rita; Winfrey added ten million dollars of her own to the cause. In 2007, Winfrey donated forty million dollars to open the Oprah Winfrey Leadership Academy for Girls in South Africa. In 2014, Winfrey donated $12 million to the Smithsonian's new National Museum of African American History and Culture. In 2018, Winfrey donated $500,000 to the March for Our Lives student demonstration in favor of gun control in the United States.

Significance

Winfrey's rags-to-riches story remains a powerful testament to the power of self-reliance and perseverance. She

Winfrey receiving the Presidential Medal of Freedom from President Barack Obama. (Wikimedia Commons)

built on her speaking ability and innate empathy to become a television icon, media mogul, and powerful tastemaker. She has built a business empire whose reach extends throughout popular culture. Although the scope of her influence has drawn criticism at times, and she has promoted controversial products and people, her power as a trendsetter is unquestionable. Among her numerous awards and honors are an Emmy Lifetime Achievement Award (1998), a Global Humanitarian Action Award (2004), a George Foster Peabody Individual Achievement Award (1995), and induction into the Broadcasting Hall of Fame and National Association for the Advancement of Colored People (NAACP) Hall of Fame. In 2013, Winfrey was the recipient of the Presidential Medal of Freedom from Barack Obama.

Marylane Wade Koch, updated by Micah L. Issitt

Further Reading

Cotten, Trystan T., and Kimberly Springer, eds. *Stories of Oprah: Oprahfication of American Culture*. Jackson: University Press of Mississippi, 2009. Collection of essays focusing on Winfrey's influence over American culture.

Farr, Cecilia Konchar. *Reading Oprah: How Oprah's Book Club Changed the Way America Reads*. Albany: State University of New York Press, 2004. Describes how Winfrey influenced reading comprehension and popularized the concept of reading for pleasure.

Harris, Jennifer, and Elwood Watson, eds. *The Oprah Phenomenon*. Lexington: University Press of Kentucky, 2007. Collection of essays examining the economics and power of Winfrey over American culture through her influence on entertainment, politics, and national opinions.

Noel, Jennifer. "Lights! Camera! Oprah!" *Ebony* 40, no.6 (April, 1985):100-105. Detailed, well-illustrated profile of Winfrey written when she anchored *A.M. Chicago*.

Paprocki, Sherry Beck. *Oprah Winfrey: Talk Show and Media Magnate*. New York: Chelsea House, 2006. Written for young-adult readers, this biography offers a concise overview of Winfrey's life and accomplishments.

Stone, Tanya Lee. *Oprah Winfrey: Success with an Open Heart*. Minneapolis, Minn.: Milbrook Press, 2001. Written for younger students, this biography provides insight into Winfrey's life challenges and successes.

Winfrey, Oprah. "Oprah Winfrey's Official Biography." http://www.oprah.com/pressroom/OprahWinfreys-Offcial-Biography. Winfrey's official Web site includes this detailed, illustrated biography as well as information on her many business and charitable interests.

ANNA MAY WONG

Actor

Born: January 3, 1905; Los Angeles, California
Died: February 3, 1961; Santa Monica, California
Areas of achievement: Film, theater, television

A popular actor during the early twentieth century, Anna May Wong overcame typecasting and the prejudices of her time to become a highly respected artist. She managed to challenge negative stereotypes with her own projects and inspired a generation of Asian American actors to follow her into the world of film and theater.

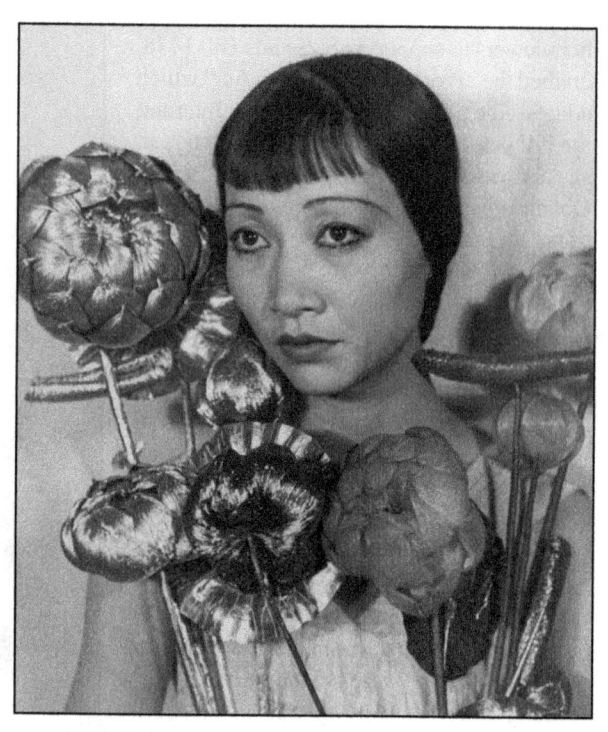

Anna May Wong (Library of Congress)

EARLY LIFE

Anna May Wong was the second child of Wong Sam Sing and Lee Gon Toy, both second-generation Chinese Americans. The family lived near Chinatown in Los Angeles. Wong Sam Sing was a laundryman, a typical occupation for his family, and as their children grew up, they joined their parents in the family business. Liu Tsong (as Wong was called as a child) and her older sister were the only Chinese children at their school; they were constantly teased and sometimes even physically abused by their classmates. To protect his daughters from bullying in school, Wong Sam Sing sent them to a Presbyterian Chinese school; they also attended Chinese language school on Saturdays.

During the early days of the film industry, major studios were in the process of relocating from New York to Los Angeles. In spite of her family's disapproval, Wong became a great fan of the short silent films being shown in nickelodeons. She started to position herself around the studios and use her English name, Anna May. Soon she landed her first role as an extra in the 1919 silent film *The Red Lantern*. After more experience, she dropped out of high school and at the age of sixteen secured her first role, as the wife of Lon Chaney's Asian character in the film *Bits of Life* (1921).

LIFE'S WORK

The following year, Wong was cast in a leading role in *The Toll of the Sea* (1922), the first Technicolor film to be made in Hollywood. The plot was a variation on Italian composer Giacomo Puccini's tragic opera *Madame Butterfly*, in which the Asian heroine commits suicide because of her non-Asian lover's infidelity. The popularity of the plotline reflected general fears of racial mixing. This fear also interfered with Wong's career, as studios were afraid of casting an Asian American actor as a love interest alongside European and American costars. Nevertheless, Wong won critical acclaim for her acting.

Her next major project was *The Thief of Bagdad*, produced in 1924 and starring Douglas Fairbanks, in which she played a beautiful Mongol slave girl. Loosely based on a story from the *Arabian Nights*, the film was a huge success. Her next major film, released as *The Dragon Horse* in 1927, was set in Ming China, and had an Asian cast. Although not well known, the film provided a welcome relief from typecasting. In her next film, *Old San Francisco*, Wong played another kind of stereotypical character–an evil, manipulative role later termed the "dragon lady." Soon afterward she decided to pursue her career in Europe.

Wong is presented a book on the history of Boston by Deputy Mayor John McMorrow and former Fire Commissioner Russel Codman. (Wikimedia Commons)

> "*This is such a short life that nothing can matter very much either one way or another. I have learned not to struggle but to flow along with the tide. If I am to be rich and famous, that will be fine. If not, what do riches and fame count in the long run?*"

In Germany and throughout Europe, Wong was treated with respect, but she also experienced the isolation of being away from the Chinese American community. She and her sister Lulu first went to Berlin, where Wong studied German and acted in the film *Schmutziges Geld* (1928; titled *Show Life* in English). She met many German intellectuals, including the philosopher Walter Benjamin. She used her newly acquired German language skills in Vienna, where she played the title character in the operetta *Tschun Tschi*. Wong also appeared on stage in London in *The Circle of Chalk* with Laurence Olivier. She starred in five English films.

English broadcaster Eric Maschwitz fell in love with Wong, and upon their separation he composed the wistful lyrics of the song "These Foolish Things (Remind Me of You)," which would become a jazz standard. With her international stardom assured, Wong confidently returned to the United States in 1930, starring in the successful Broadway play *On the Spot*, which was later adapted as the film *Dangerous to Know* (1938).

Signing a contract with Paramount, Wong could not escape the typecasting and pervasive racism that infected Hollywood and popular culture at large. In *Daughter of the Dragon* (1931), she played the daughter of Fu Manchu, another predictably evil character. In 1932, she appeared with her friend Marlene Dietrich in Josef von Sternberg's *Shanghai Express*. Wong was insulted when she was passed over in favor of Caucasian actors for MGM's adaptation of Pearl S. Buck's *The Good Earth* (1931), which follows a Chinese family.

During this period, Wong became a spokesperson for Chinese resistance to the invasion of China by Japan, which culminated in the outbreak of the Second Sino-Japanese War in 1937. In spite of Wong's loyalty to the cause, Chinese audiences resented her for her portrayals of Chinese characters. During her 1936 tour of China, Wong experienced this hostility firsthand. In the late 1930s, however, Wong was able to make a few films in which she portrayed more positive characters, including *Daughter of Shanghai* (1937). Wong continued acting in film and on television until her death in 1961. She was given a star on the Hollywood Walk of Fame in 1960.

Significance

Like many actors of ethnic minority descent in twentieth-century Hollywood, Anna May Wong was forced to conform to racial stereotypes and exaggerate her ethnicity. Wong persevered, challenging professional and cultural conventions, and was able to transcend these limitations. Film historians have increasingly recognized Wong's role in cultural history and her considerable talents as an actress. Asian Americans in particular have been inspired by her courage. *Anna May Wong: In Her Own Words*, a documentary film by Korean American filmmaker Yunah Hong, was shown in 2010 at the Pusan International Film Festival. Several recent biographies have also examined her personal story and life's work.

Alice Myers

Further Reading

Chan, Anthony B. *Perpetually Cool: The Many Lives of Anna May Wong (1905–1961)*. Lanham: Scarecrow, 2003. Print. Detailed biography provides a great deal of historical context; illustrated, with filmography and index.

Hodges, Graham Russell. *Anna May Wong: From Laundryman's Daughter to Hollywood Legend*. New York: Palgrave, 2004. Print. Comprehensive biography covers childhood and entire career; illustrated, with bibliography, filmography, and index.

Leibfried, Philip, and Chei Mi Lane. *Anna May Wong: A Complete Guide to Her Film, Stage, Radio, and Television Work*. Jefferson: McFarland, 2004. Print. A well-researched guide providing details on all of Wong's works; illustrated, with bibliography and index.

Leong, Karen J. *The China Mystique: Pearl S. Buck, Anna May Wong, Mayling Soong, and the Transformation of American Orientalism*. Berkeley: U of California P, 2005. Print. Study of American orientalism in 1930s and 1940s; shows how Wong created an identity embracing both Chinese and American cultures; illustrated, with bibliography and index.

Environment

America's self-identity has always resonated with ideas about nature, wilderness, and the natural environment. It wouldn't be too much to say, along with historian Leo Marx, that from the time of the colony of Jamestown, founded in 1607, to the date of the closing of the Western frontier, usually given as 1890, "the encounter of white settlers with what they perceived as wilderness—unaltered nature—was *the* defining American experience." The term "nature" meant various things to different settlers across that span of time. It's well-known, for example, that the Puritans brought with them an early modern belief in the depravity of the wilderness and its innate connection to evil. Later, under the influence of the Romantic movement, a cohort of writers, painters, and even explorers took a different view. For them, the natural world was seen in terms sometimes approaching an immanent divine: being in the presence of nature could be both uplifting and transformative.

As the Western frontier, once seemingly limitless, began to dwindle with westward expansion, a movement arose to preserve large tracts of wilderness. John Muir, born in Scotland in 1838, spent his adult years exploring the North American continent and writing books and many articles about his experiences. Muir was influential in founding Yosemite National Park in 1890, one of the great national parks in the American West. (Yellowstone, founded in 1872 by President Ulysses S. Grant, is widely recognized to have been the first national park not only in the United States but in the world.) The Grand Canyon, the Petrified Forest, and others national preserves and parks would follow.

The modern environmental movement began in the 1960s and 1970s to address widespread problems like air pollution and water pollution. On April 22, 1970, twenty million people attended rallies across the United States to celebrate the first Earth Day. Soon, environmental awareness would become an everyday concern for most Americans. The movement continued earlier efforts at conservation but it also tried to alter the nation's patterns of production and consumption. It did this through advocacy and legislation. In the time since, the environmental movement has often had to learn to negotiate across political divides and between groups with disparate interests. Those interested in conservation in Alaska, for example, are not always like those who are impacted by air pollution in urban environments. Drawing lines between seemingly different groups, interests, and dynamics has become a strong suit for some activists in the environmental movement, a virtue rather than a vice. The writings of activists like Vandana Shiva and Winona LaDuke inspired millions of people precisely because they made clear the fascinating and surprising inter-connectedness of apparently disparate things, such as women's issues, the environment, race, class, and other concerns.

King Range National Conservation Area in Northern California. (Bob Wick, Bureau of Land Management)

Rachel Carson

Biologist

Born: May 27, 1907; Springdale, Pennsylvania
Died: April 14, 1964; Silver Spring, Maryland
Areas of Achievement: Biology, conservation and environmentalism, literature, natural history

A marine biologist and conservationist, Rachel Carson is most remembered for her 1962 book Silent Spring, *an exhaustively researched exposé that sparked a national furor over the use of pesticides in the United States.*

Early Life

Rachel Carson was born in Springdale, Pennsylvania, in 1907 to parents Robert Warden Carson and Maria McLean Carson, who instilled a love of language, music, and nature in their three children. Rachel's long walks with her mother in the nearby orchards and woods awakened in her an awe for the natural world that lasted her entire life.

At a young age Carson conceived the goal of becoming a writer. When she was ten years old her story "A Battle in the Clouds," which won a $10 prize, was published in *St. Nicholas*, a children's magazine. She continued to write throughout her teenage years and at the age of eighteen she entered the Pennsylvania College for Women (later Chatham College) as an English major. During her first two years there, Rachel contributed many works to the school newspaper's literary supplement.

Despite her success as a budding writer, Carson changed her major from English to biology midway through her undergraduate career. One of Carson's mentors, a biology instructor named Mary Skinker, encouraged Carson to think about graduate school. Carson applied to graduate school at Johns Hopkins University in Baltimore, Maryland, for the fall of 1929 and was accepted. Before beginning her program at Johns Hopkins, Carson studied under a scholarship at the Marine Biological Laboratory at Woods Hole Oceanographic Institution on Cape Cod, Massachusetts.

The following year saw many changes in Carson's life; her parents moved to Baltimore to live with her, and she received a teaching assistantship at Johns Hopkins Summer School. Carson completed her master's degree in marine zoology in 1932, and continued to teach until 1936.

In 1935, Carson's father died. Under pressure to support her family, she went to work part-time at the Bureau of Fisheries (later the US Fish and Wildlife Service), writing and editing radio scripts. She took the Civil Service examination and accepted a full-time appointment as an assistant biologist at the bureau. Carson continued her work for the bureau for the next sixteen years, eventually rising in rank to become editor in chief of the publications department.

Rachel Carson (Wikimedia Commons)

> "*Those who dwell among the beauties and mysteries of the earth are never alone or weary of life. Those who contemplate the beauty of the earth find reserves of strength that will endure as long as life lasts. The more clearly we can focus our attention on the wonders and realities of the universe, the less taste we shall have for destruction.*"

Life's Work

Carson's government work led to her first article about the ocean, titled "Undersea," published in the *Atlantic Monthly* in 1937. As lyrical as it was informative,

"Undersea" attracted the attention of an editor from Simon & Schuster, who encouraged Carson to expand it to book length; therefore, in 1941, Carson published *Under the Sea Wind: A Naturalist's Picture of Ocean Life*. Although the book received excellent reviews, its publication was lost in the aftermath of the Japanese attack on Pearl Harbor and the entrance of the United States into World War II. Despite its effect on the sales of her first book, the war effort not only provided Carson with a wealth of new information about the ocean but also

---

Rachel Carson Publishes *Silent Spring*

The publication of *Silent Spring* in 1962 is often considered the beginning of the modern environmental movement. Through her subject—the threat to the Earth through the unrestricted use of chemical pesticides—Rachel Carson captured international attention as she turned a debate mostly held among scientists into a public political issue.

Carson was working for the US Bureau of Fisheries and decided to write a book after receiving a letter from a friend, Olga Huckins of Duxbury, Massachusetts. In the summer of 1957, a state-hired airplane had flown over Huckins's land, spraying dichlorodiphenyltrichloroethane (DDT) for mosquito control. The following day, Huckins found seven dead songbirds in her yard and wrote to Carson asking for help.

DDT is extremely poisonous to many different kinds of insects and does not degrade quickly in the environment. Although first made in 1874, DDT was not found to be an effective insecticide until 1939—in time to be used during World War II to dust the clothing of soldiers for protection against typhus (spread by lice) and malaria (spread by mosquitoes).

The rest of her book provided scientific evidence to show the seriousness of the threat of pesticides such as DDT. She described how hundreds of chemicals had been created to kill pests and how the fittest insects had built up tolerances to these chemicals, forcing the creation of even more lethal compounds to kill the insects that survived. Carson also argued that chemical pesticides often caused severe damage to wildlife, in addition to having long-term effects on human health.

Carson called attention to examples of reckless use of insecticides by the United States Department of Agriculture (USDA). The USDA eliminated pests by spraying land with DDT; after the treatment, fish, songbirds, and beneficial insects such as bees were found dead, leaf crops were badly damaged, vegetables were coated with spray residue, and milk was contaminated by pesticide residues on the grass eaten by dairy cattle.

After the publication of *Silent Spring*, President John F. Kennedy requested a study of the pesticide issue. A panel was formed from the President's Science Advisory Committee; in 1963, the committee released its findings in a report called "The Use of Pesticides." The report credited Carson with having alerted the public to the problem. It recommended that the government inform people of both the hazards and the benefits of pesticides. The report supported Carson's argument that pesticides should be tested for safety before they are allowed to be used.

After reading Carson's book, Senator Abraham A. Ribicoff set up Senate committee hearings to study all federal programs related to environmental pollution, including pesticides. When Carson testified before the Ribicoff Committee, she explained how chemicals from aerial spraying could attach to particles of dust and drift for long distances. DDT residues were found even in Antarctica, where the pesticide had never been used. The committee's 1964 report, "Pesticides and Public Policy," urged federal support for research on the environmental and human health effects of pesticides.

In 1969, the National Cancer Institute released a study showing that continuous exposure to low levels of DDT could produce cancer in laboratory animals. This study caused officials to regard DDT as "potentially" carcinogenic to humans, an important part of the decision to ban the chemical. Carson's book prompted calls for a complete overhaul of the nation's environmental policies. In 1969, Congress officially recognized the importance of environmental quality when it passed the National Environmental Policy Act.

Carson conducts Marine Biology Research with Bob Hines. (Wikimedia Commons)

provided the nation with many new pesticides that were developed as a result of research into chemical warfare. As early as 1942, when she unsuccessfully proposed an article on the effects of the pesticide dichlorodiphenyltrichloroethane (DDT) to *Reader's Digest,*

Carson was interested in the issues involving the use of untested pesticides. At this time in her life, however, she could not bring herself to believe that human-made chemicals could fundamentally affect what she called the "stream of life" on the land, in the skies, or in the oceans. Thus, she returned to her first love and wrote the book *The Sea Around Us,* published in 1951. One chapter, "The Birth of an Island," was published in 1950 in the Yale Review and won the George Westinghouse Science Writing Award. The book was enormously popular, winning the National Book Award in 1951 and the John Burroughs Medal in 1952; it remained on bestseller lists for more than a year. She was awarded a Guggenheim Fellowship, but returned the money after receiving substantial royalties from commercial sales of the book. Carson's resulting financial independence allowed her to resign from her government post and devote herself to her writing.

Just before the publication of *The Sea Around Us,* Carson had begun work on what originally was to be a field guide to the Atlantic shore but later became *The Edge of the Sea* (1955), a portrayal of "the marginal world" between ocean and land. This book also became a best seller. Carson's love and reverence for nature, together with her technical training and her expository gifts, made her the perfect person to write *Silent Spring* in 1962. Initially, Carson intended to write only an article on the effects of pesticides. However, her studies indicated that the widespread spraying of toxic chemicals such as DDT led to disastrous effects on wildlife and possible links with human diseases such as cancer; these facts, together with the incomplete information the chemical industry was releasing about its products and the ignorance of the American public about the effects of pesticides, convinced Carson that she needed to write a full-length book explaining these issues.

In *Silent Spring*, Carson suggested that scientists needed to conduct rigorous studies on the long-term environmental effects of pesticides. She documented evidence showing a pattern of increasing concentrations of pesticides in animals. She conservatively combined the results of more than a thousand technical reports to form an unassailable evidentiary foundation to support her alarming conclusions. At the same time, she encouraged love and respect for life in all its forms.

The publication of *Silent Spring* led to a national debate over the use of pesticides. Unable to discredit the scientific precision of the book, her opponents frequently misrepresented her positions, then attacked those misrepresentations as well as the author's scientific ability. Despite these attacks, the public outcry over Silent Spring led President John F. Kennedy to appoint a special commission charged with studying the pesticide controversy. This Science Advisory Committee eventually supported most of Carson's conclusions and duplicated many of her suggestions. Carson's work and her testimony before the US Senate played an important role in the formation of the Environmental Protection Agency (EPA) in 1970. Carson died of cancer and heart disease in 1964, approximately six years before the EPA opened its doors.

SIGNIFICANCE

As the beloved author of three well-researched and beautifully written books about the sea, Carson was able to draw a large reading audience for her final book, *Silent Spring*. As a well-trained scientist who was able to consult with specialists in many fields, Carson was able to write with precision and confidence about the technical issues surrounding the use of pesticides. She was also able to hold her audience's attention through understandable explanations and suggestions written in a graceful, accessible style. *Silent Spring* incited a national debate over the cavalier use of pesticides, leading to the growth of the American environmental movement and the formation of the EPA. In 1980 Carson was posthumously awarded the Presidential Medal of Freedom—the highest civilian honor in the United States. Her profound influence on grassroots environmentalism and the green movement persists in the twenty-first century.

Katherine Socha

Further Reading

Brooks, Paul. T*he House of Life: Rachel Carson at Work.* 2nd ed. Boston: Houghton, 1989. Print. A biography of Carson written by her editor; based on Carson's private papers, with samples of her public and private writings.

Lytle, Mark Hamilton. *The Gentle Subversive: Rachel Carson, Silent Spring, and the Rise of the Environmental Movement.* New York: Oxford UP, 2007. Print. An updated examination of Carson's influence in sparking the environmental movement.

Marco, Gino J., Robert M. Hollingworth, and William Durham, eds. *Silent Spring Revisited.* Washington: Amer. Chemical Soc., 1987. Print. A collection of essays including a summary of Silent Spring, as well as an essay about Carson's motives and the reaction to her book by a personal friend of Carson's; further essays explore the scientific, political, and environmental issues surrounding the use of pesticides.

Murphy, Priscilla Coit. *What a Book Can Do: The Publication and Reception of Silent Spring.* Amherst: U of Massachusetts P, 2005. Print. Examines the significance of Silent Spring; describes Carson's approach to the book and the response of her opponents, the media, and the public.

Van Jones

Lawyer; writer; civil rights and environmental activist

Born: September 20, 1968; Jackson, Tennessee
Areas of Achievement: Environmentalism, journalism, law, politics, writing

From September 2007 to March 2009 Jones, an attorney, writer, and activist, served as the founding president of Green for All, a national environmental-justice organization. Through Green for All Jones worked with activists, organizations, policymakers, and business, labor, and community leaders to establish programs to train low-income and minority members of society for "green-collar jobs."

Early Life

Anthony "Van" Jones and his twin sister, Angela, were born in 1968 in Jackson, Tennessee, a small town about 90 miles east of Memphis. His father was the principal of a junior high school, and his mother was a high-school

Van Jones (Wikimedia Commons)

teacher. His grandfather was the leader of the local Methodist Episcopal Church, and Jones often accompanied him to religious conferences. In an interview with *The New Yorker*, Jones told Elizabeth Kolbert that as a child he was "bookish and bizarre," and his sister added that Jones was "the stereotypical geek—he just kind of lived up in his head a lot." As a boy, when Jones received action figures of Luke Skywalker and Han Solo, characters from the *Star Wars* films, he played with them by pretending that they were running for public office.

After graduating from high school, Jones enrolled at the University of Tennessee at Martin. He changed his name the first day of his freshman year, having decided that "Anthony Jones" was too dull. He chose the first name "Van" because "it has a little touch of nobility, but at the same time, it's not overboard," as he told Kolbert. Hoping to become a journalist, Jones majored in communications and political science. During his time at the university, Jones founded several student newspapers, with the goal of building a network of black college students in Tennessee. According to the Web site of Ashoka, an organization devoted to what it calls social entrepreneurship, Jones's college journalism work "took him to Louisiana, where he saw racism and poverty as he had never seen before. He knew then that, to achieve the kind of change he wanted, he would have to be more than a writer." Additionally, internships at a few newspapers convinced him that a career in journalism was not for him. After graduating, in 1990, and serving an internship with the Tennessee state legislature, he enrolled at Yale Law School, in New Haven, Connecticut.

During his years at Yale, Jones witnessed events that helped to shape his worldview and further spurred him to activism. In March 1991, during his second semester, he was particularly disturbed by the infamous police beating of Rodney King, an African-American who, while intoxicated, was pulled over for speeding by Los Angeles police officers. When he resisted arrest, the officers violently subdued him, first with a Taser and then with repeated baton beatings. A bystander captured the event on video camera, and a portion of the footage was broadcast nationally. Jones had taken a semester off from law school and was working as an intern for the Lawyers' Committee for Civil Rights (LCCR) in San Francisco when, in April 1992, a jury whose members included no blacks acquitted the four officers charged with police brutality in the King case. The acquittal sparked widespread outrage, leading to a week of violence and mayhem that became known as the Los Angeles Riots of 1992. Jones, who observed those events for the LCCR, was arrested during the riots, along with many other young men, most of them members of minority groups. His arrest incident underscored for him that African-American men were often victims of wrongful arrest and police abuse. Jones had witnessed similar injustices in New Haven. "I was seeing kids at Yale do drugs and talk about it openly, and have nothing happen to them, or, if anything, get sent to rehab," Jones told Kolbert. "And then I was seeing kids three blocks away, in the housing projects, doing the same drugs, in smaller amounts, go to prison."

> "*If the road to social transformation can be paved only by saints who never make mistakes, the road will never be built. The upside is that we don't have to be perfect to save our communities and restore the Earth. We just have to try hard and be as honest as we can be about the processes we are going through. So I share the mistakes and failures, as well as the successes, because that is the truth of my journey – and of anyone's journey.*"

LIFE'S WORK

After graduating from law school, Jones moved to San Francisco, where in 1995 he founded the Bay Area Police Watch. That group used computer software in an attempt to track unjust practices on the part of officers and precincts and make the information available to lawyers, watchdog groups, and the media. Jones's organization soon received up to 15 complaints per day on its police-misconduct hotline, from residents of San Francisco and neighboring Oakland. In 1996 the Bay Area Police Watch expanded its focus to become a civil rights organization, renamed the Ella Baker Center for Human Rights, in honor of the activist who had pressured the national Democratic Party to confront racial discrimination and, in 1957, helped found the Southern Christian Leadership Conference. One of the center's main goals was to help youths avoid prison and secure good jobs. Through news conferences and sit-ins or other public demonstrations, the center also worked to publicize and protest police and government violations of civil rights.

The first major case the center took on was that of Aaron Williams, a young black man who on June 4, 1995 was arrested for burglary after a violent struggle with San Francisco officers and died while in police custody. Reading a news account of the incident, Jones noticed the name of one of the officers involved in it: Marc Andaya. "At the time I read that story, I had a file several inches thick sitting in my cabinet on Marc Andaya," he told Ken Garcia for the *San Francisco Chronicle* (March 12, 1998), "and when I saw his name in connection with the Aaron Williams death, I made a commitment to myself that I was not going to rest until people knew about this police officer and his record." In 1984 Andaya had shot to death a person whom Jones described to Garcia as a "mentally ill, unarmed black man"; the following year Andaya had been suspended for 30 days for choking a handcuffed suspect; and in 1993 the Oakland Police Citizens Review Board judged that Andaya had used excessive force and racial slurs against an African-American suspect. He had been hired by the San Francisco Police Department in 1994. At the Police Commission disciplinary hearing concerning Williams's death, several witnesses testified to having seen Andaya kick Williams in the head after he was subdued. The charges of police brutality were dismissed, however, when a medical examiner concluded that Williams, a crack-cocaine abuser, had died not from the beating he received from officers but from a heart attack triggered by drugs. Thanks to Jones's efforts to publicize Andaya's record, pressure mounted, mainly from the African-American community, to oust the officer. In 1997 Andaya was fired for lying on his police application about his previous record. For his advocacy work, Jones was honored with a Next Generation Leadership Fellowship from the Rockefeller Foundation and a Reebok Human Rights Award.

In another major accomplishment, the Ella Baker Center prevented an expansion of California's sprawling juvenile-incarceration system. In 2000 Jones learned about a state plan to construct a 540-bed juvenile-detention center in Alameda County, which would have been one of the largest facilities of its kind in the nation. Though the project was presented to the public as a way to improve conditions for young offenders, he saw it as a step that would inevitably lead to many more black teenagers' being incarcerated. Jones began a campaign to stop the construction of the center, using the tag line, "Stop the Superjail." He organized demonstrations involving local teenagers, and the public-awareness campaign worked: in 2003 the construction plans for the center were halted.

For Jones, that triumph was tarnished by what he feared was the selfishness of his motivation for community activism. "I certainly wasn't motivated only by love for the people," he told Kolbert. "I was trying to find some kind of community, or some sense of belonging, or some sense of redemption through heroic deeds. I wasn't being honest with myself about it, and it all just proved to be incredibly fragile." One day Jones attended a lecture at a San Francisco bookstore by Julia "Butterfly" Hill, the environmental activist best known for living in the canopy of a 600-year-old California redwood tree, from December 1997 to December 1999, to prevent Pacific Lumber Co. loggers from cutting it down. Hill saved the tree and later founded a nonprofit organization called Circle of Life. "There was no guarantee she was going to win...," Jones told Kolbert. "I was always looking for clever things I could game out, and she just stepped out on faith, and did it... I wanted to do my work like she had done her work." Jones was also amazed that Hill had felt no bitterness toward those who had opposed her efforts. Jones and Hill became friends and, realizing that they shared similar goals, began delivering lectures together. Hill told Kolbert about Jones, "We fit together like pieces of a puzzle. I brought the piece that we are not separate from this planet. His piece was we need to uplift everyone." "We could see underneath all of it was the idea of disposability," Jones told Kolbert. "The idea that you've got disposable people, a disposable planet."

Jones suggested that the Ella Baker Center work to link civil rights and environmentalism, which he saw as related issues. By involving the poor and minorities—the groups most affected by pollution, excluded from the benefits of technological advances, and in need of jobs—in the environmental movement and training them for jobs "greening" the infrastructure of the U.S., Jones believed that he could address three societal problems at once: poverty, racial inequality, and environmental degradation. His plan was to create a Green Job Corps in Oakland that would train poor and underserved city residents for such jobs as weatherizing buildings and constructing and installing solar panels. Though Jones's suggestion to expand the scope of the Ella Baker Center was not popular among the group's board members, who deemed it unrealistic, he began speaking to environmental organizations and applying for grant money to bring green jobs to Oakland. In 2004 Jones received $215,000 from the New York-based Nathan Cummings Foundation, which he used to fund organizational meetings and retreats. Jones was disappointed, however, when no jobs resulted from all his planning. He applied for and received another $215,000 grant from the foundation, which he again spent on planning meetings and research. Feeling as though he had wasted time and money, Jones realized that changing public policy was the only way he was going to bring green jobs to Oakland.

In February 2007 Jones was invited to a roundtable discussion of global climate change hosted by one of San Francisco's representatives in Congress, House Speaker Nancy Pelosi. Because the invitation specified that each guest was to deliver a brief self-introduction, Jones tried to be as succinct as possible, but as other invitees stood up and introduced themselves with lengthy speeches describing their work and goals, Jones realized he had missed an opportunity to articulate his vision. When Pelosi asked for questions at the end of the meeting, after which there was to be a press conference, Jones said, as quoted by Derrick Z. Jackson in the *Boston Globe* (September 29, 2007), "My question is, at the press conference, will you say four words?" He asked Pelosi to say the words, "Clean Energy Jobs Bill." Jones then launched into an engaging oration, asking Pelosi and all of the invitees to support the passage of a bill to provide funding for the creation of jobs that would contribute to a clean-energy economy. At the press conference Pelosi commended Jones's idea and stated that everyone at the roundtable meeting had agreed that a clean-energy jobs bill should be introduced in Congress.

Pelosi's endorsement inspired local and national support for bills that linked the creation of jobs for minorities with the quest for a green economy. Jones helped form the Oakland Apollo Alliance, a coalition of labor unions and environmentalists that seeks green-collar jobs in Oakland. In June 2007 Oakland became the first city in the nation to pass a law creating a Green Job Corps, a program geared toward building a green economy. The Oakland city government provided $250,000 to the Green Job Corps to create a program to train unemployed residents for jobs in such areas as solar energy, organic food, and wind power. They were also trained to bring existing buildings up to the energy-efficiency standards required by California state law. The first class of 40 graduated from the program in 2007. Jones sees those jobs as valuable because they rely on local labor and, therefore, cannot be outsourced. "You can't take a building you want to weatherize, put it on a ship to China and then have them do it and send it back...," Jones told Thomas L. Friedman for the *New York Times* (October 17, 2007). "Those green-collar jobs can provide a pathway out of poverty for someone who has not gone to college." Also in June 2007 then-U.S. representative Hilda Solis of California (now the U.S. secretary of labor) introduced a measure authorizing the U.S. Department of Labor to spend $125 million to train low-income workers for green jobs. The bill, called the Green Jobs Act, was put under the umbrella of the Energy Independence and Security Act, approved by Congress and signed into law by President George W. Bush in December 2007. While Bush's 2009 budget proposal not only lacked funds for the act but also cut or eliminated money allocated for a range of existing job-training programs, the economic stimulus package passed by Congress in early 2009 and the budget proposed by President Obama in late February set aside billions of dollars for greening the economy.

In September 2007, while remaining the president of the Ella Baker Center, Jones founded Green for All, a national organization aimed at promoting green jobs and environmental justice. He partnered with other organizations with similar goals, including the New York City-based environmental-justice organization Sustainable South Bronx and the American Council on Renewable Energy (ACORE); he delivered many lectures throughout the U.S. to raise public awareness of the potential for green-collar jobs to transform the economy. Jones advocated banning the construction of new coal plants, establishing a national Clean Energy Corps, creating incentives to trade in traditional cars for hybrid cars, and establishing a loan program for "emergency efficiency measures." In October 2008 Jones published *The Green Collar Economy: How One Solution Can Fix Our Two Biggest Problems*, which makes the case for improving the failing U.S. economy and a damaged environment by investing in green-collar jobs. The book became a *New York Times* best-seller and was generally praised, though some critics contrasted Jones's considerable gifts as a public speaker with his workmanlike prose.

Many have questioned the premise of Jones's argument that combating climate change is a good way to lift people out of poverty. For instance, some economists have expressed doubts that the alternative-energy industry would provide more jobs than the number that would be lost in industries such as coal-mining; others question whether a green economy would succeed in providing permanent jobs for the chronically unemployed, a historically difficult task. Matthew Kahn, an economics professor at the Institute of the Environment of the University of California at Los Angeles (UCLA), is among those who have asked whether environmentally oriented public-works programs would be any better run than their traditional counterparts, which have often proven to be inefficient. According to Jones, the way to avoid such pitfalls is to make sure the plan pursues both goals: providing jobs for the poor and creating a greener society.

"You can pass all the bills you want to; you can appropriate all the bills you want to," Jones told Kolbert. "You can even start retrofitting buildings. But if I go there and the people who are doing the retrofits are just the people who used to have the jobs anyway, and they're mostly all one color and mostly all one kind of people, then I'm not going to be satisfied."

Jones's ideas soon received support from many Democratic legislators, including Senate majority leader Harry Reid; several dozen governors; and more than 900 U.S. mayors, who expressed their support by signing the U.S. Conference of Mayors' Climate Protection Agreement. In Barack Obama's first months in the White House, the president expressed his support for the allocation of $15 billion per year on renewable energy, weatherization for low-income housing, and carbon-capture and -storage projects. In March 2009 Obama hired Jones as a special adviser for green jobs, enterprise, and innovation in the White House's Council on Environmental Quality. (That month Phaedra Ellis-Lamkins became the chief executive officer of Green for All.) During the six months he held his position in the administration, Jones focused on improving the energy efficiency of Americans' homes. According to VanJones.net, "Toward this end, he led a 12-Department inter-agency process, which designed proposals to weatherize and retrofit millions of American homes, including by leveraging private capital." Jones also headed an interagency group to help Democrats better implement the stimulus programs contained in the American Recovery and Reinvestment Act of February 2009; he worked to tailor the stimulus programs to address the needs of minorities and rural Americans.

Jones had been with the Obama White House for only a few months when he came under attack by conservative pundits, especially the Fox News analyst Glenn Beck, and several congressional Republicans, regarding several of his past associations and statements. Jones was criticized for signing a 2004 petition, sponsored by the controversial 9/11 Truth Movement, calling for an investigation into the actions of President George W. Bush with respect to the September 11, 2001 terrorist attacks; for using a derogatory word to describe congressional Republicans during a speech he delivered a month before he was appointed to his federal position; and for his association in the 1990s with a neo-Marxist organization called Standing Together to Organize a Revolutionary Movement. In the summer of 2009, Color of Change, an Internet-based advocacy organization that Jones co-founded in 2005 with James Rucker, formerly of MoveOn.org, initiated a boycott of Glenn Beck's show after Beck accused Obama of harboring a "deep-seated hatred for white people"; the boycott resulted in several companies' pulling ads from his show. In response to the boycott, Beck stepped up his criticisms, calling on Jones to resign. Congressional Republicans followed suit; Representative Mike Pence of Indiana was widely quoted as calling for Jones's resignation because "his extremist views and coarse rhetoric have no place in this administration or the public debate." As criticism from the right heightened, Jones defended his record and apologized for some of his past statements.

On September 6, 2009 Jones announced his resignation. "On the eve of historic fights for health care and clean energy, opponents of reform have mounted a vicious smear campaign against me," he said in a statement, as quoted on KTVU.com. "They are using lies and distortions to distract and divide." Jones stated, however, that he did not want the administration's efforts to defend his record to interfere with the president's agenda. That sentiment was echoed by the White House press secretary Robert Gibbs, who stated, "What Van Jones decided was that the agenda of this president was bigger than any one individual." The seeming reluctance of the administration to defend Jones angered many of Jones's supporters, who thought that his resignation served to legitimize what they called the false and distorted claims advanced by conservatives. "The Obama Administration should have acted like the victors they are and made sure Van Jones stayed just where he was," John McWhorter wrote for the *New Republic*. "I understand that Obama can't rule as the outright lefty many of his fans would prefer. But Jones' presence was a laudable representation of progressivism in the Administration... If the Obama folks are going to throw even people like this off the train just because some silly people make some silly noises, then the bloom really is off the rose." Since he left the administration, Jones has reportedly been working in an office lent to him by the progressive Washington, D.C. think tank the Center for American Progress, where he previously served as a senior fellow; he does not have a salaried position there.

In June 2011 Jones launched an advocacy project called Rebuild The Dream. It was intended "to give the progressive mass movement that rose up to elect Barack Obama a new banner to march under." The launch included performances by The Roots and a DJ set by artist Shepard Fairey. In August 2012, Prince announced a series of concerts in Chicago to support Rebuild the Dream. Prince went on The View with Jones and Rosario Dawson to promote the concerts.

In early 2015 Jones launched #YesWeCode, an initiative aiming to "teach 100,000 low-income kids to write code". Again, Prince lent his support and appeared at the Essence Festival to help support the launch. Jones credits Prince with the idea to form #YesWeCode. #YesWeCode has hosted several hackathons, including one in Detroit in partnership with MSNBC, and Oakland. In an interview on CNN on April 21, 2016, hours after the musician Prince's death, Jones revealed that Prince had secretly contributed to the funding of #YesWeCode.

In 2015 Jones launched #cut50, an organization focused on bi-partisan solutions to criminal justice reform issues. In March 2015 #cut50 hosted a "bi-partisan summit" with Republican Newt Gingrich, former Speaker of the House, to promote bi-partisan solutions. Their goals are to reduce prison populations, as the US has the highest rate of incarceration in the world, and to end mandatory minimum sentencing and mandatory lengthy sentences for certain crimes. #cut50 received much celebrity support from "100 A-List celebrities" including Amy Schumer, Steph Curry, Ed Norton, Jesse Williams, Chris Pine, Russell Simmons, Shonda Rhimes, Russell Brand, Jessica Chastain, and Piper Kerman. In May 2018 Jones and other members of #cut50 met with Jared Kushner and President Donald Trump at the White House to discuss a criminal justice reform bill.

SIGNIFICANCE

Jones has served on the boards of organizations including the National Apollo Alliance, Social Venture Network, Rainforest Action Network, Bioneers, and Circle of Life. His honors include the International Ashoka Fellowship (2000), the World Economic Forum's Young Global Leader Award (2008), the Paul Wellstone Award from the progressive think tank Campaign for America's Future (2008), the Aspen Institute Energy and Environment Award in the category of individual thought leadership (2009), the Hubert H. Humphrey Civil Rights Award (2009), the NAACP President's Award (2010), the Vanguard Award from the Rainbow Push Coalition (2015), and the David E. Glover Vanguard Award (2015). Over the years Jones has made a number of lists, including *Essence* magazine's 25 Most Inspiring African Americans (2008), *Time* magazine's 100 Most Influential People in the World (2009), *Ebony* magazine's Power 150 (2011), *Rolling Stone* magazine's 12 Leaders Who Get Things Done (2012), and *The Root* magazine's 100 Honorees (2013).

A talented public speaker, Jones is known for his ability to relate to audiences ranging from unemployed urban youth to business and political leaders. "Green values are very consistent with African and indigenous values in the first place," he told Alwin Jones for *Black Enterprise* (May 2008). "Western society is coming back around to values that were and are a part of our core, our heritage, our history. We shouldn't think about it as jumping on a white bandwagon because it's our bandwagon in the first place." Jones lives in Oakland with his wife, Jana Carter, an employment lawyer, and their two young sons.

FURTHER READING:

Ambinder, Marc. "A Hundred Ways Of Looking At Van Jones." *The Atlantic*, Atlantic Media Company, 8 Sept. 2009, www.theatlantic.com/politics/archive/2009/09/a-hundred-ways-of-looking-at-van-jones/24600/.

Friedman, Thomas L. "The Green-Collar Solution." *The New York Times*, The New York Times, 17 Oct. 2007, www.nytimes.com/2007/10/17/opinion/17friedman.html.

Garofoli, Joe. "Bay Area Activist Van Jones Back in Limelight." *San Francisco Chronicle*, Houston Chronicle, 25 May 2010, www.sfchronicle.com/politics/joegarofoli/article/Bay-Area-activist-Van-Jones-back-in-limelight-3188067.php.

Jones, Alwin. "A Just Cause." *Black Enterprise*, 25 Nov. 2008, www.blackenterprise.com/a-just-cause/.

Jones, Van. *Beyond the Messy Truth: How We Came Apart, How We Come Together*. Ballantine, 2018.

---. *The Green-Collar Economy: How One Solution Can Fix Our Two Biggest Problems*. HarperCollins, 2009.

---. *Rebuild The Dream*. Nation Books, 2012.

Kolbert, Elizabeth. "Greening the Ghetto." *The New Yorker*, The New Yorker, 12 Jan. 2009, www.newyorker.com/magazine/2009/01/12/greening-the-ghetto.

Roberts, David. "It's Not Easy Becoming Green." *In These Times*, 27 Dec. 2008, inthesetimes.com/article/4114/its_not_easy_becoming_green.

Staff, The New Republic. "Prison Reform May Be The Last Bipartisan Issue Left in D.C." *The New Republic*, 29 July 2014, newrepublic.com/article/118891/prison-reform-bipartisan-issue-says-cnns-van-jones.

Winona LaDuke

Native American (Ojibwe) activist

Born: August 18, 1959; Los Angeles, California
Area of Achievement: Native American advocacy; Environment

A charismatic writer, speaker, environmentalist, economist, and activist, Winona LaDuke has been a tireless voice for Native American issues, human rights, green and rural economies, and grass-roots organizing. She is a member of the Ojibwe, or Anishinaabe, people of North America.

Early Life

Winona LaDuke was born in 1959 in Los Angeles. Her father, Vincent LaDuke, is a Native American from the Ojibwe White Earth Reservation in Minnesota. He worked as an actor in Los Angeles playing supporting roles in Westerns. Later, using the name Sun Bear, he became active in the New Age spirituality movement. LaDuke's mother was Betty Bernstein, an art teacher originally from the Bronx, New York. LaDuke's parents separated when she was about five years old and LaDuke was raised by her mother in Oregon. In high school, LaDuke had both poise and intelligence. She discovered she had a knack for public speaking, and she enjoyed being on the school's debate team.

After high school, LaDuke went to Harvard University. It was there that she began to explore in earnest her Native American heritage, joining a group of Native American activists on campus. She studied economics, and was particularly interested in rural development. When she was eighteen years old, she had the opportunity to speak at the United Nations on Native American issues, and this helped to cement her interests in activism, policy, and public speaking.

Life's Work

After Harvard, LaDuke made a very unusual move. Instead of seeking a traditional career, she took her Harvard degree and moved onto the White Earth Indian Reservation in Minnesota—the reservation her father had been raised on. At first, she struggled to be accepted there. She took a job working as the principal of the reservation's high school, and she began learning the Ojibwe language. She also started work on a master's degree through a distance learning program offered by Antioch University.

Winona LaDuke (Wikimedia Commons)

She eventually graduated with a master's degree in economic development, writing a thesis on her reservation's subsistence economy. A subsistence economy is one that doesn't use money and isn't focused on producing goods for the market to be sold for profit; it focuses on using natural resources to produce food, clothing, and shelter—products that can be either consumed directly or bartered.

> "*Mother Earth needs us to keep our covenant. We will do this in courts, we will do this on our radio station, and we will commit to our descendants to work hard to protect this land and water for them. Whether you have feet, wings, fins, or roots, we are all in it together.*"

LaDuke was strongly influenced by a group of radical economic thinkers who were convinced that the programs that were then being espoused by mainstream economists for developing economies in poor regions were making a big mistake by not recognizing the validity of these societies' traditional subsistence economies. This included what were then still called "third world" countries, but also Native American communities in North America. Most development programs sought to impose Western and "modern" methods of agricultural production and distribution, for example, that would replace the subsistence agriculture of traditional societies. This essentially forced them to adopt a capitalist, money-based economy and to be integrated into the global market system.

In the 1970s and 1980s, when LaDuke was at Harvard working on her master's degree, the debate about development was also impacted by the environmental movement and the then-new concept of achieving *sustainable* development. LaDuke thought that by gaining wider awareness for Native American ideas and practices, especially pertaining to ecology and subsistence economic practices, she could impact the debate about the environment and sustainable development.

LaDuke also wanted to help her people and the reservation. She knew that over 860,000 acres had originally been reserved for the White Earth Indian Reservation in 1867. Feeling that the land had been taken from them illegally (more than 90% of it was in the hands of non-Indians by the 1980s), LaDuke started legal proceedings against the United States government. When that avenue failed to produce results, in 1989 she founded the White Earth Land Recovery Project, a nonprofit dedicated to buying back the land that was originally the reservation's. To date the project has recovered almost 1,400 acres. As a result, they have reinvigorated the traditional cultivation of wild rice on the recovered land—a staple food of the Ojibwe—and initiated several other large-scale farming projects.

In the 1990s, LaDuke's public profile grew by leaps and bounds. In 1993, she founded Honor the Earth with the popular folk-rock group the Indigo Girls. Honor the Earth is dedicated to raising awareness about Native American environmental issues through the arts, music, and other media. In 1996 and 2000, LaDuke was selected by Ralph Nader to be the vice-presidential candidate on the Green Party ticket. This brought more attention to LaDuke and to her causes. She became a frequent voice on Amy Goodman's progressive radio news program *Democracy Now!* and, in 1998, she was *Ms.* magazine's Woman of the Year. In 1997, LaDuke published her first novel, *Last Standing Woman*.

LaDuke has published a number of nonfiction books about Native American spirituality, culture, and progressive politics. Among them are *Recovering the Sacred: the Power of Naming and Claiming* (2005), *The Militarization of Indian Country* (2013), and *All Our Relations: Native Struggles for Land and Life* (2016). Between 2013 and 2016, LaDuke was active in fighting the Sandpiper pipeline, a proposed underground oil pipeline that would have carried crude oil from North Dakota through Minnesota to Superior, Wisconsin. LaDuke argued that the pipeline's path crossed the reservation's land, and she fought the proposal. The pipeline project was eventually shelved by Enbridge Energy Partners in 2016.

SIGNIFICANCE

LaDuke has been indefatigable and eloquent as an activist, author, and public speaker. She connects such diverse issues as anti-colonialism, the environment, women's issues, and economic development to the concerns of Native Americans. In turn, she has tried to articulate ideas that address those issues derived from indigenous traditions and emphasizing harmony and sustainability. She has argued that indigenous ecological knowledge and land management practices can be reinvigorated and sustained in the modern era.

LaDuke has also initiated concrete efforts to realize this vision. As the director of the White Earth Land Recovery Project for the Ojibwe White Earth Reservation, she has reclaimed traditional farming practices, like the cultivation of wild rice, and promoted a mixed economy for the reservation that respects indigenous subsistence practices and combines them with modern ones, like the production of goods for market. Her most concrete work has been with the White Earth Reservation, and this flows not only from her commitment to her roots as a Native American but from her commitment to the spirit of localism and grass roots action. LaDuke's vision for the future may be a radical one, but, paradoxically, it is rooted in the most traditional of American values and practices.

D. Alan Dean

FURTHER READING

LaDuke, Winona. *All Our Relations: Native Struggles for Land and Life*. Haymarket Books, 2016.

---. *The Winona LaDuke Chronicles: Stories from the Front Lines in the Battle for Environmental Justice*. Spotted Horse Press, 2016.

---. *The Winona LaDuke Reader: A Collection of Essential Writings*. Stillwater, MN, Voyageur Press, 2002.

Goodman, Amy, and Winona LaDuke. "Native Activist Winona LaDuke: Pipeline Company Enbridge Has No Right to Destroy Our Future." *Democracy Now!*, 23 Aug. 2016, www.democracynow.org/2016/8/23/native_activist_winona_laduke_pipeline_company.

Silverstone, Michael. *Winona LaDuke: Restoring Land and Culture in Native America*. New York: The Feminist Press, 2001.

JOHN MUIR

Scottish-born American naturalist

Born: April 21, 1838; Dunbar, Scotland
Died: December 24, 1914; Los Angeles, California
Area of Achievement: Conservation and environmentalism, writing

Combining his skills as a scientist, explorer, and writer, Muir played a significant role in the conservation movement and in the development of the United States National Park system and left a legacy that has kept his name honored in the twenty-first century.

EARLY LIFE

John Muir (mewr) was the eldest of three sons and the third of eight children of Ann Gilrye Muir and Daniel Muir. His father grew up under the harshest poverty imaginable but eventually gained stature as a middle-class grain merchant and became a Presbyterian of severe Fundamentalist religious beliefs. He worshiped a God of wrath who found evil in almost every childish activity. Typically, John and his playmates would leave the yard, and his tyrannical father would fly into a rage and punish the innocent lad. When his father did not have the total devotion of his entire family, he would punish them with the greatest severity.

In 1849, at the age of eleven, John and his family immigrated to the United States in search of greater economic opportunity. The Muirs moved to Portage, Wisconsin, an area that had a fine reputation for wheat growing, where they purchased farmland. John marveled at the beauty of the countryside. He kept busy with farm chores and read at night when he was thought to be asleep. He also developed an early love of machinery and began the practice of waking at one in the morning to go to his cellar workshop to build things out of scraps of wood and iron. His father considered his inventions a waste of time, but John built a sawmill, weather instruments, waterwheels, and clocks. In 1860, at the age of twenty-two, he displayed his inventions at the state fair in Madison. His gadgets were well received, but his dour father only lectured him on the sin of vanity.

At this juncture in his life, John decided to leave home to make his own way. First, he moved to nearby Madison and attended the University of Wisconsin. He followed no particular course of study; he took classes that interested him. He seemed more concerned with learning than with earning a degree. Muir excelled in the sciences and also enjoyed the outdoor laboratory of nature. A tall, disheveled, bearded man with penetrating, glacial-blue eyes, Muir eventually grew tired of the regimentation of college. He liked books, but he loved experience more. Some men from the university were leaving to fight in the Civil War. Muir was twenty-five years old and in his junior year of school, but he decided to leave also.

From Madison, he journeyed into Canada to take odd jobs and to study the botany of the area. Later, he turned up in Indianapolis, Indiana, working in a carriage shop. With his inventive mind, he proved a success in the factory environment until one day he suffered an eye injury while working on a machine. The puncture wound

John Muir (Library of Congress)

affected both eyes, and soon he lost his eyesight. After a month of convalescence in a darkened room, his vision slowly returned. With a new lease on life and his eyesight fully restored, Muir decided to abandon the factory world and enjoy nature.

LIFE'S WORK

In September of 1867, Muir began a walking tour that would take him from Louisville, Kentucky, to the Gulf Coast of Florida. He found the wildlife and plants of the South fascinating. His travels took him through Kentucky, Tennessee, Georgia, and Florida, until he reached the Gulf at Cedar Key. He had no particular route planned, other than to head south. He was not disappointed in what he found on his four-month trek and decided to continue his journey. He had often read the exciting travel accounts of Alexander von Humboldt, who had explored widely in South America. Such exploration was Muir's dream also, but it was interrupted by a three-month bout with malaria. When he was almost recovered, he set off for Cuba, but, upon reaching that tropical island and after waiting for a southbound ship for a month, he settled on a new destination.

President Theodore Roosevelt (left) and Muir on Glacier Point in Yosemite National Park. (Library of Congress)

> "*I will follow my instincts, be myself for good or ill, and see what will be the upshot. As long as I live, I'll hear waterfalls and birds and winds sing. I'll interpret the rocks, learn the language of flood, storm, and the avalanche. I'll acquaint myself*"

Muir believed that California offered the best climate for his malarial disorder and also afforded an environment of substantial botanical interest. He made the long journey to the West and settled in beautiful Yosemite Valley, which was snuggled in the Sierra Nevada. At times, he worked as a sheepherder and at a lumber mill, but he spent most of the time exploring the beautiful countryside, taking notes of his findings, and looking for one more glorious site of the wondrous Sierra. In 1869, Muir and a friend built a one-room cabin of pine logs near Yosemite Falls, and this became his home. He had famous visitors such as Asa Gray, the Harvard botanist, the novelist Therese Yelverton, and the renowned Transcendentalist Ralph Waldo Emerson. With all, he shared the exhilarating scenes of the high country.

After four years in Yosemite Valley, Muir moved to San Francisco and dreamed of other trips. He traveled up the coast to Oregon and Washington and climbed Mount Shasta and Mount Rainier. He also made six excursions to Alaska, where he climbed mountains and studied glaciers. His favorite area was Glacier Bay in southern Alaska, but he loved any place where he could find a mountain to climb. During his stay in Alaska, he also studied the customs of the Tlingit Indians.

Muir also found time for romance. A friend introduced him to Louisa Strentzel, daughter of horticulturalist Dr. John Strentzel and owner of a large fruit ranch east of San Francisco, near the town of Martinez. Louisa and John were married on April 14, 1880. At the same time, he became the overseer of the Strentzel ranch and introduced changes that brought production to peak efficiency. Muir grafted one hundred varieties of pears and grapes onto the best strains. His effective management of the ranch provided him with economic security. For the next ten years, he neglected his writing and mountain climbing, but he and his wife grew reasonably prosperous and reared their two daughters, Wanda and Helen.

Nine years after his marriage, Muir took an important trip back to Yosemite. With him was Robert Underwood Johnson, an old friend and editor of the influential *The*

Muir and climbing party at summit of Mount Rainier, 1888. (Wikimedia Commons)

Century. The two were dumbfounded by the changes that had taken place in the Sierra during such a short time. Sheep and lumberjacks had created great devastation in the valley and high country. Forest land was bare, and grass root structures were severely damaged by the sharp hoofs of the sheep. Johnson was moved to action. He promised to lobby influential congressmen, and he encouraged Muir to convince the American public of their conservationist cause and the need to take action before it was too late. Muir accepted the challenge and, in two well-argued articles published in *The Century*, he convinced many readers of the desperate need to preserve some of the natural wonders of the California highlands.

In 1890, the federal government rewarded the efforts of Muir, Johnson, and other conservationists by creating Yosemite National Park. Other victories followed when Congress established Mount Rainier, the Grand Canyon, the Petrified Forest, and parts of the Sierra as national preserves. The following year, Muir worked for the passage of legislation that eventually allowed President Benjamin Harrison to set aside thirteen million acres of forest land and President Grover Cleveland, twenty-one million acres more. Muir continued the conservationist cause by helping to create the Sierra Club in 1892. He became the club's first president, and the members vowed to preserve the natural features of the California mountains.

With the total support of his wife, Muir decided to abandon the ranch work and concentrate on furthering his writing career. In 1894, he published *The Mountains of California* and followed it with *Our National Parks* (1901), *Stickeen* (1909), *My First Summer in the Sierra* (1911), *The Yosemite* (1912), and *The Story of My Boyhood and Youth* (1913). In these works, he richly illustrated the growth of a conservationist mind and presented forceful arguments for preservation and ecological protection.

In his last years, Muir traveled to Europe, South America, and Africa, always learning and experiencing what he could. Seventy-six years of life and accomplishment came to an end in December of 1914, when Muir died in Los Angeles on Christmas Eve.

SIGNIFICANCE

For John Muir, it had been a full life. Forced to make a decision at an early age between machines and inventions on one hand and nature and conservation on the other, he chose the path of mountains, flowers, and preservation. In nature, he found his cathedral, and there he preached the gospel of conservation, preservation, and ecology. He walked the wilderness paths with Ralph Waldo Emerson and Theodore Roosevelt; in the end, he convinced many of his contemporaries of the rightness of his ideas.

Muir lived at a time when the United States was becoming a great industrial leader in the world. Nevertheless, he was able to point to the wisdom of preserving many natural wonders of the American West. Although an earlier generation had plundered the East, his efforts and those of others helped to save significant portions of the West, to create large national parks and forest preserves, and to protect the ecological systems so necessary for the survival of nature.

John W. Bailey

FURTHER READING

Badè, William Frederic. *The Life and Letters of John Muir.* 2 vols. New York: Houghton Mifflin, 1924. The best collection of Muir's letters.

Ehrlich, Gretel. *John Muir: Nature's Visionary.* Washington, D.C.: National Geographic Society, 2000. Insightful biography, containing many quotations from Muir's unpublished journals and his other writings. Well illustrated with landscape photographs.

Fox, Stephen R. *John Muir and His Legacy: The American Conservation Movement.* Boston: Little, Brown, 1981. This is a biography of Muir, a chronological history of the conservation movement from 1890 to 1975, and an analysis of what conservation means in historical terms.

Melham, Tom. *John Muir's Wild America*. Washington, D.C.: National Geographic Society, 1976. A good place to begin the study of Muir. Beautiful illustrations and sound background history.

Smith, Herbert F. *John Muir*. New York: Twayne, 1964. Approaches Muir through his writings as literary works and places him in the context of Transcendentalist literature.

Turner, Frederick. *Rediscovering America: John Muir in His Time and Ours*. New York: Viking Press, 1985. A good, sound coverage of Muir's life in the context of his times and the development of the United States.

Williams, Dennis C. *God's Wilds: John Muir's Vision of Nature*. College Station: Texas A&M University Press, 2002. Examines Muir's views of nature, morality, and conservation, locating their source in his nineteenth century Calvinist upbringing.

Wolfe, Linnie Marsh. *Son of the Wilderness: The Life of John Muir*. New York: Alfred A. Knopf, 1945. Reprint. Madison: University of Wisconsin Press, 2003. A well-written biography based on solid research that shows the many-faceted dimensions of Muir's personality.

MARGARET MURIE

Naturalist and writer

Born: August 18, 1902; Seattle, Washington
Died: October 19, 2003; Moose, Wyoming
Also known as: Mardy Murie
Area of achievement: Environment

Sometimes called the "grandmother of the conservation movement," Murie was a key figure in establishing the Arctic National Wildlife Refuge in Alaska. She also lobbied to pass important environmental legislation like the Wilderness Act of 1964 and the Alaska National Interest Lands Conservation Act of 1980. She lived to be 101 years old.

EARLY LIFE

Margaret (Mardy) Thomas was born in 1902 in Seattle, Washington. When she was still an infant, her family moved to Fairbanks, Alaska. She spent much of her childhood—from the age of nine until she left for college—living in a log cabin just outside Fairbanks. There she learned to tend the cabin's wood stoves and how to do laundry by hand and hang it indoors to dry. When she was fifteen years old, she set off on a trip to visit her father in Anchorage. She traveled with United States mail carriers on dogsleds and horse-drawn sleighs for more than four hundred miles across the frozen Alaskan landscape, seated atop the mail bags.

After high school, she attended Reed College in Portland, Oregon, for two years. On break one summer and at home in Fairbanks, she met a wildlife biologist of Norwegian descent named Olaus Murie. Olaus was studying the migration patterns of Alaskan caribou for the United States Bureau of Biological Survey, later called the U.S. Fish and Wildlife Service. He was twelve years her senior. The two fell in love almost immediately, and they married in 1924. Margaret meanwhile had completed college at the Alaska Agricultural College and School of Mines, now called the University of Alaska, with a degree in business administration. She was the first women to graduate from the school. They were married in an unusual wedding at dawn in Anvik, Alaska (it was three a.m.

Margaret Murie (Wikimedia Commons)

because of the latitude). After the wedding, they put on heavy fur parkas and boots made of animal skins and set off on their honeymoon: a three-month dogsled journey across the wilderness.

LIFE'S WORK

In 1927, Olaus took a job studying wildlife in the Teton region in Wyoming. They moved to a home in Jackson Hole, Wyoming, but Margaret preferred to remain with her husband in the field camps where she became his assistant studying elk in the wilderness. By this time, the couple had three young children, and Margaret allowed them to play freely around the camp and in the wilderness. She became skilled at lashing branches together to create makeshift tables and chairs, and she cooked meals on an open fire. In 1945, the couple bought a dude ranch of seventy-seven acres near Moose, Wyoming. There Margaret put her business degree to use, managing the ranch while her husband traveled for his research. Olaus had been instrumental in founding the Wilderness Society in 1937, and their ranch became its headquarters. Olaus's success as a scientist—he published a number of important studies during his career with the United States Biological Survey—and his commitment to preserving the wilderness made him a persuasive figure in the early days of the conservation movement. Both he and his wife were active in persuading the federal government to enlarge several national park boundaries and to found new ones. Starting in the late 1950s, the couple conceived the idea for the Arctic National Wildlife Range, an area of eight million acres in Alaska to be set aside as a wildlife refuge. Their concept was new: to preserve a complete ecological system rather than just a parcel of land.

Murie with her husband Olaus by their home in front of Grand Tetons, 1953. (Wikimedia Commons)

> "Do I dare to believe that one of my great grandchildren may someday journey to Sheenjek and still find the gray wolf trotting across the ice of Lobo Lake? Yes, I do still dare to believe!"

Olaus died in 1963, some months before the passage of the act that made the Wildlife Range a reality. Margaret went to Washington, D.C. when President Johnson signed the Wilderness Act of 1964, a document whose text was written by the Wilderness Society. After signing the document, Johnson handed the pen to Margaret Murie; the law established the Arctic National Wildlife Refuge in Alaska. Today, the act protects over one hundred million acres of wilderness from coast to coast.

When Olaus died, Margaret was sixty years old. She could have retired, but instead she became more active than ever. Over the next several decades, she took over the wildlife conservation efforts that the couple had previously worked on together, and she quickly became a figure to be reckoned with. She wrote books, pamphlets, and articles about the conservation movement and about her own life. She traveled the world to give speeches, and she attended many government hearings to speak her piece before committees. She was a consultant for the Wilderness Society, the National Park Service, and the Sierra Club, and she helped persuade President Jimmy Carter to double the size of the Arctic National Wildlife Refuge in Alaska. Her first book, *Two in the Far North* (1962), was autobiographical and told the story of her adventures in Alaska with Olaus. Its sequel, *Wapiti Wilderness* (1966), was co-written with her husband and tells about their lives together in Wyoming.

Margaret was given many awards and medals over the years, including the Presidential Medal of Freedom in 1998 when she was ninety-six years old. The Murie Center was founded in 1997 at the Murie ranch in Wyoming; it is a non-profit organization dedicated to carrying on the work of the Muries. She died in 2003, at her home, at the age of 101.

SIGNIFICANCE

Margaret Murie, who led an unusually courageous and focused life, was notable for her down-to-earth demeanor and personal warmth. These qualities, together with her undying love both for her husband Olaus and for the conservation movement in the United States, have made her a legendary American figure, and she is sometimes called the "grandmother of the conservation movement." As a conservationist and author, she helped preserve millions of acres of wilderness both in Alaska and across the United States.

D. Alan Dean

FURTHER READING

Murie, Margaret. *Two in the Far North*. Anchorage, AK: Alaska Northwest Books,. 2007. With a foreword by Terry Tempest Williams.

Murie, Margaret and Olaus. *Wapiti Wilderness*. New York: Alfred A. Knopf, 1966.

Ostlind, Emilene. "The Muries: Wilderness Leaders in Wyoming." *Wyoming State Historical Society.* wyohistory.org. https://www.wyohistory.org/encyclopedia/muries-wilderness-leaders-wyoming

Wellock, Thomas. *Preserving the Nation: The Conservation and Environmental Movements, 1870 – 2000*. Hoboken, NJ: Wiley-Blackwell, 2007.

HENRY DAVID THOREAU

Philosopher, essayist and naturalist

Born: July 12, 1817; Concord, Massachusetts
Died: May 6, 1862; Concord, Massachusetts
Area of Achievement: Environmentalism, philosophy, writing

As essayist, naturalist, social critic, and editor, Thoreau has come to be recognized as a major figure in the Transcendentalist movement and is now one of the most widely studied, read, and respected American authors of the nineteenth century.

EARLY LIFE

David Henry Thoreau (THOH-roh), who, characteristically, chose to reverse the order of his first and middle

Henry David Thoreau (Wikimedia Commons)

names, traveled widely in his imagination but spent most of his forty-four years in the remarkable New England town of Concord, Massachusetts, in which he was born. His mother, née Cynthia Dunbar, was a forceful, socially conscious woman of Scottish ancestry. His father, John Thoreau, came of French Huguenot stock; a reticent man, he was not successful in business until he became a pioneer manufacturer of lead pencils. Henry was close to his older brother John, whose death in 1842 affected him deeply. His sister Helen died in 1849, but his other sister, Sophia, survived him to serve as the guardian of his reputation.

After his graduation from Harvard, Thoreau taught briefly in a Concord school, but he resigned rather than be required to flog his pupils. From 1838 to 1841, he ran his own, relatively progressive, school in Concord, teaching Latin, Greek, and science. He spent 1843 in Staten Island, as a tutor in the household of Ralph Waldo Emerson's brother William. He also worked at various times as a house painter, carpenter, mason, surveyor, and pencil maker. During the years he lived with Ralph Waldo Emerson and his wife, Thoreau served as a kind of handyman.

He also helped Emerson edit the Transcendentalist magazine *The Dial*.

Thoreau gave his first public lecture in the Concord Lyceum in 1838, and he continued intermittently as a lecturer for the remainder of his life. He was uncompromising toward his audience, particularly on the subject of slavery, and the reaction to his presentations was mixed. At Emerson's instigation, Thoreau began to keep a journal, which, published posthumously, serves as a valuable source for his experiences, observations, and reflections.

At five foot seven, he was slightly taller than average for his time, with longish hair and a prominent nose. He was striking, though not especially handsome, in appearance, and he made no effort to dress stylishly. Thoreau's only proposal of marriage, to a seventeen-year-old woman in 1840, was rejected, and he recoiled in horror from another woman's offer to him. He died, an equable bachelor, of the tuberculosis that first struck him in 1836 and that afflicted several members of his family.

> "The law will never make men free; it is men who have got to make the law free."

LIFE'S WORK

From August 31 to September 13, 1839, during a break from their school, Thoreau and his brother John traveled by canoe along the Concord and Merrimack Rivers. Over the course of a decade, Thoreau transformed their experiences into *A Week on the Concord and Merrimack Rivers* (1849), one of only two Thoreau books published during his lifetime. A short work, *A Week on the Concord and Merrimack Rivers* reshapes a fourteen-day excursion into a Saturday-Friday rhythm. In addition to recording the flora, fauna, and people that Thoreau encountered along the way, the book is a miscellany of poems and essays on a variety of topics, including friendship, local history, fishing, Christianity, Oriental religion, quackery, and Geoffrey Chaucer. Thoreau published one thousand copies of the work at his own expense, and he noted in his journal that 706 of them remained unsold in his attic.

On July 4, 1845, Thoreau moved into a cabin that he had built on land belonging to Emerson, along the shores of Walden Pond, two miles from Concord. He lived there, alone, for more than two years, until September 6, 1847, but in his account of his stay, the experience is translated into the natural cycle of a single year. Because of the indifferent response to *A Week on the Concord and Merrimack Rivers*, Thoreau did not rush into print with his second book. Instead, between 1846, when he first began writing it, and 1854, when he finally published it, he reshaped his material through journal entries, essays, poems, lectures, and more than half a dozen successive manuscript drafts.

The result of Thoreau's efforts, *Walden: Or, Life in the Woods* (1854), is his supreme achievement and one of the most accomplished works in American literature. Written in a baroque, epigrammatic style, *Walden* is not simply the record of one man's eccentric sojourn in a sylvan setting; it is an allegory of the deliberate life, a crafty provocation to its readers to awaken from the torpor and the quiet desperation of their lives. Thoreau describes his solitary existence beside Walden Pond as an experiment, and so, too, is his prose reenactment.

Thoreau is intent on clearing his life of the unnecessary encumbrances that materialism and a lack of self-reliance encourage. His book, which concludes with the exuberance of spring revivifying the pond, would have readers undergo a similar process of purifying enlightenment. *Walden* demands a careful reader, one alert enough not to dismiss it as a naïve effusion over nature, one sensitive to its author's extravagant, incendiary wit compounded of puns, paradoxes, and hyperboles.

In July, 1846, Thoreau spent one night in the Concord jail because of his refusal to pay a local poll tax. In a lecture first delivered in January, 1848, he explained his actions as a refusal to collaborate in the injustices of a government whose conduct of the Mexican War and whose perpetuation of the institution of slavery he stubbornly opposed. First published under the title "Resistance to Civil Government," the essay into which it evolved is best known as "Civil Disobedience" and is Thoreau's best-known essay. It proclaims the primacy of the individual and insists that if governmental policy cannot pass the muster of conscience, it ought to be resisted.

In 1857, Thoreau met abolitionist John Brown and was enormously impressed. He had earlier lectured in opposition to slavery, but Brown's arrest, following his raid on Harpers Ferry, Virginia, to incite a slave insurrection, inspired Thoreau to write his impassioned "A Plea for Captain John Brown." Though Thoreau's strenuous defense of Brown's actions did not save Brown from execution, the essay was probably the most widely read Thoreau work during his lifetime. "Slavery in Massachusetts," which he had written in 1854, calls for the state to secede from the nation and the individual from the state rather

Thoreau's cove at Walden Pond. (Library of Congress)

than acquiesce in an oppressive system. Published in William Lloyd Garrison's *The Liberator*, "Slavery in Massachusetts" also had a relatively large readership.

Though he was more closely tied to Concord than were any of its other major authors, Thoreau undertook a few brief excursions elsewhere—to Maine, Cape Cod, New Hampshire, Quebec, and Minnesota. These trips provided material for several works that were not published in their entireties until after his death. *Cape Cod* (1865), for example, is a cheerful report on the environment and the local lore of what was then an exotic region. *The Maine Woods* (1864) is a fairly straightforward and perceptive description of the people, plants, and animals in the northeastern frontier of the United States. Thoreau's final excursion came on May 6, 1862, in the family home in Concord; according to his sister Sophia, his last sentence was: "Now comes good sailing."

SIGNIFICANCE

Thoreau was a friend of several of the most important New England authors of the mid-nineteenth century, among them Ralph Waldo Emerson, Nathaniel Hawthorne, and Bronson Alcott. He was not widely known outside the Concord circle during his lifetime, however, and within it he was generally condescended to as someone who had never accomplished anything beyond a local interest. Both *A Week on the Concord and Merrimack Rivers* and *Walden* were out of print by the time of his final illness. However, those two books were reprinted within weeks of his death, and five volumes of Thoreau's unpublished writings were brought out during the early 1860's. His reputation began to expand, first as a nature writer. Despite his crusty insistence, in *Walden* and in the pugnacious essay "Life Without Principle," that he refused to be exemplary of anything but fierce independence, he even attracted disciples.

Late in the nineteenth century, Thoreau attracted the admiration of British critics, particularly Laborites, as a social critic. Early in the twentieth century, Mahatma Gandhi was so impressed by "Civil Disobedience" that he published it as a pamphlet. Gandhi credited Thoreau's ideas on nonviolent resistance to illegitimate authority as being a principal inspiration behind the movement for Indian independence. In the United States, Martin Luther King, Jr., was a fervent champion of Thoreau's political ideas. "Civil Disobedience" has continued to be invoked not only by opponents of racism but also by those objecting to nuclear armaments and nuclear power. More than one protester has spent more than one night in jail, convinced that he or she was a genuine Thoreauvian.

The ascendancy of Thoreau's literary reputation was more gradual, but, with more than two hundred editions of *Walden* in existence and his face on a postage stamp, the recluse of Walden Pond is now one of the foremost celebrities of American literature, as widely studied, read, and respected as any other author of his time. He has even eclipsed his Transcendentalist mentor Emerson in popularity. *Walden* is acknowledged as Thoreau's masterpiece, and it is read not as a series of naïve nature descriptions but as a complex and sophisticated literary performance. The delights of its dazzling style have drawn attention to the craftsmanship of many of his other writings.

Despite Thoreau's posthumous apotheosis as master of observation, of political principles, and of the English language, he remains a difficult writer. His rich prose is elusively allusive and often deliberately abrasive. Those who would keep pace with the brisk movement of his prickly mind are those who have learned, and earned, the serenity of self-reliance.

Steven G. Kellman

Further Reading

Bloom, Harold, ed. *Henry David Thoreau*. Philadelphia: Chelsea House, 2003. Aimed at literature students, the book features a biography of Thoreau and analysis of his writing, including essays by Ralph Waldo Emerson and Thoreau biographer Walter Harding.

Glick, Wendell, ed. *The Recognition of Henry David Thoreau: Selected Criticism Since 1848*. Ann Arbor: University of Michigan Press, 1969. An anthology of historical commentaries documenting the growth in Thoreau's reputation—from obscurity and condescension to veneration.

Hahn, Stephen. *On Thoreau*. Belmont, Calif.: Wadsworth/Thomson Learning, 2000. A brief overview of Thoreau's ideas designed to introduce students and other readers to his work.

Harding, Walter. *The Days of Henry Thoreau: A Biography*. New York: Alfred A. Knopf, 1965. The standard full-scale biography by the most respected specialist in the field.

———, ed. *Thoreau: Man of Concord*. New York: Holt, Rinehart and Winston, 1960. A compilation of recollections of Thoreau by dozens of his contemporaries, it provides testimony to the life within its nineteenth century contexts.

Lebeaux, Richard. *Thoreau's Seasons*. Amherst: University of Massachusetts Press, 1984. An application of psychologist Erik Erikson's theory of personality development to Thoreau's life from his Walden Pond experiment until his death.

Matthiessen, Francis O. *American Renaissance: Art and Expression in the Age of Emerson and Whitman*. New York: Oxford University Press, 1941. With extensive chapters on each of its major figures, this is the pioneering study of the Transcendentalist movement, the one that set the agenda for future studies of the period.

Porte, Joel. *Consciousness and Culture: Emerson and Thoreau Reviewed*. New Haven, Conn.: Yale University Press, 2004. A study of Thoreau and Emerson as writers, portraying them as complementary literary geniuses whose ideas moved provincial New England readers into a broader international culture.

Richardson, Robert D., Jr. *Henry Thoreau: A Life of the Mind*. Berkeley: University of California Press, 1986. A biography, concentrating on Thoreau's intellectual development from age twenty until his death.

Shanley, J. Lyndon. *The Making of Walden*. Chicago: University of Chicago Press, 1957. A fascinating analysis of the stages in the composition of Thoreau's most celebrated work; it demonstrates that, far from a spontaneous record of actual experiences, *Walden* was in fact a carefully contrived work of art.

Wagenknecht, Edward. *Henry David Thoreau: What Manner of Man?* Amherst: University of Massachusetts Press, 1981. A brief, literate overview of the major themes in Thoreau's life. Wagenknecht proceeds topically rather than chronologically.

Exploration

Exploration of the world's environments and of distant parts of the globe, including the deep seas, was always more than a dry scientific enterprise or a rapaciously commercial one. In the period of the great explorers, discovery was a noble, supremely human endeavor. America is itself a product of European exploration in the early modern era, and so it's not surprising that we might consider explorers to be not only historically interesting figures but heroes as well.

The era called the Age of Exploration, sometimes also the Age of Discovery, began in the early fifteenth century and lasted into the seventeenth. In this period, Europeans began to explore the world by sea in search of new trading routes, wealth, and knowledge. In addition to creating vast empires and either decimating or forever changing the indigenous cultures that were encountered, the era of discovery would permanently alter both modern science and European self-understanding. Disciplines like anthropology grappled with the variety of ways in which human societies could be organized, and European morals and manners were reevaluated and reformulated in relation to new ideas about the Other.

A second great Age of Discovery began in the eighteenth and nineteenth centuries, this one characterized not only by empire-building and the search for resources, but by a model of scientific research, often conducted with support from the same governments and nations that had funded the earlier discoveries. Charles Darwin's five years aboard the research ship the H.M.S. Beagle is a great example of exploration under this second paradigm. In the twentieth century, when Olaus and Margaret Murie set off to explore the wilderness of Alaska with funding from the United States Biological Survey (later called the United States Fish and Wildlife Service), they were among the last explorers in this tradition.

American Progress *by John Gast, 1872.*

ROBERT D. BALLARD

Undersea explorer

Born: June 30, 1942; Wichita, Kansas
Area of Achievement: Exploration, underwater archaeology

As a pioneering undersea explorer, Ballard made several remarkable discoveries, including the resting place of the Titanic and other ships, new life-forms along hot spots in the undersea Earth crust, and evidence supporting the theory of plate tectonics.

EARLY LIFE

Robert D. Ballard was born in Wichita, Kansas, a distant relative of the gunslinger William "Bat" Masterson, who was for a time in the nineteenth century the sheriff of Wichita. When Ballard was still a young boy, his family resettled to Pacific Beach, a suburb of San Diego, California, where his father worked developing the Minuteman missile. Ballard began what would become a lifelong fascination with the world under the sea. He spent countless hours exploring along the shore, dreaming of submarines, and poring over the illustrations in an edition of his favorite book, Jules Verne's science-fiction novel *Vingt mille lieues sous les mers* (1869-1870; *Twenty Thousand Leagues Under the Sea*, 1873). When he was a senior in high school, he won a competition that enabled him to spend a summer training at the Scripps Institute of Oceanography in La Jolla, California.

Ballard's parents taught him to work hard to set and achieve his goals, and that lesson served him well while he was still a college student. At the University of California, Santa Barbara, he earned a degree in both chemistry and geology and completed the university's Reserve Officers' Training Corps (ROTC) program, earning a commission as an Army lieutenant doing intelligence work.

After graduation, Ballard began graduate study in oceanography in Hawaii, where he also took a part-time job as a dolphin trainer at Sealife Park. This job helped him develop his skills as a writer and public speaker. In 1966 he transferred to the Navy and took a job helping to design and develop missions for submersibles for the Ocean Systems Group of his father's employer, North American Aviation. Ballard liked this work because it combined his passions for applied science, or technology, and pure science. The next year the Navy sent him to Boston to serve as an oceanographic liaison officer in the Office of Naval Research. His duties included serving as the Navy's liaison to the Woods Hole Oceanographic Institution on Cape Cod, Massachusetts.

> "*I am really dedicated to understanding the planet/creature on which we live and know that means I must go beneath the sea to see 72 percent of what is going on.*"

LIFE'S WORK

On his first tour of Woods Hole, Ballard was attracted to *Alvin*, an experimental miniature research submarine capable of taking three divers to a depth of 6,000 feet, where the water pressure exceeds one ton per square inch. Ballard spent as much time as his position allowed at Woods Hole, helping map the geology of the ocean floor in the Gulf of Maine. In September, 1969, he left the Navy and joined the staff at Woods Hole; three months later he descended in a submersible for the first time as part of a team studying the continental shelf off the coast of Florida.

During these years, Ballard was also a student in the Ph.D. program in marine geology and geophysics at the University of Rhode Island. For his doctoral dissertation research, Ballard attempted to advance the plate tectonics theories of Professor Patrick Hurley of the Massachusetts Institute of Technology. He used *Alvin* to make some forty

Robert D. Ballard (Wikimedia Commons)

dives in the Gulf of Maine and surrounding areas, helping develop the techniques that made it possible to use the vessel's remote manipulator arm to drill for and collect samples of bedrock. With data taken from these samples and the results of his earlier mapping work, he provided hard evidence that the continents sit on movable tectonic plates and that the American, European, and African continents were once connected. At the same time, his work helped the *Alvin* team demonstrate and expand the capabilities of the submersible, attracting much-needed interest and funding from both government and private agencies.

By the fall of 1971, *Alvin* had been rebuilt with a titanium pressure sphere, making it capable of descending to 12,000 feet, the average depth of the seafloor. This improvement made it possible for Ballard and others to explore the undersea mountain range known as the Mid-Atlantic Ridge in 1973 and 1974, in a project called the French American Mid-Ocean Undersea Study, or Project FAMOUS. With the French scientist Jean Francheteau, Ballard posited a new theory about the composition and activity of the Mid-Atlantic Ridge. By this time the capabilities of both Ballard and the submersibles were drawing scientific and popular attention, and Ballard found himself something of a celebrity. He was now chief scientist on many expeditions and was able to obtain the funding he needed for further exploration.

In 1977 Ballard led a team from Woods Hole in an exploration of the Galapagos Rift area of the Pacific Ocean near Ecuador. The team intended to study the vents that expelled warm water from beneath the ocean floor. These vents were so far beneath the ocean's surface that no sunlight could penetrate to them, and it was supposed that no living things would be found there. Surprisingly, the researchers discovered various forms of life, including clams, crabs, bacteria, and giant tube worms, many more than eight feet long, living near underwater geysers. Oceanographers were excited by the discovery, which spurred extensive research to learn more about the chemical and biological processes that make life possible in this unlikely environment.

Ballard's next major expedition took him to the ocean floor off the coast of Baja California, Mexico. There, in 1979, he was part of a research team that discovered "black smokers," underwater volcanoes spewing black fluids reaching temperatures of 350 degrees Celsius through chimneys made of sulfide mineral deposits.

With improvements to *Alvin* continually being made, Ballard began to think that an old dream of his might become a reality: He might be able to locate the giant ship *Titanic* on the ocean floor. *Titanic*, which had sunk in 1912 on its first voyage from England to New York City, was thought to lie some 13,000 feet below the surface too far for divers or previous submersibles to go. Government and industry figures were eager to find the sunken ship, knowing the publicity would provide a tremendous public relations boost to the finders. The military hoped that technology developed for undersea exploration could also be used for submarine warfare. Private adventurers had been searching for the ship for years. Ballard was able to gather funding and the support of the Navy, and in 1982 he established the Woods Hole Deep Submergence Laboratory (DSL). The lab team developed *Argo*, a sophisticated video sled about the size of a car, with floodlights and three cameras, and *Jason*, a smaller tethered robot vehicle that could be sent into tighter spaces than *Argo* could enter. The *Argo-Jason* system enabled a research crew onboard a ship to send and steer cameras out into the dark depths, and receive and interpret video pictures.

When testing of the *Argo-Jason* system was completed, Ballard and a team of French scientists launched a joint effort to locate the *Titanic*. The French, who had sophisticated sonar technology, would map the ocean floor in the area where the *Titanic* was thought to lie, and determine a smaller area for *Argo* to search. For five frustrating weeks, the French covered a 100-mile target area but did not locate the ship. A few days before the French left the area, Ballard and his team arrived. Drawing on the French data, the Americans limited their search to a narrower area and located the *Titanic* late in the night of August 31, 1985. A year later, Ballard returned to *Titanic*, and this time he sent the smaller *Jason* robot into the ship itself to photograph the interior. The pictures of the ship, with its recognizable central staircase and unopened bottles of wine, captured the imaginations of viewers around the world.

Ballard continued his exciting work, in 1989 establishing the JASON Project, a program that sent live images from *Jason* video robots to students at museums and science centers so that they could experience through "telepresence" some of the wonders of the undersea world. Greatly expanding the possibilities of distance learning, Ballard made it possible for more than a million students each year in thousands of classrooms around the world to work interactively with underwater cameras and other equipment far below the surface of the ocean. Ballard also pursued the interest in undersea archaeology he had demonstrated in his search for the *Titanic*: In the

View of the bow of the RMS Titanic photographed in June 2004 by the ROV Hercules during an expedition returning to the shipwreck of the Titanic. (Wikimedia Commons)

1990's he located and photographed the German battleship *Bismarck*, American and Japanese warships sunk during World War II at Guadalcanal, the luxury ship *Lusitania*, and several trading ships from the Roman Empire, some as old as two thousand years.

Ballard retired from Woods Hole in 1997 and founded the Institute for Exploration, dedicated to expanding the fields of underwater archaeology and deep-sea geology. Two years later, the institute merged with the Mystic Aquarium in Connecticut to form the Sea Research Foundation's Institute for Exploration, with Ballard as president. The institute developed underwater vehicles that carry sensing and imaging equipment to depths far beyond where humans could safely go and that send data back to researchers at the surface.

In 1998, Ballard again set out to locate sunken ships, this time in the Pacific Ocean near the island of Midway, where an important battle was fought between the Japanese and the Allies during World War II. Using the latest technology for undersea exploration, Ballard and his crew found and photographed four Japanese carriers and the American aircraft carrier the USS *Yorktown* more than three miles below the surface.

Ballard's explorations continued into the twenty-first century. In 2002, working with the National Geographic Society, he located wreckage from John F. Kennedy's PT-109, which was sunk off the Solomon Islands during World War II. Ballard also managed to find and interview the two Solomon Island natives who rescued Kennedy and his crew after they had been shipwrecked. He and archaeologist George Bass led a group of marine archaeologists to explore ancient artifacts and mollusk remains 7,000 feet down in the Black Sea, using *Argus*, a remotely operated tethered underwater vehicle with optical cameras. The presence of shells from freshwater species identified during this expedition lent support to a much-debated theory that the Black Sea was settled by human beings before a large-scale flood devastated the area. In 2003 he returned to the wreck of the *Titanic* to document the decay that had befallen the ship in the eighteen years since Ballard had found it on the ocean floor.

Ballard's twin passions for exploration and for teaching led him to an active parallel career as a public speaker, television host, and teacher. He was awarded the Cairn Medal of the National Maritime Museum in 2002 and was invited to speak at the John F. Kennedy Presidential Library in 2005. In 2004, he became a professor of oceanography and director of the Institute for Archaelogical Oceanography at the University of Rhode Island.

SIGNIFICANCE

Throughout a career of more than thirty years, Ballard participated in more than one hundred dives and ventured out in more deep-diving submersibles than anyone else in the world. His explorations contributed greatly to knowledge of what lies beneath the surface of the oceans. Some discoveries, such as evidence in support of plate tectonic theory or the finding of life near hot vents on the ocean floor, were primarily of interest to other scientists and were presented in dozens of articles Ballard contributed to scientific journals. Ballard's discovery of the *Titanic* and the other lost ships thrilled people all over the world both scientists and nonspecialists alike in part because of his talent for making science and technology accessible to general audiences. Ballard wrote or cowrote more than a dozen books (including a juvenile biography and a children's pop-up book), as well as magazine articles and television programs.

Ballard also made great technological contributions, helping develop and refine submersibles, underwater video cameras, and robots to hold and move the cameras. Through his writing, speaking, and photography, and through the "telepresence" of the JASON Project, Ballard shared his discoveries with the world.

Cynthia A. Bily

Further Reading

Allen, Christina G., Pat Cummings, and Linda C. Cummings, eds. *Talking with Adventurers: Conversations with Christina Allen, Robert Ballard, Michael Blakey, Ann Bowles, David Doubilet, Jane Goodall, Dereck and Beverly Joubert, Michael Novacek, Johan Reinhard, Rick West, and Juris Zarins*. Washington, D.C.: National Geographic Society, 1998. Ballard and the other scientists explain their jobs, including a typical working day and their most frightening experiences. This volume is intended for younger readers; the information it contains is useful and accessible.

Ballard, Robert D., and Rick Archbold. *The Lost Ships of Robert Ballard*. San Diego, Calif.: Thunder Bay Press, 2005. A large coffee-table book that celebrates several glorious sunken ocean liners and warships, including the *Titanic*, *Bismarck*, *Lusitania*, and *Andrea Doria*, that Ballard located on the ocean floor. Includes high-tech underwater photographs, as well as paintings and historical images.

---. *Return to Midway*. Washington, D.C.: National Geographic Society, 1999. Ballard's exploration of ships sunk during the World War II battle at Midway, including the aircraft carrier USS *Yorktown*, which was found more than three miles below the surface of the ocean. Richly illustrated with photographs and paintings.

Ballard, Robert D., with Will Hively. *The Eternal Darkness: A Personal History of Deep-Sea Exploration*. Princeton, N.J.: Princeton University Press, 2000. Ballard provides an account of his own explorations and the efforts of other twentieth century explorers to investigate the ocean depths. Includes photographs, charts, and maps.

Ballard, Robert D., with Malcolm McConnell. *Explorations: My Quest for Adventure and Discovery Under the Sea*. New York: Hyperion, 1995. A complete account of Ballard's entire career in marine geology, this best-selling autobiography offers accessible explanations of his scientific achievements. This volume is more memoir than science and is thought by many to exaggerate Ballard's contributions to some projects, but it is lively reading, telling its story with dialogue and beautiful descriptive passages.

Hecht, Jeff. "20,000 Tasks Under the Sea." *New Scientist* 147 (September 30, 1995): 40-45. A description of Ballard's post-*Titanic* explorations of the Mediterranean Sea, looking for more than two-thousand-year-old sunken ships from the Roman Empire. For this feat of underwater archaeology, Ballard had the use of a U.S. Navy nuclear submarine, the NR-1, designed originally for deep-sea military surveillance and able to withstand high pressure and stay underwater for up to one month.

Daniel Boone

Explorer and settler

Born: November 2, 1734; Berks County, Pennsylvania
Died: September 26, 1820; St. Charles County, Missouri
Area of Achievement: Exploration, settlement

In addition to opening Kentucky to settlement, Boone became a legendary symbol of the early American frontier and is considered a national hero.

Early Life

Daniel Boone was the sixth of eleven children. His father, Squire Boone, was the son of an English Quaker who came to Philadelphia in 1717; his mother, Sarah Morgan, was of Welsh ancestry. Young Boone received little, if any, formal schooling, but he learned to read and to write, although his spelling was erratic. His real interest was in the forest, and as a boy he developed into an excellent shot and superb woodsman.

Squire Boone left Pennsylvania in 1750, and by 1751 or 1752, the family was settled on Dutchman's Creek in North Carolina's Yadkin Valley. Daniel hunted and farmed, and he was a wagoner in General Edward Braddock's ill-fated 1755 expedition against Fort Duquesne. He may have been a wagon master three years later, when General John Forbes took the fort. During the 1750's, Boone met John Finley, who captivated him with tales of the lovely land called Kentucky.

In young adulthood, Boone was about 5 feet, 9 inches in height and had broad shoulders and a broad chest. Strong and quick, he possessed marvelous endurance and calm nerves. He had blue eyes, a Roman nose, a wide mouth with thin lips, and dark hair that he wore plaited and clubbed. Boone detested coonskin caps and always wore a hat. Mischievous and fun-loving, he was a popular companion, but Boone was happiest when alone in the wilderness. Honest, courageous, quiet, and unpretentious, he inspired confidence, and he accepted the leadership roles thrust upon him.

On August 14, 1756, Daniel married Rebecca Bryan, four years his junior. Between 1757 and 1781, they had

Daniel Boone (Wikimedia Commons)

ten children, and Rebecca carried much of the burden of rearing them during Daniel's long absences. One child died in infancy, and sons James and Israel were killed in Kentucky by American Indians. Rebecca ended Daniel's interest in Florida by refusing to move there in 1766. Boone, sometimes accompanied by brother Squire and brother-in-law John Stuart, explored westward, always tantalized by stories of the fine lands and bountiful game to be found in Kentucky.

> "May the same Almighty Goodness banish the accursed monster, war, from all lands, with her hated associates, rapine and insatiable ambition!"

Life's Work

On May 1, 1769, Daniel Boone, John Finley, John Stuart, and three hired hands left Boone's cabin for his first extended visit into Kentucky. A successful hunt was spoiled by a band of Shawnee, who took their catch and most of their equipment. Stuart was later killed, and when the rest of the party went back for supplies in 1770, Boone remained behind to hunt and explore westward. In 1771, some hunters investigated a strange sound and found Boone, flat on his back, singing at full volume for sheer joy. The seizure of another catch by Native Americans was a small price to pay for such delights.

In September, 1773, Boone attempted to take his family and other settlers into Kentucky, but they turned back after an American Indian attack in which Boone's son James was among those killed. On the eve of Lord Dunmore's War in 1774, Boone and Michael Stoner were sent to warn hunters and surveyors in Kentucky of the impending danger. In sixty-one days, they covered more than 800 miles of wilderness, although Boone paused at the incipient settlement at Harrodsburg long enough to claim a lot and throw up a cabin. During the short Indian war, Boone's role as a militia officer was to defend some of Virginia's frontier forts.

During these years, Boone became associated with Judge Richard Henderson, who dreamed of establishing a new colony (to be called Transylvania) in the western lands claimed by the North Carolina and Virginia colonies. Boone helped persuade the Cherokees to sell their claim to Kentucky, and agreement was reached at Sycamore Shoals on March 17, 1775. Anticipating that result, Boone and thirty axmen had already started work on the famed Wilderness Road that brought thousands of settlers into Kentucky and helped destroy the wilderness solitude that Boone loved.

Boonesborough was soon established on the south bank of the Kentucky River, and crops were planted in hastily cleared fields. When Henderson arrived with a larger party, a government was set up with representatives from the tiny, scattered stations. Boone introduced measures for protecting game and improving the breed of horses. American Indian raids frightened many of the settlers into fleeing eastward, but during the summer of 1775, Boone brought his family to Boonesborough. Had he joined the exodus, the settlements probably would have been abandoned. Even the capture of a daughter and two other girls by American Indians did not shake his determination to hang on. Henderson's grandiose scheme failed when Virginia extended its jurisdiction over the region by creating a vast Kentucky County in December, 1776.

The American Revolution was fought largely along the seaboard, but the British used American Indians to attack the Kentucky settlements; the war in the West was fought for survival. Boone accepted the new nation created in 1776, but he was later charged with Toryism and treasonable association with the enemy. A court-martial cleared him of all charges, and he received a militia promotion.

During a raid led by Shawnee chief Blackfish, Boone's life was saved by young Simon Kenton, one of his few peers as a woodsman. The indigenous peoples' incursions brought the settlers near starvation, given the danger of both hunting and farming. When Boone was captured near Blue Licks by a large Shawnee raiding party on February 7, 1778, he persuaded his twenty-six salt makers to surrender to save their lives. Boone then convinced Blackfish to return home and that Boonesborough would capitulate in the spring. Boone was adopted by Chief Blackfish, who refused to sell him to the British in Detroit. Big Turtle, as Boone was called by the Shawnee, enjoyed American Indian life, but he escaped in June, 1778, to warn Kentuckians of an impending attack. First by horse, and then on foot, Boone covered 160 miles in four days with only one meal, and upon his arrival Boonesborough's defenses were hastily improved. In any event, the attacking party of four hundred American Indians and one dozen French Canadians did not arrive until September 7. The settlers prolonged negotiations, hoping help would arrive, and the nine-day siege was one of the longest in American Indian warfare. All hostile stratagems failed, and Boonesborough survived.

George Rogers Clark's 1778-1779 campaign in the Illinois country and later expeditions against American Indian towns eased some of the danger. Indeed, Boonesborough was becoming too crowded for Boone, and in October, 1779, he moved to Boone's Station, a few miles from the fort. Boone had acquired some wealth, but he and a companion were robbed of between $40,000 and $50,000 when they went east in 1780 to purchase land warrants. Boone felt honor-bound to repay the persons who had entrusted money to him.

His hunting exploits, escapes from American Indians, and other feats of skill and endurance made him a legend in his own time. Kentucky was divided into three counties in November, 1780, and Boone's importance was recognized by appointments as Fayette's sheriff, county-lieutenant, lieutenant-colonel of militia, and deputy surveyor, and by election to the Virginia legislature. Captured by the British in Charlottesville in 1781, Boone soon escaped or was paroled.

In August, 1782, after a failed American Indian attack on Bryan's Station, Boone's warnings went unheeded,

Painting by George Cumberland showing Boone escorting settlers through the Cumberland Gap. (Wikimedia Commons)

and the rash pursuers were ambushed near Blue Licks; Boone's son Israel was among the sixty-four non-Indian casualties. Boone participated in expeditions across the Ohio River to curb the indigenous, but he criticized Clark for not moving his headquarters to the eastern settlements for better protection. This criticism failed to take into account Clark's responsibilities for the Illinois country as well as for Kentucky: Louisville was a central location from which Clark could move quickly in either direction.

About 1783, Boone moved to Livestone (Maysville) on the Ohio River, where he opened a store, surveyed, hunted, and worked on prisoner exchanges with the indigenous. His fame spread throughout the nation and to Europe after 1784, following John Filson's addition of a thirty-four-page Boone "autobiography" to *The Discovery, Settlement, and Present State of Kentucke* (1784). In 1789 or 1790, Boone moved to Point Pleasant, in what became West Virginia, but he was in the Blue Licks area by 1795. By then, defective land titles had cost him most of his good lands, and Boone ceased to contest any claims brought against him. Disappointed by his treatment and convinced that Kentucky, a state since 1792, was becoming too crowded, Boone decided to move to Missouri, where Spanish officials welcomed him. In 1799, just before he was sixty-five years old, Boone led a party across the Mississippi River and settled on land some 60 miles west of St. Louis.

The next few years were happy ones. Despite rheumatism, Boone could still hunt, and the wilderness lured him into long journeys westward, perhaps as far as the

Yellowstone. He received large land grants, and as a magistrate he held court under a so-called Justice Tree. The old pioneer was incensed in 1812, when he was rejected as a volunteer for the War of 1812; he was seventy-eight years old but ready to fight. His wife Rebecca died in 1813, and Boone probably made his last long hunt in 1817. He had a handsome coffin made and stored for future use. After the Louisiana Purchase, through carelessness and a series of misunderstandings, he lost most of his Missouri land, just as he had earlier lost his holdings in Kentucky.

Boone probably made his last visit to Kentucky in 1817; he was reputed to have only fifty cents left in his pocket after he paid the last of his creditors. Two years later, Chester Harding painted Boone's only life portrait. Boone died at a son's home near St. Charles on September 26, 1820, after a brief illness. In 1845, his and Rebecca's remains were re-interred on a hill above Frankfort, Kentucky.

SIGNIFICANCE

Despite his preference for the wilderness, Daniel Boone contributed mightily to the end of the Kentucky frontier–by opening roads, building settlements, surveying land, and fighting American Indians. Without his leadership, Kentucky's settlement would have been delayed, for he inspired trust that kept settlers from fleeing to safety. This clash between the idea of wilderness as paradise and the restrictions of civilization has been a common theme in the history of the American frontier; it remains an issue still.

In addition to his notable accomplishments, Boone became the symbol of the American frontier during the first half-century of nationhood. James Fenimore Cooper and Lord Byron were only two of many authors whose work includes depictions of Boone. Both his character and his exploits made Boone a natural hero, and they marked a way of life, believed virtuous, that was rapidly vanishing.

Lowell H. Harrison

FURTHER READING

Boone, Nathan. *My Father, Daniel Boone: The Draper Interviews with Nathan Boone.* Edited by Neal O. Hammon, with an introduction by Nelson L. Dawson. Lexington: University Press of Kentucky, 1999. Historian Lyman Draper interviewed Boone's only surviving child, Nathan, and Nathan's wife, Olive, in 1851, as part of Draper's research for a biography of Boone. This is an updated transcript of those interviews.

Chaffee, Allen. *The Wilderness Trail: The Story of Daniel Boone.* New York: T. Nelson and Sons, 1936. An account that tells much more about Boone than his connection with the Wilderness Trail, one of the major routes for pioneers who entered Kentucky.

Draper, Lyman C. *The Life of Daniel Boone.* Edited by Franklin Belue. Mechanicsburg, Pa.: Stackpole Books, 1998. Historian Draper died in 1891, leaving a massive but unfinished biography of Boone. Belue has transcribed and annotated Draper's manuscript. Although Draper presents a hagiographic account of Boone, his work was based on extensive research and interviews, and he vividly re-creates many details of Boone's life. Belue's chapter notes correct Draper's romanticism, and the seventy-six period drawings, engraving, photos, and maps enhance the text.

Eckert, Allan W. *The Court Martial of Daniel Boone.* Boston: Little, Brown, 1973. This well-researched and well-written historical novel reconstructs the charges brought against Boone and his successful defense. The trial record disappeared, but Eckert's version sounds plausible.

Filson, John. *The Discovery, Settlement and Present State of Kentucke: . . . To Which Is Added . . . the Adventures of Col. Daniel Boon.* Wilmington, Del.: James Adams, 1784. This rare book has been reprinted many times. Although the "autobiography" was written by Filson and contains many errors, he did interview Boone and a number of other Kentuckians.

Lofaro, Michael A. *Daniel Boone: An American Life.* Lexington: University Press of Kentucky, 2003. Lofaro published an excellent biography, *The Life and Adventures of Daniel Boone*, in 1979. This updated biography is more detailed and is based upon thirty years of research. Lofaro explains why Boone is considered the quintessential frontiersman and why the idea of the frontier remains a part of the American experience.

Thwaites, Reuben Gold. *Daniel Boone.* New York: D. Appleton, 1902. Despite its age, this book provides a generally accurate biography. The author was one of the first Boone biographers to make use of the Lyman Draper manuscripts.

Richard Byrd

Aviator and explorer

Born: October 25, 1888; Winchester, Virginia
Died: March 11, 1957; Boston, Massachusetts
Area of Achievement: Polar exploration, aviation

Byrd played a central role in the development of naval aviation and was a major figure in Arctic and Antarctic exploration.

Early Life

Richard Byrd (burd) was the son of Richard Evelyn Byrd, a lawyer, and Eleanor Bolling Flood. The families of both his parents were active in Virginia politics, and Richard's brother, Harry, became an influential U.S. senator. Small and slender, Richard was nevertheless strong and athletic. Playing war games with his brothers Harry and Tom and exploring the woods and hills near Winchester increased Richard's desire for adventure. When he was twelve, he was invited to visit a family friend who was serving as United States circuit court judge in the Philippines. Richard had his parents' permission to go to Manila by himself. He remained a year, writing about his experiences for a Winchester newspaper. He then completed his journey around the world alone. It was about this time that he wrote in his diary that he wanted to be the first person to reach the North Pole.

Three years at the Shenandoah Valley Military Academy prepared him for admission to Virginia Military Institute, where he studied from 1904 to 1907, before transferring to the University of Virginia for a year. In 1908, he was appointed to the U.S. Naval Academy at Annapolis, from which he was graduated in 1912, sixty-second in a class of 155. As a midshipman, he played tennis and football, wrestled in the 135-pound class, and specialized in the rings in gymnastics. While engaging in these sports, he suffered injuries that would later cause him to terminate his active duty with the Navy. He broke bones in his ankle playing football and broke them again in a fall during a gymnastics routine. Shortly after receiving his commission, he fell down a hatchway on the USS *Wyoming*, reinjuring his right foot and causing him to walk with a slight limp. Despite this setback, he served with distinction in the Caribbean, twice saving men from drowning. It was at this time, in the summer of 1914, that he took his first airplane ride.

In 1915, Byrd married his childhood sweetheart, Marie D. Ames. Secretary of the Navy Josephus Daniels asked Byrd to serve as his aide on the USS *Dolphin*, but after a few months Byrd asked to be retired on a medical disability because his injured foot prevented him from performing regular naval duties. The political influence of his family enabled him to be promoted to lieutenant jg (junior grade) and assigned as administrator of the naval militia of the state of Rhode Island on his retirement. As a retired officer on active duty, he served in various posts for the next forty years.

Life's Work

During World War I, Byrd persuaded the Navy to allow him to enter flight training at the naval air station in Pensacola, Florida. He received his pilot's wings on April 7, 1917, and began making plans to be the first person to fly across the Atlantic. Wartime duties took him to Nova Scotia, where he helped to establish naval air stations. When the Navy was slow in supporting his plan for a transatlantic flight, he turned to his friend Walter Camp, the popular football coach at Yale University. With Camp's help, Byrd convinced the Navy to create the Transatlantic Flight Section of the Bureau of Aeronautics. Navy regulations prohibited Byrd from accompanying the flight he had organized, so he failed to share the glory of the crew of the NC-4 flying boat when it reached Lisbon, Portugal, on May 27, 1919. Undaunted, Byrd

Richard Byrd (Library of Congress)

began planning a solo flight across the Atlantic. Navy orders again thwarted his dream when he was sent to England to assist in navigating a British-built dirigible to the United States. He was fortunate, however, when he missed a trial flight that ended in a fatal crash.

Byrd spent the next three years on aviation duty with the Bureau of Navigation. In 1925, he commanded a naval unit on an expedition to northern Greenland. Encouraged by his success in using airplanes in the Arctic, Byrd decided to enter the aerial race for the North Pole. Norwegian explorer Roald Amundsen and the American aviator Lincoln Ellsworth flew to within a few hundred miles of the pole during the summer in which Byrd was in Greenland. Knowing that Amundsen, Ellsworth, and the Italian adventurer Umberto Nobile all had plans to fly to the pole, Byrd moved quickly. After being released from active duty with the Navy, he secured financial backing from Edsel Ford, organized a team of pilots and mechanics, and sailed for Spitzbergen Island. On May 9, 1926, he and Floyd Bennett flew north in a Fokker monoplane named *Josephine Ford* in honor of Edsel's daughter. Fifteen hours later, they returned with the news that they had flown over the pole. Although their claim would later be disputed, Byrd and Bennett returned to the United States as heroes. Both were awarded the Congressional Medal of Honor. In his book *Skyward* (1928), Byrd explains that they were considered heroes because "in us youth saw ambition realized."

Franklin D. Roosevelt, as governor of New York, presents Byrd with a Distinguised Service Medal. (National Archives and Records Administration)

> "*I am hopeful that Antarctica in its symbolic robe of white will shine forth as a continent of peace as nations working together there in the cause of science set an example of international cooperation.*"

In June, 1927, less than a month after Charles A. Lindbergh's transatlantic flight, Byrd finally flew across the Atlantic. Flying with Bert Acosta, Bernt Balchen, and George Noville in a Fokker trimotor, Byrd demonstrated that regular commercial transatlantic flights were practical, despite the fact that his plane was forced to crashland on the French coast because of heavy fog in Paris. The energetic and ambitious Byrd now turned his attention to the South Pole. Receiving financial support from Ford, the Rockefellers, the Guggenheims, and others, Byrd sailed with forty-one men, ninety-four dogs, a Ford snowmobile, and three airplanes on two ships, the *City of New York* and the *Eleanor Bolling*.

On January 1, 1929, the party began building a base camp, Little America, on the ice shelf at the Bay of Whales. Eleven months later, on November 28 and 29, Byrd, Balchen, Harold June, and Ashley McKinley flew their Ford trimotor to the South Pole and back. In addition to the historic flight, the expedition mapped and photographed a large section of the unexplored continent; made geological, meteorological, and zoological observations; and proved the feasibility of a permanent base in Antarctica. Byrd again returned home to a hero's welcome, and Congress promoted him to the rank of rear admiral.

Three years later, in the depths of the Depression, Byrd organized a second Antarctic expedition, this time with fifty-five men, three airplanes, an autogyro (a forerunner of the helicopter), and several snowmobiles. After reestablishing Little America, Byrd sent a small party to build an advance base more than one hundred miles south, where he planned to station three men to make weather observations through the winter (April through August) of 1934. When storms prevented the planes and sledges from transporting enough supplies, Byrd decided to remain at Bolling Advance Base alone. Although he nearly died from inhaling carbon monoxide leaking from his

Poster for the 1930 film With Byrd at the South Pole. (Wikimedia Commons)

stove, Byrd made most of his daily observations. The scientific achievements of the second expedition surpassed the first in many ways. The thickness of the ice was measured in several places, the outline of the continent was mapped more accurately, new astronomical and meteorological observations were made, and oceanographic data were collected.

The four-and-one-half-month struggle for survival at Advance Base left Byrd exhausted mentally and physically, and his career after 1935 was less spectacular than it had been. On the eve of World War II, President Franklin D. Roosevelt recalled Byrd to active duty and put him in command of the first government-sponsored Antarctic expedition since the voyage of Charles Wilkes in 1838-1842. During the war, Byrd helped find new air routes in the Pacific. In 1946, he returned to Antarctica with Operation Highjump, a naval exercise involving four thousand men, the largest expedition ever sent to that area. In 1955, he visited Antarctica for the fifth and last time during the International Geophysical Year (IGY) activities involving thirteen nations. He died two years later secure in the knowledge that he had contributed significantly to America's awareness of the importance of Antarctica and the need for international cooperation in scientific exploration.

Significance

Byrd was a complex and controversial person. His drive and success aroused strong feelings, and he was never without his critics. In a sense, Edwin Hoyt was correct in calling him "the last explorer" of the generation of Amundsen, Robert Scott, and Robert Edwin Peary, a person driven by the desire to be the first to stand on uncharted ground and to survive incredible hardships. Certainly his failure to be the first to fly the Atlantic and the little accidents that plagued his early naval career drove him to seek recognition in Antarctic exploration, but there is also a mystical side to Byrd's character. He confesses in *Alone* (1938) that he chose to remain at Bolling Advance Base by himself less for science than "for the sake of experience." He compared himself to Henry David Thoreau at Walden and to Robinson Crusoe. Ultimately he found a harmony with the universe in the freezing Antarctic night.

Byrd's plans for the first two Antarctic expeditions were as much an experiment in social organization as in natural science. There was a traditional American utopianism in the "constitution" he drew up for the government of Little America. "We have no class distinctions as in civilization," he wrote in *Alone*. "He who may have failed back there has his chance to make good here; and he will not be judged by the position he holds so much as by the way he plays the game and does his job, however humble it may be. . . ." Byrd played the game of life in the context of the social and economic upheavals of World War I and the Depression. The failures of the old world made the exploration of a new one all the more urgent. Utilizing the advances in airplane technology, aerial photography, and meteorological instruments, Byrd may also be called the "first explorer of the modern age."

Bernard Mergen

Further Reading

Bertrand, Kenneth J. *Americans in Antarctica, 1775-1948*. New York: American Geographical Society, 1971. A scholarly history that places Byrd's expeditions in a larger context. Excellent Further Reading.

Bryant, John H., and Harold N. Cones. *Dangerous Crossings: The First Modern Polar Exploration, 1925*. Annapolis, Md.: Naval Institute Press, 2000. Before he went to Antarctica, Byrd was part of an American naval contingent that explored the area north of Canada. This was the first polar expedition to use both aircraft and shortwave radio in its explorations, and the book focuses on the technology that Byrd and others employed during their expedition.

Byrd, Richard E. *Alone*. New York: G. P. Putnam's Sons, 1938. Reprint. Los Angeles: Jeremy P. Tarcher, 1986. The most interesting of Byrd's books because it is the most personal. Byrd describes his struggle to survive alone for four and a half months in Antarctica. More than a diary, this book is a discussion of the reasons for seeking extreme hardships. Obviously written to establish the author's reputation as a literary adventurer, it bears comparison to Charles Lindbergh's *We* (1927) and Joshua Slocum's *Sailing Alone Around the World* (1900).

---. *Discovery: The Story of the Second Byrd Antarctic Expedition*. New York: G. P. Putnam's Sons, 1935. Reprint. Detroit, Mich.: Tower Books, 1971. Detailed history of the expedition of 1933-1935, omitting discussion of the solitary four and a half months at Advance Base. Good on equipment-testing and life in Little America.

---. *Little America: Aerial Exploration in the Antarctic, the Flight to the South Pole*. New York: G. P. Putnam's Sons, 1930. Details of the first Byrd expedition, 1928-1930, and the building of the base Little America.

---. *Skyward: Man's Mastery of the Air as Shown by the Brilliant Flights of America's Leading Air Explorer: His Life, His Thrilling Adventures, His North Pole and Trans-Atlantic Flights, Together with His Plans for Conquering the Antarctic by Air*. 1928. Reprint. Chicago: Lakeside Books, 1981. Hastily written first book; the subtitle shows how Putnam promoted Byrd. Portions of this book had already appeared in magazines.

Hoyt, Edwin P. *The Last Explorer*. New York: John Day, 1968. Written without access to Byrd's private papers, but still a complete account of the great explorer's life.

Parfit, Michael. *South Light: A Journey to the Last Continent*. New York: Macmillan, 1985. Updates Bertrand and describes conditions in Antarctica in the late twentieth century. Good discussion of the 1956 treaty under which more than a dozen nations maintain dozens of year-round scientific stations without relying on territorial claims.

Rose, Lisle A. *Assault on Eternity: Richard E. Byrd and the Exploration of Antarctica, 1946-47*. Annapolis, Md.: Naval Institute Press, 1980. Detailed account of Operation Highjump, a naval training and scientific mission in which Byrd was marginally involved.

MERIWETHER LEWIS AND WILLIAM CLARK

Explorers

MERIWETHER LEWIS
Born: August 18, 1774; Albemarle County, Virginia
Died: October 11, 1809; Hohenwald, Tennessee

WILLIAM CLARK
Born: August 1, 1770; Ladysmith, Virginia
Died: September 1, 1838; St. Louis, Missouri

Area of Achievement: Exploration

The Lewis and Clark expedition was the first organized exploratory expedition to cross the North American continent from the Atlantic to the Pacific coast within the geographical limits of the present United States. After serving as coleader of the expedition, Clark was for three decades one of the most important administrators of Indian affairs in the nation's history.

EARLY LIVES

Meriwether Lewis was born on a Virginia plantation. His father was William Lewis, who married Lucy Meriwether, after whom the future explorer was named. Meriwether had an older sister and a younger brother. The first Lewises in America, who were Welsh, migrated to Virginia during the mid-seventeenth century, where the family became planters. Meriwether's father was a lieutenant during the Revolutionary War, but he drowned while on leave in 1779. Six months later, Lucy married Captain John Marks. After the war, the Marks family moved to Georgia, but Meriwether soon went back to Virginia to live with his relatives. There he attended several small schools taught by parsons and received some tutoring, but his chief interest and delight was in rambling in the woods, hunting and observing nature. Although

Meriwether Lewis and William Clark (Wikimedia Commons)

rather stiff and awkward as a child, Meriwether grew up to be a handsome young man.

When John Marks died in 1791, his widow returned to Virginia. She brought with her, besides Meriwether's brother and sister, a son and daughter she had borne her second husband.

A short time after his mother's return, Lewis became a soldier, as he was to remain most of his life. In 1794, he enlisted in the Virginia militia to help suppress the Whiskey Rebellion in western Pennsylvania. Liking this taste of military life, Lewis stayed in the militia until May, 1795, when he became an ensign in the United States Army. A few months thereafter, he was assigned to the "Chosen Rifle Company" that William Clark commanded, and during the short time that the two men were together, they became fast friends. Later that year, Lewis joined the First Infantry Regiment, and for the next four years he was engaged in a number of noncombatant duties, mainly on the Western frontier. In December, 1800, he was promoted to captain and became regimental paymaster.

It was while he was thus occupied that, in February, 1801, President-elect Thomas Jefferson wrote to invite Lewis to become his private secretary, probably with a view to naming him to command a transcontinental exploring expedition. Jefferson had thought about, and even planned for, such an undertaking since the United States had won its independence in 1783. In 1792, Lewis, then only eighteen years old, had volunteered for the assignment. Jefferson chose someone else, however, who failed to go.

Soon after coming to Washington, Lewis, under the president's direction, began to plan and prepare for the expedition. He obtained scientific and technical training from members of the faculty of the University of Pennsylvania; collected, with their advice, various kinds of equipment and supplies; and gathered information on his proposed route. Following congressional approval and funding of the mission and his formal designation as its commander, Lewis, early in 1803, with Jefferson's concurrence, invited his friend William Clark, with whom he had maintained contact since they served together in the army, to be its co-leader.

Clark was also born on his family's plantation in Virginia. He was the youngest of six sons and the ninth of ten children of John and Ann (Rogers) Clark. The Clarks had emigrated from England some time in the seventeenth century and, like the Lewises, had become planters. When the Revolution came, the Clarks were staunch patriots, and all of William's older brothers fought as officers in the War for Independence. The most famous was Brigadier General George Rogers Clark, who was the conqueror of the Illinois Country. William, who was too young to fight, stayed home. He received a little formal schooling and acquired the rudiments of learning, but mainly he developed the skills of a frontiersman: the ability to ride, hunt, and shoot.

> "As we passed on, it seemed those scenes of visionary enchantment would never have an end."

When he was fourteen years old, Clark moved with his family to a new plantation near the falls of the Ohio at Louisville. As a young Kentucky frontiersman, Clark, a big, bluff redhead, served with the militia in several campaigns against the hostile Indian tribes living north of the Ohio River. In March, 1792, he was commissioned a lieutenant in the United States Army, and two years later he fought under General Anthony Wayne in the famous Battle of Fallen Timbers. In July, 1796, however, Clark resigned his commission and returned home, where for the next seven years he managed his aged parents' plantation. It was there that, in July, 1803, he received Lewis's invitation to join him in leading a transcontinental exploring expedition and quickly accepted it.

LIVES' WORK

About the time Clark received his letter, Lewis, in the East, completed his preparations for the expedition and received final detailed directions from the president. The mission's purpose, as stated by Jefferson, was to explore the Missouri River up to its source in the Rocky Mountains and descend the nearest westward-flowing stream to the Pacific in order to extend the American fur trade to the tribes inhabiting that vast area and to increase geographical knowledge of the continent. With these instructions, Lewis left Washington for Pittsburgh. Descending the Ohio River by boat, he picked up Clark at Louisville, in late summer 1803. Together with a few recruits for the expedition, the two men proceeded to Wood River, Illinois, opposite the mouth of the Missouri, where they encamped early in December. During the next five months, Lewis and Clark recruited and trained their party and finished their preparations for the journey.

With everything in readiness, the expedition set out on May 14, 1804, for the Pacific. Lewis, still a captain in the First Infantry, was the expedition's official commander. Although commissioned only a second lieutenant of artillerists, on the expedition Clark was called "captain" and was treated in every way as Lewis's equal. During the journey, Lewis, a rather intense, moody introvert, spent much of his time alone, walking on shore, hunting, and examining the country. Because Lewis was better trained scientifically and the more literate of the two officers, he wrote most of the scientific information recorded in the expedition's journals. Clark, a friendly, gregarious individual, spent most of his time with the men in the boats. He was the expedition's principal waterman and mapmaker, and he was better able to negotiate with the Indians. Together, the two officers' dispositions, talents, and experience complemented each other superbly. Despite the differences in their personalities, they seem always to have enjoyed the best of personal relations.

In its first season's travel, the expedition advanced some sixteen hundred miles up the Missouri and went into winter quarters in a small fort, named Mandan for the nearest Indian tribe, situated in modern North Dakota. The following spring the expedition proceeded to the headwaters of the Missouri, made a portage of the Rocky Mountains, and descended the nearest westward-flowing tributaries of the Columbia as well as the Columbia itself. Lewis and Clark reached the Pacific by mid-November, 1805. After wintering a few miles from the ocean, in a post they called Fort Clatsop, for a nearby tribe, in March, 1806, the explorers set out for home and arrived in St. Louis in September, having long since been given up for lost by virtually everyone but Jefferson.

As rewards for their great achievement, the president appointed Lewis governor of Louisiana Territory and Clark its principal Indian agent and brigadier general of the territorial militia. Detained in the East by business related to the expedition and other matters, Lewis did not actually assume the governorship of the territory until March, 1808. He soon proved to be unsuited for the office by temperament and experience and quickly ran into trouble. He quarreled with Frederick Bates, the territorial secretary, and became unpopular with many of the people of the territory. He seldom reported to his superiors in Washington and failed to consult them on his policies and plans. As a result, he fell under their severe criticism, and he probably would not have been appointed to a second term of office had he survived the first.

In September, 1809, after only about a year and a half in office, Lewis left St. Louis for Washington, in order to try to straighten out his affairs with the government and to renew his efforts to get the expedition's journals published. On the way, while stopping at a tavern on the Natchez Trace, he was either murdered or committed suicide. Although the evidence is inconclusive, there is reason to believe, as did Clark

The Lewis and Clark Expedition being guided by Sacagawea. (Wikimedia Commons)

and Jefferson, that Lewis died by his own hand. Thus at the age of thirty-five ended the life of this great pathfinder.

Clark, in the meantime, was mainly concerned with improving relations and promoting trading activities with the Indian tribes of the territory and protecting the white settlers against the tribes of the Upper Mississippi who were allied with the British in Canada. Following Lewis's death, he was offered the governorship of Louisiana, but he declined it because he felt he lacked political experience. In June, 1813, however, the governorship of the Territory of Missouri, as the Louisiana Purchase was called after 1812, again became available, and this time Clark accepted it. During the War of 1812, which was then raging, Clark's chief responsibility was to defend the territory against the hostile Indians of the Upper Mississippi. After the war, Indian relations and the economic and political needs of the white settlers pouring into Missouri absorbed his time and interest.

Following Missouri's admission to the Union in 1821, Clark (an unsuccessful candidate to be the state's first governor) was appointed superintendent of Indian affairs at St. Louis and retained responsibility for the tribes of the Missouri and Upper Mississippi. Clark held this office until his death on September 1, 1838. As superintendent of Indian affairs, he played a major role in effecting the removal of Indians living east of the Mississippi and in Missouri to new lands in modern eastern Kansas.

Unlike Lewis, who never married, Clark was an affectionate family man. In 1808, he married Julia Hancock, with whom he had five children. Following Julia's death, in 1821 he married her cousin Harriet Kennerly Radford, a widow, who bore him two sons. Four of his sons lived to adulthood.

SIGNIFICANCE

Lewis and Clark's fame rests almost entirely on the success of their great expedition, one of the most extensive explorations undertaken in their time. They and their companions were the first American citizens to cross the continent and the first white men to traverse it within the area of the modern United States. During a journey that lasted a little more than twenty-eight months, the expedition traveled more than eight thousand miles. On the entire trip, only one man, Sergeant Charles Floyd, lost his life, and he died from a cause almost certainly unrelated to his exploring activities.

In their contacts with thousands of Indians, Lewis and Clark had only one minor violent encounter, which cost the lives of two Indians. The total expense of the undertaking was a little less than forty thousand dollars. Although Lewis and Clark did not find a commercially feasible route across the continent, as Jefferson hoped they would, they did make a significant contribution to the existing knowledge of the geography of a great part of North America. They also took a historic step toward opening the Trans-Mississippi West to American trade and subsequently to American settlement, thus providing the basis for one of the strongest U.S. claims to the Oregon Country. Their great achievement stimulated the pride of the American people and served to make Americans aware of the vastness of the continent on which they lived.

Although Lewis's career after the expedition was short and hardly noteworthy, Clark's was long and eminently successful. In three decades of dealing with the tribes of the Upper Mississippi and the trans-Mississippi West, he carried out the policies of the federal government faithfully and effectively, helping to adjust relations peacefully between the Native Americans and the whites. In doing so, by the standards of his own time, he treated the American Indians fairly and sympathetically and, in return, had their respect and confidence.

John L. Loos

FURTHER READING

Ambrose, Stephen E. *Undaunted Courage: Meriwether Lewis, Thomas Jefferson, and the Opening of the American West*. New York: Simon & Schuster, 1996. Best-selling account of the expedition by a prominent historian. Ambrose traveled along the expedition's route to the Pacific and painstakingly re-creates the activities and discoveries of the journey. The book also chronicles Lewis's tragic life in the years following the expedition.

Cutright, Paul Russell. *Lewis and Clark: Pioneering Naturalists*. Urbana: University of Illinois Press, 1969. This volume contains a wealth of detailed information on the scientific and technical aspects of the expedition, including fauna and flora discovered, topographic features discovered or named, and Native American tribes encountered.

Dillon, Richard. *Meriwether Lewis: A Biography*. New York: Coward-McCann, 1965. A noteworthy biography of Lewis, this somewhat sentimental and romantic work provides a relatively comprehensive treatment of the subject with emphasis on the expedition.

Jackson, Donald D., ed. *Letters of the Lewis and Clark Expedition, with Related Documents: 1783-1854*. Urbana: University of Illinois Press, 1962. A comprehensive collection of meticulously edited letters, memoranda, and other documents dealing with all aspects of the expedition, gathered from widely scattered sources.

Jones, Landon Y. *William Clark and the Shaping of the West*. New York: Hill & Wang, 2004. Focuses on Clark's private life and public career in the thirty years following his expedition with Lewis. Includes discussions of Clark's duties in the Kentucky militia, his service as governor of the Missouri Territory, and his role as superintendent of Indian Affairs at St. Louis.

Lewis, Meriwether, and William Clark. *The Journals of Lewis and Clark*. Edited by Bernard De Voto. Boston: Houghton Mifflin, 1953. Based on the eight-volume Thwaites edition of *The Original Journals of the Lewis and Clark Expedition*. Edited by Rubengold Thwaites. 8 vols. New York: Dodd, Mead, 1904-1905. This single volume provides a good, readable narrative of that great enterprise that retains its flavor.

Ronda, James P. *Lewis and Clark Among the Indians*. Lincoln: University of Nebraska Press, 1984. An important, sophisticated, and engaging ethnohistorical study, this work chronicles the daily contact between the explorers and American Indians and shows that the expedition initiated important economic and diplomatic relations with them.

Slaughter, Thomas P. *Exploring Lewis and Clark: Reflections on Men and Wilderness*. New York: Random House, 2003. A revisionist view of the expedition, with Slaughter attempting to correct the myths and legends that he believes have surrounded it.

Steffen, James O. *William Clark: Jeffersonian Man on the Frontier*. Norman: University of Oklahoma Press, 1977. Steffen selectively and briefly sketches Clark's life, making an occasional reference to the intellectual framework that he believes explains it.

Invention

Inventors, like entrepreneurs, are archetypal American heroes in large part because they are archetypal capitalist figures. Inventors bring a genius for creativity to that entity called the commodity. Seeing inventors as heroes actually predates seeing entrepreneurs that way. This might be because the figure of the inventor was easier for observers to give heroic status to; in the nineteenth century, the great business owners were often accused of foul play or greed, but invention was something different. In the words of Alexander Graham Bell, "The inventor... wants to improve whatever he sees, he wants to benefit the world; he is haunted by an idea. The spirit of invention possesses him, seeking materialization."

In reality the two roles—inventor and entrepreneur—often overlapped. One of the great examples of this is Thomas Alva Edison. Credited with the invention of the electric light, the phonograph, and early motion picture devices, he also worked hard to create the massive infrastructures necessary for those inventions to saturate American life, including public utility companies (for the distribution of electric lighting) and production and distribution channels for exhibiting motion pictures using his Kinetoscope machines. At peak, Edison employed 10,000 people at his West Orange lab and factory complex and he managed thirty companies. Edison was also influential in creating the popular discourse about inventors as creative American heroes and role models. Through interviews and other public relations tools, he extolled his own work ethic while dispensing easily repeatable maxims like, "What it boils down to is one percent inspiration and ninety-nine percent perspiration."

This section on inventors includes some expected historical figures such as Edison, Alexander Graham Bell, and Maxwell Eastman (the inventor of the Kodak camera). It also includes several lesser-known African American inventors—such as Patricia Bath, Garett Morgan, and Thomas L. Jennings—whose creativity and innovation, while not as widely celebrated, has also made a positive impact on our lives today.

George B. Selden Road engine patent drawing, 1879. (Wikimedia Commons)

Patricia Bath

Ophthalmologist

Born: November 4, 1942; New York City, New York
Area of Achievement: Medicine and medical technology
Primary invention: Laserphaco probe

A lifelong advocate for the blind, Bath introduced a safe and accurate laser surgery device and method for the removal of cataracts.

Early Life

Patricia Era Bath was born to Rupert and Gladys Bath in Harlem, New York. Rupert Bath was an immigrant from Trinidad, British West Indies, and her American mother was the descendant of African slaves and Cherokee Native Americans. Her father worked in a variety of jobs; he served as a motorman for the New York City subway, a merchant seaman, and a newspaper columnist. Her mother was a housewife who also worked as a domestic, one of the few positions open for African American women in the 1940's, in order to save money for her children's education.

Bath was interested in problem solving from childhood. This interest was encouraged at Charles Evans Hughes High School in New York, where she took biology courses that first sparked her interest in the sciences. She excelled in school and earned numerous awards. She applied for a National Science Foundation Scholarship and was chosen in 1959 to work in a summer program for high school students at Yeshiva University. She was also able to work with the university and Harlem Hospital on cancer research. During this time, she worked with Rabbi Moses D. Tendler and Dr. Robert O. Bernard; it was her job to collect and analyze information in an effort to forecast the progression of cancer cells. She coauthored a research report presented at the Fifth Annual International Congress on Nutrition in Washington, D.C., on September 2, 1960. That same year, she won a Merit Award from *Mademoiselle* magazine. Bath completed high school in just two and a half years.

Bath's higher education began at Hunter College in New York, where she graduated with a bachelor's degree in chemistry in 1964. She continued her graduate education at Howard University Medical School, graduating with a medical degree in 1968. This was followed by an internship at Harlem Hospital (1968-1969), a fellowship at Columbia University (1969-1970), and a residency at New York University (1970-1973).

Patricia Bath (Wikimedia Commons)

> "Do not allow your mind to be imprisoned by majority thinking. Remember that the limits of science are not the limits of imagination."

Life's Work

In 1967, while at Howard, Bath traveled to Yugoslavia to study children's health issues. A year later, she joined the Poor People's Campaign as they marched in Washington, D.C., for economic rights. After graduating from Howard, she studied ophthalmology at Columbia and became an assistant of surgery at hospitals throughout New York. During the following years, she traveled to Africa to serve as chief of ophthalmology at Mercy Hospital in Nigeria. She also worked with the White House Counsel for a National and International Blindness Prevention Program for two years.

Bath became interested in working with the visually impaired while she was at Columbia University. While serving at the Eye Clinic in Harlem, she observed a large number of African Americans suffering from vision

> **The Laserphaco Probe**
>
> *Dr. Patricia Bath began work on an invention for laser cataract surgery in 1981. Unable to find the appropriate lasers in the United States, she traveled to Berlin, Germany, where she studied the latest laser technology as she designed her "apparatus for ablating and removing cataract lenses," later called the laserphaco probe. Once the invention was complete, she successfully tested it on human cadavers. Her device was first used on live human subjects seven years after she began experiments, and she was awarded a patent for her laserphaco probe in 1988.*
>
> Bath's procedure uses a laser to destroy and remove the cataract coating of the eye. A flexible line (less than one millimeter in diameter) is inserted through an incision in the lens until it is next to the cataract. Low amounts of coherent radiation then blast the cataract by an optical fiber in the line. The line also contains a tube for irrigating the eye and a tube for removing the ablated pieces of the cataract during the procedure. A new lens is then inserted into the eye to replace the lens that held the cataract.
>
> Bath's laser probe method was revolutionary in its ability to remove cataracts safely. It replaced traditional methods, the most common of which used a drill-like device to grind the cataract. This outdated technique was sometimes inexact and potentially harmful.

problems. In a well-received report, she concluded that African Americans were twice as likely as the general population to suffer from blindness. Moreover, the study showed that African Americans were eight times more likely than whites to suffer from glaucoma-related blindness. Her work prompted her to create the practice of community ophthalmology, in which volunteers visit underserved communities to screen for vision problems.

In 1973, Bath completed her residency in ophthalmology at New York University. That year, she moved to California to join the faculty at the University of California, Los Angeles (UCLA), and Charles R. Drew University. In 1976, she cofounded the American Institute for the Prevention of Blindness. In 1983, she cofounded and chaired the Ophthalmology Residency Training Program at UCLA-Drew.

One of Bath's main areas of interest was cataract disease. A cataract is a clouding of the lens of the eye that can impair vision and sometimes cause blindness. Bath began researching laser surgery as a treatment for vision problems, and her research took her to Germany to study the latest technology. By 1986, she had designed a laser instrument for removing cataracts and successfully tested it. Bath's laser surgery method was faster, safer, and more accurate than traditional methods of cataract surgery.

Bath was granted U.S. Patent number 4,744,360 on May 17, 1988, for her laserphaco probe, becoming the first African American woman to be awarded a patent for a medical invention. The laserphaco probe works with a concentrated beam of light that breaks up and destroys the cataract. In the following years, she improved the invention and received three more patents: a method for breaking down and removing cataracts (number 5,843,071), in 1998; another laser product used for surgery on cataract lenses (number 5,919,186), in 1999; and an ultrasound method for the breaking and removing of cataracts (number 6,083,192), in 2000. She has also received patents in Europe, Japan, and Canada.

Dr. Bath is a professor emeritus and was nominated to the National Inventors Hall of Fame by the American Intellectual Property Law Association. After retiring from UCLA in 1993, she continued to promote vision care outreach, especially for the underprivileged. A picture book on her life and work in science was published in 2017, and was cited by both the National Science Teachers Association and the Chicago Public Library's list of best children's books of the year.

Significance

As the first African American woman to receive a patent for a medical device, Bath is a role model for African Americans, women, and other minorities. Her laser cataract surgery method has been used throughout the world, including India, Italy, and Germany. Bath's advocacy work with organizations such as the American Institute for the Prevention of Blindness was groundbreaking. Even after retirement, she has maintained a busy schedule, giving speeches to young people, promoting community ophthalmology, and traveling around the world doing surgery. It is her deepest wish to be able to eventually eliminate blindness. She has also promoted telemedicine, the use of electronic communications to deliver medical services to remote regions where medical care is limited or unavailable.

Theresa L. Stowell

Further Reading

Apple, David J. *Intraocular Lenses: Evolution, Designs, Complications, and Pathology*. Baltimore: Williams and Wilkins, 1989. A technical discussion of the intraocular lens. Important as it relates to Bath's life work and inventions.

Henderson, Susan K. *African-American Inventors III: Patricia Bath, Philip Emeagwali, Henry Sampson, Valerie Thomas, Peter Tolliver*. Mankato, Minn.: Capstone Press, 1998. A set of short biographies written for a juvenile audience. Contains photographs, illustrations of the inventions, and copious references.

Pursell, Carroll W., ed. *A Hammer in Their Hands: A Documentary History of Technology and the African-American Experience*. Cambridge, Mass.: MIT Press, 2005. A collection of essays about African American achievements from colonial times to the twenty-first century. Though the book does not specifically address Bath, it is an invaluable source.

Sullivan, Otha Richard, and James Haskins. *African American Women Scientists and Inventors*. New York: Wiley, 2002. A simple, straightforward presentation of African American women who have influenced science and technology. Contains a chapter on Patricia Bath. Written for a juvenile audience.

Young, Jeff C. *Inspiring African American Inventors: Nine Extraordinary Lives*. Berkeley Heights, N.J.: Enslow, 2008. A juvenile book about African American scientists and mathematicians.

Alexander Graham Bell

Scottish-born scientist and engineer

Born: March 3, 1847; Edinburgh, Scotland
Died: August 2, 1922; Beinn Breagh, Canada
Areas of Achievement: Communications; electronics and electrical engineering
Primary invention: Telephone

Bell was a prolific inventor and renowned teacher of the deaf, but he is best known for his invention of the telephone. What began as a crude prototype quickly became a useful tool that revolutionized communications.

Early Life

Alexander Graham Bell was born to Alexander Melville and Eliza Grace Bell in Edinburgh, Scotland, in 1847. His

Alexander Graham Bell (Wikimedia Commons)

father, grandfather, and uncle were elocutionists. Bell's father had invented Visible Speech, a system that uses written symbols to teach the deaf how to articulate words. Bell demonstrated his inventiveness at the age of twelve, when he built a wheat-dehusking device for his neighbor, who used it for a number of years. Together with his brother, Bell built an automaton head that could "speak" a few words. Bell attended Edinburgh's Royal High School for two years and left at the age of fifteen. At sixteen, he secured a job as a pupil-teacher of elocution and music. He studied at Edinburgh University in 1864 and later at University College in London.

After his two brothers died from tuberculosis, Bell moved with his family to London and then to Brantford, Ontario, Canada, in 1870. At the Six Nations Reserve, he learned the Mohawk language and translated its vocabulary into Visible Speech symbols. For his work, he was awarded the title of honorary chief. In 1871, Bell provided an in-service program for instructors of the deaf at the Boston School for Deaf Mutes (now the Horace Mann School for the Deaf and Hard of Hearing) in Boston, Massachusetts. The program was repeated at the American Asylum for Deaf-Mutes in Hartford and the Clarke School for the Deaf in Northampton. The next year, Bell opened a school for deaf pupils (among them Helen Keller) in Boston. Named the Vocal Physiology and Mechanics of Speech, the first class had thirty students. He became a professor of vocal physiology and elocution at the Boston University School of Oratory in 1873.

Though he was busy during the day, Bell stayed up late every night doing research in sound, attempting to find a way to transmit musical notes and articulate speech. (In his late teens, he had begun work on the transmission of sound using tuning forks. He was greatly influenced by the German physicist Hermann von Helmholtz, who had conveyed vowel sounds using a tuning fork.) The device Bell worked on was called a harmonic (or musical) telegraph, and he tried to build one that could send several messages at once through a single wire. He thought he could send multiple messages by varying their musical pitch. When his experiments led nowhere, he decided to concentrate on research and spend less time on his private practice. He had been suffering from severe headaches, and his health deteriorated. He retained only two students—George Sanders, deaf from birth, and Mabel Hubbard, who had lost her hearing because of scarlet fever at age five. Sanders's father provided Bell with free room and board and made arrangements for his son to live near Bell's boarding house. Ten years younger than Bell, Hubbard became the object of his affection.

LIFE'S WORK
During the summer of 1874, Bell made experiments on a teaching aid for the deaf called the phonoautograph, which was made from a dead man's ear. Speaking into this device caused the ear membrane to vibrate and move a lever, which wrote a wavelike pattern of speech on smoked glass. Bell thought it might be possible to use a membrane to vary an electric current in intensity with the spoken word. He also thought that multiple metal reeds (or springs) tuned to different frequencies could be used to convert the electric current back into sound. When Bell revealed his secret work on his harmonic telegraph to his two students' parents—Gardiner Greene Hubbard, a lawyer and the president of the Clarke School for the Deaf, and Thomas Sanders, a prosperous businessman—both showed interest in funding his research. In February, 1875, Hubbard, Sanders, and Bell signed an agreement that supported Bell financially in return for equal shares from any patent he developed. Anthony Pollok, Hubbard's patent attorney, would handle patent matters. Bell hired Thomas A. Watson, an experienced electrical designer and mechanic, as his assistant. In the following month, Bell met with Joseph Henry, who had pioneered electromagnetism and helped Samuel F. B. Morse with the telegraph. The scientist advised Bell to get the necessary electrical knowledge, drop the work on his harmonic telegraph, and concentrate on transmission of speech by electricity.

In June, 1875, Bell and Watson were working on the harmonic telegraph when he heard a sound come through the receiver. Watson had accidentally plucked one of the reeds. Also, one of the contact screws had been set too

---

The Prototype Telephone

The first telephone that Thomas A. Watson built for Alexander Graham Bell used a transmitter with an acid-water mixture. The telephone consisted of a funnel, a diaphragm, a cup, and a receiver. A wire attached to the diaphragm floated in the liquid in the cup. Another wire attached the cup to the receiver. Speaking into the funnel caused the diaphragm at the bottom to move, which in turn moved the wire in the liquid. When the wire moved, it changed the resistance within the liquid. The varying current sent to the receiver caused the diaphragm to vibrate and produce sound.

Although this crude prototype proved that speech could be transmitted electrically, the device was not practical, and Bell did not use it in his public demonstrations. Instead, he used a prototype that used an electromagnet instead of liquid. The design consisted of a transmitter, receiver, and magnet. Attached to the transmitter and receiver was a metal diaphragm. Speaking into the transmitter caused the diaphragm to move and the phone line to transfer this motion to the receiver. When the diaphragm of the receiver vibrated, sound was produced. The drawback to this design was that it used a single microphone: The user spoke into it and then put it to the ear to listen. There was also a time lapse in the transmission. Thomas Alva Edison later improved the telephone by dividing it into two pieces: a movable earpiece and a stationary speaking tube. Another drawback to this prototype telephone was that it was voice-powered: The user had to shout into the transmitter to be heard as well as to overcome noise and distortions. Other inventors, notably Francis Blake, Jr., contributed to improving the telephone. Blake, like Edison, invented a transmitter that improved the sound clarity of the device.

Bell on the telephone in New York (calling Chicago) in 1892. (Library of Congress)

tightly, allowing current to run continuously. Bell realized that only one reed, not multiple ones, was needed, and that continuous current was essential for transmission of sound. Watson built the first telephone the next day. Called a "gallows" telephone because of its frame, it had a diaphragm substituted for the reed. It was able to transmit a few odd sounds, but not clear speech. Bell was very much disappointed, and his experimenting slowed through the rest of the year. He spent some time writing a patent application to protect his ideas even though he had not built a working model for his telephone. Fortunately, the U.S. Patent Office at that time did not require that a working model accompany a patent application.

On February 14, 1876, while Bell was in Boston, his patent application was filed by Pollok with the Patent Office. On the same day, Elisha Gray filed his caveat for a telephone using a water transmitter. A professional inventor, Gray, together with Thomas Alva Edison, had been contracted by Western Union to find a way to send multiple messages using only a single line on the telegraph. Who filed first is still a debate, and what happened that day is still a mystery. Bell's patent was eventually challenged by some six hundred lawsuits, five of which went to the Supreme Court. Even the U.S. government wanted to annul Bell's patent based on the grounds of fraud and misrepresentation. Gray's challenge to the patent was based on the rumor that Pollok had access to his caveat and copied the principle of variable resistance and the description of the liquid transmitter onto Bell's application. However, Bell won every case. The Patent Office issued to Bell U.S. Patent number 174,465 on March 7, 1876, for his electric speaking phone. In late 1877, Gray applied for a patent for the same invention, but the Patent Office determined that "his failure to take any action amounting to completion until others had demonstrated the utility of the invention deprives him of the right to have it considered."

Three days after his patent was issued, Bell was experimenting with a transmitter when he succeeded in getting his telephone to work. The liquid that Bell used for the transmitter was a mixture of acid and water. According to legend, when he accidentally spilled some of the liquid on his clothes, he called his assistant for help. Watson heard Bell's words clearly in the next room.

In August, 1876, Bell demonstrated that his telephone could work over long distances. His first message was sent from the telegraph office in Mount Pleasant to Brantford five miles away. Bell introduced his invention to the scientific community and the general public and also at the 1876 Centenary Exhibition in Philadelphia. Pedro II of Brazil ordered one hundred telephones for his country. Bell, Hubbard, and Sanders wanted to sell the patent to Western Union for $100,000, but the company's president declined the offer. (Afterward, he regretted his decision, saying that paying $25 million for the patent would have been a bargain.) In 1877, the Bell Telephone Company was established, and a few days later Bell married Mabel Hubbard. They had four children: two girls, and two boys who died in infancy.

> "*The inventor...looks upon the world and is not contented with things as they are. He wants to improve whatever he sees, he wants to benefit the world; he is haunted by an idea. The spirit of invention possesses him, seeking materialization.*"

In 1880, the French Academy, representing the French government, presented Bell the Volta Prize of 50,000 francs ($10,000) for his invention. With this money, Bell established the Volta Laboratory in Washington, D.C.

Other honors included the Albert Medal from the Royal Society of Arts in London, an honorary Ph.D. from the University of WÃ¼rzburg (Germany), the Edison Medal from the American Institute of Electrical Engineers, and induction into the Legion of Honor. Named after Bell, the decibel (dB), equal to 0.1 bel (B), is a unit for measuring sound intensity. Also named for him is the IEEE Alexander Graham Bell Medal, established in 1976 to award contributors in the fields of telecommunications.

Bell was issued fourteen patents for the telephone and the telegraph and four patents for the photophone, which transmits speech by light rays. He shared twelve other patents with his collaborators for the phonograph, aerial vehicles, hydroairplanes, and selenium cells. Other inventions included the audiometer, which measures acuity in hearing, and the induction balance, used to locate metal objects in human bodies.

Bell became a naturalized U.S. citizen in 1882. He alternated between two homes—Washington, D.C., and his private estate Beinn Bhreagh ("beautiful mountain" in Gaelic) in Baddeck, Nova Scotia. Bell has been claimed as a "native son" by the United States and Canada. Canada maintains the Alexander Graham Bell National Historic Site in Nova Scotia, the historic Bell Homestead, and the world's first telephone company building. Collections of Bell's documents reside at the U.S. Library of Congress, Manuscript Division, and at the Alexander Graham Bell Institute at Cape Breton University in Nova Scotia.

Bell died of pernicious anemia at his private estate on August 2, 1922, survived by his wife and two daughters.

SIGNIFICANCE

Improvements to the prototype telephone helped develop it into a successful product. The use of the telephone spread quickly after the first commercial switchboard was set up in New Haven, Connecticut, in 1878. Four years later, 60,000 people owned telephones; the number jumped to 150,000 in 1886. Thanks to Thomas Alva Edison's invention of the carbon microphone, the telephone became a practical long-distance tool. In 1884, the first long-distance line was built, connecting Boston and New York. With the perfection of insulation, 11,000 miles of underground wires were used in New York City by 1889. By the turn of the century, the telephone had become a necessity, connecting people and paving the way for an interconnected world market and future developments in information technology. With 14,000 miles of copper wire strung across the country, the first transcontinental call was made in 1915.

Anh Tran

FURTHER READING

Brown, Travis. *Popular Patents: America's First Inventions, from the Airplane to the Zipper*. Lanham, Md.: Scarecrow Press, 2000. The telephone is one of eight inventions presented. Each narrative includes a profile of the inventor and a discussion of how the invention has found its way into American culture.

Grosvenor, Edwin S., and Morgan Wesson. *Alexander Graham Bell: The Life and Times of the Man Who Invented the Telephone*. New York: Harry N. Abrams, 1997. Chronicles Bell's most famous invention, from its roots in deaf education to the growth of AT&T. Covers experiments later in his career and includes historical and family anecdotes.

Pasachoff, Naomi. *Alexander Graham Bell: Making Connections*. New York: Oxford University Press, 1996. Concentrates more on his work as an educator and inventor than on his personal life. Illustrations.

Shulman, Seth. *The Telephone Gambit: Chasing Alexander Graham Bell's Secret*. New York: W. W. Norton, 2008. Examines the race to build the first telephone and uncovers potential bombshells. Provides evidence of Bell's stealing Elisha Gray's research.

GEORGE WASHINGTON CARVER

Scientist, inventor, and educator

Born: c. 1864; Diamond, Missouri
Died: January 5, 1943; Tuskegee, Alabama
Also known as: George Carver (birth name)
Areas of achievement: Business; Education; Invention; Science and technology
Primary invention: Peanut and soybean byproducts

Best known for the many products that he derived from the peanut, soybean, and other crops, Carver also helped to revive southern agriculture devastated by decades of over-farming and to advance African American education.

EARLY LIFE

George Washington Carver was born a slave sometime shortly before or during the Civil War; considerable uncertainty exists about his early years. His mother, Mary, was an African American slave who had earlier given birth to another son, Jim; both boys took the last name of

George Washington Carver (Wikimedia Commons)

their owners, Moses and Susan Carver. Carver said that his father was a slave on a neighboring plantation who died in a log-rolling accident. Moses Carver's Union sympathies led to tragedy when Confederate raiders kidnapped Mary and George from his farm and took them to Arkansas. Moses was eventually able to find George and barter a horse for the boy, but he was never able to discover Mary's fate. When the Civil War ended, Moses and Susan Carver legally adopted Mary's two sons. The brothers formed a contrasting pair, Jim hearty and healthy, Carver frail and sickly. Some scholars have attributed Carver's lifelong health problems and high-pitched voice to castration during his captivity. Carter exhibited reluctance to discuss his early life, although he did explain that a disastrous event in his past prevented his ever marrying.

Carver's vulnerable constitution suited him for household tasks rather than field work, but he did exhibit an early fascination with garden plants, and his skill at nursing sickly plants to health earned him the nickname "plant doctor." Significant changes in his life occurred when he was ten years old. He became a Christian and began attending a school for African American children in Neosho, where he did chores for a black family in exchange for room and board. He continued as a part-time student and laborer, traveling first to Fort Scott, then to Olathe, and finally to Minneapolis, Kansas, where he worked and attended high school for four years. Eager for a college education, he applied to and was accepted by a Presbyterian college in Highland, Kansas, but his hopes were crushed when, upon arrival, he discovered that the college excluded African Americans.

After failed attempts at farming on the Kansas frontier, Carver traveled to Iowa, where he became the first African American student at Simpson College. Here he found encouraging mentors for his interests in art and botany, and his successes led to his transfer to Iowa State College of Agriculture and Mechanic Arts (now Iowa State University), where he worked in the college's greenhouse and agricultural laboratory to pay his college costs. He received his bachelor's degree in 1894, becoming the college's first African American graduate, and stayed on to obtain his master's degree. His graduate research bore fruit; for example, he found a new fungus that was later named after him.

> "*Fear of something is at the root of hate for others, and hate within will eventually destroy the hater. Keep your thoughts free from hate, and you need have no fear from those who hate you.*"

LIFE'S WORK

Having learned of Carver's successes, Booker T. Washington, an African American educational leader who had founded the Tuskegee Normal and Industrial Institute for Negroes in Alabama, believed that he would be the ideal person to head his school's recently established department of agriculture. Carver accepted Washington's invitation and spent the next forty-seven years of his life at the institution. Carver faced daunting challenges when he arrived at Tuskegee in 1896. Facilities and funding were inadequate, and he had a heavy teaching load, which meant that he was not able to devote as much time to research as he would have liked. Nevertheless, through hard work and inventiveness, he was able to create a program well suited to producing excellent graduates and important research. For example, he trained students to construct their own laboratory equipment, and he lobbied state officials to pass a special bill in support of an agriculture facility at Tuskegee.

As director of this Agricultural Experiment Station, Carver was able to show how struggling southern

Carver at work in his laboratory. (Wikimedia Commons)

agriculture could be revived. Decades of constantly growing cotton and tobacco had depleted the soil of its basic nutrients, but Carver showed how crop diversification, crop rotation, and the cultivation of such legumes as peanuts, soybeans, peas, beans, and alfalfa could serve the dual purpose of enriching exhausted soil and providing poor families and their farm animals with protein-rich foods. Through his bulletins, newsletters, and other popular publications, he was able to convince farmers to alternate plantings of cotton and peanuts, and they witnessed a dramatic increase in the quantity and quality of their harvests. However, their successes soon resulted in saturated markets and reduced prices for peanuts, soybeans, and sweet potatoes. This stimulated Carver to find ways to expand markets for these crops.

During this period, Carver came into conflict with his colleagues and Washington over his neglect of administrative duties and his cavalier treatment of department budgets. Washington relieved him of his director's post at Tuskegee in 1910. This event gave Carver much more time to develop derivatives from various food products. Over the next thirty years, he became famous for the many products he derived from peanuts, including beverages, cheeses, dyes, inks, paints, plastics, cosmetics, and medicinal oils. He eschewed publishing his discoveries in scientific or technical journals, preferring to publicize his recipes in periodicals accessible to farmers and housewives. He also exhibited his products at state fairs.

Carver's life changed dramatically with the death of Washington in 1915 and the installation of Robert Moton as his successor. Moton excused Carver from all classroom obligations and encouraged him to devote himself fully to agricultural research. By this time Carver's discoveries had become sufficiently well known that he was elected the first African American member of the Royal Society of London. He studied soil and how to make it more fertile, but he devoted most of his energies to creating a wide variety of products from peanuts, soybeans, sweet potatoes, beans, pecans, cotton, cowpeas, and plums. Carver rarely patented his discoveries or subjected them to peer review; he favored making his recipes and products freely available to all who might benefit from them. At a hearing before a congressional committee in 1921, he exhibited the flour, dyes, milk, and cheeses that he had made from peanuts in order to persuade lawmakers to pass a bill instituting a protective tariff on imported peanuts. His fame as the "peanut man" led to job offers; for example, Thomas Alva Edison, another trial-and-error inventor, wanted Carver to work for him, but Carver decided to remain at Tuskegee.

In 1923, Carver formed the Carver Products Company to develop processes for manufacturing foods, dyes, stains, and paints from clays and crops for sale to other companies, but this enterprise failed, as did the Carver Penol Company a few years later. These commercial ventures did lead to Carver's only patents for his discoveries. Despite these disappointments, Carver was successful as a consultant to several companies who made use of his expertise on plant products. In the 1930's, he participated in the chemurgy movement, which focused on the development of commercial chemicals from agricultural products. In 1937, he met Henry Ford at a chemurgy conference and they became friends. Indeed, Ford considered Carver the patron saint of the movement. Even with his growing fame and influence, Carver found that his work at Tuskegee suffered because of the lack of funding brought on by the Depression. Although his health began to decline, he was able to accept many awards that came his way, and he established a foundation to continue his work at Tuskegee. When he died from anemia early in

1943, the Tuskegee Institute received numerous messages of condolence from all over the world.

Significance

Estimates of Carver's significance have varied in the decades since his death. The recipient of many awards during his lifetime for the many ways he improved southern agriculture, Carver continued to be honored after his death. His Missouri birthplace was made into a national monument, and he was the first African American scientist commemorated on a U.S. postage stamp. A nuclear powered submarine was named in his honor, and in 1990, he became a member of the National Inventors Hall of Fame. Many hagiographical biographies have been published, particularly for young people. Carver became revered as a saintly scientist and inventor who used his knowledge to improve the lives of poor farmers. On the other hand, revisionist scholars have noted discrepancies between these idealized portraits and the harsh realities of Carver's life and work. His refusal to publish in refereed scientific journals or attend scientific meetings meant that his claims of discoveries and inventions largely escaped scientific scrutiny. When scholars gained access to his records, they found that many of his recipes and inventions derived from the work of others. Hence, his claims to hundreds of by-products derived from various crops have been drastically reduced. Nevertheless, his importance to the field of agriculture has been reemphasized, particularly his environmental philosophy that humans constitute an inextricable part of the community of living things, necessitating the wise and respectful use of the land and its plants.

Robert J. Paradowski

Further Reading

Gates, Henry Louis, Jr., and Cornel West. *The African-American Century: How Black Americans Have Shaped Our Country.* New York: Free Press, 2000. Analyzes Carver's work as important to both African American and American history. Bibliography and index.

Holt, Rackham. *George Washington Carver: An American Biography.* Rev. ed. Garden City, N.Y.: Doubleday, 1963. Carver handpicked Holt to write his authorized biography, and this book profits from the author's interviews with Carver, his friends, and colleagues. Bibliography and index.

Kremer, Gary R., ed. *George Washington Carver: In His Own Words.* Columbia: University of Missouri Press, 1987. A collection of important and interesting letters and speeches by Carver. Bibliography. Mackintosh, Barry. "George Washington Carver: The Making of a Myth." *Journal of Southern History* 42, no. 4 (November, 1976): 507-528. An early example of a revisionist account of Carver's life and work. Primary and secondary references.

McMurry, Linda O. *George Washington Carver: Scientist and Symbol.* New York: Oxford University Press, 1981. A revisionist biography that attempts, by using primary sources, to separate the man and scientist from various myths and idealizations. Detailed notes and index.

Lee De Forest

Radio engineer and scientist

Born: August 26, 1873; Council Bluffs, Iowa
Died: June 30, 1961; Hollywood, California
Areas of Achievement: Communications; electronics and electrical engineering
Primary inventions: Audion (triode vacuum tube); talking motion pictures

De Forest's pioneering work in developing the technology for wireless reception paved the way for the development of radio, and his efforts to perfect the process for printing sound on film were instrumental in launching the era of "talking" motion pictures.

Early Life

Lee De Forest was born in Council Bluffs, Iowa, in 1873, the eldest child of a Congregationalist minister. When he was six years old, his father accepted the presidency of Talladega College in Alabama, an institution founded in 1865 to educate newly freed African Americans. Life in the Deep South was hard on a boy whose family was shunned by the white community, and De Forest spent much of his time on his own. At an early age, he showed an interest in science and engineering, and he was especially fascinated by the work of America's best known inventor, Thomas Alva Edison. When he was seventeen, his father, assuming his son would pursue studies to become a minister, sent him to a preparatory school in Boston to ready him for entrance to a university. In 1893, De Forest entered Yale, but instead of matriculating at Yale College, he enrolled at Yale's Sheffield Scientific School. While an undergraduate, he developed an interest

Lee De Forest (Wikimedia Commons)

in electricity and electrical engineering. After graduation in 1896, he stayed at Yale to pursue a doctorate. He chose as his dissertation topic a study of the action of short Hertzian waves (radio waves)—exceptionally good preparation for a young man intent on making a name for himself in the newly developing field of wireless technology.

After receiving his Ph.D., De Forest headed to Chicago and found a job with Western Electric, where he proved to be a mediocre employee but an inveterate tinkerer. The new field of wireless communications was just then achieving worldwide attention, as the Italian Guglielmo Marconi had only recently demonstrated that it was possible to send and receive signals through the air over relatively long distances. De Forest was determined to make his mark in that arena. Though officials at Western Electric saw no future for the company in wireless communications, De Forest spent considerable time (much of it after-hours) developing a responder that might be used to receive sound waves sent from some distance away. Let go by Western Electric in 1900, he spent the next year working as a teacher and translator of scientific publications, devoting his spare time to perfecting the device he called a "Sponder." He considered his device ready for public testing in 1901. With two associates as partners, he set off to make his fortune in wireless telegraphy.

Life's Work

In 1901 at the America's Cup yacht races, De Forest demonstrated to the world the practicability of his responder, transmitting results from the race course to New York as Marconi had done two years earlier. In that year, he organized his first corporation, the Wireless Telegraph Company of America, the first of what would eventually be more than two dozen firms set up to promote his inventions. Although most in the community of inventors and investors were still skeptical of the device's reliability, one man stepped forward to serve as a backer: Abraham White. In 1902, White became De Forest's principal champion, helping organize a number of business enterprises that, in reality, were little more than shell corporations designed to allow White and several unscrupulous investors to take advantage of the notoriety of the new communications medium and De Forest's business naïveté. De Forest was given a modest salary and set up in an office where the public could see him working on his inventions. His principal residence became New York City, where he lived for more than two decades.

> "Unwittingly then had I discovered an Invisible Empire of the Air, intangible, yet solid as granite, whose structure shall persist while man inhabits the planet."

In 1904, De Forest's equipment was featured at the St. Louis World's Fair. All the while, White was making outrageous and sometimes blatantly false claims about the success of the company and De Forest's inventions, selling stock to gullible investors. Little of this income was invested in research; most went to further advertising gimmicks and into White's pockets. De Forest may not have been aware of the extent to which his partner was defrauding the public. The two had a falling out in 1906 when legal challenges were made to De Forest's rights to market some of his equipment. De Forest eventually lost his company and was once again nearly penniless. To make matters worse, in 1906 he entered into a disastrous marriage that lasted only a few months. He would marry and divorce twice more between 1907 and 1928.

By 1906, De Forest had begun experimenting with a new form of receiver based on the work of British inventor John Ambrose Fleming. Convinced that a two-electrode vacuum tube filled with gas could be used to detect and amplify radio waves, he modified one that

> ## The Audion
>
> *The development of the audion, or triode vacuum tube, has been called one of the most significant technological inventions of all time. While Lee De Forest is generally credited with this invention, his work actually was closely linked to the earlier invention of a diode tube by John Ambrose Fleming and the later creation of a feedback circuit by Edwin H. Armstrong—although De Forest claimed to have been solely responsible for adapting Fleming's diode and for indirectly creating the feedback circuit. Interested in improving receivers for wireless telegraphy, De Forest began experimenting with improvements on Fleming's diode almost immediately after Fleming received his U.S. patent in 1905. In just a little more than a year, De Forest applied for his own patent, claiming his device was notably different from Fleming's and a significant advance in receiving telegraph signals via sound waves sent from locations miles away from his receiver.*
>
> Technically, De Forest's audion worked on the principle of radio waves' ability to affect electrical current. The first audion was a diode tube quite similar to Fleming's. It consisted of a gas-filled glass cylinder containing a filament, an arrangement similar to an incandescent light bulb, into which a second metal plate was inserted. The positive terminal of a 22-volt battery was connected to the metal plate, and a pair of headphones added to the circuit; the negative terminal was connected to the lamp filament. Almost immediately after De Forest obtained his first patent for the audion in 1906, he began making modifications to his device. The most significant alternation consisted of the insertion of a thin metal wire, bent in the shape of a gridiron, between the filament and the plate. Doing so allowed him to regulate the flow of electrical current being generated by the action of the radio waves, permitting a continuous flow of electricity and making it possible to "tune" the receptor to achieve greater audibility. De Forest did not progress further with his invention at the time, satisfied that he could receive and detect telegraphic signals with sufficient accuracy to make the audion commercially successful as a receiver for wireless telegraphy. He did take steps to demonstrate how the audion could be used to transmit voice and music, "broadcasting" programs as early as 1907. Soon, a method for achieving sufficient amplification was available, attained by linking a number of audions in sequence. The original headphones were soon replaced by speakers, and the radio industry was born.

Fleming had designed and filed for a patent, which was granted in 1906. Not fully satisfied with his device, he continued to tinker with it, eventually adding a third component to his tube, a gridiron-shaped piece of metal inserted between the original electrodes. This tiny piece of metal allowed him to control the flow of electrons in the tube and amplify sounds sent to a listening device. Patented in early 1908, the audion, as De Forest would call it, would be the invention that assured him a place among the world's most important inventors, as it was the device that would eventually allow reception and amplification of the human voice and other sounds—the basis for modern radio.

Curiously, De Forest did not realize the significance of his discovery. Working on wireless technology, he was satisfied that the device provided sufficient amplitude to allow listeners to pick up telegraphic signals sent through the air. Since 1902, De Forest had invested considerable energy and time marketing his wireless system to the U.S. Navy and later to the United Fruit Company. Both organizations saw the benefit of being able to communicate by wireless to ships at sea, and for a time De Forest was successful in raising capital and generating profits from his venture. Unfortunately, the Panic of 1907 had caused investors to look warily at wireless telegraphy, and over the years that skepticism turned into efforts to seek legal recourse against inventors and companies that had not delivered on promises of improved technology and handsome dividends.

In 1912, De Forest and several associates in his new company were sued for fraud. To raise capital, he tried to sell several of his patents to American Telephone and Telegraph Company (AT&T) for $500,000, but AT&T's representative eventually negotiated a deal to purchase them for a mere $50,000. The same story was repeated in numerous instances throughout De Forest's career, as one grand idea after another brought him only a fraction of the millions he thought he deserved for his hard work and ingenuity. Although De Forest was acquitted two years later, he was once again without sufficient financial support to continue as an independent entrepreneur. To make matters worse, his claim to have invented a device to amplify sound was challenged in 1914 by Edwin H. Armstrong, who had developed and patented a similar device two years earlier. The ensuing litigation was not settled until 1926, long after De Forest had lost interest in wireless telegraphy and turned his attention to a new topic, the possibility of producing motion pictures with sound.

Beginning in 1913, De Forest concentrated on perfecting a system for capturing sounds that could be attached in some way to motion-picture film. In his view, this would not only allow viewers to hear actors as they spoke their lines but also permit filming of events such as concerts and operatic performances, which could then be viewed in movie theaters by thousands who for reasons of money or location could not attend live performances. For nearly a decade, De Forest sought ways to imprint sound directly on film, and by 1922 he had managed to do so. In that year, he began demonstrating his new invention publicly. Calling his products "Phonofilms," De Forest recorded speeches, short dramas, symphonies, and operas (including a performance by renowned tenor Enrico Caruso). Unfortunately, he was not able to interest the major movie studios in his process, and since these controlled most movie houses in America, he was forced to show his Phonofilms in small independent theaters. Nevertheless, those who saw his productions marveled at this new phenomenon. It was not long before Hollywood took notice, although studio officials decided not to purchase De Forest's sound-on-film technology. Instead, they opted to develop their own systems, initially settling on one that used a disc for sound that accompanied the film. Once again, De Forest failed to profit substantially from his invention.

As with all his other business ventures, De Forest's Phonofilm Corporation failed to generate sufficient capital to remain solvent. His various radio companies eventually went bankrupt as well, and their assets were

Lee de Forest (left) and another man experimenting with an early AM radio transmitter using De Forest's audion vacuum tube.

purchased by the Radio Corporation of America (RCA). By 1929, De Forest's financial situation appeared dire, and he determined he would no longer try to make a living in New York. In 1930, he moved to California to restart his career as an inventor for the movie industry. He married for a fourth time in 1930, and that union proved lasting.

The last years of De Forest's life brought mixed success. Beginning in 1930 with his election to a one-year term as president of the Institute of Radio Engineers, De Forest waged a campaign against what he considered the overcommercialization of radio during the 1920's. Believing the medium was best used for transmission of high-quality programming with limited commercials, he spoke and wrote against the trend toward excessive advertising and the inclusion of programming that catered to what he considered lower-class tastes (including jazz, which he excoriated on more than one occasion). He declared bankruptcy in 1936 but continued working on inventions and filing for patents on devices aimed at improving movie production and projection. He even developed some rudimentary devices that would eventually be used to launch the television industry. During World War II, he made himself available to the government, assisting the Navy by constructing a terrain altimeter that allowed pilots to determine their positions over the ocean with greater accuracy.

By the 1940's, the radio industry began to acknowledge De Forest's role in launching the medium. He received several tributes, and media began referring to him by the title he had long used to describe himself, the "father of radio." In 1959, he received an honorary Oscar from the Academy of Motion Picture Arts and Sciences for his pioneering work in the industry. All the while, however, he was struggling to make a living by selling some of his inventions and working at various radio schools. Although he was granted more than two hundred patents during his lifetime, none proved substantially remunerative. He never retired, instead continuing to go to his laboratory in Hollywood every day to investigate new ways to improve products and processes for the electronics industry. He died on June 30, 1961, believing (with some justification) that he had played a major role in ushering in the electronic age worldwide.

Significance

Determining the true extent of De Forest's contributions to technological advancement requires considerable skill in sorting out myth from fact. Throughout his life, De Forest made great claims for himself as the "father of radio" and insisted that he had done more than any other inventor to advance the development of this new medium. Not everyone agreed with him then or later, and many scientists and historians have downplayed his contributions by pointing out his deficiencies as a theorist. Nevertheless, there is no question that the audion he designed in 1905-1906 and improved in 1907 by adding a grid that permitted better reception and amplification of sound was a key component in allowing for the future development of radio. At the time, De Forest himself did not realize the significance of his invention, and it was not until Edwin H. Armstrong modified De Forest's original design to improve amplification that commercial radio became feasible. In a similar fashion, De Forest's work in perfecting a mechanism for producing talking movies by imprinting sound on film to allow for synchronous transmission of picture and sound was revolutionary. Unfortunately, the major studios refused to work with him or to adopt his technology, choosing instead to develop other methods for generating talking pictures. By the time the movie industry adopted his sound-on-film method years later, the "talkies" had become standard fare at movie houses across the United States.

What is clear, however, is that De Forest's pioneering work in developing the audion made radio possible. Similarly, his efforts to market his Phonofilms during the mid-1920's spurred major movie studios into action to move from silent films to talking pictures, if only as a means of capitalizing on the public's curiosity with the films De Forest was presenting to limited audiences. There is also strong evidence to suggest that De Forest's work with the federal government, particularly the Navy, advanced the military's ability to communicate at sea and conduct air warfare more effectively. While claims advanced by some that he should be considered the "father of the electronic age" may be exaggerated, it is not too much to say that his work was vital to the emergence of new methods of communication that materially improved the lives of American citizens and radically changed lifestyles throughout the country.

Laurence W. Mazzeno

Further Reading

Douglas, George H. *The Early Days of Radio Broadcasting*. Jefferson, N.C.: McFarland, 1987. History of the early days of commercial radio, focusing on the decade between 1920 and 1930. Includes a brief sketch of De Forest's career and contributions to the industry.

Douglas, Susan J. *Inventing American Broadcasting, 1899-1922*. Baltimore: The Johns Hopkins University Press, 1987. Detailed examination of early attempts to develop commercially viable wireless technology. Extensive analysis of De Forest's contributions to the industry, as both an inventor and entrepreneur.

Hijiya, James. *Lee De Forest and the Fatherhood of Radio*. Bethlehem, Pa.: Lehigh University Press, 1992. Biography focusing on De Forest's character. Searches for the sparks that motivated him as an inventor and entrepreneur.

Maclaurin, William Rupert. *Invention and Innovation in the Radio Industry*. New York: Arno Press, 1971. Discusses De Forest's career in the context of a larger survey of technological advancements in the radio industry. Explores the causes for these developments and examines the Significance of the new medium on American society.

Riordan, Michael, and Lillian Hoddeson. *Crystal Fire: The Birth of the Information Age*. New York: W. W. Norton, 1997. Traces the growth of the electronics industry resulting from the development of the transistor, an advance on the audion. Explains the importance of De Forest's invention to spurring the growth of the radio industry and leading to advances in communications technology.

Schubert, Paul. *The Electric Word: The Rise of Radio*. New York: Arno Press, 1971. Reprint of a 1928 book detailing the emergence of the radio industry, tracing the development of wireless technology and placing De Forest's career in the context of worldwide efforts to commercialize this new method of communication.

Weightman, Gavin. *Signor Marconi's Magic Box*. Cambridge, Mass.: Da Capo Press, 2003. Describes De Forest's contributions to the development of radio and sketches his relationship with the inventor Guglielmo Marconi, with whom he had a brief rivalry.

Zouary, Maurice H. *De Forest: Father of the Electronic Revolution*. Rev. ed. Bloomington, Ind.: 1st Books Library, 2000. Highly dramatic retelling of De Forest's career, celebrating his achievements in ushering in the electronic revolution. Includes clippings of news stories and other documents that attest to his accomplishments.

JOHN DEERE

Manufacturer

Born: February 7, 1804; Rutland, Vermont
Died: May 17, 1886; Moline, Illinois
Areas of Achievement: Agriculture; manufacturing
Primary invention: Steel plow

Deere developed a revolutionary steel plow that facilitated agriculture on the Great Plains in the United States, and he oversaw the growth of a company that eventually became a world leader in producing farm machinery.

EARLY LIFE

John Deere, the fifth child of William and Sarah Deere, was born in 1804 in the farming hamlet of Rutland, Vermont, where his father worked as a merchant and tailor. William left the family in 1808 for a business trip to England and was never heard from again. Raised by his mother and older brothers, Deere apprenticed as a blacksmith at age fifteen and went to work as a journeyman four years later. Sometime during his apprenticeship, he began courting Demarius Lamb; they married in 1827. For more than a decade, Deere struggled to make his living as a blacksmith, sometimes hiring out to local shops, on other occasions attempting to run his own business. The glut of blacksmiths in the region, however, made it difficult for him to obtain sufficient work to pay off his debts, and fire damaged his shop on more than one occasion. Frustrated and unable to settle his financial obligations, in 1836 Deere sold his business and headed west. His pregnant wife and three young children remained behind, joining him a year later after he had established himself in the town of Grand Detour, Illinois. The tiny settlement on the Rock River needed a blacksmith, and there Deere began what would become a series of business ventures that would transform him from a simple tradesman into the head of a thriving farm implements manufacturing enterprise.

> *"I will never put my name on a product that does not have in it the best that is in me."*

LIFE'S WORK

From the day he opened his shop in Grand Detour, Deere had all the work he could handle. One of the common tasks required of blacksmiths in the region was that they manufacture and repair farm implements, including plows. In the 1830's, most of the cutting edges on both breaking plows (large instruments used to make first cuts

John Deere (Wikimedia Commons)

> **The Steel Plow**
>
> *The legend surrounding John Deere's "invention" of the steel plow has many elements of typical American folklore. Ostensibly, Deere took a piece of discarded steel blade from a commercial sawmill, chiseled off the teeth, and shaped the flat steel into a shining plowshare that would slide through thick, sticky prairie soil, creating long, straight furrows. Almost overnight, farmers discarded their old wrought iron plows for those manufactured from steel, thereby creating a revolution in American agriculture.*
>
> There are elements of truth in the story, but the actual creation of Deere's plow is somewhat more prosaic. Deere did, in fact, fashion his first plow from a piece of discarded steel. Knowing that midwestern farmers were having to stop frequently to clean off parts of their plows that were constantly being clogged by the heavy black humus they were trying to cultivate, Deere imagined that a plowshare (the cutting blade) and its attendant moldboard (the device that turned over the soil to create neat furrows for planting) might be more effective if made from a material that would resist such contamination. Already familiar with the properties of polished steel, Deere took advantage of the opportunity presented to him by reshaping the steel and fashioning the wooden handles and shafts himself. One of his principal innovations was to shape the moldboard into a parallelogram that permitted the farmer to turn the soil more easily as it was cut.
>
> Properly speaking, however, Deere did not invent the steel plow; others had experimented with steel in constructing plows before Deere manufactured his instrument. His principal contribution was to create a plow that was effective in reducing the amount of clogging farmers experienced when plowing the rich prairie soil. Although the first plows Deere created have been lost, early versions still available suggest he often combined steel and wrought iron in his designs—probably depending on what materials he had available at the time. As he became more successful in his business, he was able to use more steel, which he obtained from mills in the eastern United States. An additional key to his success lay in the combination of inventiveness with a strong belief in the principle of constant improvement. Never fully satisfied with a product once he had begun to market it, Deere was continually consulting with farmers to learn how he might modify his plows to perform even better.

in previously untilled soil) and cultivating plows (smaller ones used to prepare soil for planting) were then being made from wrought iron. Deere discovered that by creating blades from polished steel, he could provide farmers with a tool that would cut through the thick, clay prairie soil without becoming caked up, thus reducing time spent cleaning off the equipment. Deere began manufacturing steel plows in 1837, and for the next decade his skill in producing these implements, coupled with his zeal in promoting their use by farmers throughout the region, allowed him to increase his sales steadily. By 1846, he was turning out a thousand plows a year in his Grand Detour shop. In 1848, he decided to move his operations to Moline, seventy-five miles west on the banks of the Mississippi River. There he built a factory that took advantage of the latest innovations in manufacturing technology, allowing him to grow his business exponentially. Then and later he was aided by a workforce that consisted largely of immigrants who brought with them skills they had learned in Europe and a work ethic that helped the company meet the ever-increasing demand for a variety of plows and other farm machinery. Over the years, Deere developed exceptional loyalty among his workers, who appreciated his hands-on approach to business and his concern for their personal welfare.

Unfortunately, Deere's ability as a craftsman was not matched by a keen business sense. He tried on several occasions to establish partnerships, both in Grand Detour and Moline. At one time or another he was a principal in companies that bore names like L. Andrus and Company; Deere, Atkinson, and Company; Deere, Tate, and Gould; John Deere and Company; Deere and Company; and the Moline Plow Factory. Throughout his years as an active businessman, Deere struggled with credit problems—sometimes as the one in debt but just as often as the one to

John Deere equipment is still manufactured today. (Wikimedia Commons)

whom money was owed. He also had to deal with competition that frequently pirated his innovations (although on occasion he, too, was accused of stealing ideas from others), and he found himself involved in numerous lawsuits over patent and trademark rights. The most famous of these lawsuits involved a rival company set up by former associates of Deere who called their business the Moline Plow Company. That name was similar to the one Deere was then using to identify his product, "the Moline Plow." Customers were often confused by the similarity and sometimes sent business to the rival company. In a suit lasting more than four years, Deere finally won a judgment that gave him public credit for his work in developing his special line of plows. An appeals court judge reversed the decision, however, forcing Deere to abandon the generic name for his plow and identify it more closely with Deere and Company.

One of the most significant events in Deere's career occurred in 1858, when his son Charles, who had joined the firm in 1854, became general manager of his father's company. Trained in business and innately adept at management and strategic planning, the younger Deere moved quickly to reorganize operations to take advantage of the growing demand for farm implements not only in the region but throughout the country as well. John Deere's sons-in-law and a few key associates joined Charles in running daily operations. By the second half of the century, Deere's company was selling plows, cultivators, harrows, drills and planters, and even wagons and buggies. John Deere even experimented with development of a steam-driven plow to replace those dragged by animals; unfortunately, this primitive tractor was too far ahead of its time to be of practical value.

In the years after the Civil War, Deere withdrew from active management of the company that bore his name, spending more of his time working his own farm outside Moline and becoming more involved in civic and philanthropic affairs. Although he was designated as president of the newly formed corporation Deere and Company in 1868, he watched from the sidelines as Charles led the firm to a position of national prominence as one of America's leading manufacturing firms for farm equipment. In 1873, Deere and Company introduced a new trademark: the leaping deer. By 1875, company revenues exceeded $1 million, and it had established branch offices in places like Kansas City, St. Louis, Minneapolis, and Council Bluffs, Iowa, to help respond more quickly to the needs of the population in areas far removed from Moline.

Deere's wife died in February, 1865. A year later, he went back to Vermont to marry her sister Lusena, bringing her back to Moline to run his household. In April, 1873, Deere was elected for a one-year term as mayor of Moline, during which he found himself at the center of a battle to impose temperance ordinances throughout the city. He worked diligently to upgrade the city's infrastructure, especially street improvements and fire protection. Deere also found time to make frequent trips back to Vermont and out to the West Coast. In 1885, Deere's health began to fail, and despite trips to resort areas designed to aid in recovery, he continued to decline steadily. He died in May, 1886.

Significance

Deere's innovations in the design of plows and other agricultural equipment aided in the emergence of the Midwest as the breadbasket of America. Most immediately, his plow provided farmers a way to till more acreage without having to stop frequently to clean their equipment, which constantly accumulated clods of the sticky soil characteristic of the region. Additionally, Deere's constant effort to improve the quality and functionality of his products led to the development of new and better machines that allowed farmers to cultivate and harvest larger tracts of land. Although not a shrewd businessman himself, Deere managed to surround himself with family and associates who understood how to organize and grow a company in what was sometimes a hostile business climate. Despite his personal limitations, Deere served as a model for those with whom he worked; his determination to succeed as a business owner in a highly competitive market led to the eventual growth of his company into one of the country's leading manufacturing enterprises.

— Laurence W. Mazzeno

Further Reading

Broehl, Wayne. *John Deere's Company: A History of Deere and Company and Its Times*. New York: Doubleday, 1984. Comprehensive account of the founding and growth of John Deere's business, from its inception to the 1980's. Contains numerous photographs, charts, and other pertinent business data.

Clark, Neil M. *John Deere: He Gave the World the Steel Plow*. Moline, Ill.: Desaulniers, 1937. Illustrated narrative dramatizing Deere's life and accomplishments as an inventor and businessman, commissioned by the Deere company to commemorate the one hundredth anniversary of the creation of the steel plow.

Dahlstrom, Neil, and Jeremy Dahlstrom. *The John Deere Story: A Biography of Plowmakers John and Charles Deere*. De Kalb, Ill.: Northern Illinois University Press, 2005. Well-researched and highly readable biography of the two men who transformed John Deere's idea for a useful, marketable plow into one of the world's great manufacturing companies.

Magee, David. *The John Deere Way: Performance That Endures*. Hoboken, N.J.: Wiley, 2005. Examines the business climate of John Deere's company at the turn of the twenty-first century, explaining how the values and vision of its founder have been preserved and strengthened by successors who transformed the original company into a highly successful worldwide enterprise.

Charles Richard Drew

Physician and medical researcher

Born: June 3, 1904; Washington, D.C.
Died: April 1, 1950; Burlington, North Carolina
Area of Achievement: Medicine and medical technology
Primary invention: Blood bank

Drew developed a system of collecting and storing blood plasma in what is known as a blood bank, which was utilized for Allied fighting men in World War II. Whereas previously blood could be preserved for only about seven days, Drew's method made it possible to store the plasma for much longer periods of time.

Early Life

Charles Richard Drew was the first of five children born to Richard (a carpet layer) and Nora (a teacher) Drew. He was an exceptional student and athlete, earning four varsity letters in high school. Voted best overall athlete in both his junior and senior years, he graduated from Dunbar High School in 1922 with honors and a partial athletic scholarship to play football at Amherst College. As the scholarship paid only some of his expenses, he took a part-time job as a waiter. Between his athletic activities and his job, his grades suffered during his first two years of college but improved by his junior year. His athletic career continued to be outstanding. He was an all-American halfback and captain of the track team.

Upon graduation in 1926, Drew took a position at Morgan State University in Baltimore, Maryland. He wanted to become a doctor but was unable to pay for medical school at the time. He worked at Morgan, saved his money, and after two years resigned to enroll in the McGill University Medical School in Montreal, Canada. In 1933, he was awarded a medical degree and a master of

Charles Richard Drew (Wikimedia Commons)

surgery degree from McGill, where he had won first prize in physiological anatomy and two fellowships in medicine. From 1933 to 1935, he interned at the Royal Victoria Hospital and completed his residency at Montreal General Hospital. He returned to the United States to teach pathology at Howard University College of Medicine in Washington, D.C. In 1939, he married Minnie Lenore Robbins, with whom he had four children.

Life's Work

Drew's life work began in earnest after he earned his doctorate from Columbia University in 1940. He was a General Education Board fellow in surgery at Columbia from 1938 to 1940 and a resident in surgery at Presbyterian Hospital. His research on blood plasma and transfusions discussed methods for separating red blood cells from plasma to preserve them for later reconstitution and use.

Conventional blood-preservation methods at the time focused on whole blood, which could be stored for only about seven days. Drew found that plasma could be stored much longer. In his two-hundred-page doctoral dissertation titled "Banked Blood: A Study in Blood Preservation," he showed that blood could be preserved longer if the red blood cells were separated from the plasma and frozen separately. When a blood transfusion was needed, the separated elements could be reconstituted.

World War II was under way in Europe, and doctors needed blood supplies for wounded soldiers and civilians. Aware of Drew's findings, one of Drew's former teachers, then living in England, requested that he send ten thousand glass containers of dried plasma to England to be used in transfusions. This required an all-out effort to collect blood at New York hospitals for export to England. Because the United States might also soon be drawn into

The Blood Bank

While Charles Richard Drew was a student at McGill University, he worked with visiting British professor Dr. John Beattie on his research in blood transfusions. It was understood that to avoid negative reactions in a blood transfusion, the donor and recipient blood types (A, B, AB, and O) have to match. Otherwise, the patient's immune system will attack the donated blood cells. At that time, whole blood was usually transfused, and therein was another problem: Whole blood was impossible to preserve for long periods of time, so a method was needed to preserve blood for transfusions so it would be available whenever needed.

Drew found that the red blood cells had a rapid deterioration rate. They are the blood components that carry hemoglobin, which combines with oxygen from the lungs and distributes the oxygen throughout the body. With the red blood cells removed, the liquid portion of blood, the plasma, could be stored practically indefinitely. Plasma, with no red blood cells (which contain the substance that determines blood type), could be used in transfusions without having to match donor and recipient blood types. This was particularly valuable in emergency cases. Drew transformed the test tube method of separating red cells from plasma into a mass-production technique.

Although blood plasma is not a substitute for whole blood in certain kinds of transfusions, it remains in the circulation for a much longer period than the previously used saline or glucose solutions, and it helps prevent or cure shock. In cases of burns, shock (without blood loss), or some cases of anemia in which the main concern is increasing the volume of circulating blood, plasma has been found to be highly valuable.

Using a dehydration process, Drew dried plasma for preservation and convenient transportation. To prepare it for transfusion, the plasma was simply reconstituted with distilled water just before it was to be used. In its reconstituted form, it stays fresh for about four hours. Plasma was found to be viable even a year after storage.

Drew's process of collecting, preserving, and using plasma was invaluable during the years of World War II. Because the demand for plasma was extremely high during the war years, Drew also pioneered the use of trucks equipped with refrigerators ("bloodmobiles") to carry the plasma to those who needed transfusions. Thanks to his work, hundreds of thousands of lives have been saved with blood plasma and its ability to stabilize injured people, regardless of blood type.

the war and need a large blood supply, Drew devised a new mass-production technique to separate the blood components and stockpile them.

British scientists were using modified cream separators to separate plasma from red blood cells, a system far more productive than spinning off the red cells using test tubes and centrifuges or simply allowing the cells to separate and settle apart from the plasma over a period of several days. Drew ordered two of the modified cream separators from England and, with his associates, constructed similar machines to mass-produce clear plasma from the whole blood being collected by the American Red Cross and the National Research Council. This new system produced the volume of plasma likely to be needed when America went to war.

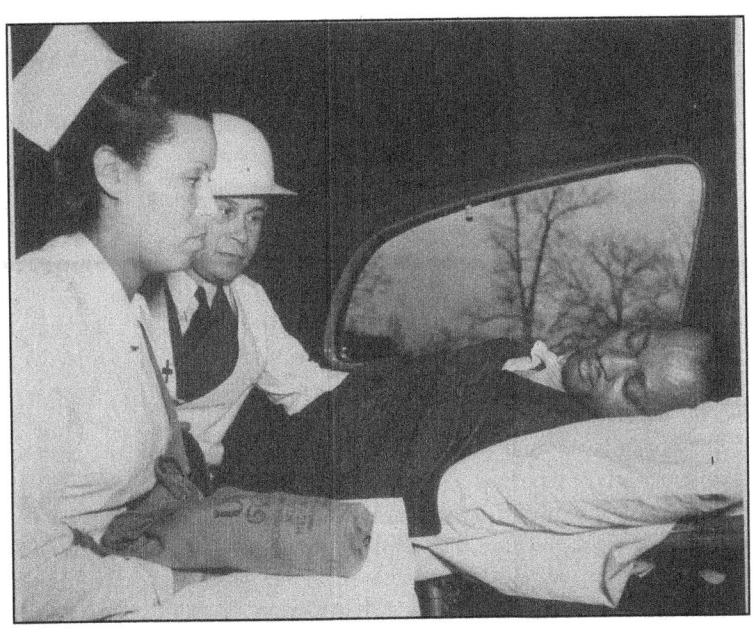

With war imminent, the American Red Cross named Drew director of its blood bank, and he was made assistant director of the National Research Council to manage blood collection for the American armed services in early 1941. Throughout the war, Drew's collection and preservation process was used; mobile blood banks were used at the front lines to treat wounded soldiers and stabilize them sufficiently to get them to hospitals.

Drew and a nurse practice first aid on a "victim" in a simulated air raid scenario. (Wikimedia Commons)

> "*I feel that the recent ruling of the United States Army and Navy regarding the refusal of colored blood donors is an indefensible one from any point of view. As you know, there is no scientific basis for the separation of the bloods of different races except on the basis of the individual blood types or groups.*"

One negative development occurred when the military ordered that all collected blood be separated by the race of the donor. Drew and other scientists and medical professionals tried unsuccessfully to convince the military that there was no difference between the blood of black and white people. They argued that men could die unnecessarily while waiting to receive the "right" blood, but they could not persuade the military to change the policy, which remained in force through the war.

In May, 1941, when Drew resigned as director of the American Red Cross, it was rumored that he left in protest over the segregated blood issue. Years later, however, his widow denied this rumor, saying that he returned to Howard University because he missed working as a teacher and surgeon. That same year, he was made head of Howard University's surgery department and chief surgeon at Freedman's Hospital. By 1944, he had become chief of staff at the hospital, a position he held until 1948.

Drew received numerous awards and prestigious appointments for his exemplary career. Among them were honorary degrees from Virginia State College in 1945 and from his alma mater, Amherst College, in 1947. He held membership on the American Board of Surgery, the first African American to do so. In 1944, he was awarded the Spingarn Medal by the National Association for the Advancement of Colored People (NAACP) for his outstanding achievements.

On April 1, 1950, while driving through North Carolina with a small group of students and colleagues to the annual meeting of the John A. Andrews Clinical Association in Tuskeegee, Alabama, Drew fell asleep at the wheel, and the car struck a soft shoulder and overturned. His injuries were the most serious: a closed head wound, a chest crushed by the steering wheel, and severe injuries to his arms and legs. He was taken to Alamance County General Hospital in nearby Burlington, where, according to urban legend, he was refused treatment because of his race. In fact, he received immediate care but was too badly injured to survive.

SIGNIFICANCE

Drew was a pioneer in blood collection and plasma processing. His experimentation turned biological research into mass-production methods that resulted in a new way to produce large quantities of transfusible blood. His work saved the lives of thousands of World War II servicemen and servicewomen and created a system of blood transfusion that saved lives in other wars and calamities. He devised a quantitative procedure for separating blood cells from plasma and preserving the components for longer periods of time than had previously been possible. His blood bank was a revolutionary advancement in modern medical practice, and the American Red Cross blood program today is a direct result of his groundbreaking work in mass-producing human plasma.

Jane L. Ball

FURTHER READING

Haber, Louis. *Black Pioneers of Science and Invention*. New York: Harcourt, Brace & World, 1970. Includes fourteen chapters on African American innovators, inventors, and scientists. The final chapter is devoted to Drew.

Hudson, Wade. *Book of Black Heroes: Scientists, Healers, and Inventors*. East Orange, N.J.: Just Us Books, 2003. Includes a short biographical sketch of Drew written for a juvenile audience.

Love, Spencie. *One Blood: The Death and Resurrection of Charles R. Drew*. Chapel Hill: University of North Carolina Press, 1997. An extensively researched, insightful discussion of how rumors and opinions affect history, with focus on how Drew died, medical care and race relations in America at the time of his death, and some of the myths surrounding his death.

Schraff, Anne E. *Dr. Charles Drew: Blood Bank Innovator*. Berkeley Heights, N.J.: Enslow, 2003. Biography of Drew written for a juvenile audience.

Trice, Linda. *Charles Drew: Pioneer of Blood Plasma*. New York: McGraw-Hill, 2000. Discusses Drew's life and work as inventor of large-scale production of human plasma. Young adult reading level.

GEORGE EASTMAN

Businessman

Born: July 12, 1854; Waterville, New York
Died: March 14, 1932; Rochester, New York
Area of Achievement: Photography
Primary inventions: Roll film; Kodak camera

Eastman invented roll film, making it possible for photographs to be taken more speedily without using breakable glass plates and hazardous chemicals. His invention allowed ordinary people to indulge in photography and opened the way for the rise of the motion-picture industry.

EARLY LIFE

George Eastman was born to George Washington Eastman and Maria Kilbourn. He had three older siblings, one of whom died in infancy. In 1865, his family moved to Rochester, New York, after his father established the Eastman Commercial College there. His father died in 1867, the college failed, and an older sister died in 1870. At the age of fourteen, Eastman quit high school to support his mother and sister as a messenger boy for an insurance company, earning three dollars per week. He eventually went to a different insurance company, where he

George Eastman (Library of Congress)

made five dollars per week and was soon in charge of filing and writing policies. He was ambitious and bright, studying accounting at night, hoping to get a better-paying job. By 1874, he was working at a bank and earning fifteen dollars per week.

At age twenty-four, he developed an interest in photography when he planned a vacation trip to Santo Domingo and it was suggested that he make a photographic record of his trip. He was irked to find how complicated that would be: The paraphernalia required to take photographs was very complicated. He needed not only a huge camera that required a heavy tripod to support it but also chemicals, tanks, a jug of water, glass plates, and a tent in which to make and apply the emulsions for the glass plates and in which to develop the exposed plates before they dried. In addition, he had to take lessons, at a cost of five dollars, to learn how to use all the gear for the picture taking. He did not go to Santo Domingo, but he continued to be fascinated with photography. Even as he continued working in the bank, he began what would become his life's work—finding new and simpler ways to make photographs.

> *"What we do during our working hours determines what we have; what we do in our leisure hours determines what we are."*

LIFE'S WORK

About 1878, Eastman was inspired to find a way to eliminate much of the gear needed to take photographs. He probed journals dealing with photography and learned of a British emulsion process that kept the treated glass

---

Roll Film

George Eastman's primary goal was to simplify the photographic process and reduce the amount of gear, time, and effort needed to take a picture. When he first set this goal, photographers had to go through a complicated process. A glass plate had to be coated with a liquid emulsion just moments before the picture was to be taken. Then, once the exposure was made, the picture had to be developed immediately. This required having a mobile darkroom to accommodate all the chemicals and paraphernalia right on the site where the pictures were to be taken.

Eastman, along with collaborators, first developed a dry, pre-coated plate that could be used in much the same way as the wet one, but with the convenience of being already prepared for exposure for the picture taking. However, in order to use a small camera that would not need a tripod, he worked to produce a dry, transparent, flexible film and a small camera to use it. The film he developed took pictures in black and white. He used paper as a light and flexible support for the needed emulsion. He coated the paper with layers of a soluble gelatin followed by layers of insoluble, light-sensitive gelatin.

The layers of gelatin had different roles to play in the making of a photograph. Some filtered light or controlled the chemical reactions that took place. Others, that made the actual image, contained silver-halide crystals, which underwent a photochemical reaction when exposed to light through the camera lens and thus captured the photographic image. Once the film was exposed, it was developed using chemicals that broke down the crystals into silver, enhancing the image. Another chemical was then used to halt the light sensitivity of the film and to set the negative image so that a picture could be printed.

This new flexible film, mounted on a spool, needed a new kind of camera, and Eastman invented the Kodak camera. A rectangular box with a fixed-focus lens, his camera could hold the spool of film and a take-up spool that allowed as many as one hundred exposures to be made without the need to unload or reload the camera.

These two inventions took photography out of the exclusive purview of professional photographers and introduced it to the masses as a way to record and save precious memories. They also opened up a new and lucrative business that made millionaires of Eastman and his associates. A direct by-product of Eastman's work was the development of the motion-picture industry, which owes much to Eastman's invention of transparent roll film.

plates sensitive enough to take pictures even after the emulsion dried. He experimented with gelatin emulsions of his own design based on British formulas, working at night in his mother's kitchen after he had put in a day's work at the bank. It took him three years, but he finally produced a formula that worked. By 1880, he developed and patented a machine that would prepare the plates in greater numbers than previously possible. He decided to start his own company, the Eastman Dry Plate and Film Company, to make dry plates to sell to photographers.

On a leased third floor of a building in Rochester, he started making his dry plates. As the business grew, he saw the need for a product that would serve both professional photographers and amateurs. To make photography more convenient and accessible, Eastman worked to find a component to produce the photographic images that was lighter and more flexible than the bulky and breakable glass plates. After some experimentation, he found that an emulsion-coated paper on a roll could be used in cameras instead of glass plates. The paper roll film was successful even though the quality of the pictures taken with the film was not very satisfactory because the grain of the paper showed on the developed pictures. Eastman continued to experiment, using layers of gelatins that ultimately allowed the photographic image to be recorded on one of the gelatin layers instead of on the paper. This gelatinous flexible film eventually evolved into the familiar roll film.

Shortly thereafter, Eastman, along with associate William Hall Walker, designed and began the manufacture of a smaller, lighter-weight camera that could use the roll film. The result was the first Kodak camera, initially called the "roll holder breast camera." People who bought and used the camera got their pictures developed and printed by sending the entire camera back to the Eastman Company along with a $10 processing fee; they received back their printed pictures and their camera reloaded with a new 100-exposure roll of film, ready to use again.

By 1900, Eastman was interested in further increasing the burgeoning interest in photography. To make it a hobby for the masses, he introduced a camera costing one dollar, the Brownie, which he ostensibly intended for children. His earlier camera cost around $15 and was therefore out of the reach of many ordinary people. By 1901, the Brownie's price had dropped to 25 cents. Owners no longer had to send the camera to the manufacturer for processing; they bought and loaded the film, took the pictures, and needed to send only the film to the company for development and printing.

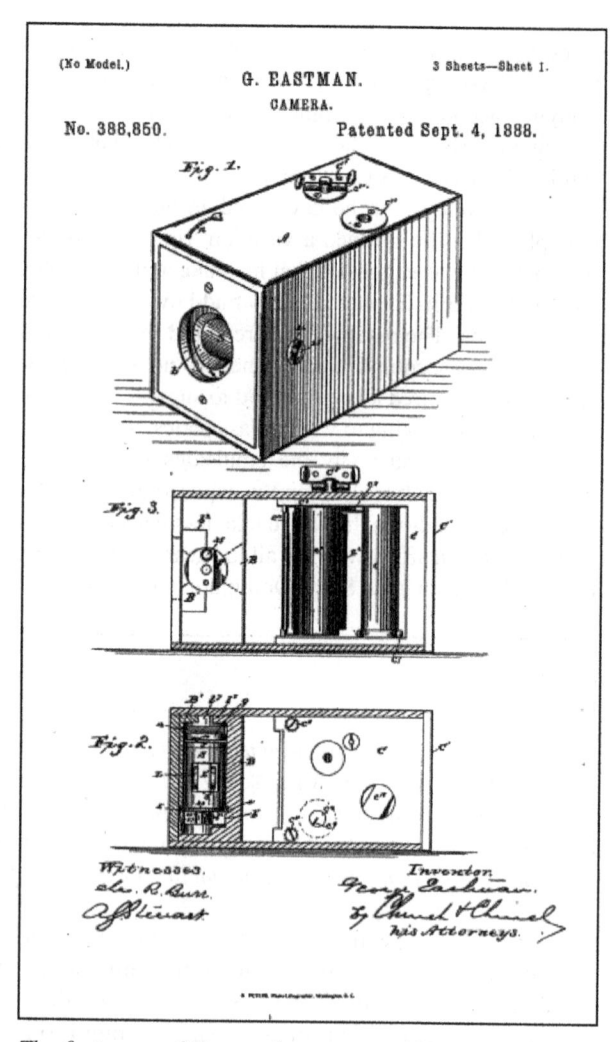

The first page of Eastman's patent no. 388,850, for his film camera and roll film. (Wikimedia Commons)

The Brownie was a fixed-focus lens box camera made of wood or metal (after 1930, plastic). Eastman's company also manufactured a folding camera that was compact and portable. Unlike other such cameras marketed around the country at the same time, the Brownie was both efficient and inexpensive; it was even capable of producing the popular postcard-size pictures.

Eastman's company became one of the most lucrative in the country. He stepped down from day-to-day management of the business by 1925 and became chairman of the board. He shifted his sights to philanthropy, becoming one of the most generous philanthropists of his time, an era that included such philanthropic giants as Andrew Carnegie and John D. Rockefeller. He donated more than

$75 million over the years to various causes, including wage dividend benefits (profit-sharing) as incentives for his employees at the Eastman Kodak Company, setting up dental clinics in Rochester, and supporting the city's theater and symphony orchestra. Other recipients of his largesse were the University of Rochester, which he endowed with funds for a school of music and a school of dentistry; the Massachusetts Institute of Technology, which was given buildings; and Tuskegee and Hampton Institutes, which received some of the $30 million he earmarked just for educational institutions.

By 1930, Eastman had begun to experience poor health. He suffered from a degenerative spinal disorder, which may have been spinal stenosis (resulting from calcification in the vertebrae). His beloved mother had suffered the same kind of disease and was confined to a wheelchair during the final two years of her life. Having always been a very active person who traveled, often to Europe, and was involved in business and civic affairs, Eastman became increasingly depressed as he foresaw his coming incapacitation. Never married, though long involved in a platonic relationship with the wife of a business associate, he never really got over the loss of his mother when she died in 1907. He remembered how painful her last two years were and did not want the same end for himself. On March 14, 1932, he put his affairs in order and wrote a final note that read, "My work is done. Why wait?" and committed suicide with a pistol.

Significance

Eastman's inventions changed American photography, making photography something the masses could enjoy, where before only a few professionals could deal with its complexities. His roll film eliminated the fragile, cumbersome glass plates needed to catch the images in the bulky cameras of the time. Instead of relying on the slow, complicated process that produced one picture at a time using several procedures, Eastman's roll film sped up the process and allowed numerous images to be captured in fairly rapid succession. After roll film, he produced a camera to use the film, one that was smaller than its predecessors, easier to use, and certainly cheaper to buy. He said in his Kodak advertisements, "You press the button, we do the rest."

The Eastman Kodak Company made photography an easier business for professional photographers as well as an affordable, fun hobby for amateurs, and Eastman's work made him a millionaire. The wealth that he acquired because of his inventions was shared with others. He became involved in many philanthropic endeavors. Even before he became a millionaire, he began sharing his fortune with the employees of his company: He was one of the earliest businessmen to set up pension plans and insurance plans for workers. Once his fortune was made, he shared it in several different areas, particularly to the advantage of his hometown of Rochester, and to educational and medical institutions all over the country.

Jane L. Ball

Further Reading

Ackerman, Carl W. *George Eastman: Founder of Kodak and the Photography Business*. Washington, D.C.: BeardBooks, 1930. A biography that gives an intimate view of Eastman's life, based on free access to Eastman's files and correspondence. Discusses events of the era affecting Eastman.

Brayer, Elizabeth. *George Eastman: A Biography*. Rochester, N.Y.: University of Rochester Press, 2006. A scholarly biography that shows the many facets of Eastman: cold, modest, generous. Discusses his business endeavors and personal life, including those private affairs that are either admirable or dubious, and insights into the patent infringement lawsuits he dealt with. Several rare photographs.

Tedlow, Richard S. *Giants of Enterprise: Seven Business Innovators and the Empires They Built*. New York: HarperBusiness, 2001. The histories of seven business leaders, with chapters devoted to each. Eastman's chapter (about thirty pages long) tells how he accomplished his business success.

West, Nancy M. *Kodak and the Lens of Nostalgia*. Charlottesville: University of Virginia Press, 2000. Concerned mostly with the advertising strategies of the Kodak Company and how important they were to the company's success, as well as how they helped lure the American consumer to the hobby of photography. Many ads are reproduced; some of Eastman's inventions, the Brownie camera especially, are discussed.

Thomas Alva Edison

Technologist, scientist, and businessman

Born: February 11, 1847; Milan, Ohio
Died: October 18, 1931; West Orange, New Jersey
Areas of Achievement: Invention, manufacturing
Primary inventions: Light bulb; phonograph; kinetoscope

Edison is mainly known as the inventor of the phonograph and the light bulb. During his lifetime, he obtained more than one thousand U.S. patents. His other inventions include a motion-picture camera, a stock ticker, an electric pen, and numerous types of telegraphs, telephones, and electrical equipment. He also developed complete power systems, business organizations, commercialization strategies, and the modern research laboratory.

Early Life

Thomas Alva Edison was born to Samuel and Nancy Elliott Edison in the small town of Milan, Ohio, in 1847. In 1854, the family moved to Port Huron, Michigan. Like Milan, Port Huron was small but served as a local center for commerce and industry. From an early age, Edison absorbed the local culture of artisans and workshops and read extensively in his father's library. He also inherited an entrepreneurial spirit from his father. He attended school for only three months in his youth and was then educated at home by his mother.

> "Many of life's failures are people who did not realize how close they were to success when they gave up."

From an early age, Edison, called "Al" in his youth, loved to experiment and investigate. He set up a laboratory in his parents' basement. In 1859, he took a job selling candy, magazines, and newspapers on the Grand Trunk Railroad running between Port Huron and Detroit. He spent his layover time in Detroit reading at the Detroit Public Library and performed chemistry experiments in the baggage car. One mishap in his chemical "laboratory" nearly burned the car. In his later writings, Edison states that it was during this time that he first noticed his hearing problem. As an adult, he became almost completely deaf.

Thomas Alva Edison (Wikimedia Commons)

In April, 1862, Edison demonstrated an entrepreneurial instinct that would serve him well later. News of the Civil War had increased his newspaper sales. On the day of the Battle of Shiloh, he saw the bulletin boards at the Detroit station surrounded by large crowds reading the announcements that 60,000 soldiers were killed and wounded. He decided that, if the same excitement were present at the small towns on the railroad, sales of papers would increase. He had the telegraph operator at Detroit telegraph the news on the battle to each station on the route to Port Huron. With the approval of the editor of the paper, Edison took along one thousand papers rather than the usual hundred. At one station where he normally stopped, he sold thirty-five papers. Edison raised the price of the newspaper at each station because there were crowds awaiting news. The papers he usually sold for five cents had gone up to twenty-five cents by the time he reached Port Huron. He made a great deal of money and began learning telegraphy the next day.

After Edison rescued the son of a telegraph operator from the path of a freight car in 1862, the operator rewarded him by giving him telegraph lessons. Edison first took a part-time job as a telegrapher in Port Huron. He eventually became an itinerant telegrapher and quickly became known as an expert receiver. He worked in several midwestern cities and continued his reading in technical and scientific literature. He spent much of his time thinking about how to improve telegraphy, which was a crude communication system at that time. To send a message from Boston to St. Louis required a chain of six operators.

In 1868, Edison moved to Boston and took a job with Western Union. He found financial backers in the telegraph community and worked on improving the telegraph. He obtained his first two patents—a vote recorder, which the state legislature would not buy, and a printing telegraph for stock quotations. The stock ticker proved more successful, and Edison left his job and devoted himself full-time to inventing.

LIFE'S WORK

Edison's professional career as an inventor took off when he visited New York City in 1869 to test an improved telegraph. After meeting Franklin Pope, a prominent telegraph engineer, Edison moved to New York. Pope and Edison set up a series of businesses to invent and promote printing telegraphs, which played a key role in the distribution of financial information. Edison sold a printing telegraph, or stock ticker, to Western Union. The profits

---

The Light Bulb and Its Power System

Thomas Alva Edison invented an electric light and an electric distribution system to power it. This invention began with a search for a lamp to replace gas lighting, which could be dangerous with the open flame. Another alternative, arc lighting, had proven more successful for outdoor lighting than for indoor, where it could give off dangerous sparks and provided too intense a light for small spaces. Others had tried unsuccessfully to develop an incandescent light bulb. However, Edison's "invention factory" system at Menlo Park, New Jersey, proved equal to the task.

The first problem with inventing a practical incandescent bulb was the filament. Most materials burned up too fast and could not give long, steady light. Edison and his team tried thousands of materials for more than a year. They began in September, 1878, with platinum wire filaments, which had a high melting point. To deal with this problem, they enclosed the filament in a vacuum bulb. However, a platinum filament would make the bulbs too expensive for wide use and require large and expensive copper-wire conductors in the power distribution system because of platinum's low resistance to the electric current. Edison realized that a system of incandescent lighting required high-resistance lamps in order to reduce the size and cost of copper conductors. With a good vacuum bulb, Edison turned to carbon for filaments. The successful choice of filament came by accident when Edison abstractedly rolled a piece of compressed lampblack between his fingers until it became a slender thread. Seeing this, he tried it as a filament. With a few further experiments, he found the right composition of materials. On October 21-22, 1879, Edison and his team tested the first successful incandescent lamp in a vacuum with a piece of carbonized thread as filament. Soon they began demonstrating it, but they continued to work on improving the filament. Within a year, Edison's company began producing commercial bulbs with a filament of carbonized Japanese bamboo.

Meanwhile, Edison focused more on inventing the electrical distribution system to power the bulb. His light bulb would only succeed commercially if numerous homes and offices had access to electricity to use the new light source. Edison modeled his distribution system on that of gas lighting, which included central stations, underground conductors, meters, and lamp fixtures. He also designed almost everything in the system, including a new electrical generator, new screw sockets to hold the bulb in the fixtures, and fuses to prevent electrical overloads.

The first permanent central station opened in Manhattan in 1882. It served Wall Street and many of the major newspapers. Edison invented a new lamp and electric distribution system that would change the world. However, eventually his system shifted from direct current, which Edison strongly defended, to alternating current. Edison's direct-current system worked efficiently in densely populated cities. However, alternating current could travel longer distances. By 1891, Edison had left behind the industry that he had helped found. His company merged into General Electric.

allowed him to set up a large laboratory in Newark, New Jersey.

Between 1870 and 1876, Edison worked on telegraph improvements such as an automatic telegraph system, which did not require an operator to take down the message. He also developed a quadruplex telegraph, which would allow two messages to be sent in one direction and another two in the opposite direction over a single wire. This increased the capacity of a wire fourfold. He invented an electric pen, which made an exact copy of something that a person wrote. Both the quadruplex telegraph and the electric pen brought substantial profits, with which Edison expanded his laboratory and business.

In 1871, Edison married Mary Stilwell. Between 1873 and 1878, they had three children: Marion, Thomas, and William. However, Edison's work remained the most important aspect of his life. His work habits included long hours away from his family. He often worked late, took short naps rather than sleeping through the night, and ate around midnight.

In 1876, Edison took his family and his work to Menlo Park, New Jersey. There he built a new home and a laboratory solely for conducting experiments. This became an unparalleled facility for invention. Edison enjoyed the mental work, the creative part of the process of invention. He would have an idea, draw up a rough sketch, and discuss it with his assistants. They would examine the sketch and work with it until they could turn it into a workable machine.

The "invention factory" set up at Menlo Park produced the phonograph, the light bulb, a power distribution system that would bring electricity into homes, and a greatly improved telephone. Western Union, for which Edison continued to do work on improving the telegraph, was concerned about the competition from the telephone and asked Edison to work on an improvement. He improved the quality of the sound and made the telephone much easier to use by providing a separate mouthpiece and earpiece. He also developed a transmitter that would carry over longer distances and that was used for nearly a century. The telephone improvements netted Edison's company over a quarter of a million dollars.

An unexpected outcome of the telephone research was the invention of the phonograph in 1877. The telephone was originally envisioned as a way for telegraph companies to transmit messages between operators. However, speech was too fast to be written down. Edison devised a way to record the vibrations in the receiving instrument and play them back slower to record the words. This led Edison and his staff to realize that they could record

Edison and his early phonograph. (Library of Congress)

sound, and the invention of the phonograph followed. The phonograph recorded and played back both words and music. While the phonograph made Edison an overnight celebrity (he was billed in the press as the "Wizard of Menlo Park"), he was unable to turn his early exhibition machine into a commercial product.

Edison brought together everything he had learned about invention and business in the development of the light bulb and the electric light and power system, beginning with a search for a lamp to replace gas lighting. Edison pulled together financial backing, numerous researchers, an expanded laboratory and shop facilities, factories, and marketing. The search for a filament took an enormous amount of time and resources. However, the demonstration of the first working light bulb in 1879 was only the beginning. Most homes did not have access to the electricity necessary to use the light bulb. Edison's laboratory then developed an electric power distribution system and opened the first electric power plant in New York in 1882. By the end of the nineteenth century, there would be over five hundred Edison plants in the United States and at least fifty in other countries.

In 1884, Edison's wife died after a long period of illness. Although work had always taken first place with Edison, he was devastated by her death. Within a year, he moved the family away from Menlo Park. In 1886, he married Mina Miller and moved his family and business to West Orange, New Jersey. There he created a laboratory that would set the example for research and development laboratories in the twentieth century.

With the invention of the kinetoscope in the late 1880's, Edison founded the American motion-picture industry. Edison and one of his trusted assistants, W. K. L. Dickson, began experimenting with celluloid film and found a way to do for images what they had done for sound. They recorded a series of images, each showing a tiny move forward. When viewed in rapid succession, the images gave the impression of movement. They developed a camera and the "peep-show" kinetoscope for viewing the films.

Although Edison's work as a businessman decreased over time, his inventive work continued for decades. Inventions included an improved phonograph, dictating machines, an improved storage battery, and a method for ore separation. Inventions such as the improved battery provided financial stability to Edison's laboratory and companies. Others, such as his magnetic ore separator, failed. Nevertheless, Edison persevered. He eventually became the nation's "inventor-philosopher," with reporters seeking his opinion on everything from diet to the existence of God.

Edison died at his home, Glenmont, in West Orange, New Jersey, on October 18, 1931. President Herbert Hoover asked the nation to dim its lights in his honor.

Edison and his searchlight cart in 1915. (Wikimedia Commons)

SIGNIFICANCE

Edison changed the lives of Americans by bringing sound and light into their homes and businesses. While he became nationally and internationally famous upon his invention of the phonograph, some of his later inventions had a greater Significance. The power distribution system that Edison developed to supply electrical power to his light bulb changed American homes forever. It not only provided light but also made possible the invention and use of numerous small household devices. Edison's inventions affected and sometimes created industries, including motion pictures, music, and electric power.

Edison's greatest contribution may have been the "invention of the method of invention," as Alfred North Whitehead called the greatest invention of the nineteenth century. Having begun his professional life as an independent inventor, Edison ended with perhaps the first modern research and development laboratory and team. His vision included what the twentieth century would term "innovation"—invention, research, development, and commercialization.

Linda Eikmeier Endersby

FURTHER READING

Baldwin, Neil. *Edison, Inventing the Century*. New York: Hyperion, 1995. Engaging biography with information on Edison's inventions (no technical knowledge necessary). Includes information on Edison's prowess in business, promotion, and commercialization. Illustrations, bibliography, index.

Essig, Mark R. *Edison and the Electric Chair: A Story of Light and Death*. New York: Walker & Company, 2003. Focuses on Edison's argument in favor of his direct current (DC) rather than alternating current (AC). Recounts details of Edison's condemnation of AC through his promotion of its use in the first electric chair, which showed that AC was too dangerous for common use. Illustrations, index.

Israel, Paul. *Edison: A Life of Invention*. New York: John Wiley & Sons, 1998. Scholarly work that provides technical detail on Edison's inventive work in the nineteenth century and some biographical details. Relies heavily on documents annotated and published by the Edison Papers Project in New Jersey. Illustrations, bibliography, index.

Jonnes, Jill. *Empires of Light: Edison, Tesla, Westinghouse, and the Race to Electrify the World*. New York: Random House, 2003. Focuses on Edison's defense of his direct current against George Westinghouse's alternating current, which Nikola Tesla supported and for which he invented. Provides good information on the marketing, promotion, and commercialization after an invention. Illustrations, bibliography, index.

Melosi, Martin V. *Thomas A. Edison and the Modernization of America*. New York: Longman, 2008. Scholarly work detailing Edison's life and work. Focuses on the business side of invention and Edison's creation of systems of research, invention, and commercialization. Illustrations, bibliography, index.

Stross, Randall E. *The Wizard of Menlo Park: How Thomas Alva Edison invented the Modern World*. New York: Crown, 2007. Engaging account of Edison's life that focuses on Edison's invention of celebrity rather than on his technical inventions. Highlights Edison's self-conscious use of the rising popular press and what Stross calls Edison's launch of the first successful branding campaign. Illustrations, note on sources, index.

THOMAS L. JENNINGS

Businessman

Born: 1791; New York City, New York
Died: February 11, 1859; New York City, New York
Area of Achievement: Chemistry
Primary invention: Dry cleaning

Jennings innovated a dry-cleaning technique to wash stains from garments without using water immersion and agitation. He submitted an application registering that procedure with the U.S. Patent Office, obtaining the earliest-known patent issued to an African American.

EARLY LIFE

Thomas L. Jennings was born during the last decade of the eighteenth century in were chosen. Most sources state his birth year as 1791, based on two obituaries written soon after his death in winter, 1859, which say that Jennings was sixty-eight years old. According to the 1850 U.S. Census, Jennings was fifty years old as of August 1, 1850, and he was fifty-five when the New York State census was taken in 1855, suggesting he was born around 1799. Neither record indicates who provided Jennings's age to census enumerators and how they knew that information.

Sources describe Jennings as a free African American without clarifying if he or his parents were ever enslaved and, if so, how Jennings secured his freedom. They do not tell who Jennings's parents were, nor do they specify what name his middle initial represents. In 1790, near the time of Jennings's birth, 1,011 free blacks and 2,369 slaves lived in New York City, composing 9.7 percent of that city's population. Jennings was free in 1820 when he applied for a patent.

Few details about Jennings's childhood are known, except that as a boy he began working as an apprentice to a New York tailor who, sources vaguely commented, was an acclaimed man. Jennings acquired skills to create and modify clothing to meet customers' specifications. No facts confirm that Jennings attended school, but his activities as an adult reveal that he was knowledgeable and literate, writing documents discussing legal issues. During the War of 1812, he dug trenches on Long Island to protect the city.

Jennings married a woman named Elizabeth, who had been born in New Jersey and was five years younger than him. They lived at 167 Church Street in the Fifth Ward of New York County and had two daughters, Elizabeth and Matilda, and two sons, Thomas and William. In addition to earning income from making clothes, Jennings operated a boardinghouse.

LIFE'S WORK

Jennings concentrated on a tailoring career after being employed in several other positions. He offered his services to customers who sought alterations for their clothing or desired new garments, which he designed and fitted. The quality of his craftsmanship attracted more clients, both in the city and elsewhere, who traveled to hire Jennings to assist them with their clothes, as people recommended him and promoted his work. Profiting from his sewing talents and entrepreneurial abilities, Jennings invested his income to establish a clothing store located on Church Street that developed into a prominent garment business.

In the late 1810's, Jennings contemplated how to resolve a common complaint his customers voiced regarding their clothing becoming stained. Instead of keeping their dirty clothes, some people replaced them if they could afford to do so, although many customers did not have that option. Jennings sought ways to clean and restore garments, stressing that he wanted to assist less prosperous clients and to prevent people from discarding clothes he had invested his time and skills to make. He realized that regular washing techniques using water might damage fragile materials.

Jennings evaluated the effectiveness of applying chemicals used by tradesmen for cleaning tasks in other professions to remove stains from diverse fabric samples. He mixed chemicals together in varying ratios until he probably determined that turpentine was the most useful cleaning fluid to lift greases and oils from fabrics without harming materials. No available information reveals whether he constructed machinery for his process. Jennings offered his innovative cleaning procedure, referring to it as dry scouring, to his clientele. This early form of dry cleaning pleased Jennings's customers and secured him more business producing clothes and cleaning them.

Aware that customers spread news of his successful dry scouring work, Jennings sought to protect his invention from other people appropriating his techniques without reimbursing him. In 1820, he submitted a patent application to the U.S. Patent Office. Sources do not indicate whether Jennings initiated the patenting process alone or whether he had legal counsel who assisted him, nor do they identify witnesses who signed his application. At the time Jennings applied, patents did not state the race of individuals patenting inventions, and the Patent Office did not discriminate against inventors based on ethnicity. The 1793 patent law in effect at that time permitted both free and enslaved African Americans to secure patents.

Jennings received a U.S. utility patent on March 3, 1821, for his invention entitled "Dry Scouring Clothes." He framed the certificate, which bore the signatures of

Dry Scouring

Thomas L. Jennings developed a practical dry-cleaning technique in response to his customers' demands. Because a fire burned Jennings's patent record, his description of dry scouring and specific information regarding his invention are unavailable. Historians hypothesize Jennings recognized that turpentine, a fluid many craftsmen used for cleaning tasks to remove greases and oils, could be used to launder fabric. Jennings probably evaluated different quantities of turpentine to determine the minimum amounts that would be effective when used on diverse materials. He possibly also combined turpentine with other chemicals to strengthen his cleanser. Jennings's dry-scouring technique might have relied on turpentine evaporating and lifting dirt from fibers.

Histories of dry cleaning do not mention Jennings's patent or acknowledge whether it inspired any other inventors in the United States or elsewhere. Instead, accounts comment that some nineteenth century Europeans used lamp fuels composed of turpentine spirits to clean cloth. After turpentine brushed on stained material dried, grime disappeared. In 1855, a Parisian, Jean Baptiste Jollyâ€"often credited as the founder of commercialized dry cleaningâ€"established a laundry based on using turpentine and chemicals to clean fabrics. Nineteenth century chemists created such solvents as benzene, which dissolved oils and fats that water could not disintegrate. Fibers did not swell when exposed to these solvents, preventing garments from shrinking as they did when laundered in water. Solvents did not damage most materials or alter their colors. Dry cleaners realized that they could expose entire garments, curtains, and other fabric items to solvents instead of just dabbing areas.

Knowledge of dry-cleaning technology and methods extended internationally, and more businesses offered dry-cleaning services to generate income from a process that was not as time-intensive as traditional laundry methods, which appealed to customers. By the early twentieth century, many dry cleaners used petroleum-based solvents, which increased risks of fires and explosions. Professional organizations, including the National Association of Dyers and Cleaners, established standards such as using dry solvents, which were replaced with synthetic solvents developed in the 1970's. Perchloroethylene, a frequently used synthetic solvent, was safer and nonflammable. In the late twentieth century, scientists continued to develop dry-cleaning solvents to be more environmentally sound, such as those patented by GreenEarth Cleaning. The U.S. Patent Office approved patents for dry-cleaning devices, solvents, and techniques from the 1880's through the early twenty-first century, but none, even New York City resident James Baker's 1912 dry-cleaning machine patent (number 1,028,317), reference Jennings's invention.

Secretary of State John Quincy Adams and Attorney General William Wirt. The Patent Office listed Jennings's invention in a contemporary publication noting registered patents. Although most historians credit Jennings as the first African American to receive a patent, there could have been prior African Americans who achieved patents who have not yet been identified. Jennings's patent became well known because Frederick Douglass mentioned it in a eulogy praising Jennings in the April, 1859, issue of *The Anglo-African Magazine*.

The Patent Act of 1836 resulted in patents receiving numbers listed chronologically from the time they had been first issued, assigning patent number 3,306x to Jennings's invention, with the *x* indicating that the patent had been registered before 1836. A December 15, 1836, fire at the U.S. Patent Office burned most patent records stored there, including Jennings's application and any associated materials supporting it. Without that application, specific information and Jennings's description of his invention remain uncertain. His dry scouring invention was the sole U.S. patent he obtained. Sources do not mention if he sought foreign patents or ever attempted inventing any other processes or objects useful to his business.

Jennings generated ample income from his patent, although records do not specify any monetary amounts. Some sources claim that Jennings initially used profits to purchase enslaved relatives, suggesting that perhaps his parents or his wife's family were slaves. In 1820, 10,368 free African Americans and 518 slaves resided in the New York City area. Jennings invested his patent earnings into bettering his community, particularly funding abolition efforts. He promoted suffrage for African Americans and educational opportunities and participated in civic groups devoted to political, economic, and intellectual activities. Jennings helped the Phoenix Literary Society provide clothes to impoverished children so they could attend schools.

After New York ended slavery in 1827, Jennings voiced his opinions regarding issues that many free African Americans experienced, especially prejudices and animosity. *Freedom's Journal*, the first African American newspaper in the United States, printed one of his speeches in its April 4, 1828, issue. He was a delegate to People of Color conventions in the 1830's. In 1837, Jennings took petitions demanding African American suffrage to the state legislature. He organized the Legal Rights Association in 1854, serving as president, to seek equal transportation services for blacks after his daughter experienced discrimination on a public omnibus. When Jennings died at his home on February 11, 1859, his framed patent was displayed by his bed.

SIGNIFICANCE

Jennings's inventiveness achieved professional and personal results. In addition to providing a useful cleaning service to his community, Jennings gained financial means to enhance his business and lifestyle and reinforce his efforts to seek legal changes to improve conditions for African Americans. Whether Jennings was aware the process of inventing and patenting would assist him economically and socially is unknown. Sources do not reveal whether Jennings had any access to other inventors who might have motivated him to pursue innovative efforts and suggested potential benefits, both immediate and future.

Although Jennings's contemporaries were aware of his invention, or at least of the novel dry scouring he offered, no records indicate how Jennings might have inspired other African American inventors or convinced skeptics of African Americans' technological and scientific abilities. Other dry cleaners might have appropriated aspects of Jennings's invention for variations they developed but for which they did not seek patents, which might have confirmed his influence.

Many antebellum African American craftsmen and laborers devised objects or methods to resolve problems they encountered. Often, those inventors did not seek patents, or other people, particularly slave owners, claimed patents for those inventions. The U.S. Patent Office first identified an African American inventor thirteen years after Jennings's received his patent when the race of Henry Blair, a free African American, was included on his 1834 and 1836 patents for agricultural tools. No records connect Blair and Jennings or suggest that Jennings inspired Blair to file for patents. Many sources incorrectly identify Blair as the first African American patent holder.

African American congressman George Washington Murray did not include Jennings in his list of African American inventors for the *Congressional Record* in 1894, nor did Henry E. Baker, an African American patent examiner, who published information he compiled regarding African American inventors. Those omissions could have occurred because Jennings's patent was overlooked because of destroyed records, because his race was unknown to those men, or because his invention achievements were no longer publicized after his family, customers, and peers died.

Elizabeth D. Schafer

Further Reading

Bolden, Tonya. *Strong Men Keep Coming: The Book of African American Men*. Foreword by Herb Boyd. New York: John Wiley & Sons, 1999. The section about Jennings consists mostly of Frederick Douglass's 1859 tribute memorializing Jennings, which includes information about Jennings and his patent unavailable in other sources.

Freeman, Rhoda Golden. *The Free Negro in New York City in the Era Before the Civil War*. New York: Garland, 1994. Historical depiction of Jennings's community, noting Jennings's civic work and providing statistics, contemporary perceptions regarding free African Americans, and diverse ways slaves obtained freedom. Illustrations include an 1855 city map.

Harris, Leslie M. *In the Shadow of Slavery: African Americans in New York City, 1626-1863*. Chicago: University of Chicago Press, 2003. Discusses groups and activities in which Jennings participated, especially conventions and relief organizations, to promote abolition and suffrage efforts for African Americans. Citations identify useful primary sources.

Hewitt, John H. "The Search for Elizabeth Jennings, Heroine of a Sunday Afternoon in New York City." *New York History* (October, 1990): 386-415. Presents biographical details about Thomas Jennings, identifying him as a tailor and merchant, not inventor, and depicts how his contemporaries reacted to his daughter's trial and his efforts to integrate transportation.

Sluby, Patricia Carter. *The Inventive Spirit of African Americans: Patented Ingenuity*. Westport, Conn.: Praeger, 2004. Comprehensive history written by a patent agent and expert emphasizes Jennings's significance as a pioneering patent holder. Appendixes, bibliography, and illustrations, many from the author's collection.

Hedy Lamarr

Austrian-born entertainer and inventor

Born: November 9, 1913; Vienna, Austria-Hungary
Died: January 19, 2000; Casselberry, Florida
Area of Achievement: Entertainment, science and technology
Primary invention: Frequency-hopping spread spectrum

Lamarr starred in dozens of films during the golden age of Hollywood, and she co-invented a communications method, involving the basic technology used in cellular telephones, that was utilized successfully during World War II.

Early Life

Hedy Lamarr (HEH-dee la-MAHR) was born November 9, 1914, in Vienna, the only child of Emil and Gertrude Kiesler. Lamarr lived a secure life as the daughter of the director of the Bank of Vienna. Lamarr's mother was a concert pianist, but she gave up her career to raise her daughter. Lamarr's family was Jewish, but in later life, particularly after immigrating to the United States, religion became less important to Lamarr. She did not renounce her Judaism, but she did not practice it.

> "Hope and curiosity about the future seemed better than guarantees. That's the way I was. The unknown was always so attractive to me... and still is."

Lamarr's exotic looks made her a natural for the film industry. She started with a bit part in a silent film when she was fifteen, and by the time she was seventeen, she had made the film that changed her life, *Ecstasy* (1933).

Hedy Lamarr (Wikimedia Commons)

> **The Invention of Spread Spectrum**
>
> Though women everywhere would have traded almost anything for Hedy Lamarr's film-star status and beauty, she was more than an actor and more than a pretty face. Highly intelligent, she had learned a lot about the mechanisms of remote-controlled torpedoes by listening to business discussions while she socialized with her first husband, Fritz Mandl, a munitions maker and Nazi sympathizer.
>
> During World War II, torpedoes were easily intercepted because the enemy could pick up the frequencies involved in deploying them. Lamarr believed that distributing the remote-control device over several frequencies would make it undetectable. Born Jewish in Austria, she deeply opposed Adolf Hitler and the Nazis. When she met like-minded George Antheil, the classical pianist and composer, the two teamed up to invent a communications method called spread spectrum, or frequency hopping. Patents were issued, and the technology was a rudimentary form of that used in cellular telephones.

She first refused the director's request that she run naked across the screen, but she relented when he promised to film the nude sequence from a great distance so that it would appear more an illusion than real. She agreed, then she insisted that everyone but the cameraman leave the set. It was not until she saw the final film footage with her parents that she realized she had been misled, and a telephoto lens had been used. *Ecstasy* became a sensation in Europe, but it was banned in the United States.

In 1933, at age nineteen, she married Fritz Mandl in Vienna. He was a wealthy munitions manufacturer. Two years later she left him because she found his pro-Adolf Hitler leanings frightening and because she disliked his controlling temperament. She escaped by drugging her maid's coffee, then driving the maid's car to the railroad station and boarding a train for Paris. From Paris she moved to London.

That first marriage would lead to five more, all ending in divorce, and the longest lasting but seven years. Lamarr had numerous affairs over the years, including a few brief encounters with women. Even so, she operated on her own strict moral code, which forbade her to enter a sexual liaison for the purpose of advancing her career, because, she believed, that would be prostitution. Her openness about her sexuality led some to say she was ahead of her times.

Despite being unable to sustain a marriage, she enjoyed being a mother and raised her three children with love and tenderness. She adopted one son, James, with her second husband, Gene Markey. With third husband, Anthony Loder, she had a second son, Anthony, and a daughter, Denise. She became a naturalized United States citizen in 1953, but she always considered Austria home.

Life's Work

However humiliated Lamarr felt about *Ecstasy*, it is what brought her to the attention of Louis B. Mayer, Hollywood film mogul of the studio Metro-Goldwyn-Mayer (MGM). He gave her a contract and brought her to Hollywood, where he changed her name to Hedy Lamarr.

She soon felt hampered by the "studio" practices in Hollywood at the time. Studios had actors under contract and thus limited their opportunities. Lamarr was an astute bargainer, however, and she was able at times to circumvent the system to her own advantage. With skillful manipulation, she convinced Mayer to loan her to Paramount Studios to star in *Samson and Delilah* (1949), which many consider the best performance of her career.

Lamarr became restless and wanted artistic control over her work. MGM had a contractual obligation to use her in a fixed number of films, and too often they were dismal flops. The only way around the problem was to select and to produce her own films. She won a release from her contract to produce and to star in the films *Strange Woman* (1946) and *Dishonored Lady* (1947); in the latter she persuaded her about-to-be-ex-husband John Loder to be her costar. Neither film was a box-office hit, but both earned a profit.

While raising money for another project, *L'eterna femmina* (1954), to be filmed in Rome, she met and married Texas oilman W. Howard Lee, a marriage that lasted seven years. Her sixth and final marriage was to Lewis J. Boies, one of the lawyers she engaged while divorcing Lee.

One thing that always bothered Lamarr was the conventional wisdom that a woman could not be both beautiful and intelligent. She was quoted as saying, "Any girl can be glamorous. All you have to do is stand still and look stupid."

Lamarr was not stupid. Her superior intellect enabled her to, with George Antheil, invent a means of scrambling radio signals that was used in World War II. After the

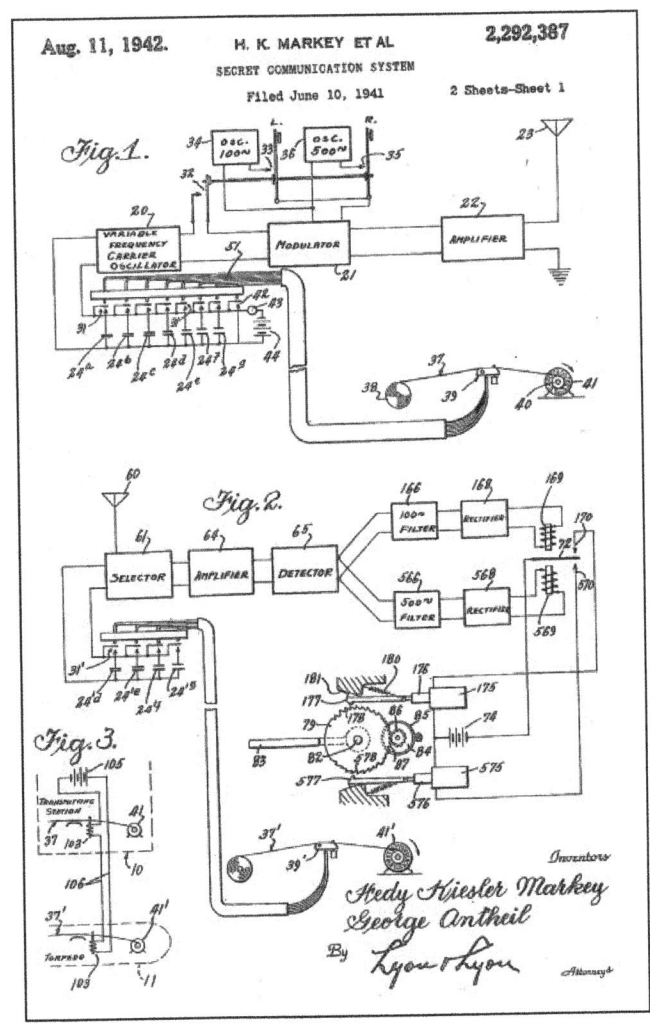

Schematics from Lamarr's patent for a frequency hopping device. (Wikimedia Commons)

Japanese attack on Pearl Harbor, Lamarr became heavily involved in the war effort with volunteer work in the United Service Organization (USO) clubs and selling war bonds. Though the technology used in her invention is still widely utilized, she and Antheil never profited from their efforts because their patents expired.

Regarded by many as "the most beautiful woman in the world," Lamarr sometimes felt that her stunning looks took too large a toll on her personal life. She reveled in her role as a mother, and she regretted her inability to create a lasting marriage. She married impulsively, which led to poor choices and sometimes to financial ruin.

However, she always bounced back. When *The Sound of Music* was filmed in 1965, the mansion that served as the Von Trapp family home was owned by Lamarr. Established after Lamarr's death of natural causes at eighty-five, the Hedy Lamarr Foundation was created to provide educational and inspirational information to promote self-discovery and social accountability.

SIGNIFICANCE

Lamarr wanted to be known for more than her extraordinary beauty, and she continually strove to improve her acting skills. She left a body of work that included about thirty films, some of them considered cinema classics, including *Samson and Delilah*, *Algiers* (1938), *Crossroads* (1942), *Ziegfeld Girl* (1941), *Comrade X* (1940), and *Boom Town* (1940). Her range extended from torrid dramas to light-hearted comedies and musicals. Perhaps her most significant contribution occurred off screen, when she co-invented a technique called spread spectrum. That invention, for which she was issued a patent, allowed the Allied forces of World War II to scramble radio communication signals to avoid enemy interception.

Norma Lewis

FURTHER READING

Gomery, Douglas. *Hollywood Studio System: A History*. London: British Film Institute, 2005. A history of the system in place during Lamarr's career that kept actors under contract to the studios, thus limiting their ability to manage their own careers.

Hill, Devra Z. *What Almost Happened to Hedy Lamarr*. San Antonio, Tex.: Corona Books, 2008. Hill, one of the few writers granted access to the screen icon, reports previously unknown episodes in Lamarr's life.

Jewell, Richard B. *The Golden Age of Cinema: Hollywood, 1929-1945*. Hoboken, N.J.: John Wiley and Sons, 2007. Describes the film industry during the time Lamarr was at the peak of her career.

Lamarr, Hedy. *Ecstasy and Me: My Life as a Woman*. New York: Macfadden-Bartell, 1966. Fascinating and unabashed account of her six marriages and her many affairs.

Garrett Augustus Morgan

Businessman

Born: March 4, 1877; Claysville, Kentucky
Died: July 27, 1963; Cleveland, Ohio
Areas of Achievement: Civil engineering; fire science
Primary inventions: Automatic traffic signal system; safety hood (gas mask); hair-straightening cream

Morgan is best known for two inventions. His breathing device, or safety hood (a precursor to the modern gas mask), was initially used by fire departments and later modified for military use, and his three-armed traffic signal was a forerunner of the modern tricolor traffic light.

Early Life

Garrett Augustus Morgan was born in Paris, Kentucky, on March 4, 1877. His father, Sydney Morgan, was the biracial son of a slave and the Confederate colonel John Hunt Morgan, leader of Morgan's Raiders in the Civil War. Garrett's mother, Elizabeth Reed Morgan, was the biethnic daughter of a Native American woman and the black Baptist minister Garrett Reed. Garrett Morgan was the seventh of eleven children.

As a young child, Morgan attended the Branch School located in the African American community of Claysville. By the age of fourteen, he had left school and the family farm and moved north to Cincinnati, Ohio, where he worked as a handyman for a wealthy landowner. To assist him in his efforts to improve his academic skills, Morgan hired a tutor. In 1895, he moved to Cleveland, where he worked for various sewing machine manufacturers and eventually became the only African American sewing machine adjuster, not only making necessary mechanical repairs but also inventing and patenting new machine parts. Among his first inventions were a belt fastener and a zigzag stitching attachment for manually operated sewing machines. In 1896, Morgan married Madge Nelson, but after two years their relationship ended in divorce.

Morgan lived during a period of institutionalized segregation in the United States. As a young man, he realized that even the most talented African Americans had very limited career opportunities. For such individuals, self-employment enabled them to utilize more fully their talents and to earn a worthwhile income. Although African Americans had gained the right to patent inventions, they encountered challenges in manufacturing and marketing them. However, through strong business networks and creative advertising strategies, many minority businessmen were successful in developing, patenting, and marketing their inventions.

> *"If you can be the best, then why not try to be the best?"*

Life's Work

In 1907, Morgan opened his first business to sell and repair sewing machines. One year later, he married Mary Anne Hassek, a Bohemian seamstress, with whom he had three sons. That same year, Morgan helped found the Cleveland Association of Colored Men, an offshoot of the National Negro Business League founded by Booker T. Washington. Morgan's commitment to promoting African American businesses and fighting racial prejudice was demonstrated by his active membership and service as an officer. When the Cleveland group merged with the National Association for the Advancement of Colored

Garrett Augustus Morgan (Wikimedia Commons)

People (NAACP) in 1914, he became an NAACP member and maintained membership until his death in 1963.

In 1909, Morgan launched a business with thirty-two employees to manufacture coats, dresses, and suits. As a garment manufacturer, he sought a way to reduce fabric damage by reducing friction on the sewing machine needle. While experimenting with a liquid lubricant for the needle, he discovered that the liquid straightened the fibers of a coarse piece of cloth. After further experimenting, he found that the liquid also smoothed human hair, and he developed it into the firsthair-straightening cream. In 1913, he started the G. A. Morgan Hair Refining Company to market the cream and additional cosmetics he developed.

Morgan invented a safety hood in 1912 and patented it two years later as a "breathing device." Worn over the head of a person, the canvas hood had two tubes in front that extended downward to encircle the body and join to form a single tube in the back. Hanging close to the ground, the bottom of the single tube was lined with a moist sponge to filter the incoming air. A metal tube inside the hood included a mechanism that prevented smoke from entering as the user inhaled and exhaled air. A nonpressurized air supply was available from a backpack reservoir. Morgan intended the device to be used by firemen, engineers, chemists, and others whose jobs placed them in danger of inhaling toxic fumes or air that contained hazardous dust particles. The National Safety Device Company, with Morgan as its general manager, was established to manufacture and sell the hood. In 1914, at the Second International Exposition of Safety and Sanitation in New York City, the device won first prize, Morgan was awarded a gold medal, and sales increased as fire departments of many cities adopted the hood for general use. Morgan received a U.S. Navy contract for the devices one year later. When gas masks were needed by soldiers to protect them from the effects of poisonous gases such as chlorine, a modified Morgan Safety Hood was among the

---

Traffic Signals

As an inventor and businessman, Garrett Augustus Morgan was financially successful. He was among the privileged Cleveland residents to own an automobile and experience the chaotic road conditions resulting from pedestrians, bicycles, horse-drawn carriages, and automobiles vying for the right of way. After witnessing a terrible accident, Morgan realized that better traffic signals were needed to prevent future catastrophes.

Prior to Morgan's traffic signal, most of the existing signals featured only two positions: stop and go. Manually operated, these two-position traffic signals were an improvement over no signal at all, but because they allowed no interval between the stop and go commands, collisions at busy intersections were common.

Another problem with the two-position traffic signals was the susceptibility to human error. Operator fatigue invariably resulted in erratic timing of the stop and go command changes, which confused both drivers and pedestrians. At night, road conditions were often chaotic because no traffic officers were on duty and motorists simply ignored the signals.

Morgan's mechanical traffic signal was a T-shaped pole unit that featured three positions: stop, go, and an all-directional stop position. The third position halted traffic in all directions before it allowed travel to resume on either of the intersection's perpendicular roads. This feature not only made it safer for motorists to pass through intersections but also allowed pedestrians to cross more safely.

At night, or at other times when traffic was minimal, the lighted Morgan signal could be positioned in a half-mast position, warning approaching motorists to proceed through the intersection with caution. Morgan also included optional bells that could be used as alarms. The half-mast position had the same signaling effect as the flashing red and yellow lights of modern traffic signals. The device made streets safer for pedestrians and was also used at railroad crossings.

Morgan's traffic management technology was used throughout North America until it was replaced by the red-, yellow-, and green-light traffic signals currently used worldwide. Morgan eventually sold the rights to his traffic signal to General Electric for $40,000. Shortly before his death in 1963, Morgan was awarded a government citation for the traffic signal.

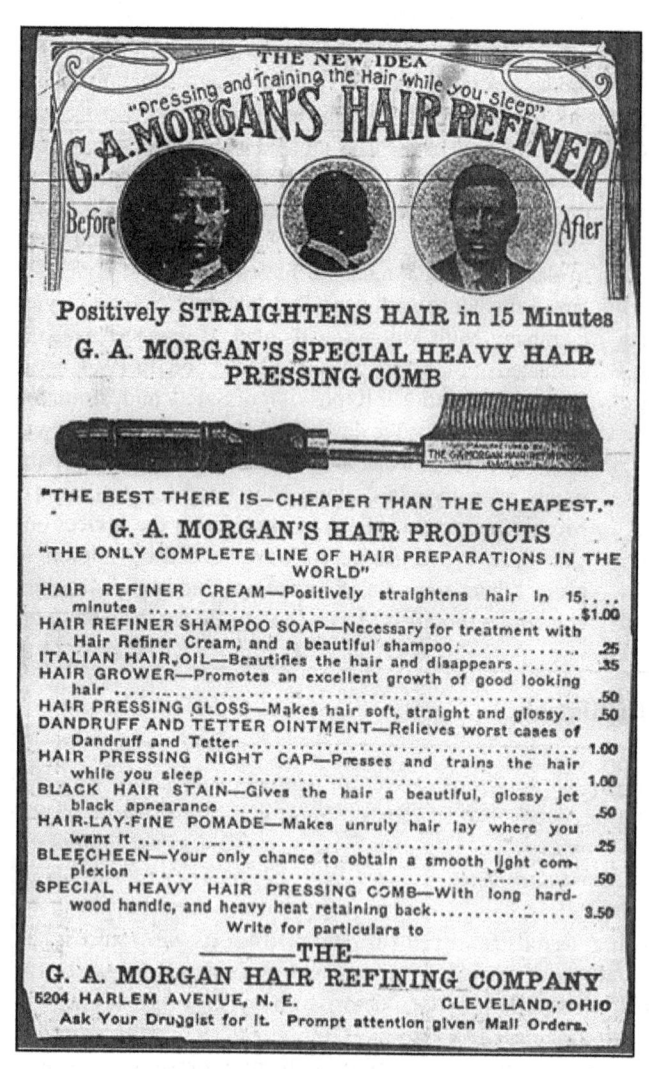

A 1913 advertisement for Morgan Hair Refining Company. (Wikimedia Commons)

devices tested and used by the British government during World War I.

On July 24, 1916, an explosion occurred in a Cleveland Water Works tunnel 250 feet below Lake Erie. The tunnel quickly filled with smoke, dust, and poisonous gases and trapped thirty-two miners. After several rescue attempts proved futile, Morgan was contacted. With the help of his brother Frank and a neighbor, William Roots, Morgan gathered safety hoods and rushed to the scene of the disaster. At the site, the Morgan brothers, initially unable to convince the discouraged rescue workers to join them, slipped on the hoods and entered the tunnel. Once the brothers began to successfully retrieve bodies, others donned hoods and rejoined the recovery effort. Although the men were unable to save all of the victims, they were able to save many who otherwise would have died. While Morgan's heroism and safety hood were impressive and photographically documented, little mention of his role appeared in Cleveland news reports, and he did not initially get the credit he deserved. Morgan eventually received awards from several civic organizations and honorary membership in the International Association of Fire Engineers. However, he never received the Carnegie Medal for heroism that had been awarded other rescue workers he had assisted and provided with safety hoods.

Morgan lived during the era when automobiles were becoming the preferable mode of transportation. After witnessing a terrible accident between an automobile and a horse-drawn carriage, he sought to develop a way to automatically direct traffic without operator intervention. Morgan was the first inventor to apply for and acquire a U.S. patent for an automatic three-position traffic signal. His device included a position for an all-directional stop and a position that permitted motorists to proceed with caution. The T-shaped signal post also had lights and alarms. The patent was granted on November 20, 1923. Morgan later had the technology patented in Great Britain and Canada. Although he formed the G. A. Morgan Safety System Company to manufacture the traffic signal, he later decided to sell the patent to General Electric.

Morgan was active in Cleveland's African American community. He founded a newspaper, the *Cleveland Call*, which he published from 1920 to 1923. The newspaper, now known as the *Call and Post*, is published in Cleveland, Columbus, and Cincinnati. Morgan purchased land in Wakeman and founded the Wakeman Country Club, the first African American country club in Ohio. He was awarded an honorary degree from Western Reserve University and helped found a black fraternity, Alpha Phi Alpha, on its campus. In 1931, he ran as an independent candidate for Cleveland's city council but was not elected. Morgan developed glaucoma in 1943 and eventually lost 90 percent of his sight. In spite of the disease, he persisted in working on his inventions. One of his last was a self-extinguishing cigarette. He died in Cleveland on July 27, 1963.

Significance

During his life, Morgan was a respected entrepreneur and inventor. His most notable inventions, the safety hood and the traffic signal, helped to resolve safety issues of his time. The safety hood was adopted for both fire department and military use. Morgan's traffic management technology was used throughout North America until it was replaced by the red-, yellow-, and green-light traffic signals currently used around the world. He served as a catalyst to promote transportation education and the development of intelligent transportation systems (ITS). Morgan received many awards for his contributions to public safety and has been recognized in the United States as the "father of transportation safety technology."

Although he was from a poor family, had little formal education, and lived during an era of overt discrimination in the United States, Morgan was self-taught and steadfast in the pursuit of all of his diverse goals. As an inventor, businessman, newspaper publisher, and politician, he inspired many African Americans to overcome economic, educational, social, and political inequities based on race.

Several public schools in cities around the United States, including Chicago, Cleveland, and New York City, were later named in his honor. The district of Claysville, Kentucky, was renamed Garrett Morgan Place. Garrett A. Morgan Boulevard in Prince Georges County, Maryland, and the Washington Metro Morgan Boulevard Station are also named in his honor.

Elizabeth D. Schafer

FURTHER READING

Chowdhury, Mashrur A., and Adel W. Sadek. *Fundamentals of Intelligent Transportation Systems Planning*. Norwood, Mass.: Artech House, 2003. Introduces the basics of ITS, with emphasis on traffic-flow issues and principles. Examples of successful ITS applications are provided. Index.

Kerner, Boris S. *The Physics of Traffic: Empirical Freeway Pattern Features, Engineering Applications, and Theory (Understanding Complex Systems)*. New York: Springer, 2004. To facilitate the analysis of complex traffic patterns and roadway congestion by traffic scientists and engineers, Kerner discusses a three-phase traffic theory, the empirical spatiotemporal behavior of traffic based on his own research, and mathematical modeling and engineering applications. Bibliography.

King, William M. "Guardian of the Public Safety: Garrett A. Morgan and the Lake Erie Crib Disaster." *The Journal of Negro History* 70, nos. 1/2 (Winter/Spring, 1985): 1-13. This research article highlights the role of Morgan in the Lake Erie recovery efforts and details his efforts to gain recognition for his heroism.

Mahoney, Gene. *Introduction to Fire Apparatus and Equipment*. 2d ed. Saddle Brook, N.J.: Fire Engineering Books, 1986. Provides a detailed examination of modern fire apparatuses and equipment.

Purcell, Carroll, ed. *A Hammer in Their Hands: A Documentary History of Technology and the African American Experience*. Cambridge, Mass.: MIT Press, 2005. This scholarly publication provides a collection of primary sources that document African American technological achievements.

Sluby, Patricia Carter. *The Inventive Spirit of African Americans: Patented Ingenuity*. Westport, Conn.: Praeger, 2004. Presents a history of African American inventors and scientists based on a review of patents issued. Appendix of inventor names, inventions, and patent numbers.

Spangenburg, Ray, and Kit Moser. *African Americans in Science, Math, and Invention*. New York: Facts On File, 2003. Outlines the lives of 160 African American scientists, highlighting the challenges and difficulties the subjects encountered in their scientific pursuits, including barriers to formal education and training. Bibliography, special categorical index, and black-and-white photographs.

Journalism

The primary role of a journalist is to convey timely and accurate information—to provide the "news." This sounds uncomplicated enough, but because information is so important in a democratic society, journalists are tasked with an extremely important role. In many ways, the history of America as a democracy is linked to the history of journalism. Some of the foundational principles of a free press originated with historical events that predate the drafting of the Bill of Rights, whose First Amendment guarantees free speech. In 1735, for example, Peter Zenger, the publisher of the *New York Weekly Journal*, was put on trial for allegedly printing libel about the British government. His lawyer argued that Zenger's articles were not libelous because they were rigorously factual; Zenger was eventually found to be not guilty. The case is important because it established that negative or apparently harsh statements are not libelous when they are true, and this principle enables journalists to fulfill their role in society.

By the late nineteenth century, the nation's major newspapers had developed most of the elements of quality reporting that we recognize today. Long-form investigative journalism was still in its infancy, however. Journalists were already understood to play an important role in shaping public debates about issues like slavery, abolition, and other topics of the day. Only with the development of so-called "muckraking" journalism in the late nineteenth and early twentieth centuries did journalists begin to take on a heroic status for many Americans. One of the most important of these was Ida Tarbell, a great pioneer of modern investigative journalism. Her reporting on the misdeeds of the Standard Oil Company for *McClure's Magazine*, collected in a 1904 book, *The History of the Standard Oil Company*, documented the company's shady and destructive business practices and ultimately led to the dissolution of the company's monopoly. Her reporting spurred the creation the Federal Trade Commission as well as anti-trust legislation.

In the twentieth century, journalism's great figures helped the nation navigate tumultuous political developments during the Cold War and beyond. They often took great personal risks to report on things like the consolidation or abuse of power in corporations, government and the military, and in that peculiar fusion of these entities that President Dwight D. Eisenhower called the "military-industrial complex." From reliable nightly authorities like Walter Cronkite on television, to investigative journalism at the *Washington Post* during the Watergate scandal, to the work of Seymour Hersh, who exposed to the public the My Lai massacre that occurred in 1968 in Vietnam and, much later, the torture that occurred at Abu Ghraib in 2004, America's journalists played—and continue to play—an essential role in shaping the national dialogue and American politics.

Newsstand at the National Press Building in Washington, D.C., circa 1940. (Library of Congress)

Walter Cronkite

Journalist

Born: November 4, 1916; St. Joseph, Missouri
Died: July 17, 2009; New York City, New York
Area of Achievement: Journalism, radio and television broadcasting

Cronkite, a television journalist and anchor for, most famously, CBS Evening News with Walter Cronkite *from 1962 to 1981, earned the title "the most trusted man in America" from his viewing audience for his objective and judicious coverage.*

Early Life

Walter Cronkite (KRON-kit) was born in St. Joseph, Missouri, to Walter Cronkite and Helen Fritsche Cronkite. His paternal forebears were Dutch, descending from Hercks Seiboutzen Krankheidt. Cronkite grew up in Houston, Texas, where his family had moved when he was ten years old. As a student at San Jacinto High School, he worked on the school's newspaper, *Campus Club*, and won a Texas Interscholastic Press Association newswriting contest. The young Cronkite worked hard to earn his own spending money by selling newspapers and *Liberty* magazines. He was influenced by *American Boy* magazine, leading him to pursue a career in journalism.

Cronkite enrolled at the University of Texas at Austin (1933-1935) and worked on the *Daily Texan* (the university's newspaper). He also worked as a cub (novice) reporter for major newspapers in their respective capital bureaus during the Depression. His mentors, such as Gordon Kent Shearer, bureau chief for United Press (now United Press International, or UPI) in Austin, influenced Cronkite to be accurate and fair. Cronkite accepted a full-time position with the *Houston Press* in 1935, then moved to the *Houston Post*. He became a news writer and editor for Scripps-Howard and UPI in Houston, Kansas City, Dallas, Austin, El Paso, and New York. He worked in radio broadcasting in Oklahoma City for an affiliate of NBC (station WKY), covering football games, then joined the United Press in 1937 and earned a good reputation as a World War II correspondent covering military action in North Africa and Europe from 1942 to 1945.

Cronkite also assisted in reopening the United Press news bureaus in postwar Amsterdam and Brussels as a foreign correspondent and went to Nuremberg, Germany, as chief correspondent to report on the Nazi war crimes trials. He then worked in Moscow as the UP bureau manager from 1946 to 1948 and was a lecturer and magazine contributor in 1948 and 1949. In 1940 he had married Mary Elizabeth Maxwell (who died in 2005), and he had three children with her Nancy Elizabeth, Mary Kathleen, and Walter Leland III.

Walter Cronkite (Wikimedia Commons)

> "*The first priority of humankind in this era is to establish an effective system of world law that will assure peace with justice among the peoples of the world.*"

Life's Work

Cronkite became a national network correspondent in 1950 with CBS News in Washington, D.C. His program, *CBS Evening News with Walter Cronkite*, was a well-respected broadcast that ran from 1962 to 1981 and was headquartered in New York. Cronkite also hosted the *CBS*

Cronkite reporting from Vietnam. (Wikimedia Commons)

Morning Show. His reputation as a respected journalist was sealed because of his coverage of the major news events of the 1950's and 1960's: the Korean War; the 1952 presidential election; summit meetings in Vienna, Paris, and Moscow; the Cuban Missile Crisis; the Vietnam War; the assassination of President John F. Kennedy; the Medgar Evers story; the assassination of Robert F. Kennedy; Martin Luther King's assassination and the Civil Rights movement and struggle; the Apollo 11 landing on the Moon; the Watergate scandal and trial; and the anniversary of D day, which he had covered originally as a UP war correspondent in 1945.

Cronkite traveled the globe to get his stories. He journeyed to war theaters in Vietnam and returned after the Tet offensive convinced that the United States should negotiate an end to the Vietnam War. Soon after Cronkite's return, and after his news report on Vietnam, President Lyndon B. Johnson decided not to run for reelection and attempted to end the war.

Cronkite also narrated the historical documentary television series *You Are There* (1953-1957), *Twentieth Century* (1957-1967), and *Eyewitness to History* (1961-1962). As anchor of the *CBS Evening News* in 1962, Cronkite competed with the NBC team of Chet Huntley and David Brinkley, but by the late 1960's he surpassed them in television ratings and viewer numbers. He had become an icon with a reputation for truthfulness and honesty, came to be known as Uncle Walter, and ended each evening's program with the now-iconic phrase "and that's the way it is." His calm, firm, and assured baritone voice informed his viewers of national and world news.

During many news-making moments Cronkite often reported nonstop. One example was his twenty-seven-hour coverage of the Moon landing of Neil Armstrong and Buzz Aldrin. He believed the Moon landing to be one of the biggest stories of the twentieth century and the one event that would be remembered five hundred years later. Cronkite traveled to the Middle East and was instrumental in bringing Egypt's Anwar el-Sadat and Israel's Menachem Begin together to negotiate a peace agreement.

Cronkite hosted several television specials, including the following: *Vietnam: A War That Is Finished* (1975); *The President in China* (1975); *In Celebration of US* (1976); *Our Happiest Birthday* (1977); *Why the World* (1981) for the Public Broadcasting Service (PBS); *Universe* (1982) for CBS; *Solzhenitsyn: 1984 Revisited* (1984); *Dinosaur* (1991); and *The Holocaust: In Memory of Millions* (1993) for the Discovery Channel. He received the Peabody Award in 1962 and won several Emmy Awards. He received the William A. White Award for journalistic merit in 1969 and the George Polk Journalism Award in 1971. He won the Gold Medal from the Radio and TV Society in 1974 and the Alfred I. Dupont-Columbia University Award in broadcast journalism in 1978. He was awarded the Presidential Medal of Freedom by Jimmy Carter in 1981.

Following his retirement as anchor for CBS on March 6, 1981, he wrote a news column through King Features Syndicate. He took on special assignments, such as anchoring news coverage of the second space flight of John Glenn in 1998 (as he had of Glenn's first flight), and returned periodically as a special correspondent for CBS and for Cable News Network (CNN). He broadcast a series of commentaries for National Public Radio (NPR) on historic events such as Dwight D. Eisenhower's role in the D day campaign, as well as the Gulf of Tonkin incident, the 1968 Democratic Convention, the war in Vietnam, and the terrorist skyjacking in 1970.

Cronkite believed journalists held a great responsibility because they reported what was to become "history" a nation's collective memory. His news commentary, too, was deeply meaningful to his audience. On March 9, 2004, Cronkite broadcast a reflective commentary on NPR that recalled an earlier CBS television show produced by Fred Friendly and Edward R. Murrow that questioned the bullying tactics of Senator Joseph R. McCarthy, who engineered a campaign of terror against alleged communists in government and in the

President Ronald Reagan meets with Cronkite in the Diplomatic Reception Room. (Wikimedia Commons)

entertainment industry. Cronkite applauded his news colleagues' refusal to be politically intimidated, and he praised their justice-seeking reportage. His professional ethics and his own pursuit of the truth set the standard for the type of news reporting he described in his 2004 NPR commentary.

After retiring from CBS as anchor, Cronkite served on the board of directors of CBS and continued to work for several networks as a news correspondent. He even performed the voice of Benjamin Franklin for the children's animated series *Liberty's Kids*. He also created a series of historical videotapes, CDs and DVDs for *The Vietnam War with Walter Cronkite* (1985-1987), *Walter Cronkite Remembers the Twentieth Century* (1997-1998), *All You Want to Know About the United States Constitution* (1998), and *You Are There* (2004). Cronkite received the Harry S. Truman Good Neighbor Award for his "truth in broadcasting" in 2004.

Among Cronkite's many books are *Vietnam Perspective: CBS News Special* (1965), *The Challenge of Change* (1971), *Eye on the World* (1971), *A Reporter's Life* (1996), and *Around America* (2001). He wrote the commentary to CBS photographer Irving Haberman's *Eyes on an Era* (1995) and contributed book forewords to *The Rise of the Computer State* (1983), *Places of Power* (2000), *The Heart of Success* (2000), and *Architects of Peace* (2002), as well as to several children's books on U.S. presidents. The Walter Cronkite School of Journalism and Mass Communication was established at Arizona State University in recognition of Cronkite's life achievements as a journalist, critic, and author.

SIGNIFICANCE

Cronkite pioneered television news, elevated broadcast journalism to the highest levels of honesty and integrity, and increased the popularity of broadcast news among television viewers during the turbulent 1960's and 1970's and into the early 1980's. His voice was one of reason, recording some of the twentieth century's most memorable events. His stature and style provided a strong role model for future commentators in print and on radio and television.

Cronkite also was an excellent researcher who checked his facts. He was an affable and photogenic television personality, and his broadcasts were clear, genuine, authoritative, and accurate. He deftly worked within the time constraints of television, which broadcasted his image around the world. He strived to maintain objectivity, and he shunned bias in reporting.

Barbara Bennett Peterson

FURTHER READING

Aaseng, Nathan. *Walter Cronkite*. Minneapolis, Minn.: Lerner, 1981. A well-written, praising, yet factual biography.

Cronkite, Walter. *Eye on the World*. New York: Cowles, 1971. Cronkite surveyed the previous decades' major historic events at home and abroad, selecting certain events for comment.

---. *A Reporter's Life*. New York: Alfred A. Knopf, 1996. A most valuable autobiographical source, giving anecdotes from Cronkite's personal life and professional career and revealing the friends who contributed to his success.

---. *Vietnam Perspective: CBS News Special Report*. New York: Pocket Books, 1965. Cronkite's name will forever be linked to reporting the Vietnam War, which he accomplished with informed analysis and historical clarity in this small primer.

Westman, Paul. *Walter Cronkite: The Most Trusted Man in America*. Minneapolis, Minn.: Dillon Press, 1980. This work discusses Cronkite's credibility and his career with CBS.

Ann Curry

Journalist, activist, and philanthropist

Born: November 19, 1956; Agana, Guam
Also known as: Ann Curry Ross
Areas of Achievement: Journalism, social issues, philanthropy

Curry's presence on television since 1978 as a news broadcaster has helped change the face of the American media, not only serving as a very visible role model for women journalists, but also serving as a pioneer for Asian Americans striving to overcome negative stereotyping by the mainstream media.

Early Life

Ann Curry was born in Agana, Guam, on November 19, 1956, to Bob Curry and Hiroe Nagase Curry. Curry's father, a career naval officer, met Curry's mother, the daughter of poor rice farmers, in Yamagata, Japan, while stationed in occupied Japan after World War II. Curry, the oldest of five children, lived as a child on the Sasebo military base in Japan, where she attended elementary school. Curry moved to the United States when her father was transferred to Virginia and then California. The family finally settled in Ashford, Oregon.

As a child, Curry was frequently the victim of racism, prejudice, and bullying. Taught early on by her family to stand up and defend herself, Curry often found herself in the principal's office at school for fighting.

After graduating from Ashland High School in 1974, Curry entered college. Although her family had little money for her education, Curry paid her own way, working as a hotel maid, cocktail waitress, and bookstore clerk. Curry was the first member of her family to attend college, graduating from the University of Oregon School of Journalism in 1978. That same year, she became an intern at KTVL television station in Medford, Oregon, where she was told by the executive producer that she had no future in journalism because, as a woman, she was too weak to carry a camera. Curry went on to become the station's first female news reporter.

Life's Work

After three years at KTVL, Curry relocated to Portland, Oregon, where she worked at NBC-affiliate KGW as a news reporter for three years. In 1984, Curry moved to Los Angeles to work for CBS-affiliate KCBS television

Ann Curry (Wikimedia Commons)

as a news anchor. While working at KCBS, Curry received two Emmy Awards, the first for her live coverage of the October 1987 Los Angeles earthquake and the second for her live coverage of a San Bernadino gas explosion in 1989.

In 1990, Curry returned to NBC, relocating to Chicago to become NBC's Chicago news correspondent. By 1991, Curry was promoted to the NBC morning-news show, *News at Sunrise*, where she served as anchor until being promoted again in 1997 to anchor of NBC's national morning-news program *The Today Show*.

> "*I try to do stories that make a difference - stories that affect the way people think, stories that people need to hear - and usually what drives me is to do stories about people who have no voice, people who have no political power, people who are overlooked by society.*"

Curry has often covered difficult circumstances. She received worldwide recognition for her reports from Macedonia in 1999, covering the refugee crisis precipitated by the genocide in Kosovo. In 2001, Curry reported live from the USS *Roosevelt* during the US-led invasion of Afghanistan, and in 2003, she reported live from the USS *Constellation* during the US-led invasion of Iraq. Curry reported extensively from Southeast Asia after the 2004 tsunami killed over 250,000 people. She reported on AIDS, poverty, and malaria in Africa as she traveled in 2005 with First Lady Laura Bush. Curry received her third Emmy for her reporting from Darfur, Sudan, in 2006, which focused on the crimes against humanity and genocide taking place in that region. In 2007, she traveled to Antarctica, where she documented scientists' climatology research. She reported live from Haiti in 2010 after an earthquake devastated the country's population and infrastructure.

U.S. Navy Adm. Mike Mullen, chairman of the Joint Chiefs of Staff, walks with Curry during an interview on Forward Operating Base Walton, Kandahar, Afghanistan, April 24, 2009. (Wikimedia Commons)

In 2005, Curry became anchor of the primetime program *Dateline NBC*. She has also substituted as anchor on the evening *NBC Nightly News* since 1997.

After her younger sister, Jean, was diagnosed with breast cancer in 1998, and her mother, Hiroe, died of gall bladder cancer in 2001, Curry has worked as an advocate for numerous charities seeking a cure for cancer. On December 17, 2007, *The Today Show* broadcast live coverage of Curry as she bungee jumped off the Transporter Bridge in Middlesbrough, England. The event raised ten thousand dollars for charity.

In 2011, NBC rearranged its news staff, and Curry became co-host of *The Today Show*, replacing longtime co-host Meredith Vieira. It was widely reported in June 2012 that Curry would be replaced as co-host of *Today*. Curry hired attorney Robert Barnett to represent her in her discussions with NBC. On June 28, 2012, Curry announced in an emotional broadcast on the show that she was leaving *Today*. She signed a new multi-year contract with the network as NBC News National and International Correspondent/Anchor and *Today* Anchor at Large. Her departure had led to some discussions about racism, particularly as one of the few prominent Asian-American journalists on the national stage.

On January 13, 2015, it was announced that Curry would be leaving NBC News after nearly 25 years. After leaving NBC News, Curry founded her own multi-platform media startup. She continues to conduct major news interviews on network television, most recently securing an exclusive interview with Iranian Foreign Minister Javad Zarif about the Iran nuclear talks. In January 2018, Curry returned to television with her six-part PBS series, *We'll Meet Again*. Developed by her own production company, the series focused on 12 stories of people searching for individuals who changed their lives. She then appeared on The View as guest co-host on January 23, 2018 where she addressed the controversies surrounding her departure from TODAY.

Significance

Curry has earned a worldwide reputation as a fearless reporter who regularly broadcasts from remote locales, many of which are dangerous and volatile. Curry's commitment to speak for those who have no voice has transformed her from a media personality to a spokesperson for the global community. Her own experiences as a victim of racism, bigotry, prejudice, and sexism have made her sensitive to similar injustice experienced by others throughout the world. Curry is recognized both as a media personality and as a humanitarian. From Kosovo to the Sudan to Haiti, she is renowned for her empathy and sensitivity in reporting on the plight of those in despair.

Mary E. Markland

Further Reading

Carter, Bill, and Brian Stelter. "NBC Expected to Pick Curry as 'Today' Co-Host." *New York Times* 1 May 2011:B1. Print. An article detailing the then-anticipated changes in NBC's news shows, including discussion of Curry's career and popularity with viewers.

Sachs, Wendy. "Surviving the Crunch." *How She Really Does It: Secrets of Successful Stay-At-Work Moms*. Cambridge: Da Capo, 2009. Print. Includes discussion with Curry about balancing motherhood with career, raising her children while being an early morning news anchor for NBC's *Today Show*.

Spragins, Ellyn. *What I Know Now: Letters to My Younger Self*. New York: Broadway, 2008. Print. Contains an entry in which Curry recalls her early life and her relationship with her father.

Margaret Fuller

Journalist

Born: May 23, 1810; Cambridgeport, Massachusetts
Died: July 19, 1850; Fire Island, New York
Area of Achievement: Journalism, social reform

A pioneering feminist far ahead of her time, Fuller was a perceptive literary and social critic, and the first American woman to work as a foreign journalist.

Margaret Fuller (Wikimedia Commons)

Early Life

Sarah Margaret Fuller was the first of the nine children of Timothy Fuller and Margaret Crane Fuller. Her father, a prominent figure in Massachusetts politics, was a graduate of Harvard College and the absolute authority in his household. Keenly disappointed that his first child was a girl, Timothy Fuller nevertheless determined to educate her according to the classical curriculum of the day—an experience usually afforded only to boys.

Even as a small child, Margaret was directed by her father in a rigorous schedule of study. She learned both English and Latin grammar and, before she was ten years old, read Vergil, Ovid, and Horace as well as William Shakespeare. At the age of fourteen, Margaret went briefly to Miss Prescott's School in Groton but soon returned home to immerse herself again in study. Although Margaret was intellectually developed far beyond her years, the girl's intensity caused trouble in friendships, a pattern that continued throughout her life. Margaret was also uncomfortable with her physical appearance. Therefore, she decided to cultivate her intellect, spending fifteen-hour days reading literature and philosophy in four languages, breaking only for a few hours of music and walking each day.

By the late 1820's, Margaret was forming strong friendships with Harvard students such as James Freeman Clarke and Frederic Henry Hedge, many of whom would later become involved, as she did, with the Transcendentalist movement. She was becoming known in intellectual society in Cambridge and at Harvard as a formidable conversationalist. The same determination that brought her such success, however, also brought criticism. Margaret tended toward sarcasm, offending even close friends in intellectual discussions, and the great demands that she placed upon herself she also placed upon others.

In 1833, Timothy Fuller moved his family to a farm in Groton. Margaret taught her younger siblings and, when her mother's health declined, took over the household. She continued to read, particularly German literature and philosophy, but her life at that time was a strain. Early in 1835, Margaret fell seriously ill, then recovered; in October of that year, her father died.

At this turning point, Margaret's future seemed uncertain and difficult. She had planned a European trip to expand her horizons but had to cancel it in order to support the family. After a three-week visit at the home of Ralph Waldo Emerson (a Transcendentalist and a literary figure) in Concord, she decided to take a teaching position at Bronson Alcott's experimental Temple School in Boston.

In 1837, Margaret accepted a teaching position in Hiram Fuller's (no relation) Greene Street School in Providence, Rhode Island.

During her two years in Providence, Fuller also continued her scholarly work—often at the expense of her health—translating Johann P. Eckermann's Conversation with Goethe, for example, and publishing poems and international literature reviews in a liberal, Unitarian journal edited by James Freeman Clarke. In addition, she wrote her first piece of important criticism, which was published a year later in the first issue of the Transcendentalist publication the Dial. Although Margaret was a successful teacher, she missed the intellectual stimulation of Boston, so in 1839 she moved back to Jamaica Plain, a Boston suburb, where she was joined by her mother and younger siblings.

LIFE'S WORK

When Margaret Fuller moved back to Boston, her involvement with Transcendentalism (which began when she met Emerson in 1836) increased. As a movement, Transcendentalism focused around a common perspective on religion and philosophy rather than any particular doctrine, and intellectuals met regularly for discussion about the nature of freedom and spirit. In 1840, Fuller became the first editor of the Transcendentalist literary quarterly the *Dial*. She also wrote much of the copy and kept the periodical alive—almost single-handedly—until she resigned her editorship two years later.

> "*Let no one dare to call another mad who is not himself willing to rank in the same class for every perversion and fault of judgment. Let no one dare aid in punishing another as criminal who is not willing to suffer the penalty due to his own offenses.*"

Fuller supported herself during this time by conducting "Conversations," highly successful weekly discussions attended by the society women of Boston. Fuller believed that women were not taught how to think, and she determined to remedy this with discussions of topics from Greek mythology to ethics to women's rights. Through these "Conversations," which continued until she moved to New York in 1844, Fuller became known as a powerful speaker and intellectual critic. During this time, she was also involved with *Brook Farm*, a Transcendentalist experiment in the nature of ideal community that began in 1841 (she did not actually live there).

Fuller was frequently Emerson's houseguest in Concord. She said of Emerson, "From him I first learned what is meant by the inward life." They had a strong friendship, and through their discussions, both were able to develop their knowledge and appreciation of literature. The friendship was complex, however, and Fuller and Emerson were not always comfortable in each other's presence, much less with each other's ideas.

During this period, Fuller traveled outside the boundaries of New England. Her journey to the Midwest is recorded in her first book, *Summer on the Lake* (1843), in which she investigated the relationship between nature and society, focusing on people and social manners. While conducting research for this book, Fuller became the first woman to receive permission to enter the library at Harvard University. The book also brought Fuller to the attention of Horace Greeley, editor of the *New York Tribune*. He invited her to become the newspaper's literary critic, and—against the advice of friends such as Emerson—Fuller accepted. In December, 1844, she moved to New York, leaving the constraints of family and friends behind, to become the first female member of the working press in the United States.

Horace Greeley said that Fuller was, in some respects, the greatest woman America had yet known, and he gave her almost a free hand with her writing. Fuller's style became more solid, and her thinking deepened even further as she wrote regularly on major authors and ideas of her time. While at the *Tribune*, Fuller also became concerned about public education and social conditions. She visited prisons, poorhouses, and asylums, and her front-page articles about them moved people's feelings and laid the foundation for reforms. In 1845, Greeley published Fuller's *Women in the Nineteenth Century*, the first American book-length discussion of equal rights for men and women. The book became a public sensation and made Fuller's name known throughout the English-speaking world. A classic in American feminist literature, it combined the spiritual focus of a transcendental vision with the need for practical action and was influential in the Seneca Falls conference on women's rights in 1848. In 1846, Fuller published *Papers on Literature and Art*, a compilation of her critical reviews that set a high standard for American literary criticism.

The strain of writing on deadline made Fuller's chronic headaches worse, however, and she was also trying to recover from a broken romance. In August, 1846, Greeley commissioned her as the first American foreign correspondent, and she visited first England, then France, and finally Rome, in April, 1847. Everywhere she went, Fuller met with major figures of the time and sent dispatches back to the Tribune. Fuller was disturbed by the misery that she saw around her, particularly that of working-class women. More and more, life—not art—became her preoccupation, and Fuller's articles on the common worker appeared prominently in the *Tribune*.

In the summer of 1847, Fuller made an extended tour of Italy. She was drawn into the Italian struggle for independence, and in the course of her travels she met Giovanni Angelo Ossoli, a young Italian count who was committed to the liberal cause. Ossoli and Fuller became lovers and, it seems, planned for a life together. Because Ossoli would have been disowned by his aristocratic family for marrying a non-Italian and a non- Catholic, however, the marriage was delayed for more than a year.

Ossoli and Fuller spent the winter of 1848 involved in the Republican struggle in Rome. Fuller continued to send detailed articles about the revolution to the *Tribune*, but she kept her relationship with Ossoli a secret for a long time, even from family and friends in America. Fuller was expecting a child, so she moved to Rieti, outside Rome, where she gave birth to a son, Angelo, on September 5, 1848. Fuller stayed with the child until April, then left him with a nurse and returned to Ossoli and the fighting in Rome, where she directed an emergency hospital and ran supplies to her husband's fighting unit. When the Italian liberals were finally defeated in July, 1849, Ossoli and Fuller were forced to leave Rome. They took Angelo and fled to Florence, where Fuller wrote what she thought was the most important work she had done to date: a history of the Italian revolution of 1848.

Fuller wanted to publish the manuscript in the United States, so the family set sail for New York City on May 17, 1850, despite Fuller's deep foreboding about the journey. Difficulties started soon after they set sail: The ship's captain died of smallpox; then Angelo became sick with the disease, and he almost died. On July 17, just after land was sighted, a storm came up and the inexperienced captain ran the ship aground near Fire Island, New York. Whenever the storm abated, people tried to swim to shore, only a few hundred feet away, but Fuller resigned herself to death and refused to leave the ship. She eventually allowed a sailor to try to save the baby, but Fuller and her husband stayed on board as the ship was pulled apart by the sea. Angelo's body finally washed ashore, but Fuller, Ossoli, and Fuller's manuscript were never found.

SIGNIFICANCE

Those who remember Margaret Fuller most often do so within the context of her association with New England Transcendentalism, but her most significant contributions were in the areas of literary criticism and social reform. Despite the fact that her own writing style was inconsistent, Fuller is nevertheless considered to be one of the two real literary critics of the nineteenth century, along with Edgar Allan Poe. She developed a theory of criticism that combined perspectives of realism and romanticism, and she held to high standards that did not fluctuate with the prevailing winds of the times.

Fuller was also a pioneering journalist and perceptive social critic on both the national and the international levels. In Tribune columns, her commentary on public education and social conditions looked deeply into American values. She visited and wrote about Sing- Sing and Blackwell's Island prisons, for example, and her visits led to the establishment of the first halfway house for newly released female convicts. Her dispatches from Europe—especially her account of the Italian revolution—helped Americans grow in their understanding of the world around them.

Although Fuller did find fulfillment as a wife and mother, her powerful character was not circumscribed by these traditional female roles. In her behavior, Fuller questioned economic, social, and political assumptions about women; in her writing, she propagated her belief in equality through. Her major work, *Women in the Nineteenth Century* (1845), is generally considered to be the first important feminist work by an American woman. Fuller fascinated the readers of her day and challenged their ideas about what a woman could and should be. More than a century later, her argument that people should be able to express themselves as individuals, not simply as representatives of their gender, continues to offer insights into the unlimited potential of human nature.

Jean C. Fulton

FURTHER READING

Allen, Margaret Vanderhaar. *The Achievement of Margaret Fuller*. University Park: Pennsylvania State University Press, 1979. This biography presents a strikingly feminist perspective on Fuller's life and work. Allen concludes that Fuller was easily the equal of Ralph Waldo Emerson and Henry David Thoreau.

Blanchard, Paula. *Margaret Fuller: From Transcendentalism to Revolution*. New York: Delacorte Press, 1978. This biography is written from a clearly feminist perspective, but with a more subtle voice than Margaret Allen's (see above). It has helped to make Fuller more accessible to the general reading public.

Capper, Charles. *Margaret Fuller: An American Romantic Life.* 2 vols. New York: Oxford University Press, 1992, 2006. This stunning narrative deals comprehensively with Fuller's identity as a female intellectual, the primary issue in her life. Based on sources, many of which have never before been used, this volume covers her early years and her beginnings as an American prophet and critic.

Chevigny, Bell Gale, comp. *The Woman and the Myth: Margaret Fuller's Life and Writings.* Old Westbury, N.Y.: Feminist Press, 1976. This major study changed Fuller scholarship during the mid-1970's and is essential reading for anyone who is seriously interested in Fuller.

Edwards, Julia. *Women of the World: The Great Foreign Correspondents.* Boston: Houghton Mifflin, 1991. Presents a lively and vivid account of Fuller's activities in Europe and quotes liberally from her communiques to the Tribune. The book gives a real sense of Fuller within the context of her times.

James, Laurie. *Why Margaret Fuller Ossoli Is Forgotten.* New York: Golden Heritage Press, 1988. An actor, James has done extensive research in preparing her original one-person drama about Fuller, which has toured internationally. In this sixty-five-page book, James presents her thesis that Fuller has been buried in history because the authors of her "definitive" biography Memoirs of Margaret Fuller Ossoli (1852) intentionally misrepresented her life and works. James builds quite a case against Ralph Waldo Emerson, William Henry Channing, and James Freeman Clarke. She elaborates further in her Men, Women, and Margaret Fuller (1990).

_____, ed. *The Wit and Wisdom of Margaret Fuller Ossoli.* New York: Golden Heritage Press, 1988. This selection of quotations is organized around topics such as "love," "equality," "revolution," "toys," and "faith and soul." Fuller's astute, often wry observations have not gone out of date, and the reader can get a real taste of Fuller from this small book. It also includes a list of Fuller's major achievements and a bibliography.

Myerson, Joel, comp. *Critical Essays on Margaret Fuller.* Boston: G. K. Hall, 1980. These articles represent Fuller criticism from 1840 to the date of this publication. As Myerson observes, it is obvious that from the start, critics were more interested in Fuller's personality than in her work. The fifty-three mostly short selections make interesting reading.

Steele, Jeffrey. *Transfiguring America: Myth, Ideology, and Mourning in Margaret Fuller's Writing.* Columbia: University of Missouri Press, 2001. Traces the development of Fuller's feminist consciousness and social theories, showing how she combined her personal experiences and cultural criticism to create a new vision for American society. Includes detailed analyses of her major texts, including her Dial essays and her correspondence with Ralph Waldo Emerson.

Von Mehren, Joan. *Minerva and the Muse: A Life of Margaret Fuller.* Amherst: University of Massachusetts Press, 1994. A biography, tracing Fuller's evolution from child prodigy to New England intellectual. Focuses on her character, including the relationship of her private life to her ideas about personal development and democratic culture.

Watson, David. *Margaret Fuller: An American Romantic.* New York: Berg, 1988. This is a useful account of Fuller's life, work, and reputation. Watson examines Fuller's roles as romantic, feminist, and socialist, suggesting that she deserves to be taken seriously as a contributor to historically important bodies of thought. Of particular interest is Watson's examination of modern feminist Fuller scholarship. He concludes that modern attempts to "rescue" Fuller do not always escape the myopic traps to which they are opposed.

WILLIAM LLOYD GARRISON

Journalist and abolitionist

Born: December 10, 1805; Newburyport, Massachusetts
Died: May 24, 1879; New York City, New York
Area of Achievement: Journalism, social reform

A crucial figure in the abolition of American slavery and the coming of the Civil War, Garrison combined Protestant evangelicalism, Jeffersonian liberalism, and Quaker humanism into a radical antislavery doctrine that called for the immediate end of the institution of slavery.

EARLY LIFE

In his 1913 biography of William Lloyd Garrison, John Jay Chapman described his subject's emergence as a radical abolitionist in 1830 as a streaking, white-hot meteorite crashing into the middle of Boston Common. However, little in Garrison's background would have foretold of his career as a professional reformer and founder of a radical antislavery movement. His parents, Abijah and Frances (Fanny) Maria Lloyd Garrison, had once lived simply and obscurely in wealthy Newburyport, Massachusetts. By the summer of 1808, however, President Thomas Jefferson's embargo had nearly destroyed New England's merchant marine, inflicting immense suffering upon lower middle-class sailing masters such as Abijah.

During that same summer, the Garrisons' five-year-old daughter died from an accidental poisoning. Abijah Garrison could not withstand the pressure and grief of this period. He took to heavy drinking and then deserted his struggling family of three. The childhood of young William Lloyd was then an even greater ordeal, and he often had to beg for food from the homes of Newburyport's wealthy residents.

In 1815, Lloyd, as he was called, was apprenticed to a Maryland shoemaker, but the young boy simply lacked the physical strength to do the work. In 1817, Lloyd found himself back in Newburyport, alone and apprenticed to a cabinetmaker. That work also proved unsuitable. When he was thirteen, his luck began to change when he secured an apprenticeship with the editor of the Newburyport *Herald*. Lloyd feared another failure, but within weeks he displayed remarkable skill and speed. The editor quickly made him shop foreman. Garrison had found his life's work.

After mastering the mechanics of the trade, Lloyd was eager to print his own writing. Like Benjamin Franklin a century before, he submitted editorials under a pseudonym (Garrison used "An Old Bachelor") that his boss liked and published. "An Old Bachelor" gained much attention, even from conservative political leaders. In 1826, with a loan from his former employer, Garrison purchased his own newspaper, which he immediately named the *Free Press*. Seeking respectability and entrance into the ruling elite of Massachusetts, Garrison advocated the conservative politics and social ideas of the Federalist Party. The *Free Press* became bellicose in its political stands, denouncing everything that smacked of Jeffersonian democracy. During his brief tenure at the paper, Garrison discovered the poet John Greenleaf Whittier, published his first poetry, and also made some oblique criticisms of the institution of slavery, but he revealed nothing that gave the slightest indication of what lay only four years in the future.

William Lloyd Garrison (Wikimedia Commons)

Following this relatively conservative initiation into his journalistic career, Garrison became more and more strident in his style and radical in the opinions he voiced in editorials, to the extent that he lost subscribers, defaulted on his loan, and lost his paper. In 1828, he drifted to the *National Philanthropist*, a temperance paper, and attacked dancing, theatergoing, dueling, and gambling. The fiery editor denounced war and began to display a more thoroughgoing disdain for the institution of slavery by decrying a South Carolina law outlawing black education. Garrison soon repeated his familiar pattern and within six months found himself without a job. He managed to secure a position at the *Journal of the Times* in Bennington, Vermont, and there railed at intemperance and advanced his ideas concerning peace and gradual emancipation.

In 1829, Garrison had become radicalized on the issue of slavery, about one year after reading Benjamin Lundy's newspaper, the *Genius of Universal Emancipation*. Garrison had met Lundy, a Quaker abolitionist, in 1828 and had adopted his views on the gradual emancipation of American slaves. On July 4, 1829, again unemployed, Garrison delivered his first antislavery speech, indicting the North for its racism and declaring that gradual emancipation was the only possible way to end slavery. Then, after reading the works of black Americans such as David Walker and English abolitionists such as James Cropper, Garrison decided to dedicate his life to ending what he viewed as the greatest abomination in American history. He went to work for Lundy and moved back to Baltimore, Maryland, where he co-edited the *Genius of Universal Emancipation*.

Before the end of 1829, Garrison had abandoned gradual emancipation—Lundy had not—and called for the immediate end of slavery. He lashed out against slaveholders and even against New Englanders who countenanced the institution. On April 17, 1830, he was confined to a Baltimore jail for criminal libel against a New England merchant. Word of Garrison's imprisonment circulated throughout the North and eventually reached the ears of the wealthy New York merchants and reformers, Arthur and Lewis Tappan. They bailed Garrison out of jail and paid his fines. He wandered back to Boston and decided to set up a new paper there.

> "*Every slave is a stolen man; every slaveholder is a man-stealer. By no precedent, no example, no law, no compact, no purchase, no bequest, no inheritance, no combination of circumstances, is slaveholding right or justifiable. While a slave remains in his fetters, the land must have no rest.*"

On October 16, 1830, Garrison advertised a series of public lectures on the subject of slavery and the American Colonization Society. The ACS, established in 1817, claimed to oppose slavery and favored black uplift and the evangelization of Africa, but Garrison sought to expose it as a tool of the slaveocrats who actually perpetuated slavery. At the October lectures, Garrison denounced the ACS as a racist organization that intended to expel free black Americans if they refused to leave voluntarily. Boston's liberal and conservative clergy alike reacted to the lectures with disgust. Other thinkers, such as Samuel Joseph May, a renegade Unitarian minister and reformer, Bronson Alcott, a Transcendentalist educator and May's brother-in-law, and Samuel E. Sewall, May's cousin, became captivated by Garrison's moral vigor and earnestness. They instantly converted to radical abolitionism and pledged to aid the young editor. Emergence of *The Liberator* the following year established Garrison as the leader of the radical antislavery movement.

Life's Work

William Lloyd Garrison stood about five feet, six inches tall. His slender, almost fragile frame supported a massive bald head, and his powerful blue eyes were framed by tiny, steel, oval-shaped spectacles. Although relentless on the lecture platform, in private Garrison comported himself with great dignity and grace. Like many reformers, he married late. While lecturing in Providence, Rhode Island, in 1829, he met Helen Benson, the daughter of the Quaker philanthropist George Benson. Timid in the presence of women and lacking a stable career, Garrison initiated a long courtship, finally marrying Helen on September 4, 1834.

On January 1, 1831, Garrison published the first issue of *The Liberator*. It angered northerners as irrational and incendiary and struck fear in slaveholders as an uncompromising condemnation. Garrison, as a pacifist, eschewed violent rebellion, but his strident language—something entirely new in the long history of American antislavery thought—inaugurated a new era in American history. He denounced slavery as sin, called upon all true Christians immediately to abandon it no matter what the cost to the Union, and blasted those who thought slavery might be gradually abandoned. What, gradually stop sin? Tell a man to rescue his wife from a rapist gradually? Garrison thundered. Why complain of the severity of my language, he cried, when so unutterable an evil abounded. Ignoring his critics, Garrison lashed out: "I *will be* as harsh as truth, and as uncompromising as justice.... I will not excuse—I will not retreat a single inch—AND I WILL BE HEARD."

Garrison's antislavery appeal fused the evangelical fervor of the Second Great Awakening, which had begun during the 1790's, with the long-standing Quaker opposition to slavery. He had tapped an essential root of American thought, and if he could convince Americans that slavery was, in fact, sin, then they would have to accept his second proposition that it be immediately abandoned. Southerners understandably recoiled from his rhetoric, but they were horrified when, eight months after appearance of *The Liberator*, Nat Turner turned Virginia inside out by fomenting a slave rebellion and killing dozens of whites, including women and children. Southerners connected the two events, blamed Garrison for the killings, put a price on his head, and demanded that Massachusetts suppress the newspaper and its editor.

In January, 1832, Garrison and twelve men—antislavery apostles—founded the New England Anti-Slavery Society. In June, he published his influential *Thoughts on African Colonization* (1832), and, for the

Image of the front page of The Liberator *(15 December 1854).* (Wikimedia Commons)

next three years, Garrison and his associates dedicated themselves to destroying the credibility of the American Colonization Society. He helped found the American Anti-Slavery Society on December 4, 1833. Between 1833 and 1840, two hundred Auxiliaries of the American Anti-Slavery Society were organized from Massachusetts to Michigan with about 200,000 members. They sent antislavery agents throughout the North to whip up controversy and support for the cause.

The growth of radical antislavery thought caused great consternation. Between 1830 and 1840, abolitionists suffered from personal and physical abuse. Rocks, bricks, and the contents of outhouses were thrown at them. They were denounced as anarchists who would destroy the Union if it suited their whim. In 1836, southern states requested Governor Edward Everett of Massachusetts to suppress Garrison and his friends. On November 7, 1837, Illinois abolitionist editor Elijah P. Lovejoy was assassinated by a rampaging mob determined to destroy his newspaper, the *Alton Observer*. The attacks on abolitionists and the murder of Lovejoy sparked unprecedented sympathy for the antislavery advocates, who could now justifiably claim that abolitionism and a defense of a free press and free speech were inseparable.

To Garrison, abolitionism was only the most important of a collection of reforms, from women's rights to temperance, connected by a liberal Christian faith in a benevolent God and the rejection of all forms of force and violence. In 1836, Garrison learned of two extraordinary women from Charleston, South Carolina. Sarah and Angelina Grimké, born into a slaveholding family, had rejected their home and human bondage, converted to Quakerism, and moved north. In 1837, Garrison arranged a speaking tour for them in New England. Huge crowds turned out for the sisters, who risked their reputations to ignore the social restrictions against women speaking in public. Indeed, during the course of their tour, the Grimkés became ardent exponents of women's rights, having seen how prominent clergymen denounced their violation of women's restricted sphere. Garrison supported the sisters and opened up the Massachusetts Anti-Slavery Society to women, urging his conservative colleagues to do the same.

Garrison's support for women's rights brought howls of protest from other abolitionists, who urged him to avoid "extraneous" issues and stick to antislavery work. He refused to compromise and answered his critics by becoming even more radical. At the September, 1838, meeting of the American Peace Society, Garrison, May, and Henry C. Wright, a radical Garrisonian, attempted to gain the society's acceptance of nonresistance thought. They wanted to outlaw as utterly unchristian all forms of war, force, and violence, even denying one's right to defend oneself. When faced with an attacker, according to nonresistance thought, one could only respond with Christian meekness and manifestations of love. Garrison, May, and Wright all claimed that they had personally disarmed robbers or criminals with love. Conservatives refused to accept the new doctrine or to permit women to participate in their society, and they left the meeting. In response, Garrison and his friends formed the New England Nonresistance Society to spread what they saw as true Christian principles.

Garrison's extreme ideas fractured his own Massachusetts Anti-Slavery Society in 1839 and the American Anti-Slavery Society in 1840. Although the antislavery movement seemed to be crumbling, Garrison responded in typical fashion. While many of the best young male abolitionists avoided Garrison's organizations and went into politics, Garrison damned the political system. In 1842, he advocated the dissolution of the Union. The nation had become so corrupt, so dominated by slave power that no hope existed for slavery's end so long as the South remained in the Union.

Although Garrison's critics argued that no hope for the end of slavery existed if the South left the Union, Garrison ignored them. In 1843, *The Liberator* adopted its most radical stand yet. The "compact which exists between the North and the South is 'a covenant with death, and an agreement with hell'—involving both parties in atrocious criminality; and should be immediately annulled." On March 17, 1843, Garrison began placing the slogan "NO UNION WITH SLAVE-HOLDERS!" on the masthead of his newspaper, where it remained until the Civil War.

Split over women's rights and nonresistance ideas, the antislavery movement nearly ended by the mid-1840's. Little money flowed in and few Americans could accept dis-unionism, no matter how much they hated slavery. Passage of the Fugitive Slave Act in 1850 boosted the American Anti-Slavery Society's prospects, because most northerners came to hate the law as an infringement of constitutionally protected rights. As the nation moved toward civil war during the 1850's, Garrison increased his attacks on slavery, the Constitution, and the Union.

With the firing on Fort Sumter in April, 1861, Garrison supported Abraham Lincoln and the Union cause. Although many of his associates thought the South ought to leave the Union peacefully, Garrison saw the war as perhaps the only opportunity to end slavery, even if it did violate his peace principles. He thus supported the Lincoln administration's war policy, all the while urging the president to abolish slavery. When Lincoln signed the Emancipation Proclamation in 1863, Garrison was ecstatic, and when the nation adopted the Thirteenth Amendment, abolishing slavery, in 1865, he felt vindicated. Believing his life's purpose fulfilled, Garrison retired from activism, though he continued to support the Republican Party and causes such as temperance and women's rights. He died in New York City on May 24, 1879.

SIGNIFICANCE

Although Garrison harbored some racial prejudice, he was a pioneer of racial justice. He argued that racism and slavery worked hand-in-hand and that northern prejudice and southern intransigence shared equally in the responsibility for perpetuating slavery. Garrison's message of racial justice and abolitionism threatened the nation's class system, which exploited northern free blacks as well as southern slaves and endangered the tenuous bonds that had kept the Union together since the formation of the Constitution. Public reaction to Garrison did not change until passage of the Emancipation Proclamation in 1863. Before the war's end, he became a prophetic figure to Americans. The Boston mobs that tried to lynch him in 1834 raised statues to him in 1865. Modern historians have recognized Garrison's indispensable role in the ending of American slavery and have hailed him for his simple claim that the Declaration of Independence ought to speak for everyone, black and white, male and female.

Donald Yacovone

FURTHER READING

Chapman, John Jay. *William Lloyd Garrison*. New York: Moffat, Yard, 1913. A sympathetic early biography by the son of one of Garrison's associates.

Friedman, Lawrence J. *Gregarious Saints: Self and Community in American Abolitionism, 1830-1870*. New York: Cambridge University Press, 1982. Representative of the best modern studies of the abolitionist movement. Gives an inside look at the subtle distinctions the reformers made on a variety of topics related to voting, the Constitution, and how distinct groups of reformers sprang up around charismatic figures such as Garrison, Gerrit Smith, or the Tappan brothers.

Garrison, William Lloyd. *The Letters of William Lloyd Garrison*. Edited by Walter M. Merrill and Louis Ruchames. 6 vols. Cambridge, Mass.: Harvard University Press, 1971-1981. The best way for the student to become acquainted with Garrison is to read the activist's own work. These are copiously annotated personal and public letters that fully display the thinking and the sometimes idiosyncratic personality of *The Liberator*'s chief editor.

---. *William Lloyd Garrison and the Fight Against Slavery: Selections from "The Liberator."* Edited with an introduction by William E. Cain. Boston: Bedford Books of St. Martin's Press, 1995. Includes forty-one selections from the newspaper dealing with issues related to slavery. The introduction provides historical background on slavery and the abolition movement in the United States and the events in Garrison's career.

Kraditor, Alieen S. *Means and Ends in American Abolitionism: Garrison and His Critics on Strategy and Tactics, 1834-1850*. New York: Pantheon Books, 1969. Far and away the best book on Garrison's movement and thought. Kraditor fully explores the controversy of the "woman question" and argues convincingly that, in order for Garrison to gain acceptance of a minimum of antislavery thought, he had to remain more radical than the nation and many of his antislavery brethren.

Merrill, Walter M. *Against Wind and Tide: A Biography of William Lloyd Garrison*. Cambridge, Mass.: Harvard University Press, 1963. A thorough and often critical examination of the abolitionist's career. The text emphasizes Garrison's personality, which could be extremely abrasive and unforgiving. The author recognizes, however, that it took an abrasive personality to challenge the foundations of American society.

Perry, Lewis. *Radical Abolitionism: Anarchy and the Government of God in Antislavery Thought*. Ithaca, N.Y.: Cornell University Press, 1973. The most sophisticated treatment of antislavery thought, concentrating on Garrison and his nonresistance colleagues. Perry examines the origins of Garrison's thinking and connects it to wider trends in Western Christian thought.

Rogers, William B. *"We Are All Together Now": Frederick Douglass, William Lloyd Garrison, and the Prophetic Tradition*. New York: Garland, 1995. Describes how Douglass and Garrison drew on the tradition of Biblical prophecy in their struggle against slavery, intemperance, and the oppression of women and minorities.

Stewart, James B. *Holy Warriors: The Abolitionists and American Slavery*. New York: Hill & Wang, 1976. A good, readable survey of the antislavery movement, emphasizing Garrison's role and the religious nature of the movement that stemmed from the influence of the Second Great Awakening.

Thomas, John L. *"The Liberator": William Lloyd Garrison—A Biography*. Boston: Little, Brown, 1963. The best study of Garrison; it appreciates his central role in the movement but remains critical of his tactics and personality. Thoroughly researched, and more detailed than Merrill's biography.

KATHARINE GRAHAM

Publisher

Born: June 16, 1917; New York City, New York
Died: July 17, 2001; Boise, Idaho
Area of Achievement: Business and industry, communications, journalism

The only woman to serve as publisher of a major American newspaper during the twentieth century, Graham built The Washington Post into a national institution and helped end the presidency of Richard M. Nixon after the newspaper's reportage of the Watergate scandal.

EARLY LIFE

Katharine Graham (GRAY-uhm) was born into a family with wealth, financial power, social privilege, and public notoriety. The fourth child of Eugene Meyer and Agnes

Katharine Graham (Wikimedia Commons)

Ernst Meyer, Graham had almost limitless options when she graduated from the University of Chicago in 1938. By numerous accounts, her father was one of the more remarkable Americans of his time, who consciously chose to marry a white Anglo-Saxon Protestant (WASP) so his children would not have to fight the anti-Semitism that stung him at an early age. He had amassed a fortune of more than $50 million through careers in merchandising and investment by 1917, when he liquidated his holdings to embark on government service. He had successfully pursued more than a half-dozen different careers by 1933, when at fifty-seven years old, and almost as a hobby, he purchased at a bankruptcy sale a discredited newspaper, *The Washington Post*.

As her father pursued the task of bringing *The Washington Post* to a level of journalistic respectability, Graham alone among the Meyer children chose journalism as a career, working initially as a reporter with the *San Francisco News* for a year before joining *The Washington Post* in 1939. According to Carol Felsenthal's 1993 biography of Graham, her father had mailed her daily issues of *The Washington Post* throughout her stay at the University of Chicago, where she had gone to pursue her interest in journalism after two less-than challenging years at Vassar College. Her year on the West Coast served as something of a first and last apprenticeship before joining her father's paper.

Although Graham's entry in *Who's Who in America* indicates that she served on the editorial staff of *The Washington Post* from 1939 to 1945 when she retired to devote herself to raising her family and although she did throw herself wholeheartedly into that job upon her initial arrival there, Felsenthal maintains that Graham's interest in a career in journalism ended the moment she met her future husband, Philip L. Graham. He was one of Washington's most eligible bachelors, endowed with a commanding presence and one who could be engagingly charming. They married on June 5, 1940, within six months of their first meeting. Graham had found a mainline WASP to marry. More important, in Philip Graham, a former editor of The Harvard Law Review, she had also found the person whom her father would turn to manage *The Washington Post*.

Graham's marriage lasted for nearly a quarter of a century, but few of those years appear to have been easy. Her husband allegedly thought of her and his father-in-law in terms of vile ethnic slurs even as he loved the one and respected the success of the other. Over time, he became a philanderer and separated from Graham, only to return to her later. In the meantime, he took over *The Washington Post* as its publisher in 1946, when Meyer temporarily left it for a six-month stint as head of the World Bank. Upon Meyer's return, Philip assumed responsibility as chair for the paper's day-to-day operations, significantly expanding its operations over time; in 1957 he opened its overseas bureaus. The son of a political father and the brother of a future U.S. senator, Philip also threw himself into national politics as an undisguised booster of Lyndon B. Johnson in the latter's struggle with John F. Kennedy for the Democratic Party's 1960 presidential nomination. At the same time, bouts of depression and self-doubt, coupled with his mania, became so severe that he sought institutionalized treatment for what was subsequently diagnosed as bipolar disorder.

For her part, Graham concentrated on retiring from the paper and entering into private life, hosting parties of Washington's elite for her husband and, above all, rearing their four children: daughter Elizabeth and sons Donald, William, and Stephen. On August 3, 1963, Philip checked out of the Chestnut Lodge treatment center, spent the day with Graham, and then killed himself while she napped. With her husband's death, Graham assumed the role of publisher of *The Washington Post*.

LIFE'S WORK

Graham ran *The Washington Post* for most of the next thirty years. In addition to publisher, she was its president (1963-1973, 1977), board chair (1973-1993), and chief executive officer (1973-1991). During those decades, she continued and improved upon the efforts of her father and her husband to build *The Washington Post* into a great journalistic institution and, eventually, into a profitable Fortune 500 company.

> "*To love what you do and feel that it matters: how could anything be more fun?*"

Kenneth Berents, a respected newspaper analyst, wrote in *The New York Times* (September 10, 1993) while covering Graham's formal retirement as *The Washington Post's* board chair, that Graham often spoke of herself as "an oddity [in a world dominated by men], and looked upon as such." Breaking down gender bias took time and diligence; however, as time passed, she gained confidence both in her ability to manage the newspaper and in the people she chose to run it. By the time she began cutting back on her involvement in the operations of *The Washington Post* and turned the publisher and chief executive responsibilities over to her son Donald (in 1979 and 1991, respectively), The Washington Post had become not only a world-class newspaper but also the centerpiece in a respected media conglomerate including the *International Herald Tribune* (on which Graham served as cochair), *Newsweek* magazine, and cable and broadcast television properties. Not surprisingly, during those years in Berents's words Graham came to be viewed as "one of the industry's great ladies." Indeed, she had become the only woman to head a major American newspaper, and her autobiography *Personal History* (1997) would win a Pulitzer Prize in 1998.

Just as Graham broke new ground as a woman heading a media empire, so her newspaper constantly broke new ground in covering the news under her steadying influence, her care in selecting *The Washington Post's* management team, and her willingness to support her staff even when pressured to do otherwise.

To write of these developments is to relive the America covered by *The Washington Post* during Graham's leadership. The 1960's was a turbulent decade for the United States, with Washington, D.C., serving as center stage in a changing America. Just months after Graham's husband committed suicide, President John F. Kennedy was assassinated in Dallas. Then came the Lyndon B. Johnson-Barry Goldwater campaign of 1964 and the buildup of U.S. military forces in Vietnam the following year. There followed a decline in civil rights marches but the rise of antiwar protests and the cities began to explode with antiwar anger. Activism, peace; Vietnam War The Tet Offensive in Vietnam in early 1968 persuaded President Johnson not to seek reelection, and Robert F. Kennedy, the former president's brother, was assassinated in June in Los Angeles while campaigning for the Democratic Party's nomination for president. Also, Martin Luther King, Jr., was assassinated, and the Washington riots that followed his death provided *The Washington Post* with a fastbreaking story, literally on its doorsteps and complete with photo opportunities of machine-guns on the steps of the Capitol. The paper's coverage of the event was perhaps the key moment in the emergence of *The Washington Post* among the elite national newspapers in the United States.

The Washington Post continued its newfound publishing status with its openly critical coverage of both the Johnson and Nixon administrations and their respective conduct concerning the Vietnam War. In June of 1971, *The Washington Post* published secret Pentagon Papers, publication of, despite being advised not to do so by its own lawyers. In fact, and much to the annoyance of Ben Bradlee, Graham's hand-picked editor, *The New York Times* broke the story two days before *The Washington Post* obtained its own copy of the documents chronicling the role of the U.S. government in choreographing its own entry into the Vietnam War. By the time the case reached the U.S. Supreme Court to test the government's ability to squelch the publication of the documents on the grounds of national security, *The Washington Post* had become an equal party to the action.

Graham's greatest impact on the newspaper and in the realm of public affairs, however, was still to come in The Washington Post's investigative coverage of what was initially considered a minor break-in during the early morning hours of June 17, 1972, at the headquarters of the Democratic National Committee at the Watergate complex in Washington, D.C. *The Washington Post* would stay with that story long after other news organizations and newspapers had abandoned it. Requests to drop the story would come from important persons such as Graham's sometime moviegoing companion, Henry Kissinger, who was Nixon's national security adviser and later secretary of state. Veiled and not-so-veiled threats of action against *The Washington Post* and its media empire came from the offices of Nixon's special counsel, Charles Colson, and from former Attorney General John Mitchell, who threatened to revoke *The Washington Post's* television station licenses. Nonetheless, with the same determination she would later show in facing down strikers at her newspaper, Graham never wavered in her support of her staff, and she refused to cower to the threats.

Graham went ahead with the story, and the trail led from Watergate to the White House. The reportage of Bob Woodward and Carl Bernstein cemented *The Washington Post's* growing reputation for journalistic respectability and independence, and it set a standard for investigative journalism. It also made celebrities of Graham, Bradlee, and Woodward and Bernstein. President Nixon resigned from office in disgrace, and *The Washington Post* received a Pulitzer Prize for Public Service for its work.

Significance

The highwater mark for not only *The Washington Post* but also Graham's career was the paper's coverage of the Watergate affair. Watergate, however, did not mark the end of Graham's affiliation with the newspaper and its growing communications empire. She remained its chief executive officer for another twenty years, during which time the value of a share of stock in *The Washington Post* increased more than 3,000 percent, ten times the growth rate of the Dow Jones average during the same period.

Graham turned over the principal executive duties to son Donald Graham in 1991, but she remained the chair of its executive committee until her death on July 17, 2001, in Boise, Idaho. She died shortly after suffering a fall while attending an annual gathering of communications and Web and Internet professionals in Sun Valley, Idaho.

Joseph R. Rudolph, Jr.

Further Reading

Bernstein, Carl, and Bob Woodward. *All the President's Men.* 2d ed. New York: Simon & Schuster, 1994. No study of Graham and The Washington Post would be complete without this now-classic rendition of the Watergate affair, first published in 1974. Crucial decisions at the newspaper were not made by Graham directly but by the executives she trusted and supported.

Bradlee, Benjamin C. *A Good Life: Newspapering and Other Adventures.* New York: Simon & Schuster, 1995. Well worth reading in its entirety. Includes an especially interesting commentary on the publisher of The Washington Post from the paper's former editor.

Davis, Deborah. *Katharine the Great: Katharine Graham and Her "Washington Post" Empire.* 3d ed. New York: Sheridan Square Press, 1991. Originally published in 1979, this book was updated to cover Graham's years in semiretirement that followed her 1979 decision to turn over publishing duties to her son Donald.

Felsenthal, Carol. *Power, Privilege, and the "Post": The Katharine Graham Story.* New York: G. P. Putnam's Sons, 1993. Something of an unauthorized biography of Graham. Reputedly written without interviews of Graham (who was working on her memoirs), this work was published shortly before her official retirement from The Washington Post.

Gerber, Robin. *The Leadership Journey of an American Icon.* New York: Portfolio, 2005. An interesting study of Graham that uses leadership theory to argue that Graham always possessed innate leadership qualities.

Graham, Katharine. *Personal History.* New York: Knopf, 1997. The starting point for any research on Graham and her tenure with The Washington Post. Personal History won a Pulitzer Prize in 1998.

Liebovich, Louis W. *Richard Nixon, Watergate, and the Press: A Historical Retrospective.* Westport, Conn.: Praeger, 2003. Drawing from newly available sources that help shed new light on the Nixon administration's role in Watergate, this book reexamines the scandal and demonstrates how the administration attempted to battle and manipulate the press.

Ware, Susan. *Letter to the World: Seven Women Who Shaped the American Century.* Cambridge, Mass.: Harvard University Press, 2000. A collection of individual studies. Places Graham's influence on publishing on the same plateau as the influence exerted by Eleanor Roosevelt, Margaret Mead, and Babe Didrikson Zaharias in their respective careers.

The Washington Post Staff. *The Fall of a President.* New York: Delacorte Press, 1974. An excellent collection of *The Washington Post's* coverage of the Watergate affair, from its early, limited reporting on the Watergate break-in to the House of Representatives' consideration of Articles of Impeachment against Nixon.

MARIA HINOJOSA

Mexican-born journalist

Born: July 2, 1961; Mexico City, Mexico
Area of Achievement: Journalism

A broadcast journalist, producer, and author, Hinojosa has won numerous awards during a career that has included stints with National Public Radio, CNN, and CBS. The author of two books, Hinojosa has been recognized as one of America's most influential Hispanic women.

EARLY LIFE

Maria de Lourdes Hinojosa (EE-noh-HOH-sah) was the fourth child of Raul and Berta (Ojeda) Hinojosa. Raul was a doctor and Berta a social worker. When Hinojosa was eighteen months old, her family immigrated to the United States. At first living in New England and then settling in Chicago, Hinojosa attended the University of Chicago High School, where she founded a group called Students for a Better Environment. With an eye toward being an actor, she enrolled at Barnard College, part of Columbia University.

While at Barnard, Hinojosa landed a job at Columbia's student radio station, WCKR-FM, where she was producer and host of *Nueva cancion y demas* and later became the station's program director while earning a degree in Latin American studies, political economy, and women's studies. Hinojosa graduated *magna cum laude* from Barnard.

> "*I always saw myself as building bridges. So it wasn't just about Latino stories. It was telling untold stories of many different communities.*"

Hinojosa took an internship with National Public Radio (NPR) in Washington, D.C., in 1985 and worked as associate producer on *Enfoque nacional,* NPR's weekly Spanish-language news program, which aired out of San Diego. For this assignment Hinojosa lived in nearby Tijuana, Mexico. NPR's first Latina correspondent, Hinojosa returned to Washington in 1988 to report and produce stories for *Morning Edition* and *All Things Considered.* In 1989, she won a Corporation for Public Broadcasting Silver Award for her report "Day of the Dead."

Maria Hinojosa (Wikimedia Commons)

Life's Work

In 1990, Hinojosa was the first Latino to host a primetime public-affairs television show in New York when she hosted *New York Hotline* on WNYC. In 1993, she launched *Latino USA*, an NPR program heard in several U.S. markets. The program introduced Latino issues to the rest of America and helped Latinos learn about topics relevant to themselves and their communities.

From 1997 to 2005, Hinojosa worked for CNN's New York City bureau, where she reported on urban issues. In 2001, she reported a weeklong series for CNN and *Time* magazine about the United States-Mexico border. Two years later, she covered the *Columbia* space shuttle disaster for CNN as a reporter and anchor.

Hinojosa has authored two books. In 1995, she released the young-adult book *Crews: Gang Members Talk with Maria Hinojosa,* based on a 1990 story she reported for NPR. This book gave a voice to gang members, an element of society whose point of view is rarely explored in the popular media. Hinojosa's 1999 title, *Raising Raul: Adventures Raising Myself and My Son,* is a serious departure from her previous title. In this book, she examined inequalities in the minority community and the disappointments and the happiness involved in conception and childbearing.

As the head of the Futuro Media Group in New York City, Hinojosa leads journalists in developing stories that reflect the rich cultural diversity of the United States. Once the senior correspondent for *NOW* on PBS, Hinojosa became a contributing correspondent to its successor, *Need to Know.* Hinojosa and her husband, artist German Perez, create altars for Day of the Dead observances. This artwork gives the journalist a different outlet for her creativity.

Over the years, many awards and honors have been bestowed upon Hinojosa for her work as a broadcast journalist, including the prestigious Leadership Award from the National Association of Hispanic Journalists. In 1999, *Working Mother* magazine named her one of the Twenty-five Most Influential Working Mothers in America. She also won the 2002 Latino Heritage Award from Columbia University and the Ruben Salazar Award from the National Council of La Raza for outstanding work in her career. In 2007, she was honored by the Paley Center in a program that recognized women's contributions to media. *Hispanic Business* magazine has named her among the One Hundred Most Influential Latinos in the United States three times.

Significance

Hinojosa has covered a wide range of important news stories in her years as a journalist. She provides a positive Latina presence in news media and brings insight and acumen to her work. She also is an accomplished author and advocate for women and Latinos.

Randy L. Abbott

Further Reading

Hinojosa, Maria. *Crews: Gang Members Talk to Maria Hinojosa.* San Diego, California: Harcourt Brace, 1995. Aimed at the young adult market and based on an NPR report for *All Things Considered*, this book presents candid and disturbing interviews with gang members.

---. *Raising Raul: Adventures Raising Myself and My Son.* New York, N.Y.: Viking, 1999. This book covers the author's conflicting attitudes toward having her own family, the difficulties and complications involved in the process of having and rearing children in modern America.

Rodriguez, Marissa. "The Binds of Marriage: Journalist Maria Hinojosa Travels the World to Document the Shocking Practice of Child Marriage." *Hispanic* 20, no. 11 (November, 2007): 34-36. Discusses Hinojosa's reporting on child brides.

Fabrizio, Doug, and Maria Hinojosa. "The Realities of Diversity: A Conversation With Maria Hinojosa." RadioWest, National Public Radio, Salt Lake City, Utah,

22 Oct. 2018. A discussion with Hinojosa about the nature of racism and having difficult conversations about race.

Edward R. Murrow

Broadcast journalist

Born: April 25, 1908; Guilford County, North Carolina
Died: April 27, 1965; Pawling, New York
Areas of Achievement: Journalism, radio, television

Murrow, the pioneer of news broadcasting, set the standard for objective reporting while warning against the potential for manipulation by electronic journalism.

Early Life

Egbert Roscoe Murrow, called "Egg" by family and friends, changed his name to the more common "Edward" as a young man. When he was still a child, his family moved to the Pacific Northwest, where Murrow spent summers working in the logging camps. In high school, he was a super-achiever on several levels: a successful athlete, valedictorian of his class, student body officer, and, prophetically, star of the debate team. Following his graduation, the rangy, six-foot two-inch young man returned to the logging camps. In 1926, after one year of this hard labor, he had saved sufficiently to enroll at Washington State University.

His popularity continued in college, enhanced by his dark, handsome looks a physical appearance that would prove useful in his final career choice. In college, he majored in speech, honing his communication skills; he also added acting to his list of credits and began to cultivate the taste for elegant, expensive clothes for which he would later be known.

As the president of the student government, Murrow was a delegate to the annual convention of NSFA, the National Student Federation of America, of which he was elected president. Immediately following his graduation with a B.A. in speech, he moved to New York City to undertake his new, unpaid responsibilities. His tenure with the NSFA afforded him travel throughout Europe, where he began to establish a network of friends and acquaintances that would eventually encompass the most influential people of the time. During these early Depression years, he also traveled frequently within the United States; these experiences were to affect his developing social and political conscience. Murrow resigned from the NFSA in his second year as president (1931) to take a salaried position with the Institute of International Education.

Edward R. Murrow (Wikimedia Commons)

In this position, he was assistant to Stephen Pierce Duggan, director of the institute, a reformer who believed in the betterment of humankind and in the principle of noblesse oblige. Duggan and the Eastern Establishment, to whom he introduced his young protégé, further contributed to Murrow's political development as well as adding to his list of valuable contacts.

> "*It seems to me that any action that arbitrarily limits the citizen's access to sight, sound and print, upon which opinion can be based, is, in the true sense of the phrase, un-American.*"

In 1934, Murrow married Janet Brewster. He was earning five thousand dollars a year, a comfortable sum by Depression standards, when he accepted a position at

Columbia Broadcasting System (CBS) Radio. Eventually, he was made European director for CBS in London. This posting marked the beginning of the CBS wartime news team and Murrow's own beginning as the major influence in broadcast journalism.

LIFE'S WORK

For an energetic, talented, and idealistic young reporter, there could have been no better vantage point from which to view the ensuing struggle than prewar London. By 1939, Murrow had established a crew that included Eric Sevareid, Bill Henry, William Shirer, and Cecil Brown, among others. Murrow charged them to report the human side of the news, not only the facts but also how the average person reacted to the facts. He also urged them to speak naturally, to be honest, and to be neutral. One of his greatest achievements was the training of this impressive group of reporters, who could communicate over the air a sense of the drama unfolding around them. For the first time, broadcast journalism eclipsed print in popularity. Without endless rewrites, copy editors, layouts, and printings, it was demonstrated that the electronic medium could accurately report the news and do so faster.

As radio's most recognizable personality, Murrow himself did not realize the extent of his influence or his huge listenership until a 1941 trip to the United States. At a banquet in his honor, the poet Archibald MacLeish, commenting on Murrow's reports on the attack on London, acknowledged his achievement.

> You burned the city of London at our doors and we knew that the dead were our dead . . . were mankind's dead . . . without rhetoric, without dramatics, without more emotion than need be . . . you have destroyed . . . the superstition that what is done beyond 3,000 miles is not done at all.

Never content to sit back and be the London bureau chief, Murrow needed to face danger, to be present to absorb the flavor of the events he reported. He stood on a rooftop and watched the bombing of London. He flew twenty-five bombing missions, refusing even the president of CBS's plea that he cease such a dangerous practice. He was in Vienna when the city was occupied by the Nazis and saw at first hand the atrocities of which they were capable. He walked among the half-dead inmates of the concentration camp at Buchenwald soon after it was liberated. His harrowing broadcast describing this experience was reprinted in the media and replayed over and over on the air.

Many years previously, Murrow had begun smoking. As early as 1942, this pleasure had become an addiction; he was smoking up to three packs of unfiltered cigarettes a day. He was already exhibiting a "weak chest" and other pulmonary problems. His restless nature, probing mind, need for experience, and inability to relax all led him to periodic exhaustion, requiring hospitalization.

On November 6, 1945, Janet Murrow, at age thirty-five, gave birth to a son, Charles Casey Murrow. With the war over, it was time for the family to return to New York. Murrow took the position of vice president and director of public affairs for CBS.

This was a difficult period of adjustment. Postwar New York was brash and wealthy, in stark contrast to war-torn London; Murrow missed his old friends and colleagues and the excitement of covering the war. After eighteen months in the position, Murrow resigned to return to broadcasting the news. He settled into a comfortable life, doing what he knew and loved best at a salary of $125,000 a year, an amount necessary for a man who enjoyed fine clothes, a good address, fast cars, and the best restaurants.

President Johnson meets with Murrow in the Oval Office. (Wikimedia Commons)

Augmenting this income were royalties from the *Hear It Now* recordings. This record was the brainchild of Fred Friendly, a colleague whose partnership would span the remainder of Murrow's broadcast career. Released in 1948, the record brought together the actual recorded speeches of such personalities as Winston Churchill, Franklin D. Roosevelt, Adolf Hitler, Huey Long, Will Rogers, and Edward VIII, with Murrow narrating. A quarter of a million copies were sold in the first year.

See It Now, the documentary program that established Murrow's reputation as a television journalist, debuted on November 18, 1951, the result of another partnership with Fred Friendly. A precursor to the present-day documentary, the program was improvised and rife with technical problems: blackouts, loss of picture, and so on. The show explored contemporary issues, from what it was like underground with coal miners in West Virginia to the experience of riding a school bus following desegregation in the South. A particularly moving segment was on Korea at Christmas. Rather than focus on military strategies, Murrow interviewed average soldiers and their reactions to the war. Before being canceled, his show won three Peabodys, four Emmys, and various other awards from *Look*, *Saturday Review*, the New York Newspaper Guild, and others.

Along with *See It Now*, Murrow's other venture into television was *Person to Person*, a program that took cameras into the homes of the rich and famous while Murrow interviewed them by remote from the studio. *Person to Person* was an enormous commercial success, widening his audience to include millions of viewers who would never have watched *See It Now*. Through *Person to Person*, Murrow became as familiar as the celebrities he interviewed, vastly increasing his credibility. The show also served to document an era, featuring interviews of such diverse subjects as Marilyn Monroe, Fred Astaire, Fidel Castro, and John F. Kennedy and his wife, Jacqueline.

In early 1953, Murrow was targeted by the House Committee on Un-American Activities. He had been too consistently critical of Joseph McCarthy; he was prominent and, through his activities in the 1930's, he was vulnerable. Murrow fought back with a segment of *See It Now* entitled "A Report on Senator Joseph R. McCarthy." His strategy was to catch McCarthy in his own contradictions by splicing together his various speeches with Murrow's voice-over narration. Murrow ended with a speech spoken directly to the camera, not read as was his normal practice.

Murrow with Israeli prime minister David Ben Gurion. (Wikimedia Commons)

> He [McCarthy] didn't create this situation of fear, he merely exploited it; and rather successfully. Cassius was right. "The fault, Dear Brutus, is not in our stars, but in ourselves."

By the following morning, CBS had received one thousand telegrams applauding the telecast. Murrow, returning from lunch the next day, was mobbed on Fifth Avenue. *Variety* labeled him "practically a hero." McCarthy's power was beginning to wane.

In 1961, exhausted from his years in broadcasting and disillusioned with CBS, Murrow accepted the directorship of the United States Information Agency in the Kennedy administration. His tenure ended after three years, after surgery for cancer of the lung. Awarded the Presidential Medal of Freedom in 1964, Murrow died at his farm in New York on April 27, 1965, at the age of fifty-seven.

Significance

Murrow spent his life following the dictates of his conscience: struggling with the top executives at CBS, with Kennedy, with McCarthy, and even with his adoring

> **Look Now, Pay Later**
>
> *On October 15, 1958, Edward R. Murrow delivered the keynote address at the Radio-Television News Directors Association's convention in Chicago, criticizing the television networks for their failure to provide programming about serious and controversial subjects.*
>
> Our history will be what we make it. And if there are any historians about fifty or a hundred years from now, and there should be preserved the kinescopes for one week of all three networks, they will there find recorded in black and white, or color, evidence of decadence, escapism and insulation from the realities of the world in which we live. I invite your attention to the television schedules of all networks between the hours of 8 and 11 p.m., Eastern Time. Here you will find only fleeting and spasmodic reference to the fact that this nation is in mortal danger.... If this state of affairs continues, we may alter an advertising slogan to read: look now, pay later.
>
> For surely we shall pay for using this most powerful instrument of communication to insulate the citizenry from the hard and demanding realities which must be faced if we are to survive.... This instrument can teach, it can illuminate; yes, and it can even inspire. But it can do so only to the extent that humans are determined to use it to those ends. Otherwise it is merely wires and lights in a box.

public. With a profound commitment to fair reporting, Murrow set the standard for broadcast journalism.

He became a dedicated antifascist in the early 1930's, working with the Emergency Committee to bring out of Europe ninety-one scholars whose lives and works were endangered. These activities would figure prominently in smear tactics made against him by the House Committee on Un-American Activities. Although his head-on collision with McCarthy was considered by many to be television's "finest hour," Murrow himself agonized over its production. His objectivity and his dedication to balanced presentation were lacking. He called it a "half hour editorial."

In a career-long relationship, flawed at times with serious bitterness, CBS found the perfect vehicle in Murrow. Not only had nature bequeathed him a mellifluous baritone voice and dark good looks, but he was also a trained and skillful debater. His speaking ability, his passionate social conscience, and his dedication to providing the truth infused his broadcasting with a rare vitality. Yet Murrow was taxed by television in a way that his audiences would never guess: He was incredibly camera shy. He had been nervous on the radio, but television added the dimension of the camera. His hands trembled, the heat of the lights made him perspire and squirm; under the table, his nervous leg jumped.

Murrow's most enduring battle was with broadcasting itself, to see that it upheld its integrity. Repeatedly to colleagues, in speeches, and in articles he warned of the potential of broadcasting to manipulate the news and the public. At the same time, he believed that broadcasting had the potential to be "a real aid in keeping the light of Western Civilization burning." In his lifetime, he saw that light burn dangerously low.

Terrill Brooks

Further Reading

Edwards, Bob. *Edward R. Murrow and the Birth of Broadcast Journalism.* Hoboken, N.J.: Wiley, 2004. Edwards chronicles Murrow's career, describing how his broadcasting innovations affected radio and television newscasts.

Kendrick, Alexander. *Prime Time: The Life of Edward R. Murrow.* Boston: Little, Brown, 1969. Kendrick was one of the so-called Murrow Boys, trained in his tradition. This training gives him an insider's view in this profusely illustrated and anecdote-rich biography. Often insightful, he captures Murrow's involvement and his conscience but stops short of any criticism. Good for an overview of the sins of commercial television.

Murrow, Edward R. *In Search of Light: The Broadcasts of Edward R. Murrow, 1938-1961.* Edited by Edward Bliss, Jr. New York: Alfred A. Knopf, 1967. These selections were made from five thousand broadcasts, which spanned Hitler's seizure of Austria to Kennedy's inaugural address. Bliss, a longtime CBS staffer, has chosen broadcasts that add dimension to history or show Murrow's perspective on the development of his style.

---. *This Is London.* New York: Simon & Schuster, 1941. Texts of his London radio broadcasts from August, 1939, to December, 1940, when he was chief of the European bureau for CBS. The broadcasts read well because Murrow was not only a good speaker but also a sensitive writer with a good grasp of the language. An excellent source for a historical perspective.

Seib, Philip. *Broadcasts from the Blitz: How Edward R. Murrow Helped Lead America into War*. Washington, D.C.: Potomac Books, 2006. Describes how Murrow covered events in Britain during World War II and how his reporting rallied Americans to support the British by entering the war.

Sperba, A. M. *Murrow: His Life and Times*. New York: Freudlich Books, 1968. Exhaustive biography. Almost obsessive in its documentation of each detail of Murrow's life. In this well-balanced, critical presentation, Sperba penetrates the reasons for Murrow's actions and the sources of his beliefs while communicating Murrow's passion for proper news reportage. The definitive biography.

IDA TARBELL

Journalist

Born: November 5, 1857; Erie County, Pennsylvania
Died: January 6, 1944; Bridgeport, Connecticut
Area of Achievement: Investigative journalism, social reform

Tarbell became a prominent leader in American magazine journalism in a period when women were almost entirely absent from the field. She is especially known for her investigative series on the Standard Oil Company in 1902, a report considered the first great work of the muckrakers of journalism.

Ida Tarbell (Wikimedia Commons)

EARLY LIFE

Ida Tarbell was born on her grandfather's farm in western Pennsylvania four years before the Civil War began. Her father, Franklin Sumner Tarbell, had earlier struck out for Iowa and its richer farming prospects; he would not see his daughter until she was eighteen months old. Ida's mother, Esther McCullough Tarbell, was a descendant of Massachusetts pioneers and had taught school for more than a decade before her marriage. She would ultimately bear four children, of whom Ida was the eldest.

When Tarbell was three, her father moved the family to the Pennsylvania oil region to take advantage of financial opportunities there. After the Civil War, the family would follow the oil boom to several towns in western Pennsylvania, settling ultimately in Titusville when Tarbell was thirteen. While her father made an increasingly comfortable living building wooden oil tanks, Tarbell studied in the local schools and attended Methodist church services and revival meetings with her family. When the time came for her to continue her studies, her father naturally selected Allegheny College, the Methodist coeducational college in nearby Meadville.

For the next four years, Tarbell combined diligent study in biology and languages with social activities, class offices, literary magazine editing, and public speaking. She was romantically linked with at least one young man, but the relationship did not survive college and Tarbell never married. After her graduation, she embarked on a short-lived career as a teacher at the Union Seminary in Poland, Ohio. A low salary and high expectations placed on her ability to teach all subjects led to her return to Titusville after two years.

The opportunity that led to Tarbell's career in journalism appeared a few months after her return. She was hired as an editor for the *Chautauquan*, a magazine published to promote adult education and home learning by the Chautauqua Literary and Scientific Circle. Although the editorial work she was assigned initially was stultifying, she gradually expanded her responsibilities to include translating, reviewing manuscripts, and writing her own articles. The workload at first was light, and the magazine was located in Meadville, which enabled her to complete a Master of Arts degree at Allegheny College.

When Tarbell left the *Chautauquan* in 1891, she sailed to France determined to immerse herself in Parisian culture, support herself by submitting articles to American newspapers, and write a biography of Madame Manon Philipon de Roland, a hero of the French Revolution. She did all of this and more. After reading some of her work, Samuel S. McClure, the publisher of *McClure's* magazine, personally visited her in Paris to offer her a job. In the fall of 1894, she accepted his offer, which included money for the passage home.

> "There is no man more dangerous, in a position of power, than he who refuses to accept as a working truth the idea that all a man does should make for rightness and soundness, that even the fixing of a tariff rate must be moral."

Life's Work

Tarbell's first work at the magazine was the surprising assignment of producing a series of articles on the life of Napoleon, whose hundred-year-old military exploits produced a flurry of activity in the popular press of the 1890's. She had not expected to do a work of that sort, and she was astonished to be asked, after returning from Paris, to undertake a biography of a French subject using the comparatively limited sources to be found in American libraries. Nevertheless, her labors at the Library of Congress resulted in a distinctive and popular *McClure's* series that was subsequently published as a book, as was the practice at the time.

The resources of the Library of Congress were excellent, as Tarbell discovered, and so were the human resources in the nation's capital. She remained in Washington, D.C., until 1899, during which time she met influential politicians and public servants. She wrote articles about them and ghost-wrote the memoirs of other famous men. Her major work during her Washington years was another *McClure's* assignment, a biography of Abraham Lincoln. She conducted interviews in Washington and Illinois and established a wide network of correspondents who provided her with information. Her study of Lincoln's early years was published in 1896, with a complete two-volume biography following in 1900, after its serialization in the magazine.

Called to the *McClure's* New York staff in 1899 as managing editor, Tarbell joined a talented group of writers and editors. Although McClure himself was seldom in the office, his partner, John Phillips, shrewdly managed the publisher's affairs. Among the writers McClure and Phillips published regularly were Ray Stannard Baker and William Allen White, both of whom were poised on the brink of fame as preeminent journalists of their time. Also on the staff then or shortly thereafter were Willa Cather, Finley Peter Dunne, and Lincoln Steffens. This group took the lead in a new journalistic enterprise muckraking and Tarbell's series on the Standard Oil Company was in the forefront of that type of work.

The series that would later be published in book form as *The History of the Standard Oil Company* was launched in the November, 1902, *McClure's* magazine. Tarbell had undertaken it in response to McClure's idea of detailing the rise of the trusts in the late nineteenth century; she had formulated the idea of tracing the history of one such enterprise and the great entrepreneur associated with it, John D. Rockefeller. Growing up in the oilfield districts had acquainted her with the industry and the geographic area in which the boom began. Her industrious methods of working and her indomitable spirit in researching her subject ensured a thorough product. If anyone in *McClure's* talented group of writers could master such a vast (and elusive) body of information, it was Tarbell.

The Standard Oil series established two things: The first was that Tarbell was a formidable author and one of the outstanding journalists of her time; the second was that muckraking (as the reform journalists' movement was labeled in 1906 by Theodore Roosevelt) was a responsible enterprise that could produce thorough and dispassionate analyses of problems. Because of the efforts of Tarbell and her cohorts, *McClure's* became the leading voice of protest among the popular magazines.

This preeminence was short-lived, however, and Tarbell became the leader of a staff revolt against the magazine in 1906. At the center of the controversy was the mercurial McClure. The publisher was famous for his ability to produce ideas for articles at a rapid-fire pace, but his erratic behavior in 1905 and 1906 seemed to Tarbell, Phillips, and others to threaten the magazine they had helped to build. They questioned his new, risky publishing ventures and wondered whether his commitment to reform had been undercut by his commitment to making money. Tarbell resigned from the magazine in April, 1906.

By June, the old *McClure's* group had formed a new venture. They founded the Phillips Publishing Company, raised money to purchase a failed magazine, and launched it in the fall as their own, *The American Magazine*. Tarbell remained a regular staffer and contributor until the group sold its interests in 1915, although she also submitted articles to other magazines. Her major series in *The American Magazine* covered diverse topics: the protective tariff, the American woman, and the "golden rule" in business.

The first series highlighted the author at her best. She explained the complexities of the tariff to the general public, clarified controversies, and produced a reasoned analysis that clearly explained the costs of high tariffs to working people. Her golden rule series, her last extended writing for *The American Magazine*, was a defense of scientific management in industry, a work that demonstrated how efficiency could blend with humane treatment of labor. The third series on the American woman proved to be the most controversial and caused a rift between Tarbell and some of her suffragist friends.

Like many reformers during the early years of the twentieth century, Tarbell believed that the government, through protective legislation, could act in the general interest of laborers, women, and minorities. Revolutionary change in the social or political system was not necessary. She was never truly a feminist. She did not support the woman suffrage movement, since she believed that a woman's influence was best exerted in the home, not in areas that were traditionally male preserves. Thus, for working women, she favored legislation that would limit their hours to allow them more time in the home. Raised by a suffragist mother, and herself a dominant force in a traditionally male profession, Tarbell espoused an apparently contradictory philosophy relating to women and their roles in society.

After the sale of *The American Magazine* in 1915, Tarbell remained active as a freelance writer. She also traveled and lectured on topics about which she had written earlier. She worked briefly in Washington during World War I until she was sidetracked by a diagnosis of tuberculosis and by the subsequent treatment. She spent much time during her later years tending to family members, often at her farm in Connecticut, which she had purchased in 1906 with her book earnings. Projects she completed in her sixties and seventies included biographies of steel magnate Elbert Gary and General Electric head Owen D. Young, a history of American business during the late nineteenth century, and her autobiography, *All in the Day's Work*. Her major magazine writings were series on the Florida land boom and on Italian dictator Benito Mussolini.

Tarbell's work progressed more slowly as she aged, but she doggedly kept at it. In her eighties, she used her own declining health as the subject of a work she never completed, *Life After Eighty*. Old age, Parkinson's disease (diagnosed about two decades earlier), and pneumonia brought about Tarbell's death in early January of 1944. At her request, she was buried in Titusville.

SIGNIFICANCE

Tarbell exerted both a specific and a general influence on her times. The specific influence related to Standard Oil, whose illegal operations she documented as thoroughly as if she were preparing a legal brief. Legal action, in fact, was the result. When the attorney general filed a 1906 case against Standard Oil for violation of the Sherman Antitrust Act, the charges were essentially those that Tarbell had made and documented in her book. The case was heard and appealed; when the U.S. Supreme Court made its ruling in 1911, it ordered the dissolution of the giant corporation.

Tarbell's general influence concerned the status of women in public life. Although she, ironically, did not participate in feminist or suffragist activities, her whole career exemplified what activist women attempted to achieve the opportunity for women to enter the professions.

Richard G. Frederick

FURTHER READING

Brady, Kathleen. *Ida Tarbell: Portrait of a Muckraker*. New York: Seaview/Putnam, 1984. The most thorough treatment of the contradictions in Tarbell's writings and of the contrast between her own achievements and her views on women and public life.

Conn, Frances G. *Ida Tarbell, Muckraker*. New York: Thomas Nelson, 1972. Written especially for juveniles, the book is anecdotal but informative. There is no systematic discussion of Tarbell's works, but there are numerous quotations from her writings.

Lyon, Peter. *Success Story: The Life and Times of S. S. McClure*. New York: Charles Scribner's Sons, 1963. Discusses Tarbell's writings in the context of the magazine muckraking movement generally considered to have begun in *McClure's* magazine. Examines the complex relationship between Tarbell and McClure.

Tarbell, Ida M. *All in the Day's Work: An Autobiography.* New York: Macmillan, 1939. An unassuming autobiography made rather bland by the author's saccharine approach to describing the controversies in which she was involved.

---. *The History of the Standard Oil Company.* 2 vols. New York: Macmillan, 1904. Tarbell's magnum opus was not only the first great work of the muckrakers but also a solid history of the development of the oil industry in the United States. It is the main work on which her literary reputation rests.

Tomkins, Mary E. *Ida M. Tarbell.* New York: Twayne, 1974. This book in Twayne's United States Authors series mainly considers Tarbell's writings and evaluates her contributions to literature.

Treckel, Paula A. "Lady Muckraker." *American History* 61, no. 2 (June, 2001): 38. A tribute to Tarbell, focusing on her investigation of Standard Oil.